CW00607322

THE POLITICAL CLASS IN ADVANCED DEMOCRACIES

The Political Class in Advanced Democracies

edited by

JENS BORCHERT

AND

JÜRGEN ZEISS

OXFORD

UNIVERSITY PRESS

OXFORD
UNIVERSITY PRESS

Great Clarendon Street, Oxford OX2 6DP

Oxford University Press is a department of the University of Oxford.
It furthers the University's objective of excellence in research, scholarship,
and education by publishing worldwide in

Oxford New York

Auckland Bangkok Buenos Aires Cape Town Chennai
Dar es Salaam Delhi Hong Kong Istanbul Karachi Kolkata
Kuala Lumpur Madrid Melbourne Mexico City Mumbai Nairobi
São Paulo Shanghai Taipei Tokyo Toronto

Oxford is a registered trade mark of Oxford University Press
in the UK and in certain other countries

Published in the United States
by Oxford University Press Inc., New York

British Library Cataloguing in Publication Data
Data available

Library of Congress Cataloging in Publication Data
Data available

ISBN 0–19–926036–2

1 3 5 7 9 10 8 6 4 2

Typeset by Newgen Imaging Systems (P) Ltd., Chennai, India
Printed in Great Britain
on acid-free paper by
Biddles Ltd., Guildford and King's Lynn

Acknowledgments

Most of the chapters in this volume were originally presented and discussed in a first draft at a conference held at the University of Göttingen. Comments given by Heinrich Best, Klaus von Beyme, Peter Lösche, and Michael Minkenberg greatly helped in the multiple revisions of manuscripts. For organizational help we would like to thank Torsten Denkmann, Kerstin Diehl, Andreas Flegel, Ralf Henke, and Jürgen Mischke. The workshop was unbureaucratically financed by the Fritz Thyssen Foundation. The preparation of the book has been supported by the Volkswagen Foundation through financing the Research Group on Politics as a Profession. An earlier German version was published by Leske + Budrich in 1999. For critical remarks and the highly supportive working atmosphere they collectively provide we would like to thank our colleagues in the research group and within the Center for European and North American Studies at the University of Göttingen. For their help in preparing the manuscript we would like to thank Anke Reinhardt and Almut Stoletzki. At OUP we would like to thank Dominic Byatt for his continous support and patience. To Claire Croft, Stuart Fowkes, and Alison Heard we are grateful for taking care of the project in its various stages.

J.B.
J.Z.

Contents

List of Figures

List of Tables

List of Contributors

Jens Borchert: Director, Research Group "Politics as a Profession" and Lecturer in Political Science, Center for European and North American Studies, University of Göttingen, Germany.

Marleen Brans: Professor, Public Management Institute, Department of Political Science, Katholieke Universiteit Leuven, Belgium.

Gary Copeland: Director of the Carl Albert Congressional Research and Studies Center and Professor of Political Science, University of Oklahoma, Norman, USA.

Claudia Derichs: Assistant Professor of Political Science at the Institute of East Asian Studies, University of Duisburg, Germany.

Lieven De Winter: Professor and Director, Center for Comparative Politics, Université Catholique de Louvain, Senior Lecturer, Katholieke Universiteit Brussel, Belgium.

David C. Docherty: Associate Professor, Department of Political Science, Wilfrid Laurier University, Waterloo/Ontario, Canada.

Michael Gallagher: Associate Professor, Department of Political Science, Trinity College, University of Dublin, Ireland.

Lutz Golsch: Managing Director, Ahrens & Behrent, Financial Dynamics GmbH, Frankfurt, Germany.

Magnus Hagevi: Senior Lecturer in Political Science, School of Social Sciences, Växjö University, Sweden.

Torben K. Jensen: Associate Professor, Department of Political Science, University of Aarhus, Denmark.

Uwe Jun: Assistant Professor in German and Comparative Politics at the University of Potsdam, Germany.

Harold R. Kerbo: Professor of Sociology in the Social Sciences Department at California Polytechnic State University, San Luis Obispo, USA.

Marcus Kreuzer: Assistant Professor of Political Science at Villanova University, Villanova/Pennsylvania, USA.

Monique Leijenaar: Associate Professor of Political Science, Faculty of Management Studies, University of Nijmegen, Netherlands.

Ian McAllister: Director of the Research School of Social Sciences at the Australian National University, Canberra.

Elizabeth McLeay: Associate Professor of Political Science, School of History, Philosophy, Political Science and International Relations, Victoria University of Wellington, New Zealand.

José M. Magone: Senior Lecturer in European Politics at the Department of Politics and International Studies, University of Hull, UK.

Peter Matuschek: PhD candidate at the Center for European and North American Studies (ZENS), University of Goettingen, Germany.

Hanne Marthe Narud: Professor of Political Science, Department of Political Science, University of Oslo, Norway.

Kees Niemöller: Associate Professor in Methodology and Statistics, Faculty of Social Sciences, University of Amsterdam, Netherlands.

Uri Ram: Senior Lecturer in Sociology, Department of Behavioral Sciences, Ben Gurion University, Beer Sheva, Israel.

Ettore Recchi: Associate Professor of Sociology, Department of Political Science and Sociology, Università degli Studi di Firenze, Italy.

Ilkka Ruostetsaari: Senior Assistant Professor, Department of Political Science and International Relations, University of Tampere, and Senior Reseach Fellow, Academy of Finland.

Ina Stephan: Consultant, Hamburg, Germany.

Luca Verzichelli: Associate Professor of Political Science at the University of Siena, Italy.

Reto Wiesli: Head of the Bureau for Health Policy, Bern, Switzerland.

1

Professional Politicians: Towards a Comparative Perspective

JENS BORCHERT

INTRODUCTION

In all western democracies today we have a group of professional politicians who, in Max Weber's memorable terms, do not only live "*for* politics"—like the old notables used to—but try to make a living "*off* politics" (Weber 1958: 84). Politics then is not only a struggle for power, a striving for the common good, or the shaping of the collective conditions of life, but also a profession (cf. Borchert 2003). Historically, this has not always been the case, but rather has been the result of a nationally specific process of professionalization. This process and its—as Weber so clearly foresaw—far-reaching implications are all too often ignored in studying politics. One goal of this volume hence is to create a sense for the importance of this topic.

As a result of political professionalization, we find a heightened interest in making the political career a permanent one (Schlesinger 1966). But it has also produced vastly different career patterns. Thus, in the US political careers at the national level more or less are congressional careers. In many European countries—especially those with proportional representation electoral systems—the career within the party apparatus is at least as important, if only because it most often is a prerequisite for a safe position on the party list for parliamentary elections. This is only one of many significant national differences recorded in this book. What is undertaken here is an attempt to map out the terrain of professional politics under different political systems. A truly comparative analysis is beyond the scope of this volume and thus has to be postponed to another occasion.[1]

Earlier versions of this chapter were presented at the American Political Science Association and at the Carl Albert Center for Congressional Research and Studies of the University of Oklahoma. Financial support was provided through a fellowship of the German Marshall Fund of the United States who since then unfortunately has decided to discontinue this fellowship program (hopefully not based on an evaluation of this work). For critical comments I would like to thank Michael Berkman, Susanne Borchert, Gary Copeland, Linda Fowler, Kim Geiger, Lutz Golsch, Stephan Lessenich, Ron Peters, Klaus Stolz, Juergen Zeiss, and the participants in the Goettingen workshop.

[1] The call for a historically grounded and internationally comparative approach is hardly new. Pippa Norris (1993, 1997), Linda Fowler (1994), and before them Donald Matthews (1985) have argued quite similarly. Especially Fowler's very inspiring paper contains a call for a much broader approach to political recruitment.

What needs explanation is the overall approach of this book. If the structure and composition of the political class and its attachment to positions in governments, legislatures, parties, and interest groups as well as to the local, regional, and national levels is taken as contingent, why then is the focus of analysis on national parliaments? This seeming contradiction may be explained by two factors: on the one hand the reader of the individual chapters on countries will quickly realize that while the role of national parliaments in political careers differs greatly, it always plays a role— be it as the highest goal of a career or merely as a springboard to other, more highly valued positions. The second reason for focusing on national legislatures is that it is them who regulate the professional life of politicians and thus control the conditions of political professionalism.

In order to establish the basis for comparative analysis and to give readers the chance to draw meaningful comparisons for themselves, the chapters on countries follow a common scheme. In what follows, I will try to highlight the implicit theoretical and conceptual background of this scheme. In my understanding a comparative approach to "politics as a profession" must take into account:

1. the different *historical processes* of political professionalization,
2. the varying *institutional contexts* in which the political class emerged,
3. the *national patterns* in terms of class size, career paths, income opportunities, and scandalization that have evolved (including the functional equivalents that are involved in different political systems from the view of potential professional politicians), and
4. the impact of the political class and its self-interest on any major *institutional reform*.

The notion of *political class* is a theoretical concept which is both concise and empirically open enough to provide a link not only between American and European approaches, but also between hitherto segmented fields of research. This includes fields such as recruitment, representation, careers, political finance, professionalization, legislative institutionalization, reform, and policy-making style—and even larger segments of the discipline like legislative research, elite analysis, and studies of political parties (cf. programmatically Borchert and Golsch 1995).

In the remainder of this chapter, I will first outline the concept of political class, its origins, and its theoretical implications. Then the four aspects of "politics as a vocation" mentioned above will be discussed one by one. Overall, my goal is to demonstrate the analytical usefulness of the concept by developing a categorical framework for analyzing the political class within a comparative framework.

INTO A CLASS FOR ITSELF: THE CONCEPT OF POLITICAL CLASS

The *classe politica* is, maybe appropriately so, an Italian invention. It was Gaetano Mosca who introduced the term into social science. For him the political class was synonymous with the ruling class—with a twist: not only did this class strive for power; it also provided for its own "material means of subsistence" (Mosca 1939: 50). While the identity of the ruling and the political class is a historically obsolete phenomenon, the collective interest in a reliable income from politics and in a reasonable chance for career maintenance and advancement constitute the modern political class as a collectivity.

This point has been made most forcefully by Max Weber who did not use the concept yet, especially in "Politics as a Vocation" (1958),[2] described very insightfully the process of political professionalization. Those traditional politicians—essentially local notables—who "lived for politics" were increasingly replaced by new-style politicians, party functionaries who lived "off politics".[3] Weber thought that this tendency he observed in the Germany of his day (1918) would continue and also become a universal trend. This was only partly correct, as indeed professionalization continued and spread all around western democracies (and moved further down *within* countries), while the party bureaucrat did not become the archetype of a professional politician.

The notion of a "political class" itself was buried for a long time in international political science. It always remained present in Italian political and academic discourse (cf. Sartori 1963; Farneti 1972; Cotta 1979, 1982; Mastropaolo 1984), thanks to Mosca, but was only rather loosely defined. This was even more true for some social scientists in other countries who from time to time used the term, as for example Ralf Dahrendorf (1965), but did not differentiate it systematically from "political elite". The French political scientist Georges Burdeau in 1958 took up the term "political class" and connected it to criteria that are commonly associated with the notion of "class" (Burdeau 1975). In particular, he emphasized the elements in the way of life and thinking that are common among all modern politicians and thus transcend differences of party, ideology, and social background (Burdeau 1975: 258–60). He also pointed out that being a member of the political class is not necessarily connected to having power (Burdeau 1975: 263). Accordingly, for him the political class "consists of the totality of those persons or groups who—apart from the goals they pursue—share in the privileges linked to political authority" (Burdeau 1975: 258).

While this definition certainly is too broad for our purposes—it would include everybody benefiting from political patronage, for example—Burdeau's conception is very useful, because it (*a*) draws a clear line between political elite and political class and (*b*) goes beyond Weber's sociological definition of professional politicians by linking a structurally defined category to a collective consciousness and collective

---

[2] The classical translation by Gerth and Mills is still most widely used, although it is highly problematic (cf. Borchert 2001).

[3] Weber (1958: 84–7) was perceptive enough to note that the difference was conceptual rather than exclusive. Even professional politicians do in some way live "for politics". The decisive difference, however, is, as Weber emphasized "economic," namely the main source of income. Is it provided directly or indirectly through political activity, or is it not?

	Living for politics (power versus public interest)	Living off politics (self-interest versus professionalism)
Class in itself (structure)	Political elite	Professional politicians
Class for itself (structure + agency)	Power elite, ruling class	*Political class*

Figure 1.1 *A taxonomy of approaches to studying politicians*

action. This points back to Marx' distinction between a "class in itself" and a "class for itself," the former being "objectively" defined, while the latter is a real actor (also cf. Beyme 1993: 156). If the political class is to be an analytically useful concept, it has to be understood as a class for itself, because it is only this way that one avoids conspiracy-like ascriptions of a common interest.

Of course, there is more than a bit of irony in the fact that Marxist class theory has always been found wanting precisely because it was not able to make the link between structurally defined collectivities and real collective actors, and now we should find professional politicians to be a group that fulfills all the criteria to be considered a class. Combining the criteria that have been introduced by Marx and Weber, we can more easily distinguish between the various categories to study politicians (see Fig. 1.1). One has to keep in mind, however, that these categories are distinct only in an analytical sense and hence the persons included may and do overlap considerably. The distinction here is about perspectives, not about people.

The debate on the political class, especially in Italy and Germany, at first was a popular and journalistic debate with "political class" being used as a derogative term holding professional politicians responsible for crisis symptoms of the political, economic, social, and moral systems. Political scientists have only belatedly joined the debate. In Germany, the major proponents of the concept have been Dietrich Herzog (1992, 1993) and Klaus von Beyme (1993, 1996).

Beyme's approach in particular is for the most part compatible with the concepts outlined here. Specifically, he draws a clear analytical boundary between political class and political elite (Beyme 1993: 25–32). He contrasts the most basic interests of the two as "steering" or decision-making (political elite) versus "self-preservation" (political class). Thus, the two groups have overlapping yet not identical memberships in that not everybody involved in political steering is a professional politician and not every professional politician has a say when it comes to important decisions. The political class is much more self-referential and geared towards its own autonomy in regulating itself (Beyme 1993: 31).

The one major problem with Beyme's approach is that he insists on relating the political class to party democracy. Hence, by definition there would be no political class in the United States. This, however, is an unnecessary and unwarranted narrowing of a concept that seems capable of accounting for political professionalization and its impact in vastly different institutional settings. The central role of parties in Western Europe more generally should be considered as one of several empirically discernible—and thus comparable—cases. The institution to look at, however, remains in all cases the national legislature, because of its central role for professional political careers and because of its being the eye of the needle through which any institutional reform structuring political careers has to pass. That this research perspective in no way belittles the role played by political parties for professional political careers in most countries, and is demonstrated by the following chapters on countries.

To sum up the argument made here, beneath the tides of research interests in professional politicians, there is a common ground linking them. This common ground is all too often ignored. Hence the disparate research traditions should be brought together by one or more integrative concepts. Much the same could be said for the integration of broader research fields such as legislative studies, research on political parties, or on political elites. Different emphases here often coincide with nationally distinct research agendas and perspectives.

Thus, in the US research on professional politicians has been conducted almost exclusively within the realm of legislative, or more precisely, congressional research.[4] The assumption is that "progressive ambition" (Schlesinger 1966) will lead most professional politicians at some point in their career to run for Congress. Some might not—but these will be covered by scholars studying state legislatures. The US professional politician by definition is a legislator. The European perspective on politicians rather focuses on party politicians. This emphasis is partly justified, as is the Americans', by the obvious realities of the corresponding political systems. A career within the party is not conceivable in the United States; running for parliament and staying there without having a home base within one's party is equally unthinkable in European-type party democracies.

While these differences are real, it makes no sense to keep the analysis of what are otherwise quite similar developments confined to the narrow compartments of either legislative or party research. This is even more true when we look back in history and recognize that today's state of affairs was far from clear when the process of political professionalization started—with strong parties in the United States and weak parties in Germany (Borchert 1997). That is why I propose the concept of political class as a term that comprises professional politicians with whatever career paths available to them in the given institutional setting. It is with this concept that we could integrate theories and findings in different fields. For example, the cartel party model developed in a very suggestive way by Richard Katz and Peter Mair (1995) highlights the same historical process of institutional molding according to the collective interests of political actors that I am focusing on. Yet viewing that model

---

[4] An important exception to the rule is Martin Shefter's (1994) comparative analysis of the historical development of political parties and state structures in France, Italy, and the United States explicitly using the category of political class.

within a basic understanding of political class would enable us to compare the European experience with developments in the United States.

One common denominator of career paths everywhere is that the national legislature is the prime goal of political pros and would-be pros. The way to get there differs greatly, but being there and remaining there—at least for some time—is for the most part the key to a successful professional career in politics. It offers prestige, contacts, a guaranteed income, further career opportunities, often generous pension plans, and the unique chance to regulate one's own profession. This last property of national legislatures—its extensive control over the shape of the institutional environment in which politics, and not only legislative politics, is conducted—turns them into something like a "central committee" of the political class. The political class clearly is much larger than the national legislature; yet it is here that the fortunes of all members are most effectively influenced. The Members of the national legislature may be seen as the core in a model of concentric circles representing the political class. Hence it makes much sense to start—but not end—research on the political class with a focus on the national legislature, even under conditions of party government.

As I hope to have demonstrated, the concept of political class could be an instrument to overcome a segmentation of research that is understandable in terms of the academic division of labor and of the historical development of political science in different countries, but that is not very helpful in understanding the phenomenon and the impact of professional politics. To cite but one example: American congressional research has come to the conclusion that a certain institutional impasse has been reached, because the post-reform institutional order serves the interests of Members of Congress so well that they do not want to change it—and it is they who are in control of the reform process (Mayhew 1974: 81–2). Much the same conclusion has been reached by German research on political parties: "Institutional innovations that would lead to a restriction or long-term destruction of the party privilege ... cannot be expected from the parties, as that would contradict their interests. On the other hand, it is only through them or by them that reform could become real" (Greven 1992: 290–1).

Now this sounds like a converging analysis of institutional deadlock and at the same time provides an interesting explanation of the crisis of confidence that professional politics is currently experiencing. But as these conclusions have been reached in different fields in different countries, they are not being considered in the same context.

CLASS FORMATION: POLITICAL PROFESSIONALIZATION AND THE HISTORICAL EMERGENCE OF A POLITICAL CLASS

According to my definition, the political class "lives off politics" and acts as a "class for itself". In practice then, studying the political class means determining a point— or, at least, a period—in the history of each country we study at which the political class emerged. That in turn depends on (most of) its members being fully aware of their common interests and acting correspondingly. In other words, we have to analyze the *formation of the political class*. Here we can learn a great deal from work on the formation of the working-class. In a conceptually rich article, Ira Katznelson (1986: 13–22) has distinguished five levels of class formation, namely its structural existence (in our case, professionalization), patterns of life (only partially applicable; for example, amount of time spent in the capital, that is, within the group), disposition towards collective action (group consciousness, social and cultural cohesion), collective action (political reforms, mode of policy-making), and the "process of connection" between the other four levels.

In any case the emergence of a political class is by necessity based on a prior process of political professionalization—no political class without professionalization. The reverse is not true, however, there may be, and probably are, processes of political professionalization that do not result in the formation of a political class (in this volume the chapter on Denmark provides an example). This is the case when either the necessary coherence of professional politicians is hindered because of historically caused antagonisms between competing parties or political camps, or if politicians do not succeed in differentiating their occupation clearly enough from society at large and in isolating themselves from society's control.

Studying the political class by definition will mean undertaking some historical and comparative research into the professionalization process that is central to the notion. This research could build on quite a number of prior studies especially for the United States. Concerning European countries there is hardly any political science literature on the subject, but some work done by historians and historical sociologists. Also, there are only very few comparative studies (Putnam 1976; Eliassen and Pedersen 1978; Graham 1982; Schlesinger 1991; Somit *et al.* 1994; Best and Cotta 2000). Hence there clearly is a need for a volume like this that lays the groundwork for more comparative analyses of political professionalization, political career patterns, and their institutional framework.

Professionalization in my view should not be reduced to any simple one-dimensional concept such as reelection rates or average length of service in the legislature. After all, it could conceivably be a particular *pattern*—rather than a lack—of political professionalization to move from one position to the next and then on to a third one within short time-spans. Rather, one should analyze at what time politicians seized the opportunity to make politics not only their pastime but their job. As this formulation suggests, the process has two analytically distinct parts: arising opportunities and making use of them. Structural preconditions for political professionalization—that is, both the historical emergence of political professionalism as a new phenomenon and the recurrent individual decision to pursue a political career—would include:

1. A *reliable source of income* in politics (which could come from parliamentary service, party positions, interest groups, patronage jobs, or any combination thereof). The income has to be high enough to make a living and to render a political career attractive in comparison with other options. Given that politics

as a profession has certain specific attractions (closeness to power, opportunity to express and pursue ideological convictions, media prominence, etc.), these may serve as a partial compensation for giving up the chance to get a higher income in other fields. In the historical analysis of legislators, there are three good indicators for professionalism: (*a*) the time when per diems are transformed into salaries, (*b*) the time these salaries are raised to professional levels (to be determined), and (*c*) the introduction of legislative pensions.

2. A realistic chance of maintaining a job in politics or moving on to something more attractive (this could mean anything from little electoral opposition and hence a safe seat to a well-established game of musical chairs). The danger of an abrupt end to the career has to be limited, either by a relatively safe reelection[5] or by a security net of other attractive positions within politics (or in related areas) to fall back upon if one is not reelected or has to resign. The optimal choice of politicians, of course, is a combination of these two *mechanisms of career maintenance*.

3. A chance of a career, that is, of moving further up the ladder (an established career pathway). As ambition tends to be progressive, there should be *chances for career advancement*, either within the institution (party leadership, committee chairs) or between institutions (involving legislative, executive, party, and interest group positions on the local, regional, national, and supra-national level of government). This implies that there are rather clearly defined shared hierarchies of political positions.[6]

Professionalization as a macro-development only becomes real, however, with the decision of a rising number of people to make politics their profession under the prevailing conditions, to remain in politics for longer periods of time, and to further adapt those prevailing conditions to their needs. At this point, it is important to note that there are four separate yet related levels at which political professionalization occurs and thus has to be analyzed: on the level of individual politicians, on that of particular political offices, on that of institutions, and finally on the level of the political system as a whole.

Individually, professionalization nowadays refers to the process whereby the cherished citizen is transformed into the pariah politician. The opportunity structure is defined by the availability, accessibility, and attractivity of a political career. On the way to professionalization, would-be politicians both choose a new profession and are "resocialized" into its collective beliefs, its ethos. The creation of a new profession, of course, is a singular historical event.

While individual professionalization necessarily is a recurring process, it generally takes place within a predefined setting and according to established patterns. As long as newcomers to the trade adapt to the prevailing rules, the individual pursuit of politics

---

[5] Even a safe reelection can be provided by one of several functional equivalents. If incumbents can rely on superior financial and other resources and thus contribute to the vanishing of marginal seats, the effect is much the same as if party lists provide a safe haven for most incumbents against fickle voters.

[6] There may be several coexisting hierarchies in a given polity.

as a vocation is a rather repetitious and hence uninteresting thing. However, those historical moments when professional politicians emerge for the first time in a given institutional setting are critical junctures that merit closer attention. Equally interesting are times of transition, when patterns of professionalization or even professional politics *per se* are being questioned. One indicator for individual professionalization could be the emergence of a new type of politician whose social background simply requires some income to be derived from politics. Another could be the adult years spent in political office.

The professionalization of *political offices* is a historical process whose results are passed on from one office-holder to the next. Even while the newcomer is still adapting to his new environment, he or she already holds a professionalized political office. This is typically indicated by the resources at hand: salary, staff, privileges, etc. These attributes of professionalization very seldom come as a total surprise to those who are newly elected or politically appointed. More often than not, this has at least been part of the reason to run for this particular office as opposed to one that is clearly non-professional. As very few incumbents work to dismantle the very office they are holding, the professionalization of political offices generally consists of one take-off point (the first instance of individual professionalization) and then a long period of consolidation and expansion. Indicators for the professionalization of a political office are the income derived directly from the office and the time that has to be spend for political work. For example, the professionalization of the office of national legislator could be assumed once meaningful salaries are introduced and the time in session increases notably and to a point where it becomes difficult to pursue a "civil" profession besides.

Much the same is true for the professionalization of *political institutions*. Yet the two have to be distinguished. An office that is part of an institution may be professionalized either earlier or later than the institution at large. Thus, it is conceivable that some constituent parts of a legislature (state delegations, parliamentary parties) professionalize before that becomes common elsewhere. Also, it is at least theoretically possible that non-professional offices continue to exist within a professionalized environment. Had term limits for Congressmen been approved by the Supreme Court in the United States, we might very well have seen a development, where some state delegations consisted of amateurs. Yet Congress would still have been a professional legislature. In the extreme case, one might even imagine a Congress under term limits where all members are amateurs and so are their offices, but the institution remains professional due to the central role professional staff could play under such an arrangement. Typically however, the disjuncture of office and institution in terms of their professionalism should be a period of transition, during which precisely those disjunctures provide the fuel for the institutional changes to come.

Very important in this context is the pattern of institutional professionalization. This pattern can differ vastly between an institution that is a springboard for other office and one that tends to retain its members for longer periods of time. Generally speaking, however, a professionalized institution should be characterized by a high percentage of professionalized members, by a differentiated internal structure and time-consuming internal procedures, and finally by a notably larger budget for its operation than is typically the case for amateur institutions.[7]

Last, but by no means least, there is the professionalization of *the political system*. This is above all a matter of degrees and patterns. The number of positions in a given political system which are professionalized (in relation to the population at large)—the prime indicator for systemic professionalization[8]—varies greatly as does the accessibility of these positions. For example, in a federal system many offices may be professionalized but are simply not an option for somebody from another state, as residency is a formal or informal requirement. At the same time, however, federal systems tend to have more professionalized political positions. Other indicators for system-wide professionalization are the existence of clearly structured career patterns and the overall amount spent for party and campaign finance as well as for the operation of political institutions.

Different patterns of professionalization on the level of the political system can be detected according to the way different offices tend to be linked up and held by the same person—either concurrently (cumulation of offices) or successively (succession of offices). The cumulation of political offices on different levels of government or on the governmental and the party and interest group level is the most important indicator for the prevailing pattern of systemic professionalization. On the other hand, it is precisely the absence of a cumulation of offices that American political scientists mean when they are talking about "institutionalization" and institutional professionalization (Polsby 1968). In Europe, on the other hand, a personnel overlap between different institutions and different levels of government is regarded as an indicator and evidence for political professionalization. Hence, it is only by comparison that we realize how the boundaries between offices and institutions are very important indeed, but indicate different patterns of political development rather than different stages (also cf. Hibbing 1999).

POLITICAL CLASS AND INSTITUTIONAL ORDER: THE STRUCTURE OF OPPORTUNITY

Overcoming National Idiosyncrasies: Integrating the Individual and the Institutional Level

As I named the integrative function of the category "political class" as its major analytical potential, it should come as no surprise that I regard the integration of hitherto separated fields of research as another demand for further research. I would suggest that the most fundamental perspectives to be integrated are those of *the individual politician* versus *the institutional context* (Norris 1993: 25; also cf. Cooper and Brady 1981).

---

[7] For a very interesting attempt to measure the degree of professionalization along these lines cf. Z'graggen (2002).

[8] The number of professionalized positions should be checked against population size so as to account for countries of varying size.

American researchers tend to focus on legislatures and here on the individual agency of ambition-driven legislators structuring their own careers.[9] Either rooted in the rational choice paradigm like David Mayhew's seminal work (1974) or based on the participant observation approach pioneered by Richard Fenno (1978), these studies tell us a great deal about Congress and its Members. The rational choice approach has hardly found any other field on which it can so nicely display its analytical power: where else do you have such a delimited group of individuals, whose fortunes are based to a considerable degree on their independence from group-ties? In a comparative perspective, the approach is rather peculiar: The institution is understood mostly as a composite of individual members, their interests and goals. Institutional constraints and rules—as well as institutional resources—are mostly relegated to the sidelines.

European social scientists on the other hand emphasize party politics and the institutional properties within the polity as a whole. Especially in Germany, one finds an unbroken tradition of old style institutionalism emanating from the normative approach of public law (appropriately called *Staatswissenschaften*—"state sciences"). Institutional realities are largely deduced from and functionally linked to the constitutional order, thus leaving little room for change. Individual members of the legislature merely fulfill roles prescribed by that order. The legislator—just as the parliamentary parties or the opposition—is present in most of the standard literature on the German *Bundestag* merely as a void. He (or she) is given certain tasks and functions; if the legislator lives up to these expectations, fine. If not, he is to be blamed. The very concept of a self-interested legislator is anathema to this line of research.

One useful way of understanding the basic differences between American and European legislative research is Norris' distinction between supply- and demand-side approaches (Norris 1993: 2–4; also cf. Fowler 1994: 3–13). Americans tend to look at the supply of potential legislators, their recruitment, their ways of being elected and re-elected, and the interests they develop in the process. Europeans look at the institutional demands imposed on would-be legislators, their selectivity, their power in determining legislators' behavior.

It should be clear that both perspectives—while geared to reflect the respective political reality they are analysing—are deficient; it is only together that they make a whole. This is increasingly, though by far not universally, recognized on both sides of the Atlantic:

The analysis of political personnel should not be separated from the analysis of its socio-institutional context of action. This is also true in the reverse sense; the analysis of political institutions or organizational units requires taking into account the actors working in and through them. (Herzog 1993: 125)

Far more appropriate (...) is an attempt to see recruitment as a mutually reinforcing interaction of private motivations and public contexts. After all, candidates are goal-maximizing individuals as well as products of a particular time and place; they pursue their personal ambitions in a socially and institutionally determined setting. (Fowler 1993: vi)

[9] This is based on Joseph Schlesinger's classical work (1966). Also cf. Loomis (1988), Fowler and McClure (1989), Ehrenhalt (1991), Hibbing (1991), and Prinz (1993) among others.

Individual career-building and institutional maintenance are inextricably linked together in an interactive relationship where one inevitably influences and (re)forms the other—especially, as both have co-developed historically (see Dodd 1977, 1981). Individual legislators have to be seen as being politically embedded in an institutional context (also cf. Norris 1993: 33). They also have to be perceived as—at least potentially—a collective actor capable of adapting this very context to their own needs. It is this collective actor that I call the political class.

Class Structure: Institutional Context and Structure of Opportunity

The institutional context of political careers—the "structure of opportunities" (Schlesinger 1966)—can be broken down into six components that capture the essential considerations of professional politicians and those thinking about a career in politics within a comparative framework.

State structure refers above all to the territorial organization of a state. Which levels are there below (or, with the transnational integration in Europe, also above) the national level? How are these levels of government integrated politically? Is a career that moves from one level to another possible and customary or are there serious obstacles? Clearly, federal systems like the United States or Germany in general offer more and different career paths than unitary systems where the political game basically is concentrated in the capital in an almost courtly manner. There are exceptions, though: if the federal and the state level are as autonomous of each other as in Canada, moving freely between them might be seriously impeded. In unitary systems as well, the relations between the national and the local level are contingent, leading to the interlocking of the levels in terms of political careers as in France, or to a separation as in Britain.

The *role of the national legislature* is a matter of obvious concern to any would-be politician, as the attractiveness of serving—in terms of prestige as well as of practical impact—cannot be estimated without reference to the legislature as a whole. How strong (and how autonomous) is it *vis-à-vis* the executive? What is its policy influence? Is Parliament the principal site of law-making or are bills normally formulated in the bureaucracy? Is the legislature in charge of patronage jobs? As is made clear by these questions, legislators also have to take some interest in the legislature as an institution—a point to which we will return later. It should also be clear that depending on how these questions are answered, a politician might opt for a career outside the national legislature, or might regard the national Parliament as but a stepping-stone to other career goals.

The *internal structure of the legislature* will necessarily influence the choices any prospective candidate will make and be the focus of the reform efforts of legislators, as it is this factor which determines their daily life and their career options. The number of elected chambers (one or two) and the number of seats determine the chances of becoming a legislator and of having the option to move upward within Parliament. Rules and procedures structure the role of parliamentary parties, committees, and individual legislators. It is the distribution of power and influence among these three levels that to a large extent delimits the available role models of legislators. Further-more, the resources the legislature and individual legislators have at their disposal differ greatly in various countries and thereby also structure the passable routes of action.

The *electoral system* determines how one gets in and remains there. In a "first-past-the-post" electoral system with candidate selection taken away from parties as in the United States, the electoral point of reference is the constituency and hardly anybody else—besides the political action committees providing campaign finance. If candidate selection within the same electoral system is controlled by local parties, this point of reference shifts quite strongly to the local party. As a result we will find a comparatively strong involvement of potential political professionals in party politics. In proportional representation systems nomination and renomination—which in many instances virtually guarantee reelection—are handled by national or state parties which necessarily changes the allegiances of legislators.[10]

Parties and interest groups are the other major political players outside the official state system. Their role, their historical successes in hijacking parts of the state, may provide alternative career paths for political hopefuls. Also, they may offer fallback

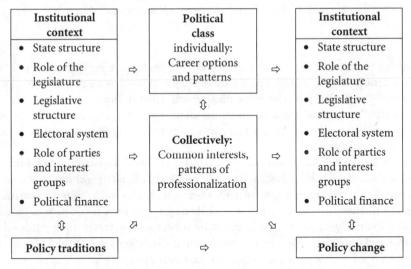

Figure 1.2 *The political class as an independent and a dependent variable: an integrated model*

---

[10] In Germany, for example, local and sub-state party organizations are relatively influential, because the former nominate the district candidates—normally a prerequisite for getting on the state list of a party—whereas the latter usually agree on quotas for intra-state regions before the state convention in order to avoid open conflict. Hence, controlling that level of intra-party decision-making becomes paramount to reelection.

	Entrepreneur	Backbencher
State structure	Federal	Unitary
Role of legislature	Strong	Weak
Legisl. structure	Two chambers	One chamber
	Strong committees, weak parties	Strong parties, weak committees
	Individual legislators influential	Individual legislators influential
Electoral system	First-past-the-post	Proportional Representation
Role of parties/ interest groups	Weak parties, fragmented interest groups	Strong parties, centralized interest groups
Political finance	Campaign finance, essential, mostly non-state provided	Campaign finance appendix of party finance

Figure 1.3 *Prototypes of legislators and institutional context*

positions if an incumbent is not reelected or chooses to leave parliamentary politics. Retirement is made much easier once there is a job at hand as a well-paid lobbyist or an equally well-paid job within the party reach. Historically, parties have come to dominate the field of political organizations except for the United States and Switzerland where interest groups still play an important role in political recruitment and political finance.

Questions of *political finance* center around party and campaign finance, through the specific constellation of which access to political campaigns is either restricted or opened up. The most important questions here concern the availability of state funding, the treatment of incumbents and challengers, and the dependence on parties and/or interest groups. A special question concerns the intertwining of political finance and politicians' income: in some countries, legislators are "strongly expected" to give a fixed part of their salary back to their parties.

These six elements provide the basic institutional context for the political class, and at the same time are the possible objects of reform efforts that seek to alter the rules in the collective interest of that class (see Fig. 1.2). The following country chapters focus on the relations displayed in the left-hand part of the figure—with the political class being the dependent variable—whereas institutional change can only be hinted at, but not really analyzed in the confines of this volume. The same is true for the link to policy-making that also is alluded to in the figure.

As a context providing both selective incentives and imposing restrictions, these elements produce systematically different types of professional politicians (see Fig. 1.3). We might call the prototypes at the two ends of the spectrum the "entrepreneur" (or professional legislator) and the "backbencher" (or professional party politician). While the former largely constructs his career on his own, the latter is provided with a career by a party. It should not come as a surprise that the resulting behavior can be expected to be vastly different. Thus we can expect that there is an interdependent relationship between the structural properties of a democratic system and the course of action pursued by political practitioners.

The "entrepreneur" needs a corridor for independent action in order to distinguish himself in front of his constituency. Thus, a political class composed of entrepreneurs has to "agree to disagree": individuals have to portray themselves as being in opposition to one another and to the institution at large, but this interest is beyond contention. A political class of "backbenchers," on the contrary, shares a consensus in emphasizing inter-party difference and intraparty coherence. Individual distinction is a burden rather than an asset, as it may cause internal opposition. The impact for institutional reform should be clear: entrepreneurs need a much more decentralized institutional context for furthering their careers than backbenchers for whom fragmentation carries the considerable risk that the front-bench might no longer be able to deliver the prerequisites for a safe and sustained career.

Hence, prototypes of professional politicians and the institutional contexts which facilitate their emergence tend to reinforce each other. Usually, it takes major political and/or social upheaval to overthrow structures as deeply embedded as these. That is, major changes from one pattern to the other could only be expected when there is strong exogenous pressure on the political class that translate into a reform of central features of the institutional order. Otherwise, political reforms only tend to deepen existing institutional arrangements and to further sharpen the profile of a particular type of politician, because the reform process is largely controlled by members of the legislature. Reforms in this case largely are the result of a clash between the *opportunity structure* provided by the political system and the *career interests* of individual politicians (also cf. Berkman, De Boef, and Poggione 1995: 27–8). This self-referentiality is further reinforced by the relatively low salience of many reform issues that are very important to politicians but normally rather obscure to the public at large.

As the "entrepreneur" and the "backbencher" are prototypes, they are hard to find in the real world. As the present volume shows, most countries fall in between these two extremes. Yet American politicians come very close indeed to the "entrepreneurial" type, while, for example, the Dutch or Swedish member of the political class fulfills most, though not all criteria for the "backbencher" model. So if we are to reformulate Sombart's question in asking "why are there no backbenchers in the United States?," the answer this time around is fairly straightforward: because the current institutional setting does not allow for backbenchers—faithful party soldiers would spell electoral disaster here.

STUDYING THE POLITICAL CLASS IN A COMPARATIVE FRAMEWORK: POSITIONS, CAREER PATHS, SOURCES OF INCOME, AND POLITICAL INSULATION

Class Boundaries: Who is a Member of the Political Class?

But how are we to determine who belongs to the political class and who does not? Using the concept empirically would have to be based on a working definition that effectively delimits the members of the political class from non-members. This inevitably will be a matter of contention. The clearer cases are members of the national legislature, elected officials and political appointees in the executive branch, professional party officials at the federal, state, and local levels, many though not all state legislators, cabinet members of state governments, full-time assistants of legislators and parliamentary parties. At the local level one would have to include big-city mayors, city managers, and sometimes also other council members and officials, the decisive criteria being the income derived from that position and the degree of its politicization.

The tougher choices come with the judiciary. If Supreme Court judges are politically selected as in the United States and in Germany, they should be considered part of the political class there, but not necessarily in other cases. The election of judges, district attorneys and the like at all levels of government in the United States poses a serious problem of drawing the line, especially since many of these offices are proven stepping-stones for a further political career. In the European party democracies the greatest problem arises because of the parties' colonialization of so much territory within state and society: the managers and members of the board of public enterprises are in effect political appointees as are the directors of public broadcasting systems, the heads of many foundations, the lay heads of churches, the directors of private charities, and others.

Drawing the line between the political class and other professions and thus also determining the approximate size of the political class in different democratic political systems is itself an important goal of research in the field. Here a collaborative effort with country specialists applying a common analytical framework as in this volume is most appropriate. This way we get to know more not only about the size and the specific composition of national political classes, but also about the interlocking of different positions typical for each country and time (see below).

Recruitment and Career Paths: How to Get in and Where to Go from there

The question of social background has long been a focus of attention of elite research.[11] It is only recently, however, that researchers have turned to the points of entry to professional politics, to questions of political recruitment (Gallagher and Marsh 1988;

---

[11] Recently, this topic has been gained in prominence because it was linked to the adequate representation of women and ethnic minorities (cf. among many studies Swain 1993; Thomas 1994; Phillips 1995; Young 1997; Williams 1998; Canon 1999).

Fowler 1993; Norris and Lovenduski 1995). What do professional politicians do before they turn pro and who selects them for their new career? Is there a pre-professional field like local politics or party youth organizations in which newcomers typically learn the skills needed to enter the professional field? Also one would contrast a pattern of candidate self-selection like the one prevailing in the United States with one of co-optation that is more dominant in party democracies. In the latter case the group of selectors becomes an important subject in its own right. At what level and by whom are prospective candidates for professionalized political offices screened and selected (cf. Norris 1997)?

Analysis of the selection (and the re-election) process should also enable us to say more about political representation. Where could possible challenges to a politician's career come from? In what ways is the relation between the voters and the office-holders a mediated one in which selectors pose the real danger? Who could positively terminate a politician's career and who could not? Which structures of dependence are typically created in a given political system? The answers to these questions, I think, could help us to find out more about the systematic differences and similarities between institutional orders.

In most established democracies the career from the entry to the first professional office on to other tasks follows certain fixed patterns. That is, public and party offices are not randomly sought but fall into a rather clear, nationally and historically specific hierarchy. Politicians, on the other hand—unless their ambition is non-existent or static (they just want to remain where they are)—are striving for even higher office. What is considered higher, however, is highly contingent. There is not necessarily an order of things that privileges the national over the state or regional level, and the latter over the local one. In some countries a move from national legislator to the state executive or even the regional legislature or to big-city mayor is considered a rational upward move,[12] whereas in others such a move would be regarded as an inconceivable degradation. About phenomena surrounding the patterning of careers we know very little yet (cf. Schlesinger 1966, 1991; Prinz 1993; Francis and Kenny 2000)—and even less in terms of transnational comparison.

Much the same is true for the cumulation of political offices. Depending on the institutional structures of the political system, politicians engage in horizontal and/or vertical cumulation of offices. Horizontally, they combine legislative mandates with party functions at the same level—or with executive positions where that is not precluded by incompatibility rules. Vertically, positions at the national, regional, and local level are held simultaneously. The rationale usually is the same for all these forms of cumulation: the political career is safeguarded against possible challengers, and personal links with influential selectors are maintained. It would be more than worthwhile, however, to track down these specific patterns and relate them to the institutional features of the respective system. The cumulation of offices and positions also depends on the interdependence between different political and semi-political institutions which in party democracies is concurrent with the degree

---

[12] For the importance of the regional level cf. Stolz (2001).

to which parties have successfully colonialized state and society and hence are able to distribute positions outside their original domain.

Income: How to Live off Politics

Income is an obvious incentive for most professions. Few people are willing to lose money by being a professional politician—which does not preclude fictitious "losses" by comparison to positions one might have held theoretically. Thus, material rewards include not only the legislative salary—which is conspicuously absent from most legislative studies although this, of course, is one rather important element of the institutional incentives to become and remain a professional politician.[13] Also the chances for extra income, the pensions provided, non-monetary benefits, beneficial side-effects on a civil profession, or the prospect of obtaining a much better paid position in the private sector after ending the political career have to be taken into account. The income provided at different points on the career path clearly influences career-planning: if state or regional legislatures provide an income that is close to what one could make in the national legislature, but offer more chances for internal career advancement, more people will be likely to consider a long-term career within the state legislature (Squire 1993; Bell 1994).

In most cases, legislators are in the enviable position of being able to regulate their own income—or at least the mechanism by which it is raised. How this is done is another point that merits attention. Is there a recourse to rather technical formulas, are raises decided upon rather quietly, or is there a big public debate surrounding each attempt to increase the incomes derived from politics?

Analytically, politicians' income also is relevant, because it is an important indicator of professionalization. However, there is no historically comparative analysis yet of legislative salaries. Moreover, numbers on salary development often are only of limited use, as they are not controlled for inflation, thus giving a distorted image. The best overviews on legislative salaries have been provided by Beyme (1993: 141–6, 1999: 193) and by Hood and Peters (1994). On that base we may distinguish parliaments (but not politicians, since they may well have other sources of income) according to their level of professionalization.

CLASS ACTION: THE POLITICAL CLASS AND INSTITUTIONAL REFORM

Scandals, Corruption, and Political Alienation: Mistrust in Professional Politicians

While politician-bashing is a very fashionable business in most western democracies these days, the crisis of confidence in politicians is real and it should not be

---

[13] In the 1990s, however, some scholars have looked at "avarice" (Hall and Houweling 1995) and the "rewards at the top" (Hood and Peters 1994).

attributed solely to voters demanding too much of their representatives (cf. Craig 1993, 1996; Kaase and Newton 1995; Mény 1998; Norris 1999; Pharr and Putnam 2000). The reasons for political discontent vary a great deal. Generally, they include an increasing sensitivity towards scandals—centering around issues of morality— and cases of political corruption that focus on improper material rewards (della Porta and Vannucci 1999; Thompson 2000; Heidenheimer and Johnston 2002). That is remarkable because there is no reason other than historical romanticism to assume that politicians "used to be better" in the old days (cf. Polsby 1968: 167–8 for some illustrations to the contrary with regard to the United States).

On the other hand, there is a clear tendency on the side of the media in many countries to "scandalize" politics, to emphasize personal shortcomings at the expense of covering policy differences. This tendency is further reinforced when candidates for political office themselves downplay differences in substance and instead raise the "character issue" as is common in American politics these days. There more incumbents fall victim to this depoliticized way of campaigning than to ideological challenges. The question is whether this is an American peculiarity or a rather uniform trend.

Another related reason for political alienation is professional politics itself. Professional politicians are increasingly perceived for what they indeed are: a clearly delineated group with common interests and a privileged position to further their common good. The reason for the process of delegitimation, however, is not that analysis in itself, but rather the comparison with a rather abstract ideal of direct democracy and self-rule in which the public sphere should be removed from professionalism. The result is a much greater vulnerability of politicians (King 1997). Again, the criticism of professionalism varies considerably and thus is an interesting topic for cross-national comparison.

The Dual Quest for Reform: Self-Interest and External Pressure

The prominence of scandals and political corruption as well as the general skepticism toward political professionals have led to a new wave of debates on institutional reform in most western democracies. Clearly, institutional reform is a central topic for any discussion of the political class. Due to the conjunctures of political research, however, this has recently not been paid as much attention as it used to—at least in the United States—shortly after the Congressional reform era of the 1970s.[14] Thus, the impact of individual ambition and career interests on institutional structure is still an under-researched subject (Matthews 1985: 42; Fowler 1993: 153–78).

Yet again a look back in history cautions against an overdose of institutional determinism. Otherwise institutional change would be incomprehensible. The change in the predominant career patterns and the subsequent institutional reforms in the

---

[14] There has been, however, one particularly noteworthy attempt to systematically link individual representatives' interests and legislative reform. Peters, Copeland, and Mott (Peters *et al.* 1994; Copeland *et al.* 1994) have not only defined legislative reform in a very careful and concise way, they also take an empirical look at the impact of turnover on such reforms. Important conceptual contributions to the older debate on legislative reform were, above all, Davidson and Oleszek (1976) and Dodd (1977).

United States during the 1910s are a case in point (cf. Swenson 1982 and Chapter 21, this volume). It was only when more and more legislators—mostly independent-minded politicians from the West who had been elected in primaries—were seeking a durable career *within* Congress that they changed the system in a very dramatic way during the legislative revolt of 1910/11 and its aftermath. This raises a fundamental question: when are reforms with as much impact as this one likely to occur? In other words: when do politicians leave the beaten track of institutional politics as usual and opt for radical change?

It seems quite logical to assume that they do so once their individual career interests unite in a collective interest as a political class that transcends internal divisions of party or region. It is only with professionalization—and with the ensuing emergence of a political class—that transcending the divisions of party and region becomes conceivable. For example, German legislators for a long time remained wedded to their respective political milieu (social democratic, catholic, liberal, conservative) to an extent that effectively precluded any cross-party alliance to further the collective self-interest which was one reason for the political weakness of the German *Reichstag* (Best 1989). On the other hand, Lijphart (1968: 103–38) has shown how the parties representing the Dutch pillars of socialism, catholicism, liberalism, and protestantism reached a compromise in 1917. That compromise characteristically reconciled both the policy goals and the career interests of those involved.

Peters, Copeland, and Mott (1994: 2) define "reform" as change that is characterized by intentionality, reaction (to some perceived grievance), and value (underlying the judgment and the intended direction of change). Hence reform efforts related to the collective interest of the political class are most often reactions to institutional obstacles in maintaining or advancing political careers. As already indicated, in rarer occasions they might also be reactions to external pressures on the institution at large that is threatened with delegitimation or loss of power. Here Dodd's (1994) suggestion to regard institutional development as a process of collective learning could be very helpful. He distinguishes between "short-term cycles of political adjustment and reform" and "metacrises of the collective epistemology" that can only be resolved by way of very basic changes in that collective understanding of politics and society (Dodd 1994: 336–7). The former would allow for institutional reforms in the collective self-interest of the actors involved—the political class—whereas in the latter case crises are too large to be contained within an autonomous group (e.g. during the ongoing crisis of Italian political institutions). Thus, exogenous pressure under these extraordinary conditions is able to neutralize or even overcome the self-interest of professional political actors. Yet, historically the reforms triggered by this latter motivation have tended to be far less successful than those driven by—or at least translatable into—immediate self-interest.

What are the possible bases for the judgment of legislators that reform is needed? In general, deficiencies are diagnosed with reference to one or more of four institutionalized relations:

- between the electorate and the elected,
- between the legislators and the legislature,

- between the parties and the state,
- between the center and the periphery (state and/or local level).

It is to these relations that the three fundamental interests of the political class as a collective actor are applied. While income is a point in itself, the interest in career maintenance suggests keeping a close eye on those actors that might be a danger to this interest: the voters, the selectorate, parties, and, last not least, possible challengers. Politicians have to have a chance to please voters and the selectorate; they need either a party that secures their re-election or that leaves them enough leeway to do that on their own; and they want to deter potential challengers. In these points interests tend to converge across party lines. There is a "cartel of (and for) incumbents" that can be observed very clearly, for example, when there is a need for legislative redistricting. Also, the politics of career maintenance has to be concerned with the politics of legitimation—it has to address others outside the legislature. This refers to the problems of political accountability and of maintaining a certain level of trust (cf. Przeworski, Stokes, and Manin 1999; Warren 1999). In contrast, the politics of career advancement is largely an internal affair of the political class and refers to institutional changes that offer the chance of climbing up the ladder. The 1979 introduction of select committees in the British House of Commons is a case in point. Before, the only possible pathway up was to wait for one's chance to join the cabinet. With the select committees a new avenue for legislators' activities and career hopes was established (Judge 1981; Jogerst 1993). Overall, the endogenous causes for institutional reform clearly are an issue that warrants further research.

THE OUTLINE OF COUNTRY CHAPTERS

From the beginning, the conception of this volume was that of a handbook. That implied two requirements for (*a*) the selection of countries covered and (*b*) the structure of chapters. As to the selection, we wanted to cover all of the more important advanced industrial democracies. Unfortunately, neither the ambiguous category of "importance" nor the notion of advanced industrial democracies offer any clear-cut advice on which countries to include and which to ignore. For this volume we tried to include all advanced industrial countries having had a democratic system of government for at least 20 years and having a population of a million or more.

However, two countries that do fulfill these criteria—Austria and Greece—have not been included for very pragmatic reasons. Coordinating a book like this brings all kinds of difficulties the most severe of which is to get the chapters within a certain time-span that does not render the rest of the book outdated by the time the last contributions arrive. In that dilemma we have decided to leave out those two countries for now.

The individual chapters follow a common format in order to give users a chance to read this book comparatively. This does not mean, however, that the peculiarities of countries are disregarded. Quite the contrary, which also implies a different emphasis on particular aspects of professional politics in individual chapters. It is thus that the varieties of professionalism in advanced democracies emerge. The hope associated with this volume is that it would induce many to conduct their own comparative research using this book as a point of inspiration and departure.

REFERENCES

Bell, Francis X. (1994). "Has the Primary Springboard Stopped Springing? The Effects of Legislative Professionalism in the American States on Political Career Decisions", unpublished manuscript, presented at the Annual Meeting of the APSA, New York.

Berkman, Michael, De Boef, Suzanna, and Poggione, Sarah (1995). "Legislative Modernization in Comparative Perspective: Economic Change, Political Ambition, and American State Legislatures", unpublished manuscript, presented at the Annual Meeting of the APSA, Chicago.

Best, Heinrich (1989). "Mandat ohne Macht: Strukturprobleme des deutschen Parlamentarismus 1867–1933", in H. Best (ed.), *Politik und Milieu*. St. Katharinen: Scripta Mercaturae, pp. 175–222.

—— and Cotta, Maurizio (eds) (2000). *Parliamentary Representatives in Europe 1848–2000*. Oxford: Oxford University Press.

Beyme, Klaus von (1993). *Die politische Klasse im Parteienstaat*. Frankfort: Suhrkamp.

—— (1996). "The Concept of Political Class: A New Dimension of Research on Elites?" *West European Politics*, 19: 68–87.

—— (1999). *Die parlamentarische Demokratie*, 3rd edition. Opladen: Westdeutscher Verlag.

Borchert, Jens (1997). "Pathways to Political Professionalism: Institutional Context and the Emergence of a Political Class in the U.S. and Germany", unpublished manuscript, presented at the Annual Meeting of the APSA, Washington, D.C.

—— (2001). "Max Weber's Political Sociology and the Professionalization of Politics", unpublished manuscript, presented at the Annual Meeting of the APSA, San Francisco.

—— (2003). *Die Professionalisierung der Politik*. Frankfort: Campus.

—— and Golsch, Lutz (1995). "Die politische Klasse in westlichen Demokratien: Rekrutierung, Karriereinteressen und institutioneller Wandel". *Politische Vierteljahresschrift*, 35: 609–29.

Burdeau, Georges (1975). "Die politische Klasse", in W. Röhrich (ed.), *Demokratische Elitenherrschaft*. Darmstadt: Wissenschaftliche Buchgesellschaft, pp. 251–68.

Canon, David T. (1999). *Race, Redistricting, and Representation*. Chicago: University of Chicago Press.

Cooper, Joseph, and Brady, David (1981). "Toward a Diachronic Analysis of Congress". *American Political Science Review*, 75: 988–1006.

Copeland, Gary, Mott, Jonathan, and Peters, Ronald (1994). "Turnover and Reform in the U.S. House: An Empirical Assessment, 1899–1992", unpublished manuscript, presented at the Meeting of the Western Political Science Association, Albuquerque; NM.

Cotta, Maurizio (1979). *Classe Politica e Parlamento in Italia 1946–1976*. Bologna: Il Mulino.

—— (1982). "The Italian Political Class in the Twentieth Century: Continuities and Discontinuities", in M. Czudnowski (ed.), *Does Who Governs Matter?* DeKalb, IL: Northern Illinois University Press, pp. 154–87.

Craig, Stephen C. (1993). *The Malevolent Leaders*. Boulder: Westview.

—— (ed.) (1996). *Broken Contract*. Boulder: Westview.

Dahrendorf, Ralf (1965). *Gesellschaft und Demokratie in Deutschland.* Munich: Piper.

Davidson, Roger H., and Oleszek, Walter J. (1976). "Adaptation and Consolidation: Structural Innovation in the House of Representatives". *Legislative Studies Quarterly,* 1: 37–66.

della Porta, Donatella, and Vannucci, Alberto (1999). *Corrupt Exchanges: Actors, Resources, and Mechanisms of Political Corruption.* New York: Aldine de Gruyter.

Dodd, Lawrence C. (1977). "Congress and the Quest for Power", in L. Dodd and B. Oppenheimer (eds), *Congress Reconsidered.* New York: Praeger, pp. 269–307.

—— (1981). "Congress, the Constitution and the Crisis of Legitimation", in L. Dodd and B. Oppenheimer (eds), *Congress Reconsidered,* 2nd edition. Washington, DC: CQ Press, pp. 390–420.

—— (1994). "Political Learning and Political Change: Understanding Development Across Time", in L. Dodd and C. Jillson (eds), *The Dynamics of American Politics.* Boulder: Westview, pp. 331–64.

Ehrenhalt, Alan (1991). *The United States of Ambition: Politicians, Power, and the Pursuit of Office.* New York: Times Books.

Eliassen, Kjell A., and Pedersen, Mogens N. (1978). "Professionalization of Legislatures". *Comparative Studies in Society and History,* 20: 286–318.

Farneti, Paolo (1972). "Problemi di Ricerca e di Analisi della Clase Politica Italiana". *Rassegna Italiana di Sociologia,* 13: 79–116.

Fenno, Richard F. (1978). *Home Style: House Members in their Districts.* Boston: Little, Brown.

Fowler, Linda L. (1993). *Candidates, Congress, and the American Democracy.* Ann Arbor: University of Michigan Press.

—— (1994). "Theories of Recruitment in Comparative Perspective", unpublished manuscript, presented at the Meeting of the International Political Science Association, Berlin.

—— and McClure, Robert D. (1989). *Political Ambition.* New Haven: Yale University Press.

Francis, Wayne L., and Kenny, Lawrence W. (2000). *Up the Political Ladder: Career Paths in U.S. Politics.* Thousand Oaks, CA: Sage.

Gallagher, Michael, and Marsh, Michael (eds) (1988). *Candidate Selection in Comparative Perspective.* London: Sage.

Graham, James Q. (1982). "Legislative Careers in the French Chamber and U.S. House, 1871–1940". *Legislative Studies Quarterly,* 7: 37–56.

Greven, Michael Th. (1992). "Die Parteien in der politischen Gesellschaft sowie eine Einleitung zur Diskussion über eine 'allgemeine Parteientheorie'", in O. Niedermayer and R. Stöss (eds), *Stand und Perspektiven der Parteienforschung in Deutschland.* Opladen: Westdeutscher Verlag, pp. 276–92.

Hall, Richard, and Houweling, Robert Van (1995). "Avarice and Ambition in Congress". *American Political Science Review,* 89: 121–36.

Heidenheimer, Arnold J., and Johnston, Michael (eds) (2002). *Political Corruption,* 3rd edition. New Brunswick: Transaction.

Herzog, Dietrich (1975). *Politische Karrieren.* Opladen: Westdeutscher Verlag.

—— (1992). "Zur Funktion der Politischen Klasse in der sozialstaatlichen Demokratie der Gegenwart", in T. Leif, H.-J. Legrand, and A. Klein (eds), *Die politische Klasse in Deutschland.* Bonn: Bouvier, pp. 126–49.

—— (1993). "Politik als Beruf: Max Webers Einsichten und die Bedingungen der Gegenwart", in H.-D. Klingemann and W. Luthardt (eds), *Wohlfahrtsstaat, Sozialstruktur und Verfassungsanalyse.* Opladen: Westdeutscher Verlag, pp. 107–26.

Hibbing, John R. (1991). *Congressional Careers: Contours of Life in the U.S. House of Representatives.* Chapel Hill: University of North Carolina Press.

Hibbing, John R. (1999). "Legislative Careers: Why and How We Should Study Them". *Legislative Studies Quarterly*, 24: 149–71.

Hood, Christopher, and Peters, B. Guy (eds) (1994). *Rewards at the Top*. London: Sage.

Jogerst, Michael (1993). *Reform in the House of Commons: The Select Committee System*. Lexington: University Press of Kentucky.

Judge, David (1981). *Backbench Specialisation in the House of Commons*. London: Heinemann.

Kaase, Max, and Newton, Kenneth (1995). *Beliefs in Government*. Oxford: Oxford University Press.

Katz, Richard S., and Mair, Peter (1995). "Changing Models of Party Organization and Party Democracy: The Emergence of the Cartel Party". *Party Politics*, 1: 5–28.

Katznelson, Ira (1986). "Working-Class Formation: Constructing Cases and Comparisons", in I. Katznelson and A. Zolberg (eds), *Working-Class Formation*. Princeton: Princeton University Press, pp. 3–41.

King, Anthony (1997). *Running Scared*. New York: Free Press.

Lijphart, Arend (1968). *The Politics of Accommodation: Pluralism and Democracy in the Netherlands*. Berkeley: University of California Press.

Loomis, Burdett A. (1988). *The New American Politician*. New York: Basic Books.

Mastropaolo, Alfio (1984). *Saggio sul Professionismo Politico*. Milan: Franco Angeli.

Matthews, Donald R. (1985). "Legislative Recruitment and Legislative Careers", in G. Loewenberg, S. Patterson, and M. Jewell (eds), *Handbook of Legislative Research*. Cambridge, MA: Harvard University Press, pp. 17–56.

Mayhew, David (1974). *Congress: The Electoral Connection*. New Haven, CT: Yale University Press.

Mény, Yves (1998). "The People, the Elites, and the Populist Challenge", in M. Greven (ed.), *Demokratie—eine Kultur des Westens?*, Opladen: Leske + Budrich, pp. 289–303.

Mosca, Gaetano (1939). *The Ruling Class*. New York: McGraw-Hill.

Norris, Pippa (1993). "Through the Eye of the Needle: Comparative Legislative Recruitment in Western Democracies", unpublished manuscript, presented at the Annual Meeting of the APSA, Washington, DC.

—— (ed.) (1997). *Passages to Power: Legislative Recruitment in Advanced Democracies*. Cambridge: Cambridge University Press.

—— (ed.) (1999). *Critical Citizens: Global Support for Democratic Governance*. Oxford: Oxford University Press.

—— and Lovenduski, Joni (1995). *Political Recruitment. Gender, Race and Class in the British Parliament*. Cambridge: Cambridge University Press.

Peters, Ronald M., Copeland, Gary, and Mott, Jonathan (1994). "Turnover and Reform in the U.S. House: An Historical and Conceptual Analysis", unpublished manuscript, presented at the Meeting of the Southwestern Political Science Association, San Antonio, TX.

Pharr, Susan J., and Putnam, Robert D. (eds) (2000). *Disaffected Democracies*. Princeton: Princeton University Press.

Phillips, Anne (1995). *The Politics of Presence*. Oxford: Clarendon.

Polsby, Nelson W. (1968). "The Institutionalization of the U.S. House of Representatives", *American Political Science Review*, 62: 144–68.

Prinz, Timothy S. (1993). "The Career Paths of Elected Politicians", in S. Williams and E. Lascher (eds), *Ambition and Beyond*. Berkeley: Institute of Governmental Studies, pp. 11–63.

Przeworski, Adam, Stokes, Susan C., and Manin, Bernard (eds) (1999). *Democracy, Accountability, and Representation*. Cambridge: Cambridge University Press.

Putnam, Robert D. (1976). *The Comparative Study of Political Elites*. Englewood Cliffs, NJ: Prentice-Hall.

Sartori, Giovanni (1963). "Dove Va il Parlamento?", in G. Sartori (ed.), *Il Parlamento Italiano 1946–63*. Naples: Edizioni Scientifiche Italiane, 279–386.

Schlesinger, Joseph A. (1966). *Ambition and Politics*. Chicago: Rand McNally.

—— (1991). *Political Parties and the Winning of Office*. Ann Arbor: University of Michigan Press.

Shefter, Martin (1994). *Political Parties and the State*. Princeton: Princeton University Press.

Somit, Albert, Wildenmann, Rudolf, Boll, Bernhard, and Römmele, Andrea (eds) (1994). *The Victorious Incumbent*. Aldershot: Dartmouth.

Squire, Peverill (1993). "State Legislative Careers", in S. Williams and E. Lascher (eds), *Ambition and Beyond*. Berkeley: Institute of Governmental Studies, pp. 145–66.

Stolz, Klaus (2001). "The Political Class and Regional Institution-Building: A Conceptual Framework". *Regional and Federal Studies*, 11: 80–100.

Swain, Carol M. (1993). *Black Faces, Black Interests*. Cambridge, MA: Harvard University Press.

Swenson, Peter (1982). "The Influence of Recruitment on the Structure of Power in the U.S. House of Representatives". *Legislative Studies Quarterly*, 7: 7–36.

Thomas, Sue (1994). *How Women Legislate*. New York: Oxford University Press.

Thompson, John B. (2000). *Political Scandal*. Cambridge: Polity.

Warren, Mark E. (ed.) (1999). *Democracy and Trust*. Cambridge: Cambridge University Press.

Weber, Max. 1958 (first published 1918). "Politics as a Vocation", in H. Gerth and C. W. Mills (eds), *From Max Weber*. New York: Oxford University Press, pp. 77–128.

Williams, Melissa F. (1998). *Voice, Trust, and Memory: Marginalized Groups and the Failings of Liberal Representation*. Princeton, NJ: Princeton University Press.

Young, Iris M. (1997). "Deferring Group Representation", in I. Shapiro and W. Kymlicka (eds), *Ethnicity and Group Rights*. New York: New York University Press, 349–76.

Z'graggen, Heidi (2002). "Professionalisierung von Parlamenten im internationalen Vergleich", unpublished manuscript, Bern.

2

Australia: Party Politicians as a Political Class

IAN MCALLISTER

Perhaps more than in any of the other established democracies, professional politics in Australia is linked to political parties. The hallmark of Australian politics is the predominance of the political party: the vast majority of voters identify with and vote for one of the major political parties; gaining state or federal election to the lower house is next to impossible without the benefit of one of three party labels—Liberal, National, or Labor; and minor parties or independents have played little part in shaping the development of the party system. Within the legislature, party government operates in every sense of the word, with the enforcement of rigid discipline among elected representatives. Not least, the party political elites have been highly effective in adapting political rules and institutions to serve their collective interest. Placed against this backdrop, it is perhaps hardly surprising that the political class in Australia—the elected representatives in the federal, state, and territory parliaments—has roots which are firmly within the major political parties.

Strong party control of the political system has its origins in the country's political culture, and this also serves to reinforce both support for and the role of the political class. Louis Hartz (1964) has argued that the cultural development of Anglo-American colonial societies is determined by the values and beliefs that were dominant during the period in which they "split" from the host society, Britain. Since Australia split from Britain in the nineteenth century, the colonial "fragment" that emerged was imbued with the utilitarian ideas of Jeremy Bentham and his followers. As a result, Australian political culture has been avowedly utilitarian in its orientation, and utilitarian values have infused all aspects of the political system and its institutions (Collins 1985; Hancock 1930).

The expression of utilitarianism in politics has been seen as "the reliance on an instrumental view of the political process" (Hughes 1973: 142), so that the state exists primarily in order to resolve problems and disputes, not to preserve individual liberty. In Hancock's (1930: 69) famous words, "Australian democracy has come to look upon the state as a vast public utility, whose duty it is to provide the greatest happiness for the greatest number." Examples include the extensive use of the law to regulate society and ensure proper social conduct, from industrial relations to minor aspects of individual behavior, to the system of compulsory voting.[1] Within this context, it is seen as entirely logical for the public to support a political class, which provides a link between government and public policy on the one hand, and the political parties on the other.

This chapter examines the origins, extent, and development of the political class in Australia, with particular emphasis on the strong party–political dimension. The group of professional politicians that are the subject of the chapter are defined as those who have gained election to national office in the federal Parliament, or election to one of the six state or two territory assemblies. While this definition covers a large number of people—just over 800, at the present time—in practice much of the chapter is concerned with the group of national representatives, who currently number 224. Any in-depth examination of the state and territory political systems would require considerably more space than is available here, because of their diversity, complexity, and very different histories.

POLITICAL PROFESSIONALIZATION IN HISTORICAL PERSPECTIVE

The early establishment of strong, disciplined mass political parties in Australia resulted in a range of democratic innovations, leading contemporary commentators to regard Australia as a "democratic laboratory" (Aitkin and Castles 1989). Throughout the 1850s, many political reforms were introduced in the colonies[2] which were far ahead of those of any other country in the world. By 1859 all but two of the colonies had introduced universal manhood suffrage. This compares with 1870 for its introduction in the United States, 1879 in New Zealand, and 1884 in Britain.[3] New Zealand led the world in granting votes to women (1893) with most of the Australian colonies following shortly after. Once again, the United States (1920) and Britain (1928) lagged behind their Australian counterpart.

From the perspective of establishing a professional political class, the principle of payment for elected representatives was also established early in Australia—in 1870 in Victoria, with most of the remaining having followed by 1890. By contrast, payment for Members of Parliament was not introduced in Britain until 1911, with the effect that Members either had to have substantial personal wealth or had to rely on extra-parliamentary organizations, such as the trade unions, for financial support (Goot 1985). The payment of elected representatives in Australia had the consequence of

---

[1] Australia is one of the few democratic countries in the world to force citizens to vote. Outside of Latin America, the only major democracies with compulsory voting are Belgium, Greece, and Australia. The Netherlands abolished it in 1971.

[2] The colonies were the administrative and political units that existed prior to federation in 1901, when the modern Australian political system was established. The colonies were effectively self-governing in respect to their internal affairs, with Britain assuming responsibility for such matters as defense, trade, and foreign relations.

[3] In Britain, the franchise was extended in 1884 to working men, but it was not properly universal until 1918, almost 60 years after its introduction in Australia.

making them more independent as well as more egalitarian, but it also ensured strong party control of legislative recruitment, a pattern which has continued to the present day. It was the payment of members, along with the other democratic innovations introduced in the late nineteenth century, which led James Bryce (1921: 181) to comment that Australia "has traveled farthest and fastest along the road which leads to the unlimited rule of the multitude".

Although the payment of elected Members was introduced at an early stage, by international standards, the Australian Parliament has comparatively few sitting days. In 2002, for example, the House of Representatives sat for eighty-six days and the Senate for eighty-four days. The average, however, is usually lower: in 1995, the House of Representatives sat for seventy days. This compares with about double the sitting days for the British and Canadian Houses of Commons, respectively. Nor has there been any significant change in the number of sitting days during the course of the century, with the exception of the period during the Second World War, when Parliament sat less frequently. The greater pressure of work in the postwar years has been accommodated by increasing the length of sittings. In the first decade of the century, the average sitting day was about 7.5 h; in the 1950s just over 9 h; and between 1990 and 1996 about 10.5 h (Barlin 1997: appendix 16). This "deliberation deficit", as it is sometimes called, is clearly illustrated by the relative absence of parliamentary scrutiny over legislation. In 1995 an average of 2.5 bills per day were scrutinized by the House of Representatives, compared to well below 0.4 bills per day in Britain and Canada (Uhr 1998: 239). There is no constitutional requirement for a minimum sitting period; the constitution simply requires that Parliament must arrange for a sitting "once at least in every year". Members themselves have argued against any increase in sitting days; their view is that they need to spend time in their electorates, and in many cases that requires travelling considerable distances.

Detailed legislative scrutiny and deliberation takes place through a series of committees. In the Parliament elected in November 2001, there are eleven joint committees, combining members from both houses; eight are administered by the House of Representatives and three by the Senate. In addition, the House of Representatives has eighteen standing committees and the Senate thirteen standing committees and two select committees, covering a wide range of topics. Traditionally, committees have been chaired by a member of the party in power, thus ensuring strong party control over their work. In 1994 this principle was abolished in the Senate, thus giving the committees more independence from the government of the day. The result has been considerably more scrutiny of government policy and decisions; one of the Senate's select committees in 2002, for example, was concerned with inquiring into events surrounding whether or not asylum seekers had threatened to throw their children overboard a boat in order to gain entry to Australia.

THE INSTITUTIONAL CONTEXT

Since the establishment of the Commonwealth in 1901, Australia has had a federal system of government, consisting of legislatures in the six states and two territories, and the federal legislature based in Canberra. Five of the six states (New South Wales, Victoria, South Australia, Western Australia, and Tasmania) have bicameral legislatures, with Queensland operating a unicameral system.[4] The two territories, the Northern Territory and the Australian Capital Territory, have both unicameral legislatures, the former established in 1980, the latter in 1989. The federal (or Commonwealth) Parliament in Canberra has a lower House of Representatives and an upper house, the Senate. The constitution requires that the lower house be "directly chosen by the people of the Commonwealth", a provision designed to exclude the indirect choice of members through an electoral college. The Senate is also directly elected.

The broad pattern of state and territory governments is that they are appointed by the State Governors and are responsible to lower houses of parliaments.[5] The powers exercised by the states are those not granted to the Commonwealth by the federal constitution. Each state has its own constitution and while there are differences in detail, the broad pattern is uniform. Except for Tasmania, the constitution of each state makes a general grant of power to make laws for the peace, welfare, and good government of the state. The powers of the Commonwealth, as set out in the constitution, are largely those of taxation, trade and commerce, defense and foreign affairs, and communications.

The electoral systems of the states and the Commonwealth vary widely, both across the states and territories and over time. In most cases, as Table 2.1 illustrates, upper house members are elected by proportional representation and lower house members by single member electorates. However, during the course of the century, the electoral systems of most states and the Commonwealth have experienced significant change. For example, in the case of the Commonwealth, the House of Representatives has seen three separate electoral systems: in the first Commonwealth election in 1901, the various electoral systems in use in the colonies were applied; between 1903 and 1918 a first-past-the-post system based on single member constituencies was adopted; and since 1918 preferential voting has been in use. In the Senate, no less than five separate systems have been used; since 1984 proportional representation with ticket preferences has prevailed. On constitutional matters referendums are obligatory. A total of forty-six referendums have been held since 1901, twenty-one of them in conjunction with federal elections. A majority of voters in a majority of states and territories must agree to any change; all but nine of the forty-five proposed changes have been rejected.

Just as important as the type of electoral system is the frequency with which elections are held. Federal elections must take place every three years for the lower and

---

[4] The appointed upper house in Queensland, the Legislative Council, voted itself out of existence in 1921.

[5] The Governor-General represents the British Crown in Australia and therefore carries out the functions of the head of the state. One of his most important competences is to appoint the government, even when, according to common law, the majority party is in charge of forming the executive. Besides, the Governor-General also decides the dissolution of the Parliament. In the states, the respective functions are carried out by the State Governors.

Table 2.1   *The electoral systems of Australian parliaments*

	Upper house members			Lower house members		
	Number	PR[a]	SME[a]	Number	PR	SME
Commonwealth	76	X		150		X
New South Wales	42	X		93		X
Victoria	44		X	88		X
Queensland	—	—	—	89		X
South Australia	22	X		47		X
Western Australia	34	X		57		X
Tasmania	19		X	35	X	
Northern Territory	—	—	—	25		X
ACT	—	—	—	17	X	
Total	237			601		

[a]PR = proportional representation; SME = single member electorates.

Source: McAllister *et al.* (1997); and updates from state and Commonwealth parliamentary libraries.

every six years for the upper house; in the states, the same rule applies, except in New South Wales where the period between elections is four years.[6] In practice, however, elections are held much more frequently. Of the twenty-two federal elections in the postwar years, seven have been conducted less than two years after the previous election. The net effect is that the average Australian voter must attend the polls around once every 12–18 months, an unprecedented level of voting among the advanced democracies.

Despite the many changes in the electoral systems at the state and federal levels, the party system has remained remarkably stable. The parties that compete for electoral support at the close of the twentieth century are very much the descendants of the parties that existed at the beginning of the century. Moreover, with the exception of some comparatively minor splits and fissures, parties outside the major Labor vs. Liberal-National division[7] have gained little electoral success. Of the forty federal elections that have been held between 1901 and 2001, only eight have produced a non-major party vote that has exceeded 10 percent of the first preference vote[8] and in only one federal election—1990—has a single minor party gained more than 10 percent of the first preference vote.[9]

---

[6] Upper house elections may be held more frequently if there is a "double dissolution" election, whereby both houses are dissolved simultaneously. This may occur if certain constitutional provisions are met.

[7] The coalition between the Liberal and National parties has remained in existence since the 1920s, except for short periods in 1973–4 and 1987. Despite the permanent nature of the arrangement, there has been little pressure for a merger; two conservative parties, one catering for urban dwellers, the other appealing to farmers living in the "bush", has suited those on the anti-Labor side of politics.

[8] Namely, 1943 (16.3%), 1958 (10.6%), 1977 (12.2%), 1990 (17.2%), 1993 (10.8%), 1996 (14.3%), 1998 (20.2%), and 2001 (19.2%).

[9] In the 1990 federal election the Australian Democrats won 11.3% of the first preference vote.

Parties therefore occupy a central role among voters, who use them to minimize their information costs at elections which, as noted above, are both complex and frequent. This is reflected in the high proportion of voters who maintain a party identification. At the same time, frequent visits to the polls ensure that their partisanship remains salient. Parties also play their role in reinforcing the system by giving "how to vote cards" to their intending voters outside polling stations; in the 2001 federal election, 50 percent said that they followed a "how to vote" card, compared to the same proportion who said that they decided based on their own preferences. Party identification is therefore the basis for party stability. As Aitkin (1982: 1) argues, "the causes of stability are to be found in the adoption, by millions of Australians then and since, of relatively unchanging feelings of loyalty to one or other of the Australian parties."

Opinion polls demonstrate that, with the exception of the late 1960s—a period of Labor decline—no more than four percentage points separated the proportions identifying with the two major parties.[10] Although the vast majority of voters identify with one or other of the major parties, there has been an increase in the number of those with no party attachment. Indeed, this group has increased threefold in size since 1987, reaching 15 percent in 2001. Party identification is not only expressed in direction but also in strength. There has been a decline in the strength of party identification. Those who see themselves as very strong identifiers have declined by almost half, from 34 percent in 1979 to 18 percent in 2001. Conversely, those who are "not very strong" partisans now make up just over one-third of all voters.

Central to maintaining the salience of the parties has been the system of compulsory voting. Writing nearly half a century ago, the eminent American observer Louise Overacker (1951) commented that "the character of the party battle and the behavior of the voters are affected by the compulsory franchise and preferential voting". Compulsory voting was seen as a logical (and uncontentious) extension of compulsory enrollment, introduced in 1911. It was first practiced in Queensland for the 1915 general election, and over the next three decades the other states and the Commonwealth followed suit. In all cases, the move to compulsion was bipartisan since it suited the parties. The effect on turnout before and after the introduction of compulsion was dramatic, as intended. In the Commonwealth, turnout increased from 58.0 percent in the last election under voluntary voting to 91.3 percent in the first election held under compulsory voting. Ordinary citizens accepted the new system with little complaint, and as a consequence the system has been easy to administer.

But the consequences of compulsory voting have extended far beyond merely increasing voter turnout. For the political parties, they have relieved them of the need to mobilize the vote, perhaps their most ubiquitous function in modern democracies.

---

[10] The 1967 and 1979 Australian National Political Attitudes surveys were conducted by Don Aitkin, the 1987–2001 Australian Election Study surveys by Clive Bean, David Gow, and Ian McAllister, and the 2001 Australian Candidate Survey by Rachel Gibson and Ian McAllister; all were funded by the *Australian Research Council*. The data are available from the *Social Science Data Archive* at the *Australian National University* (http://www.ssda.anu.edu.au).

This has reduced the parties' operating costs and freed resources so they can be devoted to voter conversion. Increasingly, conversion has been conducted through the electronic media, with more traditional forms of campaigning, such as door-to-door canvassing, becoming ever more rare as the organizational bases within the electorate have declined.[11] Compulsory voting has also had the indirect effect of making parties less concerned about the quality of their candidates, since the personal vote is small (Bean 1990) and candidates rely on party labels for election. The net effect is that the political class of elected representatives is often not drawn from the ranks of those candidates most attractive to voters.

The emphasis on voter conversion over mobilization is illustrated by the money the parties spend on election campaigning. The adoption of modern campaigning techniques in the 1980s, mainly relying on the electronic media, have seen election costs for the major parties spiral (Mills 1986). The 1983 election campaign was the first in which Labor spent more than AU$1m (€0.56 m),[12] and costs have escalated since. The 1993 election, the last for which expenditure data are available, saw some reduction in costs, reflecting the problems the parties were encountering in paying off their debts.

While the parties are not restricted in the amounts that they can spend in elections, there are stringent financial limits for individual candidates. In federal elections, funding is granted to candidates and Senate groups who have received at least 4 percent of the formal first preference vote in the previous election, and the level of funding is indexed to the consumer price index; in 2001 the subsidy stood at AU$1.62 (€0.91) per House and Senate vote. The arrangements for each of the states and territories vary considerably. In South Australia, Western Australia, and the Northern Territory there are no restrictions on funding for candidates; the remaining states and the ACT have arrangements which are similar to those of the Commonwealth.

Notions of governance and accountability in Australia have followed Westminster conventions, with the British model forming the basis for the 1901 constitution that established the federation (Butler 1973; Crisp 1983). However, a distinctive Australian approach to representation has been molded by two factors, in addition to the introduction of a federal system. The first is the size of the country. With seventeen million people in an island continent that exceeds the size of Europe, elected representatives often have to travel long distances between their electorates and the federal capital in Canberra. Even within their constituencies, the distances are often considerable: the Western Australian district of Kalgoorlie, for example, exceeds the size of France. Within these vast electorates, voters are often very remote, physically and politically, from their chosen representatives. At the same time, elected representatives often have to spend considerable time travelling between their constituency and Canberra.

---

[11] Unfortunately, we lack any concise over-time data concerning the proportions exposed in Australia to different forms of party campaigning. In 2001, only 2% of those interviewed in the Australian Election Study said that they had attended a meeting or rally conducted by an election candidate.

[12] Conversion from AU$ to Euro are based on the exchange rate of 6 November 2002 (AU$1 = €0.5601).

A second modification to the Westminster model of responsible party government is the level of discipline that the Australian parties enforce on their members. Labor was the first to achieve effective discipline at both the electoral and parliamentary levels, but the Liberals, of necessity, soon followed (Rydon 1986: 188). Dissent from the party line within the House of Representatives is almost unheard of, and the party machines have a variety of means by which they can enforce discipline among their Members, not the least of which is the threat of "deselection"—the removal of the person as the party candidate in an electorate. As Jaensch (1994: 239) puts it, "legislative voting is redundant, except on the rare 'conscience votes' or the ever rare case when a member of the Liberal or National parties has come under pressure from constituents or the local or state party base."

THE POLITICAL CLASS

Size and Composition

The size of the political class, defined as state, territory, and federal elected representatives, has grown considerably during the course of the century. The size of the federal Parliament is currently 150 Members in the lower house and seventy-six in the upper house, making a total of 226; this is more than double the figure at the start of the century (Table 2.2). A major change occurred in the House of Representatives in 1949, when the size was increased to 121. This change was based on a recommendation by a Royal Commission and was intended to ensure more equal representation; the same Royal Commission also recommended an increase in the size of the Senate, from thirty-six to sixty members. The changing population balance between states has meant that there have been more adjustments since to the size of the House

Table 2.2 *The size of the Commonwealth House of Representatives and Senate, 1901–2002*

House of Representatives		Senate	
1901	75	1901	36
1949	121	1949	60
1974	127	1975	64
1984	148	1984	76
1993	147		
1996	148		
2001	150		

Note: Dates are given when a major change in the size of the chambers took place.

[13] Each of the states is represented equally in the Senate, starting with six members each in 1901, and since 1984, twelve members each, with an additional two members from each of the two territories.

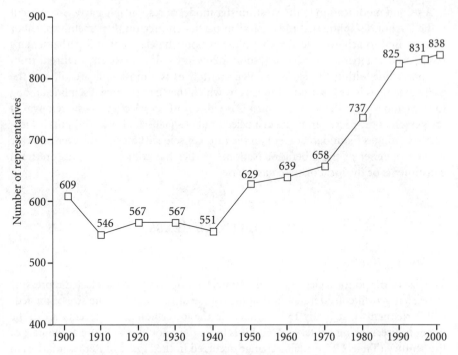

Figure 2.1 *The size of the political class in Australia, 1901–2001*

Notes: The political class is defined here as elected representatives to the federal Parliament and to state and territory Parliaments, including appointed members to upper houses.

Source: see Table 2.1.

of Representatives than that of the Senate.[13] Redistricting is based on the latest available census statistics of the population of the state or territory. It takes place every 10 years.

The size of the state and territory Parliaments has also varied widely. The smallest lower house is the Tasmanian Legislative Assembly, which currently has thirty-five members, and the largest that of New South Wales with ninety-three members, followed closely by Victoria's with eighty-eight members. The size of the upper houses has also varied considerably and is further complicated by the fact that, in the early part of the century, many upper house members were appointed rather than directly elected, with members holding their position for life. However, the size of the political class in Australia has not increased as rapidly as might have been expected (see Fig. 2.1). While it has grown by about one quarter, the population has increased more than fivefold, from 3.7 million in 1901 to 19.7 million in 2002.

Perhaps surprisingly, the number of elective offices actually decreased after federation in 1901. This was the result of many of the state Parliaments reducing their size on the creation of the Commonwealth, when some of their powers were transferred to the new federal Parliament. For example, the size of the New South Wales lower

Table 2.3 *Social characteristics of the political class, 2001*

	House of Representatives	Senate
Women (%)	25	29
Men (%)	75	71
Age group (%)		
<35	5	1
35–44	22	23
45–54	41	30
55–64	28	37
65 or more	3	9
Mean age (years)	48.3	51.9
Born overseas (%)	17	18
(N)	(150)	(76)

Note: Overseas birth excludes New Zealand and Papua New Guinea.
Source: Commonwealth Parliamentary Library.

house was reduced from 125 to 90 Members in 1904, and the Victorian lower house from ninety-five to sixty-eight members. Most of the states have gradually increased their numbers of elected representatives since; the main exceptions are South Australia, which had forty-two members in 1901 and has forty-seven at present, and Western Australia, which has grown by just seven members, from fifty to fifty-seven. This reflects the relatively small increases in the populations of the two states compared to the nation as a whole.

The social composition of the federal Parliament following the November 2001 election is shown in Table 2.3. There are comparatively few differences in social composition between the two houses, with the exception of gender, where the Senate has a slightly higher proportion of women compared to the House of Representatives. While the numbers for female representation are low, Fig. 2.2. shows that they represent a substantial increase over previous Parliaments; in 1980, for example, just two of the then 125 lower house members were women (McAllister and Studlar 1992). The rapid increase since then has been caused by pressures within the major parties to promote women as candidates for winnable seats. This has had a particularly marked impact in the Liberal Party, where the number of female MPs increased from four in 1993 to seventeen in 1996 (fifteen in 2001). The Australian Democrats, who have no lower house seats but gain representation in the Senate because of the electoral system,[14] have been the foremost promoters of women: five of the Democrats' nine Senators in 2001 were women.

Most elected representatives are in their 40s or 50s; less than one in twenty were younger than 35 in 2001, with the mean age standing at 48 for the lower house, or four years older than the mean for the electorate as a whole, and just under 52 for the

---

[14] The Senate system of single transferable vote proportional representation favors minor parties, particularly when in a "double dissolution" election all Senate seats become vacant.

McAllister

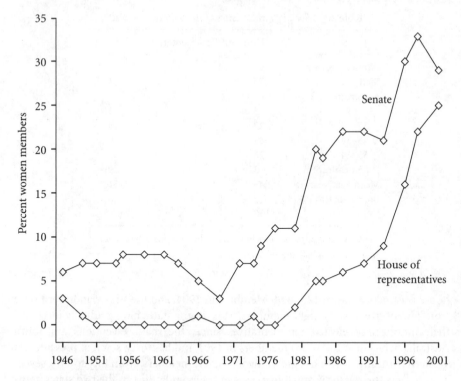

Figure 2.2   *Share of female representatives in Australia, 1946–2001*

Source: Commonwealth Parliamentary Library.

upper house. The youngest member of the lower house is a Labor representative, who was born in 1973, and the oldest a Liberal who was born in 1935. In the upper house, the oldest member was born in 1932, while the youngest member, Natasha Stott-Desjopa, was born in 1969 and leads the Australian Democrats.

   In a country where one in five of the population has been born overseas and more than half of those in a non-English speaking country, the ethnic composition of the political class assumes great importance. Traditionally, the political class has been drawn from the ranks of the Australian- or British-born, and the major political parties made little effort to recruit non-English speaking immigrant members (Jupp 1992). That changed in the early 1970s with the Whitlam Labor government's policy of multiculturalism, but it has still to make an impact on the composition of the political class: although around one in six has been born overseas, more than half of those were born in the United Kingdom or Ireland.

Political Recruitment and Political Careers

Studies of legislative recruitment consistently demonstrate that elites differ considerably from the citizens they represent on most characteristics, particularly socio-economic ones. As Table 2.3 illustrated, legislators are likely to be older than the citizens they represent, overwhelmingly male and Australian born. They are also about five times more likely to have a university degree than voters, confirming Putnam's (1976: 27) observation that a high level of formal education is the single most important characteristic for recruitment into a political elite. In Australia as elsewhere, elected representatives are disproportionately drawn from the ranks of the teaching and legal professions. Socialization into politics is also important: in the 2001 election, around one quarter of the candidates standing for the major parties had some prior family political involvement, through having a close family member who had stood for election.[15]

In Australia, the centrality of political parties within the political system presents a further set of barriers to ensure that the political class differs from the electorate that they represent. While membership of a major political party is an essential criterion for election in almost all of the advanced democracies, in Australia a high level of participation in the party organization is an additional requirement and, preferably, some form of employment with the party. The form of participation in the party organization is determined mainly by the type of organization in question (Panebianco 1988). The strongly disciplined Australian parties ensure that participation in centrally-organized party activities in the states or in federal politics will bring the greatest rewards in terms of selection for a winnable seat.

Such party service can be defined in many ways. There is a basic distinction, however, between party service which is of a voluntary and unpaid nature, and party service which involves holding a regular, paid job. While the former implies loyalty, it also suggests a degree of amateurism; if individuals are recruited into politics through this path, it may involve a conditional commitment, since most will have had a regular job which could be taken up again if their political careers prove not to be successful. By contrast, holding a paid job implies professionalism and a high level of commitment to making politics the individual's chosen career. If the political career fails, there may be no other skill to which the party professional may turn (McAllister 1997).

Voluntary party service is defined here in terms of strictly party-related activities, such as holding local or branch office, and by an extended period of party membership. All of these branch-centered activities demonstrate a level of party commitment, particularly at the local level. Professional party service is concerned with employment by the party, either directly in the national headquarters or in a regional office, or in a minister's or elected representative's office. Both types of party service are, of course, not mutually exclusive and may overlap in significant ways; voluntary party service can (and often does) provide a path to professional service, and vice versa.

The 2001 Australian Election Study[16] candidate survey asked election candidates a range of questions about their level of party political involvement at different stages

---

[15] Estimated from the 2001 Australian Election Study survey, candidate sample.

[16] Data from the Australian Elections Study available from the *Social Science Data Archive* at the *Australian National University* (http://www.ssda.anu.edu.au)

Table 2.4   *Party service by chamber, 2001*

	House of Representatives	Senate
Elected party position (%)		
Conference delegate	86	57
Local official	46	67
State official	20	52
Federal official	6	49
Party activity		
Length of membership (years)	7.7	11.2
Party activity (hours per month)	15.4	35.1
Party employment (percent)		
Employed by MP, minister	9	11
Employed by party	3	11
(N)	(469)	(63)

Note: Party activity refers to activity prior to election if an incumbent.

Source: 2001 Australian Election Study, candidate sample.

during their lives; the figures reported here are based on the 469 candidates who stood for election to the House of Representatives and who responded to the survey and the sixty-three respondents who stood for the Senate.[17] Table 2.4. shows that most of the candidates had held some form of elected party office. The most common type of party office-holding for lower house candidates was acting as a conference delegate, a position most candidates had held at some point, followed by-election as a local branch official, which was mentioned by about half of the candidates. Senate candidates reported generally higher levels of office-holding, with the exception of acting as a conference delegate. About two-thirds of Senate candidates had acted as a local party official, and half had held a state party position.

The candidates were asked how long they had been a party member: the average was just under eight years for lower house candidates and over eleven years for Senate candidates. The time spent on party affairs varied from just over 15 h per month to over 35 h, reflecting a significant commitment to the party organization. In contrast to voluntary party service, professional party service was much rarer among the candidates. About one in ten of both groups said that they had been employed in an MP's or minister's office. Three times more Senate than lower house candidates had been employed by their party.

In addition to their work for the party, election candidates must also demonstrate a commitment to the voters within their constituency. Although the size of the personal vote in Australia is comparatively small, the majority of House of Representatives

---

[17] There are fewer candidates for the Senate because it was a half Senate election. A total of 713 candidates stood for the lower house; the 469 respondents represent a response rate of 66.8%. A total of 125 candidates stood for the Senate, of whom sixty-three responded to the survey, representing a response rate of 50.4%.

candidates live in the constituency within which they stand, and have done so for a substantial period of time (McAllister 1992: 213).[18] Involvement within the community is also important, through active membership of a range of social organizations. In the survey mentioned above, the most popular organizations were community groups, sports organizations, and trade unions or staff associations. How important were the various aspects of party service and community involvement in winning election in 2001? This question can be addressed by a multivariate model predicting whether or not the candidate was elected, using the range of party service measures together with community involvement. Since the dependent variable is dichotomous—whether or not the candidate in question gained election—logistic regression techniques are used. The party factors which were most important in winning election to the House of Representatives were length of party membership and employment by the party. Both can be regarded as a resource, providing aspirants to the political class with political experience, confidence, and knowledge, which makes them more effective career politicians. However, the main value of these experiences is to ensure selection for a winnable seat; their influence on electoral outcomes is therefore indirect, rather than direct, by making the individual a better candidate. In contrast to party activity, having gained an elected party position or being actively involved in community organizations within the electorate do not significantly influence the outcome. Within the Senate, only length of party membership influences the outcome.[19]

Party service is therefore of major importance in winning federal elections in Australia. The mechanism by which party service assumes such importance in the political class is through party selectorates, which play a decisive role in choosing candidates who possess particular social or other characteristics. These are usually characteristics that they themselves value, believe that their party values, or which they consider to be attractive to the wider electorate (Bochel and Denver 1983; Gallagher and Marsh 1988).

Living off Politics

Payment for elected representatives was stipulated in the federal constitution in 1901, although, as noted in the first section, the principle of payment was established earlier in the colonial Parliaments. Section 48 of the constitution states that, until otherwise provided by Parliament, "each senator and each member of the House of Representatives shall receive an allowance of four hundred pounds a year, to be reckoned from the day on which he takes his seat". Under section 66 it was provided that ministers would receive "an annual sum which, until the parliament otherwise provides, shall not exceed twelve thousand pounds a year". The history of Members

---

[18] In the 2001 elections, the Australian Election Study candidate survey found that 85% of all lower house candidates lived in the constituency within which they were standing for election, and of this group, the mean period of residence was 19 years.

[19] The small number of cases for the Senate does not enable the replication of these estimates for Senate candidates.

Table 2.5   *Income of national MPs, 1901–2001 (in AU$)*

Year	Salary	Allowance urban constituencies	Allowance rural constituencies
1901	800	—	—
1920	2,000	—	—
1938	2,000	—	—
1952	3,500	1,100	1,400
1959	5,500	1,600	2,100
1968	9,500	2,650	3,350
1977	24,369	6,000	7,500
1986	45,543	17,329	20,605
1990	58,300	22,685	32,895
1994	69,693	24,558	35,611
1997	81,856	26,076	37,813
1999	85,500	27,300	39,600
2000	90,000	27,300	39,600
(2000 in €)	(50,400)	(15,290)	(22,180)

Notes: Electorate expenses allowances are the same for Senators as for Members of the House of Representatives with urban constituencies. Pounds became dollars in 1966. The figures are not adjusted for inflation.

Source: McAllister *et al.* (1997); Commonwealth Parliamentary Library.

of Parliament salaries is set out in Table 2.5. The figures prior to 1952 are not strictly comparable with later ones, since in 1952 the electorate expense allowance was introduced to reimburse Members and Senators for expenses legitimately incurred on parliamentary and electorate work. A stamp and travel allowance had previously existed but was replaced by an all-embracing expense allowance. Salaries and allowances have usually been those recommended by independent tribunals.

In 2001, the annual salary for a federal Member or Senator was AU$90,000 (approx. €50,410), with an additional AU$27,300 (€15,290) by way of allowances for a city member, and AU$39,600 (€22,180) for a country member. Ministers and the Prime Minister gain extra remuneration, in addition to their parliamentary salaries and allowances. In 2001 it was AU$65,250 (€36,550) for a government minister, while the Prime Minister received an additional AU$144,000 (€80,660). Along with these salaries, all members and ministers receive generous superannuation, which is based on their length of service in Parliament, as well as travel and other allowances when they leave Parliament. Former Prime Ministers receive generous office and clerical allowances.

There are no formal restrictions on elected representatives earning money outside Parliament, but rules have been introduced to minimize any conflicts of interest that might arise with their political role. A register of House of Representatives members' pecuniary interests was introduced in 1984, which includes information such as company directorships, gifts and donations, and share holdings. A failure by a member to

list an interest is regarded as contempt of Parliament and therefore subject to sanction, which can include suspension. A similar register was introduced in the Senate in
1994, and a committee established to ensure compliance, consisting of a majority of
non-government members. A more serious concern has been conflicts of interests
involving government ministers. A register of ministers' interests and a set of guidelines for ministerial conduct were introduced in 1996. The new guidelines strictly regulate ministers adjudicating on matters where they might have a potential conflict of
interests.

THE POLITICAL CLASS AND INSTITUTIONAL REFORM

As a country with a well-entrenched and innovative democracy, most of the conditions
of service of the political class in Australia, as well as the nature of their work, is governed by the law, the constitution, or by the expectations of the political parties they are
members of. There have been demands for greater parliamentary efficiency, more rig-
orous scrutiny of legislation, longer parliamentary sessions, and less party control of
the parliamentary process (for reviews, see Lovell 1994; Uhr 1998). In most cases, however, there are few demands from parliamentarians for these reforms, and the arguments emanate from small groups of academics and specialized observers, rather than
from voters. To the extent that voters have any major interest in parliamentary reform,
it is in establishing a code of ethics for legislators. Between 1901 and 2001, there were
ninety-six ministerial resignations or dismissals, of which eight could be traced to
ministerial impropriety. However, seven of those eight occurred since 1992.

The ethical standards of the political class in Australia have become a major issue
for voters. This follows a trend in many democracies, most notably Britain, where
voters have become concerned about the standards of conduct in public life
(McAllister 2000). Based on responses to eight questions about the importance of
certain forms of behavior by parliamentarians, Table 2.6. shows that voters have
much higher expectations of conduct among their representatives than the representatives themselves. Judged over all eight types of conduct, the average of voters saying "extremely important" is 65 percent. However, among the elected representatives,
the average is 49 percent. Elected representatives exceed voters in the importance
they attribute to acting honestly—although only by one percentage point. On the
remaining seven types of conduct, voters exceed parliamentarians, most notably on
refusing gifts and using public resources economically. Given the disjuncture
between the views of voters and parliamentarians on the importance of ethical
conduct, it is perhaps not surprising that this has become a major political issue.

The federal Parliament has responded to these popular demands for higher standards by seeking greater public disclosure of members' interests. An all-party working group was established in 1994 to draft a code of ethics, and a report was
published in 1997, at the same time as a companion report concerning the ethical
standards required of ministers. This has not yet resulted in the establishment of any
form of administrative oversight to ensure compliance with these standards.

Table 2.6 *Perceptions of ethical conduct by politicians, voters, and parliamentarians, 1996*

	Percent saying "extremely important"		
	Voters	MPs	Difference
Important for federal politicians to:			
Act honestly at all times	74	75	−1
Always put public interest ahead of their personal interest	73	60	13
Always behave in a dignified manner	60	47	13
Refuse to accept gifts of any kind	46	24	22
Not favor specific interests	49	25	14
Always tell the truth in public	73	53	20
Use public resources economically	74	51	23
Respect the dignity and privacy of members of the public	74	51	23
Mean	65	49	
(N)	(1,795)	(103)	

Note: Elected representatives are candidates elected to either the House of Representatives or the Senate in the 1996 federal election.

Source: 1996 Australian Election Study, voter and candidate samples.

CONCLUSION

One factor which is common to candidates in national elections in almost all liberal democracies is membership of and sponsorship by a political party. Once the legal eligibility criteria have been met, a minimal requirement for legislative recruitment is to be a party member. But once this precondition has been filled, it is also evident that party service can be a significant factor. Parties often reward their loyalists, particularly in political systems which have substantial numbers of safe seats or where there are opportunities for co-option or for indirect election. Moreover, with the increasing professionalization of politics, there exists a growing pool of party professionals who seek (and sometime expect) such electoral rewards. Indeed, without such incentives, it might be difficult for parties to meet the required level of recruitment to sustain their full-time, professional staff.

In Australia, the political culture, and even more so the political system, are conducive to the activities of strongly disciplined political parties. Strong party control is reflected in the composition, outlook and behavior of the political class—the more than 800 elected representatives in the federal Parliament in Canberra and the state and territory Parliaments. These individuals are rooted in parties, represent party interests in their respective legislatures, and make institutional rules and procedures to ensure the continuity of parties. Nowhere is party control more evident than in the federal Parliament. Here the parties operate rigid discipline to the extent that dissent from the party line is virtually unheard of, and the real decisions concerning legislation are arrived at within the party room. Labor was the first to achieve effective discipline at both the electoral and parliamentary levels, but the Liberals, of necessity, soon followed, making legislative voting redundant (Rydon 1986: 188; Jaensch 1994: 239).

The political class in Australia is, therefore, very much a *party* political class. Moreover, it is difficult to see how this circumstance might change, given the difficulty that minor parties and independents find in gaining election, at least to the lower House of Representatives. To the extent that there is any pressure from the electorate for change in these formal and informal political rules, it is with respect to higher standards of conduct among the political class. As we have seen, Parliament has begun to respond to those demands, but it seems unlikely that it will enforce the standards of conduct among its members that voters clearly demand, at least in the medium term.

REFERENCES

Aitkin, Don (1982). *Stability and Change in Australian Politics*, 2nd edition. Canberra: ANU Press.
——and Castles, Francis G. (1989). "Democracy Untrammeled", in: K. Hancock (ed.), *Australian Society*. Cambridge: Cambridge University Press, pp. 208–27.
Barlin, L. M. (1997). *House of Representatives: Practice*, 3rd edition. Canberra: Australian Government Publishing Service.
Bean, Clive (1990). "The Personal Vote in Australian Federal Elections". *Political Studies*, 38: 253–68.
Bochel, John, and Denver, David (1983). "Candidate Selection in the Labour Party: What the Selectors Seek". *British Journal of Political Science*, 13: 45–69.
Bryce, James (1921). *Modern Democracies*. New York: Macmillan.
Butler, David (1973). *The Canberra Model*. Melbourne: Macmillan.
Collins, Hugh (1985). "Political Ideology in Australia: The Distinctiveness of a Benthamite Society". *Daedalus*, 114: 147–69.
Crisp, Leslie F. (1983). *Australian National Government*, 5th edition. Melbourne: Longman Cheshire.
Gallagher, Michael, and Marsh, Michael (eds) (1988). *Candidate Selection in Comparative Perspective: The Secret Garden of Politics*. London: Sage.
Goot, Murray (1985). "Electoral Systems", in D. Aitkin (ed.), *Surveys of Australian Political Science*. Sydney: Allen and Unwin, pp. 179–264.
Hancock, Keith W. (1930). *Australia*. London: Ernst Benn.
Hartz, Louis (1964). *The Founding of New Societies*. New York: Harcourt, Brace & World.
Hughes, Colin A. (1973). "Political Culture", in H. Mayer and H. Nelson (eds), *Australian Politics*. Melbourne: Cheshire, pp. 133–48.
Jaensch, Dean (1994). *Power Politics: Australia's Party System*. Sydney: Allen and Unwin.
Jupp, James (1992). *Immigration*. Melbourne: Oxford University Press.
Lovell, David (1994). *The Sausage Makers: Parliamentarians as Legislators*. Canberra: Parliamentary Research Service.
McAllister, Ian (1992). *Political Behaviour: Citizens, Parties and Elites in Australia*. Melbourne: Longman Cheshire.

—— (1997). "Australia", in P. Norris (ed.), *Pathways to Power: Legislative Recruitment in Advanced Democracies*. Cambridge: Cambridge University Press, pp. 15–32.

—— (2000). "Keeping Them Honest: Public and Elite Perceptions of Ethical Conduct Among Australian Legislators", *Political Studies*, 48: 22–37.

——, Mackerras, Malcolm, and Boldiston, Carolyn B. (1997). *Australian Political Facts*. Melbourne: Macmillan.

—— and Studlar, Donley T. (1992). "Gender and Representation Among Legislative Candidates in Australia". *Comparative Political Studies*. 25: 388–411.

Mills, Stephen (1986). *The New Machine Men*. Ringwood: Penguin.

Overacker, Louise (1951). *The Australian Party System*. New Haven, CT: Yale University Press.

Panebianco, Angelo (1988). *Political Parties: Organization and Power*. Cambridge: Cambridge University Press.

Putnam, Robert D. (1976). *The Comparative Study of Political Elites*. Englewood Cliffs, NJ: Prentice Hall.

Rydon, Joan (1986). *A Federal Legislature: The Australian Parliament, 1901–80*. Melbourne: Oxford University Press.

Uhr, John (1998). *Deliberative Democracy in Australia*. Cambridge: Cambridge University Press.

3

Belgium: Political Professionals and the Crisis of the Party State

LIEVEN DE WINTER AND MARLEEN BRANS

The professionalization of the *political class* remains an understudied theme in Belgian political science. Only a few attempts were made to study parliamentary elite characteristics in a longitudinal way (Van Hassel 1959; Schmidt 1970; Beaufays 1972; Brans 1999; Fiers 2000), to which one can add a few surveys focusing on a particular legislative "class".[1] One of the reasons for the lack of scientific attention is the taboo character of the income of politicians, which is part of a more generalized attitude of secrecy about the income and wealth of ordinary citizens. A second reason is the complex character of the political class in the Belgian partitocracy (Deschouwer *et al.* 1996), given the fact that parties have invaded the public sector to such an extent that a large number of public positions are available to party politicians and are to some extent used to reward or "park" party mid- and upper-level elites. Until recently these positions included the entire judiciary, the top of public enterprises and financial institutions, and most parts of the civil service. The federalization process has also created a new professional political class at the level of the regions and communities (see below).

For reasons of practical feasibility and comparability, we will focus on Members of Parliament (MPs), and especially the members of the House of Representatives (*Chambre des Représentants* or *Kamer van Volksvertegenwoordigers*), for which official information and scientific research are less scarce than for the Senate, a chamber whose utility is more and more questioned.

POLITICAL PROFESSIONALIZATION IN HISTORICAL PERSPECTIVE

The constitution drafted by the Belgian founding fathers in 1831 granted members of the House of Representatives a modest allowance whereas it explicitly denied such an

---

[1] See Debuyst (1967), De Bakker (1969), ISCOP-IMSA (1986), Baufay (1991), De Winter (1992), Dewachter *et al.* (1997), Depauw 2000, and the Belgian part of the Loewenberg survey, an encompassing comparative analysis of elites' attitudes in Belgium, Italy, and Switzerland (see Dierickx 1978; Frognier 1978; Deridder, Peterson, and Wirth 1978).

allowance to Senators (Brans 1994, 1999). While it imposed no property conditions
for eligibility to the House, it did for the Senate. As established in 1831, the character
of parliamentary pay involved no more than a compensation for travel and lodging
expenses. In 1893, allowances for Members of the House were slightly upgraded,
changed from variable monthly to standardized annual payments, and free rail travel
was added. As yet, senatorial office remained non-remunerated.

The constitutional revision of 1920 constituted a major step forward to professionalization, as it tripled the allowance for representatives. It also offered the possibility of granting the Speaker of the House an additional yearly allowance as well as
pensions for all members. A year later the issue of senatorial pay was settled: although
this revision still denied Senators the right to a salary or even an allowance, it
entitled them to a reimbursement of expenses. Opponents to these reforms had wanted
to see the level of Representatives' pay set at a lower level to prevent the allowance to
lose its character of an indemnity rather than a salary. Their arguments referred to
the dignity, honor and disinterestedness of the mandate. Defenders used the same
argument and hinted at the Weberian principles of "pay for democracy" and "pay for
independence". In addition, they referred—but not literally[2]—to the professionalization of the parliamentary office: The growing workload of Representatives both
in- and outside Parliament had turned their office into their prime occupation, leaving
them little time to make a living elsewhere.

But was the level of parliamentary pay as set in 1920/21—Belgian Francs (BEF)
12,000 for Representatives and BEF4,000 for Senators[3]—really enough to allow for a
modest living off politics, as parliamentary discourse suggested? Clearly not for
Senators, but in principle, it was enough for Representatives, as nominally, their base
allowances stood at 100–200 percent of the annual salary of skilled workers in the
food and construction industries (Scholliers 1985). Compared with civil service pay,
MPs' allowances were situated within the lower salary ranks. However, given the
expenses parliamentary office entailed and the intrinsic future insecurity, the parliamentary pay structure only offered a modest income for candidates, should they be
denied to make a living elsewhere. Thus, the income of Parliamentarians was strongly
characterized by outside earnings. It would remain that way for the future, even when
in 1967 parliamentary allowances were linked to the level of salaries of magistrates at
the Council of State, the highest administrative court (see below).

After 1921, no constitutional revision of parliamentary pay took place, but a range
of separate decisions eventually made the constitutional difference between
Representatives and Senators insignificant. In the following decades, basic parliamentary allowances were modified in three ways: first, straightforward increases, then
followed by indexation, and, finally, linkage. In the inter-war and immediate post-war
period, pay raises were justified with the "cost of living argument". The first substantial

---

[2] See Kamer van Volksvertegenwoordigers. *Parlementaire Annalen* (1919–20), 17 June 1920: 1722.

[3] Note from the editors: Adjusted for inflation (in 1988 BEF) the payments amounted to approximately
BEF132,000 (€3,270) for Senators and BEF396,000 (€9,820) for Representatives (calculation based on
Mitchell 1992).

pay raise in both houses took place in 1927, to make up for the pay erosion due to inflation and devaluation. By 1930, Representatives' pay stood at 3.5 times its constitutional
level, that of Senators at seven. In the 1930s, parliamentary pay was subjected to the
same deflationary politics as all other salaries were. In the immediate post-war period,
a new wave of substantial pay modifications took effect: In 1945, the Senate copied the
inter-war level of the House but by two more consecutive decisions in 1946 and 1947,
it more than tripled this sum. The House in turn established the sum at 1.5 times its
inter-war level, but two decisions in 1946 and 1947 tripled the initial post-war level.
Between 1947 and 1964, basic levels were raised on two occasions in the House and
three in the Senate.

Meanwhile, allowances were linked to the index of consumer prices (Senate 1959;
House 1962) which also changed the nature of future pay raises: they became
straightforward pay raises. In 1964, the Senate finally caught up with the House by
copying its level and from then onwards, allowances would be raised simultaneously.
In 1967 both chambers informally took the salaries of magistrates at the Council
of State as a reference point for the first time. With this linkage the basic allowance
also came to include other employee benefits like holiday pay and end of year
premium.

It is not possible to give a clear-cut statement about the historical development of
parliamentary work. The total number of hours the plenary assembly of the House
met since its creation in 1831 does not indicate a trend towards more time-consuming
plenary session work. Of course, the bulk of intraparliamentary activity takes place
in committees and parliamentary group meetings. Unfortunately, the records of the
House only provide data on the number of committee meetings since 1949. Here we
do notice a trend towards increasing activism, but basically this upward trend has
started after 1967.

Seniority has decreased considerably in the post-war period. With an overall average of 9.4 years of parliamentary experience for Representatives in the 1946–95
period, and 7.9 for Senators (Fiers 1998, 2000), after the 1995 elections, average seniority was 5.5 years for the House and 6.9 years for the Senate (Depauw 1997: 209).
After the 1999 elections average seniority was 5.7 years for the House and 6.6 years
for the Senate.[4] This is partly due to the growing fragmentation of the party system
which not only brings candidates of new parties into Parliament for the first time,
but also makes more seats marginal in each constituency given the unpredictable way
of allotting second (provincial) tier seats to various constituencies.

The Belgian Parliament is characterized by scarce institutional resources. The
House maintains only 533 permanent employees (in 2000), of which about a quarter has a university degree. Of the latter, only a few dozens provide intellectual assistance to individual MPs.[5] The Judicial Service—currently with six advisors—can
give individual legislators technical assistance in drafting private member bills.

---

[4] Data refer to the composition of the chambers one month after the elections, thus when those
promoted to ministerial rank were replaced by their substitutes (which usually are newcomers).

[5] Mainly those working for the Services of the Library of Parliament.

Each committee has one secretary who—time permitting—can also act as research assistant. Apart from these services, no collectively provided staff accessible to individual members is available.

The introduction of individual staff is relatively recent. In 1980 each MP was indirectly allocated funds to employ a half-time assistant, remunerated at the level of a clerk. From January 1981 onwards, this system was extended so that MPs could now employ one full-time assistant or two part-time assistants. Given the salary level, these assistants were mainly used for secretarial work (De Winter 1992). While secretarial assistants are individually attributed to MPs, university-trained assistants were allocated to political groups at a proportion of one per eight Representatives in 1988. In 1993, it was decided to have one assistant per two MPs and in 1995 one per MP. By now, the Senate enjoys the same level of assistance. Most political groups in both House and Senate pool these staff resources (De Winter and Dumont 2000).

Up to 1987—when an extra building was erected—the Parliamentarians had to cope with considerably strained working conditions, because the plenary areas of the two chambers and the MPs' offices were housed in an eighteenth century palace, which combined luxury and prestige with a lack of comfort and space.

THE INSTITUTIONAL CONTEXT

Since the 1960s, the Belgian unitary state has gradually moved into the direction of federalism. In 1993, the fourth (but not last) major revision of the constitution completed the organization of a *sui generis* federal structure based on the overlapping of three linguistic Communities (the Flemish majority, the French minority, and the tiny German minority) and three socio-economic Regions (Flanders, Brussels, and Wallonia), with numerous intersections (like the fusion of the Flemish Community and Flanders Region into a new political entity).

Under pressure of public opinion, the authors of the 1993 constitutional reform found that it was not politically feasible to expand the number of professional politicians at the levels of the federal state and the regions and communities taken together. Up until the reform, the members of the regional and community assemblies were also seated in the federal Parliament, but the 1993 revision put an end to this "double mandate" by splitting federal from regional/community offices. Hence, after long and tiresome discussions between parties and parliamentary groups, each trying to keep the number of members of their preferred assembly as high as possible, a compromise was reached that only marginally increased the overall number of members of the three types of assemblies. That was only possible by way of a drastic reduction in size of the House and the Senate. Hence, the federalization process not only reduced the size of the national political class, it also created an entirely new class of professional politicians at the level of the regions and communities, which all have their directly elected legislature, an executive team of ministers headed by a *minister-president* (Prime Minister), a full-fledged civil service, and a public financing system of parties and parliamentary groups.

The 150 members of the current House of Representatives are elected through proportional representation in twenty multi-member constituencies (with a minimum of two and a maximum of twenty-two seats). Parties in each constituency normally draw up lists that include a number of candidates equal to the number of Representatives to be elected. The ordering of candidates on the electoral lists is of particular importance, because in practice voters only determine the number of seats a party will receive. Thus, the parties themselves decide in advance who will obtain these seats (De Winter 1988), in spite of the increasing use of preferential voting (60 percent for the House, 64 percent for the Senate; Smits and Wauters 2000). The rules for distributing seats strongly favor those candidates placed high on the lists. Thus MPs still remain not directly accountable to their voters.[6]

Before the 1993 reforms, the Senate was composed of three categories of Senators:

- 106 (in 1991) "directly elected Senators", elected in twenty-one constituencies;
- 51 "provincially elected Senators", appointed by the provincial councils,
- and "nationally co-opted Senators", equal to half the number of the provincial Senators.

They were co-opted by the directly elected and provincially elected Senators. After the reforms the Senate is composed of seventy-one members, forty of whom are directly elected in one Flemish (twenty-five) and one Francophone (fifteen) constituency. The Flemish Council and the Francophone Community Council each delegate ten members, and the Council of the German-speaking Community one. They can be considered as representatives of the Communities to the federal Parliament. Finally, the remaining ten Senators are co-opted by the first two categories of Senators.

The post-war Belgian party system has undergone dramatic changes in the 1970s. After remaining the two-and-a-half-party system it had been from the moment of the introduction of general suffrage in 1919 well into the 1960s, it became the most fragmented European party system within a relatively short period of time (De Winter and Dumont 1999). The number of parties in the House rose from four (1949) to fourteen (1981). Since then, the degree of fragmentation has not declined. Therefore, one of the crucial features of the Belgian party system is that there are no "Belgian" parties any more—they are homogeneously Flemish or Francophone and only present themselves in the Flemish or Francophone constituencies.[7] In fact, although the types of parties are quite similar, Belgium has two quasi-autonomous party systems, each with different balances of power between the main parties, and a different evolution of their electoral fortunes. This fragmentation creates a strong centrifugal force in party competition (Deschouwer 1996).

The role of the Belgian Parliament in decision-making is extremely restricted in terms of legislation, government control, and government formation, as the fragmentation of

---

[6] The central party organizations decide whom they will back as candidates for the thirty-one non-directly elected senatorial seats. In most cases, these are candidates who failed to win a seat at the general elections, while some do not even run at all in any type of election.

[7] With the exception of the bilingual Brussels–Halle–Vilvoorde constituency in which the Flemish and Francophone systems overlap.

the party system and the executive makes the political system inherently unstable (the average government lasted 1.51 years in the 1944–2003 period; Dumont and De Winter 1999). Therefore, government support has become a permanent duty for majority MPs as far as voting on legislative projects, investiture declarations and motions of confidence or censure are concerned. This also stems from the complexity of the process of coalition-building: Usually only after several months, a *formateur* will eventually manage to conclude an encompassing and detailed coalition agreement and then will be nominated as Prime Minister (De Winter, Timmermans, and Dumont 2000). After the debate on the governmental program, the new government has to win the investiture vote. Before this final stage, the parliamentary groups as such are not involved in the formation process. As the coalition program and configuration are approved by the national party conferences of the respective coalition parties before the government seeks the investiture by the Parliament, a negative vote by majority MPs would openly defy the decisions of their party's supreme decision-making body. The role of parliamentary groups and individual MPs is equally limited concerning coalition maintenance and collapse. Since 1947, not a single cabinet fell due to a defeat on a vote of confidence in Parliament.

As far as the legislative function is concerned, the large majority of bills approved by Parliament are introduced by the government rather than by individual MPs. Yet, one observes a steady increase in the annual number of private member bills introduced in the House (De Winter 1998). However, their success rate is very low, while a large majority of bills introduced by the government become effective law. This can be explained by the detailed and extensive governmental agreements reached between the majority parties, which predefine to a large extent the legislation to be initiated by the government and to be enacted by Parliament in the following legislative term. The MPs of the majority parties have very little leeway to amend these proposals, as this would destabilize the delicate agreement reached between governing parties.

The House has become more active in controlling governmental decisions. Especially since the doubling of the parliamentary staff in 1995 the number of interpellations and parliamentary questions has risen (De Winter 1998). Yet the majority's duty of permanent government maintenance considerably undermines the effectiveness of this increasing oversight activity. Finally, there are the committees of parliamentary investigation, which were traditionally quite uncommon to Belgian parliamentary life, given the attitude of majority MPs, who—in solidarity with the government—were reluctant to allow investigations that could embarrass a specific minister or the entire government. However, since the end of the 1980s, committees of inquiry are used much more frequently, on the average of about one a year per chamber. They somehow have developed into an alternative means of parliamentary oversight and some have gained high visibility—still, not a single minister has been forced by them to resign.

Given the limited policy role of the Belgian Parliament and the permanent pressure on majority MPs to unconditionally support the government, MPs still encounter strong difficulties in responding to their constituents' policy preferences. Thus most MPs try to circumvent this handicap by generating support through symbolic, non-policy related representational behavior, by increasing their efforts with regard to clientelist case work, and through "pork barrel politics". Belgian MPs spend about half of their working time in the constituency and attend numerous meetings and social gatherings organized by a wide variety of local organizations, groups and institutions (De Winter 1997). Two out of three MPs also hold local public office, which facilitates their contact with constituents (see below). This high level of activity outside Parliament also explains the traditionally high levels of absenteeism in the chambers (De Winter 1992).

The constitutional founding fathers of 1831 opted for a bicameral system, in which the Senate originally constituted the more aristocratic and conservative element. From the beginning, both chambers were symmetrical in terms of their main functions (government-formation, legislation, control) and internal organization. Owing to the democratization of the suffrage even their party composition has become highly similar. After the 1993 constitutional reforms the Senate was reduced drastically in size from 185 to 71 seats, the House from 212 to 150. The Senate has also lost several of its competencies and is evolving into a "chamber of deliberation" and meeting place between the federal and regional/community levels of government.[8]

Committees in both chambers are predominantly of the permanent and specialized type, usually corresponding to the main executive departments. Committee membership and leadership positions are allocated in a proportional way among the parliamentary groups. The main role of committees in the Belgian Parliament is the passage of government legislation (including budget bills). Until 1985, all committee meetings were held behind closed doors. Since the 1993 statutory reforms, public meetings have become the rule, rather than the exception. Although committees can gather advice and ask documentation from persons or institutions not belonging to the Parliament, the number of hearings remains extremely low (De Winter 1998).

Apart from the financing of operational expenses and personnel of parliamentary parties since 1970 (see above), the comprehensive system of public financing of the extra-parliamentary parties at the national[9] level started only in 1989 (Van Bunder 1993). Before, tax-deductible gifts were allowed to the party research centers only. In 1985, this possibility was extended to donations up to BEF 2 million (approx. €49,600),[10] made to a specifically created party treasury fund. The 1989 comprehensive legislation on the public financing of parties envisaged a lump sum for each party (with at least one MP in each chamber) and an additional sum for each voter

---

[8] Now only the House can invest or dissolve a government, vote on the budget, and allow interpellations of ministers. All government bills are introduced in the House. Yet, the Senate remains equally competent for constitutional reforms, regional and community matters, ratification of treaties and the organization of the judiciary. It is exclusively responsible to deal with conflicts between the national and regional/community legislatures.

[9] As there are only regional parties, in principle one should also include the financing of operational expenses and personnel of parliamentary parties within the regional and community assemblies in order to calculate the overall sum at the disposal of the "national" or highest level of party organization in Belgium. However, data for this level is hardly available.

[10] Converted according to the fixed EMU rate (BEF1 = €0.0248).

at the last legislative elections. Added were a number of regulations intended to decrease the overall cost of campaigning per party (which had more than quadrupled in the period 1974–87) as well as per candidate, and also prohibiting a number of campaign techniques. Furthermore, the use of tax-deductible donations was first limited to a much lower level, and then altogether prohibited in 1993. The control of these campaign restrictions is in the hands of a parliamentary committee. The law of 1993 also filled some lacunae and blocked some loopholes, but more importantly, it quadrupled the total amount of subsidies. These state subsidies are all given to central party offices that then decide how to allocate these funds to different candidates. Hence, also in terms of campaign resources MPs have grown more dependent on their national party.

Other sources of party income are membership fees (the overall rate of membership is still at 7.5 percent of the population), contributions from elected officials (see below), and from parliamentary parties. Finally, political parties in office can "claim" a considerable number of the members of the so-called *cabinets ministériels*, the personal but mainly party-appointed staff of ministers and secretaries of state. In the 1980s, their overall number was around 3,000 (Van Velthoven 1987), but their number has decreased in the 1990s, as a partial compensation for the expenses of the public financing of central party offices and in accordance with the shift of policy competencies to the regions and communities. However, this decrease has been entirely balanced by an increase of cabinet personnel at the substate level (Suetens and Walgrave 1999).

Interest groups are quite influential in Belgium, working through a well developed set of several hundred formal advisory and co-decisional bodies, where the groups are consulted and often participate in the decision-making and even the implementation process. Clearly, these consultative and (co-)decisional networks undermine the Parliament's and the executive's competence in many policy sectors with the former ratifying and the latter executing decisions taken in the neo-corporatist network (Dewachter 1992: pp. 138–9). The importance of these pressure groups is related to the consociational or pillarized character of Belgian society. In fact, the predominance of the traditional political parties (Christian Democrats, Socialists, and Liberals) is partly due to the fact that they aggregate, articulate, defend and implement the interests of a wider network of organizations. These organizations are constituent elements of a pillar, a "societal segment" or a "sociological world", each including trade unions, farmer and "middle class" organizations, socio-cultural organizations, educational and health service networks, press networks, etc.

Pressure groups have been particularly influential in the CVP (*Christelijke Volkspartij*—Christian People's Party, since 2001 rebaptized into *Christen-Democratisch & Vlaams*). The CVP is a Flemish catholic catch-all party which appeals to catholic workers, farmers, and "middle classes" (i.e. shopkeepers, artisans, liberal professions, and entrepreneurs). These three socio-economic categories are highly organized, and together with the catholic educational network, health sector, and cultural and recreational organizations, form the most influential catholic "pillar". All three categories have active sections at the constituency level and are represented as *standen* (estates) in the constituency parties and control the selection of political personnel at all levels— the local, constituency, provincial, and national one (Smits 1986). In fact, nearly all CVP representatives obtained their seat because one of the *standen* offered them a safe place on an electoral list. Most of these groups organize regular meetings between "their" MPs and the leadership of the groups at the federal and constituency level, where the MPs are briefed about the issues at stake in Parliament and the party that are important to the estates.

In the other parties, the impact of pressure groups on candidate selection and internal decision-making is less predominant by now, as these parties are not the political representatives of a "pillar" (Greens, *Volksunie, Vlaams Blok*), or their pillar organizations are more loosely linked with the party (Liberals, Socialists, and Francophone Christian Democrats). Still, given the relative irrelevance of Parliament in the decision-making process, most influential pressure groups directly contact members of the government and the leaders, executives, and the party research centers of the extra-parliamentary party of the majority, but rarely individual MPs or the parliamentary groups (De Winter and Dumont 2000).

THE POLITICAL CLASS

Size and Composition

The political class in Belgium, that is those that gain a sufficient income from politics, includes the holders of elected and executive positions at the national and regional/community level, the governors and the permanent deputies of the ten provinces,[11] and the mayors of large cities.[12] In addition, one finds the members of the personal staffs of national and regional ministers (*cabinet ministériel*). Many of these members shift back and forth between cabinets and (higher) civil service, whereby "cabinet service" assures fast promotion in the civil service, and the civil service also serves as a waiting chamber for politicized civil servants (because their supporting party is in opposition) before they can take up a new mission in a cabinet (Dewachter 2001: 293). A similar circulation of elites occurs between ministerial cabinets on the one hand and the judiciary and public enterprises on the other hand. In this chapter, however, we will only focus on the national parliamentary elite.

By European standards, the proportion of women in Parliament is low. However, in a long-term perspective, there has been a gradual increase of the proportion of female representatives, from 1.5 percent in 1946 to a peak of 23 percent in 1999 (for the House). In the 1960s and 1970s, several parties installed overall quotas for women on their candidate lists, but usually female candidates were not put on the

[11] Permanent deputies are members of the executive in the provinces. Each province counts six deputies, which are paid at the level of a Senator. Since the 2000 elections, the overall number of members of the provincial councils (provincial legislature) is 738.

[12] Since 2000, the salaries for mayors and aldermen have been increased considerably, expanding the number of local office-holders that can make a living from politics.

Table 3.1 *Socio-political background of MPs, 1999*

	House	Senate
Total number	150	71
Women (%)	23.3	28.2
Men (%)	76.7	71.8
Average age (years)	47.0[a]	48.3
Language groups (%)		
Flemish	60.7	57.7
French	39.3	42.3
Occupation (%)		
Liberal professions	24.7	25.4
Educational professions	27.3	23.9
Civil service	14.7	22.5
Entrepreneurs	10.0	9.9
Employees	19.3	11.3
Media	1.3	2.8
Pensioners, other	2.7	4.2
Cumulation of local offices (%)[a]		
Mayor	23.3	7.0
Alderman (local executive)	6.7	2.8
Councilor	31.3	19.7

[a] See notes.

Notes: Given the incompatibility of parliamentary and ministerial functions, many elected officials resign to take up executive office at the federal or regional level. They are then replaced by persons from the "list of substitutes" that accompanied the list of effective candidates in each constituency. Data given mostly present the situation after the formation of the federal and regional governments in 1999, apart from those indicated by an [a], that refer to the composition right after election day (13 July 1999).

Source: See note 13.

eligible places. Since 1995, a minimum presence of one third of either gender group on the lists has become gradually obligatory for different type of elections.

In the 1970s, the Belgian parliamentary class clearly became younger as the post-war generation was gradually replaced by a much younger one (Debuyst 1967). The average age—around 47 years—is remarkably stable (since at least 1978). This rejuvenation is partly due to the inscription of maximum age limits (usually 65) for elected office in party statutes at the end of the 1960s, although most age limits have been abolished or relaxed since the relative success of "pensioners parties" in the first half of the 1990s (Smeets 1994).

The most common occupational background is in the teaching and liberal (mostly legal) professions, each representing about one quarter of representatives (of those elected in 1999).[13] Also in the Senate, this background is equally common, but so is

[13] Figures are based on data presented in the annual report of activities of the House, based on the self-declared professional background of MPs. Senate figures were provided by the Section Historiography of the Service Documentation and Statistics. Some figures were calculated by Stefaan Fiers (2000), Departement Politieke Wetenschappen, KU Leuven.

public service. On the basis of a more detailed survey regarding the profession held prior to the first parliamentary mandate,[14] one can conclude that in 1996 about half of the representatives and two thirds of the Senators already worked in politics or in public service before becoming a MP (if we include interest organizations and party officials, economists and social scientists, and journalists working in the public media). This common "public background" might facilitate MPs' growing inclination to see parliamentary income as a regular public service salary, rather than a privilege, a honorary indemnity, or a mere reimbursement of expenses.

Finally, since 1970, all MPs are constitutionally obliged to indicate at the beginning of each legislative term—by taking the oath either in Dutch or French—whether they belong to the Dutch or French-speaking linguistic group, as some specific policies require "linguistically qualified" majorities. In the 1999 House, ninety-one MPs adhere to the Dutch-speaking and fifty-nine to the French speaking group. In the Senate the figures are forty-one and thirty respectively.

Political Recruitment and Political Careers

Candidate selection in most Belgian parties is situated at the level of the constituency party organization. In all traditional parties—except for the *Parti Socialiste* (PS)— a gradual shift away from the poll procedure—a type of primary which involved all party members—has occurred between 1960 and 1990 (De Winter 1980, 1988). In most parties, the process is now in the hands of the local and constituency party activists, while in the Flemish Christian Democrats (CVP) it is largely supervised— even at the constituency level—by the three intra-party pillars. However, some parties have re-introduced general member participation in the 1980s: the Greens and Francophone Christian-Democrats using "open lists"; and since 1992 the Flemish Liberals (VLD—*Vlaamse Liberalen en Democraten*) using "model lists" which contain the order of candidates as preferred by the constituency party leadership and in practice are hard to modify by the members (Jagers 2002).[15]

Selectors not only have preferences concerning the background characteristics of the candidates, they also hold strong expectations with regard to the behavior their candidates display inside and outside Parliament.[16] The selectorates usually

---

[14] Survey conducted by Lieven De Winter within the project of Representation in Europe (Schmidt and Thomassen 1999). Response rate was 58% for Members of the House and 63% for Senators. Respondents could give more than one profession.

[15] Of the Representatives which responded to our 1996 survey, about one out of ten was selected through an "open list" poll, three out of ten through a "model list" poll, and one third through a constituency party congress of delegates from the local parties. Another 20% were selected by the constituency party executive and only in a few cases was the national party formally involved. Given the very large constituencies, Senators are much more likely to be selected by national party headquarters. Still, in about half of the cases they were selected through a poll, although in most cases it was on the basis of a model list.

[16] The strongest common expectations reported by the 1996 respondents (House) are, in decreasing order of importance: activities in Parliament; in the national, constituency and local party organization; nursing the collective needs of the constituency; an exemplary private life-style; individual case-work; and nursing one's local mandate. For selectors' expectations in the 1980s, see De Winter (1988).

Table 3.2   *Current and past experience in organizations, 1996 (% of respondents)*

	House		Senate	
	Current	Past	Current	Past
Local/regional party branch	72.2	20.7	68.5	25.8
National party organization	48.3	25.9	66.7	12.1
Professional organization	5.9	16.5	8.2	22.7
Trade union	7.3	19.9	0.0	14.7
Business organization	6.6	6.4	9.2	5.2
Women organization	7.1	4.9	23.7	3.3
Environmental group	5.7	8.3	8.6	14.6
Religious organization	5.3	7.7	4.6	6.1

have—through de-selection—the means to sanction an MP who does not live up to their expectations.

Table 3.2. presents the percentage of MPs that either held a position in different recruitment reservoirs at the moment of the survey (1996) or did so only in the past. It shows that holding a local or regional party office is an experience a very large majority of MPs shares. In fact, less than one out of ten MPs has never held a leadership position in local or regional party organizations. Also offices in the national party are important. Only about one out of four MPs never had that experience. Yet, Representatives seem to abandon this position more often than Senators once elected (only half of the Representatives currently hold this office, against two out of three Senators). Having held leadership office in the socio-economic pressure groups (trade unions, business, and professional organizations) constitutes an experience shared in the past by more than four out of ten Representatives and Senators. However, these are activities which most of them give up when becoming MP, given the fact that only one out of five currently holds such a position. Finally, non-economic pressure group offices (women, environmental, religious, or spiritual organizations) are or have been held by few Representatives (less than one out of ten). However, nearly one of four Senators currently exercises a function in a women's organization. This difference is mainly due to the better representation of women in the Senate and the importance of these organizations in the political career of female politicians.

All in all, pressure group offices are held only by a small number of MPs. In comparison with the previous survey (reference year 1980) the involvement of Representatives in pressure groups and other organizations of civil society has declined considerably (De Winter 1992). This points to a further increase of parliamentary professionalization as the office of MPs becomes more and more detached from other positions.

Belgian MPs hold offices in the leadership of pressure groups for a variety of reasons. First, this is one of the prominent career paths, which lead to a seat in Parliament, especially for MPs with socio-demographically less advantageous backgrounds. It serves as an apprenticeship and a power base for the further political career. Second, particularly in the CVP intra-party pressure groups not only control the (de-)selection of candidates, but also sponsor the actual election of their candidates in terms of campaign costs (before the introduction of public financing of campaigns), by promoting them in their membership periodicals and affiliated newspapers, and by offering them a chance to meet the members and activists of the organization. Finally, in the case of non-election, they can lobby within the party for providing their candidate with a soft landing as a co-opted Senator or a member of a ministerial cabinet. Otherwise they can offer a fallback position within their organization. Intra- and extra-party pressure groups can also provide important resources relevant to intra-parliamentary work (De Winter 1992): Pressure groups are important sources of assistance with regard to the drafting of bills and amendments, interpellations, and parliamentary questions. The holding of a pressure group office also provides for secretarial staff and equipment, helps covering parliamentary expenses and serves as an additional source of income.

The *cumul local*, that means holding a local elected office together with a seat in Parliament, is one of the traditions of Belgian parliamentary behavior and represents a wider tendency towards localism within the political culture. Table 3.1. shows that in 1999 about six out of ten Representatives combined their parliamentary mandate with a local office,[17] against only three out of ten Senators. Of those Representatives half were members of the local council, while the other half held offices at the executive level, as mayor or alderman (the latter are directly elected by the city council, the mayor is appointed by the Minister of Interior upon proposal of the city council). Apart from the Greens, all parties tried to exploit the dual mandate, as far as the recruitment reservoir and statutory arrangements permitted.[18] As a consequence, Representatives tend to spend a considerable proportion of their time—nearly eight hours per week—on their local duties.

There are many reasons why Belgian MPs combine their parliamentary mandate with a local office. First, many MPs already held a local office before getting elected to Parliament, and this was often one of the reasons why they were recruited and got elected (De Winter 1992: 194–5). The local office in fact offers visibility and notoriety within the constituency, often more than the seat in Parliament, unless one belongs to the elite of the party. In addition, the exercise of important local offices (like that of mayor of a big city) can serve as an effective preparation for ministerial office (De Winter 1990).

The combination of the salaries of local and national office makes it even more attractive to become a full-time professional politician. Furthermore, given the limited role of MPs in decision-making, local executive office is often a more creative and resourceful job than that of a backbencher. It includes executive as well as legislative aspects, with relatively high prestige and large personal resources (office, staff, car, budget, patronage). It gives the power to allocate substantive material and

---

[17] The same share is true for the period 1960–88 (De Bondt 1971; Ronsmans 1985; Ackaert 1988).

[18] Some parties made the parliamentary office incompatible with the office of mayor or alderman of a commune of more than 30,000 (CVP) or 50,000 (PS) inhabitants (Deschouwer 1992).

non-material public resources. In addition, the public standing of mayors is often higher than that of legislators (IMADI 1989). Consequently, the local mandate is often psychologically more rewarding than the parliamentary one.

About one third of the Representatives exercise a (part-time) job outside Parliament (in 1996, against nearly half in 1980). For those "part-time MPs" their job consumes more than 12 h a week, of an average total working time budget of nearly 60 h a week. Thus, even "part-time MPs" are usually almost full-time politicians. The combination of a private occupation with a parliamentary mandate is most common amongst liberal professions, academics, and entrepreneurs. The advantage of this professional *cumul* is the additional income, and often also the additional resources like office, staff, and information. It can also offer a fallback cushion in case voluntary or involuntary withdrawal from politics.

The circumstances of the end of parliamentary careers have not yet been studied longitudinally. Of the respondents to the 1980 survey who were not running any more in the 1981 general election, only one out of five referred to unfavorable treatment at the selection process as a reason for not running. More than one third mentioned the practical incompatibility of a parliamentary mandate with public or private occupations, or party imposed age limits. One out of five referred to disagreement with the (changes in) ideology of their party and as many to the fact that they "had been in Parliament long enough". Very few MPs seem to lose their mandate because they have been deselected due to voter rebellion (Depauw 2000: 437).

In order to identify MPs office goals, we asked our respondents how much they would like to occupy different kinds of political and non-political offices in the future (Table 3.3). The data shows that MPs' first office ambition is static: re-election as a national MP. Second come—if taken together—executive positions at the local or provincial level. Third we find—especially amongst Senators—the position of minister in the national government. The exercise of a liberal profession is attractive for one out of six Representatives and one out of four Senators. In-House career paths are also commonly sought after (leadership of parliamentary group or a parliamentary committee chair). Positions at the European level include membership of the European Parliament, while some Senators also see themselves as future members of the Commission.

Hence, Belgian MPs' progressive office ambitions focus in the first place on subnational government (or Europe and the private sector), rather than massively seeking the higher offices at the national level (in government, the legislature, and party) that legislators are traditionally supposed to aspire. These "localist" career ambitions explain why so many reforms aimed at reducing the local *cumul* have failed (see below).

Living off Politics

The 1996 income structure of MPs comprised a base allowance, intrinsic office rewards in cash and kind, formal post-service benefits such as pension and severance

Table 3.3 *Office ambitions of Belgian MPs, 1996 (% of respondents, several answer possible)*

	House	Senate
National Parliament		
Ordinary member	64.9	55.9
Parliamentary group leader	26.5	23.9
Committee chair	12.8	12.7
Party leader	13.0	6.1
European Parliament/Commission		
Member of EP	13.9	21.3
Chair EP group	1.7	4.7
Chair EP committee	1.6	4.7
Commission member	3.1	16.7
Executive positions		
National government	23.5	45.3
High civil servant	1.9	0.0
International service/diplomacy	4.6	4.7
Local government		
Mayor large city	19.9	20.1
Mayor small town	24.9	14.6
Alderman large city	9.2	25.0
Alderman small town	2.9	2.6
Governor province	6.2	0.0
Deputy province (executive branch)	2.9	2.8
Other		
Socio-cultural sector/media/education	8.4	2.8
Entrepreneur	6.2	7.5
Leader interest group	3.4	2.8
Liberal profession	16.7	26.9

pay, and outside-earning opportunities (Brans 1994, 1999). In 1996, the base allowance stood at €62,696 (2002: €69,219), and up to that year half of this allowance was exempt from taxes, as a means to offset members' professional expenses. In response to the recurring controversy around this perceived tax privilege, allowances are now fully taxed, but this was compensated for by a lump sum expense reimbursement (of 28 percent of the basic allowance). In the House, both allowances are linked to attendance: Members who attend less than 80 percent of plenary meetings lose part of their income.[19] There are three further deductions from the base allowance: pension contributions, a "solidarity contribution", and party contributions, the latter ranging from 8 percent for the Francophone Socialists to as much as 50 percent for the Francophone Greens. Besides, MPs receive a range of

---

[19] Only a handful MPs have suffered from the absenteeism regulation.

intrinsic office rewards.[20] Legislative leadership office-holders, such as the Speaker, the Vice-Speakers, the Questors, parliamentary secretaries, and group leaders[21] receive additional functional allowances, ranging from 15 percent to 72 percent of the parliamentary allowance, which were also tax-exempt until 1996. The special allowances provide substantial add-ons to the ordinary backbenchers' allowances. They are also complemented with additional office facilities.

Pensions for Representatives were introduced in 1920 and for Senators pension contributions became compulsory in 1946. The conditions of eligibility to a full or partial pension differ slightly for the two chambers. In the House, all members have the right to a pension at the age of 55 and they must have been seated for at least 20 years to draw the maximum pension, set at 75 percent of the allowance. Senators are eligible for a pension at the age of 58 and they need eighteen years of service to draw a full pension, set at the same percentage as the one for the House.[22] Severance pay, introduced in the mid-1970s, gives ex-members one month of the parliamentary allowance per year of service, but with a minimum of twelve months if they have served at least one year. Since the mid-1970s, both chambers also have a "social assistance fund", providing financial help to ex-members and their spouses, in case they are not eligible for a parliamentary pension or widower/widow pension.

Until 2002, formal post-service rewards were clearly limited, as few people served long enough in Parliament to draw a full pension and to receive more than a year severance pay, let alone two years.[23] Lack of research on careers after parliamentary office prevents a conclusive evaluation of informal post-service rewards. However, the distribution of post-service earning opportunities is supposedly unequal across parties and individuals and in addition they may be insecure and characterized by scarcity. In this respect, the continuation and extension of part-time earning opportunities seemed to provide members a better way of securing future rewards. The reward structure of MPs traditionally emphasized outside and part-time earnings. These rewards are variable; on the one hand they depend on legal regulations of incompatibilities of office (which apply equally to all MPs) and on the other hand on

[20] These rewards include a travel allowance, which supplements the constitutionally guaranteed free rail pass. They enjoy a partial remission of postal costs. Members can phone for free from within the Parliament building and are entitled to free coffee, tea, beer, soft drinks, cakes, and fruit—and they can eat in two subsidized restaurants. Other perquisites include a free visit to the state opera and a number of insurance schemes (terrorism, third party liability, travel and luggage, car, and housing).

[21] The College of Questors is in charge of measures relating to the parliamentary building, logistics personnel, and ceremonial aspects, as well as to the budget of their chamber. The Vice-Speaker replaces the chairman of the respective chamber in case of absence and the secretaries primarily control voting procedures. These three offices—together with the leaders of the parliamentary groups—constitute the *Bureau*.

[22] Both chambers have transitory measures. Representatives can already retire at the age of 52, but their pension will be reduced by 5% for each year they retire before age 55. The same reduction rule applies to Senators, but here the age is 55, and they must have contributed to the pension fund for at least five years.

[23] Only 9.9% of the male and 7.5 % of the female Representatives served longer than twenty years. In the Senate, the respective number is only 6% (Fiers 1998). For the same reason, only a very small minority enjoys the two years of severance pay. As the average age of Representatives is around forty-seven years, they are in office in the prime of their professional lives. Therefore parliamentary office has less the character of a *fin de carrière*.

the different affiliations of individual MPs and on party-imposed rules. Until 1999, there were few legal restrictions on outside earning opportunities,[24] but there were some party-imposed restrictions—differing widely in scope and exceptions. Most political parties have incompatibility rules regarding the combination of a parliamentary seat with local offices in large districts, but when political opportunities arise, exemptions are often granted (Brans 1999). Only the *Volksunie* party, the Greens, and the Flemish Liberals forbid their members offices in pressure groups. Furthermore, Green MPs are not allowed to hold another paid job, whether public or private. The principle of a register of members' outside earnings and personal wealth has been introduced in 1995, but is still not implemented due to the lack of enabling legislation.

In 1999, the opportunities for part-time earnings from combining public offices was restricted by law, followed by a decision of the House *Bureau* in 2002 to improve severance pay. This supports the assumption that these components of the reward structure for MPs are interrelated: formal post-service rewards and outside earning opportunities act as alternatives for reducing the financial insecurity of parliamentary office. Outside earning opportunities were restricted in two ways: by limiting the number of public offices MPs can combine and by installing a financial threshold. MPs can now take on only two other non-executive public offices (e.g. board of public utilities; local councilor) or one executive office (e.g. mayor or alderman), and their combined income cannot exceed more than 1.5 times the sum of the parliamentary allowance. Severance pay in turn, has been improved in several ways. The maximum is raised from 2 to 4 years and MPs have less difficulty getting more than one year severance. They now get 2 years of severance pay when having served fifteen years, compared to 24 years before 2002.[25]

For more than 70 years, decisions on legislative salaries and other benefits were "depoliticized". They were removed from the ordinary political process to make them more immune to cross-party competition and public scrutiny. First, this was done through linkage, with allowances automatically following the salaries of magistrates at the Council of State. Other decisions were made in small and non-transparent intra-parliamentary decision-making units, which facilitated consensual decision-making and even allowed for bypassing the constitution. Only in 1996, most elements of the income structure were settled by law, making them more transparent. But decisions on allowances for intra-parliamentary leadership offices, intrinsic office rewards, and severance pay are still taken by the Houses' Bureau, and prepared

---

[24] Legal political incompatibilities prevent MPs to sit in both chambers. After the 1993 Reform of the State, this legislative incompatibility was extended to membership of sub-national legislatures as well as to ministerial office. A diffuse legislation—over fifty special laws and decrees—regulates incompatibilities of parliamentary office with memberships or directorships in a number of para-governmental agencies, regulatory institutions, and advisory boards. Most of these rules date from 1936, when incompatibilities in the economic, financial, and commercial sphere were introduced to counter allegations of conflicts of interests. There are no legal incompatibilities of parliamentary office with private occupations or with positions in pressure groups.

[25] The maximum of four years is only arrived at after 27 years of service.

and implemented by their College of Questors. Decision-making in these units is characterized by low publicity of debate and low transparency.

Overall, the location of decision-making allows for large autonomy between the two chambers and versus the executive, which is only restricted by two constraints: The first are party rules governing members' party contributions and outside earning opportunities. The second is the responsibility of the Minister of Finance regarding the fiscal treatment of MPs' allowances.

The income differentials for top positions in both the public and private sector are substantial. Cabinet members earn twice as much as ordinary backbenchers; top civil servants earn one third and top judges two thirds more than MPs. Overall though, civil servants and judges have few outside earning opportunities and so do cabinet members.[26] The gap to top private pay is clear, as the "average" manager earns almost twice as much as an MP, with bonuses and performance premiums further widening the gap. However, contrary to suggestions of recent, cross-national executive remuneration studies (Hood and Lambert 1994: 39–40), it cannot be said that the gap has widened over the last decade.

THE POLITICAL CLASS AND INSTITUTIONAL REFORM

Since the 1991 "Black Sunday" elections, in which the extreme right and other protest parties made significant progress, the issue of institutional reform and refining democracy has moved high up on the agenda of Belgian politics. This has produced a great number of reform proposals concerning a wide range of institutions and procedures. Therefore it is impossible to give a comprehensive survey, and we can only address the main initiatives.

Within a working group co-ordinated by the Speaker of the House,[27] a consensus was reached in 1997. The issues that were implemented in the years following included: improving the income status of local office holders; a modest restriction of the *cumul local*;[28] the closing of some loopholes of party finance by the private sector; the lowering of the maximum campaign cost limit for individual candidates; the prohibition of the use of commercial publicity boards for campaigns; the extension of consultative referendums at the local level; the re-evaluation and simplification of existing legislation; an increasing accessibility of public administration; the enhancing

---

[26] In 1991, the incomes of Senators, BEF2,281,000 (€56,568), and Members of the House, BEF2,269,000 (€56,271), were nearly the same. High civil servants got BEF2,878,000 (€71,370) and higher judges BEF3,507,000 (€86,970). At the top were the salaries for ministers with BEF4,535,000 (€112,470), which are even above the ones for top managers in the private sector with BEF4,230,000 (€104,900). Data provided by the Financial Services of the House; for more data and references, see Brans 1999.

[27] This group comprised the four majority parties (the Flemish and Francophone Socialists and Christian Democrats) and the Francophone Liberals.

[28] From 1999 onwards, MPs can combine their mandate with only one executive office at the local/provincial level, while before they could combine several. The total amount of income from all public mandates generated this way may not exceed 150% of the parliamentary pay, which would be topped off in case of excess income. Still the income stemming from private sector activities is not limited at all.

of transparency, responsiveness, responsibility and efficacy of public administration; the depolitization of civil service recruitment and promotions; and the drafting of a code for MPs that would curtail their clientelistic interventions in public administration.[29] Also many parties have drafted codes of proper conduct, which are usually more strict than the current consensus, and in which each party to some extent tries to put into practice for its own elected officials the principles they would like to impose on the entire political class (De Winter and Dumont 2000).

The new red-blue-green Verhofstadt government (1999) put political reform high on its agenda. It established a bicameral commission for political renewal, whose agenda covered an enormous range of topics. Up until now, it has produced two excellent extensive reports about referendums and electoral reform. However, the main proposals for renewal did not emerge out of this commission. It was bypassed by the government, under strong leadership of the prime-minister. The commission was also heavily affected by absenteeism.

Hence, the new government has reached political agreements about the following issues: large province-based constituencies; the introduction of a provincial 5 percent threshold; increasing the impact of preference voting; direct election of the mayors; gender parity on candidate lists, with assured presence of women on safe places. The Senate is to be reformed dramatically, but it is doubtful that the current Senators will agree to the disempowerment of their assembly.

CONCLUSION: PROFESSIONALIZED POLITICS IN A DELEGITIMIZED PARTITOCRACY

Belgium, together with Italy, is often labeled a partitocracy (De Winter, Della Porta, and Deschouwer 1996). Whenever political power is delegated, political parties play a predominant role. They channel the delegation of power from voters to MPs, from Parliament to the cabinet, from the collective cabinet to individual ministers, and from ministers to their civil servants (De Winter and Dumont forthcoming). The parties have developed a large number of *ex ante* and *ex post* controls and permanent monitoring mechanisms in order to maintain their control over MPs as well as ministers and civil servants.

Survey research indicates that a large majority of Belgian citizens believe that parties and politicians are not responsive to the policy preference of ordinary citizens (ISPO-PIOP 1999 post-electoral survey). This public disaffection with Belgian parties reached alarming degrees at the end of the 1980s, as reflected in the breakthrough of the extreme right and other protest parties. Yet, while the Italian *partitocrazia* suddenly imploded in the early 1990s, the Belgian *particratie* underwent a number of gradual adaptations, which reduced (the negative consequences of) the grip of political parties

[29] The Flemish Parliament has recently accepted such a code, drafted by one of the authors (Lieven De Winter), which gradually becomes the standard for similar codes being drafted by other legislative assemblies at the national, provincial, and local level.

on central government and thus prevented a full collapse of the partitocratic system. To some degree they restored the governability of the country. Still, even while major corrections have been made, one can wonder whether these are sufficient to cope with the strong outburst of public dissatisfaction with the way parties have run the country in the past decades. The heavy burden of the repayment of the gigantic public debt will remind the population for decades of the excesses of the Belgian partitocracy and for a long time will undermine the legitimacy of the main political parties. Their chances of survival will eventually depend on the scale of the *mani pulite* operation recently launched by the Belgian judiciary and the delegitimizing effects of the handling of the pedophilia, dioxin and other scandals (De Winter and Rihoux 1998).

However, while satisfaction with democracy took a dramatic dip in 1997 (minus 34 percent to 19 percent, the lowest in the European Union), it has recovered surprisingly quick, to even above the European average (De Winter and Türsan 2001). Trust in political institutions has followed this trend (with trust in government, Parliament, the parties, and public administration approaching again the European average), but trust remains dramatically low for the judiciary, police, army, and the Church.

Hence, restoration seems to have started. Survey research indicates that political reform has dropped from the citizens' agenda, but it remains high on the political agenda, due to the reform-thrive of the blue-red-green coalition parties (De Winter 2003). If the next elections of 2003 blacken another Sunday (due to the primacy of security, anti-immigration, anti-muslim paranoia due to 9/11, declining economy and budgetary margins, and government policy incohesion) institutional reform may vanish from the overall political agenda for the next decade.

REFERENCES

Ackaert, Johan (1988). "Nationale schaduwen over de gemeentepolitie". *Kultuurleven*, 55: 629–35.

Baufay, Vincent (1991). "La stratification sociale du parlementaire belge: Mis à jour des thèses de M. Debuyst", unpublished M.A. thesis, Brussels: Université Libre de Bruxelles.

Beaufays, Jean (1972). "Tentative d'analyse sociologique du député catholique belge". *Courrier Hebdomadaire du CRISP*, 573.

Brans, Marleen (1994). "Belgium: Public Office—Private Rewards", in C. Hood and G. Peters (eds), *Rewards at the Top*. London: Sage, pp. 106–19.

—— (1999). "The Dynamics of Material Reward Systems for Legislators: A Comparative Study of Material Rewards for Legislators in the Netherlands and Belgium", Ph.D. thesis, Florence: European University Institute.

De Bakker, Bert (1969). "Bijdrage tot een sociografie van de Belgische politieke tegenstellingen", unpublished M.A. thesis, Leuven: Departement Politieke Wetenschappen.

De Bondt, Hedwig (1971). "Stratificatie van de Belgische Parlementsleden bij middel van hun extraparlementaire bindingen", unpublished M.A. thesis, Leuven: Departement Politieke Wetenschappen.

Debuyst, Frédéric (1967). *La fonction parlementaire en belgique: Mécanismes d'accès et images*. Bruxelles: CRISP.

Depauw, Sam (1997). "Een huis met een grote tuin", in W. Dewachter, I. Thomas, and S. Depauw (eds), *Afscheid van het laatste dubbelparlement*. Leuven: Acco, pp. 207–23.

—— (2000). "Cohesie in de parlementsfracties van de regeringsmeerderheid: Een vergelijkend onderzoek in België, Frankrijk en het Verenigd Koninkrijk (1987–97)", Ph.D. thesis, Leuven: Departement Politieke Wetenschappen.

Deridder, Martine, Peterson, Robert L., and Wirth, Rex (1978). "Images of Belgian Politics: The Effects of Changes on the Political System". *Legislative Studies Quarterly*, 3: 83–108.

Deschouwer, Kris (1992). "Belgium", in R. Katz and P. Mair (eds.), *Party Organizations*. London: Sage, pp. 141–98.

—— (1996). "Waiting for the 'Big One': The Uncertain Survival of the Belgian Parties and Party System(s)". *Res Publica*, 48: 295–306.

—— De Winter, Lieven, and Della Porta, Donatella (eds) (1996). "Partitocracies between Crises and Reforms: The Cases of Italy and Belgium". *Special Issue of Res Publica*, 48: 215–494.

Dewachter, Wilfried (1992). *Besluitvorming in Politiek België*. Leuven: Acco.

—— (2001). *De mythe van de parlementaire democratie: Een Belgische analyse*. Leuven: Acco.

—— Thomas, Inge, and Depauw, Sam (1997). *Afscheid van het laatste dubbelparlement*. Leuven: Acco.

De Winter, Lieven (1980). "Twintig jaar polls, of de teloorgang van een vorm van interne partijdemocratie". *Res Publica*, 32: 563–85.

—— (1988). "Belgium: Democracy or Oligarchy?", in M. Gallagher and M. Marsh (eds), *Candidate Selection in Comparative Perspective*. London: Sage, pp. 20–46.

—— (1990). "Parlement et parti politique comme trajectoire de la carrière ministérielle en Belgique". *Les Cahiers du CRAPS (Université de Lille II)*, 12: 40–54.

—— (1992). "The Belgian Legislator", Ph.D. thesis, Florence: European University Institute.

—— (1997). "Belgian MP's between Party and Voters". *Journal of Legislative Studies*, 3: 128–54.

—— (1998). "Parliament and Government in Belgium: Prisoners of Partitocracy", in P. Norton (ed.), *Parliaments and Executives in Western Europe*. London: Frank Cass, pp. 97–122.

—— (2003). "Political corruption in the Belgium" in M. Bull and J. Newell (eds), *Corruption in Contemporary Politics*. London: Macmillan, pp. 33–105.

—— Della Porta, Donatella, and Deschouwer, Kris (1996). "Comparing Similar Countries: Italy and Belgium". *Res Publica*, 38: 215–36.

—— and Dumont, Patrick (1999). "The Belgian Party System(s) on the Eve of Disintegration", in D. Broughton and M. Donovan (eds), *Changing Party Systems in Western Europe*. London: Pinter, pp. 183–206.

—— and Dumont, Patrick (2000). "Belgium: Subjects of Partitocratic Dominion", in K. Heidar and R. Koole (eds), *Parliamentary Party Groups in European Democracies*. London: Routledge, pp. 106–29.

—— and Dumont, Patrick (forthcoming). "Belgium: Delegation and Accountability under Partitocratic Rule", in K. Strøm, W. Müller, and T. Bergman (eds), *Delegation and Accountability in Western Europe*. Oxford: Oxford University Press.

—— and Rihoux, Benoit (1998). "From Segmented Loyalty and Distrust, to Voice and Exit? The Belgian Regime Crisis". *ECPR-News*, 9/3: 22–3.

—— Timmermans, Arco, and Dumont, Patrick (2000). "Coalition Formation and Governance in Belgium: Of Government Gospels, Evangelist, Followers and Traitors", in W. Müller and K. Strøm (eds.), *Coalition Government in Western Europe*. Oxford: Oxford University Press, pp. 300–55.

—— and Türsan, Huri (2001). *The Belgian Presidency 2001*. Notre Europe, Research and Policy Paper, 13. Paris.

Dierickx, Guido (1978). "Ideological Oppositions and Consociational Attitudes in the Belgian Parliament". *Legislative Studies Quarterly*, 3: 133–60.

Dumont, Patrick, and De Winter, Lieven (1999). "La formation et le maintien des gouvernements belges (1946–1999)". *Courrier Hebdomadaire du CRISP*, 1664.

Fiers, Stefaan (1998). "Partijvoorzitters in België", Ph.D. thesis, Leuven: Departement Politieke Wetenschappen.

—— (2000). *Vijftig jaar volksvertegenwoordiging. De circulatie onder de Belgische parlementsleden 1946–1995*. Brussels: Koninklijke Vlaamse Academie van België.

Frognier, André (1978). "Parties and Cleavages in the Belgian Parliament". *Legislative Studies Quarterly*, 3: 109–32.

Hood, Christopher C., and Lambert, Sonia (1994). "Mountain Tops or Iceberg Tips?", in C. Hood and G. Peters (eds), *Rewards at the Top*. London: Sage, pp. 25–48.

ICSOP-IMSA (1986). *Le rôle du parlementaire en Belgique*. Brussels: ICSOP-IMSA.

IMADI (1989). *Studie naar het vertrouwen dat de Belgische bevolking heeft in de eerlijkheid en bekwaamheid van een aantal (overheids-) organisaties en maatschappelijke sleutelfiguren*. Antwerpen: IMADI.

ISPO-PIOP (1999). *Codebook Belgian General Elections*. Leuven-Louvain-la-Neuve: ISPO-PIOP.

Jagers, Jan (2002). "Eigen democratie eerst! Een comparatief onderzoek naar het intern democratisch gehalte van de Vlaamse politieke partijen". *Res Publica*, 44: 73–96.

Mitchell, B. R. (1992). *International Historical Statistics, Europe 1750–1988*, 3rd edition. New York: Stockton Press.

Ronsmans, Myriam (1985). "De cumulatie van mandaten door de Belgische parlementsleden", unpublished M.A. thesis, Leuven: Departement Politieke Wetenschappen.

Schmidt, Detlef (1970). "Die Beteiligung der Nationalitäten in der Politischen Elite in Belgien 1944–1968", dissertation, Kiel: Christian-Albrechts-Universität.

Schmitt, Herman, and Thomassen, Jacques (eds) (1999). *Political Representation and Legitimacy in the European Union*. Oxford: Oxford University Press.

Scholliers, Pieter (1985). *Loonindexering en sociale vrede: De koopkracht en klassestrijd*. Brussels: VUB, Centrum voor Hedendaagse Geschiedenis.

Smeets, Réné (1994). *Ouderen en Politiek*. Leuven: Davidsfonds.

Smits, Jef (1986). "Les standen dans les partis sociaux-chrétiens", *Courrier Hebdomadaire du CRISP*: 1134–5.

—— and Wauters, Bram (2000). "Het gebruik van de voorkeurstem bij de parlementsverkiezingen van 13 juni 1999". *Res Publica*, 42: 265–304.

Suetens, Marc, and Walgrave, Stefaan (1999). "Leven en werk van de kabinetslede". *Res Publica*, 41: 499–528.

Van Bunder, Dirk (1993). *De officiële inkomsten van de politieke partijen en hun parlementaire fracties*. Brussels: Vrije Unviersiteit Brussel, Centrum voor Politicologie.

Van Hassel, Hugo (1959). "Sociografische aspecten van de Belgische Senaat, 1919–1958". dissertation, Leuven: Departement Politieke Wetenschappen.

Van Velthoven, Louis (1987). *De ministeriële hofhouding*. s.l.: s.n.

4

Canada: Political Careers between Executive Hopes and Constituency Work

DAVID C. DOCHERTY

Conventional wisdom suggests that most political careers in Canada are simply time-outs from careers outside the political world (see Franks 1987; Ferejohn and Gaines 1991; Laponce 1992). It is true that the high levels of turnover in federal elections—anywhere from one to two thirds of the House of Commons is replaced at election time—means that the Canadian political career tends to be short when compared to careers in other nations (such as the United States and Great Britain). It is also true that the executive-centered nature of the Canadian Parliament places a disproportionate amount of authority within the cabinet, and that the majority of Members of Parliament (MPs) are effectively shut out of initiating public policy and legislation. Additionally, continual election studies have shown that most voters place party and leader ahead of the local candidate when casting their ballots at election time.

It is not surprising then that the political career in Canada is viewed, at least by academics, as a particularly unattractive one. Most MPs have spent their careers entirely on the backbenches, away from the levers of power. There is little opportunity for promotion. The size of cabinet has declined since the 1980s, and the choice of who sits in cabinet rests entirely with the Prime Minister. Yet despite the seemingly unpromising opportunity structure, the number of applicants seeking entry into the political class increases at each election. And while most successful candidates are content with the existing structures, a new political party that has tapped into increasing public cynicism has emerged. Among other things, the new Canadian Alliance has been leading the call for changing the existing rules (both formal and informal) that govern the members of the House of Commons.[1] As a result, the federal political class is at something of a crossroads.

The author gratefully acknowledges the financial support this research received from a grant partly funded by Wilfrid Laurier University Operating funds, and partly by the SSHRCC General Research Grant awarded to Wilfrid Laurier University.

[1] The Canadian Alliance was created in 1999 in an attempt to unify right of center parties in Canada under one banner. Although new, the party is largely constructed from the Reform Party of Canada itself a grassroots party that was created in the late 1980s out of a sense of disenchantment with the then Progressive Conservative government.

This chapter examines the present state of the political class in Canada. It argues that the political class has three predominant characteristics:

- First, all MPs enjoy certain benefits and privileges of office, privileges they in fact created and maintain.
- Second, at least until recently, not all backbenchers are the unhappy warriors that many academics have painted them to be. Many MPs have found satisfying careers by ignoring an institutional context that does not favor promotion or the realization of personal ambition.
- Third, recent elections (1993, 1997, and 2000) have produced sizeable cohorts of MPs unafraid of challenging the existing institutional rules and norms. Many of these members can be found on the government backbenches.

The combination of these factors has produced a parliament where traditional assumptions about party discipline and strong hierarchical leadership are being increasingly challenged.

POLITICAL PROFESSIONALIZATION IN HISTORICAL PERSPECTIVE

The holding of federal elected office in Canada did not develop into a full-time, professionally paid position until well into the late 1950s and early 1960s. Prior to this, most MPs were considered political amateurs for several reasons: they were not professional politicians who made politics their full-time job; they did not see politics as a life's calling; they had little experience in the political world; and they did not stay in office for long periods of time. The notable exception to this rule were members of the political executive. In particular, starting in the Depression, and especially during and after the Second World War, being a member of cabinet was a full-time job, even if the remuneration was not sufficient to make ends meet. As a result, up until the 1960s most members of cabinet were individuals successful in other lines of work who could afford a full-time political career. Most backbenchers only came to Ottawa when the House sat, and were expected to have paying jobs at home, albeit positions that could afford them generous time off to deal with the nation's business.

Beginning in the 1950s, the House of Commons began to increase both its number of sitting days and its remuneration to members. For many political scientists and politicians, the "modern" parliament began with the election of John Diefenbaker in 1957 (Atkinson and Thomas 1993). According to former veteran MP and then Senator C. G. "Chubby" Power it was during the latter part of the 1950s that MPs "metamorphosed" from part-time legislators into full-time, professional politicians. In reminiscing on his own political past, Power describes how the House of Commons was transformed from a place where individuals went to further their own business interests to one where individuals had to give up their other businesses to become full-time career politicians (Power 1957: 479).

The transformation of the federal politician from part-time dabbler to full-time legislator was more evolutionary than revolutionary. The increase in the number of sitting days which began in the late 1950s and early 1960s meant that MPs began spending less time in their ridings and more time in Ottawa. During this period, increasing Ottawa demands were coupled with an increased demand from members' constituencies. Members could no longer handle all constituency concerns with a Friday and Saturday "surgery," using their spouse as a constituency assistant. Full-time constituency staff in a formal office became essential. Lawmakers could no longer be part-time legislators.

The rate of pay for members began to increase to meet the growing time demands and allow them to treat elected office as a profession. Today, all MPs are full-time paid politicians with salaries and additional indemnities that take most of them over the CA$130,000 (approx. €84,940)[2] mark each year, with staff, caucus resources, and offices in Ottawa and their constituencies. Some members even move to Ottawa with their families and consider it as their primary residence. Members of Parliament in Canada, therefore, now all consider themselves (although they might choose not to admit it) professional politicians.

At the same time, the federal legislature itself began a slow move toward professionalization. By the late 1960s, an increasingly full agenda caused the executive to delegate some of its responsibilities to backbench members via a renewed committee system. While done in the interests of making the cabinet more efficient, the effect was to give more authority (and responsibility) to non-cabinet members (Jackson and Atkinson 1980; see also Jewett 1966). In order to help facilitate these new responsibilities, opposition parties (in 1969) and the government party (in 1970) were provided funds for caucus research staff (Franks 1987: 85–8). At present, any political party with twelve sitting members in the 301-seat House is recognized as an official party and receives funding for research and administrative staff.

In this regard, whether members of the political elite or not, all MPs share in the privileges of the political class. Simply by dint of being elected, a member is provided up to four full-time office employees, funding for constituency offices, and resources in the capital. However, given the dominance of political parties in Canada, it is not surprising that further resources are provided to parties that meet the twelve member threshold. The cost of leaving a party to sit as an independent includes giving up access to these additional research and administrative privileges.

The House of Commons, while always de facto independent of the executive, has, in the past two decades, increased its autonomy from cabinet. A Board of Internal Economy, with members representing all officially recognized parties and chaired by the Speaker of the House, sets administrative and budgetary policy for the Commons. Since 1988 the Speaker of the House is elected by all members in a secret ballot vote, and nominees for the job of Speaker now seek support from all MPs, not just the Prime Minister. After each election, an independent commission reviews and establishes members' salaries, though Parliament must vote to approve the commission report.

---

[2] All Euro amounts converted as of 27 October 2002 (CA$1 = €0.653) and rounded.

The Commons has also become more "professionalized" in more subtle yet just as important ways. For example, after each election, the Commons holds orientation sessions for all new MPs. Beyond helping rookies literally find their way around the legislative complex, these sessions help to reinforce existing norms and values about the legislative environment in Ottawa. This, coupled with the fact that new members turn to veteran legislators (and staff that may have preceded their arrival) for advice and direction, helps to reinforce existing institutional practices. In becoming more professional, the Commons has also become a more dominant feature of members' lives.

THE INSTITUTIONAL CONTEXT

The Canadian Parliament is a Westminster-style parliament in a federal state, which, when combined with the single member plurality electoral system, produces some interesting consequences for governance in Canada. First, the bulk of authority for national governing rests within a small segment of the national Parliament, the executive. Yet the executive must be seen to represent the entire country and all its regions. While the choice of who makes it to cabinet is vested entirely with the Prime Minister, there are a number of practical political constraints on this freedom of choice. In particular, the cabinet must be seen to represent the different regions of the country (Atkinson and Docherty 2000). Historically, this meant that the cabinet was dominated by regional "barons," individuals who were regarded as the chief spokesperson for their region in cabinet. Regional patronage and government contracts were all dispensed, at least informally, through this regional minister (Bakvis 1991). While the strength of regional ministers has declined, they still exist and remain a potent force in policy and political decision making.

Beyond region, Prime Ministers are also encouraged to ensure that every province has a representative in cabinet. While this is not difficult for larger provinces (Ontario, for example, has just over one third of the 301 federal seats), it can become troublesome in the case of smaller provinces, such as Prince Edward Island which has only four seats in the House of Commons. An MP who is the sole government representative of a smaller province, therefore, has an almost automatic berth at the cabinet table regardless of individual talent and ability, while many talented members from larger provinces have less opportunity for promotion. The need for gender, linguistic, and ethnic balance at the cabinet table also influences the Prime Minister's choices.

The single member plurality system has often caused distortions between the percentage of votes a party receives and the percentage of seats they win (Cairns 1968). More than once a Prime Minister has faced the unpleasant prospect of forming a government with little or no representation from one or more regions. The 2000 general election, for example, returned the Liberal Party to power with 174 of the 301 seats in the House of Commons. However, the Liberals nearly elected three-quarters of their caucus from Ontario and Quebec. The Liberals elected only fourteen members out of a possible eighty-eight in Western Canada.

When this type of situation occurs, Prime Ministers are not adverse to turning to the upper house (or Senate) to ensure regional representation. The Senate is an appointed body with limited power. Senators are appointed by the Prime Minister, sit uncontested, and are well paid until the age of seventy five when they must retire.[3] The Senate can stop legislation sent to it from the House, but cannot initiate any legislation on its own. The primary political purpose of the Senate, beyond filling regional vacancies in the cabinet, has been to serve as a repository for the party faithful of the government of the day. Prime ministers have traditionally used the Senate either to reward long serving MPs who are retiring or to create vacancies in the Commons (Docherty 2002). Given the sinecure of senators, it is hardly surprising that more than one MP has decided to turn his or her back on elections and move to Canada's upper chamber.

Senators sit in their respective party caucuses and often play an active role in organizing their party's election strategy. Senators are, therefore, members of Canada's political class, despite the fact that most of their work is done behind the scenes. Calls for Senate reform in Canada have become more frequent in the last decade, but are unlikely to come about as they would require substantial constitutional changes. Given the lack of public support for the Senate, and the failure of successive attempts at constitutional change, Prime Ministers have tried to deflect attention from the Senate by using their power to appoint Senators to cabinet only when other options are not available.[4]

While Senators do participate in their respective party caucuses, their roles are not as well defined as those of members of the Commons. There are many strong legislative oriented Senators, but this is more a personal choice than a formal job requirement. For some members of Canada's upper house fund-raising and election preparedness can take precedence over an interest in policy and legislation. In this sense, senators are more party operatives than professional politicians. The most active members of the political class remain the elected MPs.

For Members of the House of Commons, the increasing professionalization of their chamber and the increasing resources placed at their disposal, have not lessened the still dominant role played by political parties and party leaders. Paul Thomas (1985: 43) suggests that the strength of parties in Parliament is so great that "in Canada, legislative behaviour is party behaviour." Party leaders enjoy great discretion in running the parliamentary wing of political parties. The two related reasons for this leader dominance inside Parliament can be traced to the historically strong emphasis on party discipline and the control leaders have in choosing who sits in cabinet or the opposition front benches.

---

[3] Like for MPs, the "average" remuneration for senators is difficult to determine. Senators, however, earn over CA$100,000 (€65,340) a year for their efforts.

[4] Attempts to change the Senate have been made several times in the past two decades. However, as with most attempts at constitutional reform in Canada, these changes become tied up in other proposals for constitutional amendments and inevitably fail.

The Canadian legislature takes a more restricted view of confidence than does the British House of Commons. Canadian Prime Ministers are loath to lose any vote, and as a result are always anxious to have the undivided loyalty of members of their caucus when it comes to voting. The notion of confidence is directly related to the need for strong party discipline in the Canadian House of Commons. Party discipline and caucus solidarity are, therefore, hallmarks of the Canadian legislative system. Challenges to the existing arrangement of formal rules and informal practices are thus challenges to the notion of party dominance in all aspects of legislative life.

THE POLITICAL CLASS

Size and Composition

Delineating the size of the political class in Canada is a difficult task. Like many things in Canada, the ability to live off politics, either as a professional politician or a paid staff person of a politician or party, differs by region and province. Members of the Parliament of Canada, both in the Commons and Senate, are almost by definition members of the political class. Further, many staff members of MPs and Senators could easily be defined as members of the political class, particularly the staff in the nation's capital. Full-time, paid constituency staff hold a less obvious political role. Their primary duties include helping individuals who get caught up in government red-tape, a less political and more ombudsperson type role.

Defining the political class at the sub-national level is even more problematic. Provincial legislatures are all professional to some degree, but in some provinces the provincial assembly meets less frequently and backbenchers have outside careers in addition to their elected ones (Moncrief 1994). Most of the large and mid-size provinces have professional legislatures and provide all members with staff and constituency resources. The opportunities for full-time political careers in these legislatures are present and there is little movement from provincial to federal office in these provinces. Only for members of provincial assemblies in the Atlantic provinces is it more common to attempt to build a national career, due in large part to the smaller size and limited opportunities in these legislatures.

For the purposes of this chapter, therefore, discussion of the political class will focus on the elected men and women in the national House of Commons. It is recognized, however, that the political class is a fluid social construct, that includes appointed officials, party activists, and legislators at the municipal and sub-national level. Yet for all of these other positions, the apex of the political career in Canada is a seat at the cabinet table gained by sitting as an elected MP.

Like in most democratic states, the demographic profile of MPs does not closely resemble the profile of the general population. Most members are white males who have greater than average education and whose careers prior to politics were more professional and financially rewarding than that of the average Canadian.

The traditionally dominant political parties in Canada (the Liberals, Progressive Conservatives, and New Democrats) have made different attempts to encourage the election of women, all with limited degrees of success. The left wing New Democratic Party has nominated more female candidates than the other parties, but has never enjoyed the national success of the Liberal, Conservative, and now Canadian Alliance parties. The number of women in the Commons has increased at each election in the past two decades, but only crept over the 20 percent level after the 1997 and 2000 general elections. Most analysts suggest that local autonomy in the nomination process and a lack of financial resources available to help women fight for competitive party nominations are the root causes of the under-representation of women (Young 1991).

The average age of most political newcomers in each Parliament (see Table 4.1) provides support to the conventional analysis that most members do not enter at an early age. In fact, it is clear that most MPs leave some other occupation they have spent some time in, to pursue their political career. The fact that most members come to Ottawa without provincial or municipal experience supports this view. For most members of the national political class, therefore, their time spent as a MP is their only elected experience.

Political Recruitment and Political Careers

The combination of party discipline and leader dominance has helped to create a federal political career in Ottawa that can be characterized as both self-contained and relatively unwelcoming for members with progressive ambition. Despite this, however, the federal House of Commons is the institution that best provides the opportunity for satisfying progressive ambition in Canada. For most politically ambitious individuals the road to success in Canada goes through the House of Commons. It is perhaps surprising then that so few members of the federal political class follow a ladder from municipal to provincial to federal service. As Table 4.1 indicates, few

Table 4.1 *Selected characteristics of the MPs in five legislative periods*

	33rd Parl. (1984–88)	34th Parl. (1988–93)	35th Parl. (1993–97)	36th Parl. (1997–2000)	37th Parl. (2000–)
Female MPs (%)	10.4	13.2	18.0	20.1	20.9
Average age entering office	42.2	43.9	46.5	45.8	49.8
MPs who served provinicially	8.6	7.1	5.2	6.5	8.6
MPs who served municipally	25.2	25.8	20.2	25.7	27.6

Note: With the exception of the 36th and 37th Parliaments, all figures are based on the membership of the House of Commons at the end of the legislative session. Municipal service includes those individuals who served as elected members of local school boards.

Sources: Docherty (1997); Canada of Parliament web site (www.parl.gc.ca).

members come with municipal experience and even fewer with provincial training. One of the reasons for this separation of offices is the lack of organized party politics at the local level in Canada. Few cities and towns are organized politically along party lines. Local politics, therefore, is not the best starting block for party politicians. Nonetheless, in the past decade a number of mayors from large urban centers have gone on to lead provincial parties and governments and to run nationally and sit in the federal cabinet. However, these individuals are often courted to run by political parties and do not see the mayor's office as a stepping stone to federal or provincial politics.

Additionally, the separate federal and provincial party organizations in Canada have helped to create barriers between the sub-national and national assemblies (Dyck 1989). What little movement from provincial office to the federal Parliament exists is more likely to occur in the smaller Atlantic provinces (New Brunswick, Nova Scotia, Prince Edward Island, and Newfoundland) than anywhere else. By and large, however, there is very little movement from the provincial to federal level.[5] Finally, federal legislation prevents individuals from running for national office while serving provincially. Once provincial members have a federal party nomination, they must give up their sub-national seat. The same rules do not apply to municipal office holders. There is less risk, therefore, in seeking federal office from a municipal seat than there is from a provincial one.

For the most part, the political class in Ottawa is a self-contained and self-recruited group. Most MPs begin and end their political careers within the parliament itself. Given the executive-centered nature of Canada's parliamentary system, opportunities for significant influence in policy are limited to those individuals in or close to the political executive. The attractiveness of a cabinet career is almost self-evident. Government policy and legislation are initiated in cabinet or cabinet committees. A cabinet position provides an MP with the opportunity to develop a national reputation and profile, and thus Cabinet becomes the ultimate goal of every ambitious federal politician. A seat at the federal cabinet table, therefore, represents the only chair that allows an individual the opportunity to satisfy both political and policy ambition. It is the only guaranteed ticket of entry into the political elite. The positions of parliamentary secretaries and legislative committee chairs are seen as informal rungs on the career ladder in the Commons. These lesser positions are viewed as just that by most MPs: lesser positions.

The importance of getting into cabinet is evidenced by how MPs themselves value these positions. Members of the thirty-fourth Parliament (1988–93) and rookie MPs in the thirty-fifth Parliament were asked how important obtaining a cabinet

---

[5] In fact, there is almost as much movement from the federal level to the provinces. Backbench MPs have left Ottawa to become provincial party leaders, where they enjoy a higher profile and a chance at leading a government. Further, the left-wing New Democratic Party (NDP) has formed governments provincially but not federally. NDP politicians, therefore, have more opportunities to become members of the political elite at the sub-national level.

Table 4.2   *Career goals of experienced members vs. rookies, 1993*

Position sought	Importance to career (% of answers)							
	Very important		Somewhat		Not very		Not at all	
	Vets.	Ro.	Vets.	Ro.	Vets.	Ro.	Vets.	Ro.
Cabinet	21	100	38	0	17	0	23	0
Shadow cabinet	33	50	46	50	11	0	10	0

Vets. = veterans; Ro. = rookies.

Note: N for veteran Members = 86, for Rookies = 18.

Source: Authors own survey of MPs, 1993.

position and/or a shadow cabinet position was in terms of their own career satisfaction (Table 4.2).[6]

A spot at the cabinet table is the brass ring of federal politics. Over 80 percent of MPs indicated it was an important career goal. All rookies felt it an important career goal. For veterans, their ambition might be tempered by a realization that cabinet might not be in their cards. Nonetheless, most ambitious MPs want to make it to the cabinet table, and this ambition runs across political parties, including the relatively new Alliance Party and the older but less successful New Democratic Party (Docherty 1997). The problem members encounter is getting to the cabinet table. As suggested earlier, Prime Ministers have the final say on who makes it to cabinet, and talent and ability must often take a back seat to loyalty and region. The problem that remains for most MPs, therefore, is how to deal with a political career that is relatively stagnant. The answer for most is to turn their attention away from the legislature and look back to their ridings.

According to Richard Price and Maureen Mancuso (1995), the opportunity structure of office in Canada encourages MPs to concentrate on the constituency aspect of their jobs in two distinct yet complementary ways. The few available cabinet positions and the relative obscurity of committee work leaves little to be gained by concentrating on parliamentary tasks over local work (Price and Mancuso: 224–6). Additionally, the provision of human and financial resources is not limited to Parliament Hill. Members are free to dedicate any or all of their global staffing allowance to personnel in their federally funded offices within their ridings, ostensibly to better serve their constituents. If members are frustrated with Parliament Hill activities, they are completely free to turn to, and have their staffs turn to, matters of a more parochial nature.

[6] Unless otherwise indicated, data used in this chapter are taken from surveys of the two Parliaments undertaken by the author for a larger study (see Docherty 1997) or from a survey undertaken by the author funded by SSHRCC Grant 1999–2002.

Table 4.3 *Interests of parliamentarians, 2001*

Duty	Rank of enjoyment
Serving constituency	1
Developing public policy	2
Helping individual constituents	3
Being an issue advocate inside caucus	4
Communicating government policy	5

Note: 1 = most enjoyable, 5 = least enjoyable.

Surveys of MPs seem to bear out this hypothesis. The combination of constituency services and lack of internal opportunities seems to encourage Members to look for satisfaction outside the legislative arena. In terms of time, constituency service takes up more of an MP's day than any other single activity. In fact, for most members it takes up more time than all other responsibilities combined (Docherty 1997; see also Eagles 1997). And as Table 4.3 indicates, local work is the type of activity that brings the most pleasure to members who are effectively shut out from parliamentary decision-making. This is true even among members who came to Ottawa with legislative work in mind and the idea of constituency work as a necessary evil.

Most MPs in Canada are first and foremost constituency members.[7] The majority of members spend the bulk of their time and energies on constituency problems. Part of this is, of course, demand-driven. Constituency offices attract attention, attention most MPs are eager to grab. They see local work as an effective way of maintaining their reputation as problem solvers. People in the riding who encounter problems with government agencies or departments expect MPs to help resolve these difficulties (Ferejohn and Gaines 1991). In the minds of most parliamentarians, this also has electoral consequences. Aware that their futures are inexorably tied to that of their leader and party, they also recognize that a failure to engage in local work will almost guarantee electoral defeat (Docherty 1997).

One interesting change can be noted. In 2001, parliamentarians ranked developing public policy ahead of helping individual constituents (though the percentages were quite close). This marks a major change from previous parliaments where helping individuals was always a close second behind serving the constituency as a whole (see Docherty 1997, 2002). It is too early to determine the cause of this change. It might reflect the arrival of the Canadian Alliance—a new right wing populist party that replaced the Reform Party and is presently the Official Opposition. But new Liberal MPs who are not in the cabinet have also indicated an increased interest in public policy formation. It is important to note, however, that while there appears to be a renewed interest in matters of policy, members still devote the largest portion of their working day to constituency matters.

---

[7] For a fuller discussion of constituency pulls see Price and Mancuso (1995) and Docherty (1997, 2002).

There is an additional benefit to be gained from concentrating on local service. For many MPs, it means avoiding any conflicts with their party leader and whip. Local service has little partisan content. Members are seen as fighting for their riding, not for their party. Acting as a local trouble shooter means avoiding conflict with the party, its leader, and the government. Instead members see voters as customers who are always right, and the bureaucracy as the obstacle to consumer satisfaction. Party discipline is removed from the equation of representation when members tackle local issues. If anything, party leaders are quick to defer to their caucus members when the latter are speaking about local concerns and issues.

In sum, the political career of most MPs often looks like the flight path of a boomerang. Members go to Ottawa hoping to engage in meaningful policy work. However, with most policy spheres being held by members of cabinet, and few chances of getting into cabinet, MPs soon look for other meaningful activities to fill their day. The one that is most constant and rewarding is local service. There is always a demand for a local problem solver and members are quite willing to react to this need.

Living off Politics: Electoral Security in the Political Class

Thus far it has been suggested that in terms of recruitment, ambition, and life inside Parliament, members of the established political class enjoy certain advantages. Income is only one aspect, even if an important one. Determining an "average" salary for MPs is difficult, since the additional indemnities vary by position. In 2000, the base salary was over CA$120,000 (€78,360). Ministers receive an extra CA$39,000 (€25,480) and also parliamentary secretaries, whips, deputies, and other members earn additional salaries.

Within the political class itself, members of the executive enjoy even more advantages than backbenchers. Individuals who make it to cabinet have negotiated an inhospitable opportunity structure and are now in a position to enjoy the fruits of their efforts. They have more opportunity to engage in policy work. They set the standard for party discipline rather than have it dictated to them by other members of their party. They also enjoy a higher level of pay, which is included in their eventual pension benefits at the end of their political career (Fleming 1992).

And the advantages of making it to cabinet in Canada's executive-centered Parliament do not end with life inside Parliament. Members of cabinet also have an easier time living off politics than do others in the political class. For one of the overarching truisms of Canadian politics is the relatively weak electoral security of MPs. Certainly compared to members of the United States Congress and the British House of Commons, the job prospects of most Canadian MPs are very much open at each election time. Simply put, Canada has few "safe electoral seats" for any political party, and the number of members re-elected based on their own reputations is relatively small. As Clarke *et al.* (1996) have consistently shown, voters consistently place party and party leader ahead of local candidate in their voting determinations. Very few MPs in Canada enjoy a personal vote, that is a strong vote base independent of the support given by their leader or party.

As a result, and given the high levels of turnover that occur with each election, any electoral advantages a MP can amass are critical. As it turns out, one of the greatest electoral weapons in an incumbent's arsenal is experience in cabinet. With positions of influence comes a more national profile, something that can be parlayed into an electoral advantage. More particularly, members of cabinet are often seen to be able to "deliver the goods" to their district. Voters are more likely to support a member if he or she is or was in cabinet, by viewing the member, and not his or her party, as being responsible for any federal largesse that has made its way to the district. Table 4.4 compares the personal vote of backbenchers to cabinet members and others in positions of authority in three elections. Members in positions of authority include sitting and former members of the executive, House leaders, party leaders, and the Speaker of the House.

In each of the five elections, the pattern is the same. It is backbench MPs (in each case the majority of members) who hold lower buffers against their national party's fate. The five-to-six point personal vote of backbenchers is almost identical to the level of incumbency effect that previous researchers have found to exist among all MPs (Lovink 1973; Irvine 1982; Krashinsky and Milne 1991). Even when governments lose, cabinet ministers are more likely to hold their seats than their ideological colleagues on the backbenches. When executives initiate public policy that is unpopular, they are often the last to pay the political price for their decisions. By contrast, backbenchers—who have had the least to say about the policy—are usually the first to go.

Of course, sometimes members of the executive and backbenchers lose their re-election bids, and with Canada's high turnover rates, this occurs regularly. In the 1993 election, for example, the governing Progressive Conservative party fell from over 150 seats to just two. In 1997 the Liberal party was returned with a second consecutive majority, but it was much reduced (interestingly, of the eighteen defeated Liberal incumbents only two were in cabinet). Yet even when losses occur, the political class establishes the rules for their departure. The Liberals were returned with a third majority in 2000, this time with an increase in the number of seats from 1997.

Table 4.4 *Personal vote by highest position held, backbenchers vs. leaders (in %)*

Election year	Backbench MP	Present or former "leader"
1984	5.3	12.1
1988	5.2	9.2
1993	6.2	8.9
1997	6.8	15.1
2000	8.3	16.7

Note: Figures are the difference in per cent between the personal vote of an incumbent and the average party vote in the respective region.

Sources: For 1984–93: Docherty (1997). 1997 and 2000 figures calculated from Elections Canada Official Voting Results.

Prior to an election call, the Prime Minister has at his or her disposal hundreds of well-paying patronage positions. Appointment to the Senate is the most popular of these posts. Those called to serve their country from the Senate hold this position until age seventy-five. To help make life in this body more bearable, Senators are provided generous pay, office and staff resources, and free phone usage. Other patronage positions include chairing various commissions, judgeships, and representing her Majesty as a Lieutenant or Governor General. Depending upon the patronage position vacating lawmakers may not have to abandon their member's pension. For some, this pension begins immediately after their exit from elected office and can be worth up to 75 percent of their best salary as an MP. The practice of receiving a patronage post while collecting a pension is referred to as "double-dipping" and has been widely criticized. Nonetheless, the only ones who can stop this practice are the legislators themselves, and they have only recently begun to offer reforms in this area.

For those who do not receive a patronage position, the resettlement entitlements for defeated and retiring members go a long way toward easing the transition back to private life. Among other benefits, members receive two months pay, career counseling, and direct assistance in job-seeking.

Members of the executive are less likely to require career counseling than backbenchers. First, cabinet ministers tend to be the beneficiaries of the better paying (and full-time) patronage positions (Docherty 2001). Second, politicians with cabinet experience are, not surprisingly, in higher demand in the private sector than are backbenchers. Most members of the executive have little problem finding post-elected work, notably on corporate boards of directors or government relations groups (Docherty 2001). Once again, the difference between the executive and the backbench is apparent. Even when leaving the political class, elite members are advantaged in a way that escapes the remainder of House Members.

THE POLITICAL CLASS AND INSTITUTIONAL REFORM

Thus far, the picture painted of the Canadian Parliament is not an encouraging one. Members of the political class enjoy certain privileges of their own making, but a substantial gulf separates the cabinet from the backbenches. As a result, backbenchers look sullenly to their ridings and find what satisfaction they can in aiding constituents. While not incorrect, such a picture would leave the erroneous impression that the Canadian Parliament and its members have not changed at all since the beginnings of professionalization in the 1960s. Nothing could be further from the truth. As Atkinson and Thomas (1993) point out, the House of Commons of the 1990s looks "nothing like the House of the 1960s." Committees have gained more authority and independence, the government has ceded more authority to members and the House, and the quality of representation has improved significantly.

The biggest change, however, has been the increasing challenge to the long-standing practice of strong party discipline. Members have been pushing for more freedom in voting. In order to circumvent the possible breaking of party solidarity, some MPs have advocated expanding the circle of legislation that is not considered a matter of confidence. This argument suggests that governments use a broad interpretation of confidence in order to keep government backbenchers in line. If members knew the government would not fall if a vote was lost, there would be less hesitancy to vote against one's party.

In 1985 the McGrath Committee examined parliamentary organization and procedure with an eye to providing private members more independence. Paramount among their recommendations was the suggestion that the definition of confidence could be narrowed (McGrath 1985). The rationale behind this advice was to allow members to act as either constituency delegates or trustees, but not as delegates to the party whip. The committee argued that a government elected with a majority should be recognized as having a mandate to govern for a full term. Defeat on any single piece of legislation does not nullify this mandate. Pointing to the Parliament in Great Britain, the committee argued that a strict adherence to confidence is not a requirement of Westminster-style assemblies.

A parliament which has narrowed its definition of confidence would presumably provide more independence for its members. If the government considered only budget bills and other major pieces of legislation as matters of confidence, the ability of members to vote in accordance with either their conscience or with their reading of their constituency views would be increased. According to the members of the McGrath Committee, and other proponents of legislative reform, such a move would be the first big step in making Parliament more representative of public desires.

Yet despite a history of such proposals, party leaders and government executives have consistently been reticent to provide MPs with this increased freedom. As a result, some members and parties have begun to use party discipline as an election issue. Foremost among these challengers of the status quo is the right wing Reform Party (now the Canadian Alliance), formed in 1986. In 1997 and 2000, the Reform/Alliance formed the Official Opposition in Ottawa. Among their populist pledges are term limits, recall of members, and the promise to act as delegates of constituency wishes even if they conflict with the party platform. Many Alliance MPs see elected office as a vehicle for changing the traditional system of representation in Canada. This conception of representation suggests a style of politics that conflicts with our traditional understanding of political representation in Canada (see Stewart 1977: 10–22). Yet despite the reasonable success of the Reform/Alliance experiment, the greatest challenge to leader dominance has come from the government side of the chamber.

During the 35th and 36th Parliaments, backbench Members of the Liberal Party voted against their government on a number of issues, including gun control legislation and legal protection to gay and lesbian Canadians. In the 37th Parliament, there has been an increased willingness on the part of backbenchers to challenge leader dominance. Members have openly criticized the Prime Minister and the cabinet over proposed legislation, cabinet appointments, and ministerial conduct (Docherty 2003). The fact that these latest challenges are public and multiple is the evidence of their strength.

However, these challenges do not necessarily signal a turning point in Canadian legislative behavior. Among other causes, their origins can be found in two unique— but coinciding—events. First, after three consecutive Liberal majorities, there is now a cohort of government backbenchers who realize they will never make it to cabinet. Once the brass ring is removed—there is less incentive to jump at the crack of the party whip. Second, since 1993 there have been four opposition parties in the Commons, not two, and none of these parties has a realistic chance of challenging the Liberal Party for power. There is nothing like a strong opposition to convince a governing caucus of the need for strong solidarity. Without the need to circle their wagons, Liberal MPs are more comfortable challenging each other, including the cabinet and Prime Minister.

Of course, until a government loses a vote, wholesale changes to our present understanding of confidence are unlikely to take place. However, the mere fact of open criticism, much of it unpunished, suggests that challenges are more likely to occur and will be accepted in some format by parliamentary leaders. For the first time since the development of the modern political class in Canada, challenges to leader rule and the need for significant parliamentary reform have become part of public discourse—even if only confined to discussions in the national media between academics, reporters, and politicians.[8]

Finally, it is interesting to reflect that all of the challenges from the backbench and opposition parties have focused on the rules governing Parliament and not the extra privileges enjoyed by the political elite. Members have challenged confidence and party discipline with mixed success, but have not struck home with calls for more say in policy initiation. In this sense at least, members are careful not to change practices they one day hope to benefit from. In perhaps a most telling indicator of the strength of institutional values successive Reform and Alliance leaders, all long-standing critics of the perks given to members of the political class, have moved into the government-sponsored residence of the Leader of the Official Opposition. The literal move was supported by most members of the Reform caucus who indicated that their leaders now had official duties of state to conduct and required a residence fitting their station.

Thus, members of the political class are divided on some aspects of elected life. Backbench Members would like to see more freedom to vote as they wish and greater input into policy making. But they are reticent to accept changes that would compromise the benefits of elected life they now enjoy. That is why any calls for less party discipline are accompanied by reminders that this should not result in more elections. And as long as members see some hope for a move to the political executive, they are careful not to challenge the benefits that go with membership in the more exclusive echelon of representative life in Canada.

[8] See, for example, Michael Bliss, "Seeking renewal for a one-party state", *National Post*, 5 May 2001. Also Jack McLeod, "What we need is a revival", *National Post*, 3 March 2001. Luiza Chwialkowska, "No room for dissent", *National Post*, 15 February 2001; and Hugh Windsor, "Saving the enfeebled parliamentarian", *The Globe and Mail*, 4 April 2001. Also Jane Taber "Backbench Rebellion Busts Open", *National Post*, 30 April 2002.

REFERENCES

Atkinson, Michael, and Docherty, David (2000). "Parliament and Political Success in Canada", in M. Whittington and G. Williams (eds), *Canadian Politics in the 21st Century*. Scarborough: Nelson Canada, pp. 5–30.

—— and Thomas, Paul (1993). "Studying the Canadian Parliament". *Legislative Studies Quarterly*, 18: 287–308.

Bakvis, Herman (1991). *Regional Ministers, Power and Influence in the Canadian Cabinet*. Toronto: University of Toronto Press.

Cairns, A. C. (1968). "The Electoral System and the Party System in Canada, 1921–1965". *Canadian Journal of Political Science*, 1: 55–80.

Clarke, Harold, Lenson, Jane, LeDuc, Lawrence, and Pammett, Jon H. (1996). *Absent Mandate: Canadian Electoral Politics in an Age of Restructuring*, 3rd edition. Vancouver: Gage Publishing.

Docherty, David C. (1997). *Mr. Smith Goes to Ottawa: Life in the House of Commons*. Vancouver: UBC Press.

—— (2001). "To Run or Not to Run: A Survey of Former Parliamentarians". *Canadian Parliamentary Review*, 24: 16–23.

—— (2002). "Citizens and Legislators: Different Views on Representation", in N. Nevitte (ed.), *Value Change and Governance in Canada*. Toronto: University of Toronto Press, pp. 165–206.

—— (2003). "Majoritarian Government and Governance: Lessons for Canada?", in F. Seidle and D. Docherty (eds), *Reforming Parliamentary Democracy*. Montreal: McGill-Queen's University Press.

Dyck, Rand (1989). "Relations Between Federal and Provincial Parties", in A. Gagnon and B. Tanguay (eds), *Canadian Parties in Transition*. Scarborough: Nelson, pp. 186–219.

Eagles, Munroe (1997). "The Political Ecology of Representation in English Canada: MPs and Their Constituencies", unpublished manuscript, presented at the Annual Meeting of the Canadian Political Science Association, St. Johns, New Foundland.

Ferejohn, John A., and Gaines, Brian (1991). "The Personal Vote in Canada", in H. Bakvis (ed.), *Representation, Integration and Political Parties in Canada*. Toronto: Dundurn Press, pp. 275–302.

Fleming, Robert J. (1992). *Canadian Legislatures 1992: Issues, Costs, Structures*. Scarborough: Global Press.

Franks, C. E. S. (1987). *The Parliament of Canada*. Toronto: University of Toronto Press.

Irvine, William (1982). "Does the Candidate Make a Difference? The Macro-Politics and Micro-Politics of Getting Elected". *Canadian Journal of Political Science*, 15: 755–85.

Jackson, Robert, and Atkinson, Michael M. (1980). *The Canadian Legislative System*, 2nd edition. Toronto: Macmillan Canada.

Jewett, Pauline (1966). "The Reform of Parliament". *The Journal of Canadian Studies*, 1: 11–5.

Krashinsky, Michael, and Milne, William J. (1991). "Some Evidence on the Effects of Incumbency in the 1988 Canadian General Election", in L. Seidle (ed.), *Issues in Party and Election Finance in Canada*. Toronto: Dundurn Press, pp. 45–78.

Laponce, Jean (1992). "Democracy and Incumbency: The Canadian Case", unpublished manuscript, presented at the Annual Meeting of the Canadian Political Science Association, Charlottetown, Prince Edward Island.

Lovink, J. A. A. (1973). "Is Canadian Politics Too Competitive?". *Canadian Journal of Political Science*, 6: 341–79.

McGrath, James (1985). *Special Committee on Reform of the House of Commons.* Ottawa: Queen's Printer.

Moncrief, Gary (1994). "Professionalism and Careerism in Canadian Provincial Assemblies: A Comparison to U.S. State Legislatures". *Legislative Studies Quarterly,* 19: 33–48.

Power, Charles Gavin (1957). "Career Politicians: The Changing Role of the MP". *Queen's Quarterly,* 43: 478–90.

Price, Richard, and Mancuso, Maureen (1995). "The Ties that Bind: Parliamentary Members and Their Constituencies", in R. Krause and R. Wagenberg (eds), *Introductory Readings in Canadian Government,* 2nd edition. Mississauga: Copp Clarke Pitman, pp. 198–220.

Stewart, John (1977). *The Canadian House of Commons: Procedure and Reform.* Montreal: McGill-Queens University Press.

Thomas, Paul (1985). "Parliamentary Reform Through Political Parties", in J. Courtney (ed.), *The Canadian House of Commons: Essays in Honour of Norman Ward.* Calgary: University of Calgary Press, pp. 43–68.

Young, Lisa (1991). "Legislative Turnover and the Election of Women to the Canadian House of Commons", in K. Meygery (ed.), *Women in Canadian Politics: Towards Equity in Representation.* Toronto: Dundurn Press, pp. 81–99.

5

Denmark: Professionalism in an Egalitarian Political Culture

TORBEN K. JENSEN

POLITICAL PROFESSIONALIZATION IN HISTORICAL PERSPECTIVE

Compared to most other societies, both the social order and the political culture in Denmark are very egalitarian. This raises two broad, if somewhat contradictory expectations about professional politicians. On the one hand, most people will not accept a situation in which a lot of people are in practice precluded from taking on political tasks, because they cannot afford it. Thus, we should expect pretty good economic compensations to political representatives elected by the people. On the other hand, egalitarians are generally skeptical of authority, leaders, and symbols of power. Thus, we should expect rather moderate allowances and a public with a critical and vigilant attitude toward their leaders. This egalitarian bias would make it difficult for professional politicians to transform into a political class.

The Danish political system is based on parliamentary government[1] and dates back to the constitution of 1849, which instituted constitutional monarchy, based on a formal tripartation of power, civic, and political rights, universal suffrage (for men over 30 years and with own household), and a bicameral Parliament, *Rigsdagen*, with a lower chamber called the *Folketing* and an upper chamber called the *Landsting*. This first constitution only lasted until 1852, because of political problems with the southern duchies. After Denmark had lost the territories of Slesvig, Holsten, and Lauenborg in a second war with the Prussians in 1864, the constitution was changed in 1866 for the second time.

When in 1872 the farmers' party (*Venstre*) won the majority in the lower chamber, while the Conservatives controlled the upper chamber and the government, and with no constitutional rules to settle possible conflicts between the two chambers, a three-decade bitter struggle over the constitution began. The conflict culminated in a period of ten years (1885–94), during which *Venstre* vetoed most of the legislation in

---

[1] The following description of the development of parliamentary government is based on Rasmussen (1972), Müller *et al.* (1977), Gundelach (1988), and Hilden and Høyrup (1995).

the lower chamber, and the government as a countermeasure dissolved the Parliament and ruled by means of provisional laws. It was not until 1901, with the so-called "change of system," that the parliamentary principle of cabinet responsibility to the lower chamber was finally accepted.

The stalemate in the political system gave rise to an extensive self-organization among *farmers* in economic, cultural, and religious life. Thus, they developed a very strong civil society, based, in the economic sphere, on the co-operative movement, and, in the cultural and religious spheres, on private associations, independent schools, independent churches, and folk high schools.[2] Independence combined with freedom (liberalism) and equality combined with participation (egalitarianism) were the basic political values in this process. So, in Denmark the democratization of the political system took place before industrialization. This modern society was created in the political fight against a conservative upper class and a highly educated political elite of government officials. The seeds of distrust toward experts were sown here. The transformation was very much the farmers' project, and this partly explains the egalitarian bias among those who later became the Liberals in the political spectrum.

In 1915 the constitution was changed for the third time. The franchise was extended so as to also include women, servants, and poor people, and the electoral system was changed from a majority system into a proportional representation system. The possibility of holding referendums on constitutional changes was also inserted. During the first half of the twentieth century, the workers organized the labor movement, and the Social Democratic Party became the dominant political force in Denmark. Through an extensive social regulation in the 1930s they laid the groundwork for the modern welfare state. Basic political values were now social security and—again, but this time in the context of industrialization—political and economic equality.

The contemporary constitution of 1953, among other things, formally laid down the principle of cabinet responsibility, abolished the upper chamber, enlarged the *Folketing* to 179 seats, and lowered the voting age to 23 years (which was later successively lowered to 18 years). Furthermore, the constitution extended the possibility of holding referendums to include laws if at least one third of the Members of Parliament (MPs) demanded it, and it introduced rules concerning the transfer of national authority to international organizations, the *Ombudsman* institution, and a 2 percent electoral threshold. The low-entrance threshold together with the proportional electoral system provided some of the important institutional preconditions for the later development of an extreme multiparty system. So, it took 100 years to develop parliamentary government in the present form and have the basic principles written into the constitution.

The third social force to fundamentally change Danish society and political culture was the *new left* conglomerate of movements in the 1960s and 1970s. The

[2] These *folkehøjskoler* were created in the nineteenth century and were a specific Danish institution, established on private initiative and economic bases. The goal was to improve the general education of the rural population in a humanistic sense; one could voluntarily attend courses in politics, literature, philosophy, history, sports, and some practical courses. The *folkehøjskoler* was an important contributor to the political and cultural mobilization of the Danish peasantry in the second half of the nineteenth century.

anti-authoritarian and anti-establishment ideas, grass-root organizations, and, not the least, the political mobilization of women added new forms of political participation and organization to the existing system. And the emphasis was—again—on autonomy, participation, and equality.

No single party has commanded a majority in Parliament since 1906. Consequently, the governments have been either minority governments based on one party, coalition majority governments or minority coalition governments—the latter being the most common form since "the landslide election" in 1973. These parliamentary conditions have probably contributed to the development of a political culture with a strong emphasis on dialogue, pragmatism, compromise, and consensus. Although it is possible to trace this trend back to the Conservative governments from before the "change of system" in 1901 (Nørgaard 1998), patterns of corporatist decision-making developed in the first half of the twentieth century, fueled by the extraordinary circumstances during and between the First and Second World Wars. These corporatist structures were further developed during the extension of the welfare state in the 1960s and maintained in a slightly altered version up to now (Christiansen and Rommetvedt 1997; Blom-Hansen and Daugbjerg 1999; Christiansen and Nørgaard 2002). They have probably both been a result of and further contributed to a pragmatic and consensus-seeking political culture.

The professionalization of the MPs is a complex phenomenon with several different but also closely connected dimensions. In their comparative analysis of long-term changes in political recruitment in Denmark and Norway, Eliassen and Pedersen (1978) interpret professionalization first as an aspect of the increasing workload of legislators. The second dimension relates to the resources the MPs command, which refers to the professionalization of the institution. As a third dimension of professionalization we have the question of income.

As the fourth dimension of professionalization Eliassen and Pedersen define intellectual and status-based (political) professionalization. *Intellectual professionalization* relates to the tendency that the orientations, perceptions, and total outlook of legislators will tend to become more and more like those of professional men. A legislator is increasingly required to be an individual with a generalist orientation and an ability to perform complex operations. Intellectual professionalization they operationalize by the proportion of newcomers to Parliament with an academic degree. *Political professionalization* refers to changes in the recruitment pattern of the legislative elite and designates a process by means of which social status gives way to political status as the basic criterion for legislative recruitment. Social status and achievement are replaced by political experience and achievement. Below, the development on all four dimensions will be discussed briefly.

(1) *Increasing workload—legislation as a full-time job.* A Danish parliamentary session normally lasts only 8 months (from the first Tuesday in October till about Constitution Day on 5th June), and most MPs in most debates do not appear in Parliament (two things that ordinary people often find offending because they think the nearly empty floor of Parliament shown on television means that the MPs

neglect their duties—in addition to having very long vacations). Nevertheless the assignment as legislator in Denmark has long been a full-time job, at least for most members.

Over the years—as Table 5.1 indicates—the level of parliamentary activity has grown considerably. This expansion of activities is probably a result of both the increasingly demanding task of maintaining and developing a welfare state with its tendencies to *Verrechtlichung*, that is to regulate more and more fields in more and more detail (external factor), and the increased level of conflict caused by the many parties in Parliament since the "landslide" in 1973[3] (internal factor). In addition to the preparation of and participation in the activities on the floor and in the committees, the MPs need to establish and cultivate relations to fellow partisans in the parliamentary party (daily meetings), legislators from other parties (especially fellow spokespersons from coalition and other parties), journalists, political representatives within their own party organization and constituency, and representatives of organizations. Observations of and interviews with Danish MPs display that the "job" as legislator—with a few exceptions—means a much-longer-than-40-h week, and that quite a few are engaged in political activities day and night, except the (few) hours when they sleep. In this sense of the term—the workload dimension—Danish legislators clearly are professionals (Damgaard 1979; Jensen 1993).

(2) *The professionalization of the institutions.* With the purpose of being able to cope more effectively with the increasing workload, different strategies have been applied. *First,* MPs simply use more time on parliamentary core activities (floor debates, committee meetings). In addition, voting and deliberations have been rationalized through—among other things—electronic voting, a substantial reduction of speech time and the introduction of bills and answering questions in writing (Damgaard 1977).

Second, over the years both the academic and the non-academic staff in the *Folketing* have increased and been reorganized. In 1990 all the permanent committees were upgraded from a half to one academic secretary, and the staff of the Finance Committee was enlarged even more. A new international division was created with the purpose of preparing the *Folketing* in general and the European Committee in particular for a more internationalized and Europeanized political world. In 2001 the international division and the IT-division were strengthened further. Also, the number of persons hired by MPs and parliamentary party groups—but financed by the Parliament—has increased over time (see Table 5.1 and the discussion of reforms below). But compared to the central administration, the parliamentary staff and the number of other assistants to legislators are small. The Danish MPs have until now deliberately refused to build up their own bureaucracy as a means to control the government and its bureaucracy. As an example, although the subject has been brought up from time to time, there has never been a majority willing to establish an independent advisory law unit in Parliament. Instead, the MPs count on

---

[3] Time consumption concerning proposals, questions, and debate all seem to increase dramatically at that time.

Table 5.1 *Indicators of the professionalization of the Danish Parliament*

	1850–70	1901–14	1953–63	1974–84	1994/95	2000/01
Sessions and sittings (average numbers)						
Length of session (days)	187	218	242	c. 245	c. 245	c. 245
Sittings per session	116	135	113	115	108	103
Hours of floor debate per sitting	3.4	2.7	2.4	4.1	4.0	6.0
Hours of floor debate per session	390	370	270	466	434	617
Activities in Parliament (average per session)						
Bills introduced		c. 95	147	292	264	239
Bills passed	c. 40	c. 60	119	164	224	216
Resolutions introduced		c. 6	18	115	123	202
Resolutions passed		c. 5	11	15	13	16
Interpellations		1	5	36	48	70
Accounts from ministers			4	12	12	21
Questions from MPs to ministers			90	1,225	2,669	4,027
Answered in writing			9	932	2,375	3,622
Answered verbally			81	293	294	405
Debates in Parliament (per session)						
Number of columns in the official records				6,678	9,766	14,520	19,908

Committee activities (average per session)	1972–74	1994/95	2000/01
Received deputations	225	388	268
Written communications received[a]	837	3,112	2.851
Written questions to ministers	3,141	8,217	8.341
Documents received	4,837	19,174	23.121
Number of meetings		625[b]	562
Consultations with ministers			773

Size of staff	1954	1974	1995	2001
Staff employed by the *Folketing*			282	378
Academically trained	12	21	51	78
Number of people employed by MPs and party groups[c]			214	273
Academically trained			91	120
Number of MPs[d]	101 (50)	114 (65)	179	179	179	179

[a] Instead of institutionalized "hearings" individuals and organizations can voluntarily hand in statements concerning current legislative bills.
[b] Data from 1997.
[c] Employed by MPs and party groups but financed by the *Folketing* (see below).
[d] Up to 1953 numbers for *Folketing* and *Landsting* (in parentheses).

Source: The years 1850–1984: Damgaard 1977 and 1992. The parliamentary year 1994/5: own data obtained from Folketingstidende 1995*a* and *b*. The parliamentary year 2000/01: http://www.folketinget.dk/ Baggrund/00000036/00679081.htm (which is the official—and very informative and recommendable— homepage for the Danish Parliament, also available in English).

"critical confidence," with reference both to tradition, the Minister Accountability Law and existing parliamentary activities (see Table 5.1) keeping the ministers to their duty of providing correct and sufficient information to the Parliament.

Third, the MPs have specialized. In 1972/73 the *ad hoc* based committee system was transformed into a system with permanent specialized committees which basically correspond to the fields of responsibility of the ministries. The current number of permanent committees is twenty-four. Most committees have seventeen ordinary members. The change to specialized committees has made it possible to schedule parliamentary activities more effectively. The reform has also made it possible for the individual MP to acquire more specialized knowledge and insight and has been an important contribution to the professionalization of the institution (Damgaard 1977, 1980). Although the committees in important ways structure the work in Parliament, they have nevertheless not developed into independent bases of power. They are most properly understood as arenas for party competition rather than as independent actors (Jensen 1995). To the extent that "power" can be said to be concentrated at any one locus, the parliamentary party groups would be the place to look (Jensen 2002). So also in this sense of the term—being part of an effective, working Parliament—Danish legislators are professionals.

(3) *The professionalization of the office—from assignment to occupation.* From the very beginning, the size of MP allowances has been part of the political struggle. In 1848 the Conservatives proposed a daily allowance of DKR4 to each member of the constituent assembly. By fixing such a low allowance, they hoped to prevent farmers and ordinary people from accepting election to the assembly. However, their proposal was not accepted. Instead, the daily allowance was fixed at DKR8. The Conservatives immediately proposed that the members of the constituent assembly should voluntarily give up half of their allowances with the purpose of paying an extra battalion of soldiers in the war against the rebels, that is, the independence movement in the southern duchies. As a countermove, the Liberals insisted on having a paragraph in the election law according to which "each MP is under an obligation to receive his fixed daily allowance" (Hvidt 1972). This rule is still in force.

The allowance—having been fixed to DKR6 as a compromise in the first ordinary session in 1849—was sufficient only for covering the extra costs incurred by the assignment, but it could not pass for an ordinary income and was not enough to support a family—and thus to "live off politics." After "the change of system" in 1901, allowances were raised in 1903, 1916, and 1918, until a major reform was introduced in 1920. The components of the new system were a salary tied to the income level of a head clerk in the central administration plus a tax-free allowance, differentiated according to the distance between the MPs home and central Copenhagen, to allow for any expenses for travel, hotel accommodation, etc. The MPs at that occasion drew the consequences of the fact that an assignment as the people's representative in the national Parliament had developed into a full-time job.

The decision-making process in the Danish Parliament concerning this important reform was very quiet: one ordinary member from each party moved an amendment to the election law. Obviously, granting themselves higher salaries was a step that the

MPs considered very controversial in relation to their voters, and the reform is one of the first clear examples of Danish professional politicians acting as a political class. On the other hand, to tie the income of full-time national political leaders to the level of a medium-ranging bureaucrat may seem rather modest.

(4) *Intellectual and political professionalization.* In their historical study of professionalization in Norway and Denmark, Eliassen and Pedersen (1978) use two indicators of *political professionalization:*

- Indicator 1: *Political professionalization* was defined as the number of newcomers to Parliament who had held positions in various political or semi-political organizations[4] at the time of their first election, and/or had some sort of political experience derived from participation in local politics as members of municipal councils.
- Indicator 2: *"Pure" political professionalization* was defined as the number of *political professionals* (indicator 1) minus any persons belonging to the higher social or educational echelons of society.

From 1849 to 1945 political experience was of growing importance for election to the Danish Parliament, while from 1945 to 1960 political professionalization has shown a downward tendency. In 1960 a little more than half of the newcomers in Parliament had political status in the broad sense (1)—almost all of them in the sense of a "pure" political professionalization (ibid.). Unfortunately, these studies have not been continued, so the present tendency is not definitely established. But as can be seen from Table 5.4, the vast majority of Danish MPs also nowadays acquire political experiences before their first election.

Concerning *intellectual professionalization,* the overall tendency is that the number of MPs with university training has increased. It is not quite clear, however, whether education increases at the expense of or as a supplement to political experience, but there are some indications that the latter is the case.

To summarize, the *Danish MPs are professionals in every respect:* Being a representative in the Danish Parliament is in practice a full-time job and is paid as such. The MPs have either political or university training, or both. The Danish Parliament and the party groups have resources of their own, and parliamentary structures (in the shape of permanent committees) have developed which allow, or compel, the MPs to specialize, thus making their work much more efficient.

THE INSTITUTIONAL CONTEXT

Denmark is a small unitary state with about five million inhabitants. The small and comparatively homogeneous population has never produced arguments for a federal structure. However, it is noteworthy that the public sector in Denmark is one of the

---

[4] National party organizations; major interest organizations; mayors; cabinet ministers; journalists; editors and media affiliates at newspapers with more or less close affiliations to political parties.

most decentralized in the world. The sixteen counties and the 275 municipalities have the right to collect taxes independently, and in addition they implement in practice most of the national welfare state programs. The local governments' share of total public expenditure has increased over the years to about 70 percent. Annual bargains take place between the national government and local government organizations on issues of macroeconomic policies in order to coordinate the numerous local government activities. So local governments, and in particular their national associations (The National Association of Municipalities and The National Association of Counties), have become important political actors at the national level (Blom-Hansen 1997, 2002).

The constitution does not mention political parties. But the election law does—and for good reason. Since the introduction of a proportional representation system based on multimember constituencies in 1920, the parties in practice have enjoyed a monopoly of nominating candidates. For a long period between 1920 and 1971, the two major cleavages in the population—poor versus rich and country versus city—together with the proportional representation system produced a rather stable party system based on four major parties: the Conservatives, the Liberals (farmers), the Social Liberals, and the Social Democrats—plus at least one small left-wing party (the Communists and from 1960 on the Socialists). But the "landslide election" in 1973 transformed the Danish party system from a moderate to an extreme multiparty system. At that occasion suddenly as many as ten parties were represented in Parliament, and since 1973 at least eight parties have been represented in the *Folketing* at any time.

In nearly all the Danish parties the nomination process is very decentralized. It is the members of the local party organizations in the constituencies who nominate candidates. In half of the parties, candidates are elected by ballot. The rest of the parties have rules that lay down some consultative procedures with the party executive committees. Over time, the trend has gone towards giving the local organization and the individual member of the party an increasing influence in the nomination process (Bille 1997).

At the same time, all the Danish parties have experienced a dramatic decline in membership. In 1960 the parties had 600,000 members altogether. By 1995 total membership had fallen to 200,000. These figures mean that while the parties in 1960 attracted 21 percent of the voters, they are now only able to organize about 5 percent (Bille 1997). Considering that not all of the party members actually participate in the nomination process, the final result is that in practice only a very small and exclusive group of voters are gatekeepers at the first gate that prospective professional politicians have to pass through.

Also the way candidates are listed on the ballot has changed over time. Unlike before, most parties in most constituencies now neither fix an order of priority of their candidates on the ballot nor accentuate a preferred candidate among the names. This has over time increased voter influence on the final result. For candidates, it means a much more competitive system where they can be defeated by fellow partisans as well as by candidates from other parties.

So, while the strongest and most active supporters of the parties guard the first gate, the second gate is much more open. This probably gives rise to two different types of persons as candidates: (1) people with a party career, with the party members so to speak choosing one of their own and (2) people the party members have reason to believe will be able to "sell the ticket," that is, draw votes, get elected and thereby give the local party a representative in Parliament it might otherwise not have. In the latter case party members think strategically and might not choose one of their own.

THE POLITICAL CLASS

Size and Composition

How many political offices are there in Denmark that are potentially within the reach of politically ambitious people? As described above, professional politicians can be defined by means of the following three criteria: (1) They achieve their political positions directly or indirectly through elections, (2) they earn their living from these jobs, and (3) they have—via legislation and institutional reforms—a privileged access to influence the conditions of their own power, career, and income.

Following these criteria, Danish MPs, including the ministers of the Danish government, constitute the most prominent group of professional politicians. The few ministers recruited outside Parliament should also be included. Though the full-time assistants to legislators do not achieve their jobs through election, and although their political influence is more indirect and more varied, their political careers, too, are closely connected with elections. Therefore, they should be included in the category of professional politicians. Although county mayors and mayors in the municipalities only fully satisfy the first two criteria above, they should be included, too; also the executive members in the national associations of municipalities and counties. In Denmark none of the positions in the central bureaucracy are politically appointed, and no civil servant is replaced because the parties in power have changed. However, the right-wing government that came to power after the last elections in 2001 has attached a PR-adviser to each of the eighteen ministers. Nine of these advisers were recruited outside the ministries. These highly influential, politically appointed spin-doctors should—for the same reasons as legislative assistants— also be included in the group of professional politicians.

So, as indicated in Table 5.2, professional politicians make up a relatively small group. Broadly defined, the group includes about 750–800 people. Below, only the MPs will be further analysed.

Political Recruitment and Political Careers

Whereas the Danish electoral system produces an extraordinarily strong correspondence between the support for the different parties in the electorate and the distribution of seats in Parliament (Elklit 1993, 1997), the electoral system does—of course—not distribute the seats so as to mirror the population in socio-economic terms. In that respect, Denmark resembles all other countries with universal suffrage.

Table 5.2 *Professional politicians, 2002*

Members of the national legislature	179
Ministers recruited from outside Parliament	2
Assistants to legislators employed by MPs and party groups	273
Members of the board of the National Association of Municipalities	17
Members of the board of the National Association of Counties	17
County mayors	14
Mayors	275
Politically appointed spin-doctors attached to ministers	9
Politically appointed civil servants in the central administration	0
Total	784

Table 5.3 *Socio-economic indicators of the Danish population and MPs (%)*

	MPs			Population
	1979	1994	2001	1999
Gender				
Female	22.9	33.0	38.0	51
Male	77.1	67.0	62.0	49
Age				
−39	25.1	18.5	30.8	53
40–49	33.5	33.5	20.1	14
50–59	30.2	40.8	35.2	14
60−	11.2	6.1	14.0	19
Average	46.8	48.1	47.0	n.a.
Education				
More than 12 years	68.4	73.3	73.7	19
Academic	37.9	39.3	40.2	5.1
Natural Science	6.7	5.0	1.7	n.a.
Social Science	19.0	20.0	20.1	n.a.
Law	8.9	7.8	6.7	n.a.
Humanities/Theology	3.4	7.8	6.7	n.a.
Other	6.1	4.5	13.4	n.a.
Teachers college	14.0	14.0	10.6	n.a.
Occupation				
Management, research, teaching	70.4	72.8	68.8	9.8[a]

[a] Numbers from 1995.

Source: Jensen (2002) and Danmarks Statistik (1994).

From Table 5.3 it appears that, compared with the population as a whole, a disproportionately large share of seats in Parliament are held by the following groups: men, 40–59-year-olds, highly educated persons, and people with occupational background in jobs with a high content of management, research, and teaching which means white-collar workers, self-employed persons, and people from the public sector.

Although the share of women has increased substantially over the years and is rather high compared to most Parliaments, still only a little more than one third of the MPs are women. The average age has fallen over the years and is now 47 years. But while the group of 40–59-year-olds constitutes only one fourth of the general population, it makes up three fourths of Parliament.

With regard to education, Table 5.3 shows that the MPs clearly constitute an elite group: only one third of the MPs have less than 12 years of schooling, but most of these have some sort of technical training or craftsmanlike education. One third of the MPs have finished long advanced studies (university degrees), and one third have short or medium-length advanced studies behind them. A remarkably large share of Danish MPs are educated at teachers' colleges, and this group—together with those educated at the faculties of theology and arts—makes up a strong humanistic component in Parliament. A sizable group is constituted by those educated in the fields of social science (20 percent). Compared to many Parliaments, the number of MPs with a law degree is rather low (6–8 percent).

If we focus on the occupational background of the MPs at the time when they were first elected, the general picture is that the MPs come from jobs where the component of knowledge is very important. Altogether, 69 percent of the representatives are recruited from the fields of management (23 percent), teaching (22 percent), and research/application of knowledge (24 percent), whereas only 10 percent of the population are occupied in these fields.

So, it is beyond doubt that on a range of dimensions—gender, age, education, occupation—professional politicians do not mirror the Danish population, and especially with regard to resources of knowledge, they clearly constitute an elite group. But it is also true, that compared to other elite groups in the Danish society— the administrative, military, legal, economic, scientific, and media elites—the elected political elite resembles the whole population most (Christiansen, Møller, and Togeby 2001).

In the previous section, we analysed the results of the recruitment process. Now the recruitment process itself will be looked at. The main questions are: What career opportunity structures do national politics offer? What does the typical, individual career path look like? From where are the MPs recruited? What kind of politician does this recruitment pattern generate?

The point of departure for our analysis is the process of political professionalization, that is, the ways in which MPs secure relevant political experiences and a base for a national political career in parties, local politics, and/or semi-political organizations. Table 5.4 shows that as many as three fourths of the MPs have held one or more posts somewhere in the party organization before being elected to Parliament; about half of the MPs have had experiences in local politics; and finally about one fourth have either been employed by or held posts in semi-political organizations. The parties clearly provide the broadest road to the national Parliament, but on the other hand, more than one fourth of the MPs have not even held a position in the

Table 5.4 *Political experience of Danish MPs, 1979 and 2001*

Party

Political offices, employment	Overall experience		Held concurrently	
	1979	2001	1979	2001
Local board of youth organization	17.3	24.0	0.0	1.7
National board of youth organization	17.9	23.5	0.6	0.0
President of party youth organization	3.4	8.4	0.0	0.0
Local board of the adult education section	6.4	4.5	1.1	1.7
National board/adult education section	7.3	5.6	1.7	1.1
Local board of the party organization	41.3	38.0	15.6	8.9
Regional board of the party organization	12.8	10.6	5.0	3.9
Member of the national party board	35.2	27.4	26.3	15.6
Member of the executive committee	10.1	7.3	5.6	2.8
Party vice president	5.0	5.6	1.7	2.2
Party president	3.4	6.7	2.2	3.9
Employment in party organization	4.5	7.3	—	—
One or more of the above assignments in the party organization.[a]	*70.9*	*69.3*	*40.8*	*31.3*
Employment[b] or one or more of the above assignments in the party organization	*70.9*	*69.8*	—	—
Local politics				
Member of municipal council	36.9	43.6	16.2	17.9
Mayor (municipality)	3.4	5.6	0.0	1.7
Member of county council	6.1	12.8	3.4	7.3
Mayor (county)	0.0	2.2	0.0	0.6
One or more of the above assignments in local politics	*40.2*	*49.2*	*19.0*	*22.9*
Organizations/Interest Groups				
Blue-collar organizations, labor unions	12.3	10.6	3.9	0.6
Employers' organizations	0.6	0.6	0.0	0.0
Farmers' organizations	3.4	2.2	2.2	0.6
White-collar organizations	6.1	0.6	1.1	0.0
Academic organizations	3.6	1.1	1.1	0.0
Trade organizations	3.9	11.2	2.8	6.7
Employment in an interest group before election	*12.8*	*14.5*	—	—
One or more of the above assignments in an interest group	*29.6*	*23.5*	*11.2*	*7.3*
Assignment or employment in an interest group	*38.0*	*30.7*	—	—

[a] Because one member typically has held more than one assignment the numbers for each type of assignment do not simply add up.
[b] An employment is defined as an ordinary, paid job in a party or an interest organization, respectively.
Source: T. Jensen (2002).

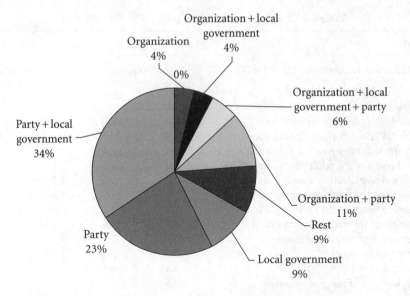

Figure 5.1   *Political experience of Danish MPs prior to first election*

local party. This means that the parties do not have a real monopoly as the MPs' experience base.

Figure 5.1 gives a more detailed picture of the different routes to Parliament. It reveals, first, that there are small paths into Parliament, which seem to make it possible to "bypass" party-work. Thus, small groups of MPs have as their sole base: organizations (4 percent), local government (12 percent), a combination of these two (4 percent), or a university degree (6 percent).[5] Second, of those who have one base only, the party is still the most prevalent (25 percent). Third, half of the MPs (49 percent) have experience from several fields before their first election. The largest group combines local government and the party organization. So, the Danish Parliament can hardly be said to consist of mere party soldiers having lived a life isolated from the rest of society.

The accumulation of posts in the Danish political system is rather unusual for MPs (see right column Table 5.4). Looking at the cumulation of posts between the *Folketing* and municipalities and counties (local level), we find that in 2001 only 17.9 percent of the MPs combined membership of local and regional councils with membership of the national legislative assembly, and only three mayors had a seat in Parliament. There are no national rules against the accumulation of posts. But according to internal rules in the Social Democratic Party—the second biggest party with fifty-two seats out of 179 in the national Parliament and about one third of the 275 mayors—combining several mandates has been prohibited since the early 1980s.

---

[5] The 6% with a university degree only derives from further analysis of the "rest" group.

This partly explains the low share of members of municipal and county councils among MPs, and local politicians sometimes refer to this as the reason for communication and coordination problems between the two levels of political life. But the link between local and national politics still seems to be strong because so many MPs start their career in local politics. The proportion of MPs with simultaneous activities in local politics tends to be very unequal between parties. Thus, in two parties, the Liberals and the Danish Peoples Party, members of municipal councils constitute one third of the parliamentary party groups.

Internal party rules in the Social Democratic Party hardly explain why so few mayors combine their job with a seat in Parliament. The Liberals—since the general election in 2001 the largest party with fifty-six seats in Parliament and with more than half of the 275 mayors—have no party rules to forbid cumulation of assignments. Still, in 2001 there were only two liberal mayors who were also Member of the national Parliament. But the fact that both the assignment as mayor and that as an MP have developed into fairly well-paid full-time jobs might count as an explanation (see below). Besides that, it is difficult in practice to fulfil the duties of both jobs, and there are indeed only few personal incentives to try to do so.

Also in relation to the EU Parliament (the supranational level), the Social Democratic Party has rules to prevent their MEPs from simultaneously being Members of the *Folketing*. The Conservatives, the Social Liberals, and the two movements against the EU have no tradition to have double seats either. So again, only the Liberal group stands out with all three out of the sixteen Danish MEPs simultaneously being Members of the Danish Parliament in the last term coming from the Liberal group. Yet, in this session there are no Danish double mandates at all.

When elected to Parliament, MPs also typically give up their assignments in interest groups. What Danish MPs do combine—on the national level—are the job as Member of Parliament and a possible appointment as minister. As a rule, ministers are recruited among the MPs. The number of ministries and ministers has in the last 30 years varied between nineteen and twenty-four. The number of ministers recruited from outside Parliament has varied between four and six in most of the periods but has recently fallen to two or three (three for the government in office). And as a rule, the MPs continue to be full MPs during their term of office as minister. But the ministers have the option to apply for a temporary leave from Parliament and give their seat to their substitute. Only one small party in government has made use of this possibility so far. In conclusion, the cumulation of political jobs is not a widespread phenomenon among Danish MPs.

As Table 5.5 reveals, for most of those elected, membership of the Danish Parliament is not a lifelong engagement. With an average share of new members near 25 percent[6] and an average length of service for Danish MPs no longer than 8.5 years,

---

[6] Since 1960 these figures have been rather constant. The four exceptions are the 1971 election, the "landslide" election in 1973 (five new parties in Parliament and nearly 38% newcomers), the 2001 election (when the Social Democrats lost, the Danish Peoples Party had their breakthrough, and power was transferred to the rightwing, 35% newcomers) and the election in 1988, only one year after the last election (8% newcomers).

Table 5.5   *Seniority of Danish MPs, 1979, 1994, 1998, and 2001*

	Seniority among Danish MPs elected in (%)				Seniority among Danish MPs who left Parliament at the elections in (%)			
Seniority	*1979*	*1994*	*1998*	*2001*	*1979*	*1994*	*1998*	*2001*
0–4 years	50.8	33.5	45.3	51.4	65.5	n.a.	31.4	30.9
4.1–8 years	21.2	29.1	15.6	16.2	8.6	n.a.	13.7	17.6
8.1–12 years	13.4	14.0	16.2	8.9	3.4	n.a.	9.8	13.2
12.1–16 years	10.1	8.9	10.1	11.2	12.1	n.a.	13.7	17.6
>16.1 years	4.5	14.5	12.8	12.3	10.3	n.a.	31.4	20.6
n	179	179	179	179	100	n.a.	100	100
					(58)	n.a.	(51)	(68)
Average years of seniority	5.5	8.4	7.6	6.7	6.0	n.a.	12.4	10.3
Reelected	65.4	69.8	70.9	62.6				
Reelected after a break	9.5	3.4	3.9	3.4				
Share of newcomers[a]	25.1	26.8	25.1	34.6				
Elected	100	100	100	100				
	(179)	(179)	(179)	(179)				
Defeated in election	14.5		19.6	18.4				
Resigned	17.9		9.0	18.4				

[a] Newcomers are defined as MPs who win a seat for the first time, not including MPs who have been defeated before and regain their seats.

Source: T. Jensen (2002).

few MPs can feel really safe in their seats. Table 5.5 also shows that the average seniority for those MPs that left the *Folketing* at the last election in 2001 was 4 years. High turnover and low average seniority diminish the possibility of professional politicians developing into a political class. But the average seniority of 8 years for all members covers a variation from 1 to 41 years, with 25 percent of representatives having been members for more than 12 years and 15 percent for more than 16 years. So maybe the true "class of professional politicians" should be found among this smaller group with a lifelong career as MPs.

Living off Politics

As described above, the institutional rules regulating the income of the politicians are few and simple. The law on parliamentary elections simply leaves it to Parliament to decide what MPs should be paid. The arrangement introduced in 1920 with salaries being tied to the income level of a head clerk in the central administration plus a tax-free allowance is still in force. In 1946 it was supplemented by pension arrangements. A specific law from 1969 regulates ministerial pay. The actual level of income in 2002 is displayed in Table 5.6.

Table 5.6 *Incomes of Danish politicians per year, 2002*

	MPs	Ministers	Mayors
Salary	€66,830[a]	€124,509[d]	€59,811–81,023[e]
	(DKR496,415)	DKR924,850	(DKR444,277–601,837)
Tax-free allowance	€6,437[a]	€6,437	—
	(DKR 47,814)	(DKR47,814)	
Accommodation compensation (if not living on Zealand)	€10,118	€10.118	—
	(DKR75,153)	(DKR75,153)	
Pension[b]	€38,094	€9,717–35,736	—
	(DKR 282,960)	(DKR71,907–264,444)	
Severance pay[c]	€66,830–133,660	€186,763–373,528	—
	(DKR496,415–992,830)	(DKR1,387,275–2,774,550)	
Fringe benefits	Free travel in public transport	Free travel in public transport	—

[a] Danish MPs are under an obligation to receive their salary and tax-free allowance. The level of the salary since 2000 has been tied to the salary of higher civil servants in the state on salary grade (*skalatrin*) 51.
[b] The level of pension differs according to seniority and the MPs obtain the full amount after 20 years in Parliament. They can receive a pension at the age of 60.
[c] Every Danish MP has a right to a so-called severance pay when he/she leaves Parliament because of electoral defeat or resignation. The compensation has the form of the regular salary for at least one and at the most two years to allow a financially secure transition period, e.g. for seeking a civil occupation.
[d] The salary of ministers recruited from Parliament is reduced by the amount equal to his/her salary as MP. The prime minister and the head of Parliament receive 125% of the ordinary minister salary. The Minister of Foreign Affairs, the Minister of Finance, and the deputy prime minister receive 110%.
[e] Depending on the number of inhabitants in the municipality.

Source: http://www.folketinget.dk/Baggrund; Bill no. 140 introduced 7 December 1999 about salary and pension for Danish ministers.

Although politicians do not formally have to negotiate their salaries with anybody outside Parliament, there are other constraints. The income they grant themselves may influence their chances of re-election. Contrary to more hierarchical or individualistic political cultures, the Danish egalitarian culture contains as some of its most essential traits principles saying that "rulers have no right to privileges," "men of power should not try to look as powerful as possible," and "even the tiniest approach to vanity or a pompous style should be discouraged" (Knudsen 1993; Jensen 1994). In such an egalitarian culture with a competitive political environment of eight parties (including one right-wing party with a rather populist platform and one left-wing party with an outspoken egalitarian world-view), and with an electorate having a somewhat distorted idea of the actual workload of their representatives, any attempt by the MPs at increasing their own level of income could very easily create political trouble and undermine public confidence in the politicians—with tangible results at the polls.

Danish MPs actually have not—until recently maybe—been very efficient when it comes to protecting their own individual economic interests. They have barely been able to maintain their real income level of the late 1960s. Inflationary pressure during the 1970s and the suspension and removal of automatic indexation in 1982 eroded their income (Christensen 1994). A controversial 37 percent increase in salaries in 1986 (see below) only compensated the loss in real income which MPs had suffered since 1969 (Christensen 1995). In 2000 it was the same old story. The salary had not been raised for 14 years, and MPs approved another controversial 23 percent increase in salaries, fixed the salary to that of high-ranking civil servants and re-introduced automatic indexation. MP salaries do not compare well with the incomes of private-sector managers, nor those of top leaders in the civil service. By comparison, permanent undersecretaries in the ministries and judges of the Supreme Court make just over €101,000 (DKR750,000) a year. So, it is about twice as profitable to have a top position in the executive and judicial branch than in the legislative assembly.

Danish ministers are not allowed to accept any paid jobs whilst in office and must leave any existing positions when appointed. No formal rules prevent MPs from seeking supplementary incomes. There are a number of positions to which MPs are appointed. Sometimes the law stipulates that the political parties, or at least the larger parties, should be represented on a particular body. And there are "representatives of the public interest" on the board of directors of banks, insurance companies, and other financial institutions. Other positions may be reserved for, or at least open to, politicians. From time to time, the prevalence of such sidelines provokes intense public debate (especially in the tabloids) about reasonable income, greediness, and conflicts of interests. In 1994 the Danish Parliament therefore introduced rules to create more transparency about MPs' sidelines and financial interests. These rules, which were prepared by the Standing Order Committee, introduced an open but voluntary registration of MPs' financial interests and jobs on the side. Thus, in recent years 69 percent of Danish MPs reported on their financial interests.

Although the Liberal Party caucus—allegedly for reasons of principle—did not accept the rules, a few members of the group nevertheless did report their sidelines, interests, etc. On the other hand, despite the fact that all other parties originally supported the registration, there is only one party group—the leftist Unity List—whose members have all reported their interests. So the registration does not give a complete picture of the supplementary activities involved. MPs are not asked to report the precise level of extra income, and nobody has tried to estimate it. As Table 5.7 shows, extra income is not unusual.

Besides parliamentary measures such as interpellations, questions to ministers, votes of no confidence in individual ministers or the government as such, Danish MPs have different types of courts and commissions of inquiry at their disposal, if they suspect serious mistakes or neglects in the discharge of a minister's office. Since 1980, eighteen cases involving ministers and civil servants have been investigated by commissions of inquiry. These affairs and (sometimes) scandals have all been about different kinds of incompetence and inefficiency among bureaucrats and consequent

Table 5.7 *Self-reported sidelines and financial interests of Danish MPs, 1995 and 1998*

Category of additional income	%/(N)		
	1994	1998	2001
Member of the board of directors of firms/institutions	26.0 (31)	30.6 (38)	23.6 (29)
Paid jobs	35.0 (43)	21.0 (26)	30.9 (38)
Self-employed	11.4 (14)	18.5 (23)	13.0 (16)
Economic support from institutions, organizations, firms, individuals	0.0 (0)	0.0 (0)	0.0 (0)
Gifts from inland givers	1.6 (2)	0.0 (0)	0.0 (0)
Trips abroad paid by others	0.8 (1)	6.5 (8)	3.3 (4)
Gifts from foreigners	0.0 (0)	0.0 (0)	0.0 (0)
Economic interests in firms	4.9 (6)	0.8 (1)	4.1 (5)
Arrangements with former employers	20.3 (25)	21.8 (27)	14.6 (18)
Arrangements with future employers	15.4 (19)	12.1 (15)	8.9 (11)
No economic interests (but accept to report)	39.3 (36)	31.5 (39)	36.6 (45)
Number of MPs who voluntary have reported	(123)	(124)	(123)

Note: Several answers were possible.

Source: The Law Secretariat of the *Folketing*. In 1994 and 1998, 123 and 124 of the 179 MPs respectively accepted to report their sidelines and economic interests, which means that 69 percent of the MPs reported.

bad counseling of ministers (Christensen 1996). None of these scandals has involved corruption, that is, in none of these cases politicians, ministers, or civil servants have let their own economic interests influence the administration of public funds or tried to enrich or favor themselves, their families or friends. Since 1908, no Danish politician, minister, or civil servant in the central administration has been involved in corruption or nepotism to an extent that has caused investigation (Christensen 1993). Neither have the political parties been involved in corruption—quite a remarkable achievement in comparative perspective.

THE POLITICAL CLASS AND INSTITUTIONAL REFORM

Since 1986 Danish professional politicians have reformed the institutional setting in three respects: (1) they have increased the salary of the representatives at both the central and local levels, (2) they have introduced direct public financial support to party organizations and at the same time increased the financial support to the parliamentary party groups, and finally (3) they have passed laws that give the public access to party accounts.

In 1986 it was decided—as mentioned above—to increase the salary of MPs while simultaneously introducing government subsidies for the political parties. Thus, the presidency of Parliament presented the increase in MPs' salaries as just one element in a broader package. The total package was intended to (*a*) break mass-media dominance regarding political parties' opportunities to present themselves to the public and (*b*) make political activities less dependent on subsidies from private firms and interest organizations. More specifically, the raise in MPs' salaries should (*c*) be a compensation for the heavy increase in parliamentary work, making it more and more difficult for MPs to combine their political assignment with other types of work, and (*d*) prevent that people abstain from standing for Parliament at elections for financial or job-related reasons (Christensen 1995). The decision-making process in Parliament followed the by now familiar pattern: the presidency presented a compromise between the major parties, and very few MPs participated in the following brief floor debate. As mentioned above, history repeated itself in 2000 when the presidency of Parliament presented a compromise package which among other things raised the salary of MPs, MEPs, and ministers, fixed the salary of MPs to that of high-ranking civil servants, reintroduced automatic indexation, increased the severance pay, but also did away with a heavily criticized lifelong pension for retired ministers.

From a modest beginning in 1965, when Parliament provided the parliamentary party groups with one secretary for every twenty-five seats the party had in Parliament, the direct financial subsidy from Parliament to the groups, fixed at the latest reform in 1996,[7] now amounts to €4,792 (DKR35,700) per month per MP, plus a general grant to each party group of €30,606 (DKR228,016) per month. These amounts now allow the individual MPs to hire university graduates as assistants and the parties to set up their own consultative groups. Altogether, public support to the parliamentary groups has increased from about €40,390 (DKR300,000) in 1966 to €5.5 million (DKR41 million) in 1987, €7.5 million (DKR56 million) in 1995, and €13.1 million (DKR97.5 million) in 2000 (Bille 1997; Jensen 2002). This explains the increase in the number of people employed by MPs and party groups between 1995 and 2000 displayed in Table 5.1.

Direct public financial support to party organizations was not introduced until 1986. First, it has been traditional in Denmark to conceive party organizations as private organizations. Second, and more importantly, a deep conflict of interests among the major parties produced a stalemate for years, even though all the major parties experienced a serious decline in membership and income based on membership fees.

The Social Liberals—a small party with few members, no strong ties to interest organizations and therefore limited means at their disposal, but at the same time the party which for decades has held the balance between left and right in Parliament— have persistently worked for the introduction of public financial support combined with a maximum of openness to party accounts and free choice concerning private contributions. The Social Democrats, with historically strong ties to the national trade unions, have considered contributions from big organizations a natural thing and therefore supported public access to party accounts. However, they have opposed any arrangement that would make it possible for individual members of the trade unions to contract out of giving financial support to parties they do not agree with. The Conservatives and the Liberals did not find the introduction of public financial support that important and considered it an ill-timed proposal; besides, in their

---

[7] The reform called *Olsen-plan* after the President of Parliament then in office, Erling Olsen—was initiated with the purpose of increasing the resources and power of Parliament against the administration, interest groups, and the media and other strong political actors.

opinion, it belongs to the private sphere which political party individuals or companies may want to support financially. Therefore, they strongly emphasized the necessity of protecting (big) contributors' names and opposed open party accounts. At the same time they found it—allegedly for the same reasons—important to protect individual members of trade unions against collective contributions to parties.

In 1986, when the law of public financial support to parties was passed, no rules of openness and free choice were attached. The Social Liberals pragmatically accepted the new rules as part of a package (including increased salaries to MPs) with the purpose of strengthening parties in general. According to the new rules, every party should receive a certain compensation for every vote obtained at national, county, and municipal elections. Altogether, this amounted to about €4.0 million (DKR30 million) every year from the taxpayers to the parties. The fact that this did not provoke much debate on the floor could indeed be taken as a clear example of professional politicians acting as a class for themselves.

But in 1990, only 3 years after these new rules had come into force, the Danish Parliament at the initiative of the Social Liberals passed regulations making it mandatory for political parties to make their accounts public and enabling individual members of trade unions to contract out. In the early 1990s, both the Conservatives and the Social Democrats began to seriously feel the decline in membership and consequently in financial resources. This is probably one of the reasons for the broad agreement among the parties in 1995 to increase public support to the parties costing the state about €10.8 million (DKR80 million) per year. This initiative was also part of the broader plan to increase financial support to the parliamentary party groups and provide them with better facilities (see above)—with a view to strengthening Parliament in relation to the media, interest groups, the central administration, local governments, and the European Union. At that occasion, a majority in Parliament also decided that the names and addresses of contributors who give more than €2,700 (DKR20,000) within one year should be made public. The amount of public support for the parties is regulated every year by the Minister of the Interior. In 2002 the subsidies were €3.21 (DKR23.75) per year per vote obtained at general elections, €0.41 (DKR3.0) per year per vote obtained at county elections, and €0.64 (DKR4.75) per year per vote obtained at municipal elections.

In conclusion, the Danish politicians have recently increased the resources available to party organizations considerably. Though the rules of public access to party accounts are not without loopholes, and although it has not been demonstrated yet how zealously the parties will enforce these rules, it seems that the strong conflicts of interests among the parties have contributed to a rather transparent system.

CONCLUSION

Compared to most other countries, Danish political culture is very egalitarian. Modern Danish political history has so far produced a political culture with a strong feeling of national unity and with a general desire for both economic and political equality, dialogue, pragmatism, compromise, and anti-authoritarianism. The attitude towards leaders therefore is very critical. This egalitarian culture constitutes the system of beliefs, attitudes, and symbols that define the political situation in Denmark.

Danish MPs are professionals in every sense of the word: Being a representative in the Danish Parliament is in practice a full-time job and is also being paid as such. Danish MPs are either politically or academically trained, or (generally) both. The Danish Parliament and the parliamentary party groups have resources of their own, and parliamentary structures have developed (in the shape of permanent committees) that allow/compel MPs to specialize, thus making their investigative work much more efficient. The 179 MPs form the core of professional politicians in Denmark. Compared with the electorate, Danish MPs represent in many respects an elite group, especially with regard to level of education. However, compared to other elite groups the elected political elite resembles the general public most closely.

Although the most common path to a seat in Parliament is via some kind of a career in a party, the parties do not have a monopoly as the MPs' experience base. About one fourth of the MPs have held no positions in their party organization prior to their first election. A career as a Member of the Danish Parliament often starts in local politics or in semi-political organizations. It is not common in the Danish political system to accumulate posts, and due to a turnover of about 25 percent in a volatile party system, nobody can count on being a member for life.

Compared to the average income among Danish wage earners Danish MPs are well paid. But compared to leaders in both the private and the public sector, the salaries of Danish MPs—now tied to the income level of a higher ranging bureaucrat in the central administration—are still modest. Some of the MPs compensate to some extent for this by having paid jobs on the side or by being members of boards of directors and governing bodies. Notably, Danish politicians, ministers, bureaucrats, or parties have not been involved in corruption for nearly a century.

If the Danish politicians can be said not to have been very successful in protecting their own individual economic interests, they have, on the other hand, recently been able to considerably increase the collective resources of the parliamentary party groups and party organizations through direct public financial support. But the analysis of the professionalization of Danish MPs, their career paths, income level, and the decision-making processes around increases in salaries and public financial support reveals a party system constituting a competitive political environment with conflicts of interests. And it seems that this competitive political system in combination with the deeply entrenched egalitarianism has actually prevented the Danish professional politicians from developing into a political class.

REFERENCES

Bille, Lars (1997). *Partier i forandring*. Odense: Odense Universitetsforlag.

Blom-Hansen, Jens (1997). "Macroeconomic Control of Local Government in Scandinavia: The Formative Years". *Scandinavian Political Studies*, 21: 129–60.

—— (2002). *Den fjerde statsmagt? Kommunernes Landsforening i dansk politik.* Aarhus: Aarhus Universitetsforlag.

—— and Daugbjerg, Carsten (eds) (1999). *Magtens organisering: Stat og interesseorganisationer i Danmark.* Aarhus: Systime.

Christensen, Jens Peter (1996). "Skandalesager og embedsmandsansvar". *Politica*, 28: 255–70.

Christensen, Jørgen Grønnegaard (1993). "Corporatism, Administrative Regimes and the Mismanagement of Public Funds". *Scandinavian Political Studies*, 16: 201–25.

—— (1994). "Denmark: Institutional Constraint and the Advancement of Individual Self-Interest in HPO", in C. Hood and B. G. Peters (eds), *Rewards at the Top.* London: Sage, pp. 70–89.

—— (1995). "Better Than Their Reputation: Danish Politicians and the Absence of Sleaze". *Parliamentary Affairs*, 48: 650–62.

Christiansen, Peter Munk, Møller, Birgit, and Togeby, Lise (2001). *Den danske elite.* Copenhagen: Hans Reitzels.

—— and Nørgaard, Asbjørn Sonne (2002). *Faste forhold—flygtige forbindelser. Stat og interesseorganisationer i Danmark.* Aarhus: Aarhus Universitetsforlag.

—— and Rommetvedt, Hilmar (1997). "Parliaments and Organized Interests in Denmark and Norway", unpublished manuscript, presented at the XVII IPSA World Congress, Seoul.

Damgaard, Erik (1977). *Folketinget under forandring.* Copenhagen: Samfundsvidenskabelig.

—— (1979). *Folketingsmedlemmer på arbejde.* Aarhus University: Forlaget Politica.

—— (1980). "The Function of Parliament in the Danish Political System: Results of Recent Research". *Legislative Studies Quarterly*, 5: 101–21.

—— (1992). "Denmark: Experiments in Parliamentary Government", in E. Damgaard (ed.), *Parliamentary Change in the Nordic Countries.* Oxford: Oxford University Press, pp. 19–49.

Danmarks Statistik (1994). *Statistisk Tiårsoversigt 1994.* Copenhagen: Danmarks Statistik.

Eliassen, Kjell A., and Pedersen, Mogens N. (1978). "Professionalization of Legislatures: Long-Term Change in Political Recruitment in Denmark and Norway". *Comparative Studies in Society and History*, 20: 286–318.

Elklit, Jørgen (1993). "Simpler than its Reputation: The Danish Electoral System 1915–20 in a Comparative Perspective". *Electoral Studies*, 11: 189–205.

—— (1997). *Danske valgsystemer: Fordelingsmedtoder, spærreregler, analyseredskaber.* Aarhus University: Department of Political Science.

Esaiasson, Peter, and Heidar, Knut (eds) (2000). *Beyond Westminster and Congress—The Nordic Experience.* Columbus, OH: Ohio State University Press.

Folketingstidende (1995*a*). *Forhandlingerne i Folketingsåret 1994–95.* Christiansborg: Folketinget.

—— (1995*b*). *Årbog og Registre: Folketingsåret 1994–95.* Christiansborg: Folketingets Præsidium, Folketinget.

Gundelach, Peter (1988). *Sociale bevægelser og samfundsændringer.* Aarhus University: Politica.

Hilden, Hans Peter, and Høyrup, Mogens (1995). "Grundlovens forudsætninger", in H. P. Hilden and M. Høyrup (eds), *Folketinget efter valget: Den 21. september 1994.* Christiansborg: Folketinget, pp. 34–40.

Hvidt, Kristian (1972). "Politiker—hverv eller erhverv: Vederlag til politikere før og nu". *Økonomi Og Politik*, 46: 357–74.

Jensen, Henrik (1995). *Arenaer eller aktører: En analyse af Folketingets stående udvalg.* Frederiksberg: Samfundslitteratur.

—— (2002). *Partigrupperne i Folketinget.* Copenhagen: Jurist- og Økonomforbundets Forlag.

Jensen, Torben K. (1993). *Politik i praxis: Aspekter af danske folketingsmedlemmers politiske kultur og livsverden.* Frederiksberg: Samfundslitteratur.

Jensen, Torben K. (1994). *The Danish Political Elite: Recruitment, Style and Culture.* Unpublished manuscript, presented at the ECPR Joint Sessions, Madrid.

——(1995). *Rapport vedrørende data og dataindsamling i forbindelse med spørgeskemaunder-søgelsen i Folketinget i forsommeren 1995.* Aarhus University: Department of Political Science.

——(2002). *MF-databasen 2002.* Aarhus University: Department of Political Science.

Knudsen, Tim (1993). "Det går nok—essay om dansk statskultur og eurokratiet". *Politica,* 25: 269–87.

Müller, Hans, Sørensen, Peter, Zillmer, Klaus, and Gullberg-Hansen, Niels (eds) (1977). *Fundamental Historie: Alfabetisk opslagsbog* (2nd edition). Copenhagen: GEC Gad.

Nørgaard, Asbjørn Sonne (1998). *The Political Origin of Corporatism in Denmark, 1890–1920: Is the Social Democratic Welfare State Founded by Bourgeois Parties?* Aarhus University: Department of Political Science.

Rasmussen, Erik (1972). *Komparativ Politik bd II.* Copenhagen: Gyldendal.

6

Finland: From Political Amateurs to Political Class

ILKKA RUOSTETSAARI

POLITICAL PROFESSIONALIZATION IN HISTORICAL PERSPECTIVE

The formation of the Finnish political class has occurred in three stages. Under Russian rule (1809–1917), and until the radical political reforms of 1906, only an assembly of the four estates existed. During this period, only Members of the Senate, that is, the cabinet, could be described as professional politicians, but not the parliamentarians. The first stage can thus be terminated from the establishment of the party system at the end of the nineteenth century up to the reforms. The following creation of an unicameral Parliament and the simultaneous introduction of universal and equal suffrage in 1906 were the preconditions for the establishment of a political class. After independence in 1917 its nucleus consisted of the President of the Republic, the MPs, and the ministers. Journalists of the party press could also be counted among members of the Finnish political class and additionally since the Second World War a growing number of party functionaries. This second phase ended with the introduction of the public financing of political parties in the 1960s. The following third stage witnessed a vastly increased number of party functionaries, assistants to the Members of Parliament (MPs), and politicized appointments within the civil service. Furthermore, when Finland became a member state of the European Union in 1995, MEPs and their assistants joined the political class.

Overall, the Finnish political class has continuously grown. The only drawback was caused by the decline of the party press since the 1980s, but the parties tried to partly compensate this by buying shares in local radio stations. The multistage growth process of the inner core of the political class, but also of its outer fringes, shall be analyzed in detail in this chapter.

THE INSTITUTIONAL CONTEXT

The roots of the Finnish Parliament can be seen in the first convening of the estates in 1809 under Russian rule. When regular meetings of the Diet began, there were no national parties in the modern sense. In the second half of the nineteenth century, parties began to take shape in the Diet along political cleavages, first around the issue of language, that is, Finnish vs. Swedish (today Finland is officially bilingual), followed by a conflict between the labor movement and the bourgeois camp at the end of the century. The second period of party activity started in the 1890s when the parliamentary parties undertook efforts to create national electoral organizations which eventually led to the formation of national parties (Rommi 1971: 373).

The main actor in the third period was the Social Democratic Party of Finland (SDP), which was founded in 1899 and can be regarded as the first modern Finnish party with a comprehensive organization. It drew support mainly from industrial workers, tenant farmers, and farm laborers who were not eligible to vote before 1906 (Pesonen 1995: 10). The reform of 1906, which meant a step from an assembly of four estates straight to an unicameral parliament elected through universal and equal suffrage, was the most radical in the whole of Europe at this time. Political parties were thus forced to form party organizations covering all parts of the country. Up to independence from Russia in 1917, however, the Finnish government was appointed by the Tsar and responsible to him and not to the Diet (Jussila, Hentilä, and Nevakivi 1995: 77–8).

The period 1917–18 was a clear turning point in Finnish political development: After the civil war ended in 1918, the Constitution of the Republic was confirmed in 1919. It combines parliamentarism with a powerful elected President of the Republic in an unitarian state. The basic structure of the Finnish party system was formed in this context and has endured to the present day with a continuity which also has characterized the other political institutions. These persistent institutional power structures also provided the context for the professionalization of politics. The formal as well as the actual power of the President of the Republic has been very strong. Since the Second World War, he has determined foreign policy and has also occupied a central power position in the domestic political arena. Within this institutional context, the role of Parliament as well as that of individual MPs was weak, especially after the late 1960s as a result of the establishment of a (neo-corporatist) income-policy. Therefore a career as a politician was not very attractive for ambitious individuals, especially since promotion was based on seniority and party discipline was strict. Parliament gained somewhat in significance in the 1990s due to minor constitutional reforms, until a new constitution was enacted in March 2000. The formal powers of the President of the Republic were cut down significantly in the fields of foreign policy and domestic decision-making: for instance, the power to form the cabinet was removed from the President and given to the Parliament. On the other hand, the powers of the Finnish national legislature were eroded as a result of EU membership in the beginning of 1995.

Proportional representation has been the dominant feature of all sorts of elections in Finland since the first democratic vote in 1907. The 200 Members of the unicameral Parliament are elected for a four-year term. Seats are allocated proportionally to fourteen multimember districts according to their total population sizes.[1] Each district is a

[1] The autonomous province of Åland has a separate fifteenth constituency with exactly one seat.

separate subunit in the electoral process. The preferential votes for individual candidates (there are no party lists and each voter has one vote) are then counted for allocating seats to parties within districts, but not nation-wide (Kuusela 1995: 24). The eventual ranking of the candidates is carried out by using the d'Hondt method.

As far as preconditions for the professionalization of party politics are concerned, the Finnish electoral system can be seen as dysfunctional because it emphasizes the role of individual candidates at the expense of party organizations—contrary to the non-preferential systems where the ranking of candidates is done by party organizations. In the Finnish electoral system the voters alone decide which candidates are elected by expressing a preference for one specific candidate in their constituency. Therefore, candidates have to compete for the mandate both with candidates from their own and from other parties—and thus the party cannot openly favor, for instance, party leaders at the expense of political amateurs (Gallagher, Laver, and Mair 1995: 285; Ruostetsaari and Mattila 2003).

The introduction of party subsidies in 1967, the Party Act of 1969, as well as the application of the new 1969 Law on the Election of Parliament had crucial effects on the functioning of the party system by successfully creating more hospitable conditions for a professionalization of politics. Since the beginning of that third stage, the political parties have financed their activities for the most part by government subsidies, supplemented by public grants to party newspapers. Although the party system in Finland is still heavily fragmented and even non-registered civic groups can nominate candidates for elections, party organizations have become much more hierarchical. Accordingly, party activity lost most of its amateur nature and became increasingly bureaucratized. This development was linked to the belief in state planning which dominated public administration at the end of the 1960s. The professionalization of campaigns since the end of this decade, when parties introduced cost-intensive TV campaigns and started to employ advertising agencies and opinion polls, only became possible because of the public financing (Sundberg 1995: 46).

External advisers and campaign specialists have become important only on the national party level because it is there that campaigns are organized and financed. In contrast, the campaigns of individual candidates are far less professionalized: On the local and regional levels, candidates must build their own support groups—consisting of individuals who are not necessarily members of their party—bring in their personal financial assets, and rely on the help of rank and file party members (Sundberg 1995: 53–5).

Local parties are hardly bureaucratized as there are only very few paid party functionaries in their organizations (all parties together have about twenty-five full-time local functionaries—for more than 400 municipalities). The Center Party, for instance, does not have any full paid functionaries on this level at all. On the regional level no directly elected representative bodies exist, and policy-making is controlled by the leading politicians of municipalities, regional party functionaries, and the civil servants of the provincial administration. Regional party organizations employ only very few full-time functionaries and their number has been further reduced due to decreasing public party subsidies in the 1990s.

The Left Alliance (former Communists), the Social Democrats, and the Center Party (KESK, until 1965 called Agrarian League) traditionally have had intimate relationships with interest groups representing social classes, that is, the blue-collar workers or the agrarian population, respectively. These interest groups are economically powerful, and their political influence is remarkable. For example, the members of the Central Organization of Finnish Trade Unions (SAK), which is dominated by the Social Democrats, number more than one million, one-fifth of the Finnish population. The SAK constitutes a significant personnel base mainly for the Social Democrats but to a lesser extent also for the Left Alliance and has also supported left-wing electoral campaigns through financial and personnel resources—even if in the 1990s the SAK declared itself to be independent of political parties. Despite its smaller membership, the Central Union of Agricultural Producers (MTK) has together with its research institution increased the resources of the Center Party respectively.

THE POLITICAL CLASS

Size and Composition

Contrary to the concept of political elite (see, e.g. Ruostetsaari 1993), the concept of political class (*classe politica*, see Cotta 1982) has not been employed in Finland, although Finnish class structures have been analyzed extensively by sociologists. The starting point for the following analyses is the argument that the scope of the concept of political class is wider than that of the political elite. The political class does not only consist of MPs and ministers—both groups being members of the inner core of the political elite, too. In contrast to the political elite, being a member of the political class is not necessarily connected to having power. Accordingly, for Burdeau (1975: 263) the political class "consists of the totality of those persons or groups who—apart from the goals they pursue—share in the privileges linked to political authority". Similarly, Beyme (1993) draws a clear analytical boundary between political class and political elite by contrasting their basic interests: "steering" or decision-making (political elite) versus "self-preservation" (political class). However, the most important point is that the political class "lives off politics".

The Finnish political class can be divided into an inner core and an outer fringe—analogous to Wright Mills' (1956) concept of the power elite. The inner core consists of elected politicians, their assistants and personal advisors, party functionaries, and journalists of the party press; all in all a quite small group of about 1,000 persons. On the other hand, specifying the size of the outer fringe is a more complicated task. Even the definition of those who "live off politics" is obscure: For instance, should a civil servant be included in the political class if he no longer participates in political activity, but was appointed to his current office mainly on the grounds of political merit? He does not formally "live off politics". However, we can estimate that at least one third of municipal civil servants and at least a quarter of central state officials can be included in the political class. The groups of actors who form the inner and outer areas of the political class will be analyzed in some detail now.

Without doubt, politicians in national executive and legislative positions, that is, the 200 national MPs, the eighteen cabinet ministers,[2] and the President of the Republic, can be included in the inner core. Furthermore, we can include the ministers' special advisors (political secretaries) as well as the five advisors to the President. In 1970 seven persons were appointed political secretaries to assist ministers due to the increased workload of the cabinet. Two years later the system was officially extended so that each of the eighteen ministers got his/her own political secretary. While their total number was twenty-three in 1989, it reached twenty-eight in 1997 (Westerlund 1990: 357). During the period 1970–89 about 260 persons held posts as special advisors or political secretaries. Before their appointment most of them worked as state or municipal officials or they were already part of the political class as party functionaries (24 percent of the special advisors; Westerlund 1990: 96).

On the parliamentary level the assistants to the parliamentary groups must be included in the Finnish political class, too. Ever since 1967 parliamentary parties were granted resources in order to hire political staff. Until then only the Communists with their large economic resources could afford to pay full-time staff (Sundberg 1996: 129; see also Noponen 1989: 178). Since then, the number of legislative assistants has increased continuously (1967: 8, 1977: 16), only declining temporarily after 1983 due to fading electoral support for the Communists and the split of their party in 1987, which heavily affected the number of party officials. All in all, in 1997 the parliamentary parties had forty-seven full-time assistants.

Simultaneously, the administrative personnel of the Parliament, which serves the parliamentary committees and MPs, has increased considerably; starting from 165 in 1970 it had reached 401 in 1988 (Noponen 1989: 58). This administrative personnel, however, is not part of the political class.

As late as spring 1997 a new system of personal assistants to MPs was established and each MP was granted FIM3,800 (€639) per month for this purpose.[3] As the modest allowance enabled only part-time employment, some MPs shared one assistant. The allowance was increased to FIM10,000 €1,682 in 1999, making full-time assistants possible. All in all, in Spring 2002, 180 personal assistants were employed by MPs. In international comparison this number is rather small (Sundberg 1996: 129). An additional enlargement of the Finnish political class occurred when Finland became a member state of the European Union in 1995 and held the first direct elections to the European Parliament in 1996. In May 1997, the sixteen Finnish MEPs were assisted by thirty-three persons.[4]

As far as political parties are concerned, it has often been argued that parties have bureaucratized and accordingly the influence of party members has weakened. This development was interpreted either as a result of the increased number and influence

---

[2] In Finland most ministers are also MPs (in December 2002 all 18 ministers).
[3] Converted according to the fixed EMU rate (FIM1 = €0.1682).
[4] *Source:* Finnish Information Office of the European Parliament, 22 May 1997.

of party functionaries or of the need for expertise that has continuously increased in policy-making. This kind of argument has its roots in Robert Michel's (1962) well-known "iron law of oligarchy"; but also Max Weber has referred to the tendency that power in political parties is concentrated in a small elite at the top of the organizational hierarchy and the wielding of power is bureaucratized (Weber 1978: 1395–6; also see Duverger 1954: 151–7). Thus, it has been presupposed that the professionalization of parties and the concentration of power goes hand in hand with a growing number of party bureaucrats—at the same time a process of de-democratization. In any case, our starting point here is that the growing number of party functionaries represents the core of the phenomenon called professionalization of politics. In Finland the system of party subsidies granted by the state since 1967 has provided the base for this professionalization. While in the beginning of the 1960s the total number of party functionaries was around sixty, the number doubled until the end of the 1980s. The Social Democrats (SDP) and the Conservatives (National Coalition Party) mostly accounted for the growth of functionaries; in these parties their number has increased three-fold. In the case of the Conservatives this can be explained by their growing electoral success and therefore increasing public subsidies; for the other parties, however, also the already mentioned strong linkages to interest groups have been important (Sundberg 1996).

Also on the regional party level we can observe a growing professionalization, that is, an increase in the amount of full-time officials, especially in the Center Party and the Conservative Party (Sundberg 1996: 125). Nevertheless, no regional political class exists because this level of government is strongly dependent on the local one. Contrary to national and regional party organizations, bureaucratization has not affected the local level of party activity (see above). However, at this level policy-making does experience a gradual professionalization. First, in the beginning of the 1990s the number of municipal committees has been reduced radically. Hence the number of people participating in municipal decision-making was cut in half and local policy-making is increasingly the task of a small local elite composed of top civil servants and leading local politicians. Second, a small part of the elected local representatives can be described as professional politicians in the sense that they have a civil occupation, but devote more and more time to municipal policy-making. As much as two fifths of the councilors are municipal or state civil servants. It is common that local civil servants are active as municipal councilors or belong to the municipal board (which is elected by the council)—and about one third of appointments to local offices are based—at least partly—on party allegiance. Therefore, in a broader sense, we can speak of a local political class—even if in 1995 the eligibility of local public servants for local political offices was limited.

This semi-professionalization, however, is not restricted to the local level. On the national level persons who do not formally "live off politics" but have leading positions in national party organizations can be included in the political class; they spend a significant part of their time on political work. Furthermore, there is a considerable number of party functionaries outside the different party levels already covered: in the parties' subsidiary organizations such as those for women, youth, students, and pensioners. And at least the major parties have their own educational associations as well as party institutes; for the left-wing parties also the functionaries of the workers' sports organizations play a certain role, although they have lost much of their influence during recent decades (Sundberg 1996: 130–2).

As far as the outlines of the Finnish political class are concerned, one of the most important as well as most difficult questions concerns the party-politicized appointments within public administration. This phenomenon, which has been regarded as diminishing the trust of the people in politicians, is not a new one: political appointments have increased especially since the parliamentary elections of 1966 both on the national and local level (see, e.g. Nousiainen 1991: 292; Aho 1996: 95). However, it is difficult to differentiate politically motivated appointments, because according to the Finnish Constitution the qualifications which the candidate for public office has to fulfil are knowledge, capability, and proven civil merit. Political activities can be counted as the latter—but political appointments mostly favor members of the party in government. Different studies have revealed that approximately one third of the appointments to higher civil service on the national level occurred due to party allegiance. The higher the office, the more common was a politicized appointment (Ståhlberg 1986). According to studies with a broader focus, about a quarter of Finnish civil servants were appointed partly on grounds of political merit—in their own assessment. Political patronage was especially frequent in local administrations; more than 40 percent stated that their political affiliation had influenced their recruitment (Vartola and Ursin 1987: 95–6). Hence, it seems evident that a part of the public officials can be included in the political class—based on the political character of their careers: one third of the municipal and one fourth of the national civil servants.

Although supervisory boards of state-owned firms are also manned on political grounds, they have not directly affected the formation of the political class (Ruostetsaari 1992). On the contrary, newspapers are closely linked to Finland's political and cultural development. In the long run and in international comparison, the characteristic features of the Finnish press have been its great variety and the large circulation (3.2 million per day in 1990; in relation to a population of 5.1 million) as well as its strong affiliation to political parties. In fact, the establishment of the press was not based on economic entrepreneurship; rather, newspapers were committed to ideological aims and political groups (Nousiainen 1991: 125–6): the organizational core of the incipient political parties was grouped around newspapers. At the turn of the century there were about eighty newspapers, of which one third was affiliated to political parties. The share of the party press increased until 1930. While the total number of newspapers remained stable afterwards, the number of newspapers controlled by political parties decreased rapidly (Jyrkiäinen 1994: 301–3). Between 1946 and 1989, thirty-five newspapers were discontinued, three quarters of them affiliated to a party. Out of currently fifty-six dailies, only eight have a formal affiliation with a political party: five belong to the Center Party, two are Social Democratic, and one is connected to the Swedish People's Party. Even massive public subsidies (1991: FIM49 million, approx. €8,24 million) could not halt this development. The share of party dailies in the total circulation was no more than 8.7 percent in 1996. On the other hand, these losses have been partly replaced by the party share of ownership in local radio stations. All in all, this development and the generally more critical attitude of journalists towards politicians has led to a depolitization of the journalistic profession and thus to a reduction in the size of the political class (Jyrkiäinen and Sauri 1997).

Besides the quantitative delimitation of the "Finnish political class" there remains the question if this formation deserves the title "class": Is the Finnish political class characterized by a collective consciousness and collective action which are seen as qualifications of the concept (e.g. Burdeau 1975)? In short, is it a "class for itself"? Since the political elite constitutes part of the inner circle of the political class, a preliminary answer can be given by studying the elite structure of the Finnish society (Ruostetsaari 1993).

The hypothesis of an exclusive, cohesive, and unanimous "power elite" governing Finland could be supported in this study. The hypothesis was based on two factors: First, different elites have been united by social integration; and second, Finnish society has traditionally been very state-centered, which has served to link social sectors and the elite groups within those sectors both with the state apparatus and with each other. The findings of the study revealed that (1) in terms of its recruitment patterns the group of people who occupy top positions in different sectors of the Finnish society can be described as fairly closed and as clearly distinguishable from other people— disadvantaging the lower strata of the society; (2) there was fairly close and intensive interaction between the people who occupy elite positions in different social sectors; (3) top decision-makers in Finland are also fairly unanimous in terms of their attitudes. Furthermore, it seems as if the gulf between the power elite's and the people's attitudes has deepened since the early 1990s, e.g. when membership in the European Monetary Union is concerned.[5]

A further manifestation of the political class' coherence may be the co-operation between the four largest political parties. Since the early 1980s, they have conducted joint opinion polls (by Gallup Finland) on a regular basis, a co-operation unthinkable between parties in any other European country (Bowler and Farrell 1992: 223–35).

Political Recruitment and Political Careers

At the end of the Diet period in 1905/6, education was clearly a privilege of the upper classes. Eight out of ten representatives came from the upper social strata and no less than nine out of ten had an education higher than the basic level (primary school), which at that time was obtained at most by 5 percent of population older than 15 years. Two thirds of the members of the last Diet had a university degree (Noponen 1964: 41–5). Due to the parliamentary reform and the introduction of

---

[5] In March 1996 only 29% of the Finnish people supported and 56% rejected joining the EMU, while almost the whole power elite insisted on it—in European comparison the greatest gap (based on Eurobarometer data, in *Helsingin Sanomat*, 30 May 1997).

universal and equal suffrage in 1906, representatives' average level of education fell significantly, but MPs were still much better educated than the population as a whole. However, the proportion of members with university degrees has again increased since the beginning of the 1950s and especially since 1970.

As far as the professionalization of politics is concerned, it is noteworthy that the share of university degrees in humanities, theology, and social sciences grew rapidly, the latter subject most closely connected to the politician's vocation. In international comparison the small share of lawyers has been a special feature of the Finnish Parliament already from the outset (Blomstedt 1967: 915). The increase in the MPs' level of education was concurrent with the expansion of the welfare state as well as with a growing GNP share of the public sector (Ruostetsaari 2000).

Politicians' competence and professionalization is not only affected by formal education, but also by their experience as elected or appointed representatives in other bodies before recruitment to Parliament. Active participation in party activities furthers upward mobility in two ways: by virtue of the education and training offered and by the relations which it creates (Dogan 1961: 82). In fact, insufficient formal education can be compensated by political activities.

The most common arena of political training has been the municipal level, that is, membership in a parish council, municipal board, or municipal council. Before Finnish independence in 1917, about half of representatives had had a local political background before entering Parliament. Until the mid-1950s the share was roughly three quarters and thereafter more than four fifths (see Fig. 6.1; in Finland there are no directly elected representative bodies at the regional level).

The second frequent arena of training have been national political positions that could be practiced besides a civic profession ("other national positions"), referring to membership of a party's executive committee, party council, or the electoral college

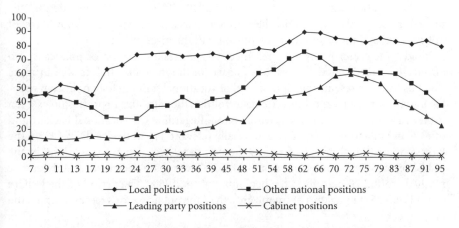

Figure 6.1. *Political background of MPs, 1907–1995 (%)*
Source: Ruostetsaari 2000, *passim.*

for the election of the President of the Republic.[6] In Finland, membership in the electoral college has commonly preceded recruitment to Parliament. The third path to Parliament is a leading party position, that is chairman or vice chairman of national, regional, or local party organizations. On the other side, a ministerial office is regarded as the top of a long political career. This resembles the United Kingdom, but is contrary to France, where part of the ministers enter the cabinet shortly after having been elected to Parliament and the greater part of a parliamentary career comes not before but after government experience. Also contrary to France, in Finland appointment to the government generally depends on parliamentary seniority (Yrjölä 1973; Dogan 1979: 20–1). This model has remained stable during the whole period of unicameral Parliament in Finland.

Considering all types of political backgrounds mentioned above, it is evident that the career of representatives became more structured in the second stage of political class formation (1906 to the 1960s). The share of MPs without any political background before recruitment to Parliament decreased from 30.5 percent under Russian rule to 18.6 percent during the period between the World Wars, and to 4.5 percent in the period 1945–62, but again increased somewhat to 7.7 percent in the period 1966–95. At the same time, accumulation of MPs' experience in several political positions before entering Parliament also increased: the share of MPs who had held three or more different types of offices increased from 7.4 percent (1907–17) to 8.1 percent (1919–39), to 25.6 percent (1945–62), and to 29.7 percent in the period 1966–95 (Ruostetsaari 2000, *passim*).

Despite this increase, the importance of political training prior to Parliament began to decline from the beginning of the 1970s onwards. This indicates a new type of politician, an "expert representative" who is highly educated but has seldom served in political functions. The average "expert representative" is mostly a well educated civil servant, more and more female, but increasingly without experience in party or labor union work, as a local elective representative, in a leading party position, or any other political experience (Ruostetsaari 2000). Thus, we can conclude that the procedural expertise of politics has been replaced by substantive knowledge of policy areas, and more and more by publicity in the mass media.

Besides the career paths just presented, the professionalization of politics is also affected by careers based on positions as party or union official. In fact, we can argue that this form represents the highest level of vocational training for a politician's profession: these persons know how to make politics; they already are professionals, even if they have not occupied an elected position. Regarding the vocational background of MPs in Finland two aspects are especially relevant: (1) In the last Diet 1905/6 the largest occupational group of representatives consisted of persons working in the public sector, 45 percent (Noponen 1964: 55). Their share decreased steadily until it reached around 20 percent at the beginning of the 1960s. The period of the welfare state (1966–95) saw again a dramatic growth of the public sector's representation; the

---

[6] Until 1988 the President was elected by a college of 301 electors, chosen through direct elections. In 1994 the President was for the first time elected directly.

share of MPs coming from the public sector doubled to 40.2 percent. (2) Important changes also occurred in the group of party and labor union officials.[7] On the average, 13.7 percent of representatives elected in 1907–17 belonged to this group and three out of ten representatives from the Social Democrats. The share of journalists and writers was 16.1 percent; most of them employees of the party press; again, almost a quarter of the SDP's parliamentarians were journalists or writers. This large share was a result of the effort at party organization triggered by the reform of 1906 (Noponen 1964: 55–6). While the share of party and union officials in the Parliament remained relatively stable between the World Wars, it began to increase considerably to over 20 percent at the end of the 1950s, thus leading to a stronger professionalization of politics. However, this occupational group steadily lost importance since that time, almost paralleled by a growing share of MPs from the public sector (see above).

Another criteria for political professionalization is electoral turnover: the longer the average stay of representatives in the Parliament, the larger the collective experience and the continuity of parliamentary work. As a general rule, turnover has been particularly extensive when a longer time than usual had elapsed since the previous elections or the number or relative power of parties varied exceptionally widely in the context of a major political crisis (Noponen 1964: 314). After the reform of 1906, which naturally led to a high exchange of parliamentarians, turnover remained quite low until the first crisis, the Civil War in 1918: a representative was elected on average 2.6 times in this period (1863–1906: 2.3 times). It is not surprising that the first Parliament (1919) elected after independence and the Civil War had a high turnover, especially among the Social Democrats. In the beginning of the 1930s alterations in the party system, particularly suppression of the Communists and the electoral successes of the extreme Right and small farmers' parties, again led to an increased rotation of MPs.

Both requirements for a high turnover were fulfilled in the first general election after the Second World War in 1945. Six years had passed since the previous elections, twice as many as normal, and Prime Minister Paasikivi stressed the importance of having "new faces" in Parliament to invent a change in the foreign policy (Tarkiainen 1971: 344). Half of the MPs elected in 1945 were newcomers. While MPs elected in 1939 had been elected on average 4.3 times, in the elections of 1945 the number went down to 3.1.

After the Second World War turnover stabilized on a low level (1945–1962: 3.2). Besides the state of peace this had one specific reason: a law was enacted in 1947, stating that a person is entitled to a legislative pension after he or she has reached the age of 60 or leaves Parliament—after 10 years of being an MP (continuously or not) receiving half the maximum amount and after 20 years the full pension (since 1992 already after 15 years of service). Therefore a third or fourth (re-)election has become an important threshold for an MP as far as the entitlement to a pension is concerned

---

[7] Both groups are merged here because of the close cooperation between left-wing parties and the Finnish labor unions.

(Tarkiainen 1971: 345). However, between 1966 and 1995—in the third formative stage of the political class—turnover increased again, on the average only 2.6 (re-)elections per MP.

Thus, for the whole time since independence we see a continuous decrease of the mean number of elections in which an MP was successful. The risk of losing a seat at the hands of voters has increased in the long run, and as the professionalization of politics presupposes a long and stable career, we can conclude that the professionalization of parliamentary politics has decreased, especially since the Second World War.

To conclude, we will look at the group of ministerial and presidential "special advisors". It has been a commonly held view in Finland that they are fast-track political careerists. This does not seem to be true. Out of the 260 advisors between 1970–89 only thirty-one were afterwards elected to Parliament, though six of them were already MPs at the moment of appointment or had been parliamentarians previously. No more than 4 percent of the special advisors in 1970–89 were afterwards appointed to the cabinet. Only the post of the Prime Minister's special advisor has been more rewarding: For instance, the political secretary of PM Mauno Koivisto (PM 1979–1982; President of the Republic 1982–1994) was Paavo Lipponen who was himself appointed Prime Minister in 1995 (Westerlund 1990: 106–8). However, about half of the advisors could advance their personal careers considerably (in politics or civil service) in a relatively short time after leaving their office. For another group, the assistants to MPs, no corresponding data is available yet.

Living off Politics

The development of parliamentary remunerations reflects the changing nature of the representative's office in Finland (Noponen 1989: 176). In the beginning, according to the Parliament Act of 1869, Members of the Diet were entitled to a sufficient living for the time the Diet convened and they got paid by their respective estates. Actually, the motive for a representative's career could not be economic profit—in most cases the income decreased when becoming a Member of the Diet. Membership of the Diet was *not* a profession because the Diet convened for no more than 4 months per year. After the parliamentary reform of 1906 the duration of the session was set to regularly 90 days and after 1918 extended to 120 days, though in practice it was longer. The salary was paid only for days the Diet was convened. As the salary of the representative was not enough to make a living, individuals who lived far from Helsinki could not afford to be nominated as candidates because they could not carry on their original profession alongside the duty of a representative. In fact, this kind of "social selection" may have been more decisive for recruitment than the stage of nomination and the behavior of the constituency (Lilius 1974: 163–4; Noponen 1989: 56, 176). According to Noponen (1964: 321–3) this selective mechanism can be seen as one of the reasons why the Parliament did neither have a greater share of the country's upper class nor did reflect the social structure of the constituency.

With increasing session length this problem intensified. Thereafter, the number of issues to be handled in the Parliament multiplied; actually, Parliament had to convene

7–8 months a year since the mid-1930s, making a civil profession alongside the parliamentary work virtually impossible. In 1947 the remuneration was changed to an annual salary—and we can argue that from then on the economic preconditions for the transformation of the task of an MP into a profession were fulfilled. Yet, at the same time the costs of election campaigns began to rise and had to be paid to a larger part by the candidates themselves. Significant consolidations of MPs standing occurred in 1956 and 1977 when their salaries were linked to the income classifications of civil servants and ministers. In principle, an MP's salary increased automatically along with those of civil servants. Hence, MPs' salaries were not raised by way of a conscious parliamentary decision for many years.

A fundamental salary reform took place in September 2000. The formal connection between the salaries of civil servants and the MPs was terminated. For instance, seniority allowances and holiday bonus were abolished. As a result of the reform, MPs' salaries increased by between 16 and 42 percent, depending on the length of service. The advantage was greatest for newcomers whose salaries increased by 30 percent; however, the salary of the Speaker was doubled. The current salary of an MP with less than 12 years of service is €4,541 and €4,877 per month when exceeding 12 years. The Speaker is monthly paid €8,073 and the vice-speakers €6,728. Thus, the Speaker can be compared to the Prime Minister and vice-speakers to ministers. For extra outlays the Speaker additionally receives €505 and the vice-speakers €303. Another innovation was that MPs' salaries are now tied to the workload and the difficulty of their tasks: the chairmen of four parliamentary committees (European affairs, foreign affairs, constitution, and finance) are paid €841 per month in addition to their basic salaries. Chairmen of other committees receive €505.

The reform was continued in July 2001. The chairman of the taxation section of the finance committee now receives €505 per month extra and other section heads €331. Chairmen of parliamentary groups get €841 if the parliamentary group has sixteen or more Members and €505 if it has between three and fifteen.

Since 1947 MPs living more than 30 km from Helsinki had been paid an extra daily allowance. This has been replaced by a yearly general allowance in 1985; it is now 30, 40, or 56 percent of the basic salary depending on the MP's place of residence. Until 2000, 80 percent of this general allowance was tax-free, now 100 percent. Furthermore, MPs have free airline, railway, and bus travel in Finland as well as free taxis in Helsinki. MPs are given mobile phones by the Parliament but calls have to be paid. However, MPs get a "communication compensation" which is €84 per month. All in all, as a result of the reforms Finnish MPs can no longer claim to be badly paid.

THE POLITICAL CLASS AND INSTITUTIONAL REFORM

It can be concluded that the office of MP became a vocation only after the Second World War, as a result of reforms regarding remuneration and pension. However, the final breakthrough came with the party subsidies granted by the state since 1967, which also decreased the dependence of party leaders on the party rank and file.

Professionalization intensified after the early 1970s: the numbers of party functionaries, assistants to political decision makers, and members of party expert
bodies increased rapidly, reflecting the bureaucratization and technocratization of
politics. With regard to all of these innovations the political class was the innovator
as well as the beneficiary. Simultaneously the formal education of MPs improved;
especially the share of university graduates increased—social sciences being the most
popular discipline. Hence, we can argue that the "vocational education" of MPs was
improved. Furthermore, the political training in public institutions and party organizations before recruitment to Parliament was increased. This kind of political professionalization occurred simultaneously with the establishment of the Finnish
welfare state as well as the quantitative growth of the public sector.

However, there have been some tendencies in Finland limiting the professionalization of politics. On the local and regional levels political amateurs are not super-
seded and replaced by professionals as far as the electoral campaigns of individual
candidates are concerned. This results from a peculiarity of the Finnish electoral system: the voters must vote directly for a candidate, not only for a party. This emphasizes the role and campaigning abilities of individual candidates at the expense of
party organizations, even more so since these campaigns are financed by the candidates themselves and their support groups. Only national electoral campaigns have
been professionalized since the early 1970s; they are planned and led professionally
by political parties in which political amateurs have no role alongside media
consultants and advertising experts.

It is evident that the attitudinal distance between the elites and the people is
reflected in political alienation and distrust in politicians. For instance, in 1994 as
many as 83 percent of Finns agreed with the statement that "political parties have
been driven further and further away from the problems of the real people" (EVA
1995: 67). The gap between the elites and the citizens is also reflected in the trust of
people into social institutions. According to the *World Values Survey 1996*, Finnish
political parties were the institution which people trusted least; only one percent had
much trust while 84 percent expressed their distrust. Thus, political parties ranked
behind the European Union, big firms, and TV. The most trusted institutions were
the church (55%), the judiciary (66%), the armed forces (80%), and the police
(84%). This mirrors the legalistic tradition which developed during Russian rule as
well as the state-centered political culture in Finland. Over time the trust in
Parliament decreased most; from 68 percent (1981) to 20 percent (1993), even if this
phenomenon appears to be contextual: trust in all institutions has increased again
after the end of the depression of 1991–3 (Nurmela, Pehkonen, and Sänkiaho 1997:
171–6). It is interesting to note that the alienation has generally increased in spite of
the preferential electoral system with its close link between voter and representative.

Evidently, political alienation and distrust in politicians were also increased by
some political scandals, which in Finland have centered overwhelmingly on financial
or economic matters, like the most significant political scandal to date which took
place in the early 1990s: The Minister of Trade and Industry was given a conditional
sentence of imprisonment by the Supreme Court for bribery while in ministerial

office. Moreover, he was dismissed from the office of MP by Parliament itself. This scandal took place in the context of a bank crisis and a general recession which had already decreased the trust of the people in the political elite.

In fact, the Finnish recession in the 1990s was deeper than that of the 1930s. The GNP decreased by more than 10 percent between 1991 and 1993, the value of the national currency fell almost 40 percent, unemployment was higher than 20 percent, and 130,000 jobs, a quarter of all industrial workplaces, were lost. In a few years Finland fell from the club of the world's wealthiest countries to below the middle level of industrial countries (Väyrynen 2000: 14–5.) As a result of the economic crisis welfare services had to be cut significantly. However, the crisis was not politicized: there were very few disagreements between government parties and opposition parties concerning welfare cuts and methods to revitalize the national economy. At that time decision-making was dominated by a policy of "no alternatives" (cf. e.g. Kantola 2002). The second joint project of the Finnish political class concerned the country's membership in the European Union: all major parties supported it. A crucial role was played by the Center Party: even though the rank and file members of the party, especially the farmers, resisted EU membership, the party leaders endorsed it.

All in all, in spite of some political scandals the Finnish political class has assumed a more cohesive and unanimous form in the 1990s. In fact, the increased cohesion of the political class brought about the radical remuneration reform, which had been delayed for several years because of anxiety concerning voters' reactions. Due to the economic context—the recession and the cutting of welfare services—it is understandable that the MPs' generous salary increase was not very popular among citizens. It seems evident that the chasm between the political class and its constituency has widened since the early 1990s.

REFERENCES

Aho, Seppo (1996). *Virkainjaon välttämättömyys: Keskustelut poliittisista virkanimityksistä 1970-luvulta 1990-luvulle.* Tampere: Tampereen yliopisto.

Beyme, Klaus von (1993). *Die politische Klasse im Parteinstaat.* Frankfort: Suhrkamp.

Blomstedt, Yrjö (1967). "Lakimiehet ja poliittinen valta itsenäisessä Suomessa". *Lakimies,* 65: 914–18.

Bowler, Shaun, and Farrell, David M. (eds) (1992). *Electoral Strategies and Political Marketing.* New York: St. Martin's.

Burdeau, Georges (1975). "Die Politische Klasse", in W. Röhrich (ed.), *Demokratische Elitenherrschaft.* Darmstadt: Wissenschaftliche Buchgesellschaft, pp. 251–68.

Cotta, Maurizio (1982). "The Italian Political Class in the Twentieth Century", in M. Czudnowski (ed.), *Does Who Governs Matter?* DeKalb: Northern Illinois University Press, pp. 154–87.

Dogan, Mattei (1961). "Political Ascent in a Class Society: French Members of Parliament 1870–1958", in D. Marvick (ed.), *Political Decision-Makers.* Glencoe, IL: Free Press, pp. 57–90.

Dogan, Mattei (1979). "How to Become a Cabinet Minister in France: Career Pathways 1870–1978". *Comparative Politics*, 12: 1–25.

Duverger, Maurice (1954). *Political Parties*. New York: Wiley.

EVA [Center for Finnish Business and Policy Studies] (1995). *Epävarmuuden Aika—Matkalla Uuteen*. Helsinki: EVA.

Gallagher, Michael, Laver, Michael, and Mair, Peter (1995). *Representative Government in Modern Europe*, 2nd edition. New York: McGraw-Hill.

Jussila, Osmo, Hentilä, Seppo, and Nevakivi, Jukka (1995). *Suomen Poliittinen Historia 1809–1995*. Helsinki: WSOY.

Jyrkiäinen, Jyrki (1994). *Sanomalehdistön keskittyminen*. Tampere: Acta Universitatis Tamperensis, Ser. A, Vol. 409.

——and Sauri Tuomo (1997). "The Mass Media in Finland: Trends in Development", in U. Carlsson and E. Harrie (eds), *Media Trends 1997 in Denmark, Finland, Iceland, Norway and Sweden*. Nordicom: Göteborg University, pp. 37–54.

Kantola, Anu (2002). *Markkinakuri ja Managerivalta: Poliittinen Hallinta Suomen 1990-luvun Talouskriisissä*. Helsinki: Loki-kirjat.

Kuusela, Kimmo (1995). "The Finnish Electoral System: Basic Features and Developmental Tendencies", in S. Borg and R. Sänkiaho (eds), *The Finnish Voter*. Helsinki: Finnish Political Science Association, pp. 23–44.

Lilius, Patrik (1974). *Säätyvaltiopäivien työmuodot*. Suomen kansanedustuslaitoksen historia, IV osa. Helsinki: Eduskunnan historiakomitea.

Michels, Robert (1962). *Political Parties*. New York: The Free Press.

Mills, C. Wright (1956). *The Power Elite*. New York: Oxford University Press.

Noponen, Martti (1964). *Kansanedustajien sosiaalinen tausta Suomessa*. Helsinki: WSOY.

——(ed.) (1989). *Suomen kansanedustusjärjestelmä*. Helsinki: WSOY.

Nousiainen, Jaakko (1991). *Suomen poliittinen järjestelmä*, 8th edition. Helsinki: WSOY.

Nurmela Sakari, Pehkonen, Juhani, and Sänkiaho, Risto (1997). "Viiltoja suomalaiseen yhteiskuntaan", in *Suomen tulevaisuus—taloudesta arvoihin*, No. 6. Helsinki: Valtioneuvoston kanlian julkaisusarja.

Pesonen, Pertti (1995). "The Evolution of Finland's Party Divisions and Social Structure", in S. Borg and R. Sänkiaho (eds), *The Finnish Voter*. Helsinki: Finnish Political Science Association, pp. 9–22.

Rommi, Pirkko (1971). *Puolueet ja valtiopäivätoiminta*. Suomen kansanedustuslaitoksen historia, IV osa. Helsinki: Eduskunnan historiakomitea.

Ruostetsaari, Ilkka (1992). *Vallan ytimessä*. Helsinki: Gaudeamus.

——(1993). "The Anatomy of the Finnish Power Elite". *Scandinavian Political Studies*, 16: 305–37.

——(2000). "From Political Amateur to Professional Politician and Expert Representative: Parliamentary Recruitment in Finland since 1863", in H. Best and M. Cotta (eds), *Parliamentary Representatives in Europe, 1848–2000*. Oxford: Oxford University Press, pp. 50–87.

——and Mattila, Mikko (2003). "Candidate-Centred Campaigns and their Effects in an Open List System", in D. Farrell and R. Schmitt-Beck (eds), *Do Political Campaigns Matter?* London: Routledge.

Ståhlberg, Krister (1986). "The Politicization of Recruitment to Central Public Administration in Finland". *Statsvetenskapliga tidskrift*, 89, 159–69.

Sundberg, Jan (1995). "Organizational Structure of Parties, Candidate Selection and Campaigning", in S. Borg and R. Sänkiaho (eds), *The Finnish Voter*. Helsinki: Finnish Political Science Association, pp. 45–65.

—— (1996). *Partier och partisystem I Finland.* Esbo: Schildt.

Tarkiainen, Tuttu (1971). *Eduskunnan valitseminen 1907–1963.* Suomen kansanedustuslaitoksen historia, IV osa. Helsinki: Eduskunnan historiakomitea.

Vartola, Juha, and Ursin, Klaus af (1987). *Hallintovirkamieskunta Suomessa.* Julkishallinnon julkaisusarja A, N: 0–2. Tampere.

Weber, Max (1978). *Economy and Society.* Berkeley: University of California Press.

Westerlund, Lars (1990). *De politiska sekreterarna i Finland.* Åbo: Åbo Academy Press.

Väyrynen, Raimo (2000). *Suomi avoimessa maailmassa: Globalisaatio ja sen vaikutukset.* Helsinki: Sitra/Taloustieto.

Yrjölä, Pentti (1973). "Ministeriura", in H. Hakovirta and T. Koskiaho (eds), *Suomen hallitukset ja hallitusohjelmat, 1945–1973.* Helsinki: Gaudeamus, pp. 61–86.

France: Enduring Notables, Weak Parties, and Powerful Technocrats

MARCUS KREUZER AND INA STEPHAN

POLITICAL PROFESSIONALIZATION IN HISTORICAL PERSPECTIVE

France's republican experiments in 1791–2 and 1848–52 were too short-lived to spur the development of professional politicians. It was only in 1870 with the beginning of the Third Republic that the professionalization of French politics started in earnest. Three elements characterized this professionalization. First, it took place within a large and centralized state bureaucracy the goals of which frequently conflicted with those of politicians. Second, French politicians quickly, and by European standards early, became skilled political entrepreneurs but their careers remained marked by a high degree of uncertainty. Third, disciplined political parties developed very slowly which delayed the professionalization of certain aspects of parliamentary and electoral politics.

In the Third Republic, the professionalization of politicians took place within an already highly institutionalized and large-scale Napoleonic state bureaucracy. Throughout the nineteenth century, this bureaucracy served various monarchical and imperial regimes. During the Second Empire (1852–70), for example, Louis Napoleon used the bureaucracy to select so-called official candidates, organized their election campaigns and obstructed vote-getting efforts of any challenger (Zeldin 1959; Kreuzer 1996). Therefore it is not surprising that this state bureaucracy retained some of its anti-republicanism after 1870. Higher civil servants, the local prefects, and army officers continued to be disproportionately recruited from the aristocracy and *haute bourgeoisie*.

The leaders of the Third Republic never managed to fully republicanize the civil service (Birnbaum 1994: 45–7). They succeeded, however, in introducing two administrative reforms that sought to reduce the bureaucracy's anti-republicanism. First, they created competitive entrance exams for all higher civil service positions in order to wrest the recruitment process from existing reactionary, old-boys' networks. Second, the founders of the Third Republic created the *Ecole Libre des Sciences Politiques*. This new and private school was designed to rigorously train prospective civil servants. Its high tuition costs, however, limited access to children of the aristocracy and *haute bourgeoisie* (Silberman 1993: 148–52). Ultimately, these two reforms isolated the administrative recruitment process from both reactionary influences and pressures of patronage. Yet, they also contributed to an inward-looking civil service with a technocratic and anti-political culture that remained hostile to the wheeling and dealing of the emerging political class.

The anti-political orientation of bureaucrats grew almost in proportion to the professionalization of politicians. In the 1870s, political professionalization was still limited. Conservative notables from the Second Empire continued to benefit from deferential voters, government-sponsored election campaigns, and various forms of electoral malfeasance (manipulation of voter registration, electoral invalidations, etc.; Garrigou 1992: 81). From the 1880s onwards, however, professional politicians began to displace the old notables. One important driving force behind this professionalization was the bitter constitutional conflicts fought between republicans and monarchists. In these conflicts, each side tried to win the upper hand by modernizing its electioneering practices and improving its local organizational infrastructure (Kreuzer 2001: 23–51). As a result, politicians could no longer win votes by relying solely on their social status and personal economic resources. They now also had to improve their rhetorical skills, build political networks, and satisfy the interests of their constituency. They became modern notables who assisted individual voters in their administrative dealings and in providing pork-barrel projects for their constituencies (Birnbaum 1994: 37).

This fairly rapid professionalization of politics, however, did not produce a large and very cohesive political class. Parliamentary pay remained modest as any increases faced stiff public opposition. Payments were first introduced in the Second Republic (1848–52) but the 9,000 francs (FRF) annual salary remained unchanged until 1909 when it finally was increased to FRF15,000—an amount about as high as the salary for a higher civil servant. Furthermore, political careers provided little security, the electoral turnover rate remained high throughout the Third Republic. On average, 41.2 percent of the Deputies were newly elected between 1870 and 1893, between 1894 and 1914 the rate was 35.4 percent and 40 percent between 1918 and 1939 (Dogan 1953: 322). These high turnover rates also kept legislative seniority fairly low at around 10 years throughout the Third Republic. According to Dogan, France developed a two-tiered political class with one tier consisting of regularly re-elected incumbents and another tier with short-lived, political "itinerants" (Dogan 1953: 332).

This high degree of professional uncertainty can partially be attributed to the weakness of France's nineteenth century parties and their consequent inability to regularize political careers. The professionalization described so far proceeded from one form of notable politics to another—without parties assuming any political prominence. The enduring, albeit altered, strength of notable politics reflects the fact that universal male suffrage was introduced before the onset of the industrial revolution in 1848. Because of this sequencing, electoral professionalization took place in the absence of well-organized interest groups, national communication infrastructure (e.g. railroads, national press), large scale urbanization and distinctly formed class identities. Such an environment kept the costs of winning votes low and facilitated local, door-to-door canvassing and informal personal networks around which notable politics was organized (Kreuzer 2001: 23–51). Once institutionalized, notable politics had greater latitude to minimize the demands generated by industrialization for more national and disciplined party organization (Huard 1996).

The weakness of parties meant that France's political class, for all its *esprit de corps*, remained atomistic and weakly organized. The atomistic quality became particularly apparent in the legislature. Deputies frequently belonged to multiple parliamentary groups, switched their memberships and rarely adhered to disciplined party voting in the *Assemblée nationale* (AN). The Third Republic's parliamentary procedures purposefully obstructed the professionalization of legislative affairs. These procedures required that committee positions be assigned by lottery and prohibited parliamentary groups from holding their meetings in the chamber of Deputies. These restrictions served to randomize legislative careers and prevent the formation of disciplined parliamentary groups. Such groups were widely considered to be incompatible with a Deputy's free mandate (Albertini 1961: 586–669; Mestre 1994: 14). The lifting of these restrictions in 1910 contributed to a modest increase in parliamentary discipline during the inter-war period. Committees became better organized and had greater continuity in their membership. They, however, still had no administrative support staff (Albertini 1959: 39).

The most notable development between 1900 and 1939 was the growing importance of parties in electoral politics. By 1914, Socialists, Republicans, and Conservatives had all transformed their informal organizational networks into permanent parties. These parties functioned as national umbrella organizations for coordinating fundraising, distributing campaign material, and strengthening voters' party identification. However, these new parties complemented rather than supplanted the personal vote-seeking style of political notables. They were loosely structured electoral organizations that were strictly tailored to the re-election needs of individual political entrepreneurs (Huard 1996: 226–89). They did not give—as it was the case in Germany—rise to party bureaucrats and still required that Deputies launch their political careers as locally elected officials and cumulate offices to support their political ambitions. Any organizational innovations that would have limited the autonomy of Deputies never got past the drawing board. During the inter-war period, only the *Section française de l'Internationale Ouvrière* (SFIO)—which was then splitting into the Socialists and the Communists—and the Radical Party (*Parti Radical*) formalized their governance mechanisms sufficiently to permit grassroots members to influence personnel and policy matters (Kreuzer 2001: 71–8, 91–7).

The German occupation and the Vichy regime constituted a contradictory break in the development of the political class. On the one hand, the parliamentarians themselves gave away their power by transferring their competencies to Marshal Pétain; furthermore, the prohibition and suspension of parties interrupted the institutionalization process that had begun in the inter-war period. On the other hand, the Vichy regime neither had well organized and trained followers—like for example the German or Italian fascist mass organizations—nor own qualified elites which could have supported the takeover at the local level and thus sustained the power apparatus. The regime had to fall back upon local elites. After the liberation of France in 1944 a new breed of politicians from the *résistance* was recruited at the national level, while the local level was marked by continuity (Höhne 2000).

During the Fourth Republic (1945–58), the importance of political parties continued to grow and that of notables to decline. The three largest parties, the Socialists, Communists, and Christian Democrats (*Mouvement Républicain Populaire*—MRP), were also the three best organized groups. They had centralized their electoral organizations, recruited sizable memberships, and established formalized governance structures. Their organizations allowed them to carry out national campaigns, control the formulation of policies and, to a lesser extent, direct the recruitment of candidates. Individual candidates consequently had less opportunity to promote themselves and were more frequently denied re-nominations if they were disloyal to their parties (Williams 1958: 348–9).

The parties even managed to organize legislative business more tightly. They set the agenda, assigned committee positions and allocated ministerial portfolios. Therefore, public "interest shifted away from the Palais Bourbon [Parliament] where decisions were formally registered to the party meeting where they were really made" (Williams 1958: 359). Party discipline was by no means as strict as in Britain or Germany but it noticeably increased after 1945. Other aspects of parliamentary work, however, remained unchanged: Deputies still received no public funds for hiring support staff. Parties instead levied a tax on the Deputies' incomes to employ legislative staffers. The salaries and pension benefits continued to be pegged to those of higher civil servants (Williams 1958: 365, 193). At the cabinet level, civil servants assumed a more prominent advisory role after 1945. Many of these member of the *Haute Administration* (ministerial bureaucracy) came from the new *Ecole National d'Administration* (ENA) which was created in 1945 (Birnbaum 1994: 59–66).

The Fifth Republic constitutes a significant break in France's political professionalization. After 1958, politics was characterized by the growing influence of technocrats, stricter party discipline in Parliament, and the renewed electoral importance of notables (Ruß *et al.* 2000).

THE INSTITUTIONAL CONTEXT

Political professionalization in France has been shaped by the enduring tensions that existed between administrative state structures and representative political institutions. Since 1870, entrepreneurial politicians with their need for particularistic benefits co-existed with a large and centralized state bureaucracy which saw itself as self-appointed defender of the national interest. These enduring tensions, however, were significantly modified by the different constitutional configurations of the Third, Fourth, and Fifth Republics. The Third Republic's political institutions exacerbated the tensions between politicians and bureaucrats. Its small, single-member districts personalized electoral contexts and created considerable demand for all sorts of particularistic benefits (Kreuzer 2001: 53–70). Its weak executive and strong committees, in turn, imposed few disciplinary constraints on Deputies to desist from endless pork-barrel projects and advocate coherent, national policies as favored by state officials (Albertini 1959). In the Fourth Republic, proportional representation and the introduction of women suffrage led parties to pursue more collective policies and the strengthening of the executive restricted the allocation of particularistic benefits.

However, it was not until the Fifth Republic that the tensions between politicians and bureaucrats were significantly reduced. De Gaulle made no secret of his dislike for the parochial politics of the Third Republic and the polarized sectarianism of the Fourth. To prevent a repetition of these experiences, he changed the representative political institutions as well as the administrative state structure. With the aim to improve the coordination of economic development policies and to curtail the power of the cities and *Departements* de Gaulle introduced various administrative reform projects. Local politicians and bureaucrats were successful, however, in obstructing and finally preventing many reforms—except the implementation of the regions (Schmidt 1990: 76–82).

With the introduction of a plurality electoral system with a second ballot Charles de Gaulle and Michel Debré—the two major figures behind the formulation of the Fifth Republic's constitution—drew upon a modified form of the old two-step voting system. Candidates wanting to participate in the second ballot for Parliament have to overcome a legal threshold (5 percent in 1958–66; 10 percent 1966–76; and since 1976 12.5 percent but since then referring to the totality of all persons entitled to vote). This threshold reduced the localizing and personalizing effects of the electoral system of the Third Republic by automatically excluding smaller parties and candidates which had regularly "sold" their withdrawal from the second ballot and/or their support to the highest-bidding remaining candidate. Furthermore, it made it easier for party elites to coordinate the withdrawal of candidates at the national level, thus diminishing the possibilities of candidates to act as free agents and representatives of local interests (Bartolini 1984: 107; Kreuzer 2000). The introduction—in a referendum (1962)—of the direct election of the President amplified these effects, because it nationalized politics and exerted an important coattail effect on parliamentary elections. Furthermore, by admitting only the two candidates with the highest number of votes to the runoff ballot (if no one gained the absolute majority in the first ballot), the election procedure contributed to the formation of two disciplined, bipolar blocs able to gain majorities and to be resistant to claims of particularized preferential treatment (Bartolini 1984: 119–20). Eventually, presidential elections did not only modernize the campaigns, but have also strengthened the political parties in respect to the mobilization of resources and the logistic organization of electoral campaigns (Cole 1993).

The Fifth Republic's electoral system and campaigning regulations reflect the continued effort to minimize the political influence of interest groups. The single member districts localize and personalize representation and make it more difficult for interest groups to co-opt political parties. Ever since 1875, French electoral law determined a wide range of economic incompatibilities between the parliamentary mandate and positions in private corporations (Liebert 1995: 415). It also restricts the ability of interest groups to use their financial resources in order to influence political parties. Political finance regulations, for example, forbade until 1988 any private contributions to parties and limited the money that could be raised from party members. A new law passed in 1990 has restricted private contributions to 20 percent of campaign expenditures. This law also established formal restrictions on print and media advertising that were intended to moderate the cost of modern election campaigns and limit the financial dependence of parties on interest groups (Kreuzer 2000; Doublet 1992: 43; Drysch 1993: 165; Benoit and Scale 1995: 33–4). However, the new and old regulations only constrained but never prevented the mobilization of private capital resources as parties resorted to various illicit forms of political financing (Mény 1995: 159–72).

A remarkable feature of the Fifth Republic's constitution is the double-headed executive with the President as the head of state and the Prime Minister as the head of government. The President has not only the right to nominate a Prime Minister as well as individual ministers (as proposed by the Prime Minister), but can also dismiss them. Furthermore, he heads the council of ministers. In times when the Prime Minister and the President are from the same political camp, as was always the case up to 1986, the President also sets the overall direction of the government's policy, the Prime Minister and the cabinet merely being instruments of implementation. In times of split affiliations (*cohabitation*) the authority shifts towards the government and thus to the Prime Minister who is constitutionally in charge of determining and guiding national policy (article 20 of the constitution). Despite the incompatibility of governmental office and parliamentary mandate, which was intended to strengthen the autonomy of the executive *vis-à-vis* the legislative, the *cohabitation* leads to an empowerment of the *Assemblée nationale* (and hence the parliamentarians and party groups). The reason is the Prime Minister's increasing dependence upon the parliamentary majority to carry through his policy—at the same time as he lacks the backing of the President. The Prime Minister tightly controls the agenda set in his cabinet. He is responsible for all ministerial decisions and continuously supervises the activities of ministers with the help of a large staff (Thiébault 1994: 139–40). He also dominates the legislative decision-making process.

In the National Assembly, committees play a subordinate role. There are only six permanent committees which all have an extremely large membership (up to 145). This limits their specialization and ability to develop expertise that could offset the informational advantages of the government. Committees also have no right to initiate legislation and only limited possibilities to modify it (Mattson and Strøm 1995). Furthermore, the constitution gives the government extensive decree powers which permit it to by-pass the National Assembly and the Senate and to circumvent the Assembly's delaying power by calling a so called package or blocked vote which is final and only contains the amendments acceptable to the government (Andrews 1978: 490–1).

This legislative disenfranchisement affects the balance between France's representative and state structures in two ways. First, it deprives Deputies and Senators of the possibility to allocate particularistic benefits. The government, for example, can automatically block any private member bills or amendments that will either increase expenditure or decrease revenues (Andrews 1978: 485, 493). Second, the weakening of the *Assemblée nationale* indirectly enhances the influence of civil servants over the legislative process. Where committees previously discussed and amended bills, now members of the executive supervise the drafting of bills (Suleiman 1973: 749–52).

The Assembly can force the government to resign by way of a motion of no confidence, which must be introduced by at least 10 percent of the Members. On the other hand, the Prime Minister has the possibility to discipline his parliamentary majority by tying a vote of confidence to a bill (article 49.3).

Finally, only the President can dissolve Parliament which gives him the ability to discipline his parliamentary majority or, lacking one, to call an early election in the hope of winning a majority. These rules regulating governmental survival all increase the autonomy of the executive from the legislature in times of political correspondence between the Prime Minister and the President. They have allowed the executive to pay little attention to the career ambitions of Deputies and appoint as ministers or cabinet advisors the allegedly apolitical civil servants that de Gaulle viewed as the most competent guardians of the national interest. However, political practice has changed since the days of de Gaulle: the ministerial bureaucracy has become politicized, the change in government in 1981 as well as the *cohabitations* have led to a different conception of the parties and to a strengthened position for the Assembly. The political system oscillates between a presidentialization on the national level and—since 1982—an increasing importance of the departmental and regional level due to the laws on decentralization (see p.137).

Overall, the semi-presidential system that de Gaulle devised significantly strengthened the executive and weakened Deputies as well as parties. The resulting asymmetry of power between these three political actors ultimately limited the importance of particularistic benefits and facilitated the growing influence of senior civil servants and technocrats.

THE POLITICAL CLASS

A political class is characterized as a professionalized, homogenous, and closed structure, living off politics. Hence it is necessary, regarding the Fifth French Republic, to enlarge the point of reference from the so called traditional *hommes politiques* to the higher civil servants and the management of the (former) public sector. "Indeed, in critical ways, the elite has become indistinguishable from the political class in France. The barriers between serving the state, serving one's personal interest, and serving political interests have been blurred to the point of becoming, for all practical purposes, nonexistent" (Suleiman 1995: 161).

Because of their common structures of recruitment and common interests— related to a distinct historical conception of the state and its centralized bureaucratic structure—one can find the core of the political class exclusively on the national political-administrative level which hardly extends beyond the boundaries of Paris (not to say the boundaries of the seventh *arrondissement*; see Chevallier 1997).

Size and Composition

By international comparison, France can surely be seen as a "Republic of office-holders" (Ruß 1993) due to its *c.* 500,000 electoral offices. But only a small part of these can be found on the national level and few allow their holders to be financially independent: most prominently the 577 members of the *Assemblée nationale* and the 321 members of the *Sénat.* Concerning the cumulation of offices (*cumul des mandats,* see below), the more than 3,800 seats of the *conseiller généraux* at the *Départements* level and the roughly 1,700 seats in the regional councils are also important because of their influence and remuneration (Knapp 1991: 18; Frémy and Frémy 1996: 2165). Looking at the governmental and ministerial level one finds a mix of political and administrative posts, the number of which Kimmel estimates to 1,000 (Kimmel 1996: 18). We have also to include the leading posts of the nationalized or formerly nationalized enterprises because they have often been filled by former members of the Assembly or other members of the political class (Birnbaum 1994: 80–1; also cf. Bock 1999).

On the other hand, the French political parties contribute little to the professionalization of their personnel in this regard (except for the *Parti Communiste Français*—PCF, see below). Their small size as well as their weak financial base generally do not allow them to finance full-time politicians; they contribute more to the professionalization of politicians in terms of recruitment, career-planning and organization of election campaigns (Ysmal 1994: 198–202).

Political Recruitment and Political Careers

Political careers in the Fifth Republic usually follow one of two paths, both of which are founded on the historical traditions of the French state: on the one hand the importance of an autonomous and centralized administration claiming political independence, and on the other hand the significance of locally established politicians acting as a "hinge" between centralism and localism.

These traditions have been reinforced both by the institutional characteristics of the Fifth Republic (majority vote, incompatibility of executive posts and Assembly seats) and by the development of the *Assemblée nationale* towards a national legislature of local office holders (a function originally meant for the *Sénat* only). At the same time, with the founding of the ENA in 1945, an elite of administrative technocratic experts has been created. This elite can fulfill a multitude of functions and is to be found on the highest levels of the state since the 1950s. The *énarchisation* has been characteristic of certain career patterns: e.g. after graduating from the ENA joining one of the *grands corps* (*Inspection des Finances, Conseil d'Etat, Cour des*

Comptes), followed by a post in a ministerial cabinet, perhaps culminating in the rise to director of a cabinet or even in a ministerial post.[1] Since access to the *Haute administration* apart from the *grandes écoles* is barely possible, this education leads to a certain uniformity of the administration. A strongly developed *esprit de corps* and a similar socio-economic background, of a bourgeois nature, support the development of a homogenous, autonomous, and self-reproducing elite, which tends to assume a class character and extends its influence beyond political boundaries (Birnbaum 1994; Thoenig 1996).

Although the Left criticized the political hegemony of the conservative and liberal parties in the 1970s as "Etat-UDF" (UDF = *Union pour la démocratie française*) and "Etat-RPR" (*Rassemblement pour la République*) no change took place after the Socialist's ascent to power in 1981. There was neither a significant exchange of administrative elites nor a renunciation of the mechanisms of recruitment. When the ENA-graduate Laurent Fabius became Prime Minister in 1983, the technocrats were also accepted by the Socialist government. After the aristocracy and the *notables* of the Third Republic as well as the civil servants of the Fourth Republic, the membership of the administrative elite became the decisive criterion: "à la République des fonctionnaires semble succéder une République d'experts en affaires économiques" (Birnbaum 1994: 161). Connected to the change of power was a certain politicization of these elites—or rather, politicization became necessary and visible. But France is not yet a party state (*Parteienstaat*) like Germany, where the "correct" party membership sometimes is more important than competence to get a post. Yet, also in France some political scientists complain about the "osmosis" of political and administrative circles (Portelli 1988: 27; Chevalier 1997: 91).

After gaining access to politics via a ministerial cabinet and other governmental posts, members of the administrative elite may continue their careers in different ways: (1) return to the former administrative office, (2) assume a leading position in (formerly) nationalized enterprises, or (3) further develop and stabilize their political career through a national mandate as Deputy or Senator (Birnbaum 1994: 84). To preserve or to enlarge their own chances of re-election, politicians may use the possibilities of *parachutage*. This means a top-to-bottom process of nomination in a (safe) constituency for politicians who are already established on the national level (Chavel 1995). But to protect the political career it is insufficient to win a constituency and a seat in the AN given the majority voting procedure. Because of the high electoral volatility, even the "stars" of the political scene can easily be voted out. Only a local anchorage with intensive effort at the base level and some more local or regional elective mandates can significantly enlarge the chances of re-election and provide an extra income. On the other hand, a strong identification of the candidates

---

[1] Under this career pattern we can also find the graduates of the *Ecole Polytéchnique* (called "X"), who are qualified for the entrance in the *Corps des mines* or the *Corps des Ponts-et-des Chaussés*, leading to the technical administration, of the *Ecole Centrale* and of the business-schools HEC, ESSEC, ESCP. But it is more important to belong to one of the *grands corps* than to have graduated from one of these *grande écoles*. For a critical view of the *énarchisation*, see Kesler 1997.

with national party politics and/or a concentration on governmental affairs can diminish the chances of re-election.

After the rules concerning the cumulation of offices (the *cumul des mandats*) were tightened in 1985, only a combination of two of the following elective posts is now possible: Deputy in the AN or Senator, Member of the European Parliament, *conseiller régional* (Deputy on the regional level), *conseiller général* (Deputy on the level of a *Département*), city councilor of Paris, mayor in a community with more than 20,000 inhabitants, *adjoint* (vice-mayor) in a community with more than 100,000 inhabitants (Knapp 1991: 35).

A second path of professionalization is a bottom-to-top process which finds its starting point in local politics. At the outset a political party commitment is not necessary. However, this becomes indispensable for national office because of the electoral system and its block-building mechanism. Depending on the importance of the town/the region in the national context, a mayor or president of the regional council may gain importance in party politics. A connection with national politics via a mandate in the Assembly or the Senate was indispensable in the years before the passing of the decentralization acts (1982) to get access to the center of power and decision-making in Paris. Via this route, local politicians could by-pass the omni potent departmental representative of state power, the *préfet*. Both career components are complementary: "Mayors seek national office either for itself or for the resources that access to Paris can deliver. Deputies seek municipal office either for itself or for the local resources—in terms of goodwill, cash and logistical—that a town hall can deliver. Thus national office reinforces local office, and vice versa" (Knapp 1991: 30).

A local mandate offers personal and material resources in campaigning, which are not immediately at the disposal of *parachutés*. Due to the absence of party- and campaign-finance laws until 1988 as well as to the weak financial situation of political parties in France, access to such resources and the illegitimate practices of party-financing (e.g. by superelevated bills from consulting companies) have been the decisive factors in campaign-financing (Ruß 1993; Doublet 1997; Mény 1997).

The coincidence between re-election as a proof of confidence in the individual, locally based Deputy and the crisis of representation of the political class as a whole is shown by poll results (Ysmal 1995; *Le Monde*, 27 February 1997): for some years, French people have trusted their mayors (1997: 68 percent), while they mistrusted their MPs and ministers (36 percent and 41 percent, respectively).

Increasing electoral volatility, changes in the party-system, and the majority vote lead to a high percentage of marginal seats. For the period from 1958 to 1991 Ysmal estimates only 99 (21 percent) safe constituencies (Ysmal 1994: 202). In every newly elected assembly, almost one-third of the MPs are freshmen; the average incumbency is about 2.6 legislative terms (cf. Ysmal 1994: 193–4). This high degree of turnover offers a possibility for the political parties to select new candidates in many constituencies. As the elections of 1993 and 1997 showed for the PS (*Parti Socialiste*) and for the RPR respectively, electoral landslides are leading to a renewal of the political personnel and to a restructuring within the parties.

The different career patterns (top-to-bottom, bottom-to-top) are also leading to different professional paths of former Deputies (Birnbaum 1994: 80–2; Dogan 1999). While locally anchored politicians, regardless of their political persuasion, often enter leading posts on the local level, where they bring in their national experience and contacts, "top-to-bottom-politicians" stay on the national level in the management of (formerly) nationalized enterprises or return to their original authorities. In any case the contacts to the administrative elite (via education or co-operation) are more decisive for this group than the party affiliation—a fact which reflects the importance of the *grandes écoles* in forming a homogenous elite (Suleiman 1995).

With regard to the social background we find two tendencies for the Deputies as well as for the political-administrative field: "le personnel politique de droite vient principalement de la bourgeoisie économique et de la haute fonction publique, et celui de gauche de la bourgeoisie intellectuelle et de la fonction publique moyenne et supérieure" (Denni 1993: 422). This tendency is confirmed by the composition of the AN with a dominance of self-employed people in the RPR and UDF and a dominance of teachers and professors on the left. To this can be added a clear dominance of males and an average age of 48–52 years in the AN (Ysmal 1995).

Only one change can be observed in the last years: the proportion of women has risen to 11 percent (sixty-three female Deputies) in 1997 and 12 percent in 2002, so that in a European comparison it is no longer France but Greece which occupies the last rank (*Le Monde*, 4 June 1997 and 18 June 2002). In 1997, this development was mainly due to the 30 percent quota in the process of nominating candidates instituted by the PS, as a result of which forty-two of the 246 socialist constituencies were won by women (17 percent). In 2002, in spite of the introduction of a *parité*-clause in the French constitution in 2000, French parties rather accepted a financial penalty than a 50 percent quota of women among nominated candidates.[2]

Living off Politics

The levels of remuneration for French office-holders (Table 7.1) are linked to the income of the higher civil service (Rouban 1994; for the following figures cf. Frémy and Frémy 2002: 1854–5). On the local level (municipalities, departments, regions) the office-holders are not allowed to earn more than FRF50,209 (€7,654) a month.[3]

On the national level Deputies, Senators, and members of the government get, beside their remuneration, considerable tax advantages, maintenance grants to keep offices, to travel etc. as well as credits at favorable terms (Table 7.2; for details cf. Frémy and Frémy 2002: 1854–5). There is also an incompatibility rule which forbids MPs to continue practicing their original occupations, except for farmers, shopkeepers,

---

[2] In 1997, 3 of the 8 Deputies of the *Verts* are women (37.5%), in the PCF 5 of 37 (13.5%), in the RPR 5 of 140 (3.57%), and 7 of 109 of the deputies of the UDF (6.42%). In 2002, only 68 of 3,284 female candidates won a seat in the AN (4 of 21 PCF, 23 of 141 PS, 1 of 3 *Verts*, 2 of 8 PRG, 1 of 22 UDF, 36 of 369 *Union pour la majorité présidentielle* [RPR], 1 of 3 Divers Droits). The total percentage of women in the AN has increased from 10.9% in 1997 to 11.8% in 2002. For the role of women in the political life of France, see Kleszcz-Wagner (1998).   [3] Converted according to the fixed EMU rate (FRF1 = €0.15245).

craftsmen, businessmen, and professionals, accounting for only 15 percent of all MPs (Ysmal 1994: 200). Beside the access to the parliamentary research office, MPs get administrative subsidies, sufficient to hire three personal assistants to support them in their work in the constituency and in Paris. But as this is left to the MPs' discretion, the personal staff can comprise from one to five persons (*Service de la Communication de l'Assemblée*, 27 May 1997).

According to their party affiliation, national MPs have to transfer different sums to their parties: as in the case of local office-holders the PCF gets the total income and pays the regular party salary to their Deputies. The Socialist Deputies have to transfer between €1,145 and €8,436 depending on their marital status and further local mandates. The UDF collects €383, the RPR €455 to €608 from their Deputies.

Table 7.1   *Remuneration for political positions on the sub-national level, 2001 (in FRF)*

Position	Monthly remuneration (before tax)
Conseiller municipaux (city councilor)	
Municipalities < 100,000 inhabitants	No functional allowance, expense allowance possible
Municipalities > 100,000 inh.	1,384
Maire (mayor)	
< 3.500 inh.	3,921–9,918
Small cities (3,500–20,000 inh.)	12,686–14,992
Medium cities (20,000–100,000 inh.)	20,759–25,372
Large cities (> 100,000 inh.)	33,445
> 200,000 (incl. Paris, Lyon, Marseille)	33,445
Conseiller généraux (*Departement*-councilor)	
< 500,000 inh.	9,226–11,533
> 500,000 inh.	13,839–16,146
Conseiller régionaux (regional councilor)	
< 2 million inh.	9,226–11,533
> 2 million inh.	13,839–16,146

Note: 1FRF = €0.1525 (fixed EMU rate).
Source: Frémy and Frémy (2002: 1854–5).

Table 7.2   *Monthly remuneration of AN Members 2002, before tax*

Basic salary	€ 5,169
Functional allowance	€ 1,331
Additional privileges: lump sum for phone bills within the constituency; free travel in the first class of the SNCF; 40 roundtrip flights from Paris to the constituency; 6 roundtrip flights within France; attractive credit (*c.* € 76,225) loan at 2 percent interest (for 10 years) to buy a flat.	

Source: Frémy and Frémy (2002: 1854–5).

Table 7.3   *Monthly remuneration for national elective positions outside the AN, 2001 (FRF, net)*

Senators	
Basic salary	42,668
Add. privileges concerning travel, telecommunication, secretaries, credits	
Members of government (basic salaries)	
Prime Minister	60,879
State ministers, ministers (remunerations of further mandates may not exceed 50% of this sum)	46,972
Add. privileges: official car + driver; rent rebate; free travels with the SNCF etc.; integration in the parliamentary system of pensions, i.e., of civil servants	
President (annual)	
Basic salary (incl. flat)	10,541,000
Office, administration, library, etc.	51,483,000

Source: Frémy and Frémy (2002: 1854–5).

During election campaigns all Deputies have to put material resources (e.g. secretaries, assistants) at the disposal of their parties (Table 7.3).

The French MPs are able to get the right to a pension in only one legislature (5 years), if they pay the double of the basis sum (1996: FRF6,721 [€1,025]) to the independent and obligatory pension system for MPs. In this case they have the right to a pension of €1,524 monthly, after 37 years of a maximum sum of €5,486.

These data show again that there are only two possibilities to live off politics: either the politicians win a national seat or they cumulate several local mandates—or preferably both. In the 1997 Assembly, 495 of 577 MPs (86 percent) held one ore more local mandates. Among these were 305 mayors, a number which emphasizes the continuity of the *député-maire* as a successful career-pattern. A look at the cumulation of offices accentuates this fact: 97 of 208 MPs (53 percent) are cumulating two local offices, combining the office of a mayor with a mandate as *conseiller général* (followed by 18 for the combination of *maire/conseiller régional* and *conseiller général/conseiller régional*). Only three of twenty-nine MPs cumulating three mandates are not holding an office as mayor (*Le Monde*, Dossiers et Documents: Elections législatives, 25 May 1997, own calculations). The importance of a mandate as mayor confirms our argument of the "enduring notables"—in a modernized version: a local basis enhances the chances of re-election through access to human and material resources, which cannot be delivered in the same way by political parties. Holding a national mandate without a local base almost seems to be impossible, at least in the long run.

THE POLITICAL CLASS AND INSTITUTIONAL REFORM

The most important reform during the political life of the Fifth Republic has been the introduction of the direct vote for President by referendum in October 1962. In spite of some criticism from within the political class, the French people approved the constitutional revision by 62.25 percent of the votes, due to the crisis of French politics (e.g. decolonization) and the charisma of de Gaulle (Chagnollaud 1993: 456–7). This direct vote has led to a presidentialization of the entire political system which in turn has resulted in a strong personalization of politics (Wahl and Quermonne 1995). There is a direct connection to a weakening of the political parties as intended by de Gaulle. After the "*régime des partis*" in the Fourth Republic he wanted to strengthen the executive as well as its support by an independent administration. This was started with the founding of the ENA and subsequently led to a technocratization of the administrative elites in the 1950s.

Further institutional reforms concerning the Senate and the question of regionalization had been rejected in a referendum in 1969, causing de Gaulle to resign from his post. Through this course of action he founded the French political tradition of taking the result of referenda as direct proof of trust and legitimation of the President. This first attempt at decentralization and Georges Pompidou's failed attempt to reduce the presidential term from 7 to 5 years (which in 1973 failed to get the three-fifths majority required for a constitutional amendment) show that two decisive structural deficiencies of the Fifth Republic were recognized early, but that reforms did not find a majority in the population or in the political class.

It was only in 1981, when the socialists took over, that decentralization was realized causing the most far-reaching structural change in the French state since its beginnings. The transfer of decision-making powers and budgetary competencies from the central to the local, departmental, and regional levels resulted in a reduction of central power as embodied by the prefect and in an upgrading of the *conseillers régionaux* and *généraux*. Also connected to this is an increase of power for local politicians who are no longer subject to prefectorial directives, but have sufficient freedom of action at their disposal and will be measured by their policies on election day (Knapp 1991; Greffet 1995). Along with a certain confusion of competencies due to the decentralization, one further accusation is that larger budgetary competencies have led to more corruption among local politicians (e.g. Alain Carrignon, Jacques Médecin; see *Le Monde*, 27 February 1997; Ruggiero 1996). Nevertheless, the French population generally has more trust in local politicians than in MPs and ministers on the national level which confirms our argument that the negatively evaluated political class is perceived to be located in Paris.

The image of a corrupt political class increasingly emerged at the end of the 1980s when the illegitimate practices of party- and campaign-financing forced the government to pass several bills concerning the public financing in these domains (cf. Ruß 1993; Doublet 1997). But the simultaneous amnesty for the involved politicians damaged the reputation of MPs and party politicians even more, reinforcing the negative evaluation of the *classe politique*. The rapid growth of parliamentary candidates is one of the consequences of the party finance acts: in 1997 there were more than 6,300 candidates for 577 constituencies (20 percent more than in 1993, 45 percent more than in 1988). This development is due to the fact that, besides the parties represented in the AN, those parties able to nominate at least fifty candidates receive state grants (in 1997 FRF11.31 [€1.72] per vote). Thus, the smaller parties heavily rely on public funding. In 1997, the FN received FRF35.5 millions (€5.4 millions), *Les Verts* FRF11.6 millions (€1.77 millions), *Génération écologique* FRF10.3 millions (€1.57 millions), and even the trotzkyist *Lutte ouvrière* received FRF2.5 millions (€0.38 millions). But also in the case of the RPR state grants made up 62 percent of the party income, in the case of the PS 45 percent (*Le Monde*, 6 May 1997).

The 1985 act limiting the *cumul des mandats* (Knapp 1991) was a first attempt to reduce the unlimited possibilities for office cumulation. It was supposed to counter-act the effects of decentralization, for example, the power of local politicians resulting from shifting competencies. But since the most attractive combinations of offices (for instance office of mayor and national mandate) were not to be touched by this bill, most of the MPs approved. As a consequence, the mandates most frequently given up have been those of *conseiller régional* or *général*, while the *député-maire* model can be found as often as ever (see above).

Another attempt to break up given structures was to be found in the plan of Prime Minister Edith Cresson (1992) to transfer the ENA to Strasbourg. Through this she wanted to separate the political and the administrative elite spatially, thereby coun-teracting the widely held opinion that the seventh *arrondissement* in Paris contains a closed, elitist and corrupt political class. However, strong criticism from political and administrative ranks doomed this reform attempt to a failure—only some phases of the educational program have been relocated.

Some further attempts at institutional reform which aroused very mixed reactions within the political class took place in 1985 and 1995. In 1985 the Socialist govern-ment introduced the system of proportional vote for the legislative elections and declared the democratization of the institutions a programmatic goal. But the gov-ernment was confronted by strong protest even within its own ranks (Michel Rocard, Minister of Agriculture at that time, resigned), because this reform was not primarily motivated by a basic change of structures in the sense of a better representation of the voter's will. Rather the Socialists intended to split up the conservative-liberal elec-torate by giving parliamentary representation to the FN with the result that the scale of the expected socialist defeat could be limited. After the re-introduction of the majority vote by UDF and RPR, the discussion about electoral reform stopped.

In 1995 the newly elected President Jacques Chirac initiated the most important constitutional reform since 1962 (*Le Monde*, 1 August 1995; Eilfort 1997: 67–71). On the one hand his aim was to improve communication between the population and the government (that is the President) through an expansion of the referendum: He sought to extend the direct vote to questions of the organization of public power, the ratification of agreements, and to economic and social policies. On the other hand, Chirac wished to enhance the status of parliamentary work (mainly through a more regular control of the executive) by introducing a single session from October to June instead of two sessions of three months in autumn and spring. Opposing the gov-ernmental proposal of a maximum of 150 days in session, the MPs agreed on a max-imum of 120 days in session which shows how little importance the Deputies themselves accord parliamentary work: "For the MPs the parliamentary work is less important than their local and regional mandates which cover their local basis" (Eilfort 1997: 69–70).

The most recent institutional reforms—the introduction of the *quinquennat* (the reduction of the presidential mandate from 7 to 5 years) and of the *parité* clause into the constitution (2000) will perhaps change the political life in France significantly—but it is too early for results. Most of the changes on the institutional level concerning the political class resulted from the change of power in 1981. Yet they are not connected to an explicit reformist intention, but are more a reaction to unexpected developments like the uncovering of the financing practices by the media.

REFERENCES

Albertini, Rudolf von (1959). "Regierung und Parlament in der Dritten Republik". *Historische Zeitschrift*, 188: 17–48.

——(1961). "Parteiorganisation und Parteibegriff in Frankreich 1789–1940". *Historische Zeitschrift*, 193: 529–600.

Andrews, William G. (1978). "The Constitutional Prescription of Parliamentary Procedures in Gaullist France". *Legislative Studies Quarterly*, 3: 465–506.

Bartolini, Stefano (1984). "Institutional Constraints and Party Competition in the French Party System". *West European Politics*, 7/4: 103–26.

Benoit, Jean-Marc, and Scale, Jessica (1995). "Les dépenses de candidats". *Pouvoirs*, 70: 33–41.

Birnbaum, Pierre (1994). *Les sommets de l'Etat: Essai sur l'élite du pouvoir en France*. Paris: Editions du Seuil.

Bock, Hans Manfred (1999). "Republikanischer Elitismus und technokratische Herrschaft: Zu einigen Merkmalen der politischen Elite im gegenwärtigen Frankreich", in M. Christadler and H. Uterwedde (eds), *Länderbericht Frankreich*. Bonn: Bundeszentrale für politische Bildung, pp. 383–403.

Chagnollaud, Dominique (ed.) (1993). *La vie politique en France*. Paris: Editions du Seuil.

Chavel, Cécile (1995). "The Structure of Opportunities in Legislative Recruitment in France", unpublished manuscript, presented at the ECPR Joint Sessions, Bordeaux.

Chevallier, Jacques (1997). "L'élite polito-administrative". *Pouvoirs*, 80: 89–100.

Cole, Alistair (1993). "The Presidential Party and the Fifth Republic". *West European Politics*, 16: 49–66.

Denni, Bernard (1993). "Les élites en France", in D. Chagnollaud (ed.), *La vie politique en France*. Paris: Editions du Seuil, pp. 418–30.

Dogan, Mattei (1953). "La stabilité du personnel parlementaire sous la Troisième République". *Revue Française de Science Politique*, 3: 319–49.

——(1999). "Les professions propices à la carrière politique: Osmoses, filières et viviers", in M. Offerlé (ed.), *La Profession Politique XIXe-XXe Siècles*. Paris: Belin, pp. 171–199.

Doublet, Yves-Marie (1992). "Financement: quel part du droit". *Pouvoirs*, 63: 39–51.

——(1997). *L'argent et la politique en France*. Paris: Economica.

Drysch, Thomas (1993). "The New French System of Party Finance", in A. Gunlicks (ed.), *Campaign and Party Financing in North America and Western Europe*. Boulder: Westview, pp. 155–77.

Eilfort, Michael (1997). "Der 'Monarch' ist tot, der 'Adel' erschüttert: Parlamentarismus im Frankreich des Bürgerpräsidenten Jacques Chirac". *Zeitschrift für Parlamentsfragen*, 28(1): 60–84.

Frémy, Dominique, and Frémy, Michèle (1996). *Quid 1997*. Paris: Laffont.

—— (2002). *Quid 2001*. Paris: Laffont.

Garrigou, Alain (1992). *La vote et la vertu: Comment les Français sonts devenus électeurs*. Paris: Presse de la FNSP.

Greffet, Fabienne (1995). "From Local Elites to National Elites", unpublished manuscript, presented at the ECPR workshop, Bordeaux.

Höhne, Roland (2001). "Das Regime von Vichy—ein europäischer Sonderfall autoritärer Herrschaft?", in H. Timmermann and W. D. Gruner (eds), *Demokratie und Diktatur im 20. Jahrhundert*. Berlin: Duncker & Humblot, pp. 473–534.

Huard, Raymond (1996). *La naissance du parti politique en France*. Paris: Presses de Sciences Po.

Kesler, Jean-François (1997). "L'énarchie n'existe pas". *Pouvoirs*, 80: 23–41.

Kimmel, Adolf (1996). "Die politisch-administrativen Eliten in Frankreich und Deutschland nach dem Zweiten Weltkrieg", in L. Dupeux, R. Hudemann, and F. Knipping (eds), *Eliten in Frankreich und Deutschland im 19. und 20. Jahrhundert*, Vol. 2. Munich: Oldenbourg, pp. 117–23.

Kleszcz-Wagner, Anette (1998). "Frauen in Frankreich: Heiß geliebt und politisch kaltgestellt", in B. Hoecker (ed.), *Handbuch Politische Partizipation von Frauen in Europa*. Opladen: Leske + Budrich, pp. 115–44.

Knapp, Andrew (1991). "The Cumul des Mandats, Local Power and Political Parties in France". *West European Politics*, 14(1): 18–40.

Kreuzer, Marcus (1996). "Democratisation and Changing Methods of Electoral Corruption in France from 1815 to 1914", in W. Little and E. Posada-Carbó (eds), *Political Corruption in Europe and Latin America*. London: Macmillan, pp. 97–114.

—— (2000). "Personal Vote, Party Vote and Electoral Institutions: Explaining Differences of Conservative Parties in Japan, France, Britain, Austria and Germany". *Party Politics*, 6: 487–504.

—— (2001). *Institutions and Innovation: Voters, Parties and Interest Groups in the Consolidation of Democracy—France and Germany 1870–1939*. Ann Arbor: University of Michigan Press.

Liebert, Ulrike (1995). "Parliamentary Lobby Regimes", in H. Döring (ed.), *Parliaments and Majority Rule in Western Europe*. Frankfort/Main: Campus, pp. 407–48.

Mattson, Ingvar, and Strøm, Kaare (1995). "Parliamentary Committees", in H. Döring (ed.), *Parliaments and Majority Rule in Western Europe*. Frankfort/Main: Campus, pp. 249–307.

Mény, Yves (1995). "Corruption French Style", in W. Little and E. Posada-Carbó (eds), *Political Corruption in Europe and Latin America*. London: Macmillan, pp. 159–72.

—— (1997). "La Corruption in France: un changement de perception", *Les Cahiers français*. 281: 45–51.

Mestre, Carole (1994). "Le statut des partis politiques en France". *Revue d'Allemagne*, 36(2): 181–242.

Portelli, Hugues (1988). "L'évolution du personnel gouvernemental". *Le Débat*, 52: 24–31.

Rouban, Luc (1994). "France: Political Argument and Institutional Change", in C. Hood and B. G. Peters (eds), *Rewards at the Top*. London: Sage, pp. 90–105.

Ruggiero, Vincenzo (1996). "France: Corruption as Resentment", *Journal of Law and Society*, 23(1): 113–31.

Ruß, Sabine (1993). *Die Republik der Amtsinhaber: Politikfinanzierung als Herausforderung liberaler Parteien am Beispiel Frankreichs und seiner Reformen von 1988 und 1990.* Baden-Baden: Nomos.

——, Schild, Joachim, Schmidt, Jochen, and Stephan, Ina (eds) (2000). *Parteien in Frankreich: Kontinuität und Wandel in der V. Republik.* Opladen: Leske + Budrich.

Schmidt, Vivien (1990). *Democratizing France: The Political and Administrative History of Decentralization.* Cambridge: Cambridge University Press.

Silberman, Bernard (1993). *Cages of Reason: The Rise of the National State in France, Japan, the United States and Great Britain.* Chicago: University of Chicago Press.

Suleiman, Ezra N. (1973). "L'Administrateur et le Député en France". *Revue française de science politique*, 23: 729–57.

—— (1995). "Change and Stability in French Elites", in G. Flynn (ed.), *Remaking the Hexagon: The New France in the New Europe.* Boulder: Westview Press, pp. 161–79.

Thiébault, Jean-Louis (1994). "The Political Autonomy of Cabinet Ministers in the French Fifth Republic", in M. Laver and K. Shepsle (eds), *Cabinet Ministers and Parliamentary Government.* Cambridge: Cambridge University Press, pp. 139–49.

Thoenig, Jean-Claude (1996). "Les grands corps". *Pouvoirs*, 79: 107–20.

Wahl, Nicholas, and Qermonne, Jean-Louis (eds) (1995). *La France Présidentielle: L'Influence du Suffrage Universel sur la Vie Politique.* Paris: Presses de Sciences Po.

Williams, Philip (1958). *Politics in Post-war France*, 2nd edition. London: Longman.

Ysmal, Colette (1994). "Incumbency in France: Electoral Instability as a Way to Legislative Turnover", in A. Somit, R. Wildenmann, B. Boll, and A. Römmele (eds), *The Victorious Incumbent.* Aldershot: Dartmouth, pp. 190–217.

—— (1995). "Les élites politiques: un monde clos?". *Revue Politique et Parlementaire*, 980: 27–34.

Zeldin, Theodore (1959). *The Political System of Napoleon III.* New York: Norton.

8

Germany: From "Guilds of Notables" to Political Class

JENS BORCHERT AND LUTZ GOLSCH

POLITICAL PROFESSIONALIZATION IN HISTORICAL PERSPECTIVE

Political professionalization in Germany occurred much later than in the United States, but earlier than in most other European countries. In Germany, the expansion of state interventionism clearly preceded full democratization and parliamentarization. Thus, political professionalization happened within a clearly defined and rather restrictive institutional context and offered only limited political scope (for an overview cf. Best, Hausmann, and Schmitt 2000).

The greatest obstacle to legislative professionalism, however, was the absence of parliamentary salaries on the *Reich* level until 1906. This last barrier against "bringing the *Reichstag* down to the lowest level of a purely democratic representative of the people"—as the Conservative member and sometime Speaker von Levetzow put it (Molt 1963: 39)—favored the *Honoratioren* (notables) so typical of German legislatures from the 1848 Assembly to the *Reichstag* well into the 1890s. The pool of conceivable candidates was small in each constituency and consisted essentially of the local notables: estate owners, clergymen, and bureaucrats, plus some professionals and businessmen in urban areas (cf. Sheehan 1968: 512–17; Weber 1972: 842; Best 1989).

All of these people were united in their living "for" rather than "off" politics to use Weber's categories (Weber 1958). You had to have a certain financial independence to run which was what Levetzow referred to as a last base defense against "pure democracy." The Prussian Junkers, the big industrialists, and the capital rentiers had no problems in reconciling the increasingly time-consuming parliamentary service with their business activities (Molt 1963: 40–4). The same was true for higher public officials (*Beamte*) who had been given the eligibility to stand for the *Reichstag* at the request of the Liberals who originally recruited many of their leading legislators from the bureaucracy. Later, however, it was the Conservatives and the Catholic Center Party that benefited from this rule.

There was no shortage of attempts to introduce salaries. Indeed, there were fourteen successful motions in the *Reichstag* from 1871 to 1906 when finally the

Bundesrat yielded to *Reichstag's* demands. The income-less situation, thus, was preserved precisely because it was seen as undemocratic. But even when parliamentary pay was introduced in 1906, it was much too low (400 *Reichsmark* a month during the legislative sessions) to grant members of the *Reichstag* a living (Molt 1963: 38–9). Hence, some members used their simultaneous membership in state legislatures, particularly the Prussian House of Representatives (*Abgeordnetenhaus*) which had introduced salaries much earlier to accumulate legislative salaries and afford their tenure in the *Reichstag*.

Overall, the most important reason for the postponement of legislative professionalization in Germany was the *Reichstag's* lack of autonomy over the question of salary. Even with a membership dominated by old-style *Honoratioren*, the *Reichstag* itself had supported salaries from its inception. Yet the *Bundesrat*, that is the representatives of the governments of the German *Länder*, refused to go along. A further obstacle was Article 32 of the *Reich* constitution that flatly declared "The Members of the *Reichstag* as such may not receive any salary or compensation"—a clause that had been included specifically at Bismarck's request in order to preserve the socially skewed character of the membership (Molt 1963: 38).

Among parties, it was the Social Democratic Party (SPD) that from 1876 on paid salaries to its members of the *Reichstag* as well as to its own functionaries. As this was considered illegal by the government, the party faced prosecution for its disobedience. But more important than the more symbolic legislative salaries paid by the party was the great number of jobs that it provided to functionaries and journalists (Molt 1963: 44–6). After 1898, the share of party functionaries in the parliamentary party never dropped below 40 percent with the unions supplying another 15–20 percent (Molt 1963: 52, 230–1). In 1920, a full 77 percent of SPD representatives were employed by the party or the unions (Meyer 1992: 180). It was this model of professionalism that prompted Weber's analysis of "politics as a vocation" in which he expected a party-based process of professionalization that would replace the legislative and partisan amateurism of earlier days (Weber 1958: 102–3).

The social democratic approach of a party-based professionalization—that was particularly salient after the end of the legal ban on socialist activities in 1890—was viewed as a decisive organizational advantage, and hence, a model by bourgeois parties (Nipperdey 1961: 394; Roth 1963: 158). It is worth mentioning, however, that due to the experience of illegality and continuing legal restrictions against national organization, the party organization was highly decentralized and so were professional positions (Nipperdey 1961: 307–18; Roth 1963: 267; Schorske 1955: 118–19).[1]

As can be studied in Weber's writings on the subject, the creation of a professional party apparatus was generally seen as an important step to modernity that was all but inevitable. As bourgeois parties, however, lacked the resources, and as a tight party apparatus would have been too alien a concept for them, they increasingly turned to that other new actor in German political life, interest groups. The rise of interest

---

[1] For further analyses of the social democratic party organization cf. Hunt (1964); Nipperdey (1961: 293–392); Schorske (1955).

groups parallels the growth of state interventionism. Issues of economic and social policy played an important role in the deliberations of the *Reichstag*, as the Imperial governments sought to keep the Parliament from discussing foreign policy, and law and order issues that were considered more important. Thus, access to or even a presence in the national legislature was an important asset for economic interests. While the strong connections between the unions and the Social Democratic Party—with a clear dominance of the party in the early days (Roth 1963: 160)—was a constitutive part of their existence, in the bourgeois camp(s) both parties and interest groups began to look for potential allies.

The most formidable if somewhat one-sided of the alliances, thus, created was the one between the Conservatives and the "Farmer's League" (*Bund der Landwirte*, BdL). Founded in 1893 as a representative of the interests especially of East Elbian big agriculture, the BdL soon achieved hegemonic status in the rural electoral districts of Prussia and some other regions (Molt 1963: 121, 283–8). It used its highly centralized, authoritarian structure and its superb financial resources to finance the increasingly expensive electoral campaigns of *Reichstag* candidates. In return, it asked candidates to commit themselves to its agrarian platform (Molt 1963: 262). While some of its leading professional functionaries joined the *Reichstag* themselves, the BdL exerted its greatest influence by totally controlling one of the conservative parties, the *Deutsch-Konservative Partei*, and also pocketing the great majority of legislators from three other conservative and national-liberal parties. In 1907, for example, the BdL managed to single-handedly send 139 legislators (of 397) to the *Reichstag* (Molt 1963: 288). This interest group certainly contributed a lot to the centralization and professionalization of German politics, while at the same time modernizing and uniting the bourgeois camp.

Industrial interest groups tried to copy the model of the BdL, but were far less successful. Some leading representatives of two industrial associations were elected to the *Reichstag* and they joined the National Liberals where they exerted considerable influence (Molt 1963: 289–94). An interest group in its own right was the Catholic Church that was allied with the Center Party for which it supplied the organizational back-bone—dubbed "Chaplainocracy" (Weber 1972: 840; cf. Molt 1963: 265–70; Nipperdey 1961: 265–92).

In sum, the roots of political professionalization in Germany are clearly visible in the polity of the *Kaiserreich*. Yet, professionalization was incomplete and Weber's (1958: 112) "guilds of notables" were still predominant. The *Reichstag* was too weak to govern even its own affairs, and parties and interest groups were only beginning to emerge as organizational entities. But as Weber so clearly foresaw, the forces of mass democracy were about to create a major rupture after which the rules of the game were altered significantly.

When the German monarchy faltered in the aftermath of the First World War and the Weimar Republic emerged out of the revolutionary struggles, the new constitution provided for one fundamental change in particular: The majoritarian electoral system with a run-off election (similar to the electoral system in France today) that had been practiced during the *Kaiserreich* was replaced by a proportional representation system. That change strengthened the hold of party leaderships over candidate nomination and overall gave a tremendous boost to centralization. The autonomy of electoral district organization was gone, and with it the possibility of a political entrepreneur-based path to political professionalization. Interest groups continued to exert strong influence but now they had to compete with equally centralized party bureaucracies built on the social democratic model.

The legislative center of professionalization was not the *Reichstag*, however, but the Prussian House of Representatives. The Weimar Republic had done away with the Prussian three-class electoral system and with the change in the electorate came a much more thorough change in membership than was true for the *Reichstag* (cf. Winkler 1994: 598). Hence, in Prussia one could see the early forms of what later would become the prevailing party-based mode of political professionalization in the Federal Republic.

While the structural preconditions for the emergence of a political class were much more hospitable in the Weimar Republic than they had been before, the presence and continuous rise of anti-system parties narrowed the base of such a development and eventually precluded it. Nevertheless, political professionalization increased particularly in the late 1920s.

The 12 years of National Socialist rule ended a 60 years' slow but continuous development towards political professionalization and mass democracy. When Germany had started and lost yet another world war, allied powers occupied its territory and started to rebuild democratic institutions in West Germany. On the other hand, old political leaders of the Weimar period tried to realize their ideas of what a democratic Germany should look like. The result was a melange that differed from what both groups had had in mind but that gave the decisive boost to political professionalization in Germany. Political parties had formed quite early after the end of the war. While the SPD was rebuilt, the bourgeois camp was thoroughly revamped with Christian Democrats and Free Democrats emerging as the two most important forces.

The Allied Powers built new political institutions on the local and state government level based on all-party government. Thus, all-party cooperation and consensus-building became the order of the day in the founding period of the Federal Republic. The new constitution was drafted by the Parliamentary Council staffed from *Länder* legislatures according to legislative party size. For the first time, parties were given constitutional status in Article 21 of the Basic Law. In retrospect, yet not necessarily in the perception of those involved, this signified symbolically the establishment of party government in Germany (Hennis 1998).

It also was a deviation from the pre-Nazi pattern of institutional competition between legislatures, parties, and interest groups. From then on, competition was resolved in favor of parties who were able to colonialize successively large parts of state and society. The *Bundestag* and later also the state legislatures became the focus of professional political careers in Germany, but the parties remained in control over the nomination process. This modifies Weber's expectation that the process of political professionalization would move from parliaments to parties: party democracy was established, just as Weber had expected, yet not at the expense of, but through the detour of parliamentary democracy.

In comparison to Weimar, the process was somewhat decentralized, however. State and local organizations used the political vacuum on the federal level in the early days of the Federal Republic to gain a firm hold that they were not willing to cease afterwards. Interest groups remained powerful, but could only rarely provide political careers. Rather, they maintained institutionalized links to parties as organizations.

As parties gradually expanded their sphere of influence, Weber's (1958: 87) recognition that "*all* party struggles are struggles for the patronage of office, as well as struggles for objective goals" was confirmed. Public administration on all levels, public radio and television, state-owned industries, local banks, utility and transportation companies, the higher judiciary, foundations, charities—all of these were considered within the legitimate reach of party democracy. Thus, Weber's distinction of professional politicians being either "entrepreneurs" or "political officials" in Germany was resolved in favor of the latter.

THE INSTITUTIONAL CONTEXT

Assessing the institutional context of the political class in Germany, one has to consider primarily two basic features which are most important for its particular composition: federalism and party democracy (cf. Lehmbruch 1998). First, compared to a unitary state like Great Britain, the federal structure of the German state multiplies the number of positions available to political professionals, and thus, broadens the structure of opportunity considerably. There are not only the seats in the state legislatures one has to take into account here, but also numerous positions within the state party organizations and the legislative staffs of the state parliamentary parties. Also, within the federal structure the local level has enjoyed a rather high degree of autonomy. Thus, some positions in local politics like big-city mayors (very often also the council party leaders of the majority party) have always been important and professionalized in their own right. In turn, professional administrative positions were politicized. This is even more true, as positions in local politics tend to be combined with others in state or national politics. Also, federalism mitigates against central control of political nominations. Thus, there are not only more opportunities but also multiple points of access.

Second, as argued above, German political parties reach far into the realms of society and state and are powerful means of patronage. Apart from electoral offices on the federal, state, and local levels, for a large number of positions in various institutions party affiliation is a necessary precondition (cf. Beyme 1993: 58–88). These "gray areas" of party influence make it extremely difficult to paint a comprehensive picture of the German political class. Yet, they are an integral part of the phenomenon, and arguably its most distinctive feature in a comparative context.

As shown in the part on professionalization, federalism is by far the older of the two phenomena while party democracy is a post Second World War development. While state and local party organizations are most important for entering professional politics and remaining there, the national level decides on overall party strength. Thus, professional politicians must keep one eye on intraparty competition on the local and state level and the other one on interparty competition on the federal level. Nomination and renomination is the most important step to election and is firmly controlled by parties. The other potential threat to reelection is a loss of overall votes for the party that could also harm the relatively well positioned candidate. Thus, we can once again quote Weber (1958: 101): "The Members of Parliament are interested in the possibility of interlocal compromises, in vigorous and unified programs endorsed by broad circles and in unified agitation throughout the country." Both, collective legitimation *vis-à-vis* the voters and individual legitimation *vis-à-vis* the party, combine in favoring a rather docile backbencher role and discouraging maverick behavior.

Of the other institutional features of the German system, the electoral system, a peculiar form of proportional representation disguised as a "mixed-member system" with half the representatives being directly elected, provides the crucial link between federalism and party government. It assures the decisive role of local and state party organizations for candidate recruitment and career-building. The importance of interest groups, which otherwise are still an influential factor in German politics, for political careers has declined proportionally to the rise of parties.

The German *Bundestag* does not play a very strong independent role in the federal party democracy. The parliamentary majority is an integral part of the government; it supports the government and functions as recruitment reservoir—the opposition is a government in waiting and the recruitment reservoir for *Länder* governments. In the legislative process the *Bundestag* is very much inferior to the ministerial bureaucracy, as in contrast to the American Congress it does not have the same resources at its disposal.

A central element of the internal structure of the *Bundestag* are the *Fraktionen* (party groups), whose leadership does overlap to a high degree with the party leadership. The committees, a second potential center of gravity, are no powerful players in their own right—apart from a few exceptions like the budgetary committee and the foreign affairs committee. The fact, that members regularly choose a leading position in the *Fraktion* rather than a committee chairmanship when given the choice, shows how both of these institutions are evaluated in comparison.

THE POLITICAL CLASS

Size and Composition

(1) *Electoral and government offices.* At the center of the political class are the currently 603 members of the German *Bundestag,* one of the largest parliaments among western democracies.[2] Historically, the number of seats in the *Bundestag* has been

---

[2] Due to the provisions of German electoral law, the number of seats in the current legislative period (2002–) adds up to 603 rather than the 598 legally provided for. The mixed electoral system grants surplus mandates if a party wins more direct mandates in a state than it would have received on the whole on the basis of its proportional share of votes. Since a directly elected member of the *Bundestag* cannot be forced to cede his mandate, the number of legislators from that state increases. This usually happens when a party wins all or most direct mandates in a state while retaining its average share of the votes.

relatively stable after the first major expansion in 1953, when the initial amount of
408 and later 419 mandates was increased to 506. From 1965 to 1990, the *Bundestag*
was composed of a regular number of 518 parliamentarians, until German unification in 1990 led to the addition of 138 seats representing the East German states
(Schindler 1999: 381). With the 2002 elections the legal number of representatives
was reduced from 656 to 598. Half of the members of the *Bundestag* are directly
elected in single member districts, while the other half is added from state party lists
according to the respective party's overall share of the votes.

It is a systemic feature of most parliamentary democracies that membership in the
federal government takes membership in the legislature for granted. This is obligatory for the Parliamentary State Secretaries in Germany. From time to time, cabinet
revisions lead to the appointment of new ministers from outside Parliament. They
then usually win a seat—often by being assigned to a safe position on the state party
list—in the next general election.

On the state level, the legislatures of the sixteen *Länder* contain a cumulated number of 1,834 mandates, which is also expanded considerably by surplus and compens-
atory mandates that several state electoral laws allocate (to about 1,950). The size of
the state legislatures varies greatly with only a vague relationship between the size of
the state's population and the number of seats in the legislature.

Legislative offices on the local level are mostly amateur positions. Although members of city councils—especially in large cities—may devote a significant portion of
their time for political activity, they merely receive a small expense allowance (Ronge
1994: 268). Mayors, on the other hand, in most states provide the sole example of a
directly elected executive in Germany. The concentration of executive power in one
hand seems to become the dominant pattern on the level of local government.

Since the first direct elections in 1979 the European Parliament also offers access
to the political class. Between 1958 and 1979 the *Bundestag* had appointed a number
of its own members to serve simultaneously in Bonn and in Strasbourg. From 1979
to 1989, German voters directly elected eighty-one members of the European
Parliament, before in 1994 the number of seats has been expanded to the current
number of ninety-nine.

(2) *Staff positions*. Apart from the occupants of electoral offices, the political class
also consists of staff members of party organizations and parliamentary parties as well
as of personal assistants of legislators and cabinet members. The available data reveals
that the staffs of legislators and parliamentary parties have expanded considerably
during the last 30 years. This is especially true for personal legislative assistants of the
members of the *Bundestag*: facing strong backbench pressure, the *Bundestag* in 1969
allocated funds for the employment of at least one personal assistant for every member. During the following decades, the overall number of personal legislative assistants
grew tremendously—from 312 in 1969 to 2,390 in 1996 (Schindler 1999: 3263–4).

Accordingly, the political staff of the parliamentary parties in the *Bundestag*
expanded considerably, though not as sharply as the personal staff of the legislators,
from thirty-four in 1966 to 315 in 1995 (Schindler 1999: 1007). During the first four
legislative periods (1949–65), only the oppositional Social Democrats had built up

some very modest staff capacity (Jekewitz 1995: 401). Similarly, on the state level appropriations for parliamentary party staff in all state legislatures increased from DM6.6 million (€3.4 Mio.) in 1965 to DM131.4 million (€67.2 Mio.) in 1995 (Arnim 1996: 138–42).[3]

Finally, one has to consider the employees of the party organizations on the federal, state, and local levels. Again, the available data is scarce. From the existing data, one can only draw the conclusion that the staff of party organizations has increased much slower than that of parliamentary parties or of individual members (Poguntke and Boll 1992: 338–40). An important reason for the comparatively slower growth of party staff might lie in the fact that tasks like supporting leading politicians have been transferred to the parliamentary party staff and the personal assistants of legislators (Poguntke 1994: 194). With the major parties facing a persistent financial crisis, the expansion of federally funded legislative staff was much easier to achieve and much safer than building up a larger party apparatus with the risk of continually high overhead costs.

(3) *The boundaries of the political class.* Looking at the boundaries of the political class, we step into a gray area of positions which are not located in the narrow realms of electoral offices or political staff jobs, but where nonetheless, nominations are party-mediated. Due to the expansive nature of the German party state, the mechanisms of proportional representation of the major parties reach far down to the levels of school headmasters or journalists in public broadcasting networks. Von Beyme has labeled this phenomenon the "colonization of society by the party state" (Beyme 1993: 58–88). Where should we draw the line demarcating the members of the political class?

One group that is easily discernible are the so-called "political civil servants" on the federal, state, and local levels. In contrast to normal career civil servants, who cannot be dismissed unless they have committed a criminal offense, political civil servants can be dismissed any time if they do not agree with the government "on basic political principles," that is, if they are affiliated with another party (Arnim 1993: 210–13). In the course of the change of government in Bonn in 1982/83, forty-four top civil servants were dismissed, and another 200 officials were transferred to non-political positions (Beyme 1993: 66). Political criteria, however, play a role in the selection of career civil servants down to the local level, although the depth and the scope of political patronage is difficult to assess (cf. Scheuch and Scheuch 1992: 98–103).

As to the high judiciary, the judges of the Federal Constitutional Court are to be chosen by a joint committee of the *Bundestag* and the *Bundesrat* with a two-thirds majority. Apart from their high legal qualification to serve as judges, each of the two major parties claims the privilege to propose half of the judges in each chamber of the court. Thus, the CDU traditionally suggests a nominee for the chair of the first, the SPD nominates the chair of the second chamber. The highly political nature of the selection is underscored by the mobility between the Court and the political realm. Thus, two of the last three Presidents of the court—Roman Herzog and Jutta

---

[3] Converted according to the fixed EMU rate (DM1 = €0.5113).

Limbach—were recruited from ministerial posts in state governments, with the
former becoming President of the Republic afterwards while the latter was repeatedly
considered as a possible candidate for the position.

There are other sectors of public life which may selectively be counted as parts of
the political class as well, for example, the positions of the directors of public broadcasting stations or the boards of public companies. There is scattered evidence that
formally amateur political positions in larger cities are sometimes rewarded with
lucrative positions on the boards of local public firms, for example, energy or transport service companies, if the demands of political work are in fact semi-professional
(Andersen 1992: 169: Scheuch and Scheuch 1992: 85–94). Moreover, one might ask
whether to include the top officials of interest groups as well. Recent examples of
high career mobility and the cumulation of offices in the political and interest group
sectors suggest that the executives of interest groups should surely be counted as
members of the political class.[4]

Political Recruitment and Political Careers

Political parties are the exclusive channels of political recruitment in Germany (on
recruitment cf. Wessels 1997). Their monopoly over recruitment of the political class
means that a career within the party organization is in most cases an indispensable
prerequisite for any political hopeful. Before we examine the career stages that politicians pass through before they finally reach a professional political position, it is useful to give a short overview of how the selection process of candidates for these
offices works.

The *selection* of candidates for electoral offices in federal and state legislatures is
essentially a privilege of local party constituencies and state parties. The process differs, though, for district nominees and list candidates. The constituency candidates
are selected either by a caucus of delegates from the respective district party organization or by a membership vote. To win the nomination, they usually have to stress
their local grassroots and their ties to the local party. As a consequence, candidates—
at least of the two large parties—often have passed through a long internal party
career on the local and regional level, where they have worked up their way through
positions on the party boards. The ability to form an alliance of supporters within
the local party organization is essential to win a majority of the delegates.
Unfortunately, there are no recent in-depth studies of the nomination process, so
that data on the competitiveness of inner-party nominations are not available.[5] But
there are ample indications that the decision on the candidate is often orchestrated
by a circle of local and regional party leaders and activists, and as a result the caucus

---

[4] During the Kohl era there were the prominent examples of the selection of the Parliamentary State
Secretary Cornelia Yzer as the new top executive of a corporate interest group in Bonn, or the appointment of a member of the CDU parliamentary party leadership, Reinhard Göhner, as the new top manager
of the Federal Association of Employer Organizations (BDA).
[5] There are some older studies which still provide a good understanding of the basic process, notably
Zeuner (1970); Kaack (1971).

delegates are confronted with a limited or no choice at all. For the 1960s and 1970s, it has been noticed that incumbents choosing to run again rarely face a challenge, while there may be much sharper competition for open district nominations (Rudzio 1987: 153–5).

The winners of local nomination contests then usually vie for a safe place on their party's list—except for those few who have been nominated in a thoroughly safe constituency. Thus, constituency candidates and party list candidates mostly consist of the same group of people. The selection process for the party lists is more complex and involves a wider array of participants. Delegates of local party organizations meet in a state party caucus to decide on the placement of nominees for the party lists. In both large parties, candidate selection involves an intricate bargaining process among regional party bosses and leaders of party factions who control blocks of delegate votes. A multitude of interests has to be balanced on the lists: geography, gender, social background, affiliation with party factions and interest groups, ideological orientation—all play a key role in the nomination process. Additionally, all parties tend to link a safe seat on the list to a simultaneous candidacy in a district to make sure that the party is represented in hopeless districts as well. Although the electoral laws for the state legislatures partly differ from the federal law, the basic principles of candidate selection apply there as well.[6]

Two developments have influenced the selection process during recent years. First, three parties represented in the *Bundestag* have now established quotas for women on the federal, state, and local level.[7] This has resulted in an improved representation of women in the parliamentary parties of the Greens and lately also in the SPD, while the center–right parties have trailed far behind. Second, as a part of an attempt to strengthen inner-party democracy and participation, the SPD has tried to open up the candidate selection process by making it possible to nominate candidates for electoral offices through a member ballot. Thus, local party members should have the possibility to participate in the process of candidate selection while local party elites were expected to exercise less power over the nomination (Jun 1996: 218–23). First assessments of the effectiveness of the new rule have pointed out that it has been rarely used since its adoption in 1993 (Mielke 1997: 44).

Two elements dominate the stages of a political career which precede the achievement of a professional position: advancement within the party is obligatory, while the assumption of an electoral office on the local level—that is, as a member of the city council or the county assembly—is optional, if certainly helpful. Thus, it is possible to distinguish roughly between two groups of politicians whose recruitment

---

[6] Bavaria, for example, allows for a preference vote for an individual list candidate in the state legislative elections. As a result, safe seats on the list do hardly exist.

[7] The Greens had been the first to implement the concept with their decision to reserve half of the nominations for women. The Social Democrats had followed suit in 1988 and adopted a rule that requires the party subdivisions to ensure a 40% representation of women in all legislatures (Kolinsky 1993: 129–34). Finally, in November 1996 the CDU altered the party statutes in a way that the first vote on a list proposal will be invalid if less than 30% of the nominations have been reserved for women. In a conceivable second vote however, the quota does not apply (*Das Parlament*, 25 October 1996).

patterns differ mainly in the length of the pre-professional political career. A study of the members of the 13th *Bundestag* (1994–98) has shown that on the average legislators had worked in their occupation for 13 years before achieving a professional political position (Golsch 1998: 128).[8] On the other hand, there is a smaller group of politicians who follow the fast track into professional politics. After finishing their academic training in their late twenties, they practice their occupation for 2–5 years at best before becoming a member of the political class. Among the members of the current *Bundestag*, their share amounts to 23 percent of the legislators.

How do politicians proceed during the amateur stage of their career (on German political careers generally, cf. Herzog 1975)? The politicians who make politics their second career tend to focus on the local level for a substantial amount of time, both within the party and within electoral offices. They take the so-called *Ochsentour*, the long and laborious route through local and regional party offices where they obtain a certain profile in their local constituency and manage to accumulate the necessary resources in party offices themselves. The strategic position for a successful bid for nomination is the office of the chairman of the county party organization (*Kreisvorsitz*), which gives them a certain degree of control over the party apparatus and name recognition among the party membership. The state party boards play a much less important role. Frequently, advancement on the lower levels of the party organization is accompanied by the assumption of electoral office in local politics. Among the members of the 13th *Bundestag*, 57 percent have asserted that they held local electoral offices before they entered professional politics, mostly seats in the city council or the county assembly. Particularly backbenchers have often chosen this path into the political class: many of them have held local electoral office for more than 15 years before crossing over into professional politics (Golsch 1998: 160–4).

The smaller group of politicians who have started their career in professional politics shortly after finishing their (academic) education also use party functions on the lower levels as a base on which they can build their career. This fact again underscores the fundamentally local character of political recruitment in Germany. As an alternative, they may proceed through the youth party organizations or the internal party interest groups, for example, the womens' associations or the organized labor groups. Through the positions reserved for these groups on the regional and state party boards and on the state party lists for the elections, they may by-pass a career on the local level. This, however, seems to be more the exception than the rule.

The length of the amateur phase of the political career is also closely connected with the type of office that serves as the entry point into professional politics. Staff positions in the executive, in the legislatures or in the party organizations are usually filled with young academics who have just finished their studies; therefore, the mean age of the current members of the *Bundestag* entering the political class through these jobs has been thirty-one. As a contrast, legislators who have started their professional career in an electoral office outside of the *Bundestag* have been thirty-six on

---

[8] If not indicated otherwise, empirical data presented in this article have been taken from Golsch 1998.

the average, and those whose professional political career began with a seat in the federal legislature have been 42 years at the time of their cross-over.

East German legislators of course deserve special attention. The primary question has been whether the members of the old political class of the former GDR on the one hand and members of the "counter-elite" of the 1989/90 citizen movements on the other hand have succeeded in pursuing a political career in unified Germany (cf. Derlien and Lock 1994; Welsh 1996; Lock 1998; Lohse 1999). The transfer of West German political institutions (e.g. state legislatures) and political parties to the East German states has furthermore raised the question whether patterns of recruitment and careers have been adapted from the old *Länder*, too.

On the whole, current evidence points to the conclusion that a substantial portion of the political class in the five new states has entered politics at the time of transition in 1989/90, while a much smaller amount of politicians succeeded in continuing careers from the lower levels of the former GDR regime. Considering the fact that both the institutional framework and the party system have been imported from West Germany, it is not surprising that career patterns increasingly resemble those of West German politicians. Turnover has decreased, and the members of the "new" political class in the East have by now become regular political professionals.

After shedding some light on the recruitment patterns and the amateur stage of political careers in Germany, it is now necessary to take a closer look at the career patterns within the political class. Are there distinct patterns leading from one office to another? Is it possible to detect a linear hierarchy of offices that directs the ambition of politicians from the local to the state and federal level?

First, and most surprising, there is probably less mobility within the political class that one might have expected. Looking again at the members of the 13th *Bundestag*, it is striking that for as much as 69 percent of the legislators the seat in the *Bundestag* has been the first professional political office at all. For this large group of politicians, recruitment to the federal legislature simultaneously meant cross-over from an amateur position into the political class. Thus, for the majority of the parliamentarians in the *Bundestag* advancement to higher office implies a career within the institution and/or the appointment to a cabinet position. Conversely, less than a third of the members has passed through a professional political career in the narrower sense of advancing from an office on a lower level to a higher one.

Studying the career paths of this group of legislators, nonetheless, allows us to establish certain facts about movements among the different kinds of office. Here, the state legislatures play an outstanding role. More than half of the members of the *Bundestag* who had acquired experience in professional political positions started their career as a state legislator; on the whole, 16 percent of all current members of the *Bundestag* have served as state legislators before. Although this movement from the state to the federal legislature is still the most significant career path, a comparison with the 1960s shows that it has sharply declined in importance: in 1965, more than 25 percent of the members of the *Bundestag* had previously held a seat in a state legislature. The (small) contingents of former members of the executive and of former staff members have remained stable. The fact that a seat in the state legislature nowadays is financially nearly as attractive as a seat in the *Bundestag* surely plays an important role (see Table 8.1). Until the 1970s, it simply had not been possible to solely rely on the income from a seat on the state level. Consequently, the reduced number of former state legislators in the *Bundestag* indicates that during the last 30 years the state level has been established as a separate career opportunity for political professionals.

A small portion of former state legislators has been appointed to positions in state government before winning a seat in the *Bundestag*. Another group of former members of the executive has started the professional career as paid mayors or as members of the political administration in city governments. Advancement from these positions to the state level and then on to the federal legislature is extremely rare. Instead, the careers of members of the local executive resemble the careers of local assemblymen and assembly-women: they are solidly rooted in local politics and in the local party.

Besides the finding that the state level has become a career in itself, other developments indicate that the hierarchy of political offices is not necessarily associated with the level of government. Between 1993 and 1999, nine states introduced local government reforms transforming the position of mayor and its equivalent on the county level (*Landrat*), which both up to that point had been mainly representational amateur positions, into professional positions with governmental responsibility and

Table 8.1 *Salaries in the* Bundestag *and the State Parliaments, December 2002 (in €)*

	Basic salary (tax-deductible)	Expense allowance (tax-free)[a]	Total
Bundestag[b]	7,009	3,503	10,512
Bavaria	5,718	2,686	8,404
Hesse	6,401	511	6,912
North Rhine–Westphalia	4,722	1,939–2,368	6,661–7,090
Rhineland–Palatinate	4,981	1,544–2,002	6,525–6,983
Lower Saxony	5,403	1,027	6,430
Baden–Württemberg	4,557	1,576–2,026	6,133–6,583
Brandenburg[b]	4,399	1,284–2,298	5,683–6,697
Thuringia	4,225	1,557–2,173	5,782–6,398
Saxony	3,943	1,718	5,661
Schleswig–Holstein	3,927	996–1,751	4,923–5,678
Saarland	4,137	1,119–1,170	5,256–5,307
Mecklenburg–Western Pomerania	3,890	1,098	4,988
Saxony–Anhalt	3,937	997	4,934
Berlin	2,951	870	3,821
Bremen	2,446	417	2,863
Hamburg	2,196	333	2,529

[a] Allowance ranges due to travel allowances depending on the distance between the capital and the district.
[b] As of 1 January 2003.

Source: Own calculations based on homepages of the legislatures.

power. As a consequence of that, a substantial number of state legislators has seized the new opportunity and launched successful candidacies for these offices, which at least in larger towns and cities as well as in the counties promised a relatively high degree of visibility and local influence.

A relatively new career path leads from the European Parliament (EP) to the *Bundestag*. Since the introduction of direct elections to the EP in 1979, there have always been federal legislators who decided to conclude their political career on the European level. Since 1987, ambitious politicians have reversed this career path and used the EP as an entry point for a successful later candidacy to the *Bundestag*. Their number is currently very small, but similar findings for Great Britain indicate that this career path might be gaining in importance (Westlake 1994).

Apart from electoral offices in the state legislatures and from executive positions on the state and local levels, staff positions have to be taken into account when talking about political careers. The data on the members of the 13th *Bundestag* shows that staff positions do in fact serve as stepping stones of political careers, with a slightly higher portion of former staffers from the party organizations. Again, the state level plays a crucial role, for a majority of staffers started the career in state party organizations or as legislative assistants in the state legislatures. There are some party-specific tendencies which are noteworthy: when the Greens, for example, during the 1980s still practiced the principle of rotation which obliged legislators to leave their office after half of the term, they used staff positions in the party and in the state legislatures as cushions for the members who had to leave their office and as an apprenticeship for the future members. Thus, one mandate provided for the professionalization of two politicians.

Apart from the horizontal cumulation of offices—for example, cabinet ministers holding a seat in the legislature—vertical cumulation frequently occurs in the way of legislators retaining local political offices. Members of the *Bundestag* use seats in the city council or in the county assembly as an additional means of assuring their presence in their home district. In the 13th legislative period, 22 percent of the legislators from the West German states indicated that they occupy one or more local electoral offices. They mostly concentrate on seats in city councils and regional assemblies and less on mayoral offices. The vertical cumulation of a seat in the federal and a state legislature is legally allowed but practically impossible.

Since seats in the legislatures are relatively safe due to the list system prevalent in German election law, the bulk of career politicians can stay in office for quite a long time. A large number of legislators vacate their seats voluntarily. Long-term office-holding is reinforced by the allocation of pension benefits which are dependent on the overall tenure of a legislator. Those who do not retire but decide to phase out through another political or public office often progress to the "gray areas" of the political class.

Living off Politics

The salaries of politicians have always been an issue with high public salience. Interestingly, the focus has been almost exclusively on the remuneration of legislators, and only lately has there been some criticism of executive salaries, too (Derlien 1994: 166).

The climax of public alienation was surely reached with the unsuccessful attempt for constitutional reform in late 1995, when the members of the *Bundestag* tried to link their financial compensation to the salaries of the judges of federal courts.

Since 1977 the rewards for parliamentarians, which up to that time formally had been labeled "expense allowances" have been accepted as a salary-like compensation for a full-time job. In a rather famous sentence, the Constitutional Court ruled that members of the *Bundestag* should receive a remuneration from the state which would allow them to live independently from outside income (Bundesverfassungsgericht 1975: 314). At the same time, the judges declared that there was a basic difference between civil servants and elected politicians which prohibited a direct coupling of members' pay and the salaries of civil servants. What is more, the Court defined transparency and publicity as the most important characteristics of the decision-making process on parliamentary pay.

Consequently, the *Bundestag* passed a "Members Law" (Abgeordnetengesetz) in which the respective height of members' income and supplemental provisions were laid down. Since from 1977 on the salaries of legislators were taxable, the level of income was adjusted accordingly and rose from DM3,850 (approx. €1,970) to DM7,500 (€3,830) per month. In addition, the three different allowances for travel, daily expenses, and costs induced by the mandate were combined in a tax-free lump sum of DM4,500 (€2,300) (Fig. 8.1).

Until the conflict over the 1995 reform plan, the salary rose to a taxable DM10,366 (€5,300) per month plus a tax-free expense allowance of DM5,978 (€3,060): this

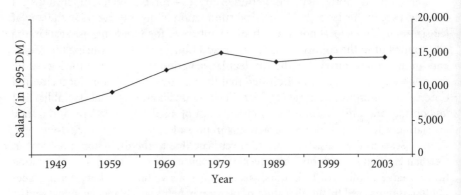

Figure 8.1 *Monthly salary of members of the* Bundestag, *at 10-year intervals (adjusted for inflation, in 1995 DM)*

Notes: The income is calculated for every tenth year and includes the basic salary (tax-free until 1977, tax deductible since then), the daily allowance, expense, and travel allowances (until 1977, respectively) and the combined lump sum (since 1977, tax-free and since 1996 with automatic correction for inflation). Since 1979 the taxable portion of the salary has been reduced by one-third to take into account taxes and to make numbers comparable.

Sources: Own calculations based on Schindler 1999: 3,215–6, 4387, and information on the consumer price index from the Federal Statistical Office (*Statistisches Bundesamt*): http://www.destatis.de/download/preis/archiv2.pdf.

added up for a combined annual income of DM196,128 (€100,280), although it has to be born in mind that the allowance is geared to cover costs for lodging in Berlin (formerly in Bonn), for a district office and other expenses related to the mandate. In addition to that, if a member left the *Bundestag*, until 1995 he was entitled to receive financial support for a maximum time of 3 years, depending on the overall time he spent in Parliament. This transitional severance pay was not reduced in the case of income from a new job inside or outside of politics, even if the member came from the civil service and used his right to immediate re-employment. The pension plan, which was introduced in 1968 (Klatt 1972: 62–72), was also tied to the time a member spent in the federal legislature. With a minimum tenure of 8 years (two legislative periods), a Member was entitled to a pension of 25 percent of the monthly taxable compensation from his sixty-fifth birthday on. After 18 years in the *Bundestag*, the pension would have reached the maximum amount of 75 percent of his remuneration from the age of 55 on (Derlien 1994: 169–70). Furthermore, legislators are entitled to free phone services in the *Bundestag*, to the use of official cars in Berlin and the free use of the German railway system.

With the 1995 reform plan, which was part of a larger attempt to reform the legislature (Lemke-Müller 1996: 3; Marschall 1999: 45–71), the salary should have been increased while the generous transitional salary and pensions were to be reduced. The main instrument was the coupling of the members' remuneration (except the lump sum) to the salary level R6 of the judges of federal courts, which in the year 2000 would have been as high as DM15,500 to DM16,500 (€7,900–8,400); in fact, the salary for the members of the *Bundestag* would have increased by approximately 50 percent over the next 3 years (Arnim 1996: 332–3). The overall goal of the reformers was to make pay increases for Members an automatic process determined by the salary increases of judges—which in turn are set by the *Bundestag*; thus, public discussion (and the usual outrage) against such measures would have been by-passed. As a compensation for the pay increase, reformers decided to cut the time the transitional salary would be paid by half. They also decreased the maximum level of pensions from 75 to 69 percent while increasing the tenure needed for this highest level from 18 to 23 years. The plan to automatize legislative salary increases failed because a constitutional amendment necessary to alter Article 48 of the Basic Law that had been passed by the *Bundestag* was defeated in the second chamber (*Bundesrat*). The reductions of pensions and transitional salaries, though, became effective in 1996 (cf. Marschall 1999: 49–55). As of 1 January 2003, the members of *Bundestag* receive a taxable salary of €7,009 plus a tax-free expense allowance of €3,503 per month.[9] This amounts to a combined annual income of €126,144. The salary (except the lump sum) of the four Vice-Presidents is 150 percent of the base remuneration, and the President of the *Bundestag* receives the double base salary.[10] Heads and other officials of the parliamentary parties receive additional payments out of the parliamentary party budgets (Arnim 1996: 264–5).

---

[9] Since the 1995 reform, the lump-sum allowance is indexed to inflation on an annual basis.

[10] In several state legislatures, the practice of paying higher remunerations goes down to the level of committee chairpersons and chairs of faction work groups (Arnim 1996: 262–3).

If we put the historical tendency of legislative salaries into perspective by controlling for inflation (cf. Fig. 8.1), we can easily see that major gains were made in the early years of the Federal Republic. In the years from 1949 to 1969 income almost doubled. The 1977 reform brought legislative salaries to a high point after which they declined. Because of public scrutiny they simply could not keep pace with inflation rates in the 1980s. By now, we can say that legislative salaries remain constant at a fairly high level.

With the exception of cabinet members, legislators may earn outside income from a private occupation or from seats on corporate boards of trustees. Since 1987, they have to publicly disclose what, if anything, they do as a private occupation beside their mandate, and they also have to publish on which boards of firms or foundations they serve as trustees. In contrast to the United States, until recently the income legislators earn from outside sources only had to be disclosed to the President of the *Bundestag*, who was in charge of overseeing whether there might arise a conflict of interest or not. There is no information available how this has been handled in practice. Attempts by a minority within the legislature to oblige members to file public financial statements failed periodically, until shortly before the 2002 elections an initiative of some younger social-democratic Members of Parliament (MPs) succeeded. In the midst of various scandals over both corrupt party finance and questionable payments to various MPs by a lobbyist, the reform measure established the obligation to publicize legislators' outside income and interests in the official handbook of the *Bundestag*.

The salaries of executive politicians are calculated on the basis of civil servants' rewards. The most striking feature of the reward system for executive politicians, however, is the fact that the Chancellor and his cabinet ministers commonly are members of the legislature, too, and thus, cumulate salaries both from their executive and their legislative functions. Their legislative salary is reduced by 50 percent, and the tax-free lump sum is diminished by 25 percent (Derlien 1994: 168–9). The cumulation of legislative and executive office has a rather strong effect in the case of the parliamentary secretaries of state, who receive the same salary as permanent secretaries (*Staatsekretäre*) in the civil service, are not yet involved in the administrative work of a ministry. They act as parliamentary deputy to the minister, which means that they also receive the aforementioned share of the legislative salary. Thus, these positions are in high demand, and we find a frequent rotation, so that many legislators of the majority can enjoy this position.

In general, the cumulation of incomes and pensions from different offices is a characteristic feature of the current reward system in Germany, and it is extraordinarily difficult to sort out the various sources of public income individual politicians do in fact have (Arnim 1996: 266–70). In the states, most of the legislatures have modeled themselves after the example of the *Bundestag*, and thus, increased their members' pay to levels which in some cases are not far from the federal legislature (Table 8.1).

On the whole, it seems obvious that the public remuneration of politicians allows them to live well off politics, especially if one considers the quite generous pension plans and the possibility of a cumulation of incomes from various public and private sources. Of course, Derlien is right when he points out that remunerations for public office are not competitive with salaries paid in equivalent positions of the private sector, which reinforces the predominance of civil servants in legislative positions (Derlien 1994: 182–3). On the other hand, comparative evidence shows that German salaries are highest for executive politicians and the second-highest behind US Congressmen for legislators on the federal level if one uses purchasing power parities as a comparative measure (Hood and Lambert 1994: 27). Furthermore, one has to consider the other elements of public financing of the political class through the financing of political parties, party foundations and parliamentary parties, which we did not take into account here (cf. Ebbighausen *et al.* 1996).

THE POLITICAL CLASS AND INSTITUTIONAL REFORM

Stability seems to be the marked feature if one looks at institutional reform in the *Bundestag*. Reform attempts have been rare, and most of these efforts have tried to strengthen the rights of the opposition against the governing coalition, or they have aimed at shifting the balance between the executive and the legislature. At first glance, the career interests of the political class did not play a significant role. The explanation is rather easy: the electoral security of members essentially depends on their ties to their local party constituencies and on their party loyalty. Individual performance in Parliament is less important. Moreover, the systemic requirements of parliamentary democracy make the cohesion of the parties in Parliament essential for the functioning of the political system. The collective performance of the parliamentary parties is seen as the key to electoral success, and the individual legislator has to accept that a relatively safe career position is provided by the party as a trade-off for deference to the party in parliament. The combined effect of these two characteristics has been that a decentralization with massive power shifts among members, like it occurred in the United States during the 1970s, was never an option to pursue.

As a consequence of that, the political class has focused on four areas of reform in which career interests become at least partly visible: the staff resources of individual legislators, their chances to promote their own public image, the public image of the institution as a whole and most of all on questions of income and financial support. Since we have dealt with the latter question above, we will focus on the other three here (also cf. Golsch 1998: 247–89).

The resources of individual legislators came on the agenda in the late 1960s. Until then, the *Bundestag* had often been characterized as a "three-class-society" (Apel 1967: 134–5), in which staff and material resources were concentrated in the hands of the parliamentary elite and in those of legislators supported by influential interest groups. The large majority of backbenchers was left to themselves. In 1969, the discontent on the back benches was organized by a number of freshmen who led a first and small rebellion against the parliamentary establishment (Thaysen 1972: 178;

Marschall 1999: 22–5). Embedded in a package of reforms later labeled "small parliamentary reform" ("*kleine Parlamentsreform*"), they succeeded in getting the authorization for at least one personal legislative assistant for each member of the *Bundestag*. For the legislators, this staff expansion proved essential for meeting the intensified responsibilities of constituency service.

The second area of institutional reform that can be considered as being stimulated by career interests has focused on the possibilities of self-promotion for individual members. It is one of the rare examples where decentralization within Parliament has been brought forward, and it has focused almost exclusively on the allocation of speech time in plenary sessions. It is important to note that the substantial decision-making process takes place in the various subgroups of parliamentary parties and in the committees, while the plenary session mainly fulfills the task of highlighting the political differences between government and opposition. Therefore, the conclusion seems justified that with the drive to decentralize the allocation of speech time, the members mainly aimed at improving their chances to gain name recognition and public standing.

During the reform debates in 1969, backbenchers complained about exclusive rights of the parliamentary leadership in the distribution of speaking time in plenary sessions. With a reduction of the maximum time to 15 min, they wanted to reach a more even distribution of speech opportunities. In this respect the backbench reformers were successful, mainly because the parliamentary leadership saw this as a means to make debates more lively and interesting for the general public, too. During the late 1980s, the restructuring of debates again came to the fore, when an interparty alliance of backbenchers and former members of the leadership around former liberal minister Hildegard Hamm-Brücher (*Überfraktionelle Initiative Parlamentsreform*) organized to strengthen the rights of individual members (Werner 1990). They proposed the so-called "open debates" in which the sequence of speakers should not be predetermined by the parliamentary party leadership but *ad hoc* by the President of the *Bundestag*. The deliberative side of parliamentary work hence should be stressed, and backbenchers should get further chances of presenting themselves to the public. Furthermore, the interparty initiative called for better staff and technical resources for individual members. In the end, both the drive for more resources as well as for a restructuring of debates failed against the resistance of the leadership.

Finally, in 1995 a moderate loosening of the strict control of debates was passed, and members were granted the possibility to react to plenary speeches by claiming a short intervention. The reason for the successful passage of this reform measure lay in the fact that the goal of improving the public image of the institution had become an important issue. As a consequence of that, the reform was less initiated by backbenchers but by the leadership, who wanted to react to a perceived crisis of legitimation by making parliamentary work more accessible and more attractive for the public. Hence, the third type of institutional reform mentioned above plays a role here: by improving the public image of the institution, the members of the political class have tried to prevent both a backlash of voters against established parties that might have hurt their career position and an increasing alienation from electoral politics altogether.

Finally, one has to consider the option that the career interests of the political class do not only become effective in intended drives for institutional reform, but also in the prevention of measures that might harm the position of the members of the political class. Here, the reduction of the size of the *Bundestag* in 1996 provides an interesting example. For the first time in history, the *Bundestag* purposefully attempted to reduce the number of mandates available, and thus, seriously acted against the career interests of a considerable number of its own members. In October 1996, the legislators voted to reduce the number of seats from 656 to 598 in the year 2002. Does this mean that the career interests of the members of the political class did not play a significant role in this process?

The answer is, both yes and no. The reduction was part of a larger reform scheme developed by the leadership that, furthermore, included a reorganization of debates and committee work and the pay increase mentioned above. The overall goal was to produce a "smaller legislature where better paid members work more attractively and more efficiently" (*Süddeutsche Zeitung*, 14 May 1995). It was, clearly, a reform effort that was pushed by the leadership, who was under pressure from both a dissatisfied and alienated public and an uneasy membership calling for a pay increase. There are ample signs that party leaderships offered members a trade-off between the down-sizing and the pay increase: The promise of higher remunerations served as an argument to "sell" the downsizing plan to the backbenchers, and vice versa the pay increase was publicly set off against the downsizing. It was only as part of a package deal that a reduction in size became feasible (Marschall 1999: 69).

A closer look at the details also reveals that the Members' interests served as a powerful barrier against a further reduction of seats. An official self-commitment of the *Bundestag* defined that the number of seats should be reduced by a hundred at the most, but in any case it should be below 600. In the end, the decision to downsize the legislature to 598 seats meant that the *Bundestag* chose the minimal solution, and the scheduling of the reduction for the 2002 elections left enough time for endangered members to secure their career position or look for alternatives on the state level. Obviously, the career interests of members prevented the *Bundestag* from opting for a more radical solution in this case as in others.

REFERENCES

Andersen, Uwe (1992). "Gemeinden", in U. Andersen and W. Woyke (eds), *Handwörterbuch des politischen Systems des Bundesrepublik Deutschland*. Bonn: Bundeszentrale für politische Bildung, pp. 163–71.

Apel, Hans (1967). "Ein Plädoyer für den Berufspolitiker". *Die Neue Gesellschaft*, 14: 129–35.

Arnim, Hans-Herbert von (1993). *Der Staat als Beute*. Munich: Knaur.

——(1996). *Die Partei, der Abgeordnete und das Geld*, 2nd edition. Munich: Knaur.

Best, Heinrich (1989). "Mandat ohne Macht: Strukturprobleme des deutschen Parlamentarismus 1867–1933", in H. Best (ed.), *Politik und Milieu*. St. Katharinen: Scriptae Mercuriae, pp. 175–222.

Best, Heinrich, Hausmann, Christopher, and Schmitt, Karl (2000). "Challenges, Failures, and Final Success: The Winding Path of German Parliamentary Leadership Groups towards a Structurally Integrated Elite 1848–1999", in H. Best and M. Cotta (eds), *Parliamentary Representatives in Europe 1848–2000*. Oxford: Oxford University Press, pp. 138–95.

Beyme, Klaus von (1993). *Die politische Klasse im Parteienstaat*. Frankfort: Suhrkamp.

Bundesverfassungsgericht (1975). *Entscheidungen des Bundesverfassungsgerichts*, p. 40.

Derlien, Hans-Ulrich (1994). "Germany: The Structure and Dynamics of the Reward System for Bureaucratic and Political Elites", in C. Hood and B. Peters (eds), *Rewards at the Top*. London: Sage, pp. 166–86.

——and Lock, Stefan (1994). "Eine neue politische Elite? Rekrutierung und Karrieren der Abgeordneten in den fünf neuen Landtagen". *Zeitschrift für Parlamentsfragen*, 25: 61–94.

Ebbighausen, Rolf, Düpjohann, Christian, Prokein, Dieter, Raupach, Joachim, Renner, Marcus, Schotes, Rolf, and Schröter, Sebastian (1996). *Die Kosten der Parteiendemokratie*. Opladen: Westdeutscher Verlag.

Golsch, Lutz (1998). *Die politische Klasse im Parlament: Politische Professionalisierung von Hinterbänklern im Deutschen Bundestag*. Baden-Baden: Nomos.

Hennis, Wilhelm (1998, first published 1992). "Der Parteienstaat des Grundgesetzes", in W. Hennis, *Auf dem Weg in den Parteienstaat*. Stuttgart: Reclam, pp. 107–35.

Herzog, Dietrich (1975). *Politische Karrieren*. Opladen: Westdeutscher Verlag.

Hood, Christopher, and Lambert, Sonia (1994). "Mountain Tops or Iceberg Tips? Some Comparative Data on RHPOs", in C. Hood and B. Peters (eds), *Rewards at the Top*. London: Sage, pp. 25–48.

Hunt, Richard N. (1964). *German Social Democracy, 1918–1933*. New Haven, CT: Yale University Press.

Jekewitz, Jürgen (1995). "Das Personal der Parlamentsfraktionen", *Zeitschrift für Parlamentsfragen*, 26: 395–423.

Jun, Uwe (1996). "Innerparteiliche Reformen im Vergleich: der Versuch einer Modernisierung von SPD und Labour Party", in J. Borchert, L. Golsch, U. Jun, and P. Lösche (eds), *Das sozialdemokratische Modell*. Opladen: Leske + Budrich, pp. 213–38.

Kaack, Heino (1971). *Geschichte und Struktur des deutschen Parteiensystems*. Opladen: Westdeutscher Verlag.

Klatt, Hartmut (1972). *Die Altersversorgung der Abgeordneten*. Tübingen: Mohr.

Kolinsky, Eva (1993). "Party Change and Women's Representation in Unified Germany", in J. Lovenduski and P. Norris (eds), *Gender and Party Politics*. London: Sage, pp. 113–46.

Lehmbruch, Gerhard (1998). *Parteienwettbewerb im Bundesstaat*, 2nd edition. Opladen: Westdeutscher Verlag.

Lemke-Müller, Sabine (1996). "Zur Parlamentsreform im Deutschen Bundestag". *Aus Politik und Zeitgeschichte*, 46/B27: 3–19.

Lock, Stefan (1998). *Ostdeutsche Landtagsabgeordnete 1990–1994: Vom personellen Neubeginn zur politischen Professionalisierung?* Berlin: Verlag für Wissenschaft und Forschung.

Lohse, Jörg (1999). "Landtagsabgeordnete in Sachsen-Anhalt: Auf den Pfaden politischer Professionalisierung". *Zeitschrift für Parlamentsfragen*, 30: 117–34.

Marschall, Stefan (1999). *Parlamentsreform*. Opladen: Leske + Budrich.

Meyer, Thomas (1992). "SPD, Politische Klasse und politische Kultur", in T. Leif, H.-J. Legrand, and A. Klein (eds), *Die politische Klasse in Deutschland*. Bonn: Bouvier, pp. 172–90.

Mielke, Gerd (1997). "Mehr Demokratie wagen! SPD-Führung im partizipatorischen Zeitalter". *Blätter für deutsche und internationale Politik*, No. 1, 38–47.

Molt, Peter (1963). *Der Reichstag vor der improvisierten Revolution*. Opladen: Westdeutscher Verlag.

Nipperdey, Thomas (1961). *Die Organisation der deutschen Parteien vor 1918*. Düsseldorf: Droste.

Poguntke, Thomas (1994). "Parties in a Legalistic Culture: The Case of Germany", in R. Katz and P. Mair (eds), *How Parties Organize*. London: Sage, pp. 185–215.

——and Boll, Bernhard (1992). "Germany", in R. Katz and P. Mair (eds), *Party Organizations*. London: Sage, pp. 317–88.

Ronge, Volker (1994). "Der Zeitaspekt ehrenamtlicher Arbeit in der Kommunalpolitik". *Zeitschrift für Parlamentsfragen*, 25: 267–82.

Roth, Guenther (1963). *The Social Democrats in Imperial Germany*. Totowa: Bedminster.

Rudzio, Wolfgang (1987). *Das politische System der Bundesrepublik Deutschland*, 2nd edition. Opladen: Leske + Budrich.

Scheuch, Erwin K., and Scheuch, Ute (1992). *Cliquen, Klüngel und Karrieren*. Reinbek: Rowohlt.

Schindler, Peter (1999). *Datenhandbuch zur Geschichte des Deutschen Bundestages 1949 bis 1999* (3 volumes). Baden-Baden: Nomos.

Schorske, Carl E. (1955). *German Social Democracy 1905–1917*. Cambridge, MA: Harvard University Press.

Sheehan, James J. (1968). "Political Leadership in the German Reichstag, 1871–1918". *American Historical Review*, 74: 511–28.

Thaysen, Uwe (1972). *Parlamentsreform in Theorie und Praxis*. Opladen: Westdeutscher Verlag.

Weber, Max (1958). "Politics as a Vocation", in H. Gerth and C. Wright Mills (eds), *From Max Weber*. New York: Oxford University Press, pp. 77–128.

——(1972). *Wirtschaft und Gesellschaft*, 5th edition. Tübingen: Mohr.

Welsh, Helga A. (1996). "Parliamentary Elites in Times of Political Transition: The Case of Eastern Germany". *West European Politics*, 19: 507–24.

Werner, Camilla (1990). "Wer sind die Rebellen im Parlament? Die Interfraktionelle Initiative Parlamentsreform im 11. Deutschen Bundestag". *Zeitschrift für Parlamentsfragen*, 21: 404–18.

Wessels, Bernhard (1997). "Germany", in P. Norris (ed.), *Passages to Power*. Cambridge: Cambridge University Press, pp. 76–97.

Westlake, Martin (1994). *Britain's Emerging Euro-Elite?* Aldershot: Dartmouth.

Winkler, Heinrich A. (1994). *Weimar 1918–1933*, 2nd edition. Munich: Beck.

Zeuner, Bodo (1970). *Kandidatenaufstellung zur Bundestagswahl 1965*. Den Haag: Martinus Nijhoff.

9

Great Britain: From the Prevalence of the Amateur to the Dominance of the Professional Politician

UWE JUN

POLITICAL PROFESSIONALIZATION IN HISTORICAL PERSPECTIVE: FROM AMATEUR TO CAREER POLITICIAN

Until late in the twentieth century Great Britain was considered to be the stronghold of the amateur politician: the aristocracy, the upper middle-class, and—with the rise of the Labour Party—trade union secretaries shaped for a long time the outlook of Westminster and Whitehall. They often lived *for* politics, but very rarely made a living *from* politics. Only a small number of them were career politicians who organized their professional activity around the political sphere.

Today, however, the pattern has changed. Both Parliament and government are now dominated by career politicians who have made politics their occupation and have no other professional aim than to remain in politics. There are many signs of this development: the rising number of those working in the political field immediately after their education and, along with that, the growing number of candidates for political posts, regularized career patterns, reliable sources of income, mechanisms of career maintenance and, not least, financial security after retirement. The political career now largely takes the path of other occupational groups. As a result, there is an increase in professionalization and—often criticized—a *separation*, or, more positively, *independence* of the political class from other professional groups. This chapter focuses on Parliament and political parties, since they form the starting point as well as the center of the political class in Great Britain.

The weight of historical continuity inhibited for a long time the establishment of a political class in the United Kingdom, so that its formation ensued rather late in

I have been fortunate to have received very useful comments on early drafts of the paper that have helped me to improve the argument I am outlining. In this regard I am indebted to Samuel Huntington, Benjamin Read, Paul Talcott, and to the participants of the Sawyer Seminar at Harvard University in Fall 1997. I am very grateful to Alan Jacobs (Harvard University) who has performed an invaluable service in reading and commenting on the final draft.

comparison to other western democracies. Only in the second half of the twentieth century did the career politician, who today dominates the House of Commons, begin to become increasingly apparent (Buck 1963). Indeed, there were career politicians in every phase of the history of Great Britain, but their number was small until the late 1960s, and they had acted more as individuals. Up to this time a common awareness was nearly nonexistent; common interests were articulated only very rarely. In his book '*The English Constitution*,' first published in 1867, Walter Bagehot describes the House of Commons as a Parliament with 658 representatives "collected from all parts of England, different in nature, different in interests, different in looks, different in language" (1964: 155). The changes of the electoral systems through the Reform Acts of 1832 and 1867, both of which enlarged the electorate, led in Parliament neither to collective behavior nor to party discipline among either the Conservatives or the Liberals. Wealthy individuals from the aristocracy and bourgeoisie gathered in the House of Commons or the House of Lords to take political decisions for the nation autonomously and with the appropriate style. "They were self-perpetuating aristocrats and gentry [...] which regard service in parliament and government as part of their inherited duties" (Riddell 1993: 266). Their object was neither a reliable source of income nor a political career.

Although the basis of representation was territorial, the individual Member of Parliament (MP) acted relatively independently of the interests of his constituency (Berrington 1985; Crewe 1985; Norton and Wood 1993; Norton 1994). Many MPs spent only a few years in Parliament; only a small group of leaders remained in office a long time or returned again and again to Westminster and Whitehall. Most of them lived in Max Weber's sense nearly exclusively for politics; even so their mandate was not merely connected with status and prestige. The single MP could and did act as an individualist as party discipline was weak and in decline.

With the Reform Act of 1884, which brought almost universal franchise for men, the structure of Parliament changed, too: social class became the crucial determinant of parliamentary behavior. The importance of social class deepened as a result of the split in the Liberal Party over Irish Home Rule (1886) and through the emergence of the Labour Party. The Conservatives saw themselves as the defenders of wealth and property against the Liberal Party's more radical ideas and, from 1906 onwards, increasingly against the ideas of the Labour Party as well. From this moment, party discipline determined MPs' voting behavior; party discipline retained the upper hand for many decades: "The iron cage of party discipline has contained Westminster MPs for more than a century" (Rose 1986: 11). But party discipline was particularly strong just after the Second World War, reaching its peak in the years between 1945 and 1970. During this era, bills received nearly 100 percent support from members of the party that proposed them. On average, the governmental party suffered defeat in a parliamentary vote only once every 2 years during this period (Rose: 10–13).

Manifest class antagonism in Parliament heightened during the 1920s and 1930s. While the upper classes dominated on the conservative side—"more millionaires served in the inter-war parliaments than in the nineteenth century" (Riddell 1993: 19)—a vast majority of Labour MPs came from the working-class: until the general election of 1922, working-class MPs comprised 90 percent of the Labour benches, and they remained a majority until 1945 (Rush 1995). Because of these social ties, neither party had an interest in joining forces to establish a political class. Most members of the Conservative Party in Parliament still regarded politics as a sideline and part-time job. They pursued other interests outside politics—and often politics helped advance their business interests. Only those in leadership positions were full-time parliamentarians. The party was hardly organized, lacking the modern structures of a mass movement, because the Conservatives' individually oriented members were uninterested in organization.

Meanwhile, on the Labour benches, the idea of solidarity was strongly held. Labour MPs considered it their main political task to forward the interests of the working-class and to serve as its direct representatives in Parliament. They were also only in rare cases full-time parliamentarians, but were predominantly employed by the trade unions. This engagement in trade union affairs led not only to self-identification as a part-time MP, but also to a high rate of turnover—a phenomenon which one could also observe among Conservatives until 1945. The Labour Party also did not build up modern organizational structures, because it understood itself merely as a parliamentary extension of the unions. Considering these preconditions, both parties did not intend on building up a political class. Because of the enormous differences between them, cross-party consensus on a set of common aims and interests—let alone a common identity—seemed almost unconceivable.

One indication of the lack of interest in creating a political class was the absence of financial incentives to embark on a political career. Until 1911 MPs received no official payment; only since 1972, has there been a clear distinction drawn between parliamentary salaries and expenses incurred while carrying out parliamentary duties. Of course, MPs were paid before 1911, but only on a private and individual basis. From public funds the MPs drew only £400 p.a., an insufficient sum to allow Members to subsist on politics, especially given that there were no further allowances for expenses such as assistants or travel. In later years salaries were increased on an irregular basis, and from 1924 onwards travel allowances were available; but only since 1969 has there been a secretarial allowance and provision for free domestic phone calls and postage.

In 1963 the British government appointed an independent committee (the Lawrence Committee) to review payments to members of both Houses and to ministers. In response to the committee's proposals, the government raised salaries. But it was only in 1971 that the recommendations of the independent Top Salaries Review Body brought substantial financial improvements for MPs. While parliamentarians set their own salaries, the government's "advisory" recommendations to Parliament carry great weight. "Since then [1911, U.J.] MPs have collectively determined their own remuneration, though subject to strong government pressure" (Adonis 1993: 7). With the passage of the Top Salaries Review Body's recommendations, it is finally possible for nearly all MPs to make a living in politics.

Another historical development should be mentioned at this point: one result of the vastly reduced power of the House of Lords is that the political class focuses its ambitions exclusively on the House of Commons. For the recruitment of significant and ambitious political positions, the House of Lords is of rather limited importance. Often it is more of a reception camp for politicians who have finished their effective political life, but would still like to participate in politics. At this moment many former top politicians from the House of Commons, former ministers, and even former Prime Ministers sit in the Lords.

Overall, then, the political class in Great Britain did not emerge until the late sixties or early seventies. Insufficient professionalization, limited career opportunities, class antagonism and, not least, low salaries have led to a marked delay in the formation of a political class in Britain. Also responsible for this were the political parties, who had no interest in establishing the necessary autonomy from society. Both main parties modernized their organizational structures relatively late to create the preconditions for the emergence of a political class—which can only develop if parties are independent actors in the political system.

THE INSTITUTIONAL CONTEXT

The most important place for the public display of party competition in Great Britain is the House of Commons. Membership of the Lower House is for this reason *the* unavoidable step along the way to higher political office, not only because it ensures access to the political decision-making process, but also because it provides the financial resources for, and access to, successive stages of a political career, particularly in government. According to this logic, the House of Commons is for some the final goal, for others the stepping stone in a more ambitious political career. The members of the House of Commons are, in any case, the core of the political class in Great Britain, even after the partial abandonment of the unitary structure of the British polity. Most important political decisions are still made in London. Decentralization measures ("devolution"), introduced via referenda in September 1997, created four new legislative bodies (the Scottish Parliament, the Northern Ireland Assembly, the National Assembly for Wales, and the Greater London Assembly; cf. Cowley 2000; Rush 2001*b*) and have resulted in new career patterns on the regional level. Thus, the structure of career opportunities has been extended. The status of Westminster has changed: it is now a Parliament for England, a Parliament for Primary Legislation for Wales, and a federal Parliament for Northern Ireland and Scotland. Even if initial studies of the devolved legislatures show that they "have opened alternative career patterns, rather than interchangeable ones" (Rush 2001*b*: 19), we will have to wait to see how the new parliaments will work in the future, how they establish themselves and what kinds of career paths they offer the political class. With the adoption of a form of proportional representation for the regional assemblies, devolution is clearly changing the party system (in particular on the regional level), strengthening the positions of regional parties and of the Liberal Democrats (Webb 2000: 15–28). In the long run it will also establish other structures of political recruitment for the political class.

However, it was the parties who created the preconditions for the emergence of a political class and shaped its composition. To get a seat in the House of Commons or in the regional assemblies or legislatures, a candidate has first to succeed within his party. Parties dominate politics in Great Britain. Since the middle of the nineteenth century, two parties have determined the structure of the British party system: on the one side the Conservatives and on the other side the Liberals before 1918 and Labour since 1918. Despite some clear indications of a weakening of two-party system since the 1970s, the two main parties remain the dominant political actors, particularly in Westminster. Though the Liberal Democrats gained in support during the 2001 general election and posed serious challenges in many constituencies, they still lack adequate parliamentary representation, with only fifty-three deputies.

The two main parties have different recruiting mechanisms, which will be described later in this chapter. But the British "first-past-the-post" electoral system, with its plurality single-member districts, requires that the two main parties nominate candidates in each of the now 659 electoral constituencies. Usually, many seats are considered relatively safe for one or the other main party, independently of the national result. In the general elections from 1945 to 1992, on average two-thirds of all electoral districts saw no change in partisan majority. In these constituencies the decisive hurdle for would-be MPs from the majority party is the inner-party nomination. In the past, only in exceptional political situations—like in the elections in 1997—was it possible to break up local strongholds. In contrast to 1997 the election of 2001 saw 85 percent of sitting MPs reelected; only 21 went down to defeat (Cowley 2001: 822). Behind this surface of stability, however, an "electoral change since 1970 almost certainly implies a more open electoral market and increasingly complex patterns of competition" (Webb 2000: 79). The increasing volatility of voting behavior has reduced the number of safe seats, with a consequent rise in career uncertainty for individual candidates and MPs. As the number of marginal seats has increased, national party competition has become more significant: "Only in marginal seats is the fate of the candidate really determined by the electorate, but that fate is largely decided by the fortunes of the party nationally" (Rush 1994: 570). In times of media dominance the national trend becomes the main force in election campaigns.

The erosion of party allegiances in the electorate has rarely progressed so far as to make the personality of local candidates the decisive factor (but see Berrington 1985: 34). The relatively high rate of re-election (1945–92: 76.2 percent) must instead be explained by the deep ties of parties in their respective constituencies (Norris and Lovenduski 1995: 31). Despite the overall erosion of party allegiance, a candidates' party affiliations remain the main factor shaping the electorate's voting behavior in Great Britain (Norris 1997: 9).

MPs are still strongly dependent on their parties and also relatively loyal to their party leadership in Parliament. Yet, with the establishment of a political class over the last 25 years, MPs' self-confidence and the number of vote defections have somewhat increased (see Rose 1986; Norton 1990: 17–23; Norton 1997: 26–9; Pattie, Johnston, and Stewart 1998). Even governmental defeats on bills have occurred, though these are still rare. The typical MP today, having been socialized under different societal conditions, is more individualistic than parliamentarians 30 years ago; and not surprisingly many MPs have reported exasperation at their lack of influence over important political decisions (Norris 1997: 27). All in all, party discipline still determines the political routine in the House of Commons. Party affiliation gives the basic, underlying motivation to almost all decisions that MPs make. In most cases their personal opinions are also in line with those of their party (Rush 2001*a*: 218).

At the same time, through occasional defiant behavior, backbenchers demonstrate yet again that the House is at least formally sovereign—a notion which includes the fiction that all central political decisions are made in Parliament and that the sovereignty of Parliament is absolute (for more details see Adonis 1993: 6–24). Since select committees were created in 1979 under pressure from career backbench politicians, parliamentary work has been partly transferred to the committees. The introduction of select committees has also contributed to the intensification of cooperation and informational exchange between Parliament and interest groups, despite the Thatcher government's efforts to curtail the influence of these organizations (Rush 1990; Norton 1994: 164–70). Those were not completely ineffective; the political influence of trade unions has been drastically reduced. But otherwise the interest groups have maintained their lobbying abilities, and cooperation with Parliament has even been intensified as a result of Thatcherism (cf. Rush 2001*a*,*b*].

Because of the traditionally tight relationship between trade unions and the Labour Party, the unions constitute a recruitment basis for the party. During recent years the linkage has become looser, and the number of trade union secretaries or trade union officials in the parliamentary Labour Party is in decline. Despite this loosening and despite Blair's moves to end trade union sponsorship of MPs, the unions still pay their contribution to party coffers and expect in return to maintain influence within the party. But Labour's financial dependence on the trade unions has been reduced remarkably: union contributions fell from 96 percent of all central party income in 1983 to just 40 percent at the end of the century (Webb 2000: 235). Nevertheless, New Labour remains dependent on money from the trade unions because of scant public funding and a relatively low number of individual members.[1] Overall, however, the influence of the trade unions in the recruitment process has diminished.

In addition, interest organizations are closely linked to the political class in Great Britain, because more and more interest groups are working together with political consultants or employ them. Thus, the interest groups open up new career possibilities or extend previously existing career paths. Some MPs who lose their seats later become lobbyists and benefit from their political knowledge and experience in parliament. Some work directly for interest organizations, others for political consultancy firms, that do work for interest groups or companies. With the introduction of select committees, political networks between lobbyists, Parliament, and government have been further strengthened and intensified. A member of the political class may change positions but remain in the network. Quantitatively, these networks are not as large as those in the United States, but in the last 20 years they have grown tremendously

---

[1] There are some exceptions: Around £2 million (approx. €3.15 million) a year are made available for opposition parties, which do not have the machinery of government to support them. And in an election campaign, broadcasts, postage, and meeting halls are available to parties free of charge.

(Grantham 1989: 505). This field of political service, relatively new in Great Britain, reinforces the effect of political professionalization.

THE POLITICAL CLASS

Since the 1970s, the firm establishment of a political class in Great Britain can be observed. By 1981 Anthony King (King 1981) could already identify the steady growth of a new generation of career politicians who spent their whole occupational lives in politics.[2] Nevertheless, this phenomenon has been relatively rarely analyzed or discussed; the most pointed and extensive analyses have been done by Peter Riddell (1993, 1995) and Michael Rush (1994, 2001a). On the process of recruitment Pippa Norris and Joni Lovenduski published a detailed study in 1995 (see also Norris and Lovenduski 1997). The next section presents an analysis of the development of the political class in Great Britain on the basis of these studies. It shows the conditions that allowed the political class to emerge and how the political parties promoted and accelerated the process of professionalization which was also driven by a self-reinforcing dynamic.

Size and Composition

It is almost impossible to state the exact size of the political class in Great Britain, but it is safe to say that it is comparatively small: "Probably a few thousand at most, but it now accounts for an increasing proportion of new MPs" (Riddell 1995: 187). While MPs are at the center of the political class, the group also includes the growing numbers of political consultants, political advisors to ministers, research assistants to MPs, as well as the staff at party headquarters, in the House of Commons, and in policy research institutes working for the parties. To this list should also be added lobbyists working for interest organizations.

On the regional and local level the class includes the members of newly established legislatures and assemblies, their staff and political advisors, and the growing number of professional councilors and members of local government. The last of these groups increasingly constitutes the pool of recruitment for the lower House of Parliament (Rush 1994: 573). Also included, are British Members of the European Parliament and representatives in the different bodies of the European Union. There are some points of intersection of career patterns at the national and European level, but these two paths have tended to diverge in recent years (see Westlake 1994; Jun and Kuper 1997; Scarrow 1997; Rush 2001b). All in all, the different spheres of the political class are bound up with each other, and members share an interest in preserving their political careers.

---

[2] King defines the career politician as someone who "is committed to politics. He regards politics as his vocation, he seeks fulfillment in politics, he sees his future in politics, he would be deeply upset if circumstances forced him to retire from politics. In short, he is hooked" (King 1981: 250).

Table 9.1 *Women elected to the House of Commons, 1945–2001*

Year (average)	1945–79	1983	1987	1992	1997	2001
Total number	24	23	41	60	120	118
% of MPs	3.8	3.6	6.3	9.2	18.2	17.9

Source: Norris and Lovenduski (1995: 103); House of Commons.

The political class in Great Britain is strongly dominated by men. In Parliament women are vastly underrepresented, even in comparison to other West European countries. Universal female suffrage, not introduced until 1928, did not lead to a distinct increase in the proportion of women in Parliament: until the 1980s their share in seats remained under 5 percent (see Table 9.1). After decades of slow progress there has been a rise, particularly in 1997, above all due to quota policies for women in the Labour Party (Perrigo 1996; Squires and Wickham-Jones 2002). The enormous increase after the election in 1997 can be explained by the modernization of organizational structures that has taken place within the Labour Party over the last 15 years (Jun 1996; Panitch and Leys 1997; Heffernan 2001). There are now quotas for women on all party decision-making committees. An important step was the vote of the party convention in 1993 that women should be candidates for half of all Labour seats where MPs are retiring and for half of all of Labour's most promising seats.[3] But because the use of all-women shortlists by the Labour Party was ruled illegal, the Blair government, if it wants to increase women's representation through quotas, must do so through different means.

There are several reasons why women are still under-represented in Parliament. First, local parties often hesitate to nominate women as candidates, especially for promising seats, because of a perception that women may be less effective campaigners (Adonis 1993: 55; Norris and Lovenduski 1995: 141)—a perception that is not confirmed by empirical research (Norris 1997: 188).

Another disadvantage for women in the recruitment process is the fact that they less often work in occupations that provide networks easing the way into political life. Therefore, the resources for political participation are lacking (Norris and Lovenduski 1995: 111). Moreover, the double burden of family work and employment that many women face limits the amount of time they have available for participation in local party activities, a precondition for becoming a candidate.

The rise to candidacy requires perseverance and financial resources; only once they have entered Parliament can politicians actually make a living from politics.

[3] This regulation was carried through by implementing "all women shortlists," that is, in certain constituencies only women could become candidates (Lovenduski 1997: 709–11). Despite still being applied in the 1997 elections, these lists had been outruled as illegal by a court in 1996, because they discriminate against men when it comes to the distribution of parliamentary seats and thus to free occupational access.

As a consequence, not only the demand for, but also the supply of female candidates is lower; significantly fewer women than men strive for a political career (Rush 1994: 572). The under-representation of women is already obvious in the organizational structure of parties: Women are represented in those structures in proportions far below their share of the population, while they are almost completely absent from leadership positions. Another peculiarity of British parliamentarism has further obstructed access for women: the House of Commons used to debate until late at night (debates often began at 2 p.m.), so that women with children were again placed at a disadvantage. But now the regular end of debate is fixed at 10 p.m., and ten times in a year there is no debate on Fridays. Besides the still open question whether and to what extent women are in fact "acting for" women (Childs 2002) so that increased descriptive representation would result in women-friendly policies, it is safe to say that the situation for women in the British Parliament is still disadvantageous in comparison with other western democracies.

The political situation for ethnic minorities in Great Britain is relatively precarious. They are also under-represented in Parliament. Until 1997 only ten representatives of ethnic minorities managed to gain a seat. Yet, after the general election of 1997, nine MPs from ethnic minority groups (all Labour) were elected; in 2001 the number rose slightly to twelve (all Labour). Even if the political situation has improved over the last 20 years, particularly in the Labour Party, ethnic minorities are still underrepresented. The main reason for this is again that local parties fear that they will be at an electoral disadvantage if they select a minority candidate. Yet, the situation is improving: In 1997 forty-four ethnic minority candidates ran in the general election; in 1992 the figure had been only twenty-four (Saggar 1997).

Competition for candidatures has become more intense in the last 15 years, with a clearly observable trend: the pool of applicants is now increasingly drawn from those who are younger, better formally educated, and working in occupations closely related to politics ("brokerage occupations"; cf. Norris and Lovenduski 1995: 122). The advantages of occupations close to politics are obvious: they offer sufficient occupational security, flexibility, and income for a political career. Lovenduski and Norris come to the conclusion that the social bias of the House of Commons is more the product of supply than of demand (Norris and Lovenduski, 1995: 113). So, the share of those MPs with occupations close to politics has grown substantially over time, and they also make up the largest share within the growing group of career politicians. By contrast, the proportion of candidates coming from occupations wholly independent of politics ("proper jobs") has fallen further (Riddell 1993: 22).

The pre-political careers of the political class are not long: the political career often begins in the early or mid-30s, sometimes earlier. A common point of entry is a consultancy to parties or government, the position of an advisory or assistant to ministers, MPs, etc. Riddell sees a steep increase in the number of MPs who aimed to become politicians from the beginning of their student days: "Many have known nothing else than politics, and earned their living mainly, if not solely, from political activities" (Riddell 1993: 186; cf. Adonis 1993: 53; Rush 1994: 573). Politics becomes their main profession, and they are full-time Members of the Parliament "in both attitude and practice" (Rush 2001a: 112). Through politics they earn their money, achieve their status in society and maintain their social security. Their career at Westminster is the professional center of their lives. Without a doubt the prospect of a reliable income shapes the career decision considerably. Even if some Conservative MPs drew higher salaries in their former professions than they do in Parliament, this does not discourage them from entering politics. Peter Riddell argues in fact that the political class lacks representatives who have had a successful career outside politics before entering the political stage (Riddell 1993: 273–80). This criticism points towards an unmistakable tendency but seems overdrawn: before getting elected to Parliament, most would-be MPs have already made their way inside or outside the political world (Rush 2001a: 131), and there remains a significant, if declining, share of MPs coming from occupations independent of politics.

Closely connected to this occupational structure of the political class is the socio-economic background of MPs. There is an obvious convergence between parliamentarians of the two main parties in this respect. Both parties recruit their candidates mainly from the new middle class, and since the 1970s there has been a noticeable homogenization of Parliament's social structure (Norton 1997: 25; Rush 2001a: 94–108). Both parliamentary parties are dominated by MPs with a university degree. Oxford and Cambridge retain their lead on the Conservative side, but over the years an increasing proportion of Tory MPs has been drawn from other universities; on the Labour side "Oxbridge" has never held a majority (for detailed data see Rush and Cromwell 2000; Rush 2001a). The relatively long period of training has the consequence that only a few begin their parliamentary careers before the age of 30; most MPs are first elected between 35 and 45.

Particularly distinct are the changes within the Labour Party: manual workers and trade union secretaries with low formal qualifications have been almost wholly replaced by graduates of public (i.e. private) schools and/or universities. After the general elections of 1997 and 2001, the percentage of manual workers in Labour's parliamentary party was the lowest in the party's history. But the parliamentary party's working-class roots have not been totally cut, as Cowley points out: "Labour MPs are often first-generation middle class, the children of working-class parents" (2001: 826). On the Conservative benches the traditional aristocracy and the upper middle-class have been replaced by private-sector professionals, lawyers, and self-employed persons.

Three trends can be identified: first, the need for potential candidates to engage in politics early and to establish themselves occupationally and financially, in order to create the preconditions for a career in politics; second, a clear decline in the number of MPs for whom a parliamentary career was a fairly late adjunct to their principal occupation; and third, an increase in the professionalization of MPs (Rush 1994: 576; Rush 2001a: 109–38). This professionalization is marked by relatively high salaries, appropriate career patterns, and "the resources to support the performance of parliamentary duties" as well as the fact that being an MP is now a full-time job (Rush 2001a: 112).

Political Recruitment and Political Careers

Members of Parliament's changed commitment to politics as a profession is mostly reflected in their tendency to enter Parliament earlier and stay longer than their predecessors. Politics means career for them—once elected, most MPs want to stay in Parliament for the rest of their professional careers and give up their seats only involuntarily (Rush 1994: 577; Norton 1997: 25). Consequently, the median length of service rose from 14 years for those leaving the House of Commons between 1945 and 1974 to 18 years for those leaving between 1974 and 1992 (see Table 9.2). The reelection rate between 1945 and 1992 was 76.2 percent and has remained very high since (Rush 1994; House of Commons).

Only landslide defeats like that of the Conservative Party in 1997 lead to a significantly lower rate of reelection. Because most MPs plan their political careers at an early stage and acquire highly specific knowledge and skills, they usually direct most of their attention toward career maintenance. "There are now more committed full time politicians, for whom their careers at Westminster are the center of their lives, both financially and socially" (Riddell 1993: 266). Only a few regard their membership in Parliament as a short-term engagement, leaving voluntarily after one or two sessions. However, many MPs who lose their seats try to return to the House of Commons. More than half of those who lose their seats stand for election again, and more than one-third have actually been successful. Because parties need qualified and professional politicians on their benches, they create the appropriate conditions for the re-entry of experienced individuals into Parliament.

Peter Riddell (1993: 267) identifies two important motivations for pursuing a career in politics: on the one hand a dedication to politics and an ambition to advance political goals, and on the other hand the prospect of making a living through politics. The rise in salaries has given MPs greater financial independence and flexibility, which is necessary for a professional career. With the introduction of a contributory pension scheme in the mid-1960s, the parliamentary career is now conforming more to a normal working life. In previous times many less well-off

Table 9.2 *Years served in Parliament (%)*

	1918–44		1945–74		1974–2001	
	Cons.	Labor	Cons.	Labor	Cons.	Labor
Less than 5 years	22.0	29.2	9.0	10.4	7.8	9.9
5–9 years	19.5	17.8	23.2	28.4	20.0	20.9
10–14 years	23.6	14.2	18.0	16.1	14.5	19.4
15–19 years	11.5	16.4	19.5	16.5	15.0	18.1
20–24 years	11.5	9.4	13.8	12.2	16.1	12.7
25 or more years	11.9	13.0	16.5	16.3	24.9	19.0

Source: Rush (1995, 2001a); own calculations.

Labour MPs could not afford to leave Parliament and sought re-election well after 65 years of age. Today, MPs older than 65 are rarely found in the House of Commons.

The duration of the parliamentary career, the growing tendency to withdraw from Parliament at a normal retirement age, and the young age at which careers are started, are indicators of the increasing professionalization of MPs. For the parties the advantage of professionalization lies in a greater knowledge of political processes on the part of politicians. Even before their entry into Parliament, most MPs gain political experience within the parties that both, MPs and parties, can use and benefit from later.

In addition, career politicians not only become familiar with communication networks in their early years, but also learn how to use them to their own benefit. These networks are growing as more and more jobs related to politics are created. The political class has expanded, and most of its members aspire to a seat in the Parliament. Greater demand has led to a greater supply of jobs close to politics, which in turn has increased the level of demand. The most important step on the career ladder is still a seat in Parliament, however, so that the demand for parliamentary mandates far exceeds the supply: "The process of recruitment is one where many run but few succeed" (Norris and Lovenduski 1995: 25). A consequence of this is also that many candidates have lost several races in multiple constituencies before finally winning a seat.

Here, the parties' influence takes effect again: they determine the constituency in which a candidate runs for election, which sometimes leads to a mid-career change of constituencies. The political parties have almost completely monopolized the function of nominating candidates. Conversely, this is the most important function of British political parties, apart from the articulation and aggregation of interests: "Placing candidates in safe seats, possibly for a lifetime political career, has more significant consequences than getting conference resolutions adopted, or supporters nominated to internal bodies" (Norris and Lovenduski 1995: 3).

While the parties have different procedures for selecting proper candidates for Parliament and ministerial positions, there are also many similarities in their recruitment processes (for details see Detterbeck 2002: 79–85). Both formal procedures and informal arrangements characterize the recruitment process, though the process has become more formalized over the last 20 years. In the two main parties, the local organization has the formal right to select candidates. Despite a centralized party system, the local parties have managed to maintain considerable autonomy in the selection of candidates for Parliament. To achieve high political office, a potential candidate has to win a majority of his or her party members in a constituency. This selection principle has remained in force, even as national party leaderships have increased their influence over the recruitment process over the last decade. With regard to the formal process, the national party leadership has only three possible ways of influencing a nomination: (1) laying down the rules by which local parties choose candidates; (2) maintaining lists of possible candidates to exercise a degree of quality control; and, finally, (3) retaining a veto-right against the local choice.

Beyond this, the National Executive Committee (NEC) of the Labour Party has exerted particularly strong influence over the selection process of candidates.

For instance, at by-elections or European Parliament elections, a special NEC task force, or panel, has been charged with coordinating the selection process (Wring, Baker, and Seawright 2000). The intraparty decision making process, thus, exhibits a centralizing tendency, giving more influence to the national party leadership, which convenes panels to oversee and monitor the selection process. In the eyes of Eric Shaw this is a development with significant consequences for the constitution of the political class: "By altering the structure of political opportunity, the new filtering devices, over a period of time, may well reinforce existing trends towards the selection of more conformist, instrumental minded and career-driven candidates" (Shaw 2001: 51).

Incumbents and those "inheriting" a safe seat have long had a head start at election time. Between 1945 and 1992 on average only 140 challengers per election won seats in Parliament, as compared with 511 incumbents and same-party successors (Norris and Lovenduski 1995: 24). This phenomenon reflects the deep roots of parties within their respective class bases and the strong anchoring role of party identification, which ensured the stability of party support in most constituencies until the early 1970s.

Nominated candidates do not form a homogenous group in their political attitudes, and even within a single parliamentary party, differences in career patterns and parliamentary behavior are readily apparent. More and more MPs are coming to Westminster with their own political agendas, with precise plans for how to achieve them, with the desire to specialize in one or two policy areas, and with the ambition to rise as high as possible within the profession. All of this constitutes a problem for the parties' chief whips: "Chief whips today see a dearth of loyal, undemanding back benchers and a plethora of ambitious, importuning MPs." As one chief whip posed the problem: "We have too many MPs—and they all want office" (Campbell and Wilson 1995: 56). Career politicians are ambitious and seek an outlet for their ambitions. Therefore, they demand a more active and influential role than their predecessors, with the result that backbench dissension has become more common since 1945 (Riddell 1993: 269; Rush 1994: 578; Hodder-Williams 1996: 290).

The ideal career develops as follows: Party nomination, successful candidacy, followed by (in sequence) membership in the House of Commons, a term as secretary to a backbench committee, time as a parliamentary private secretary to a minister, service in the Whips Office, promotion to under-secretary, service as minister of state, and then membership in the cabinet (Riddell 1993: 9). While identifying this ideal–typical path, it is important to note that not every MP aspires to become a cabinet minister. In his classification of backbench- and leadership-roles in the House of Commons, Donald D. Searing (1994, 1995) distinguishes between four informal backbench roles and four formal leadership roles (for other typologies see Adonis 1993: 63–92; Mancuso 1995). On the side of the backbenchers these are (1) Policy Advocates, who are often specialized in particular policy areas and who place a high value on committee work; (2) Constituency Members, who pursue the interests of their constituency; (3) Parliamentary Men, who are classical parliamentarians, often act as generalists, and prefer plenary debate; (4) Ministerial Aspirants, who want to become ministers later in their careers.

These informal roles of backbenchers are not to be understood as static. The MPs change the roles as a politician's the career goals and stations change, which means that a single MP can have different roles at different times in the development of his or her career. The parliamentarian seeks his role within Parliament in accordance with his own self-understanding, ambition, career expectation, and status. For example, one might favor the role of the Constituency Member, because it brings with it more acknowledgment from the constituency or because advancing constituent interests effectively provides substantial job satisfaction. Women tend to choose this role with particular frequency (Norris and Lovenduski 1995: 224). The Policy Advocate is often an expert in a policy area to which he dedicates his ambition and parliamentary work. The select committees are his or her main field of activity. To satisfy the ambitions of the career politicians successive governments have tremendously increased the number of junior ministers since 1945: they now number more than sixty. "The prime minister must take care that younger MPs, who will move up into the Cabinet in years to come are brought forward to be given their apprenticeship on the lower rungs of ministerial ladder" (Theakston 1987: 47).

Only very few MPs willingly contemplate a career outside politics. The increasing professionalization of politics has, as a result, led to a partial separation of politics from other occupational groups in both structure and substance. This fact fuels the critique of professional politicians as unable to recognize "real" society's problems: "Politicians inhabit a private intellectual and social world, largely separate from those running large companies or the professions. Their priorities are different—notably trying to stay in office or retain their seats, which can produce a short—rather than a long-term perspective." (Riddell 1993: 28).

Other scholars argue that a large majority of parliamentarians desire mainly to pursue and implement policies that they think will be in the interest of a majority of the people (Hodder-Williams 1996). Probably both assumptions are in some sense true: the political class has an interest in at least maintaining its financial and social status as well as an interest in making decisions that will benefit a large segment of the electorate, even if for no other reason than to secure its own political survival and to justify its own existence.

Living off Politics

In the 1970s, the parties created an important precondition for the establishment of the political class: the financial situation of politicians in Great Britain has improved considerably in the last 25 years. During this period there have been major improvements in pay, services, and facilities for MPs. The number of well-paid positions in parties or as political consultants or advisors has increased quickly and steadily, even though the opportunities remain far fewer than those in Germany or the United States. Not only did parties and the House of Commons expand their staff, but enterprises and interest groups also employed a greater number of political and media consultants. Increasing numbers of positions of power and influence are now available on various public bodies, quangos, or non-governmental organizations.

Table 9.3   *MPs salaries, 1911–2000, selected years (in 1,000 £)*

1911	1937	1946	1957	1964	1972	1976	1980	1984	1988	1992	1996	2000
400	600	1,000	1,750	3,250	4,500	6,062	11,750	16,106	22,548	30,854	34,085	48,371

Source: House of Commons; Rush (1994); Rush (2001*a*).

Many MPs themselves serve as political consultants. In 1989, for example, more than 180 MPs were listed in the Register of Members' Interests as consultants or advisors to organizations outside Parliament (Grantham and Seymour-Ure 1990: 45–6).

The positive financial developments for the political class can best be illustrated with the increase in MPs' salaries. MPs in 1972 earned only £4,500 (€7,090)[4] a year; by 1987 their salaries had increased to £18,500 (€29,140). Ten years later they earned £34,085 (€53,690) p.a., a near doubling within ten years. This increase followed the recommendations of the Top Salaries Review Body, a commission consisting of parliamentarians and outside experts. Despite these recommendations, the salaries remained an ongoing matter of dispute between the government and the House of Commons until 1988. Before an agreement was reached, the government had often argued that MPs' pay should be linked to civil service salaries. In the end the government got its way: since 1 January 1989, MPs' salaries have been fixed at 89 percent of the national maximum point of the Grade 6 (Old Senior Principal) pay-scale in the non-industrial civil service, excluding additional allowances. In 1995 the government allowed that the salary level be increased by a "relevant percentage", comparable to average annual salary rises in Grades 5–7 of the civil service in the previous year.

The upward trend in salaries has been steep in recent years: between 1996 and 2000 MPs' salaries rose more than 40 percent. In February 1996 the Government asked the Senior Salaries Review Body to conduct a full review of parliamentary pay and allowances. It recommended to set the salaries for MPs at a yearly rate of £43,000 (€67,740) with the provision for an annual raise tied to civil service pay bands. In its review in 2001 it recommended "that the parliamentary salary should be increased by 2,000, in addition to any increase resulting from the usual annual review mechanisms, in both 2001 and 2002, because Members' pay had fallen behind that of comparators in the public sector and elsewhere' (Walker 2001).

Since 1969 MPs have received numerous allowances in addition to their salaries. They can claim expenses up to a set limit for travel on parliamentary business as well as travel expenses for spouses, secretaries, and children under the age of 18 for journeys between home, constituency, and London. In addition, MPs have free access to the following services: domestic telephone calls, postal services, and railway services. They may also claim reimbursement for secretarial assistance, general office expenses, and the employment of research assistants. The average expenditure on the latter increased from an annual £4,200 (€6,620) in 1979 to £51,572 (€81,240) a year in 2000. This budget allows each MP to equip a constituency office and employ at

[4] Conversions from GB£ to Euro are based on the exchange rate of 14 November 2002 (£1 = €1.57).

least two full-time assistants at the going rate. Other allowances cover social security payments for MPs' staff, including pension provision, a London supplement for those with constituencies in Inner London and an overnight allowance for those MPs whose homes are far away from the capital. Outgoing deputies also have a right to severance pay, a lump sum equivalent to 50–100 percent of salary, depending on age and length of service.

One has also to keep in mind that more than two-thirds of all MPs have significant extra-parliamentary income of some kind. There are no restrictions placed on out-side earnings: since 1975, MPs are only required to declare certain financial interests, including financial sponsorships, paid directorships and employment, and substant-ial interests in land and shares to the Office of the Speaker of the House. This register of outside earnings is published every year and open to the public.

A pension scheme for MPs was first introduced in 1965 with the Ministerial Salaries and Members' Pensions Act. Pensions are related to the final salary level, since 1984 accruing at 1/50 for each year of service, compared to 1/60 before. The contribution payable by Members was reduced in 1992 from 9 to 6 percent of salary. MPs may also purchase additional pension benefits for which they receive extra contributions. The dependence of the pension on the last income and length of service fosters long-term careers. The achievement of higher positions results in higher earnings, which, along with longer tenure in office, result in higher pensions. This resembles arrangements in other professions and is a further indication of the increasing professionalization of the political class.

Even if some MPs still find it difficult to make a living from politics (Riddell 1993: 11), the financial position of the political class has greatly improved. While income is usually not individuals' only, or prime, motivation for pursuing a political career, financial security is surely a significant point. Pay reforms have allowed politicians in Great Britain to live off politics, though without accumulating great wealth. The services and facilities provided to the MPs have also been expanded and improved. There has, for instance, been a remarkable growth of the House of Commons' staff since 1972 (by 168 percent; Rush 2001a: 129).

THE POLITICAL CLASS AND INSTITUTIONAL REFORM: GRADUAL CHANGE WITHIN BROAD CONTINUITY

The political system of Great Britain has for a long time been characterized by con-tinuity. Nevertheless, the changes that *have* occurred have been significant in regard to the development of the political class and its professionalization, because they typify single indicators of this process. Three reform processes or reform attempts shall be mentioned here: (1) the introduction of select committees within the House of Commons; (2) the establishment of a new behavioral code; and (3) the decentralization of the British polity.

(1) Until 1979 there were only a few opportunities for MPs to specialize in specific policy areas or to influence government policy at a formative stage (Norton 1997: 28).

During the 1970s more and more voices were heard calling for the introduction of select committees to scrutinize and influence government policies in particular areas and to create a more extensive process of deliberation and scrutiny than had existed before (Hawes 1993; Jogerst 1993). After the general election in 1979, the new Leader of the House, Norman St. John-Stevas, and backbenchers from both main parties pushed for change, which resulted in the introduction of select committees.[5] These committees supplemented the House of Commons' standing committees, appointed to consider a series of bills on related subjects. Standing committees proceed by debate, while select committees mostly proceed by the taking of evidence and the making of reports on their inquiries.

The departmental select committees have become a well-established and much-appreciated part of the parliamentary life (Norton 1990: 20). The committees fulfill those functions that reformers expected of them: they are an important means of specialization and they take influential effect on government, allowing scrutiny of particular sectors on a continuous basis not achievable on the floor of the House. There are now sixteen departmental select committees, so that each important governmental department can be overseen by a single committee. The committees give approximately 150 backbenchers not only the opportunity to specialize in a certain area, but also the chance to generate political capital from their specialization. The committees offer MPs the possibility of pursuing an alternative path outside the typical career pattern; here he or she can specialize, present himself or herself with a clear image, attract the attention of whips and the party leadership, and qualify for further political tasks. A select committee chairmanship is considered a prized post by many MPs, in particular by "Policy Advocates." The expansion of the select committees created new channels through which parliamentarians can influence policies. They also offer MPs interesting fields of activity. As a result, MPs devote a great deal of attention to the work of these committees, a tendency that is unlikely to be reversed. Besides the departmental select committees there are other groups of select committees: the so-called domestic committees give advice to the House and the Speaker related to the administration of the House; the scrutiny committees which are concerned with proposed legislation; and select committees considering external matters, such as the Committee of Public Accounts, the Committee on Public Administration, and the Environmental Audit Committee.

(2) Since the late 1980s the behavior of the political class has increasingly been criticized in the United Kingdom. Above all, the lack of transparency of MPs' finances and their "apparent readiness cynically to abuse their positions of trust" (Hodder-Williams 1996: 285) has come under public attack. At the same time the popularity of MPs has declined to a record low. Those politicians who demanded payment from companies or interest organizations for parliamentary questions ("cash for question issues") have fallen most deeply into disrepute. These ethical problems, mentioned frequently in the *Sunday Times*, have tarnished MPs' reputations to such an extent

---

[5] Philip Norton characterizes this reform as "the most significant [...] of the last half of the twentieth century" (Norton 2001: 46).

that politicians now take last place among all professional groups in their public standing (Riddell 2000).

As a result of this development, a Committee on Standards in Public Life under the chairmanship of Lord Nolan was appointed in October 1994 to examine current concerns about standards of conduct of all holders of public office, including issues relating to their financial and commercial activities. The Committee was charged with making recommendations for remedying the existing defects and with outlining regulations that would improve incumbents' reputations. The independent panel was constituted as a standing body with its members appointed for 3 years. The Committee's first report reflected public concerns about the conduct of MPs: "The Committee identified a climate of 'slackness' in parliamentary politics" (Oliver 1995: 592). In the opinion of the Committee, the root of this problem lay in the fact that MPs were not aware of the standards of conduct expected of them or had no precise understanding of those standards. Up to that time, there existed neither a list of standards of conduct nor was any limitation or ban on outside earnings. Many parliamentarians consider outside earnings as a legal and a legitimate way of improving their financial status. After all, entry into the House of Commons, particularly on the Conservative benches, may imply a pay cut for some new MPs.

Beyond this, the Nolan Committee's report contained several recommendations for the improvement of MPs' standing, most of which have been adopted by the House of Commons (for details see Gay 2001). The Committee recommended a new Code of Conduct for parliamentarians. According to the report, MPs should give precedence to the interests of their constituencies and to the public interest over all other interests. The terms of parliamentary service should also be made more transparent to the public (Oliver 1995; Rush 1997). Paid advocacy by members should be banned.

Another aspect of the professionalization of the political class in Britain is in evidence here: the setting of professional standards, as most occupational groups have done. At the same time, these standards lay down rules that provide a basis for measuring, investigating, and criticizing the conduct of MPs outside Parliament more easily. Effective enforcement requires that MPs accept the rules and have an interest in their maintenance. For the enforcement of the standards, the Nolan Committee recommended the introduction of a new Parliamentary Commissioner for Standards and of a Select Committee on Standards in Public Life. The Parliamentary Commissioner for Standards was established to investigate the operation of the Register of Members' Interests as well as complaints about the conduct of MPs and to give advice or guidance to individual MPs and the Select Committee on Standards and Privileges about the Code of Conduct and on all matters concerning conduct, propriety, and ethics (Woodhouse 1998). MPs are accountable for their conduct only to Parliament. There are sometimes calls for external control by, for example, the courts (Woodhouse 1998: 60), but so far this merely remains a topic for further discussion.

The new Political Parties, Elections and Referendums Act, passed in November 2000, established an Electoral Commission with a wide remit (Fisher 2001). The Act covers political donations and limits campaign spending at the national level in general elections. Its most significant impacts are an enhancement of the transparency of party fundraising and an enforcement for the main parties to evaluate their financial conduct (Fisher 2001: 699).

(3) The most significant new reform in the political system of Great Britain is the move towards more decentralization ("devolution"), animated by New Labour. In referenda in both Scotland and Wales a majority of voters opted for the introduction of a directly elected regional Parliament. The pro-devolution majority in Scotland was much larger than the very bare majority in Wales; the Scottish Parliament also has more far-reaching and taxing competencies than the Welsh one. Here, a new level of career opportunities for the political class seems to have emerged, because the reform has created new jobs in politics. The regional parliaments have established career positions for assistants, advisors, secretaries, and, above all, members. In addition to this, the Blair administration has announced plans to promote the process of decentralization in England, too. Office holding in local government is already one of the main paths to national elective office in Britain, and it is to be expected that its political importance will be increased, should New Labour realize its plans. Distinct local and regional career paths, as in the United States and Germany, are not unlikely to develop.

Other important reform proposals, which concern the recruitment and composition of the political class, shall only be mentioned briefly. Reform of the electoral system is debated again and again, not only because the current system of "first-past-the post," or plurality single-member districts, disproportionately favors the two main parties in the distribution of seats, but also because it discriminates against some population groups (ethnic minorities, women, persons under the age of 30 and above 60) in the nomination process (Hodder-Williams 1996: 293–4; see also Ingle 1997: 105–6). Critics of the electoral system are even of the opinion that the competitive dualism can explain the disdain for politicians in public opinion. However, since 1945 no significant reform of the electoral system on the national level has been implemented. On the other hand, for the regional Assemblies and Legislatures a mixed electoral system has been established. Electoral procedures for British Members of the European Parliament have also been revised: in place of the single member majoritarian system, a more proportional one was adopted.

Also, often discussed but never realized are proposals to reform the relation between Parliament and government to give Parliament greater power. But in this case as well, since 1979 no substantial change has occurred, because of a lack of interest on the part of the ruling party. After the General Election of 1997 a Select Committee on the Modernisation of the House was set up, which "had recommended some useful and sensible reforms, but which altered the effectiveness of scrutiny only at the margins" (Cowley and Stuart 2001: 238; cf. Riddell 2000: 248; Norton 2001). There are now new opportunities for backbenchers with the new parallel debating chamber in Westminster Hall and greater consultation in the legislative process, but the dominance of the executive has not been jeopardized. The Blair administration has also rejected any reform that might strengthen the competencies and political role of select committees *vis-à-vis* the government.

CONCLUSION

This chapter has shown the process of professionalization of the political class in Great Britain. The parties created the crucial preconditions for the emergence and establishment of the political class, and it was in their interest to accelerate the process of professionalization. Basic conditions have been improved through the steady increase of MPs' salaries since the 1970s, an expansion of political occupations, mechanisms for career maintenance—all of these being non-partisan measures. Driving this process was a change in the membership and organizational structure of the parties, which partially lost their ties to their original social bases and which needed the career politician to manage an ever greater number of more complex tasks. The emergence of the political class has then developed its own self-reinforcing dynamic: new supply found new demand. Once established, it is almost unthinkable that the political class will give up its position voluntarily. Every reform of the political system has to take this fact into account. On the contrary, the intra-party reforms of New Labour have accelerated the process of professionalization: the renunciation of the trade unions, the deprivation of party activists of their power base, and a new pragmatic view of politics give the career politician even more opportunities to act independently.

Moreover, previous institutional reforms have not changed the composition of the political class as much as they have strengthened the process of professionalization of the *existing* political class. Political networks within different policy areas have arisen. These networks foster the development of the career politician, who early in his or her career enters politics and wants to stay there; the networks facilitate both the entry into politics and remaining there. Establishing structures of communication to the party leadership, the constituency, and the media has become all-important for securing election and re-election. The establishment of the political class enabled the parties to control the recruitment process more firmly, but the question remains whether this is an outcome valued by the public.

REFERENCES

Adonis, Andrew (1993). *Parliament Today*. Manchester: Manchester University Press.

Bagehot, Walter (1964). *The English Constitution*. London: C. A. Watts.

Berrington, Hugh (1985). "MPs and their Constituents in Britain: The History of a Relationship", in V. Bogdanor (ed.), *Representatives of the People?* Aldershot: Gower, pp. 15–43.

Buck, Philip W. (1963). *Amateurs and Professionals in British Politics 1918–59*. Chicago: University of Chicago Press.

Campbell, Colin, and Wilson, Graham K. (1995). *The End of Whitehall: A Comparative Perspective*. Oxford: Blackwell.

Childs, Sarah (2002). "Hitting the Target: Are Labour Women MPs 'Acting for' Women?" *Parliamentary Affairs*, 55: 143–53.

Cowley, Philip (2000). "Legislatures and Assemblies", in P. Dunleavy, A. Gamble, I. Holliday, and G. Peele (eds), *Developments in British Politics 6*, New York: St. Martin's Press, pp. 108–26.

—— (2001). 'The Commons: Mr. Blair's Lapdog?'. *Parliamentary Affairs*, 54: 815–28.

Cowley, Philip, and Stuart, Mark (2001) "Parliament: a Few Headaches and a Dose of Modernisation". *Parliamentary Affairs*, 54: 238–56.

Crewe, Ivor (1985). "MPs and their Constituents in Britain: How Strong are the Links?", in V. Bogdanor (ed.), *Representatives of the People?* Aldershot: Gower, pp. 44–65.

Detterbeck, Klaus (2002). *Der Wandel politischer Parteien in Westeuropa: Eine vergleichende Untersuchung von Organisationsstrukturen, politischer Rolle und Wettbewerbsverhalten von Großparteien in Dänemark, Deutschland, Großbritannien und der Schweiz, 1960–1999.* Opladen: Leske + Budrich.

Fisher, Justin (2001). "Campaign Finance: Elections under New Rules". *Parliamentary Affairs*, 54: 689–700.

Gay, Oonagh (2001). *Parliamentary Standards*. Research Paper 01/102, London: House of Commons.

Grantham, Cliff (1989). "Parliament and Political Consultants". *Parliamentary Affairs*, 42: 503–18.

—— and Seymour-Ure, Colin (1990). "Political Consultants", in M. Rush (ed.), *Parliament and Pressure*. Oxford: Clarendon Press, pp. 45–84.

Hawes, Derek (1993). *Power on the Back Benches? The Growth of Select Committee Influence.* Bristol: SAUS Publications.

Heffernan, Richard (2001). *New Labour and Thatcherism. Political Change in Britain.* Houndmills: Palgrave.

Hodder-Williams, Richard (1996). "British Politicians: to Rehabilitate or Not?" *Parliamentary Affairs*, 49: 285–97.

Ingle, Stephen (1997). "British Political Parties in the Last Fifty Years", in L. Robins and B. Jones (eds), *Half a Century of British Politics*. Manchester: Manchester University Press, pp. 87–107.

Jogerst, Michael (1993). *Reform in the House of Commons: The Select Committee System.* Lexington: University Press of Kentucky.

Jun, Uwe (1996). "SPD and Labour Party: Intra-Party Reforms in Comparative Perspective". *German Politics*, 5: 58–80.

—— and Kuper, Ernst (1997). "Funktion und Wirksamkeit von transnationalen parlamentarischen Versammlungen bei der Lösung internationaler Konflikte", in E. Kuper and U. Jun (eds), *Nationales Interesse und integrative Politik in transnationalen parlamentarischen Versammlungen.* Opladen: Leske + Budrich, pp. 341–67.

King, Anthony (1981). "The Rise of the Career Politician—and its Consequences". *British Journal of Political Science*, 11: 249–85.

Lovenduski, Joni (1997). "Gender Politics: A Breakthrough for Women?" *Parliamentary Affairs*, 50: 708–19.

Mancuso, Maureen (1995). *The Ethical World of British MPs.* Montreal: McGill-Queens University Press.

Norris, Pippa (1997). *Electoral Change since 1945.* Oxford: Blackwell.

—— and Lovenduski, Joni (1995). *Political Recruitement, Gender, Race and Class in the British Parliament.* Cambridge: Cambridge University Press.

—— and Lovenduski, Joni (1997). United Kingdom. In P. Norris (ed.), *Passages to Power.* Cambridge: Cambridge University Press, 158–86.

Norton, Philip (1990). "Parliament in the United Kingdom: Balancing Effectiveness and Consent?", in P. Norton (ed.), *Parliaments in Western Europe.* London: Frank Cass, pp. 10–31.

—— (1994). *The British Polity*, 3rd edition. London: Longman.

—— (1997). "Roles and Behaviour of British MPs", in W. C. Mueller and T. Saalfeld (eds), *Members of Parliament in Western Europe*. London: Frank Cass, pp. 17–31.

—— (2001). "Parliament", in A. Seldon (ed.), *The Blair Effect*. London: Little, Brown, pp. 43–64.

—— and Wood, David (1993). *Back from Westminster: British Members of Parliament and their Constituents*. Lexington: University Press of Kentucky.

Oliver, Dawn (1995). "The Committee on Standards in Public Life: Regulating the Conduct of Members in Parliament", *Parliamentary Affairs*, 48: 590–601.

Panitch, Leo, and Leys, Colin (1997). *The End of Parliamentary Socialism: From New Left to New Labour*. London: Verso.

Pattie, Charles, Johnston, Ron, and Stuart, Mark (1998). "Voting Without Party?", in P. Cowley (ed.), *Conscience and Parliament*, London: Frank Cass, pp. 146–76.

Perrigo, Sarah (1996). "Women and Change in the Labour Party 1979–1995". *Parliamentary Affairs*, 49: 116–29.

Riddell, Peter (1993). *Honest Opportunism: The Rise of the Career Politician*. London: Hamish Hamilton.

—— (1995). "The Impact of the Rise of the Career Politician". *Journal of Legislative Studies*, 1: 186–91.

—— (2000). *Parliament under Blair*. London: Politico's Publishing.

Rose, Richard (1986). "British MPS: More Bark than Bite?", in E. N. Suleiman (ed.), *Parliaments and Parliamentarians in Democratic Politics*. New York: Holmes and Meier, pp. 8–40.

Rush, Michael (ed.) (1990). *Parliament and Pressure Politics*. Oxford: Clarendon Press.

—— (1994). "Career Patterns in British Politics: First Choose your Party…". *Parliamentary Affairs*, 47: 566–82.

—— (1995). *Opportunity Structures in Historical Perspective: The UK Case*, unpublished manuscript, presented at the ECPR Workshop, Bordeaux.

—— (1997). "Damming the Sleaze: the New Code of Conduct and the Outside Interests of MPs in the British House of Commons". *Journal of Legislative Studies*, 3: 10–28.

—— (2001*a*). *The Role of the Member of Parliament Since 1868: From Gentlemen to Players*. Oxford: Oxford University Press.

—— (2001*b*). *Parallel but Separate: Political Recruitment at Three Levels in the UK*, unpublished manuscript, presented at the ECPR Joint Sessions of Workshops, Grenoble.

—— and Cromwell, Valerie (2000). "Continuity and Change: Legislative Recruitment in the United Kingdom 1868–1999", in H. Best, and M. Cotta (eds.), *Parliamentary Representatives in Europe 1848–2000*. Oxford: Oxford University Press, pp. 463–92.

Saggar, Shamit (1997). "Racial Politics". *Parliamentary Affairs*, 50: 693–707.

Scarrow, Susan E. (1997). "Political Career Paths and the European Parliament". *Legislative Studies Quarterly*, 22: 253–63.

Searing, Donald D. (1994). *Westminster's World: Understanding Political Roles*. Cambridge: Harvard University Press.

—— (1995). "Backbench and Leadership Roles in The House of Commons". *Parliamentary Affairs*, 48: 418–37.

Shaw, Eric (2001). "New Labour: New Pathways to Parliament". *Parliamentary Affairs*, 54: 35–53.

Squires, Judith, and Wickham-Jones, Mark (2002). "Mainstreaming in Westminster and Whitehall: From Labour's Ministry for Women to the Women and Equality Unit". *Parliamentary Affairs*, 55: 57–70.

Theakston, Kevin (1987). *Junior Ministers in British Government*. Oxford: Blackwell.

Walker, Aileen (2001). *Parliamentary Pay and Allowances: Current Rates*. Research Paper 01/43. London: House of Commons Library.

Webb, Paul (2000). *The Modern British Party System*. London: Sage.

Westlake, Martin (1994). *Britain's Emerging Euro-Elite? The British in the Directly Elected European Parliament, 1979–1992*. Aldershot: Dartmouth.

Woodhouse, Diana (1998). "The Parliamentary Commissioner for Standards: Lessons from the 'Cash for Questions' Inquiry". *Parliamentary Affairs*, 51: 51–61.

Wring, Dominic, Baker, David, and Seawright, David (2000). "Panelism in Action: Labour's 1999 European Parliamentary Candidate Selection". *The Political Quarterly*, 71: 234–45.

10

Ireland: Party Loyalists with a Personal Base

MICHAEL GALLAGHER

POLITICAL PROFESSIONALIZATION IN HISTORICAL PERSPECTIVE

The independent Irish state came into existence in 1922. Before this time, Ireland was part of the United Kingdom, and the question of professionalization of the political elite was subject to forces operating at the level of the entire United Kingdom. The franchise was narrow, and Irish Members of Parliament (MPs) tended to be landowners or businessmen, in other words men who had substantial financial resources of their own.

The Irish political elite was transformed in the period 1918–22. Prior to 1918, Ireland had sent around 100 MPs to the House of Commons in Westminster. From the 1870s, most of these had represented nationalist parties (pressing for greater autonomy for Ireland within the UK), and the rest were unionist (committed to the retention of the existing constitutional arrangements). However, a constitutional revolution took place in the period 1916–22, as a result of which the old nationalist political elite was swept away by a new party, *Sinn Féin*, which was committed to complete independence for Ireland. *Sinn Féin* won a majority of the votes in Ireland at the 1918 Westminster general election, and its elected representatives constituted themselves as the first *Dáil* (lower house of Parliament) of an independent Irish state (Coakley 1994). The twenty-six counties of southern Ireland became independent in 1922 (first as the Irish Free State, subsequently as the Republic of Ireland), so a new and predominantly young political elite found itself in control of a new state. This abrupt transformation of the power structure precluded any gradual process of "professionalization" that might have taken place in more settled circumstances. The new political elite that emerged in the early 1920s, and that was to dominate the country for the next 40 years, were in many cases "politicians by accident," who, in Weber's terms, were, initially at least, "living for politics" more than "living off politics."

THE INSTITUTIONAL CONTEXT

Ireland is a unitary state with weak local government. Power lies with the national government, which is responsible to the lower chamber of the Parliament, *Dáil Éireann*.

The 166 members of the *Dáil* (*Teachtaí Dála*—TDs) are directly elected in forty-two constituencies, whereas the sixty members of the upper house, *Seanad Éireann*, are indirectly elected. Together both chambers make up the *Oireachtas*, or Parliament. All members of the government must belong to one of the houses of Parliament, and in practice all are members of the *Dáil*—there have been only two ministers from the *Seanad* since the 1930s. The government sits in the *Dáil*, and while being answerable to it, also in effect controls it, for the Irish parliamentary system is modeled on that of Westminster, and despite some strengthening of the committee system in the past 15 years, parliamentary committees do not constitute an alternative locus of power. Establishing a political career, therefore, depends crucially on being elected to the *Dáil*.

The electoral system has a significant impact on the recruitment patterns of the parliamentarians. The *Dáil* is elected by proportional representation by means of the single transferable vote (PR-STV), an electoral system that is based on multi-member constituencies (on the average four per district) and invites voters to rank candidates in order of their preference (for the electoral system, see Sinnott 1999). Voters are not bound by candidates' party affiliation; they can allocate their preferences on the basis of any factor that is important to them, which may be party or may be an issue that cuts across party lines or locality (candidates always win most support close to their own home base). Candidates are listed on the ballot in alphabetical order, not by party, although their party affiliations are stated.

This makes elections very competitive and has major implications for recruitment to the political class. It means that every candidate is in competition with every other candidate. As in PR-list systems with the preferential vote (Denmark, Finland, Switzerland, and others), there is competition among candidates within each party to win as much personal support as possible. Incumbents of the largest party, *Fianna Fáil*, are more likely to lose their seat to a fellow *Fianna Fáil* candidate than to a candidate of another party. Incumbents of the second-largest party, *Fine Gael*, are also vulnerable to intraparty defeat; around a third of defeated *Fine Gael* TDs are ousted by a fellow *Fine Gael* candidate (Gallagher 2000: 97).

This means that there is no such thing as a "safe seat" that anyone in the party can hand to an aspirant member of the political class. While support from within the party organization may ease an aspirant's path to selection as a candidate in a particular constituency, this does not guarantee a seat precisely because he or she is in competition with the other candidates of the party. Even candidates of smaller parties, which usually nominate only one candidate per constituency, need to build up some personal base of support to be elected, because the solid party vote in the constituency is likely to be too small to ensure election.

For this reason, TDs, or aspiring TDs, must be "entrepreneurs" (see introductory chapter of this volume) in the sense that they need to establish a degree of personal support and recognition among the electorate. It is not enough merely to rely on the party vote in a constituency; to be successful, candidates need to ensure themselves of personal support within, or in addition to, the purely party vote. TDs are, thus, very active in casework, acting as brokers between constituents and the state to rectify constituents' grievances.

However, this does not mean that TDs in Ireland are not also "backbenchers." In parliamentary systems where the electoral system allows voters to express a choice among candidates (PR-list with preferential voting or PR-STV), MPs will combine elements of both entrepreneur and backbencher. Individual politicians compete electorally against others of their own party, but this does not necessarily—and certainly does not in Ireland—lead to incohesive parties. On the contrary, the parliamentary groups in Ireland are very cohesive, and voting against the party line (or even abstaining) on any issue, no matter how minor, is likely to lead to disciplinary action, most probably expulsion from the parliamentary caucus.

Many aspects of the institutional structure of the Republic of Ireland conform to those suggested in the "backbencher" model. As already observed, Ireland is a unitary state in which government dominates Parliament, and individual TDs are not active or significant in the legislative process. Political parties are highly cohesive. Whether one considers them "strong" depends on what this term means (Mair 1997: 120–54); certainly they are rather poorly funded and offer slim employment prospects, but at the same time they dominate political life. Interest groups are centralized, and while the major economic interest groups in particular are heavily involved in the formation of economic policy, interest groups are not important actors in determining elections (see Murphy 1999; O'Halpin and Connolly 1999).

THE POLITICAL CLASS

Size and Composition

Defining the political class, as always, is not straightforward, especially in countries such as Ireland, where the phrase is not common currency. In Ireland, it could reasonably be argued, the political class does not extend much if at all beyond the 166 members of the *Dáil* and the sixty members of the *Seanad*. These 226 individuals include, as we have pointed out, not only all Members of Parliament, but also all members of government.

Of course, one could object that the political class should not be defined quite so narrowly. The President of Ireland is elected directly by the people and, though in most regards fulfilling the same functions as a constitutional monarch, does have certain potentially significant political roles in specified situations (Gallagher 1999*b*). Judges of the High Court and the Supreme Court are appointed by the government, and some of their decisions inevitably have political consequences, though there is a high degree of separation between judiciary and executive, and the judges would not generally be thought of as belonging to the "political class." Likewise, the government makes a number of appointments in public enterprises—to their boards, for example, and this constitutes a modest source of patronage for party supporters. Yet, the government's appointees are, for the most part, hard to conceive as belonging to the political class in the same way as full-time politicians do.

The parties themselves have in the past been weakly funded and collectively employ only around forty people, most of whom are clerical and administrative staff

Table 10.1   *Occupations of elected deputies, 2002*

	Manual employee	Non-manual employee	Commercial	Farmer	Lower professional	Higher professional	Total
N	4	35	28	21	37	41	166
%	2.4	21.1	16.9	12.7	22.3	24.7	100

Source: Gallagher (2003: 115).

(Farrell 1994: 223). There has been some modest expansion in recent years due to annual public subsidies set at €1.27 million in 1998, increasing in line with inflation in subsequent years (Laver and Marsh 1999: 158). Even so, the parties do not have jobs in their own apparatus to offer to defeated TDs, nor is the apparatus, with very rare exceptions, a breeding ground or launching pad for a political career. Only the party general secretaries, and at most one or two others in party head offices, can realistically be seen as having any input into the political process and as playing roles that are political as well as administrative.

Because Ireland is a centralized and unitary state, it lacks provincial or regional government, and local government is not professionalized.[1] Although local government is an important recruiting ground for national politicians, as we shall see later, it is not particularly significant in itself. In other words, there are no professionalized positions in either party or government structures below the national level, and very few in party structures even at the national level.

Consequently, in the rest of this chapter we shall concentrate on members of *Dáil Éireann*, the directly elected lower house of Parliament. What type of people are parliamentarians in Ireland? We can examine their backgrounds on a number of key dimensions: occupation, education, and gender. We shall concentrate on the *Dáil* elected in 2002, the 29th *Dáil*.

We use a sixfold classification scheme for the occupations of *Dáil* deputies, in line with standard practice in studies of Irish legislators (see Table 10.1). The manual employee and non-manual employee (i.e. white-collar workers) categories are fairly self-evident; in the *Dáil* elected in 2002 the former include, for example, a printing operative and a technician, while examples of the latter category include clerical officers, laboratory technicians, and secretaries. The "commercial" category comprises mainly small businessmen or businesswomen and is needed to analyze parliamentarians in Ireland because of the significant number who hold occupations such as shopkeepers, auctioneers, publicans, and directors of small companies. Farmers are another self-evident category. Among professionals a distinction can be drawn between "lower professionals" (mainly schoolteachers) and a higher qualified group

---

[1] The local level of government in Ireland comprises five urban county boroughs and 29 rural county councils with relatively small competences. Below that level, cities and greater villages have their own governing bodies—with even fewer competences. The terms regional and local politics used in this text refer to the county councils/boroughs.

with academic training, called "higher professionals," which includes lawyers, doctors, lecturers, accountants, and architects.

In all countries, political elites are not a microcosm of those who elect them (Norris 1996: 186–7), and Ireland is no exception to the general pattern: there has always been a strikingly strong representation of TDs from the "commercial" category (men from this sector were very powerful in nationalist politics during the pre-independence period), which in analysis of most other Parliaments is not thought large enough to warrant a separate category. The explanation for this lies not in any great profusion of small entrepreneurs in Ireland—they comprise less than 5 percent of the population—but in the political resources with which their occupations endow them. Publicans or auctioneers are in daily contact with a wide range of people in their communities, something that is especially important in rural Ireland, which well illustrates Czudnowski's observation that "candidacies originate in central linkage positions in a communications network" (1975: 231). Such occupations help to increase the profile of a potential politician both among the wider public and among party activists, who play a key role in the candidate selection process. Self-employed people have the additional advantage that they can take time off work at will for political activity.

Examining the occupational patterns since the foundation of the state, five features stand out. First, the number of farmers has steadily decreased, from a peak of over a third in 1937 to fewer than an eighth in 2002; though over the past 20 years it has remained steady. This long-term drop mirrors the declining role of agriculture in Ireland, which in the 1920s accounted for over half the workforce but now makes up only 10–15 percent of it. Second, the "commercial" category, while still large, is declining in strength; it accounted for almost a third of all TDs in 1969 and 1973 but had dropped to about a sixth by 2002. Third, the number of deputies with a professional background has been increasing steadily since the 1960s, especially among "lower" professionals, who are mainly schoolteachers. Schoolteachers have the advantage that, if elected to Parliament, they can retain their job while appointing a substitute teacher, though this does not in itself explain why the trend has been so strongly upward. Fourth, the number of TDs who have had any experience in manual labor is small indeed and has varied little over the last 70 years. Here, the Irish pattern is not exceptional. Finally, the number of full-time deputies has increased greatly over the last 25 years or so. In the past, many deputies combined their parliamentary work with their previous occupation; now all but a minority are full-time politicians.

As we might expect, professionals have by far the best record when it comes to advancement to cabinet level. Of the seventy-nine professionals in the 29th *Dáil*, 28 percent have been ministers, compared with only 8 percent of deputies from the other occupational groups. A control for seniority—which makes sense since, naturally, newer TDs are less likely to have advanced far up the greasy pole—demonstrates the relationship even more starkly. We can predict that the proportion of professionals in the *Dáil* will continue to rise, given that they are, on average, younger than other occupational groups.

Education is very strongly correlated with membership of political elites in virtually all political systems (Putnam 1976: 26–8, 35–6). Ireland is not an exception to

Table 10.2 *TDs with university degree at selected elections, 1932–2002*

Election	1932	1943	1961	1973	1982(Nov.)	1992	2002
%	24	21	28	28	38	49	49

Source: Gallagher (1995: 5; 2003: 115).

this, but the proportion of deputies with a university education has always been lower than in many other countries. At most elections up to the late 1940s the proportion of university-educated deputies hovered around the quarter mark, and not until 1981 did it reach a third (see Table 10.2). By 1992 almost half of all TDs had a degree, but this proportion has not risen subsequently. Education is of course strongly related to occupation, and the increase in recent years is tied to the increase in the number of professionals in the *Dáil*. Whereas the great majority of professionals in the 29th *Dáil* (68 out of 79, or 86 percent) had an academic degree, only 15 of the other 87 (17 percent) did.

This increase in well-educated TDs with a professional background has had some impact on the nature of the *Dáil* and its relationship with government. The *Dáil* has often been derided in the past as an unusually supine Parliament, a "woefully inadequate institution" (Dinan 1986: 71). In recent years, however, it has made serious reform efforts within the limits of the "Westminster model", partly due to pressure from backbench TDs who have the ability and the desire to contribute to national political matters but who lacked any opportunity to do so under existing structures. In response to this pressure, an expanded committee system has been introduced and bills are now reviewed by relatively small, specialist committees rather than by the entire *Dáil* as before (Gallagher 1999a).

Like occupation, education is strongly related to the achievement of ministerial office. Graduates are significantly more likely than non-graduates to be promoted to the cabinet. In the *Dáil* elected in 2002, university-educated TDs were newer and about 4 years younger than non-graduates, so the increase in the proportion of university-educated TDs can be expected to continue.

Women are under-represented in virtually every Parliament (Randall 1987). It is hardly surprising that the Parliament in a strongly Catholic and—in the past—predominantly agricultural country such as Ireland should be particularly male-dominated. Over the 70-year period from 1922 to 1992, only 4 percent of the almost 4,000 *Dáil* seats won were taken by women. Moreover, for many years even those few women who did succeed in being elected to the *Dáil* tended to be preceded by a male relative, usually a deceased father or husband, who in a sense supplied them with their political credentials. Even as recently as 1977, of the mere twenty-five different women to have been elected to the *Dáil* over the previous 55 years, only five had not been preceded by a male relative (see Table 10.3). In addition, no woman was appointed to even a junior ministerial position until 1977, and none was appointed to the cabinet until 1979 (Galligan 1999; Galligan and Wilford 1999).

The change in recent years has thus been all the more dramatic because of the very low base from which women started. The percentage of women in Parliament has

Table 10.3 *Women members of* Dáil Éireann, *1977–2002*

Election	Number in *Dáil*	%	Elected for first time	Total number since 1922[a]	
				Total	Unrelated[b]
1977	6	4.1	3	25	5
1981	11	6.6	7	33	11
1982 (1)	8	4.8	1	34	12
1982 (2)	14	8.4	3	37	14
1987	14	8.4	5	42	17
1989	13	7.8	2	44	19
1992	20	12.0	9	53	26
1997	20	12.0	5	61	30
2002	22	13.3	5	68	34

[a] Total number of different women elected since 1922.
[b] Unrelated to independence figure or former TD.

Notes: One woman was elected for the first time at a by-election between the 1977 and 1981 general elections, a further three at by-elections between the 1992 and 1997 general elections, and two more between 1997 and 2002.

more than trebled since 1977, and, of the forty-three women elected for the first time since then, twenty-nine have made it to the *Dáil* without having had a trail blazed by a male relative. In comparative perspective, though, Ireland is still well behind the West European average.

Compared with male TDs in the 29th *Dáil*, women Members tend to be better educated and are more likely to have a professional occupational background—this applies to 73 percent of them, compared with 44 percent of men. They were about 7 years younger than their male counterparts at the 2002 election, which bodes well for an increase in the number of women TDs in years to come.

Political Recruitment and Political Careers

In every political system, candidate selectors play a key gatekeeping role. This role is especially powerful when the electoral system denies voters any chance to reject or amend the choices made by the selectors. For example, when the electoral system is based on PR with non-preferential lists (Germany, Israel, and Spain), the voters must either accept the selectors' rankings as they stand or reject the party list altogether. Likewise, in single-member constituency systems (Britain), there is no choice of candidate for the voters. As we have seen, matters are different in preferential versions of PR. The selectors within the party organization pick the candidates, but the voters can decide which of these individuals to support above others.

In other words, in such countries as Germany or Israel the party organization presents voters a fixed menu, and voters have only the choice of accepting it in its entirety or rejecting it. In contrast, in such countries as Ireland, Denmark, Finland,

and Switzerland, the selectors offer a menu, and party voters can choose freely from that menu (but only from that menu). In the United States of America there is no one with the power even to present a menu; any aspiring candidate for Parliament can present himself or herself as an *à la carte* option under the banner of one of the two main parties.

In Ireland, candidate selection varies little among most of the parties (Laver and Marsh 1999). The most important actors in the process are ordinary party members, who select their party's candidates in each of the 42 multi-member *Dáil* constituencies. Around a third of all party members take part directly in this process. The exceptional case is Fine Gael, in which all members have the right to participate directly, and a 1999 survey of members found that about two-thirds did so (Gallagher and Marsh 2002: 89). Naturally, aspiring candidates of the major parties do not simply sit back and hope that local members select them; they do their best to build up their own personal following in the local party organization. The national centre of the party (the national executive and/or the leadership) has two powers concerning candidate selection. First, it may veto candidates selected locally, a power that is very rarely exercised. Second, it may add names to those selected locally, a power that is more commonly used, though often the person added to the ticket is someone who failed to be selected locally and whose addition to the ticket may smooth ruffled feathers at local level. Incumbents are almost invariably reselected. Where several candidates are picked, there is little effort to produce a "balanced ticket" except with regard to locality. In other words, while a party's candidates in one constituency will usually come from different parts of the constituency, there is no attempt to balance gender, age, or social class. Occasionally a party will recruit a candidate from outside the party organization, such as from a women's or a farmers' organization, but such cases are rare. Moreover, unless they are handled carefully, such attempts to "parachute-in" a candidate over the heads of the party members can lead to resentment from the members and prove counter-productive. Thus, for a TD being reelected depends crucially on (1) being reselected as a party candidate, and (2) receiving enough personal support from the voters to be elected.

It might seem that TDs are, therefore, fairly independent of the national party leadership, and, in particular, that they can vote independently on issues in the *Dáil*—safe in the knowledge that provided they keep their local support, both among party members and voters, there is little effective sanction the national leadership can employ against them. One might expect the result to be incohesive parliamentary parties whose members respond to local rather than national imperatives. However, as we have already observed, this is decidedly not the case; the Irish parliamentary parties are extremely cohesive, with abstentions from the party line, let alone opposition to it, being very infrequent and heavily punished.

The archetypal TD enters the *Dáil* via local government. He or she—usually the former—is in the late thirties and tends to remain a local government member even after election to the *Dáil*. Looking at routes to Parliament, a near essential—especially in rural Ireland—is the possession of local roots and ideally a track record of activity within the constituency. The best way of establishing such a record is by being a county councillor. At every election since 1927, at least 50 percent of TDs have been members of local government before entering the *Dáil*. The tendency seems to have been intensifying since the 1960s, reaching 75 percent in 2002 (Gallagher 1995: 8–9, 17; 2003: 113–14). This is not, of course, unusual in a comparative context (Putnam 1976: 51). What is less usual, though by no means unique, is that even those TDs who do manage to reach the *Dáil* without first being elected to local government usually make a point of picking up the minor prize later: in the 2002 *Dáil*, for example, twenty of the forty-two TDs who were elected to the *Dáil* before they were local government members subsequently achieved election to a local authority, leaving just twenty-two TDs (13 percent of the total) who had never belonged to a local political body.

Related to this is the *cumul des mandats*. TDs usually retain their membership of local authorities after election to the *Dáil*; only ministers must resign their local seats. Remaining a county councillor after reaching the national Parliament increases the TD's opportunities to remain in the public eye, keeps the TD in close contact with his or her home area, and ensures that the local authority seat is not used by a potential rival to build up a political base. At the time of the 2002 election, 102 (61 percent) of the deputies were simultaneously members of a local authority.

The small number of TDs without experience in local governing bodies, and to some extent those who become TDs before becoming local authority members, tend to be more successful when it comes to entering government. It seems that whereas most aspiring TDs have to demonstrate brokerage abilities—that is, the ability to be effective representatives of the local and personal interests of their constituents—by work on a local council before they can hope to be elected, people of perceived ministerial ability, ideally professionals with an university education, may be exempted from this requirement; and these TDs are more likely to be appointed to government.

Although winning one's spurs by local government membership is the most common way of building up a political base, there is an easier method of acquiring one: inherit it. Studies of *Dáil* deputies have consistently stressed the high proportion of TDs who are related to previous TDs; the practice of parties nominating a relative of a deceased TD to contest the resulting by-election began as early as the 1930s. In the 2002 *Dáil*, thirty-seven TDs (22 percent) were related to one or more former or current TDs who preceded them into the *Dáil*: to be precise, there were nineteen sons, seven daughters, four brothers, three grandsons, one nephew, one granddaughter, one sister, and one son-in-law.

In the early Parliaments after independence, the age at entry often was very low because so many TDs were "politicians by accident", as already explained, but this age subsequently rose and on occasions reached the mid-forties. Recently the figure seems to have stabilized: at each of the six most recent elections the age at entry of TDs was between 37 and 39 years.

Being first elected at a young age is a great help to those hoping to become government ministers, as the prospects of entering cabinet are inversely related to age at first entry to Parliament. The reason for this is not difficult to see: with the average minister having been first elected to the *Dáil* about 12 years before being appointed

                    •

to the cabinet—the average figure for the twenty-nine TDs elected in 2002 who have at some stage been cabinet members is 11.8 years—those TDs who enter the *Dáil* at an older age find it hard to build up the required degree of seniority before they either look too old to be appointable, find themselves on the opposition benches at a crucial time, or simply lose their seats. The average age of all TDs has also been fairly stable over the past decade or more, ranging from 45 to 49 years after the five most recent elections. Most TDs are in their 40s or 50s; in the 29th *Dáil* only 15 percent were under 40, just 4 percent were under 30, and 8 percent were over 60 years old.

There is no data on the length of parliamentary careers, but job security seems reasonably high. Donnelly (1993: 8) reports that each of the 978 individuals being elected to the *Dáil* over the 1923–92 period was elected 3.9 times on average, which would mean around 12 years. Those elected in 2002 had been elected 3.3 times on average, and had entered the *Dáil* 9 years earlier. Although individual TDs can be voted out by the people, TDs have a high survival rate. On average, at the twenty-four elections of the 1927–97 period, 75 percent of TDs were re-elected, with 8 percent retiring and 17 percent being defeated (Gallagher 2000: 94). As far as is known, many of those defeated returned to their previous jobs where this was possible.

Being a backbencher is not a position of power. Given that, as we have said, government comes close to controlling Parliament, ambitious TDs want to be members of the government. Positions such as committee chairs are seen as a consolation for those not appointed to government rather than desiderata in their own right. Being re-elected is crucial, since new TDs are rarely appointed to government and, as we have seen, one has to be in the *Dáil* for quite a number of years before one can expect to enter the cabinet.

Even if the focus of this paper is on the *Dáil* as the directly elected lower house, brief mention could also be made of the upper house, *Seanad Éireann*. Its sixty Members come from three routes: forty-three are indirectly elected by an electorate body consisting mainly of members of local government, six are elected by university graduates, and eleven are appointed by the Prime Minister. The *Seanad* has few powers but can be a useful base for an aspiring TD, and, moreover, some defeated TDs seek election to the *Seanad* to keep themselves in the public eye prior to launching another bid for election to the *Dáil*. For example, at the 2002 election, ten of the sixty outgoing Senators were elected to the *Dáil*, while at the ensuing *Seanad* election, ten of those elected were ex-TDs defeated in the *Dáil* election and a further fifteen had also unsuccessfully contested the *Dáil* election (Gallagher and Weeks 2003).[2] Reform of the *Seanad* has been mooted several times in recent years; for example, in 2002 a parliamentary committee recommended that forty-eight of its Members should be directly elected with the remaining twelve appointed by the *Taoiseach* (All-Party Oireachtas Committee 2002: 38). However, past recommendations for change have not had any impact and it remains to be seen whether things are any different now.

---

[2] The legislative terms of the *Dáil* and the *Seanad* are equal in length; the elections to the Senate take place shortly after the *Dáil* is elected.

Living off Politics

Over the years, membership of Parliament has come to be accepted as a profession rather than a pastime for amateurs whose main income derived from other sources. TDs were always paid, but for many years the payment, which was very low, was termed an "allowance" rather than a salary or wage. This payment is currently about €69,000 per annum. Supreme Court judges receive €176,000 and High Court judges €166,000. About half of a TD's salary is exempt from tax. Pay rises are determined by the Review Body on Higher Remuneration in the Public Sector, which receives arguments from politicians but need not defer to them. For example, in 1996 TDs submitted a case to this body that their salary should be increased by about 30 percent, but it awarded them a rise of only 3.3 percent (Review Body 1996: 76–7). Similarly, when in 2000 MPs suggested that their salaries should be linked to a particular civil service grade, the review body agreed, but recommended a lower grade (Review Body 2000: 57, 60). The body reported that one difficulty in trying to decide a "fair" level of remuneration for the work done by TDs was that their workload varies greatly. Whereas up to the mid-1970s many TDs had a full-time occupation outside politics which they carried on simultaneously with their parliamentary duties, and there is no legal prohibition on what other work they may engage in, nowadays the great majority of them are full-time politicians.

TDs also receive allowances (at the civil service mileage rate) for travel between Parliament and their constituencies, plus a "day allowance" and overnight allowance when attending sessions of Parliament (which normally meets only on Tuesdays, Wednesdays, and Thursdays). In 1990 payments to the 131 non-office holding TDs under this heading came to €11,802 per head (Review Body 1992: 186). They are also allowed free phone calls (subject to certain constraints), and, as of 1992, free postage for up to 1,250 letters per month, and 500 free photocopies per month (Review Body 1992: 184–5). In 1990 it was estimated that the telephone facilities amounted to approximately €5,000 per TD and the mailing rights to €5,700 (Review Body 1992: 185). They also have a "constituency telephone allowance" up to a maximum of €2,500, plus a non-taxable expense allowance, of up to €5,000 to cover travel within the constituency (information from the Houses of the *Oireachtas*). They are given the necessary funding to employ one assistant, who works either in the TD's parliamentary or constituency office.

Pension rights are rather complicated (for a historical account, see Review Body 1992: 189–94). Members of the *Dáil* and *Seanad* have to contribute 6 percent of their salaries to a pension scheme, and after 3 years in Parliament they qualify for a pension—payable from the age of 50—of 2.5 percent of their final salary for each year in Parliament, up to a maximum of two-thirds of their final salary, plus a lump sum of 7.5 percent of their salary. Those with fewer than 3 years in Parliament are allowed to receive refunds of their contributions. Those members who were first elected in 1989 or before can avail of an older scheme, now phased out, under which they can draw a pension as soon as they lose their seats, regardless of their age.

Provision for severance pay was introduced in 1992. Deputies with at least 6 months' service who retire or are defeated at an election receive a lump sum equivalent to 2 months' salary. Furthermore, if they have at least 3 years' service, they receive additional monthly payments based on length of service, up to a maximum of 12 months, the first six of which are paid at 75 percent of monthly salary and the remainder at 50 percent.

TDs do not receive money from their parties; on the contrary, in many cases their party requires them to pay a proportion, perhaps a tenth, of their salary to it. Nor, as far as is known, do interest groups pay any income to TDs; however, only since the mid-1990s have TDs been obliged by law to declare their interests and extra-parliamentary income (if any). While the overall package for TDs thus puts them well above the average income, it is fair to say that the workload involved is such that very few people would enter politics merely for the financial benefits it will bring.

THE POLITICAL CLASS AND INSTITUTIONAL REFORM

Whether there is any significant degree of alienation from the political system is hard to say. Turnout at elections is low and has been declining since the 1960s; turnout at the 2002 general election was the lowest at any election since 1923. This might be taken as a sign of declining interest in and attachment to the conventional political system. On the other hand, it has been suggested that while many people might have a low opinion of "politicians" generally, they may retain a high opinion of their own specific representatives, who find it necessary to maintain a strong and active local profile and to be available and accessible to their constituents in need of assistance or advice.

Regarding public attitudes to politicians and money, Irish politics were, for long, seen as virtually untainted by corruption or scandal, but events in the mid-1990s changed this perception. After it emerged that a leading businessman had made large secret donations to two prominent politicians, one a former Prime Minister, a tribunal established to investigate the matter concluded that both had behaved improperly and, at the very least, had not declared all their income to the tax authorities. An opinion poll conducted shortly after the publication of the report found that 62 percent of those questioned believed there was widespread financial wrong-doing in the *Dáil*, and 79 percent believed in the existence of "business-political 'cosy cartels'" (Irish Marketing Services poll, cf. *Irish Independent*, 30 August 1997). A further report, issued by the Flood Tribunal (named after its chairman) which was set up to examine allegations of planning irregularities in north county Dublin, concluded in September 2002 that one of the politicians under scrutiny, the former senior minister Ray Burke, had behaved corruptly over a long period. All in all, it became possible to speak of a "crisis in the Irish body politic" (Murphy 2000).

Institutional reform rarely finds itself close to the top of the political agenda. In the mid-1990s it was highlighted by an expert committee: the Constitutional Review

Group (CRG) was established in 1995 by the government to examine the country's constitution, which dates from 1937, and make recommendations for reform. The committee produced a large report (CRG 1996) covering all aspects of the constitution. On the whole, most of its suggestions have little relevance to the present discussion, though one exception concerns the electoral system. Many TDs are opposed to the retention of PR-STV, not least because of the intraparty electoral competition that it generates, and if PR-STV were not enshrined in the constitution (which can be amended only by the people voting in a referendum), Parliament would probably have changed it by now. The CRG weighed up the pros and cons of a change, and reached a cautious conclusion: The existing PR-STV system has popular support and should not be changed without careful assessment of the consequences, and that if a change is to be made, a PR-list system or a German-style two-route system would be the most satisfactory (CRG 1996: 60).

If Ireland were to adopt a non-preferential list system, such as the electoral systems used in Israel or Spain, or the German system, it is possible that the nature of the political class would change. There would then be a certain number of safe seats that the selectors (be they ordinary party members or party leaders) could in effect award to favored aspirants. Promoters of change argue that under such a system, experts and technocrats who have no stomach for the political in-fighting that is seen as necessary at the moment to secure a party nomination could be brought into Parliament. Once there, they would not have to spend their time on constituency minutiae or internal party rivalries. Defenders of the status quo suggest that the politicians awarded safe seats are more likely to be "party hacks" than technocrats, and that such an electoral system would reduce accountability by freeing politicians from any obligation to respond to the wishes of their electors. Whatever the truth, it is a fact that the abandonment of PR-STV would reduce the voters' power to choose their representatives, and given that the voters' agreement is necessary for any change in the electoral system, this seems unlikely to take place.

The funding of political parties is another area of institutional reform that has recently received political attention in Ireland. Unusually in Europe, parties did not receive direct state funding until recently, though for many years they have received subsidies such as free party political broadcasts on television during election campaigns (for details of party funding, see Farrell 1994: 233–6; Laver and Marsh 1999; Weeks 2003). Public funding was finally introduced in 1998 as part of a package of measures that also placed limits on the level of election spending and, in addition, compelled the parties to disclose details of financial contributions over €5,000. Under the funding scheme, parties receive finance in two ways. First, a sum of around €1.5 million (the amount to be increased annually in line with inflation) is distributed annually among the parties, in proportion to the votes won by each party in the previous general election (for details of the public funds and spendings for each party, see the annual reports of the Public Offices Commission; www.poc.ie). Second, election expenses, up to a maximum of €6,349, are reimbursed for every candidate who contests a *Dáil* election and receives more than a prescribed (and low) number of votes. Reforms in this area were introduced partly in response to public pressure, when a series of political–financial "scandals" emerged in the mid-1990s. Of course, the public, while it demanded greater transparency, certainly did not call for public money being given to politicians or their parties. The effect of the revelations that emerged in the 1990s was, on the contrary, to lower the standing of parties and make them seem less rather than more worthy to be recipients of taxpayers' money. However, the parties themselves justified the introduction of public funding by arguing that the overall package of reforms should reduce the likelihood of corruption in the future.

CONCLUSION

The Irish political class is small, with the holders of very few positions outside the ranks of elected parliamentarians capable of being seen as part of it. The backgrounds of MPs are not greatly different from those of parliaments elsewhere, with women and working-class people markedly under-represented.

A number of features of the Irish political system are responsible for both the small size of the political class and the fact that MPs must combine elements of both the "entrepreneur" and "backbencher" role. The great majority of legislators are, first and foremost, representatives of their parties, for whom electoral survival and political advancement depend on remaining loyal to the party in all circumstances. But within this framework, MPs must build up a personal base of support because of the preferential nature of the electoral system. In addition, the small scale of the party organizations means that these do not provide an alternative route into politics.

REFERENCES

All-Party Oireachtas Committee on the Constitution (2002). *Seventh Progress Report: Parliament*. Dublin: Stationery Office.

Coakley, John (1994). "The Election that Made the First Dáil", in B. Farrell (ed.), *The Creation of the Dáil*. Dublin: Blackwater Press, pp. 31–46.

CRG [Constitutional Review Group] (1996). *Report*. Dublin: Stationery Office.

Czudnowski, Moshe M. (1975). "Political Recruitment", in F. I. Greenstein and N. W. Polsby (eds), *Handbook of Political Science: Volume 2*. Reading, MA: Addison-Wesley, pp. 155–242.

Dinan, Des (1986). "Constitution and Parliament", in B. Girvin and R. Sturm (eds), *Politics and Society in Contemporary Ireland*. Aldershot: Gower, pp. 71–86.

Donnelly, Seán (1993). *Partnership: the Story of the 1992 General Election, with Profiles of TDs* by Renagh Holohan. Rathcoole, Co Dublin: the author.

Farrell, David M. (1994). "Ireland: Centralization, Professionalization and Competitive Pressures", in R. S. Katz and P. Mair (eds), *How Parties Organize: Change and Adaptation in Party Organizations in Western Democracies*. London: Sage, pp. 216–41.

Gallagher, Michael (1995). "Long-term Patterns in Recruitment to the Parliamentary Elite in the Republic of Ireland", unpublished manuscript, presented at the Joint Sessions of the ECPR, Bordeaux.

—— (1999*a*). "Parliament", in J. Coakley and M. Gallagher (eds), *Politics in the Republic of Ireland*, 3rd edition. London: Routledge, 177–205.

—— (1999*b*) "Republic of Ireland", in R. Elgie (ed.), *Semi-Presidentialism in Europe*. Oxford: Oxford University Press, pp. 104–23.

—— (2000). "The (Relatively) Victorious Incumbent under PR-STV: Legislative Turnover in Ireland and Malta", in S. Bowler and B. Grofman (eds), *Elections in Australia, Ireland and Malta under the Single Transferable Vote*. Ann Arbor: University of Michigan Press, pp. 81–113.

—— (2003). "Stability and Turmoil: Analysis of the Results", in M. Gallagher, M. Marsh, and P. Mitchell (eds), *How Ireland Voted 2002*. Basingstoke: Palgrave/Macmillan, pp. 88–118.

—— and Marsh, Michael (2002). *Days of Blue Loyalty: The Politics of Membership of the Fine Gael Party*. Dublin: PSAI Press.

—— and Weeks, Liam (2003). "The Subterranean Election of the Seanad", in M. Gallagher, M. Marsh, and P. Mitchell (eds), *How Ireland Voted 2002*. Basingstoke: Palgrave/Macmillan, pp. 197–213.

Galligan, Yvonne (1999). "Women in Politics", in J. Coakley and M. Gallagher (eds), *Politics in the Republic of Ireland*, 3rd edition. London: Routledge, pp. 294–319.

—— and Wilford, Rick (1999). "Women's Political Representation in Ireland", in Y. Galligan, E. Ward, and R. Wilford (eds), *Contesting Politics: Women in Ireland, North and South*. Boulder: Westview and PSAI Press, pp. 130–48.

Laver, Michael, and Marsh, Michael (1999). "Parties and Voters", in J. Coakley and M. Gallagher (eds), *Politics in the Republic of Ireland*, 3rd edition. London: Routledge, pp. 152–76.

Mair, Peter (1997). *Party System Change: Approaches and Interpretations*. Oxford: Clarendon Press.

Murphy, Gary (1999). "The Role of Interest Groups in the Policy-making Process", in J. Coakley and M. Gallagher (eds), *Politics in the Republic of Ireland*, 3rd edition. London: Routledge, pp. 271–93.

—— (2000). "A Culture of Sleaze: Political Corruption and the Irish Body Politic 1997–2000". *Irish Political Studies*, 15: 193–200.

Norris, Pippa (1996). "Legislative Recruitment", in L. LeDuc, R. G. Niemi, and P. Norris (eds), *Comparing Democracies: Elections and Voting in Global Perspective*. London: Sage, pp. 184–215.

O'Halpin, Eunan, and Connolly, Eileen (1999). "Parliaments and Pressure Groups: The Irish Experience of Change", in P. Norton (ed.), *Parliaments and Pressure Groups in Western Europe*. London: Frank Cass, pp. 124–44.

Putnam, Robert D. (1976). *The Comparative Study of Political Elites*. Englewood Cliffs, NJ: Prentice-Hall.

Randall, Vicky (1987). *Women and Politics: An International Perspective*, 2nd edition. Basingstoke: Macmillan.

Review Body on Higher Remuneration in the Public Sector (1992). *Report No 35 to the Minister for Finance on The Levels of Remuneration Appropriate to Higher Posts in the Public Sector and the Superannuation and Severance Arrangements Appropriate to Members of the Oireachtas*, Pl 8868. Dublin: Stationery Office.

—— (1996). *Report No 37 to the Minister for Finance on The Levels of Remuneration appropriate to Higher Posts in the Public Sector*, Pn 3187. Dublin: Stationery Office.

—— (2000). *Report No 38 to the Minister for Finance on The Levels of Remuneration appropriate to Higher Posts in the Public Sector*, Pn 8907. Dublin: Stationery Office.

Sinnott, Richard (1999). "The Electoral System", in J. Coakley and M. Gallagher (eds), *Politics in the Republic of Ireland*, 3rd edition. London: Routledge, pp. 99–126.

Weeks, Liam (2003). "Appendix 5—Regulation of campaign spending", in M. Gallagher, M. Marsh, and P. Mitchell (eds), *How Ireland Voted 2002*. Basingstoke: Palgrave/Macmillan, pp. 262–4.

11

Israel: Community, State, and Market in the Shaping of the Political Class

URI RAM

POLITICAL PROFESSIONALIZATION IN HISTORICAL PERSPECTIVE

Zionist Jewish settlers began to show up in Ottoman Palestine in the last two decades of the nineteenth century. After the British conquest of the land at the end of the First World War the small Jewish community, then numbering some 60,000 souls, began to constitute itself in the framework of a political system. The political community that was shaped since 1918 turned into a state in 1948—at that point numbering about 600,000 Jews. During the War of Independence hundreds of thousands of Arabs were expelled and escaped the territory, so that after the war only about 150,000 remained within the boundaries of the new state. Today, at the beginning of the twenty-first century, the population of Israel numbers about 6.5 million people. Though close to 20 percent of the citizenry are Palestinians, the state defines itself as Jewish, yet also as democratic. The conflict between the two populations—the settlers of Jewish descent and the Arab inhabitants of the land—has had a crucial impact on the shape of the Israeli polity (Ehrlich 1987). This is expressed in the conspicuous ethnic character of Jewish nationalism, which affects both international affairs, especially the exclusion of Arab citizens from access to many public spaces and privileges, and intranational ones, especially the marginalization of the Jewish *Mizrahi* population (Jewish immigrants from Moslem countries) by the *Ashkenazi* (Jewish immigrants from Europe) national elite (see Yiftachel 1997 on Israeli ethno-nationalism).[1]

In the rather short history of Israel, its polity has gone through three historical phases, in which three distinct types of political classes may be discerned. The first type can be termed "political founders" (of the community); the second "political bureaucrats" (of the state); and the third "political entrepreneurs" (in the political

---

[1] The term *Mizrahim* (singular *Mizrahi*; literally "from the East") refers to Israeli Jews from Moslem countries, or—officially—from Asian and African countries. The appellation *Sepharadim* (literally "from Spain") is not in use anymore. The term *Sepharadim* lingered for a while after the mass Jewish immigration from Moslem countries to Israel during the 1950s, but went out of fashion in the 1970s when the presence of the *Mizrahi* population was beginning to be recognized and as the melting pot ideology started to recede.

marketplace of identities). The first era, 1918–48, is that of the formation of a political community centered around social movements and ideological political parties;
the second era, 1948–77, sees the establishment of a state and the expansion of
administration; and the third, from 1977 onwards, is that of a "political market,"
characterized by a duality which includes both "privatization" and "sectoralization"
of politics, that is, both intensified political strife among social sectors and the commercialization of electoral campaigns (obviously, the periodization should not be
taken rigidly, as processes start in one era and mature over time). The typology suggested correlates very well with the one proposed by Klaus von Beyme in analyzing
the transformation of European party systems from premodern to postmodern
times. With the exception of the aristocratic elite parties, which von Beyme dates to
the period before 1918, the trajectory of the Israeli political system resembles the
European trajectory in both chronology and character: mass parties between 1918
and the 1950s, catch-all parties between the 1950s and 1970s, and parties of professional politicians since the 1970s and 1980s (Beyme 1996).

It ought to be added, though, that since the 1990s the political culture in Israel, as
in many countries affected by globalization, is fissured between two divergent tendencies: a liberal tendency, manifested in the commercialization of politics, and a
communal (or ethnic–fundamentalist) politics, manifested by the sectorialization of
politics. The category of "professional politicians" refers to these two types, though
in different versions. In the terms coined by Benjamin Barber, Israeli politicians
today tend to affiliate either with McWorld or with Jihad (Barber 1995).

It is appropriate to comment here that the object of the current study is the structure and dynamics of the "political class" in Israel, that is, of elected political officials.
In and of itself this category should not be conflated with the "political elite," a category much smaller in size and much more powerful in authority. This distinction is
drawn succinctly by von Beyme: "political class [...] means a self-referential stabil-
ization of an income-group and a power-cartel. The other aspect—the active shaping of politics—is still in the hands of a political elite. The elite is the narrower
notion, it contains only the key decision-makers at the top of party hierarchies"
(Beyme 1996: 151; see also the introductory chapter, this volume). This distinction
has to be kept in mind throughout this chapter, though at points, especially where
citing others, the wording of the text may slip a beat.

THE INSTITUTIONAL CONTEXT

Israel is a multi-party parliamentary democracy. Its Parliament, the *Knesset*, has 120
delegates (*Knesset* Members, KMs) who are elected every 4 years in the framework of
national party lists (the whole country being one electoral district), in a proportional
representation system. Until the reforms in 1996, governments were formed by a
Knesset majority, based on an interparty agreement. Since then there are, in addition
to the parliamentary elections, direct elections to the office of Prime Minister. The
elected Prime Minister nominates his government and has to receive the consent of

the Parliament. The Prime Minister's direct election aroused great expectations for "strong leadership," but the parliamentary fragmentation and instability it created caused great dismay. As of 2002 the old system has been restored, though this may not be the last stop either.

The political system of the pre-state Jewish community, the *Yishuv*, consisted of three layers. Formal state authority over the territory, including the Arab population, was in the hands of the British mandatory government. The Jewish community had two additional layers of self-government: the top layer consisted of the international Zionist organizations, represented by the Executive Committee of the Jewish Agency for Palestine; and the lower layer of the local "national" institutions represented by the National Executive Committee (*Hanhalat Havvad Haleumi*). The local political institutions conducted more or less regularly democratic elections, based on the principles described above. One dimension of the evolvement of the local political system was the gradual rise of power of the *Yishuv* organs since the 1930s *vis-à-vis* the outside world Jewish leadership.[2]

The vehicle through which politics was conducted during the pre-state era was that of the political party, and the leading prototype was that of the mass-integration socialist party. Since the 1930s it was one political party that dominated the scene well until the 1970s: *Mapai*, which, in 1968, with two smaller parties formed the Israel Labor Party (for the history of political parties in Israel, see Neuberger 1997). The term "party" is indeed too narrow to depict the extensive nature of these movements-cum-organizations. The Israeli political system was erected from scratches by political parties. There were parties, before there was an electorate or a state. Parties—sometimes through federations of several ones—were total movements, instituting collective agricultural settlements, owning financial institutions, running industrial corporations, publishing daily newspapers, and supplying the overall economic, social, and cultural goods of their members in a stateless society in an impoverished country (Horowiz and Lissak 1978).

The founders and activists of these parties became the first political class of the early Israeli political system. The seniors among them were the immigrants of the 2nd *Aliya*, the second wave of Jewish migration to Palestine (1904–14): young, bachelor pioneers from Russia and Eastern Europe. Second in order were the 3rd *Aliya* immigrants (1919–23), albeit from the same geographic areas. These immigrants brought to their new country the nationalist fervor, socialist ideals, and communist methods of their countries of origin. In Palestine they established a peculiar political system, based on the following three premises: financial transfers from abroad through public channels; the provision of national leadership and allocation of resources to the Jewish population; and the reciprocal reception of legitimation as the political authority of most of that population (Horowiz and Lissak 1978). The system involved a formal democratic dimension, especially of competition and compromise among sectors of society (represented by different parties), as well as an authoritarian cultural dimension, especially

---

[2] A process naturally helped by the growth of the local Jewish community, but also by the grave fate of European Jewry in this period and the largely indifferent position of American Jewry towards Palestine.

regarding the relations between the "movement" and the individual. The underlying logic of the whole system was determined by the process of the Jewish colonization of Palestine—it combined the aspiration of a movement with financial resources (the Zionist movement) with the needs of settlers with labor power (the pioneers) to create an effective national settlement project (Kimmerling 1983; Shafir 1989; Ram 1993).

In 1948 the *Yishuv* community in Palestine turned into the independent state of Israel. The state inherited the operating multi-party parliamentary system under one party dominance (*Mapai*), and even on a personal level continuity was paramount. Yet, 1948 signals the transition from a community into a state, a transition which generated some processes which would eventually transform the nature of the polity and the political class. Three changes in particular have been of long-term importance: (1) the emergence of a centralized state administration and of a state-oriented political culture (*mamlachtiut*), which replaced the previous movement-centered political culture; (2) the absorption in the early 1950s of the "mass immigration", predominately from Arab and Moslem countries, which doubled the population in 3–4 years and changed its ethnic complexion; and (3) the processes of militarization and industrialization, which ushered the rapid modernization of Israeli society.

Due to the fact that all of these processes were initiated, planned, subsidized, and run by the government, or at least under its control, and above all due to the centrality of the protracted military conflict between Israel and its Arab neighbors, the 1950s and 1960s witnessed a gross centralization of power of the political class and "brought about the undisputed primacy of political considerations and the preeminence of the political elite over other elites, including economic ones" (Gutmann and Landau 1975: 168). Despite many changes that took place on the political map, well until the early 1970s, as Gutmann and Landau put it, "one can easily identify the consistent nuclei of party leaders and their constant elite supporters. These have provided the party system [and the political class; U.R.] as a whole with remarkable continuity" (Gutmann and Landall 1975: 169). Except that now the political class was closely meshed with the state administration, the army command, and the public corporations. Though a process of elite differentiation took place and professional elites emerged in all these fields, the political elite continued to play a pivotal role. As Daniel Maman put it, "despite the growing relative autonomy of non-state elites from state elites and non-elected from elected state elite, the political elites hold the pivotal position in the multiple elite structure" (Maman 1997: 34). Yet, as of recently, the new multiplicity of the social and political structure does effect the composition and practices of the political class, as is discussed below.

THE POLITICAL CLASS

Size and Composition

To begin with, the political class in the Jewish *Yishuv* pre-state community consisted of the founders and activists of that political system, the leaders who headed the political parties, especially the left-wing ones. A snapshot of its composition may be gained by a profile of the thirty-seven original signatories of the Declaration of Independence of Israel in 1948. All were Jewish, thirty-five were men, thirty-five came from Europe, twenty-nine from Eastern Europe (Russia, Poland)—only one was born in Palestine and one in Yemen. Fourteen out of the thirty-seven belonged to the 2nd and 3rd *Aliya* (9 and 5 respectively; Gutmann and Landau 1975: 163). This breakdown provides a splendid first approximation to the collective portrait of the political class of the time. Detailed information, confirming by and large, the impression brushed earlier, is provided by the meticulous study of sociologist Moshe Lissak, in whose estimation the political elite of the *Yishuv* consisted of 602 individuals (Lissak 1981).[3]

The expansion of the community and the institutionalization of its political system in the *Yishuv* period generated a process of political professionalization. For a large part of members of the political elite politics had become the major occupation and for many the major source of income. In many cases, though, livelihood was provided not directly by political organizations, but indirectly through employment in various institutions, or by affiliation with collective or cooperative settlements, linked to political organizations. A quarter of the members of the political elite were directly employed by political institutions, 14.5 percent were *kibbutzim* members, and another 11 percent were employed in public administration. All in all, for almost half of the political elite the source of living was associated with their political activity (Lissak 1981: 60–1). The figure for those who earned their living directly or indirectly from political offices is even higher for the leading strata of the elite. Once more, the tendency becomes entirely salient in the elite of the Labor sector, where all members earned their living from their political offices. Significantly, in this group members of *kibbutzim* played a major part: 20 percent in the first rank and more than 47 percent in the second rank, whereas in the population at large *kibbutzim* never exceeded 4.5 percent.[4] An interesting characteristic of the political class of the period was the fact that its mobility tended to be vertical (inside the political system) rather than horizontal (from other spheres; Lissak 1981: 74).

This collective profile of the political class, and especially of the Labor section of it, does much to explain the source of power of the Labor Movement in the pre-state period. As Lissak cogently comments:

The data on the source of income as an indication of the extent of professionalization and institutionalization of elite roles exposes the superior and advantageous position of the Labor sector [...] in terms of available cadres for professional politicians. This is due among else to

---

[3] In Lissak's account 78% of the first-rank members of the political class, and 73% of its second rank, were from Eastern Europe. This tendency even sharpens within the dominant Labor section of the political class, which was almost purely of East European descent, compared to 'only' 63% East Europeans in the non-Labor sector. The majority of the political class members were young—born after 1890 (Lissak 1981: 45–7).

[4] Another indicator of growing institutionalization and professionalization is the duration of office-holding: In the Labor sector the average duration was 8 years and in the non-Labor sectors it was 5.8 years. Twenty-seven percent of political class members from the Labor sector held positions for more than 15 years—and thus, provided much of the stability and continuity of the political system (Lissak 1981: 63).

the kibbutz movement, and to the sprawled network of companies and sectorial organizations, which served as a basis and spear-head for most political activists in the Labor sector. (Lissak 1981: 61–2)

Other sectors, especially the nationalist (revisionist) and the religious-national, emulated the political model of the Labor, though to a lesser extent and obviously with lesser success. The political prominence of Labor and its allies in that period is explainable, to a great extent, by its success in the construction of political cadres and political apparatuses, accompanied by a net of social services; these instruments facilitated its spearhead role in the Zionist colonization project.

In short, the typical member of the political class of the pre-state Jewish polity tended to display the following characteristics, and the more so the closer he was to the core of that class, that is the Labor leadership: Russian or East European in origin; young and newly immigrated when entering politics; earning his livelihood directly or indirectly from his political role; and, obviously, he is a "he."[5]

Political Recruitment and Political Careers

The first two decades of the state period saw indeed a remarkable continuity of the political class of the pre-state period. In fact, the high ranks of politics were occupied by the "founding fathers" until the mid-1970s. David Ben Gurion, chief leader of *Mapai* and of the Jewish community, and Israel's first Prime Minister, retired the post in 1963 and retired from the *Knesset* in 1970. By then, the second and third Prime Ministers of Israel, Moshe Sharett and Levi Eshkol, 2nd *Aliya* members, had already died. Ben Gurion died in 1973, and Golda Meir, a 3rd *Aliya* person, was the fourth prime minister and carried on in office until 1973. The retirement of Meir and the ascent of Yitzhak Rabin to this post in 1974 signaled the change of guards in the political class—the transition of leadership from the immigrant founders to their native descendants (*Sabra*). This, though, should be taken with a grain of salt, since the political "upheaval" of 1977 would bring the "old guard" to the fore once again, though this time around it would be the right-wing section of it—of which Prime Ministers Menachem Begin and Yizhak Shamir were typical representatives. Yet, the Prime Ministers of the 1990s were all (with the exception of a non-elected short term of Shimon Peres right after Rabin's assassination) of the *Sabra* generation: Netanyahu, Barak, and Sharon.

To be eligible for political offices or even to the high ranks of state administration or state corporations, the generation of descendants had to pass through the channels of political parties. However, its formative experience and social status emanated from a different source: military service. Between the late 1930s and the late 1960s military service had been the major recruitment base for the second generation of the Labor political class, and after a row of very successful military campaigns (1948, 1956, and 1967) it gained unprecedented prestige (Shapiro 1984; Ben-Eliezer 1995).

---

[5] Out of eighty-one names cited by Lissak (1981: 164–6) as members of the political elite only three are women.

The 1960s and 1970s saw, therefore, the new and expanding phenomenon of retired generals "parachuted" into senior political roles—among the best known are Moshe Dayan, Yigal Alon, Ezer Weizman, Yitzhak Rabin, Ehud Barak, and Ariel Sharon—and many retired officers started to move between political, administrative, and economic positions (Zamir 1977; Peri 1983; Maman 1987). This trend was accompanied by a change in the criteria for advancement in the political class from "generalist leaders" to "technocratic generals," as Gutmann and Landau put it. During the state era "a high premium [was put] on professional and technocratic proficiency" (Gutmann and Landau 1975: 172). Old ideologies like socialism or Zionism came to be seen as obsolete, and the call of the day was for performance and achievement (*bitzuiyut*).

Yet the recruitment of "new blood" to the political class was still confined to the dominant strata of the society; it was within that *Ashkenazi* (of European descent) circles that power started to pass from the generation of the founding leaders to the generation of their sons, in many cases literally speaking. Even in the 14th *Knesset* (1996–99) thirteen KMs, more than 10 percent, were second or third generation offspring of KMs (*Yediot Aharonot*, 22 January 1997).

Large sectors of the population were continuously under-represented in the political class, above all the immigrants of the 1950s, mostly from Arab and Moslem countries, who by the 1970s composed half of the Israeli population. At the time the only political channels open to this population were of second rank. Hence, some peripheral sectors which did not have due representation in the "primary" political class, formed a "secondary" political class in the 1970s, based on local mobilization. The Center for Local Authorities, which was established in 1974 and has about 225 affiliated authorities, serves as a hothouse for *Mizrahi* politicians. Likewise, Arab heads of local authorities in 1974 established a steering committee, which soon became the major representative of this sector *vis-à-vis* the state. Finally, the Jewish settlers in the occupied Palestinian territories in 1979 established a local council called *Moeztst Yesha* (Al-Haj 1993; Ben-Zadok 1993; Goldberg 1993; Grinberg 1993).

Analysis of the members of the "primary" political class by some social categories sheds light on its complexion and the degree of "representativity", or rather the lack thereof. An analysis of the birthplaces of the 374 persons who served as KMs in the period 1948–74 indicates the persistence of the old political class and its successors during the early state era. If we add gender and religion to the breakdown of the parliamentarians by country of birth and nationality, carried out by Guttman and Landau, we get an idea of the status ladder in Israeli society being reflected in the composition of the political class (see Table 11.1).

Almost half of the *Knesset* Members were born in Poland and Russia (96 and 86, respectively)—the places of origin of the 2nd and 3rd *Aliya*. The percentage of *Ashkenazim* in general, and of East Europeans in particular increases sharply at the level of cabinet ministries: 83 and 69 percent, respectively. The East European weight in the *Knesset* gradually waned, from 70 percent in the 1st *Knesset* (1949–51) to 40 percent in the 11th (1984–88). Yet the ratio of *Mizrahi* KMs rose only slowly: from 3 percent in the first *Knesset* to 10 percent in the 8th (1973–77). Regarding professionalization, it turns out that among the 374 KMs 205 were political activists before

Table 11.1   *Social categories of KMs, 1949–1974*

Category	KMs	% of KMs
Total (1949–74)	374	100
Ashkenasim[a]	250	67
Ashkenasim from Eastern Europe	215	58
Mizrahim[b]	37	10
Israel (born in Israel)	87	24
Women	79	21
Arabs	20	5

[a] Born in Europe or America (the latter category only six out of the 250).
[b] Born in Africa or Asia. The ethnic categories are sometimes ambiguous.

Source: Gutmann and Landau (1975: 185); Israel Women Network (1996: 17–8; *Hebrew Encyclopedia*).

entering Parliament, that is, saw politics as their vocation (Gutmann and Landau 1975: 183–90).

Another indicator for the lack of representativeness of the political class is its spatial dispersion. Yehuda Gradus calculated that in the period 1961–81 representation in the *Knesset* of central regions (i.e. number of KMs from such regions) was much higher than their "electoral strength" (i.e. share of statewide voting population). The salient cases of over-representation were Jerusalem, with an electoral strength of ten seats versus an actual number of twenty-three KMs rooted in the city, and Tel Aviv with twenty-three and forty-two, respectively. Accordingly, for many other peripheral regions the ratio was inverted (Gradus 1982: 15).

Israel's centralized system eroded and diminished the ties of both central government and the political parties with the grassroots, and led to the center's loss of direct contact with the periphery. [It is suggested] that the territorial dispersion of many of the new immigrants into peripheral communities retarded the genesis of a sense of common grievance and of peripheral solidarity in the face of the high level of organization and well-oiled allocative procedure of the elite cartel. (Gradus 1982: 20)

The over-representation of *Ashkenazi* male Jews from the founders' generation in the political class, and the consequential under-representation of all other groups, especially of *Mizrahim*, women, and Arabs, is dominant throughout the period from the 1950s to the 1970s. It was this emergent disparity between the (new) social structure and the (old) structure of the political class, particularly in terms of intra-Jewish ethnic division, that, among other things, brought about the "upheaval" (*mahapch*), as it came to be called, of 1977. The elections in that year brought down Labor for the first time in the country's history, and the leading coalition came to be led by Labor's major rival, the right-wing *Likud* party headed by Menachem Begin, himself a pre-state leader (immigrated in 1942) and former head of a separatist armed group called Military National Organization (IZL).[6] The following period witnessed great changes in the nature of the polity and the political class, though the exact year is again only a convenient benchmark, since some processes started before that year and some matured only recently.

The first noticeable change in the nature of the political class has been the entry into politics of *Mizrahi* politicians (of African or Asian descent, in this period mostly "second generation" individuals who were born in Israel or immigrated there at a very young age). Initially their channels of mobilization were the backbenches of the political system, such as municipal authorities, the *Histadrut* Federation of Labor, or local branches of the political parties, but eventually they made a decisive entry into the political class.

By the mid-1960s *Mizrahim* headed the majority of new local authorities, mostly poor agricultural settlements and underdeveloped towns where *Mizrahim* were the majority of the population, and about a quarter of older settlements, though none of them served as a mayor in a large or middle-sized city. By the late 1960s *Mizrahim* occupied in the various representative and governing bodies of the *Histadrut* from about one-sixth to more than one quarter of positions, the same being true for the internal representative and governing bodies of the two big parties. In the *Knesset*, the representation of Mizrahim increased only slightly, from 9.5 percent in the first term to 14 percent in the eighth term (Smooha 1978: 316–33).

While *Mizrahim* started to enter the political class significantly during the 1960s, the "ethnic cleavage" became a central issue in Israeli politics only since the mid-1970s. The *Mizrahi* sense of depravation and social protest was channeled through the *Likud*, and it stood behind its electoral successes. When in the 1990s the same vote was directed to the new *Mizrachi*-traditionalist party *Shas*, *Likud* contracted and *Shas* expanded to become the third largest party in the 15th Knesset (1999 elections). During the 1970s, as the *Likud* grew to be the largest oppositional party, it developed a two-tiered structure: the upper leadership still consisted of pre-state *Ashkenazi* founders (the "fighting family") or their successors (the "princes"), while the rank and file and mass electorate was made up to a large part of lower-class young *Mizrahim* from peripheral regions and underprivileged neighborhoods (Shapiro 1989). Research on the members of the conventions held by the two big parties in 1986 found that 32 percent of delegates in the Labor convention were from Asian or African descent, compared to 52 percent of the *Herut* party, the leading component of the *Likud* block. Moreover, breaking the common category "Asia and Africa" down in its two parts, it was found that the "Africa component" in the *Herut* made up 25 percent, compared to 14 percent in the Labor. This is significant since the Moroccan Jewry is the largest and most underprivileged, and also most militant, group among the *Mizrahim* (Herzog, Shamir, and Zuckerman 1989: 17–8). As Herzog and his colleagues put it: "Labor recruits mainly in old locales and in the center, while Herut recruits [...] mainly in the geographic and social periphery of Israel. The open ranks

---

[6] The immediate trigger was the "default" (*meachdal*) of the government in face of the surprise attack on Israel in October 1973 by the armies of Egypt and Syria, and the disastrous war that followed.

of the expanding [*Herut*] party, in addition to the challenge it posed as an alternative [to Labor's rule] were fertile ground to the entrance of political activists from new groups" (Herzog, Shemir, and Zuckerman 1989: 22).

Electoral behavior in the last two decades vindicates these findings: Low education, low earnings, *Mizrahi* descent, and religiosity are highly correlated with a vote for right-wing parties—and since the 1996 elections for the right-wing candidate for Prime Minister (Diskin 1988, 1993; Weiss 1997; Hermann 1998). While in the past all parties used to emulate the model of Labor, it became now the turn of Labor to try and emulate the *Likud* in this respect. By the 1990s the representation of *Mizrahim* in the Labor party equaled if not surpassed that in the *Likud*: towards the 1999 *Knesset* elections eight out the first twenty-five Labor candidates were *Mizrahim*, compared to seven of the *Likud*. In 2002 Labor had for the first time a *Mizrahi* head of party ("Fouad" Ben Eliezer; he was replaced by the end of the year with an *Ashkenazi* politician, Amram Mitzna). Still, the level of education of Labor candidates was much higher: of the first twenty-five Labor candidates 66 percent had 15 or more years of education, compared to 36 percent of *Likud* candidates. Both parties had four female candidates each among the first twenty-five candidates. The average age of *Likud* candidates was a little lower compared to Labor: 49.6 and 52.3 years, respectively (*Haaretz*, 6 February 1999).

However, it should be emphasized that the representation of *Mizrahim* inside the *Likud* is a matter of constant contention. One hallmark of the last two decades is the recurrent appearance of "ethnic," that is, *Mizrahi*, factions inside the *Likud* or on its outskirts, such as in the *Tami, Gesher*, and—most successfully—in the *Shas* party. Likewise, many *Mizrahi* voters have turned their allegiance from the *Likud* to the *Shas* party (a reverse move is expected in the 2002 elections). Simultaneously, *Likud* was deserted by some of the "princes", who either turned to moderate liberalism (Roni Milo and Dan Meridor) or towards radical nationalism (Benyamin Zeev Begin, son of the historical leader of the *Herut* party).

During the 1980s and especially the 1990s, the ethnic complexion of the political class in Israel has changed slowly but significantly. The number of *Mizrahi* KMs continued to grow steadily from twenty-three in the 9th *Knesset* (1977–81) to forty-one in the 13th (1992–96). Their representation also grew in the cabinet, from one minister in the first decade of the state to about a quarter of the ministers in the beginning of the 1980s and eventually to nearly half of the ministers in the late 1990s. The day 19 March 1997 may be marked as a watershed day, when a complete parity was reached between *Ashkenazi* and *Mizrahi* ministers—even if for a short while only (*Haaretz*, 10 March 1997). The initial composition of the Labor-led government of Ehud Barak was the first one in which ministers from *Mizrahi* origin outnumbered those from *Ashkenazi* origin: eleven to seven (*Yediot Aharonot*, 30 June 1999).

There has been no rise in the representation of women, whose number from 1949 to 1996 has vacillated between eight and twelve female KMs (6.6 and 10 percent; cf. Israel Women Network 1996: 15). In the 15th *Knesset* (1999) there were fourteen women. In the cabinet the number of women never exceeded two ministers and in the first composition of the Labor-led government of 1999 it decreased to one.

The number of Arab KMs has grown steadily: seven in the 9th *Knesset*, eight in the 13th and nine in the 14th (Diskin 1993: 54). It grew to a peak of twelve Arab KMs in the 15th Knesset. Until 2001 there has never been an Arab minister in the governments of Israel; in that year an Arab Druze served as minister without portfolio for a few months (he resigned under accusations of corruption, and was anyhow considered by many a poor representative of the Arab community in Israel). It must be emphasized that towards the end of the 1990s the deterioration of Israeli–Palestinian relations has also strained the relations between the state and its internal Palestinian community to the point that considering the Israeli–Palestinian politicians as part of the Israeli political class becomes questionable.

In terms of age, while in the first decades of the state the political class grew older, in recent years it gets younger. The average age of KMs of the 13th *Knesset* when elected was the lowest (50 years) since the pre-state period (Diskin 1993: 56). Of the 634 persons who served in the fourteen terms of the *Knesset* the average length of service was 2.5 terms, or 11 years (Arian 1997: 84–5).

On the whole, the Netanyahu government, which entered office in 1996 and was defeated in 1999, was interpreted by many as representing "a coalition of minorities"—Orthodox Jews, *Mizrahim*, new immigrants from Russia—struggling to push out the "old *Ashkenazi* elites" and to bring to its peak the process started 20 years earlier: transforming the old political system and its political class (for analyses of the 1996 elections and the new regime, see Ben Simon 1997; Filk 1997; Weiss 1997; Ram 1998). In the 1999 elections Ehud Barak won in a landslide, in what had been basically an anti-Netanyahu vote, yet in the terms cited above, the structure of the Parliament and of the political class has not drastically changed. The same populist anti-elite trend of the "coalition of (Jewish) minorities" has continued into the 2000s under the premiership of Ariel Sharon, and on the background of the events of 11 September 2001 and the terror attacks on Israel it has turned ever more chauvinistic.

Living off Politics, and Letting Others live off Politics too...

As far as "professionalization" refers to a steady occupation and source of income, Israeli politicians may certainly be considered a professional class. Yet, as far as "profession" also means a well bounded and distinct social category, it becomes blurred. In many cases, Israeli politicians make a living exactly from dwelling on the gray zone between state, civil society, and politics. Their income is composed of direct official remunerations, additional official allowances and benefits, and a variety of paid posts related in various ways to their positions. The terms of employment and professional ethic of elected politicians are a constant source of public attention and debate. Several state committees have dealt with such issues with regard to members of the *Knesset*.

Politicians in official positions earn salaries from the public purse. In 2002 the plain salary of a KM has been approximately US$5,500–6,000 (depends on the exchange rate; by the end of 2002 ILS4.7 = US$1). This income is directly tied to the wages of about 1,700 civil servants and another 1,300 state pensioners. The salary of cabinet ministers has been 12.5 percent higher and the salary of the Prime Minister 25 percent. The President's salary has been about US$8,000. For comparison, the average income of an Israeli wage earner was at the time less then US$1,500. The income level of KMs is decided by a *Knesset* committee, and occasionally there are public demands to form an external public committee to decide upon these matters (*Haaretz*, 22 January 1997).

On top of their base salary many politicians receive generous social benefits and reimbursement for expenses. In addition, various politicians earn more than one salary. A recent statement of external income of KMs reveals that many of them are employed as directors in public corporations (see below), lawyers, economic advisors, executives, and so on. Another source of income of successful politicians are royalties (from US publishers). Other KMs received paychecks from the *Histadrut,* from a variety of associations, from political parties, from local municipalities, and others. Zachi Hanegbi, Minister of Justice in Netanyahu's government, earned ILS113,000 (US$28,000) for an 8 months' stint as director of the Association for Fighting Car Accidents (*Haaretz*, 21 July 1997).

In 1995 the *Knesset* adopted the recommendation of an official public committee headed by the very prestigious law professor Ariel Rosen-Zvi, that as from 1997 KMs would be prohibited from having additional paid employments. In return, they should get an enhanced budget for administration and assistance, and, above all, a raise of 33 percent in their salary. The *Knesset* added, though, one clause, namely that KMs will still be allowed to have additional earnings which equal half of their parliamentary salaries. As of recently, some KMs entertain the idea that there will be a number of exceptions to the rule, and a cumulation of offices would be allowed in the cases of mayors and heads of trade unions, commercial chambers, etc. (*Haaretz*, 30 June 1997 and 2, 20, and 27 July 1997).

On top of that, members of the political class have secured for themselves very opulent pension arrangements. Up to 1996 KMs received a bonus of 4 percent of their salary for every year of membership added to the basic pension. This has been reduced to 2 percent. However, other senior politicians, like mayors, still enjoy the higher rate (Tunik 1987; Sager 1988: 95–9; *Haaretz*, 22 January, 30 June, and 4 July 1997).

Political corruption is a continuous item in the Israeli press and courts. A major scandal which has occupied public attention for years now is the trial of the head of the *Shas* party, the former minister of the interior, KM Arye Deri (another *Shas* parliamentarian, Yair Levi, has spent time in jail for corruption). It should be mentioned that corruption for the sake of one's own party or constituency is considered much more respectable then "personal" corruption of politicians, and one often hears from convicted politicians the claim that "not a penny got to my own pockets."

On the background of (1) the prominence of the political sphere and the central role of parties in Israeli society (until recently; see the following); (2) the protracted state of Israeli–Arab hostility and recurrent wars, and the necessity for constant war preparation; and (3) the extent of state intervention in the economy and the large size of the public sector (until the 1970s more than 40 percent of the economic capital belonged to the government and *Histadrut*; all under Labor political auspices), it is little wonder that the fine lines between politics, administration, and business are often transgressed. It is against this background that the practice of *protectzia* pervaded the relations between citizens and state agencies. *Protectzia* is explained in a Hebrew language dictionary as: "patronage, a recommendation for preferential treatment; support by a person of influence of someone in order to obtain for him a right to certain preferential advantage in obtaining work, and so forth" (cited from Danet 1989: 16). Exemplary in this regard is the "political appointments" issue, that is, the appointment of individuals associated with political parties or close to politicians to positions in the state administration or to boards of directors in public corporations. In 1989 the State Comptroller warned: "The phenomena of disqualified political nominations is widespread throughout the public service. The findings indicate the intervention of political considerations in part of the nominations in all ranks, starting from clerks in the beginning of their professional career and reaching directors of institutions and organizations" (Hamedina 1989: 642).

In a special investigation the State Comptroller found that in the period 1986–88 352 out of 573 nominations (61 percent) for "representatives of the public" in directories of governmental firms concerned official members of the political parties' "inner circles." In many cases all or most "public" directors were members of party centers (Hamedina 1989: 36–41). It seems that this special form of reward to politicians—by other politicians—was almost normative in the first years of the state and later gradually declined. It became widespread again after the *Likud* gained power in 1977, when its activists felt they had the right to rectify decades of being deprived from public spoils (Dery 1993).[7] In 2002, in connection with the demands by politicians to remove restrictions on their nomination as directors, it was revealed that 30 percent of the directors in governmental companies are "political nominations" (*Walla News*, 9 January 2002).

And the story does not end there. Part of the indirect benefits of political office are gained after retirement. Mayors, KMs, cabinet ministers, and others often join the private sector after completing their political career, in many cases as "advisors."

---

[7] Another illustration for a very common practice is the case of Yakov Bardugu, a young *Mizrahi* politician (born 1965) from an impoverished background. He was the closest personal adviser of David Levi, former Minister of Foreign Affairs. He started his political career as a spokesman of the head of the Local Authorities Center, Maxim Levi (former mayor of Lud, number two in the *Gesher* party, brother of the leader of the Party David Levi). Between 1991 and 1994 he was the general director of the LAC until he retired with 200% compensations. Until 1997, he was then the director of the economic company of the LAC with a monthly salary of about ILS30,000 (US$7,400). His contract guarantees him a high compensation upon retirement (value of ILS180,000; US$44,700), seven additional monthly salaries (value of ILS210,000; US$52,000), option to buy the company car for 75% of its value; and other benefits, which amount to ILS400,000 (US$99,000). His next office was general director of the National Lottery (*Mifal Hapyis*) with an expected monthly salary of ILS35,000 (US$8,700). His patrons included *Likud's* Prime Minister Netanyahu and Labor's chair Barak—both courted David Levi and his party *Gesher* as potential allies in the next political showdown (*Yediot Aharonot*, 4 July 1997). Some of the illustrations mentioned above verge on the criminal, while mostly such matters are absolutely legal. The cases described are far from exceptional or sensational; in fact they are minor, yet they rather depict widespread political class practices (Elizur and Eliahu 1973; Etzioni-Halevi 1993).

Their skills are their political connections and their ability to cut red tape by "making a phone call" to the right person. The State Attorney has recently issued a set of restrictions imposed on ministers and deputies after retirement.

As is well known, Max Weber has drawn the distinction between two types of politicians: those who live *for* politics and those who live *off* politics. In Israel, a third category has to be added: politicians who *let others live off politics too*. One of the major expectations of elected Israeli politicians is to channel government resources to their constituencies. In the first decades of the state the main beneficiary of political favoritism on a large scale was the "agricultural sector," associated with the Labor parties. However, in the last decades the main beneficiary is the "religious sector:" dozens of institutions and hundreds of thousands of individuals associated with the religious parties, who are financed by state subsidies and transactions, especially via the ministries for interior affairs, employment and welfare, culture and education, religious services, and housing. A major channel for these money transfers are the "special allocations" clauses in the state budget. The distribution of the lucrative ministries and the special allocations clauses have been, and still are, the major staple of coalitionary negotiations and agreements in Israel, despite repeated misgivings of the State Comptroller and the High Court of Justice (Gavish 1993). Furthermore, besides such special allocations, major budgetary decisions contain implicit benefits to various receptors, and they are politically determined. A case in point is the law for the encouragement of investment, by which certain development zones enjoy tax exemptions, state guarantees, and convenient credit terms. The "map" of these zones is a matter for political contestation according to party lines.

To conclude this issue, it seems that members of the political class—whether they live for politics or not—certainly live off politics and do so in a variety of innovative, direct, and indirect ways. Moreover, they secure the reproduction of their status by letting others live off politics, too. In an often quoted episode a Likud minister shouted angrily at his party members: "have we won elections in order to dispense jobs?!"—the roam from the audience was "Yes!." The state of affairs on which we glimpsed above casts some doubts regarding the degree of distinctiveness one can impute to the political class. It seems, rather, that it is well, perhaps all too well, enmeshed in both state administration and private business affairs. Yet again, it is politics itself which forms the "capital" of this class.

THE POLITICAL CLASS AND INSTITUTIONAL REFORM

On top of the transition of power from Labor to *Likud* and the evolution of a two-block political system with protracted electoral stalemate, the third period of the Israeli polity is marked by three overlapping phenomena. First, the entry into politics of new social actors, hitherto marginal to the system (or rather, marginalized by it); second, the transformation of the rules of the political game, namely changes in the electoral system; and, finally, the transformation of the political culture in two complementary directions: a growing significance of electoral competition and a growing significance of communal politics of identity, both exacerbated by the electronic mass media. The three changes together have caused an overall "marketization." or commodification, of the political system, and they radically transform the nature of the political class—a process which is still in the making.

The electoral success of the *Likud* since 1977 did not only diminish the dominance of the Labor movement and the superiority of the veteran *Ashkenazi* elite, but also has put the older communal and statist models of politics into disuse. Approaching the newly emerging model of politics, one alternates between characterizing it as "politics of identity" or "politics of the market" (commodified politics). It seems that the two coexist, negating yet complementing each other, in the same dialectical relations that Benjamin Barber (1995) defined as "Jihad vs. McWorld." Though, during the 1950s and 1960s, the *Herut* party had made an effort to emulate what was then considered as the successful model of the *Mapai* party (in terms of the diffusion of its spheres of activity and its organizational structure), in fact it had represented all along a different type of party, usually labeled a "skeleton party:" a party which does not have a standing expanded apparatus, paid cadres, and effective institutions. Yet unlike the American political parties of this type, the common bond of *Herut* had been the centrality of the "leader," Menachem Begin, who personified the founding myths of the party and was its sole authority. Moreover, since the party was in permanent opposition, it could not offer its supporters a realistic program of change or—alternatively—the spoils of government (offices, budgets, etc.). Instead, the party, and especially the rhetoric of its leader, provided symbolic compensation, a feeling of one's own importance (despite one's marginalization in the dominant political culture), and a promise of historical vision in which one's place of honor was secured. Sociologist Yonathan Shapiro (1989) labeled this the "politics of status;" politics that does not enhance one's socio-economic well-being, but raises one's sense of self-esteem.

During the 1970s this new model gradually emerged as dominant until in the 1990s it was also adopted by the deposed Labor party after a long period of electoral defeats and stalemate (thus, since *Likud* prides itself on being the "national camp," the new Labor leader Ehud Barak started to call Labor the "real national camp").

The relative decline of the political parties as the mainstay of the Israeli polity and of its political class is enhanced by the personification of politics: a process in which candidates for, and holders of, political offices are directly elected by, and connected to, the "public" and thus, bypass the mediatory services of the parties. This process has two major concrete manifestations: "primaries" and "direct elections."

"Primaries," as the process is called in Israel (in English) is the American abbreviation for primary internal party elections of party candidates for political offices. Until the 1970s candidates were nominated by a closed "arranging committee" (*vaada mesaderet*). The representative bodies of the parties later rubber-stamped full fixed lists presented to them by the committees; and no wonder politicians owed their places more to their superiors then to their constituencies (a term not yet in use then; Aronoff 1993: 41–58). Likewise the electorate was presented on voting day with a choice between closed party lists. The first open inner party contest over the party's candidacy for Prime Minister took place in 1974. The contestants were Yizhak Rabin and Shimon Peres, as in 1977, 1981, and 1992. In 1974 the electoral body had been the party "center;" by 1992, it already included all registered party members. In 1993 an open primary among registered members of the *Likud* took part for the first time for the party's Prime Minister candidate; the winner was Binyamin Netanyahu— Prime Minister of Israel in the years 1996–99. During the 1970s the *Likud* established inner-party elections of candidates for the *Knesset* list, *Dash* and Labor followed in 1977 and 1988, respectively (Brichta 1977: 103–72; Aronoff 1993: 190–205; Shapira 1996; Neuberger 1997: 230–8).

"Direct elections" means that voting for an office is personalized, whether the person stands for a party, a non-party group, or a cause. The new system was introduced first at the municipal level in 1978, and then in 1992 for the direct elections of the Prime Minister, while the parliamentary electoral system remained intact. The background for the reform on the national level was a sense of paralysis due to the protracted electoral stalemate between the two blocks, and a sense of dismay from the disproportional coalition bargaining power of small parties due to their "tip of the balance" position between the two blocks. Furthermore, there was some popular urge for a "strong leader," inflated by a neoliberal reform movement (Arian and Amir 1996; Doron 1996). The new dual parliamentary/quasi-presidential system was first exercised in the 1996 elections. Up to this point the Prime Minister would have been the head of the largest party represented in Parliament; from now on parliamentary majority and premiership were separated—in what was called ironically a "parliadential" system (Susser 1989).

Both new rules of the political game, direct elections and primaries, have been widely implemented in the 1990s; for example, Amir Peretz, the General Secretary of the *Histadrut*, intends to apply them in the trade union movement as well. Yet, they are still contested. While, since the 1970s these procedures have been depicted as an important, if not the most important, dimension of political democratization, their practical implementation has generated some second thoughts. Opinions are mixed: on the one hand, such procedures obviously involve many more people in the political process and tighten the ties between elected officials and the "common voter". On the other hand, such procedures obviously are advantageous to charismatic individuals who "pass well on the screen," but who are not necessarily otherwise politically competent. In addition, they make politicians depend more than ever before on private financial resources, their own or from contributors. Put another way, the "old system" encouraged oligarchic politics, but it involved solid party structures and ideologies and had its checks and balances; the "new system" encourages populist politics, but it opens new channels to the system, and so, these procedures are considered both positively as "more democratic" and negatively as "more populist."

The expected advantages or disadvantages for oneself are, of course, affecting one's position on these issues. It seems that the wide party membership responded very positively to the reforms. Hundreds of thousands of individuals participated in internal party elections of the two big parties, many of them just enlisted recently in the parties with this specific aim in mind. Active politicians tend to be more reserved. As

for the direct election of the Prime Minister, there emerged an across-the-board initiative by *Knesset* Members of all parties—especially the big ones, who lost power as a
result of the split vote—to abandon direct elections. The 2002 elections took place in
the old method of "one ticket" voting (i.e. for a party). As for the primaries, at the
end of 1997 the *Likud* "center" has rebelled against the election of party candidates
for the *Knesset* by all party members, arguing that it unduly reduces the role of this
party institution. Interestingly, this move was coordinated with the party's head,
Prime Minister Netanyahu, but ran against the explicit will of the senior party members. In this case, a directly elected politician, who meanwhile reshuffled the personnel of the party's institutions, showed a preference for a narrower electing body on
whom he has leverage over a wider and less controllable public of party members.
The *Likud* primaries in 2002 became a matter of police investigation, relating to
allegations of widespread buying of votes for money and the penetration of criminal
elements into the process.

Both novelties, primaries and direct elections, exerted an indelible impact on
Israel's political culture and the nature of its political class (see, for instance, Rahat
2001). They have radically transformed the life of politicians, who now have to get
up from behind their desks and court "the public." In the beginning, politicians
resorted to the traditional method of mass meetings, but later on television became
the most effective campaign tool, with the expected result of a de-ideologization
of politics. Examples for the new practices associated with the privatization and
personification of politics include:

(1) the creation of professional teams of paid advisors around chief candidates;
(2) the multiplication of one-issue "lobbies" supported by KMs to gain media
    "air time;"
(3) the creation of a *Knesset* committee for the alleviation of personal complaints
    from the public;
(4) the growing phenomenon of breaking the party discipline in *Knesset* votes by
    individual KMs;
(5) the enormous increase in private bills (from the 1st to the 12th *Knesset* 336
    private bills were submitted and forty-one enacted; from the 13th to the 15th
    Knesset more than 2,000 private bills were submitted and more than 100
    enacted, and out of the 296 first new laws submitted to the 15th *Knesset* 155
    were initiated privately by KMs; see *Wallas News*, 7 and 14 March 2002); and
(6) the seasonal ritual of public rating of individual KMs by their measured
    quantitative "productivity"—for example, the best performance in the winter
    term of the 14th *Knesset* was that of KM Tamar Gozansky, who was present in
    eighty out of ninety-one house sessions, delivered eighty speeches, twenty-two
    queries, and submitted forty-eight bills (*Haaretz*, 3 April 1997).

Yet, the most significant manifestation of privatization and personification of politics is the declining role of political parties in the process of electoral campaigns and
the mushrooming of private "associations," by which candidates bypass both
the cumbersome hand of the party cadres and the state laws which limit financial

donations to political organizations (on the Americanization of Israeli politics see Aronoff 2000; on the demise of parties see Koren 1998).

The last two decades, thus, display the transformation of the Israeli political class from a more European model, centered around ideological and apparatus political parties and the aggregation of material interests, into a more American model, centered around the commercialization of political campaigns and the enhancement of the politics of symbolic identities. This transformation of the political class should be understood against the background of the transformation of Israel's political culture (Ram 1999, 2000): the transition of Israel from a state-centered modernizing society into a globalizing market-centered and ethnicity-centered society.

REFERENCES

(Note: Hebrew titles are translated into English.)

Al-Haj, Majid (1993). "The Changing Strategies of Mobilization among the Arabs in Israel: Parliamentary Politics, Local Politics and National Organizations", in E. Ben-Zadok (ed.), *Local Communities and the Israeli Polity*. Albany: State University of New York Press, pp. 67–87.

Arian, Asher (1997). *The Second Republic: Politics in Israel*. Tel Aviv: Haifa University Press and Zmora Bitan (Hebrew; English edition 1998, Chatham: Chatham House).

——and Amir, Ruth (1996). "Transformation of Electoral Systems", in G. Doron (ed.), *The Electoral Revolution*. Tel Aviv: Hakibbutz Hameuhad, M. 37–53 (Hebrew).

Aronoff, Myron J. (1993). *Power and Ritual in the Israel Labor Party: a Study in Political Anthropology*. Armonk: M. E. Sharpe.

——(2000). "The 'Americanization' of Israeli Politics: Political and Cultural Change." *Israel Studies*, 5: 92–127.

Barber, Benjamin R. (1995). *Jihad vs. McWorld: How Globalism and Tribalism are Shaping the World*. New York: Times Books.

Ben-Eliezer, Uri (1995). *The Emergence of Israeli Militarism 1936–1956*. Tel Aviv: Dvir (Hebrew; English edition 1998, Bloomington: Indiana University Press).

Ben Simon, Daniel (1997). *A New Israel*. Tel Aviv: Aryeh Nir (Hebrew).

Ben-Zadok, Efraim (1993). "Oriental Jews in the Development Towns: Ethnicity, Economic Development, Budgets and Politics", in E. Ben-Zadok (ed.), *Local Communities and the Israeli Polity*. Albany: State University of New York Press, pp. 91–122.

Beyme, Klaus von (1996). "Party Leadership and Change in Party Systems." *Government and Opposition*, 31: 135–59.

Brichta, Avraham (1977). *Democracy and Elections*. Tel Aviv: Am Oved (Hebrew).

Danet, Brenda (1989). *Pulling Strings: Biculturalism in Israeli Bureacracy*. Albany: State University of New York Press.

Dery, David (1993). *Politics and Civil Service Appointments*. Tel Aviv: Hamachon Hayisraeli Ledemocratiya (Hebrew).

Diskin, Avraham (1988). *Elections and Voters in Israel*. Tel Aviv: Am Oved (Hebrew; English edition 1991, New York: Praeger).

——(1993). *The Elections to the 13th Knesset*. Research Studies Series, No. 50. Jerusalem: Jerusalem Institute for Israel Studies.

Doron, Gideon (1996). "The Political Logic of Reforms of Democratic Electoral Systems", in G. Doron (ed.), *The Electoral Revolution*. Tel Aviv: Hakibbutz Hameuhad, pp. 54–78 (Hebrew).

Ehrlich, Avishai (1987). "Israel: Conflict, War and Social Change", in C. Creighton and M. Shaw (eds.), *The Sociology of War and Peace*. Basingstoke: MacMillan, 121–42.

Elizur, Yuval, and Eliahu, Salpeter (1973). *Who Rules Israel?* New York: Harper and Row.

Etzioni-Halevi, Eva (1993). *The Elite Connection and Democracy in Israel*. Cambridge: Polity Press.

Filk, Dani (1997). "Post-Populism in Israel: The Latin-American Model of Netanyahu 96." *Theory and Ctritique*, 9: 217–32 (Hebrew).

Gavish, Moshe (1993). "The Spending of Public Money in Israel: Blocks and Breakdowns." *The Israeli Tax Review*, 21: 109–34.

Goldberg, Giora (1993). "Gush Emunim New Settlement in the West Bank: From Social Movement to Regional Interest Group", in E. Ben-Zadok (ed.), *Local Communities and the Israeli Polity*. Albany: State University of New York Press, 189–208.

Gradus, Yehuda (1982). *Spatial Distribution of Political Power and Regional Disparities: The Israeli Case*. Nagoya, Japan: United Nations Centre for Regional Development.

Grinberg, Lev (1993). "Pheripheral Ethnicity: Changes in Representation in Local Authorities", in E. S. Nahon (ed.), *Ethnic Communities in Israel*. Jerusalem: Jerusalem Institute for Israel Studies, pp. 103–19.

Gutmann, Emanuel, and Landau, Jacob M. (1975). "The Political Elite and National Leadership in Israel", in G. Lenczowski (ed.), *Political Elites in the Middle East*. Washington: American Enterprise Institute, pp. 163–200.

Hamedina (1989). *State Comptroller 1989 Report on the Nomination of Directors in Governmental Corporations*. Jerusalem: Hamadpis Hamemshalti (Hebrew).

Hermann, Tamar (1998). *The Electoral System and Voting Behavior in Israel*. Tel Aviv: Open University (Hebrew).

Herzog, Hana, Shamir, Michael, and Zuckerman, Alan S. (1989). *The Israeli Politician: The Social and Political Bases of Israeli Labor and Herut Parties Activists*. Research, No. 34. Jerusalem: Machon Yerushalyim Lecheker Yisrael (Hebrew).

Horowiz, Dan, and Lissak, Moshe (1978). *Origins of the Israeli Polity*. Chicago: Chicago University Press.

Israel Women Network (1996). *Facts about Women in Israel*.

Kimmerling, Baruch (1983). *Zionism and Territory*. Berkeley: University of California Press.

Koren, Dani (1998). *The Demise of Parties in Israel*. Tel Aviv: Hakibbutz Hameuchad (Hebrew).

Lissak, Moshe (1981). *The Elites of the Jewish Community in Palestine*. Tel Aviv: Am Oved (Hebrew).

Maman, Daniel (1987). "The Second Career of Senior Military Officers and the Elites in Israel, 1974–1984", unpublished M.A. thesis, Jerusalem: Department of Anthropology and Sociology, Hebrew University.

—— (1997). "The Elite Structure in Israel: A Socio-Historical Analysis." *Journal of Political and Military Sociology*, 25: 25–46.

Neuberger, Benyamin (1997). *Political Parties in Israel*. Tel Aviv: Open University.

Peri, Yoram (1983). *Between Battles and Ballots: Israeli Military in Politics*. Cambridge: Cambridge University Press.

Rahat, Gideon (2001). "Changes in the Methods of Candidates Elections", in A. Arian and M. Shamir (eds), *The Elections in Israel—1999*. Jerusalem: Israel Democracy Institute, pp. 353–81 (Hebrew).

Ram, Uri (1993). "The Colonization Perspective in Israeli Sociology: Internal and External Comparisons." *Journal of Historical Sociology*, 6: 327–50.

——(1998). "Citizens, Consumers, and Believers: The Israeli Public Sphere between Fundamentalism and Capitalism." *Israel Studies*, 3: 24–44.

——(1999). "The State of the Nation: Contemporary Challenges to Zionism in Israel". *Constellations*, 6: 325–38.

——(2000). "The Promised Land of Business Opportunities: Liberal Post-Zionism in the Global Age", in G. Shafir and Y. Peled (eds.), *The New Israel*. Boulder: Westview Press, pp. 217–40.

Sager, Samuel (1988). *The Parliamentary System of Israel*. Syracus, NY: Syracuse University Press.

Shafir, Gershon (1989). *Land, Labor and the Origins of the Israeli Palestinian Conflict, 1882–1914*. Cambridge: Cambridge University Press.

Shapira, Boas (1996). "Electoral Reforms in Israel 1949–1996", in G. Doron (ed.), *The Electoral Revolution*. Tel Aviv: Hakkibutz Hameuhad, 16–34 (Hebrew).

Shapiro, Yonathan (1984). *An Elite Without Successors*. Tel Aviv: Sifriyat Poalim (Hebrew).

——(1989). *The Road to Power*. Albany: State University of New York Press.

Smooha, Sammy (1978). *Israel: Pluralism and Conflict*. Berkeley: University of California Press.

Susser, Bernard (1989). " 'Parliadential' Politics: A Proposed Constitution for Israel." *Paliamentary Affairs*, 42: 61–81.

Tunik, Yizhak (1987). *The Committee for Additional Occupations of Knesset Members*. Report. Jerusalem (Hebrew).

Weiss, Shevach (1997). *14,729 Missing Votes: An Analysis of the 1996 Elections in Israel*. Tel Aviv: Hakkibutz Hameuhad (Hebrew).

Yiftachel, Oren (1997). "Israeli Society and Jewish-Palestinian Reconciliation: Ethnocracy and its Contradictions." *Middle East Journal*, 51: 509–19.

Zamir, Dani (1977). *Generals and Politics in Israel*. Tel Aviv: Department of Sociology, Tel Aviv University (Hebrew).

12

Italy: The Homeland of the Political Class

ETTORE RECCHI AND LUCA VERZICHELLI

As one of the country's most respected intellectuals happened to observe, in Italy "the political class forms an entity of its own and appears as a separate body with its own sphere of action, which is perceived perfectly by those who do not belong to it." "By the way," he continued, "the same perception is also shared by members of the political class themselves who, as soon as they walk through the portals of the Montecitorio or Madama palaces [seats of the *Camera dei Deputati* and the *Senato della Repubblica*], immediately become aware that they are citizens of higher rank and behave accordingly" (Bobbio 1996: VIII). Although these "elementary remarks" (Bobbio 1996: IX) cannot be taken as proof of the "class consciousness" of both the political rulers and the ruled, they are certainly a clue to the success of Gaetano Mosca's view in the Italian public debate at the end of the twentieth century—one century after the publication of his masterpiece, *Elementi di scienza politica* (1896).

Mosca first resorted to the "political class" concept when dealing with the workings of the Italian state only just unified—a state in which, as compared to older and more firmly established constitutional regimes, those in power controlled institutions rather than the contrary.[1] Such a situation made it even more clear in Italy than elsewhere in the western world that the nuts and bolts of political life can scarcely be accounted for by legal principles alone. If it is true that theoretical frameworks tend to emerge from single country anomalies, Mosca's approach turned the idiosyncrasies of late nineteenth century Italian politics into a foundational concept of modern political science and sociology (Calise 1989: 195).

Despite such historical incentives, one has to wait for Giovanni Sartori's investigation on the Italian Parliament (Sartori *et al.* 1963) to find a serious empirical study

Both authors are equally responsible for the content of this essay. Ettore Recchi wrote the historical and institutional sections, Luca Verzichelli those on the political class and institutional reform, while the conclusion was written jointly. We are grateful to Robert A. Becker for linguistic assistance.

[1] As for the original definition of the concept, Mosca was quite vague. Interpreters tend to distinguish in his works a political class in the sense of "ruling class," and a political class *stricto sensu* comprising only the top decision-makers. While the concept spread out quickly in the Italian public debate, a third and different meaning prevailed: the political class as the set of stable incumbents of political offices (Bobbio 1996: 183–4). Following in Mosca's footsteps, Robert Michels reacted against this more specific formulation (Michels 1936: p. xiv). The definition used in this book is indeed closer to the revised understanding of the concept than to the elitists' original view.

on the national political class. After Sartori's seminal book and some isolated inquiries (Spreafico 1965; Meynaud 1966; DiRenzo 1967; Sani 1967), research on the political class blossomed in the seventies. Along with theoretical analyses (Farneti 1973), we find empirical studies dealing with ministers (Calise and Mannheimer 1982; Dogan 1989), parliamentarians (Putnam 1973; Barnes 1977; Cotta 1979), party cadres and leaders (Bettin 1970; Sani 1972*a,b*), as well as with town and regional councilors (Barberis 1983).

Despite this return of interest, a full-fledged portrait of the Italian political class is still lacking to date. Far from claiming to fill this gap, we aim to provide a broad description of some aspects of the Italian political class with special reference to recent transformations. In doing this, we will attempt to grasp the social and political conditions of the process of political professionalization. To deal with such a process conceptually, we set aside the old and tried amateur–professional dichotomy. Political professionalism is regarded rather as a continuous dimension, the level of which is contingent on *the degree of economic dependence, duration*, and *intensity of involvement* of political officeholders. In historical terms, we will chiefly, albeit not exclusively, focus on national legislators, considering that usually Parliament stands out as the focal point of political careers—as a fundamental goal for emerging politicians and a necessary starting point for more ambitious ones.[2]

POLITICAL PROFESSIONALIZATION IN HISTORICAL PERSPECTIVE

The emergence of Fascism (1922–43) splits the history of the Italian democratic experience in two phases: *Liberal Italy*, a constitutional monarchy which has to be considered a proto-democracy characterized by low (although progressively inclusive) participation, and *Republican Italy*, traditionally described as a party state or, with a more negative tinge, a "partitocracy" (Maranini 1968). These phases differ sharply regarding their social and institutional contexts (see below) and, of course, the basic features of their political classes. A less dramatic, but significant change took place at the beginning of the 1990s, when the party system changed drastically and the country experienced the highest turnover of political personnel ever recorded after the regime shake-ups of 1921–24 and 1946–48 (Cotta and Verzichelli 1996; Verzichelli 1998). As we write, it is hard to predict what the outcomes of this recent turning point will be, except that the political class has undergone a relevant transformation in terms of its typical background and composition (see conclusion).

In historical perspective, the evolution of political professionalism is perhaps most visible within legislatures (cf. Mosca 1982: 1021). The rising political professionalism

---

[2] As in past research, we will use data on the lower house, the Chamber (*Camera dei Deputati*), as this was the only elective branch of Parliament in the monarchic era. In the Republican era, as both chambers share about the same electoral system and constitutional functions, the more numerous *Camera* can be considered a representative sample of the whole universe of Italian MPs.

of MPs was a central finding in Sartori's pioneer analysis of Italian Parliaments (Sartori *et al.* 1963: 323–86). The consolidation of a professional body of politicians is the result of the growing duration, intensity, and specialization of the work of parliamentarians. In Sartori's idealtypical scheme, non-professional politicians (*rentiers*, local notables) were progressively replaced by semi-professional politicians (individuals coming from non-political occupations but with strong expectations to hold political posts in the future), and these by purely professional politicians (individuals without an alternative occupation). Thus, while it would be misleading to conceive a simple law of succession from one type of Member of Parliament (MP) to another, the emergence of professionalism among parliamentarians follows, to a considerable extent, the historical trend observed in Germany (see chapter on Germany, this volume), except for the fact that in Italy the control of local resources—agrarian ownership at first, party organization later on—has always been more important than the support of central interest groups (Farneti 1973; Mastropaolo 1986).[3]

After the First World War, social and political unrest shook the political system profoundly. The liberal political class proved to be unprepared to tackle the economic crisis and the mounting protest. As a result, there was a considerable turnover of MPs in 1919. Not until the advent of Fascism, however, did changes within the political class occur in the form of "amalgamation"—to use Michels' formula—rather than in that of "replacement" of traditional notables. In particular, circulation of the ministerial elite was very limited (Cotta 1983).

As Fascism took power, many old politicians were expelled from state institutions, replaced by a younger generation of political cadres and leaders among whom aristocrats were more and more a minority. Yet, the process was less sudden and dramatic than that caused by the rise of National Socialism in Germany.[4] Although members of the fascist elites were socially somehow more varied than their predecessors, the upper class continued to be over-represented in political office. Local studies show that after 1927, when Mussolini's dictatorship had consolidated, the bulk of the fascist political class consisted of entrepreneurs, academics, army officials, and high-level civil servants (Zangarini 1978). Although it formed the main social pillar of the regime, the petty bourgeoisie was given little room at the top. Overall, Fascism set up an unprecedented political control of society, which brought about an increase in the number of political jobs as well as, of course, a larger than ever cultural homogeneity of political officeholders. As a consequence of both processes, Fascism, in its own way, helped institutionalize political professionalism in Italy.

---

[3] According to some historians, already at the beginning of the twentieth century the prominence of a large number of MPs depended on their political office rather than on extra-political status (Pombeni 1993: 70–2). The early semi-professional politicians were notables that, once elected to the legislature, used to emphasize the political identity they achieved as parliamentarians rather than their ascribed prestige in local communities. Generally speaking, thus, political professionalism was at first favored by the state appropriation of social power rather than by the democratization of political recruitment.

[4] Biographical records of the fascist political class can be found in Missori (1986). Unfortunately, to our knowledge, this data collection has not been analyzed systematically yet.

Only with the comeback of democracy and the introduction of the universal franchise could a real expansion of the social recruitment pool for Italian politicians occur. Political professionalism was then furthered by the democratization of representation. In the first instance, regime change brought with itself an almost total turnover of the political class. Only 14.6 percent of the members of the Constituent Assembly in 1946 had had previous parliamentary experience (Cotta 1979), while the large majority of MPs had entered politics through party involvement during the liberation civil war (1943–45). An instrumental union of otherwise strongly dissenting parties marked the civil war itself, which was to be reflected in the constitution of 1948. In the years to come, the surprising "constitution-worship" of politicians from all sides (Putnam 1973: 193) was proof that the pact of cooperation enshrined in the constitution continued to keep the political class unified in spite of overt ideological conflicts.

An equally widespread belief of Italian politicians in the Republican age has been that political power belonged to parties more than to any other institution—such as Parliament or government (Putnam 1973: 13). Parties, indeed, were pivotal and undisputed actors not only in decision-making, but also in political recruitment and the structuring of careers. Since the early postwar years, members of the Italian political class have typically shared a precocious involvement in party work and a subsequent long-standing career in party positions. Parties—especially the more centralized ones, such as the PCI (*Partito Comunista Italiano*)—governed these careers by establishing regular paths and timings of the progressive rise from lower to upper political offices.

In historical perspective, the mean tenure of Italian MPs stands out as a good indicator of party control of political careers (see Fig. 12.1). The average seniority of MPs decreases considerably in 1946, remaining thereafter stable around a "normal" level until the 1990s. Although this merely quantitative measurement is only a rough guideline for the analysis of parliamentary careers, its trend turns out to be in line with some other developments illustrated so far: (1) a first phase of formation of a stable parliamentary class (1861–80) and its further consolidation (1880–1900); (2) an incipient decline of notables during Giolitti's age (1900–19); and (3) a much greater change in the years following the First World War, when a large part of "gentlemen politicians" were replaced by "party professionals" (Sartori *et al.* 1963; Cotta 1983). Finally, whereas in the 1946–92 period the mean tenure is stable around 2.5 legislatures, after 1992 the average seniority sinks to an unprecedented level, because of the almost total breakup of the old political class and a subsequent, uncertain transitory phase during which a less consistent pattern of parliamentary elite circulation emerged.[5]

THE INSTITUTIONAL CONTEXT

Since its unification in 1860, liberal Italy has been marked by territorial fragmentation— in economic, cultural, and political terms. A number of regional, sub-regional, and

[5] Parliamentary turnover was already high in 1992 (around 40% both in the Chamber and the Senate). In 1994, it reached 71% in the Chamber (around 60% in the Senate). Albeit lower, the rates of 1996 and 2001 are over the average of the Republican legislatures (around 40% in both parliamentary branches).

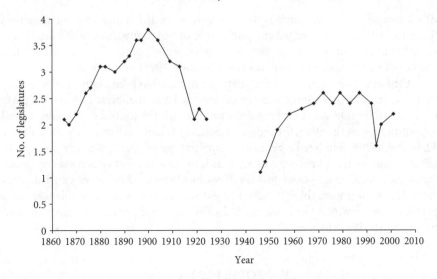

Figure 12.1 *Mean parliamentary tenure in the* Camera dei Deputati *(legislative periods)*
Source: DATA-CUBE; Parliamentary Elites Archive, University of Siena.

urban political institutions have always existed; yet a real decentralization of the state to represent these differences has never gained momentum. The 1948 constitution established a general principle of regional devolution, which was to be implemented only in 1970, often being limited by central control of economic and fiscal policies. Nonetheless, clear-cut discontinuities between pre-fascist and post-fascist democracy need to be stressed:

(1) the form of state: constitutional monarchy (1861–1948) vs. republic;
(2) suffrage: restricted (until 1913) vs. universal (extended to women in 1948);
(3) the electoral system: majority (until 1919) vs. proportional (until 1994) or mixed (after 1994);[6]
(4) party organizations and party power: erratic vs. hegemonic.

The bulk of such basic innovations finds its legal rationale in the Republican constitution of 1948.[7] This document, a long and rigid set of 139 articles, gave birth to a democratic and pluralistic parliamentary government based on a mix of liberal principles and social provisions inspired by both catholic and socialist traditions.

---

[6] In 1993, the proportional system was replaced by a mixed system, first past the post for 75% of the seats, proportionality for the distribution (with regional lists) of the remaining 25%, being valid for both the Chamber and the Senate—apart from some apparently minor differences in the proportional quota which, however, turned out to be relevant in 1994 (the first election based on the new system) and 1996. For a discussion of mixed systems, see Katz (1996).

[7] The electoral system was not included in the constitution, and this made the possibility of reforms easier thereafter, like the unsuccessful attempt to introduce a majority bonus in 1953 and the reforms of the 1990s.

Albeit in a somewhat ambiguous way in regard to their functions and prerogatives, the constitution acknowledged the public role of political parties, which had been, since the aftermath of Fascism, the gatekeepers of the political system and the real sources of policy-making (Pasquino 1987; Morlino 1991).

In the Republican age, the role of parliamentarians has been defined substantially by common constraints and resources: on the one hand, the severe influence of party (or party faction) leaders on major decisions through the control of candidacies and appointments; on the other, the legislative powers of small parliamentary committees. The first factor hindered the institutionalization of parliamentary groups as autonomous centers of decision-making, as is the case in other countries; the second factor gave back some power to MPs allowing them, as they sat in parliamentary committees, to engage in log-rolling and to form consociational alliances on a personal basis—which yielded a myriad of *ad hoc,* and sometimes contradictory, particularistic laws (*leggine*).[8]

THE POLITICAL CLASS

Size and Composition

The boundaries of the Italian political class remain, nevertheless, extremely difficult to trace (Calise 1989: 186–7). Apart from theoretical problems of boundedness, the "anti-politician" attitude of public opinion has always encouraged "hidden political professionalism" within party structures (Panebianco 1988). Much for the same reason, MPs and local political elites are accustomed to denying full-time professionalism by presenting themselves, in biographical accounts, as "free-lance journalists" or "consultants." It is likely that this self-denying attitude may even be on the rise. Thus, estimates of the size of the political class vary from some 20,000 (Sartori *et al.* 1963: 281) to half a million people (Guarino 1980: 50; Sidoti 1993: 339). Whilst, as will be pointed out, political professionalism is a growing historical phenomenon, estimates of its growth mainly differ due to the working definition of "political class" as such. In the 1991 census, 1,141 persons were recorded as "members of government and legislative assemblies" and 8,431 as "heads of collective bodies of national interest" (Istat 1995: 356). Presumably, the political class is larger but these individuals—as self-defined professionals of political and quasi-political activities—form its more conscious core.

Between 1992 and 1996, political scandals shook the Italian political class at all levels. Suffice it to say that at the end of the 11th legislature (1994), the judiciary prosecuted around 60 percent of parliamentarians and thousands of locally elected representatives. Several parties—including the oldest one, the *Partito Socialista Italiano* (PSI)—were disbanded; all the others were forced, at the very least, to change their name. Delegitimation spread rapidly. The *classe politica* as a whole, which was

---

[8] Because of this phenomenon, currently there are some 150,000 laws in Italy—about fifty times more than in Britain and thirty times more than in Germany.

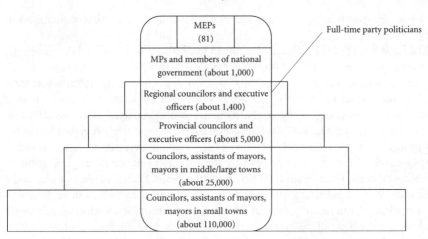

Figure 12.2   *Size and structure of the political class in Italy, 2002*

often taken as being the culprit for all national problems, was firebranded by journalists and commentators with the easily recognizable stigma of corruption. Opposition to full-time politicians entered as a primary—and successful—point in the platforms of new parties in 1994.[9] In the public debate, limits to political professionalism were proposed as a remedy against corruption and a spur to a more vital and efficient democracy (Panebianco 1993). At the same time, the political class theme was resumed by social scientists as a factor for the understanding of system-level continuities and change (Pizzorno 1993; Mastropaolo 1993*a*; Cotta and Verzichelli 1996).

Figure 12.2 shows the size and structure of the current political class in a schematic way. The size of the horizontal bars (representing the strata of the different elective and executive positions) has not changed in the last 25 years, whereas the rectangular area (representing full-time politicians) has shrunk. The top of the pyramid, the position of national representatives, never decreased in Italy, although the proposal for a drastic reduction of MPs was repeatedly discussed. In fact, the elected Members of Parliament numbered about 600 in the lower chamber before Fascism[10] and rose to 1,000 in Republican legislatures.[11] After the Second World War, the bulk of them

[9] However, the Communist Party had already launched, before the scandals, a program of organizational renewal aimed at reducing significantly the number of political professionals among its representatives (Baccetti 1997: 65–9).

[10] The precise number varied due to frequent changes in constituency boundaries. The non-elective Senate was huge and very variable in size as well, since the *Statuto* allowed the appointment of an unlimited number of Senators to represent twenty-one social categories. All attempts to reform the composition of Parliament before the rise of Fascism were unsuccessful (Merlini 1995).

[11] More precisely, there are 630 deputies and 315 elected senators—a size determined by a constitutional amendment of 1963. To this number one must add a small group of appointed senators, because every President of the Republic can appoint five *de jure* senators. In turn, heads of state become senators for life at the end of their mandates.

have been long-standing politicians and/or party professionals—that is, members of the political class.

The largest part of the political class sits in local institutions. Official data from the Interior Ministry report that 6,500 people hold office in regional and provincial councils and governments; there were 150,000 town councilors until 1993, when their number was reduced to 120,000; mayors amount to about 8,000.[12] Turnover in local institutions is always higher than in Parliament—around 60 percent in normal times, up to 80 percent in the mid-1990s. Correspondingly, among local office-holders political professionals are a minority. Yet, during their mandate, few mayors, mayoral assistants (an executive position appointed by the mayor) in major towns, and regional councilors can afford to retain their private occupations. Furthermore, one can find a hard core of local political professionals in any province, as well as in regions and municipalities. Until recently, even in the smallest communities, leadership roles were assigned on the basis of political career backgrounds. Overall, semi-professionalism appears to be the most common condition of local politicians (Caciagli 1991).

In addition, the Italian political class comprises party cadres and leaders living off politics—in central and local offices. Up to recent years, all parties used to maintain long-standing officials in their ruling bodies. Yet, their number was cut sharply in the aftermath of the scandals concerning illegal party-funding in the 1990s. According to some estimates, in 1994 the largest party organization—that of the Democratic Party of the Left (*Partito Democratico della Sinistra* (PDS), then renamed as *Democratici di Sinistra* (DS), heir of the Italian Communist Party (PCI)—counted on 670 functionaries; there used to be 3,141 in the PCI in 1976 (Baccetti 1997: 170–1).[13] By the late seventies, it was said that Christian Democrats had about 1,000 and the Socialists some 700 employed officials (Pacifici 1983: 100, 116),[14] while the right-wing *Movimento Sociale Italiano* (MSI) paid sixty-two salaries in 1980 and its successor *Alleanza Nazionale* (AN) only twenty-six in 1994, when it entered government for the first time (Tarchi 1997: 286). As traditional parties crumbled, in 1993 the Ciampi government even promoted a law that favored the pensions of party workers in order to facilitate the cut in party personnel. Seemingly, however, party professionals reacted to the perspective of retirement with a harsher intra-organizational competition for candidature to public office, thus, fostering the political professionalism of representation.

At the lowest levels, to these figures one should add an undefinable number of public employees (e.g. civil servants in local administration) who, being party members, are

---

[12] In 1993, a reform of the electoral system in local government introduced the direct election of mayors, presidents of provinces, and presidents of regions. About the impact of these recent institutional reforms see below.

[13] In the Communist Party functionaries used to earn as much as specialized blue collar workers in the metalworking industry (Pacifici 1983: 74). Communist MPs were asked to devolve to their party half of their parliamentary allowance, and local representatives to devolve their whole salary, in exchange for a wage paid by the party. This regulation was no longer applied by the PDS in all regions in the 1990s (Baccetti 1997: 215–16).

[14] Furthermore, the DC, PSI, and the minor center–left parties were highly factionalized, so that each leader had his/her own "cultural association" or "think tank" which worked as a personal apparatus.

"detached" from their routine and indulgently earmarked for political work by elected executives. Similar roles are played by *portaborse* (literally "bag-carriers")— that is, assistants to national MPs and European MPs—who certainly live off politics and, in some cases, perform their job with an eye to a future political career. Finally, other members of the political class hold offices in trade unions,[15] non-elective political authorities (e.g. public health agencies), public firms, the European Parliament, and government.[16]

Such a social dissemination, so to speak, of the political class stems from the expansionism of Italian parties, which have allegedly served as prototypes for Katz' and Mair's (1995) well-known model of "cartel party." Given this dispersion, it is hard to draw a complete sociological profile of the Italian political class. Existing research, in fact, primarily focuses on the social characteristics of parliamentarians and local elites.[17]

The average age of Italian legislators in the 1946–96 period (in the Chamber) was about 50 years; the average age at their first election was 45. The majority of the MPs had a high educational background (most often in law and humanities, even though recently business and medical backgrounds have increased), as well as middle-upper class origins. Apparently, in this respect, little has changed from the times of the old "liberal" political class. A closer look, however, reveals that many occupational categories have disappeared from the parliamentary landscape since the Second World War—that is, financial *rentiers*, army officers, and landowners. Others have been diminished, like practicing lawyers, whose numbers have dropped from about 50 percent of the MPs in the monarchic *Camera* to 32 percent in 1946 and to 11 percent in 1992. In contrast, throughout the period 1948–92, about one fourth of all parliamentary personnel was recruited from among full-time politicians—that is, people whose last occupation (if not the only one) before election was a party or trade union job.

After reaching a peak in the sixties, the proportion of experienced political professionals in the *Camera* has declined slowly until the nineties, when the precipitous fall

---

[15] The largest trade union, the left-wing CGIL, had "at least 7,000 full-time employees" in 1976; it then appeared to be the biggest trade union bureaucracy in Europe (Coi 1979: 221). Considering only full-time functionaries (i.e. excluding secretaries and administrative workers without political tasks), a more recent estimate indicates some 6,000–7,000 people as the universe of Italian trade unionists (Giovannini 1997: 180). Compared to the rest of the Italian political class, trade unionists present themselves as individuals of lower class origins and lower education. Nonetheless, less than one-third of them ever had a working-class occupation. Given their early involvement in trade unions and the mobility among different political offices (in parties, local authorities, and so on), it seems reasonable to consider them part of the political class (Giovannini 1997: 184–6).

[16] Until recently, ministers and junior ministers were almost always drawn from among Members of Parliament (Calise and Mannheimer 1982). Since the 1980s, the number of non-elected ministers has increased (most of them were, in any case, party politicians). With the "technocrat" governments of the early nineties (Ciampi and Dini cabinets especially), this phenomenon has been much more evident (Cotta and Verzichelli 1996). However, also "political" Prime Ministers like Berlusconi and Prodi resorted to some extra-political personalities, above all in the staff of junior ministers and the financial ministries.

[17] For research on MPs see Cotta (1979, 1983); Cotta and Di Palma (1986); Mastropaolo (1993a, 1996); Cotta and Verzichelli (1996); Verzichelli (1995, 1998); Cotta, Mastropaolo, and Verzichelli (2000). On local politicians see Barberis (1983); Melis and Martinotti (1988); Bettin and Magnier (1989, 1991); Cazzola (1991); Bettin (1993); Baccetti (1999); Recchi (2001); Della Porta (2002).

of many parties, the partial dismissal of the proportional electoral system, and the judicial indictment of a large part of the professional politicians, made room for less experienced representatives. In general, the stronger the party organization, the larger the number of experienced political professionals among its representatives. Hence, the PDS/DS (hereafter simply DS) and the *Partito della Rifondazione Comunista* (Refounded Communist Party, PRC) on the left wing, as well as AN on the right, can count currently on a higher proportion of political professionals in their ranks. *Ceteris paribus*, left-wing parties tend to rely on a larger number of career politicians.[18]

Party differences in the social composition of Italian MPs have always been and remain strong. The two main parliamentary groups of the winning coalition of 1996 show some continuity with the traditional party of the left (the Communist party)— in particular, the election to Parliament at a relatively early age and the predominance of political professionals, teachers, and academics among them.[19] Lawyers and other professionals are instead over-represented in the ranks of *Alleanza Nazionale*,[20] while *Forza Italia* and the *Lega Nord* rely on somewhat newer kinds of political personnel. Berlusconi's party has taken to Parliament an extraordinarily high share of entrepreneurs and managers (many working in some of the party leader's firms, especially in advertising). Among the MPs of the League, finally, artisans, salesmen, petty bourgeois businessmen, and less qualified professionals prevail.

In spite of recent changes, the gender bias in the Italian Parliament has remained substantially unaltered. In 1996 women amounted to less than 10 percent of Italian MPs, about as many as in the eighties.[21] Nor has the reshuffling of the party system affected party differences in women's under-representation—always more severe in center and right-wing parties (Verzichelli 1998, 2002*a*). Similarly, the age profile of Parliamentarians has not changed: turnover of the elite has not necessarily implied rejuvenation.

As far as can be seen from some studies on mayors (Spreafico 1965; Segatori 1992), political professionalism has advanced at a slower pace in the periphery of the Italian political system. Notables until the mid-1960s still frequently governed local communities. In contrast, political professionalism has always been more pronounced at the regional level—for instance, as early as 1971, 27 percent of the members of the Sicilian regional assembly were full-time party or trade union professionals

---

[18] In 1996, MPs with a background in both party and local elective offices made up 40% of the total in the *Rifondazione Comunista* (RCI), 59% in the PDS, and 62% in the AN. Among *Forza Italia* representatives, they counted for no more than 13%; much higher is their number among the MPs of the *Lega Nord* (44%), which thus proved to have become a party with structured career norms. For a more detailed description, see Verzichelli (1998).

[19] In general, MPs elected in the center–left cartel are more often drawn from among public employees, while their colleagues elected in the center–right coalitions are mostly recruited from the private sector (Verzichelli 1998).

[20] Also in the past, lawyers formed the largest occupational group within the ruling elite of the MSI— the extreme right-wing party from which *Alleanza Nazionale* originated (De Felice 1996: 264).

[21] The proportion of women within the constituent assembly of 1946 was only 3.6%. It rose slowly until 1979 (7.9% in the *Camera*); reached its peak in 1987 (12.5%), but slid back to 8.4% in 1992. In 1994, women MPs reached 15%, but only by virtue of a law that enforced the alternation of men and women in the rigid lists of candidates for proportional voting. Once this clause disappeared, there was a return to "normal" female under-representation.

(Mastropaolo 1993*b*: 101). In those same years, municipal councils started to become the realm of middle-aged male civil servants (Barberis 1983). The bureaucrats' "invasion" of local governments culminated in the late eighties, when four out of ten councilors in towns with more than 100,000 inhabitants were public employees (Bettin and Magnier 1989: 127).

Interestingly, their retreat began some time before—not after—the introduction of the direct election of local executives in 1993, in favor of professionals. This replacement may find a rationale in budget restrictions in local government which, since the late 1980s, reduced opportunities for the recruitment and promotion of political clientele. As parties lost the capacity to reward their activists with jobs or career advancements in public administration, civil servants somehow withdrew from political commitments. Room was, thus, created for other possible aspirants, among whom professionals frequently prevailed thanks to politically useful resources such as their wealth, prestige, specific skills, dispensability, and personal social capital.

By the mid-1990s, professionals formed the majority of politicians elected to local government—among mayors, they had grown from 13.3 percent (1987) to 23.5 percent (1993), and finally to 40.5 percent in 1995 (Recchi 2001). Although not so spectacularly, in the last few years the number of women has increased, reaching a share similar to that of female MPs—about 10 percent. In contrast, the number of young people has diminished despite the high turnover of political personnel. Finally, the social composition of party officials reflects, to a large extent, that of the rest of the Italian political class. Among them there are few women, most of whom are concentrated in the ranks of the Democratic Left.

Political Recruitment and Political Careers

Two main patterns of entry into the political class soon emerged in postwar democratic Italy: a "party-apparatus model" of recruitment close to the empirical example of the Communist Party, and a "clientele party" model close to the example of the Christian Democrats (Cotta 1979). In the first case, candidates were chosen on the basis of their work within the party organization; non-party elective offices did not constitute a crucial experience for the promotion to higher positions. In the latter case, as a considerable number of voters could be mobilized on the basis of patronage relations, parties recruited—and somehow coordinated—individual political entrepreneurs. At the end of the day, differences between the two models depended on the degree of party centralization and personnel homogeneity—both considerably higher in the PCI than in the DC (Wertman 1988; Norris 1996). All parties, however, were not only concerned with recruitment, but also with the early socialization and training of their recruits to the rules of the political game. To do this most effectively, the political class used to be formed by individuals,

(1) who entered active politics early in their lives—in 1992, two thirds of the MPs had entered the political arena before the age of 25 and average party membership was more than 20 years;

(2) who served their apprenticeship in some party office—more than half the
MPs in 1992 (Recchi 1996, 1999).

Even local politicians were not exempt from the imperative to prove their party
allegiance and respect the timing and steps of a gradual career path; for instance, in
1992, Italian mayors had accumulated—on average—30 years in political office, half
of which in party posts (Bettin 1997: 207).

The party roots of parliamentarians are reasonably well indicated by the fact of
having held party offices prior to their election to the *Camera* or not. In the long run,
by using this indicator, two moments of decline of the "partisan" type of political
professionalism emerge. The first phase, in the middle of the 1970s, followed a
moment of increasing consensus between the major parties of the Republican age
(DC and PCI). From that time on, these parties faced electoral decline, which they
tried to resist by resorting to "independent" and "expert" candidates on their lists.
The second phase of change occurred in the nineties, when the proportion of MPs
with some partisan socialization to active politics sank dramatically (but in 1996
increased slightly again). There are few doubts that this phenomenon is an effect of
the crisis of the party system. In 1994, all political forces in Parliament were new
(at least formally) since none of the labels used by previous parliamentary groups
survived. Furthermore, many of these new parties proved to be unstable and
provisional, suffering a large number of splits and mergers during the two following
legislatures (Di Virgilio 1998, 2002). The instability within the parliamentary elite
was also marked by many unprecedented shifts from one parliamentary group to
another (Verzichelli 2002b).

Nonetheless, data about the MPs elected in 2001 show that a political socialization
grounded on some party experience (often coupled with a background as local representatives) still remains the typical feature in the recruitment of national representatives. Generally speaking, the political experiences of the parliamentary elite look
very similar to those of their predecessors a couple of decades ago (see Fig. 12.3).

The effect of the change from a proportional to a majoritarian electoral system on
political recruitment is hard to assess. It seems, though, that recruitment processes
and strategies have remained heavily centralized (Di Virgilio 2002). The new system
has only brought about some rather predictable innovations—such as a more active
presence of candidates in their constituencies and the selection of personalities who
are representative of the whole coalition—but not others, such as primaries.

Research on the political careers of Italian MPs has distinguished three stages:
(1) the *pre-political*, consisting in the accumulation of resources prior to political office,
(2) the *political*, that is the set of political offices prior to election to Parliament,
and (3) the *parliamentary stage*, made up of all positions within Parliament which
create opportunities for further career development (Cotta 1979, 1983). This latter
stage deserves special attention, as it is a common concern for MPs—and a more dramatic one considering the sharp rise of parliamentary turnover in the 1990s (Cotta
and Verzichelli 1996). In fact, Parliament has rarely been a final step in the careers of
the members of the Italian political class: it was often the launching pad towards

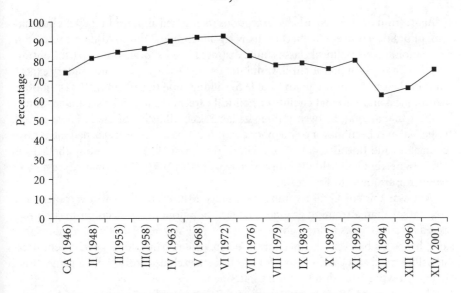

Figure 12.3 *MPs with party background in the* Camera

Note: Data refer to any type of party offices held before entering Parliament for the first time.

Source: Center for the Study of Political Change, University of Siena.

more important (such as governmental) or more secure (such as in parties or sub-governmental agencies) political appointments.

On the one hand, until 1990, practically all ministers were recruited from among MPs. Equally, in Italy, a conspicuous share of European parliamentarians was—and still is—recruited from among national MPs. Interestingly, neither ministers nor European MPs are usually giving up their parliamentary seats.[22] Resistance to leaving Parliament seems to prove, once again, the centrality of the legislature as the "natural arena" of the nation's political class.

On the other hand, classical post-parliamentary career destinies were positions in subgovernmental agencies or public firms, or in the party apparatus (Sartori *et al.* 1963: 329). The first option was more widespread in the DC and its allies, the second one in the Communist Party. According to informal party rules, Christian Democratic MPs had to maintain a high personal vote in order to run for subgovernmental positions. In contrast, the Communists used to re-enter the party organizational apparatus after two terms—with the notable exception of party leaders. While the first career pattern spread out in all parties through the years, both have survived until the 1990s—that is, for about half a century, an extraordinarily long period of continuity in a comparative perspective (Cotta and Verzichelli 1996).

---

[22] The proportion of Italian members of the European Parliament with a simultaneous mandate as national MP is the highest in Europe: 30.8 (1979), 20.9 (1984), 30.8 (1989), 45.9 (1994), and 27.6 in 1999. Dual mandates are quite exceptional in Strasbourg.

Apart from the few remarkable exceptions mentioned above,[23] in Italy the cumulation of political offices is subject to many legal incompatibilities. Also for this reason, the national-level political class is quite distinct from its local counterpart. Contrary to other cases, local politics in Italy did not use to be a necessary preliminary experience in the careers of the political elite for a long time (Guadagnini 1984). In other words, local and national circuits of political careers tended to be separated. Suffice it to say that among the twenty-three Italian Prime Ministers of the 1945–98 period, none had ever been mayor or member of any local executive; only six had sat as town councilors and one as regional councilor (Bontempi 1995: 32). Among the MPs in 1992, 18 percent had held the office of mayor (Bettin 1993: 55), a small share if compared, for example, to France.

Why was this so? Until recently, the average MP regarded local government as a trap rather than a training ground. The lack of autonomy in decision-making rendered executive roles in local government not very rewarding in terms of popularity and, hence, as bases for further career advancement. Thus, local government occasionally served as a "parking lot" for old leaders excluded from the big game rather than as an apprenticeship for future statesmen.

However, since 1993 mayors are directly elected and, as a result, wield broader institutional powers than before when they were subject to appointment by the town councils. On the whole, their popularity has grown considerably. The same has to be said concerning the executive offices at the regional level, especially after the introduction of direct election of the Presidents of the regional executives in 1999— recently often labeled as *governatori* by the media, pointing to their growing importance in an increasingly federalized political system—and the significant devolution of power triggered by a constitutional reform in 2001. Therefore, we could easily argue that success as local executives (e.g. as directly elected mayors and presidents of regional governments) is bound to be a more effective career springboard than it used to be. At the same time, we are observing an increasing process of bidirectional "level-hopping," since a significant amount of second-line national politicians (including MPs) seem to be interested in moving back to local government offices (such as mayors of big towns or regional presidents) in order to gain visibility and influence in decision-making.

Living off Politics

In Italy, a real salary for legislators was introduced only in 1948, while the small amount provided by ordinary legislation since 1880 had been nothing more than a sort of token reimbursement. Political jobs were not an institutionalized activity. The pre-Republican statute only established a formal "opening" of the annual parliamentary

---

[23] According to article 65 of the constitution, ordinary law determines the cases of incompatibility with the office of MP. Currently, members of regional councils, mayors of towns with more than 20,000 inhabitants, and presidents of provincial administrations cannot be elected to Parliament. The same is true for members of the Higher Council of Justice.

session, leaving the organization of work to internal regulations. In practice, the degree of involvement of every single deputy was, since the first legislature of 1861, relatively high, but only after 1948 was the busy agenda of the MPs formally determined by both the constitution and parliamentary norms.[24]

Describing the social profile and behavior of the Italian MPs in the first two decades of Republican history, Sartori *et al.* (1963) highlighted the emergence of an elite "living off politics." The starting point of the new era was, of course, the introduction of a real salary for every MP—an effect of the 1948 constitution.[25] Since 1965 the salary of parliamentarians is automatically tied to the income of higher judges (*presidenti di sezione di Corte di Cassazione*). A number of small changes have been introduced subsequently to permit greater tax deductions.

To date, the monthly basic parliamentary salary (*indennità parlamentare*) is €5,100 after taxes. In addition, every MP receives a daily allowance (*diaria di soggiorno*) which can amount up to €4,300 per month,[26] a standard reimbursement covering mail and telephone expenses (both in Rome and in the constituency), free train and flight tickets, and a fixed amount for recruiting a legislative assistant. On average, the parliamentary salary is about €7,500. Increases in MPs' salaries are not subject to external control: the normal inflation index, applied as to any other public sector category, determines salary dynamics, while Parliament can modify its members' other privileges autonomously. In the past, this opportunity was exploited to introduce many fringe benefits and pay rises.

In 1993, however, under the siege of a very hostile public opinion, Parliamentarians reduced the allowance for parliamentary assistants and linked its use to more detailed justifications. Some restrictions on outside income were also introduced. As a consequence, MPs cannot receive public salaries or engage in contractual relations with public administrations. Moreover, every year their total incomes and assets (as well as the tax declarations of their families) must be transmitted to the office of the chairman of their parliamentary branch who can (and usually does) make them public.

Another crucial theme, related to the salary of MPs, concerns pensions. As is common in public service, the years in Parliament can be added to a previous public sector career in order to obtain a pension. Alternatively, a period of two full legislatures is sufficient to be entitled to a life-long pension. Therefore, at least one reelection is important in order to have the chance to live off politics following parliamentary mandates. Budgetary constraints and growing anti-political feeling have recently persuaded MPs to make minor adjustments to these rules, which are perceived anyway as an important privilege for the political class.

---

[24] In the Republican constitution, article 62 sets two parliamentary sessions which start the first working day of October and February, respectively. Specific rules of duration and work organization are provided by the regulations of the Chamber and the Senate.

[25] Article 69 of the constitution simply states that every MP receives a certain amount (*indennità parlamentare*) but leaves the regulation of this issue to ordinary law.

[26] Recently, a special deduction called "absence fine" was introduced to reduce the daily allowance for those MPs who do not participate in parliamentary work.

THE POLITICAL CLASS AND INSTITUTIONAL REFORM

In the age of *partitocrazia*, there were very few proposals for institutional and constitutional reform and the majority dealt with details that could strengthen the party control of Italian politics. In particular, one of the main concerns of the political class was to update parliamentary procedures aimed at preserving the prerogatives of MPs in certain legislative sectors. The reform of the budget system of 1978 is, for instance, a good example of the efforts of Parliament to safeguard its prominence in decision-making. In the ongoing competition between legislative and executive powers, the political class defended collective bodies (Parliament at the center, local councils at the periphery) against possible institutional reforms towards a less assembly-like form of government (Cavalli 1992). This defense was, in fact, a way of defending the role of parties, which find themselves always more at ease in controlling members of assemblies rather than monocratic office-holders.

The protests against party omnipotence were, at the beginning, limited to the voices of some intellectuals (e.g. Maranini 1968) but, as time passed, demand for institutional reforms rose. In 1970, two important constitutional provisions were enacted. On the one hand, some devolution was set in motion with the introduction of regional administrations, which created new political posts and thus expanded the political class. On the other hand, the referendum for the abrogation of laws (*referendum abrogativo*) was put to work. That tool was at first used by minor and isolated parties to change some pieces of legislation (among them, the public funding of parties introduced in 1974). Later on, this instrument proved itself useful in bringing about strong innovations, after some 20 years in which the theme of constitutional reforms was raised again and again.

Before the 1990s, this theme had indeed entered the parliamentary debates recurrently but without any serious consequence due to crossed vetoes between various groups (Morel 1996).[27] Only a new wave of referenda, this time aimed at dismantling the old proportional electoral system,[28] happened to engender political change. More precisely, the referenda served as a precipitating factor, conjuring up with events like

---

[27] A first special committee (*commissione Bozzi*) for constitutional reforms was inaugurated in 1983. After 10 years (1992) another committee was formed (*commissione De Mita-Iotti*), but it could not conclude its work due to the anticipated ending of the legislature in 1994. A special committee for institutional reforms was finally appointed by both chambers after the election of 1996 (*commissione D'Alema*). This committee elaborated an organic reform of the constitution, addressing various issues from the electoral system to federalism, the organization of justice and, above all, a new form of government. Among other things, the direct election of the President of the Republic was introduced in the draft approved by the committee. Parliament, however, did not process the whole package of reforms, and even this attempt to modernize the 1948 constitution failed. Reforms are still on the political agenda: at the end of 1999, another small but significant change was made by introducing the direct election of regional presidents but political instability and volatility within the party system make the perspectives for larger reform designs very uncertain.

[28] A first referendum, held in 1991, abolished the preferential vote for election to the *Camera dei Deputati*. In 1993, another referendum abolished a significant part of the electoral law for the *Senato*. Both referenda had a very large popular participation, though some major parties explicitly invited their voters to desert the polls. The abrogations proposed were supported by an extremely wide majority of the electorate.

the restructuring of some parties (in particular the PCI) and the scandals of *Tangentopoli* (a sort of "Bribesville"). The "partitocratic" political class proved unable to defend itself from such attacks, leaving the scene to a confused alternation of emergency cabinets, non-political personalities, and unstable majorities. The most relevant reforms of these years, namely a new electoral law and a new form of government in local administration, were in fact formulated and implemented by the technocratic cabinets of Amato (1992), Ciampi (1993), and Dini (1995). In contrast, the Parliaments of the nineties, just like their predecessors, did not react to the growing social pressures for change with the energy, creativity, and courage needed to match the willingness of self-defense with the necessity of innovation.

After three legislatures being elected under the new semi-majoritarian electoral system, the political class is still unstable due to its inability to change the rules. Neither the centre–left cabinets in power between 1996 and 2001, nor the centre–right government following Berlusconi's clear victory in the 2001 election have warranted a substantial increase in political stability. The weak legitimation of the political class is particularly evident at the parliamentary level (Verzichelli 2002*b*), while local politicians, mayors from larger towns, and regional Presidents are more visible on the political stage and more trusted as "problem solvers." On the other hand, the influence of some of the outside experts temporarily replacing the political class in the nineties seems on the decline: Professional politicians are returning to Parliament, asking for the same kind of immunity that had been reduced just a few years ago. Meanwhile, technocrats are leaving the cabinet. Moreover, "democracy by referendum" has lost its appeal.[29]

In this framework, the redefinition of an accountable *political class* appears to be a necessary step. Only then could the political impasse and the distrust of "politicians" still felt by a large part of the public be overcome. The answers to the renewed claims for a number of constitutional and sub-constitutional reforms will probably be the most important test for measuring progress. In fact, at least three domains of institutional reform are still under discussion: federalism (although a "strong decentralization" already occurred with a constitutional reform in 2001),[30] the transformation of the parliamentary system; and, last but not least, the Italian contribution to a new phase of supranational integration.[31]

AFTER THE CRISIS: WHAT KIND OF POLITICAL CLASS?

Many analyses of the Italian political class have emphasized the correspondence between changes in its recruitment and composition and key innovations of the

---

[29] All the referendums proposed between 1997 and 2003 (including two concerning the electoral system for the national Parliament) did not reach the quorum of valid votes (50%) imposed by the constitution.

[30] This reform was one of the last innovations by the center-left government in charge between 1996 and 2001. The new center–right coalition, which includes the *Lega Nord*—after all a regionalist party— was promising a stronger commitment to a full federalization of the state during the 2001 electoral campaign. But the positions within the governmental majority are still quite divergent.

[31] With regard to the last two issues, the center–right coalition is showing a certain inclination to a "semi-presidential regime" and a more eurosceptical voice.

political system as a whole (Sartori *et al.* 1963; Farneti 1973; Cotta 1983). Focusing especially on MPs, two fairly stable periods were easily distinguished in the history of the political class in Italy: the age of non-professional (or "proto-professional") notables before the First World War, and the age of party professionals after the Second World War. The rise of political professionalism fits into a parallel trend of democratization and, most important for the process at hand, institutionalization of political parties.

Such a process was apparently halted in the 1990s, when Italian parties lost much of the grip they had gained on society. It would be misleading, however, to equate the crisis that occurred in the late twentieth century with previous historical phases of transformation of the Italian political class, which coincided with the transition from democracy to authoritarianism and *vice versa*. After all, tomorrow's possible changes and reforms are most likely to bring about different institutional arrangements without jeopardizing the founding principles of the polity. Yet, what can be the impact of such changes on the Italian political class? Could they bring about a sudden breakdown? Or just a turnover of personnel?

Pareto's idea that the replacement of the elite is a cyclical process involving the destiny of a whole generation of leaders has been evoked and adapted to account for the Italian case in a historical perspective (Cotta and Verzichelli 1996).[32] In line with this scheme, in the 1990s the illegal behavior of many political professionals caused the delegitimation of the whole occupational group to which they belonged—often independently from personal responsibilities. Most politicians lost credit, while societal trust shifted to non-political leaders, such as some members of the judiciary on the one hand (mainly in left-wing parties), and businessmen on the other (mainly on the right of the political spectrum). This dynamic was so rapid that change in the political class occurred as a sort of last-minute replacement. It was not a bottom-up process promoted by new aspiring elites (e.g. due to conflicts between generations), but rather a response to the need to fill a sudden vacuum at the top. Hence, at both the center and the periphery of the Italian political system, the place of political professionals was taken up by the most readily available and resourceful social actors (entrepreneurs, professionals, local notables)—natural candidates for political representation in times of weak party organizations. Some of them turned out to be *ersatz* politicians; others found politics a congenial environment for self-fulfillment and social advancement, and thus, contributed to the consolidation of a new political class.

In our view, political professionalism seems all but dead and, in the long run, political amateurs are not about to take the upper hand in Italian politics. Parties are trying hard to recover; many amateurs who succeeded in the 1990s are becoming disillusioned—and their voters, too. *Bon gré mal gré*, citizens accept the idea that politics can hardly be exempt from the ruling principle of modern societies: professionalism. Significantly, some party leaders daresay again that political professionals constitute a functional requirement of modern democracies. As Massimo D'Alema,

---

[32] As a specification of this model, Parsons' (1967*a*: 381, 1967*b*: 337–9) insight that political power may be subject to inflation could be usefully rediscovered.

leader of the DS and Prime Minister from 1998 to 2000, happened to declare: "Elsewhere nobody argues that to be in politics full time is a shame, as is the case in Italian society. Nobody blames Kohl for being a politician. [...] And nobody would go to a grocer for a medical operation saying: 'Let's get rid of surgeons!' " (Umberto Eco, *La Repubblica*, 5 November 1997: 42).[33]

Data on parliamentary candidates between 1996 and 2001 show indeed that the crisis of traditional parties has not wiped out political professionals from the scene (Di Virgilio 2002)—it has only made the resources and norms of political careers more fuzzy. Presumably, an overall expansion of political professionalism will chiefly depend on party strength, as no better device than party organizations has been invented so far to guarantee the regularity of political careers and, consequently, the occupational stability of professional politicians.

All in all, the re-professionalization of a large sector of the Italian political class is far from remote. At the same time, some other trends seem on the rise: (1) a different role of party structures in political recruitment (with an increasing weight of leaders' decisions); (2) a growing importance of local and regional offices (in particular, the mayoral office and regional government leadership); (3) a faster and broader access to political positions by economic and media elites (who occasionally resort to anti-political rhetoric). On the other hand, the emergence of a new political class can be seriously endangered by the persistence of traditional diseases, which are well known in all democratic countries and, especially, in the contexts of parliamentary, multi-party, and "consensual" systems (Pasquino 1999). Among these problems, the first one is "assemblyism" that is the spread of individualistic and opportunistic patterns of behavior among political representatives. A particular form of assemblyism is "clientelism:" a mode of interest representation based on the exchange between local consensus and private interests, which characterized a part of the political elite (especially in the Southern regions) in the early decades of the Republican age (La Palombara 1987).

But the most frequently evoked disease of the Italian political class remains *trasformismo*. Originally, the term was introduced to indicate the convergence between those MPs elected by the two main political factions (the "right" and the "left" factions in the old Liberal elite) who decided to support the same government by creating a "big center" with no real political alternative (Rogari 1998). *Trasformismo* has since become a derogatory word denoting the inconsistent nature of politicians and the dominance of political strategy over political coherence. With this meaning, the concept is once again *en vogue* among observers of Italian political life. Although new leaders have emerged, their lieutenants and counselors are disproportionately drawn from among members of the "old" political class regardless of their former party position.

[33] This argument, which D'Alema attributes to Benedetto Croce, is, in fact, much older. In his treatise *Della vita civile*, Matteo Palmieri, a Florentine political writer of the early fifteenth century, justified political professionalization in much the same way: "It is silly that the shoe-maker suggests how to make laws, how to govern the republic, or how to wage war and it is reasonable to ask physicians only about medical matters" (Palmieri 1982: 68).

The risk, however, is that by continually indulging in such an account of the behavior of the political class can lead, as with all explanations based on national culture or personal character, to a sort of fatalism. As Giovanni Sartori noted (*Corriere della Sera*, 30 December 1999), instead of simply deploring *trasformismo*, sincere reformers should rather blame the unsatisfactory performance of political institutions and rules (especially the organization of government and the electoral system), which create the favorable structural context in which this "beastly Italian plague" can develop and prosper.

REFERENCES

Baccetti, Carlo (1997). *Il Pds.* Bologna: Il Mulino.
——(1999). *Poteri locali e politiche pubbliche.* Turin: Utet.
Barberis, Corrado (1983). *La classe politica municipale.* Milan: Angeli.
Barnes, Samuel H. (1977). *Representation in Italy.* Chicago: University of Chicago Press.
Bettin, Gianfranco (1970). *Partito e comunità locale.* Bologna: Il Mulino.
——(1993). "Le ricerche sulla classe politica municipale in Italia (1978–1992)", in G. Bettin (ed.), *Classe politica e città.* Padua: Cedam, pp. 35–63.
——(1997). "Il sindaco italiano: un ruolo di governo plebiscitario?", in M. A. Toscano (ed.), *Dialettica locale—globale.* Naples: Ipermedium, pp. 197–214.
——and Magnier, Annick (1989). *Il consigliere comunale.* Padua: Cedam.
——and Magnier, Annick (1991). *Chi governa la città?* Padua: Cedam.
Bobbio, Norberto (1996; orig. 1969). *Saggi sulla scienza politica in Italia.* Rome: Laterza.
Bontempi, Marco (1995). "Le carriere dei presidenti del consiglio in Italia (1945–1993)", in L. Cavalli, M. Bontempi, and A. Perulli, *Del governo e di chi governa l'Italia.* Working Paper No. 4, Florence: Centro Interuniversitario di Sociologia Politica.
Caciagli, Mario (1991). "Vita e opere di un ceto politico". *Polis*, 5: 209–16.
Calise, Mauro (1989). "Le elites politiche", in L. Morlino (ed.), *Guida alla scienza politica.* Turin: Fondazione Agnelli, pp. 181–98.
——and Mannheimer, Renato (1982). *Governanti in Italia: Un trentennio repubblicano.* Bologna: Il Mulino.
Cavalli, Luciano (1992). *Governo del leader e regime dei partiti.* Bologna: Il Mulino.
Cazzola, Franco (1991). *Periferici integrati.* Bologna: Il Mulino.
Coi, Salvatore (1979). "Sindacati in Italia". *Il Mulino*, 262: 221–40.
Cotta, Maurizio (1979). *Classe politica e Parlamento in Italia.* Bologna: Il Mulino.
——(1983). "The Italian Political Class in the Twentieth Century: Continuities and Discontinuities", in M. M. Czudnowski (ed.), *Does Who Governs Matter?* DeKalb: Northern Illinois University Press, pp. 154–87.
——and Di Palma, Giuseppe (1986). "Cadres, Peones, and Entrepreneurs", in E. N. Suleiman (ed.), *Parliaments and Parliamentarians in Democratic Politics.* New York: Holmes and Meier, pp. 41–78.
——and Verzichelli, Luca (1996). "Italy: The Sunset of Partitocracy", in J. Blondel and M. Cotta (eds), *Party and Government.* London: Macmillan, pp. 180–201.
——, Mastropaolo, Alfio, and Verzichelli, Luca (2000). "Parliamentary Elite Transformations Along the Discontinuous Road of Democratisation: Italy 1861–1999", in H. Best and M. Cotta (eds), *Parliamentary Representatives in Europe 1848–2000.* Oxford: Oxford University Press, pp. 226–69.

De Felice, R. (1996; orig. 1980). "Il fascismo italiano e le classi medie", in S. Larsen, B. Hagtvet, and J. Mykleburts (eds), *I fascisti*. Florence: Ponte alle Grazie.

Della Porta, Donatella (2002). *Il potere locale*. Bologna: Il Mulino.

DiRenzo, Gordon J. (1967). *Personality, Power, and Politics: A Social Psychological Analysis of the Italian Deputy and his Parliamentary System*. South Bend: University of Notre Dame Press.

Di Virgilio, Aldo (1998). "Electoral Alliances: Party Identities and Coalition Games". *European Journal of Political Research*, 34: 5–33.

——(2002). "L'offerta elettorale. La politica delle alleanze si istituzionalizza", in R. D'Alimonte and S. Bartolini (eds), *Maggioritario finalmente? La transizione elettorale 1994–2001*. Bologna: Il Mulino, pp. 79–130.

Dogan, Mattei (1989). "How to Become Ministers in Italy", in M. Dogan (ed.), *Pathways to Power*. Boulder: Westview, pp. 99–139.

Farneti, Paolo (1973). *Il sistema politico italiano*. Bologna: Il Mulino.

Giovannini, Paolo (1997). "Teoria dell'élite e leadership sindacale: il caso italiano", in G. Bettin (ed.), *Politica e società*. Padua: Cedam, pp. 173–80.

Guadagnini, Marila (1984). "Il personale politico dalla 'periferia' al centro". *Le Regioni*, 4: 589–620.

Guarino, Giuseppe (1980). *Quale Costituzione? Saggio sulla classe politica*. Milan: Rizzoli.

Istat (1995). *Popolazione e abitazioni: 13° censimento generale della popolazione e delle abitazioni. Fascicolo nazionale Italia 1991*. Rome: Istat.

Katz, Richard S., (1996). "Electoral Reforms and the Transformation of Party Politics in Italy". *Party Politics*, 2: 5–28.

Katz, Richard S., and Mair, Peter (1995). "Changing Models of Party Organization and Party Democracy". *Party Politics*, 1: 5–28.

La Palombara, Joseph (1987). *Democracy Italian Style*. New Haven: Yale University Press.

Maranini, Giuseppe (1968). *Storia del potere in Italia, 1848–1967*. Florence: Vallecchi.

Mastropaolo, Alfio (1986). "Sviluppo politico e parlamento nell'Italia liberale". *Passato e Presente*, 12: 29–86.

——(1993a). *Il ceto politico: teoria e practiche*. Rome: NIS.

——(1993b). "Tra politica e mafia: Storia breve di un latifondo elettorale", in M. Morisi (ed.), *Far politica in Sicilia*. Milan: Feltrinelli, pp. 84–144.

——(1996). "Tra rivoluzione e restaurazione". *Italia Contemporanea*, 36: 497–508.

Melis, Antonia, and Martinotti, Guido (1988). "Gli amministratori comunali 1975–1987: composizione sociale e reclutamento territoriale". *Amministrare*, 28: 283–338.

Merlini, Stefano (1995). "Il governo costituzionale", in R. Romanelli (ed.), *Storia dello Stato italiano*. Rome: Donzelli, pp. 3–27.

Meynaud, Jean (1966). *Rapporto sulla classe dirigente italiana*. Milan: Giuffré.

Michels, Robert (1936). *Nuovi studi sulla classe politica*. Milan: Dante Alighieri.

Missori, Mario (1986). *Gerarchie e statuti del PNF*. Rome: Bonacci.

Morel, Laurence (1996). "Le riforme istituzionali", in M. Cotta, and P. Isernia (eds), *Il gigante dai piedi di argilla*. Bologna: Il Mulino, pp. 337–73.

Morlino, Leonardo (1991). *Costruire la democrazia: gruppi e partiti in Italia*. Bologna: Il Mulino.

Mosca, Gaetano (1896). *Elementi di scienza politica*. Rome: Bocca.

——(1982). *Scritti politici*. Turin: Utet.

Norris, Pippa (1996). "Legislative Recruitment", in L. LeDuc, R. Niemi, and P. Norris (eds), *Comparing Democracies*. London: Sage, pp. 184–215.

Pacifici, Giorgio (1983). *Il costo della democrazia*. Rome: Cadmo.

Palmieri, Matteo (1982; orig. 1431–38.). *Della vita civile*. Florence: Sansoni.

Panebianco, Angelo (1988). *Political Parties: Organization and Power*. Cambridge: Cambridge University Press.

Panebianco, Angelo (1993). "Fare a meno della politica?". *Il Mulino*, 4: 637–45.

Parsons, Talcott (1967*a*; orig. 1963). "On the Concept of Influence", in T. Parsons (ed.), *Sociological Theory and Modern Society*. New York: Free Press, pp. 355–82.

—— (1967*b*; orig. 1963). "On the Concept of Political Power", in T. Parsons (ed.), *Sociological Theory and Modern Society*. New York: Free Press, pp. 297–354.

Pasquino, Gianfranco (1987). "Party Government in Italy: Achievements and Prospects", in R. S. Katz (ed.), *Party Government*. Berlin: De Gruyter, pp. 202–42.

—— (1999). *La classe politica*. Bologna: Il Mulino.

Pizzorno, Alessandro (1993). "Le difficoltà del consociativismo", in A. Pizzorno (ed.), *Le radici della politica assoluta e altri saggi*. Milan: Feltrinelli, pp. 285–313.

Pombeni, Paolo (1993). *Autorità sociale e potere politico nell'Italia contemporanea*. Venice: Marsilio.

Putnam, Robert D. (1973). *The Beliefs of Politicians: Ideology, Conflict, and Democracy in Britain and Italy*. New Haven: Yale University Press.

Recchi, Ettore (1996). "Fishing From the Same Schools: Parliamentary Recruitment and Consociationalism in the First and Second Italian Republics". *West European Politics*, 19: 340–59.

—— (1999). "Politics as Occupational Choice: Youth Self-Selection for Party Careers in Italy". *European Sociological Review*, 15: 107–24.

—— (2001). "Vecchie e nuove strade per diventare sindaco in Italia", in A. Magnier (ed.), *Elite e comunità*. Rubbettino: Soveria Mannelli, pp. 89–104.

Rogari, Sandro (1998). *Alle origini del trasformismo: Partiti e sistema politico nell'Italia Liberale*. Rome: Laterza.

Sani, Giacomo (1967). "Alcuni dati sul ricambio della dirigenza partitica nazionale in Italia". *Rassegna Italiana di Sociologia*, 8: 126–41.

—— (1972*a*). "La professionalizzazione dei dirigenti di partito italiani". *Rivista Italiana di Scienza Politica*, 2: 303–33.

—— (1972*b*). "Profilo dei dirigenti di partito italiani". *Rassegna Italiana di Sociologia*, 13: 117–48.

Sartori, Giovanni, Lotti, Luigi, Somogy, Giovanni, and Predieri, Alberto (1963). *Il Parlamento Italiano*. Naples: ESI.

Segatori, Roberto (1992). "Assetti istituzionali e identità della classe politica in Italia", in R. Segatori (ed.), *Istituzioni e potere politico locale*. Milan: Angeli, pp. 81–102.

Sidoti, Francesco (1993). "The Italian Political Class". *Government and Opposition*, 28: 339–52.

Spreafico, Alberto (1965). "I sindaci dei capoluoghi di provincia", in A. Spreafico (ed.), *L'amministrazione e il cittadino*. Milan: Comunità, pp. 35–7.

Tarchi, Marco (1997). *Dal Msi ad An*. Bologna: Il Mulino.

Verzichelli, Luca (1995). "The New Members of Parliament", in R. Katz and P. Ignazi (eds), *Italian Politics*. Boulder: Westview, pp. 115–33.

—— (1998). "The Transition Parliamentary Elite". *European Journal of Political Research*, 34: 121–50.

—— (2002*a*). "Da un ceto parlamentare all'altro: Il mutamento nel personale legislativo italiano", in R. D'Alimonte, and S. Bartolini (eds), *Maggioritario finalmente? La transizione elettorale 1994–2001*. Bologna: Il Mulino, pp. 319–62.

—— (2002*b*). "Much Ado about Something? Parliamentary Politics in Italy amid the Rhetoric of Majority Rule and an Uncertain Party System". *Journal of Legislative Studies*, forthcoming.

Wertman, Douglas (1988). "Italy: Local Involvement, Central Control", in M. Gallagher and M. Marsh (eds), *Candidate Selection in Comparative Perspective*. London: Sage, pp. 145–68.

Zangarini, Maurizio (1978). "La composizione della classe dirigente nel regime fascista: il caso di Verona". *Italia Contemporanea*, 132: 27–47.

13

Japan: Political Careers between Bureaucracy and Hereditary Constituencies

CLAUDIA DERICHS AND HAROLD R. KERBO

POLITICAL PROFESSIONALIZATION IN HISTORICAL PERSPECTIVE

As the first nation in Asia to achieve advanced industrial status, Japan presents itself to western social scientists as an interesting and valuable test case for many of their theories. In fact, behind many of these theories we find what can only be called western biases about the processes of modernization and democratization. Modernization theories, for example, used to assume that Japan would end up with basic institutions very similar to those of the western countries. Leading theorists from the old modernization approach now recognize their ideas were far too simple.[1] The Japanese political system today has become much more democratic and "modern." Still, there are important differences to western democracies, some fairly obvious and many more below the surface.

In a volume on professional politicians and political institutions with a focus on western societies, therefore, one has to begin with a note of caution. Following Pye (1985) we must agree that knowledge about the institutional arrangements of a political system is not synonymous to understanding how it works and how actors behave. Formal political institutions in the country may look quite western and might even, like in the case of the current Japanese constitution, be written in English by Americans. But one must not infer that these political institutions actually operate exactly like western ones. Informal politics play an important role throughout East and Southeast Asia (Dittmer 2000, Derichs and Heberer 2003).

In this chapter on political institutions and the political class in Japan we will retain the structure of the other essays. Beginning with historical background information about Japan's political institutions and political professionalization, we will then examine the institutional context and political class in today's Japan, as well as

---

[1] See Bellah's new introduction to *Tokugawa Religion: The Cultural Roots of Modern Japan* (1985).

important institutional reforms that have recently taken place. From time to time, however, it will be necessary to note important differences or to show that a simple consideration of formal political institutions can be misleading.

The beginnings of political professionalization in Japan were in many respects quite dramatic. In the mid-nineteenth century the so-called "opening" of Japan was more or less a forced introduction of trade relations with western empires. Stepping out of a 250-year long, self-imposed isolation, Japan had to come to terms quickly with nation-building and modernization in order to avoid the fate of all other Asian nations around itself (with the exception of Thailand): colonization. What followed was called the *Meiji* Restoration, in reference to the new *Meiji* Emperor's installation as head of state with unrestricted executive power to increase political legitimacy for the emerging political economy. In the beginning of this process of change the new ruling class sent many of its brightest young men to western nations to bring back ideas of how to modernize all of Japan's basic institutions. Japan's former warrior class, the *samurai*, who had already served in the central and sub-national administration, were recruited for administrative service in the newly created prefectures (or states, in 1871) as well as on the national level, especially since western government structures (following both the Prussian and British models) were adopted (see also Muramatsu 1997).

Political parties emerged after the *Meiji* Restoration in 1868 and gained increasing influence with the opening of the Imperial Diet in 1890, then expanded again in the wake of the First World War. Their access to political power was constrained, however, when the military's ascendancy to the centers of decision-making was completed in the 1930s. One problem was that the constitution required a commissioned military officer to be a member of the cabinet. As the military gained more influence they also learned that they had strong leverage over civilian politicians; if they disliked the government's policies, the military would simply decommission the officer sitting in the cabinet and the government was dissolved.

Finally, disbanded and absorbed into the Imperial Rule Assistance Association in 1940, the parties had only witnessed a short period of relative democracy and influence upon cabinets composed of more or less independent politicians in the 1920s; a period referred to as the *Taisho* Democracy in reference to the short reign of the *Taisho* Emperor of the time.[2] The revival of political parties was not possible until after the Second World War when Japan came under Allied occupation and American-led reform efforts encouraged the founding of parties and labor unions in order to democratize the state.

Party politics was only one form of political engagement, though. Asking who might be considered professional politicians in early modern Japan, we find two kinds of political "activists:" One kind was composed of activists in "political associations" (*seisha*) "which arose in the 1870s and were usually couples of disgruntled former samurai, urban intellectuals, and rural landowners" (Kodansha 1993: 1212).

---

[2] A detailed discussion of democratic and non-democratic politics in prewar Japan is provided by Banno (2001).

They formed and spearheaded the Freedom and People's Rights Movement for a representative government, which became Japan's first social movement. Since this movement called for a popularly elected ("popularly" not in the sense of universal suffrage by any means, however) national assembly, their demands were sharply criticized and opposed by influential former feudal lords and court nobles, who had succeeded in forming a close-knit group of oligarchs and elder statesmen.

The second group of professionals in the political realm was composed of the so-called *Meiji* oligarchs (indicating that they stayed in office throughout the whole *Meiji* period, 1868–1912), elder statesmen, and dominant cliques who controlled the government business effectively for nearly one generation. They had already been the protagonists of the struggle to restore imperial rule in 1868 and managed to dominate politics openly as well as behind the scenes. With one exception, every Japanese Prime Minister between 1885, when the cabinet system was introduced, and 1918, when the first party cabinet was formed, had been a feudal lord. Political power was concentrated in the hands of two dozen elite members, who monopolized important government posts and extended their influence into the bureaucracy. The national administrative elite was recruited by selective appointment and promotion of protégés. And, as John W. Hall adds, these men were able to solve the critical financial problems of the young centralized state in comparatively short time (Hall 1983: 271).

The military's influence on politics increased in the 1930s, leading to a period of "Japanese style fascism". Barrington Moore (1966) argued that the evolution of democracy in Japan—much as in Germany—was hampered because all classes below the old feudal aristocracy were not yet strong enough to push for their interests, while the leaders of these old classes pursued a rapid modernization; and in Japan, the generals and admirals had an enormous say in politics not only because from 1900 onwards the custom of appointing a high ranking, active army or navy officer to the post of the Military Minister became an explicit rule (Flanagan and Richardson 1984: 10; Gluck 1985). They also had quite an ideological impact on young nationalists becoming involved in politics.

The political parties in the Diet, which was elected for the first time in 1890, were separated into two camps. Because of the pressure to modernize and to open up the country to trade and diplomacy, some form of political professionalization became necessary in the second half of the nineteenth century. Centralization of power and strong leadership were required urgently for state-building and to protect the nation against western domination. We might, thus, conclude that the oligarchs of *Meiji* Japan with their living off politics fulfilled a functional need. On the other hand, western political ideas that permeated Japanese political thought in that period stimulated all those who either felt deprived of their influence on state affairs or who noticed an opportunity to gain power under the new social order, like urban intellectuals, wealthy merchants, and well-to-do peasants. The underlying social stratification and the nature of the state in the course of modernization, however, contributed to the fact that these groups had insufficient power to push effectively for more democracy, and finally stimulated even more repression from the old elites.

Following a more traditional Asian model, it were the bureaucrats, mostly former *samurai* with a classical education, who played an important role in the modernizing, centralizing state. They were the ones who had to implement all the new policies and to spread the spirit of modernity. Knowledge and skill made them indispensable for the oligarchs, so that their future role as influential actors in politics was foreseeable.

Militarism and ultranationalism led the country to war and finally to defeat in 1945. After Japan's surrender "normal" political life had to be reorganized. There was a new constitution, imposed by the American occupation force, which introduced universal suffrage also enfranchising women. In addition, of course, the reform measures of the Allied occupation brought with them opportunities for many more ordinary people to engage in politics professionally. The reshuffling of the prewar political parties took some time but was completed in 1955, when a conservative camp around the Liberal Democratic Party (LDP) and a progressive camp consisting of the Japan Socialist Party (JSP) (later the Social Democratic Party—SDP), the formerly forbidden Japan Communist Party (JCP), and after 1960 also the Democratic Socialist Party (DSP) as an offspring of the Socialists, were consolidated. The LDP—often said to be neither liberal nor democratic nor a party—became the single dominant party throughout the postwar period, its power having been challenged only once after 38 years of governmental control: in the general elections of 1993 when a coalition of four LDP offsprings and four "old" opposition parties stripped the LDP of its majority in the Diet.

As described below, the forced democratization under the new constitution (from 1947 onwards) allowed all adults to vote and run for both Houses of Parliament. This fact and the stimulation to (re)create political parties and participate actively in local as well as in national politics gave many people, especially in urban areas, the hope of making a political career. The incentives to engage in politics were, at least shortly after the war, less of a financial than of an emotional and ideological nature, for the basic salary of Diet Members in Japan was not very attractive. The formal salary situation did not change much, so that we may ask for the motivation—apart from idealistic reasons—to become a politician. We will return to this question below.

THE INSTITUTIONAL CONTEXT

After introducing the cabinet system in 1885, the Imperial Constitution of Japan was enacted in 1889 and celebrated as a merciful "gift" of the Emperor to his people, with parties and ceremonies even though the people did not know yet what was written in the constitution (Gluck 1985: 46). And while the cabinet in prewar Japan had in fact been adapted from a Chinese predecessor called *dajokan* (Grand Council of State) and represented a deliberative system of counselors and state ministers, the new constitution was mainly an adaptation of western models. It provided for a two-chamber Parliament, specifically modeled after the Westminster system with an Upper and a Lower House. The former, called House of Counselors in Japan, was composed of court nobles and appointed nobles, thus, being a mixture of hereditary and appointive members (quite simply, the political oligarchs of the time created a peerage system modeled on the British system and made it hereditary so they could staff their "House of Lords"). The Lower House was an assembly of elected members, though suffrage was status-restricted and allowed only somewhat more than 1 percent of the population to vote (Gluck 1985: 67). There was no universal male suffrage until 1925.

The partisans of the Liberal and Progressive parties in the Lower House, devoted to popular participation in the political process, were confronted constantly by the supporters of the oligarchs who denied being a political party but can well be considered as the functional equivalent of one. Therefore, they were called "bureaucrats" parties. Since cabinet members were appointed by the Prime Minister, and the latter was nominated by the oligarchs or was at least a close affiliate of the elder statesmen after the turn of the century, the Liberals and Progressives had quite limited access to the executive. The Diet's only possibility to really take part in the legislative process except for merely approving the government's proposals was to veto the budget proposal. However, the Emperor could easily dissolve the Diet under the recommendation of the oligarchs.

The National Diet at this time can be considered a mere facade institution to legitimate the government's policies before the public and gain credibility from the West. But we should also take into account that the institution of the Diet paved the way for political professionalization, whereas in times of the Freedom and People's Rights Movement in the 1870s there was no institutional frame for that.

The political system of postwar Japan was of course shaped by the American occupation from 1945 to 1952. The constitution was rewritten with the Emperor being a mere symbol of unity of the Japanese nation and the people as the sovereign. The bicameral Diet system was not changed, but instead of an hereditary and appointive Upper House, the postwar constitution provided for the popular election of both chambers (with universal suffrage). The Upper House is still of only limited significance, although it may delay or even block legislation. Formally, this chamber is only of some importance when the majority in that House is occupied by the opposition parties—like in 1989 and 1998. In terms of political culture, the Upper House provides a forum for new parties and associations who are too small and too much focused on particular issues to win a seat in Lower House elections. The Upper House reflects more closely the current political mood of the public than its counterpart.

The access of candidates and political groups to the Upper House is easier than to the Lower House, because elections for the former take place more frequently (every 3 years half of the chamber is elected) and because individual lawmakers in this House can campaign on issues that affect people's daily life—environmental problems in certain constituencies, improvements for disabled people, and the like. The big parties in the Lower House have to perform a catch-all campaign, which does not leave much space for specific "daily life" issues.

The Lower House has a system of standing and ad hoc committees like in western systems. More striking, however, is that political decision-making is conducted through consultative, cooperative procedures, into which many interests are incorporated. This incorporation is possible through the creation of deliberative councils called *shingikai*, which are composed of academics, journalists, corporate executives, and functionaries of labor unions and federations. In 1990 there existed 212 such bodies to give advice to the ministries (Schwartz 1998). Other advisory bodies include the Policy Affairs Research Council of the LDP which has considerable influence on decision making and the *zoku*, which are groups of legislators (LDP) with expert knowledge in certain fields (due to long-time service in respective committees or in ministries) and excellent relations to the corporations in their jurisdiction. They are considered a counterweight against the strong bureaucracy but at the same time are staunch opponents to any structural reforms that would destroy their network of give and take.

We will consider below how lawmakers, in accordance with the postwar constitution, are elected to the two Houses. At this point we only briefly mention politicians below the national level. The new constitution guaranteed some autonomy to governors of prefectures and municipal mayors. However, it must also be noted that these local politicians still have very limited taxing powers and are to a great extent dependent upon the national politicians, bureaucrats, and agencies for funds. It is only in the last two decades that they have been pushing more effectively for decentralization and expanded their autonomy in several policy fields (Foreign Press Center 1997).

Finally, in the context of important political actors in the postwar setting, we must not fail to mention the national bureaucracy. As Johnson (1982) clearly shows, the ministry officials have had considerable power in Japan from the early twentieth century onwards. And their effectiveness in controlling most aspects of government was increasing up to the Second World War. In a more Asian than western tradition, the bureaucracy in Japan has always practiced considerable influence as a political actor. Much of the everyday running of government was left to unelected civil servants, with politicians giving them wide freedom to interpret and implement the law. After the Second World War, however, the power of these administrative officials even increased. It was assumed by the Allied powers that above all politicians were responsible for the war and many were purged—bureaucratic officials, however, stayed relatively untouched (Johnson 1982). Thus, these officials emerged in stronger positions of power in postwar Japan, and only in recent years was some of this power trimmed by administrative reform. For most of the time since the Second World War, though, 90 percent of the laws that passed the Diet were actually written by ministry officials, and they were written in such a way as to give these ministry officials broad flexibility of interpretation and "administrative guidance" (*gyôsei shidô*), which refers to the even greater power to decide upon rules.

THE POLITICAL CLASS

Size and Composition

The issue of size and composition of the Japanese political class is probably one of the most difficult topics from a comparative perspective. It is here that Asian value orientations have shaped the political system more than in any other area. Most importantly, throughout East and Southeast Asia we find unelected bureaucrats to be more powerful and making many if not most of the decisions carried out by elected politicians in western nations. One comparative example is useful: when the American President assumes office he can appoint up to 2,000 top officials in the federal government. These people come from all kinds of professions and usually serve only briefly in the administration—of course, at the discretion of the President. When a new Japanese Prime Minister assumes office, in contrast, he or she appoints about twenty top officials. The thousands of unelected government and ministry officials are career civil servants who can be removed from office by a politician only with great difficulty. But these officials are central actors in policy-making and management of the national government. There is no question that they are part of the Japanese political elite. The debates among Japan scholars centers on the question of who is more powerful, politicians or ministry bureaucrats, and not whether bureaucrats should be included among important political actors (Koh 1989; Kerbo and McKinstry 1995).

Due to limited space, we will not attempt anything like a "head count" of the Japanese political class. We can say that it certainly includes those politicians elected to the national Parliament (the Diet) and that the numbers are comparable to western democracies (after the 1994 reform, there are now 480 members of the Lower House and 252 of the Upper House, the latter again reduced to 247 in 2001). To this, we have to add the so called "public secretaries", between two and well over thirty per Diet Member (Feldman 2000: 34). Below the national level there are prefectural assembly members from the Tokyo Metropolitan area, from Hokkaido, Osaka, and Kyoto along with the members of forty-three other prefectural assemblies (Kishimoto 1988). And there are more than 3,000 municipal governments with elected officials. But in clear contrast to most western nations, these political actors below the national level of politics not only have much less power and influence, they usually do not act as full-time politicians (Ramsdell 1992; Curtis 1983).

Political Recruitment and Political Careers

As one might expect, there are rather different ways of recruitment into the bureaucracy compared to political office in the Diet, though as we will see the two can overlap in late career stages. Two basic points must be made about the bureaucratic elite: (1) Its members are selected upon merit, and (2) it is exceptionally well trained. From the beginning, which is to say, from the *Meiji* period when the central bureaucracy was established, the ministry elite has passed through the most respected universities in Japan. The pattern of selection from the top universities, especially Tokyo University, prevails up to the present, though with less intensity because of rising criticism and changing career patterns (Halliday 1975: 39; Koh 1989: 86; Stockwin 1999). Since the Second World War it has been even more difficult to pass the entrance exams for these universities, with Tokyo University being the most difficult. Thus, because graduation from one of the top universities is almost without exception

252 Derichs and Kerbo

required for bureaucratic elite selection, a strong element of meritocracy is involved.[3] Also among Diet Members, a university education is prevailing. In 1996 the share of university graduates ranged from 67 percent in the parliamentary group of the Social Democrats up to 95 percent in the Liberal Democrats' group—an extremely high ratio when compared to West European Parliaments (Stockwin 1999: 136, 142–3).[4]

Overall, only about 25 percent of Diet Members have been career politicians, working their way up the ladder by beginning in local politics as is common in western democratic societies. Most Japanese politicians enter late into politics, coming from other careers. Approximately half of the representatives of the Democratic Socialist Party of Japan, for example, are recruited from labor unions. It is useful to include some information on the profession prior to politics. Feldman divides the representatives of the Lower House into seven categories, including the graduates of the Matsushita Institute of Government and Management, who are trained to become political and economic leaders. The other six categories of Diet recruits are (1) second generation politicians, (2) former local politicians, (3) former government bureaucrats, (4) officials of large unions and organizations, (5) former secretaries to Diet Members, and (6) celebrity Diet Members (Feldman 2000: 22–30).

The latter are called "talents" in Japan (*tarento*) and are mostly popular figures like actors or actresses, comedians, writers, and others. The fact that over one-third of Japan's Diet Members are occupying "hereditary seats" is remarkable. In fact, the number of second generation lawmakers rose constantly since the 1980s. Like in other East and Southeast Asian political systems, these politicians do not necessarily have to be equipped with extraordinary political skills; it suffices to be a relative of a retired or dead politician. Political analysis often mentions the fact of hereditary seats as one prominent reason for political nepotism in Asia.

Ramsdell (1992: 33) has shown that during the four decades after the Second World War there was a significant decrease in the recruitment of legislators from the

---

[3] Beyond the requirement of a top university degree there are other difficulties to be overcome before access to the bureaucratic elite is permitted. Each ministry has its own exams every year to determine which graduates enter the ministry. There are, in fact, four types of exams for each ministry, corresponding to four tracks of career placement. The true elite track ("fast track") requires to pass the 'type 1' exam. Once an exam for the ministry track has been passed, and only after it has been passed, the ministry may decide who is selected. Factors such as personality and connections can enter at this point.

Recruitment from the most respected universities in Japan must still be recognized as an important factor for careers in the bureaucracy, along with the implications of this procedure. In 1991, 59% of those entering the "fast track" to top ministry positions (306 individuals) were *Todai* graduates (Koyama 1981; Ishida 1993; *Japan Times*, 9 March 1992), mostly from the law faculty. An important consequence is the creation of "old school ties" that are more widespread than in any other modern democratic society. The biased selection from Tokyo University has repeatedly come under considerable criticism from the general public. Thus, Prime Minister Miyazawa assured in 1992 that in 5 years' time the share of Tokyo University graduates among top position-holders would be reduced from the current 59 to "only" 50% (*Japan Times*, 9 March 1992). At least in regard to the selection process, this was quite successful: in 2000 only 32% of the candidates passing the top civil service exam had graduated from the Tokyo University (*Japan Times*, 17 August 2000).

[4] The dominance of *Todai* graduates is, however, less prominent than in the bureaucracy. Out of the university graduates in the parliamentary groups, between 21% (LDP) and 13% (Social Democrats) came from Tokyo University.

central government, that is, from the bureaucracy (from 21.5 percent in 1955 to 8.4 percent in 1990) as well as from the business sector (19.4–12.3 percent in the same period). In contrast, recruitment from among the political sector increased drastically (3.2–35.5 percent), which means that many aspirants started their careers as assistants to politicians or occupied posts in political parties. Business/banking and politics showed the highest rates in terms of primary occupation out of all categories. In the prewar Diet, the business sector also formed the top, but agriculture ranked still very high, whereas only 1.5 percent came from politics. Figures for the educational sector (declining from 7.0 to 3.9 percent) and the labor/socialist movement (7.4–5.5 percent) refer almost excludingly to parliamentarians of the SPJ/SDPJ and DSP (Ramsdell 1992: 27, 33).

As we will discuss in more detail below, ministry officials tend to retire rather early (during their fifties or even before) and move into corporate or political positions. Till the end of the 1980s, twelve out of sixteen Prime Ministers were from the bureaucratic elite, and most of them were also graduates of Tokyo University Law School. In other words, in 37 out the 44 years during this period, a former bureaucrat was found in the position of Prime Minister (Kitagawa and Kainuma 1985: 212).

There is another avenue of recruitment to political positions in Japan, which is also not common in the West. To put it mildly, term limits, discussed so intensely in recent years in the United States, have not exactly gained a foothold in Japan. Not only do Diet Members (especially from the LDP) seldom lose their seats until death or retirement, but the tendency to pass these seats on to family members, most often sons, is increasing. In 1987, out of 511 Diet Members of the Lower House, 305 were members of the LDP: over one-third of these LDP politicians (118) were second or third generation Diet Members. If we include the second or third generation Diet Members of the other parties, the number goes up to 130 (Maki 1987: 60). Also, twelve out of the nineteen postwar Prime Ministers, up to Miyazawa who entered this position in 1991, currently have family members serving in the Diet (Kitagawa and Kainuma 1985; Jin 1989; Blechinger 1997).

As might be expected, there are relatively few women in the Japanese political class. And because a significant number of Diet Members are men who "retired" from their ministry positions to enter politics, the mean age is rather high. The share of seats held by women for the Upper and Lower House as well as for the parliamentarians in the local assemblies occupies rank 126 in global comparison. As for 1999, the ratio of women in prefectural and city assemblies was 5.4 percent, in towns and villages 6.2 percent, in the Upper House of the national Diet 17 percent and in the Lower House a mere 5.0 percent. Since 1989, when the "Madonna boom" started with Takako Doi, the Socialist chairwoman, the percentage of elected women in both Houses has risen, but it has yet to catch up with other western democracies. In the Lower House, thirty-four out of then 474 Lower House Members (six seats were vacant at that time) were female in October 2002, which makes for a ratio of 7.2 percent (House of Representatives 2002). As for age groups, the majority of legislators has been aged between 40 and 70 years for the whole postwar period (Ramsdell 1992: 231) (Table 13.1).

Table 13.1   *Age distribution, Lower and Upper House, 1998*

Age	Lower House (1998)	Upper House (2001)
21–30	1	—
31–40	53	18
41–50	123	31
51–60	167	92
61–70	121	88
over 70	35	18

Source: IPU (2000, 2002).

Looking at the political careers and the cumulation of offices, we should begin with the ministry bureaucrats. As with major corporations in Japan, it is common bureaucratic practice that once accepted into the fast track, a person becomes a member of the "freshman class" made up of all individuals entering the ministry that year. These people are all promoted together in the first several years of their careers, and receive similar training. Then there are a couple of years spent in various divisions of the ministry, followed by a few more years as chief of a local office, before moving into higher positions that are characterized by political work. In ministries with more international responsibilities (such as the Foreign Ministry) the first 10 years will include foreign assignments as well. By the time these men reach their late forties and early fifties, the spectrum of career options begins to narrow—as it does in the world of business and industry. Not all members of an age cohort on the fast track can any longer be promoted together. At this point, selection for the highest ministry positions is made, and conflicts and infighting between factions and sections of the ministries begin.

Those who are not promoted at this time are expected to retire. But these men, of course, do not really retire; they rather pursue their careers elsewhere, and those who were promoted to the top positions such as administrative vice-minister (the highest position in a ministry within reach), will follow a few years later. Some of these ex-bureaucrats go into politics, as we have seen, but even a greater number makes a move referred to as *amakudari*: the "descent from heaven" into the corporate world. During 1991 alone, for example, 215 individuals who were members of the bureaucratic elite left their government positions for new corporate positions in companies which were regulated by the very ministry these individuals came from (Rixtel and Hassink 1998). The ruling elite is well aware of this habit working as a strong impediment to structural reform, but not even the "reform Prime Minister" Koizumi Junichiro (April 2001–) has managed to put this practice to a hold.

Living off Politics

Japan's political class in the postwar period has been able to "live off politics," much like the political class of modern western countries. But as said before, there are some interesting dimensions in which it differs from the West. The base salary for Diet Members is much above that of top ministry officials.

As of August 1998, Members of both Houses received a monthly salary of Yen (JPY) 1,364,000 (approx. €11,000), a monthly allowance for "special transportation expenses" of JPY300,000 (€2,420) if they had served for at least 25 years, and annual bonuses of about 8 million Yen (€64,500) per year.[5] Overall, the income of an average Diet Member in 1997 was about 31.2 million Yen (€251,700)—approximately 32.4 million for Lower House and 28.8 million for Upper House Members (Feldman 2000: 48).

However, there are many other sources of income. For one, politicians in Japan are not required to suspend their previous (legal) economic activity once in office. Most of their income, however, comes from other sources, legal and illegal, as soon as they attain political office, and this is especially true for those who reach high positions in the Diet.[6]

A survey on the wealth of Diet Members, required for the first time by a law which went into effect in 1993, provides an annual rough assessment of their assets to the public. This is, however, certainly an underestimate. Even with these limitations, however, the survey is quite interesting. The assets of the 749 Diet Members, including Upper and Lower House, averaged US$843,800 per member in 1992. For LDP members alone, the average was US$1.25 million per Member, so that LDP politicians accounted for three quarters of all assets of Diet Members, and provided eighty-seven of the richest Members. The twenty highest ranked LDP members alone accounted for 40 percent of all assets held by Diet members. Also, the 171 members from both Houses who were either married to daughters of (former) Diet Members or had fathers or grandfathers in the Diet had assets much higher than the average, and possessed more than half of all assets held by Diet Members (*Japan Times*, 21 June 1993).

There is no precise data on where exactly their wealth comes from, but most of it is achieved after they went into politics. The scandals of the late 1980s and 1990s shed some light on where part of the assets derives from. Significantly, it is not shrewd investment that plays the major role for increasing politicians' assets, but rather a seemingly unlimited appreciation of the bold custom of corruption, bribery, and fraud (on corruption in Japanese politics, see Blechinger 2000). These practices have since the 1990s come under harsh public criticism. The law of 1994 concerning donations to politicians was an attempt to curb the money coming into politics from the corporate world. This law prohibits donations to single politicians like faction chiefs. Instead of reaching the pocket of a single politician, the money is collected by

[5] Conversions from Japan Yen (JPY) to Euro are based on the exchange rate of 3 December 2002 (JPY1 = €0.00807).
[6] According to the *Asahi* newspaper, a member of the national Parliament had an average income of 31.2 million Yen (approx. €251,700) in 1997. These incredibly high amounts were possible, for example, through the selling of stocks, which were not always acquired legally—as some scandals revealed (*Asahi Shimbun Dahlem*, 15 July 1998).

a party office set up for this purpose. Another difference to the past is that parties get financial support now by the state. These regulations have been implemented in order to reduce the fierce fund raising races between and before elections as well as intraparty factionalism. The loophole, however, is that collecting offices for donations can be local party offices and that their number is not limited. This means that every single politician whose fund raising abilities are strong can establish his or her collecting office, declaring it simply to be a local branch office of the party.

It is, of course, not merely the politicians who are receptive to donations and opportunities for generous public spending. The bureaucrats, local and national, play their part in the game as well and nobody has managed to pull tighter strings around them yet. On the local level, citizens' campaigns have led to a stronger demand for transparency in bureaucratic decision-making. On the national level, *zoku* Diet Members and the ruling elite's "old guard" are still the major force that prevents reform-minded politicians from carrying their plans through. Scandal and economic stagnation are blamed on the current structure and power of the ministries. Until recent years, the respected ministry officials were almost untouched by scandal—this is no longer the case. Scandals, reaching from bribes to corruption in connection with building projects have grown more numerous, and the previously unquestioned system of *amakudari* has now come under increased criticism.

THE POLITICAL CLASS AND INSTITUTIONAL REFORM: STAGNATION, SCANDAL, AND STRUCTURAL CHANGE

The 1990s have brought economic stagnation and scandal to Japan. And both experiences have, in differing ways, brought pressure for major structural reform of the system of spoiling politicians as well as the bureaucrats. Political scandal, however, entered the scene much earlier: a bribery scandal brought down the Tanaka Government in the 1970s. The late 1980s witnessed one political scandal unfolding after another, bringing down two more governments and leading to an endless chain of dismissals and resignations of politicians and even bureaucrats. During the *Meiji* period already, and again during the collapse after the Second World War, major crisis led to extensive political change. Thus, many in Japan are suggesting that a third period of major change is under way. Political change first would have to remove the structural impediments to reform though, and this might well require another generational change within Japan's political class.

When the LDP finally lost its dominance over the Diet in 1993, the new Prime Minister Hosokawa was able to push through an election reform package in January of 1994. This reform reduced the number of seats in the Lower House of the Diet from 511 to 500, and created 300 new single-seat districts. The other 200 seats are now selected in 11 proportional representation districts. The idea was to reduce competition in the multi-seat districts and intraparty factionalism, which can be cited as another structural element of Japanese politics. It was also assumed that these changes would lead to two dominant parties being more competitive and strong enough to gain some real power to govern when confronted with powerful ministry officials. This new electoral system was tested for the first time in the 1996 national elections, and has since brought about little change in party competition or intraparty factionalism. Thus, reform remains on the agenda of Japanese politics.

REFERENCES

Banno, Junji (2001). *Democracy in Pre-War Japan. Concepts of Government, 1871–1937.* London: Routledge.

Bellah, Robert N. (ed.) (1985). *Tokugawa Religion: The Cultural Roots of Modern Japan,* 3rd edition. New York: Free Press.

Blechinger, Verena (1997). "Politik und Familienbande: 'Erbabgeordnete' im japanischen Parlament". *Nachrichten der Gesellschaft für Natur und Völkerkunde Ostasiens,* 159/160: 71–87.

——(2000). "Auf dem Weg zu 'sauberer Politik' und transparenten Strukturen? Korruption und Selbstreinigung in der japanischen Politik", in J. Borchert, S. Leitner, and K. Stolz (eds), *Politische Korruption.* Opladen: Leske + Budrich, pp. 145–84.

Curtis, Gerald (1983). *Japan's Political Party System: its Dynamics and Prospects.* Tokyo: The Japan Foundation.

Derichs, Claudia, and Heberer, Thomas (eds) (2003). Einführung in die politischen Systeme Ostasiens. Opladen: Leske + Budrich.

Dittmer, Lowell (ed.) (2000). *Informal Politics in East Asia.* Cambridge: Cambridge University Press.

Feldman, Ofer (2000). *The Japanese Political Personality: Analyzing the Motivations and Culture of Freshman Diet Members.* Basingstoke: Macmillan.

Flanagan, Scott C., and Richardson, Bradley M. (1984). *Politics in Japan.* Glenview: Harper Collins.

Foreign Press Center (ed.) (1997). *Japan—Eyes on the Country: Views of the 47 Prefectures.* Tokyo: Foreign Press Center.

Gluck, Carol (1985). *Japan's Modern Myths.* Princeton: Princeton University Press.

Hall, John W. (1983). *Das japanische Kaiserreich.* Frankfort o. M.: Fischer.

Halliday, Jon (1975). *A Political History of Japanese Capitalism.* New York: Pantheon.

House of Representatives 2002. *Strength of Political Groups in the House of Representatives* (Home Page). 23 October 2002 (http://www.shugiin.go.jp/itdb_main.nsf/html/index_e_strength.htm).

IPU (Inter-Parliamentary Union). 2000. *Japan* (Home Page). 12 February 2000. (http://www.ipu.org.80/cgi/multiga english/parline/parline.cnf#STAT3).

——2002. *Japan: House of Councillors* (Home Page). 23 October 2003. (http://www.ipu.org/parline-e/reports/2162.htm).

Ishida, Hiroshi (1993). *Social Mobility in Contemporary Japan.* Stanford: Stanford University Press.

Jin, Ikko (1989). *Keibatsu—shin tokken kaikyû no keifu* [Genealogy of the New Privileged Class]. Tokyo: Mainichi Shimbunsha.

Johnson, Chalmers (1982). *MITI and the Japanese Miracle.* Stanford: Stanford University Press.

Kerbo, Harold R., and McKinstry, John A. (1995). *Who Rules Japan?* Westport: Praeger.

Kishimoto, Koichi (1988). *Politics in Modern Japan: Development and Organization.* Tokyo: Japan Echo Inc.

Kitagawa, Takayoshi, and Kainuma, Jun (1985). *Nihon no Eriito* [Japan's Elite]. Tokyo: Otsuki Shoten.

Kodansha (ed.) (1993). *Japan: An Illustrated Encyclopedia* (2 volumes). Tokyo: Kodansha.

Koh, Byung C. (1989). *Japan's Administrative Elite*. Berkeley: University of California Press.

Koyama, Shigeke (1981). "Kanryo to Gakureki [Bureaucrats and Educational Credentials]", in H. Takeuchi and M. Aso (eds), *Nihon no Gakureki Shakai wa Kawaru*. Tokyo: Yuhikaku.

Maki, Taro (1987). *Nagatachou no Jouryuu Kazoku* [Leading Families at the Center of National Politics]. Tokyo: Kanki Shuppan.

Moore, Barrington (1966). *Social Origins of Dictatorship and Democracy*. Boston: Beacon Press.

Muramatsu, Michio (ed.) (1997). *State and Administration in Japan and Germany: a Comparative Perspective on Continuity and Change*. Berlin: de Gruyter.

Pye, Lucian W. (1985). *Asian Power and Politics: the Cultural Dimensions of Authority*. Cambridge, MA: Belknap.

Ramsdell, Daniel B. (1992). *The Japanese Diet: stability and Change in the Japanese House of Representatives, 1890–1990*. Lanham: University Press of America.

Rixtel, Adrian A. R. J. M., and Hassink, Wolter H. J. (1998). *Monitoring the Monitors: amakudari and Ex-Post Monitoring of Private Banks*. London: Centre for Economic Policy Research.

Schwartz, Frank J. (1998). *The Politics of Consultation in Japan*. Cambridge: Cambridge University Press.

Stockwin, James A. (1999). *Governing Japan: divided Politics in a Major Economy*, 3rd edition. Oxford: Blackwell.

14

Netherlands: Political Careers between Central Party Dominance and New Pressures

MONIQUE LEIJENAAR AND KEES NIEMÖLLER

POLITICAL PROFESSIONALIZATION IN HISTORICAL PERSPECTIVE

The French Revolution signaled the end of the Republic of the seven United Provinces of the Netherlands. They were occupied by France in 1795 and turned into a vassal state. In 1806 Napoleon installed his brother Louis Napoleon as King of the country, which then acquired the name Kingdom of Holland. Four years later France annexed the whole of the Netherlands. The Netherlands became independent again after the collapse of the Napoleonic Empire in 1813, and a power struggle between monarchists and republicans ensued, ending in favor of the former. Thus, the Kingdom of the Netherlands came into being in 1814, encompassing the present-day Netherlands, Belgium, and Luxembourg. The constitution of 1814 stated that the King should govern and the ministers should be accountable to him. It was revised in 1848 making ministers accountable to an elected Parliament, which created the basis for a constitutional monarchy with a parliamentary system.

From that time on, politics gradually became a profession.[1] Members of Parliament (MPs) were no longer dependent on whatever financial rewards or compensations they used to receive from the Provinces they represented. Ever since, MPs have been compensated by the central government, and this enlarged their independence a great deal. In the nineteenth century, however, the job was not very rewarding from a financial point of view, because only travel expenses were paid.

During the twentieth century there was a trend towards full compensation of Members of the Second Chamber (*Tweede Kamer*; together with the First Chamber—*Eerste Kamer*—named the *Staten-Generaal*). At the beginning of the

---

[1] This chapter is based on a number of authoritative publications. As many details are discussed in most of these sources, we will refer to them here in a general manner. The most important ones are Franssen and Schagen (1990); Visscher (1994); Raalte (1995, 2000); Leijenaar and Niemöller (1997); and a number of publications from the information service of the Parliament.

century the Members dedicated more and more of their time to their jobs as MPs and at least some modest level of compensation was deemed necessary. Traditionally, however, there had been many objections against financial remuneration. Many people feared that membership of Parliament would attract the "wrong" kind of people, resulting in a caste of professional politicians who could live off politics. The amount of travel expenses that was paid for was even reduced to 2,000 guilders in 1917.

On the other hand, there was a growing recognition of the undemocratic nature of such a policy. In 1917 the constitution was revised and, under pressure of the Second Chamber, the government proposed inserting into the constitution provisions for an annual compensation of 5,000 guilders (NLG),[2] a mandate to regulate travel expenses, and the rudiments of a pension scheme. Since 1937, ordinary law can settle the financial compensation of MPs, which makes it unnecessary to revise the constitution for each increase of their salaries.

THE INSTITUTIONAL CONTEXT

Government in the Netherlands comprises three levels: central, provincial, and local. The central government concerns itself with issues of national interest, while provinces and municipalities are forms of local government. The administrative structure is currently under revision: a process of decentralization is taking place, with increasing numbers of tasks and responsibilities being transferred from central to local government. The objective is to narrow the gap between the individual citizen and the authorities and to diminish bureaucracy. In urban areas, local government is increasingly becoming a matter of cooperation between the municipalities concerned, and efforts are being made to tackle problems like housing development, traffic, industrial sites, and the environment jointly. This cooperation between municipalities could have taken the form of a regional authority with its own powers, but so far no "urban provinces" have been created.

The Netherlands are made up of twelve provinces, each administered by a provincial council, a provincial executive and a Queen's Commissioner. The inhabitants of the province directly elect the members of the provincial council, which then appoints a provincial executive from among its members—being responsible for the day-to-day administration of the province. The members of the Provincial Councils also elect the Members of the First Chamber of the *Staten-Generaal*. The Queen's Commissioner, appointed by the Crown, is president of both the Provincial Council and the Provincial Executive.

The lowest governmental level is made up of 494 municipalities. The administration of each consists of a municipal council and a municipal executive (mayor and aldermen). The Municipal Council is directly elected by universal suffrage of all voters in the municipality—including foreigners who have been legal residents in the

[2] Adjusted for inflation this amounts to around US$28,300, or approx. €27,640 (inflation index according to Mitchell 1992).

Netherlands for at least 5 years. Until March 2002 each council appointed the aldermen from its members, and the alderman stayed on as member of the council. A new law, meant to establish more dualistic relations between the local council and the local executive, makes it now possible for political parties to appoint outsiders as their aldermen. After the municipal elections of March 2002, for the first time in history, a local party advertised in a newspaper for the position of alderman in the municipality of Tiel, and selected a person from about thirty applicants.

The procedures to appoint the mayor have also changed. The Crown (or the Minister of Internal Affairs) still appoints the *burgemeester* (mayor) for a period of 6 years, following a recommendation from the city council. Since 2002 larger municipalities can decide to hold a so-called mayor referendum. Citizens can then decide which of two candidates (nominated by the council) they prefer as their mayor and the elected name is then forwarded for nomination. It is to be expected that in the near future people will directly elect their *burgemeesters*. The executive is responsible for the administration and for preparing and implementing central and provincial government decisions that affect the municipality in question.

Quite a number of MPs have fulfilled, at one time in their career, one or more political functions on the provincial and local levels. However, members of the Second Chamber cannot combine these positions with their mandate. MPs sometimes have ambitions, after leaving Parliament, to be appointed as a *burgemeester* or Queen's Commissioner.

The Netherlands is a constitutional monarchy with a parliamentary system. Queen Beatrix as head of state constitutes together with the cabinet ministers the government (the Crown). The Parliament, formally referred to as the *Staten-Generaal*, consists of two houses, the First Chamber (Upper House), which has seventy-five members indirectly elected by the provincial councils, and the Second Chamber (Lower House) with 150 members elected by universal suffrage of all electors over the age of 18.

This bicameral system was introduced in 1815. The First Chamber was created mainly to satisfy southern (Belgian) aristocracy and it remained after Belgium was again separated from the kingdom. Although the First Chamber was not formally restricted to the nobility, in practice more than 90 percent of its members came from this strata. Generally, representative democracy was not an issue at that time: electors and elected alike belonged to a select elite, composed entirely of men. To be enfranchised they had to comply with all kinds of conditions, one of which was payment of a minimum amount of taxes, something that served as an automatic indicator of their wealth. Between 1815 and 1848 the members of the First Chamber were appointed for life by the King and selected from the upper echelons of society. For the King, the First Chamber was an instrument on which he could rely if the Second Chamber had passed legislation that was disagreeable to him. During this period, however, the King could not stop various amendments to the constitution, the most radical being introduced in 1848. The main consequence was that responsibility for government policy came to rest with the ministers. The King became politically inviolable. In addition, the Second Chamber acquired a series of important rights, which led to a considerable increase in its controlling power: the right of amendment, the right of interpellation, the right to institute an inquiry, and the right to approve the budget. These rights created the basis for parliamentary democracy as we now know it in the Netherlands. Since 1848, furthermore, the provincial councils choose the members of the First Chamber, while Members of the Second Chamber are chosen directly by the electorate. Since 1956 both chambers exist in their present size.

One of the main tasks of Parliament is to control the government. Another main task, together with the government, is to enact legislation and amend existing legislation to changing circumstances. The Second Chamber alone has two additional rights: the right of amending bills and the right of initiative, that is, an MP or a group of MPs may submit a bill.

Since the 1960s the extent of parliamentary activity has vastly increased. To give an example, in the parliamentary year 1960–61, 227 questions were asked by members of the Second Chamber and twenty-four motions were submitted. In the year 1984–85 the numbers were, respectively, 1,161 and 1,214 (Visscher 1994). We also see a clear increase in the number of public hearings and public inquiries organized by the Chamber.

In a formal sense the legislative power of Parliament is considerable. That seems to be confirmed by Visscher (1994) who analyzed some 3,000 parliamentary decisional processes. All cabinet proposals were delayed by the Parliament, and two-thirds of all proposals that could legally be changed were, in fact, changed. In one percent of the cases the result was more or less a completely new law and about 6 percent of the proposals were killed entirely. Furthermore, the Parliament did occasionally also exercise its right of initiative; of all laws adopted between 1963 and 1986, one percent was initiated by the legislature (Visscher 1994: 772).

The influence of Parliament is based for the greater part on the Second Chamber. The influence of the First Chamber on the legislative process is relatively small and is mainly a matter of slowing down decision-making, since it cannot amend bills. However, it can vote against a bill and by doing so it has an absolute veto. The main question, however, remains: how strong is the Dutch Parliament *vis-à-vis* the executive? Andeweg (1992: 178) points out that the Dutch case is hard to classify, because the relations between MPs and members of the cabinet seem to vary depending on the issue concerned.

Interesting in this regard is the change in the relationship between government and governmental parties with the arrival of the "purple cabinet" in 1994, consisting of three parties, PvdA (*Partij van de Arbeid*; the Labor Party), D66 (*Democraten 66*; the left liberal party), and VVD (*Volkspartij voor Vrijheid en Democratie*; the conservative liberal party). It has happened several times that one of the governmental parties did not vote with the government, and as a consequence, the bill was rejected in the Second Chamber. In the past, this would have meant a breach of confidence and a breaking up of the coalition. The fact that this time government accepted its defeat and continued its work, pointed to a "cultural" change, it was called by members of government and Parliament: the "new dualism."

Normally, the Lower House meets three times a week and committee meetings take place four times. There are three ways of voting: by parliamentary party, by person, or by secret ballot. In the first case MPs raise their hands and if the members of a parliamentary party, who are in the Chamber at the time, all vote in favor or against a bill, a motion or amendment, the Speaker assumes that the entire party group is voting that way. Every MP can, at any given moment, ask for a personal vote. This involves each MP casting a vote for or against when his or her name is called. Voting by secret ballot takes place if the House is required to propose or appoint someone, for example its Speaker.

Members of Parliament do much of their work in about twenty committees. Generally speaking, the composition of these committees is an accurate reflection of the division of power in the Second Chamber which has standing, general, and temporary committees. There are thirteen or fourteen standing committees: one for each ministry, except for the Prime Minister's Ministry of General Affairs. Further, there is a standing committee responsible for affairs pertaining to the Netherlands Antilles and Aruba. General committees deal with subjects that the Chamber considers to be of great importance and which relate to more than one ministry. For example, there is a general committee for European affairs. Temporary committees have a clearly defined, specific assignment and are disbanded as soon as that assignment has been completed.

In the first constitution of 1814, the free mandate of each individual delegate was seen as absolute, in effect precluding any form of bounded mandate or consultative process being imposed upon MPs. As a result of the emancipation of workers and religious groups towards the end of the nineteenth century, however, certain factions were formed in Parliament, becoming firmly entrenched after the introduction of a system of proportional representation in 1917. From that moment on, the Netherlands developed from a legislator-based democracy to a party democracy in which parliamentary groups rather than individual MPs are the main actors in Parliament. The distribution of time, rooms, facilities, financial and other resources, chairs and committee assignments, are all typically dependent on the size of the groups. However, this pre-eminent position of parliamentary groups is neither rooted in the constitution nor in the electoral law—constitutional law recognizes only individual representatives. As a consequence, there is a certain tension between constitutional law and the regulations concerning parties and party groups, which are subject to other laws.

In most cases close ties exist between MPs and parliamentary parties on the one hand and their party outside Parliament on the other hand. Party membership is obligatory for an MP. Some parties force candidates into a "contract" to ensure cooperation with the group or abdication of the seat in case the MP should leave the party group. This brings about a situation in which the independent position of an MP—as established in the constitution—is, to a certain extent, a judicial fiction. This is not to say that MPs are merely mandate holders for their parties. Should an MP vote against the instructions of his or her party, the legality of this cannot be disputed by anyone. The negative consequences for the political career of the person involved are, nevertheless, very real. It should be mentioned here, that in general parties make a clear distinction between the party and the parliamentary group. The major parties consider the functions of party leader and parliamentary group leader to be incompatible. The party leader takes care of the organizational matters concerning the party, while the leader of the parliamentary group is the political leader, representing the political ideas of the party.

The current electoral system goes back to 1917 when, as a result of the "pacification pact" between the political groups that had been formed by that time, the system of proportional representation was introduced together with universal suffrage (in 1917 for men and in 1919 for women). The constitution requires an election every 4 years for the Second Chamber, after which the leader of the largest party is asked by the Queen to form a majority coalition-cabinet together with other parties.

In the current electoral system the whole of the country is a single constituency. For pragmatic reasons that have to do with the administration of elections and the counting of votes, the country is divided into eighteen electoral districts, and the votes for each party list in these districts are added up. This system is one of the most proportional in the world, also because there is a very low threshold for Parliamentary representation: just 0.67 percent of votes are needed. The absence of constituencies means that candidates do not have to compete for votes in a particular district. Therefore, there is no constituency work to be done, nor is there any need for service responsiveness or symbolic responsive behavior. Strangely enough, the absence of constituencies does not mean that a territorial base is of no importance at all. Most parties in the Netherlands are structured by regions and it used to be the case that each regional branch nominated a certain number of candidates for Parliament. In the past, this meant that candidates often moved to an area in order to increase their chances of nomination (Koole and Leijenaar 1988). Yet, since the mid-1990s selection has become centralized in most parties and the regional factor has lost some of its relevance. Though, it still happens that a regional candidate gets elected by preferential votes as the result of a personal campaign in his or her own region. Preferential voting is possible, but since the majority of electors vote for the first candidate on the list it happens rarely that a candidate gets directly elected by preferential votes. In the parliamentary elections of May 2002 a woman candidate placed at number seven of the Christian Union party's list received so many preferential votes that she was elected as one of the four MPs. She overstepped the candidates placed four, five, and six on the list of candidates.

Individual politicians in the Netherlands do not need funding for personal campaigns, neither in elections to mobilize voters, nor within the party to "buy" support guaranteeing a safe seat on the list. However, political parties do need money, because all political parties represented in the Parliament have to finance a large-scale organization with full-time employees. Political parties have always had a lack of financial resources, but these days they are more dependent on a greater variety of sources. Depillarization has had the effect that parties can no longer automatically count on the support of related organizations such as labor unions and churches, support that was important, especially with regard to the mobilization of voters. At the same time parties have lost their faithful adherents, and much more effort is needed for gaining votes. The position of parties has, therefore, become more vulnerable, also financially.

Table 14.1   *Public party financing, 2000 (in €)*

Party	Total income	Public grants	MPs' payments	Donations
PvdA	7,183,109	1,582,544	886,261	240,790
VVD	4,900,203	1,290,710	0	104,453
CDA	6,234,776	991,464	282,785	522,046
D66	1,641,525	564,995	35,380	84,567
GL	2,371,921	580,720	632,997	51,568
SP	3,629,833	1,326,783	1,729,311	57,721
RPF	799,903	332,443	22,689	84,639
GPV	737,799	287,124	0	94,972
SGP	969,381	331,103	0	114,090

Notes: CDA: *Christen Democratisch Appel*; PvdA: *Partij van de Arbeid*; VVD: *Volkspartij voor Vrijheid en Democratie*; D66: *Democraten 66*; GL: *Groen Links*; SP: *Socialistische Partij*; SGP: *Staatkundig Gereformeerde Partij*; GPV: *Gereformeerd Politiek Verbond*.

Source: *Kamerstuk Financiering Politieke Partijen*, nr. 27422, vergaderjaar 2001–02.

What are the financial sources of a political party? There are three main sources: contributions of party members (46 percent of total income of parties), public grants (26 percent), and the compulsory payments by the own MPs (13 percent). Other sources are donations from individuals and from organizations and private business (see Table 14.1). Most parties, especially the left-wing ones, expect their representatives to contribute a certain percentage of their salary. For the PvdA this adds up to 12 percent of their total income, for Green Left to 27 percent, and for the SP to 48 percent.

Until very recently, political parties were not financed directly by the state, as is the case in Germany, but indirectly through their own functional institutions. Most parties, therefore, had a kind of "think-tank" institute, an educational and training institute, and specific organizations dealing for example with developing countries and/or Eastern Europe. Since 1972 each party's institute received an equal sum increased by a sum dependent on the number of seats a party had in the Second Chamber. Parties did receive, however, some direct money from the government to buy media time and in the 1970s and 1980s for special projects, such as to set up an affirmative action policy aiming to involve more women in the party. To give an indication, in 1995 the CDA (*Christen Democratisch Appel*) received NLG1,843,006 (€836,320), the PvdA NLG2,004,379 (€909,550), and the D66 NLG1,238,640 (€562,070) to keep their functional institutions running.[3] In comparison, in the same year each party received about NLG100,000 (€45,380) from the government to spend on radio and TV campaigns.

In the 1990s, party leaderships became more and more dissatisfied with this system of governmental financing, mainly because many political parties suffered financial difficulties, given the rapid loss of party members. After a debate of about 6 years

[3] Converted according to the fixed EMU rate (NLG1 = €0.4538).

and many meetings between the Minister of Internal Affairs and the chairmen of the political parties, a new law on party financing came into effect in 1999. Since then the Ministry of Internal Affairs directly finances parties and the amount is dependent on the number of seats in the Second Chamber. However, spending of this lump sum is still somewhat restricted, for example, it may not be used for campaigning. Instead, it has to be spent on providing information to the party members, for political education, contacts with associated parties abroad, or for involving more young people in politics (cf. *Kamerstuk 27422, vergaderjaar 2001–02*).

THE POLITICAL CLASS

Research on legislative recruitment in the Netherlands used to focus on party politics. If you pursued a career as an MP, you first had to become a member of a political party. Within the party you not only had to pay your dues, but you also had to become politically active: go to the meetings of the local or regional branches, become a delegate to the national party congress, subsequently chair a local or regional branch and then become nominated for the national party board. After 5–10 years of party activism there was a high probability of being asked to become a candidate for Parliament. Other—non-party—attributes such as gender or ethnic background, regional origin, professional occupation, and experience as a local or regional councilor came only into play in the process of ranking the candidates. Party service and activism used to be the primary factors facilitating legislative recruitment (Hillebrand 1992: 290; Koole 1992: 306; Thomassen, Schendelen, and Zielonka-Goei 1992: 34; Leijenaar 1993: 223–4).

During the early 1990s, however, recruitment into Parliament became less predictable. Developments such as the declining strength of old community and group identities (depillarization and individualism) caused the crumbling of the "*partitocracy*." Voters turned their back on traditional parties and on politics in general—consequently, party membership has been declining rapidly. The proportion of the electorate who carries a party membership card has fallen from 9 percent in 1963 to 2.5 percent in 2002, narrowing the recruitment base substantially. Party leadership reacted to all of this with a demand for better qualified candidates and MPs with close ties to large societal groups. Hence, the criteria for selecting candidates changed, as well as selection procedures within the parties (see pp. 269–72).

Size and Composition

Due to the availability of personal data about MPs, most studies of legislative recruitment look at whether the legislature is "an exact portrait, in miniature, of the people at large, as it should think, feel, reason and act like them" (John Adams, cited in Pitkin 1967: 60). As with most other European Parliaments, this is not the case in the Netherlands: Dutch MPs have been, and still are, recruited from the highest layers of society in terms of class, education, and income (Berg 1983: 259). Though, in the

Table 14.2   *Social background of Members of the Second Chamber, 1918–1986*

Gender	1918–46		1947–67		1968–77		1978–86	
	M	F	M	F	M	F	M	F
High social background (%)	48	77	51	70	50	82	46	90
University degree (%)	45	54	52	45	59	54	64	53
Age at entry (years)	46	47	45	45	42	41	41	41

1970s the representational nature of Parliament changed drastically, from the representation of organized interests into a "workroom for professionals." Berg explains this by referring to depillarization and democratization: both had an impact on the nomination processes within parties. Depillarization caused a looser tie between candidates and interest groups, while the demand for a more democratic party organization had the effect that a greater variety of party members became candidates which produced more diversity in opinions among the candidates. Professionalization had the effect that a political career only became possible for people with flexible jobs and enough time at their hands: mainly people working in the public sector in high level jobs (Berg 1983: 194; see also Thomassen, Schendelen, and Zielonka-Goei 1992: 351).

Before 1970, the majority of MPs came from an upper or middle class background, they lived in cities, and a large proportion had an university degree. Many of them were civil servants—often working in an educational institution—and the average age was over 60. Women were hardly represented (Berg 1983: 230). With the ongoing process of depillarization and the demand from the younger generation for more political influence, the composition of Parliament changed rapidly, starting in the 1960s. After 1963 the elderly were replaced by very young MPs, some of them in their twenties (Berg 1983: 167). Between 1968 and 1979 the number of MPs descending from a "political family" (sons and daughters of former politicians) diminished, while the number of MPs with experience in parties and as a local or provincial councilor increased (Berg 1983: 55). In the 1980s the over-representation of MPs from the large cities was corrected, while the percentage with a university degree stabilized around 60 percent, most of them having studied law. The majority of MPs were between 40 and 50 years of age (Berg 1983: 191–211). Some background statistics for the MPs represented in the Second Chamber between 1918 and 1986—100 female and 774 male—are shown in Table 14.2.

Social class is measured by coding the profession of the father of the MP.[4] Table 14.2. shows that over the whole period the percentage of MPs coming from a high-class background has remained high: about half of the male MPs and even more among women. MPs, men and women, with an academic education have always been

---

[4] For a "high social background," fathers had to have occupations like lawyer or judge. Shop owners or workers in the service sector would be indicators for a "medium social background".

Table 14.3   *Gender, age, and education of MPs (%)*

	First Chamber			Second Chamber			
	1999	1995	1990	2002	1998–2002	1994–98	1990
Gender (%)							
female	27	23	24	31	35	31	27
male	73	77	76	69	65	69	73
Age (%)							
<40	3	4	1	20	27	21	17
40–49	13	12	20	41	40	48	47
50–59	49	55	37	35	29	26	33
≥60	35	28	41	4	5	5	2
Univ. degree total (%)	73	65	59	61	61	57	63
Law	27	33	—	19	20	30	32
Humanities	1	1	—	13	13	11	—
Social sciences	14	4	—	13	14	20	20
Economics	8	7	—	4	7	17	17

Note: Numbers rounded.

Source: *Parlementair Documentatie Centrum.*

over-represented. The age at entering the Parliament was typically in the early forties, with hardly any gender differences. What has changed over time? Background data in Table 14.3 illustrates that the trends from earlier periods still persist.

The representation of women in Parliament has increased over the years from 27 percent in 1990 to 35 percent in 1998. After the parliamentary elections in May 2002 fewer women returned to the Second Chamber, mostly because in the parliamentary group of *Lijst Pim Fortuyn* (LPF) only 11 percent were female. With regard to the representation of women in Parliament, a remarkable bill passed in 2001 concerning the replacement of women MPs who became pregnant. The common practice was that they either were not replaced at all or, mainly in small parliamentary groups, by the next person on the list of candidates. However, there was no judicial guarantee that this person would step back again after the pregnancy leave. This new bill now guarantees the return of the mother to Parliament.

It is also clear that the purple parties tried to involve more young people. In the Parliament of 1998, 27 percent of the MPs were younger than 40. The Parliament that started in 2002 was much "older"—again caused by the parliamentary group of the LPF with an average age of 50 years. Not much changed over the years with regard to the educational background. In the 2002 Parliament 61 percent of all MPs had an university degree—with the LPF having the lowest average (42 percent of their MPs had university education).

Many MPs have held one or more political offices before entering Parliament. From the Parliament of 1990 we know that more than half had a senior position in the party hierarchy, more than one-third represented their party at the local and/or the provincial level, and some were MPs in the other chamber of Parliament or were (deputy) minister in an earlier government. Only a few had been mayors. In 2002, 68 percent of the MPs had previous political experience in the Parliament, government, and local or provincial councils.

Political Recruitment and Political Careers

The selection procedures of the main Dutch parties have been reported extensively elsewhere (Koole and Leijenaar 1988; Leijenaar 1993). Koole and Leijenaar (1988: 206) looked at the theory and practice of selection processes and described their changes since the 1960s. They concluded that party control over the selection of representatives grew in this period and selection procedures became more rigid, while influence of regional and local party branches over selection declined drastically. Here, we focus on changes in the main features of candidate selection in the 1990s, including the MPs' perspective on these procedures.

In the late 1980s, due to the developments mentioned before, parties started to feel uneasy with selection procedures and their outcome—the composition of the parliamentary party. Since then the parties have been changing the procedures, stimulated by the debate on institutional reform. Parties were dissatisfied with the selection process for various reasons. It was felt that the parliamentary party consisted of too many white, highly educated males of whom the majority worked in the public sector. Moreover, many believed that more effort should be put in the recruitment of young and female candidates, and it was felt that criteria such as certain professional experience, ties with interest groups, and debating skills should be valued higher than simply a long party career (Koole and Leijenaar 1988; Hillebrand 1992). The pressure for greater central involvement came, not only from inside the parties. Women's groups (inside and outside the parties) were also demanding fairer representation in terms of gender (Velde 1994). The national parties were also aware that the parliamentary parties were facing increasing public scrutiny, given the growing dissatisfaction with politics and politicians.

Accordingly, the four main parties altered their recruitment practices, providing the national party organization with a more dominant role. The PvdA introduced a higher quota for women candidates and the other large parties explicitly announced their aim of looking for more women and for younger candidates. A long party experience and previous practice in representative bodies were replaced by being young, having good communication skills and ties with civic groups and preferable with job experience in the private sector. The introduction of television in Parliament also put much more emphasis on looks and performance as a debater. As shown in Table 14.3, the parliaments elected in 1994 and in 1998 mirror these changes in criteria: about one-third of the parliamentarians were women, the average age was 46 and 44 years, respectively, and almost half of them were newcomers. In the Parliament elected in May 2002, fewer women were to be found, mainly due to the fact that the new parties selected very few women candidates.

Whereas above we gave a profile of legislators in the different Parliaments, we will now look at data from a survey among a sample of all candidates for the parliamentary election of 1994. This will provide some insight in the candidates' own experiences with the selection processes within their parties and shed more light on the background of all *candidates*, whether they became an MP or not. In a way, the profile of legislators reflects the final result of the selection process and therefore can be seen as highly indicative of the demand side. Taking into account all candidates is a useful way to analyze the supply side of political recruitment.

To determine the degree of internal party democracy, respondents were asked about the influence of specific people and groups on the selection of parliamentary candidates. Altogether eighteen different actors should be rated on a seven-point scale ranging from "little" to "much" influence. Factor analysis yields a structure of five underlying factors which together explain 69 percent of the variance:

  (1) civil society: ethnic groups, issue groups, women groups, organizations for the aged, youth groups, community groups;
  (2) work: employers, business associates, trade unions;
  (3) family: spouse/partner, other family members;
  (4) party national: national party leaders, party members, party group in Parliament, party officials;
  (5) party local/regional: party leaders.

The differences between candidates of the various parties can be seen in Table 14.4, where the mean score on each of the five factors is tabulated for each party.

The main conclusions are that the influence of civil society on the selection process is highest for the left parties, especially the Green Left. The further to the right one gets on the left–right dimension, the less salient is the influence of civic groups on the process, according to the candidates. This phenomenon is well known from other research; members of the boards of civic organizations are disproportionately adherents of left-wing parties. The influence attributed to the national party is considerable for every party except D66. Concerning the importance of the local and regional party level there exists a marked difference between the left-wing

Table 14.4 *Influence structure underlying the selection process of parliamentary candidates, 1994 (mean factor scores)*

	GL	PvdA	D66	CDA	VVD	SR	All
Civic society	0.65	0.19	−0.29	−0.03	−0.50	−0.97	−0.15
Work	−0.16	0.20	−0.31	1.17	0.49	−0.43	0.15
Family	0.08	−0.31	0.18	−0.38	0.10	0.22	−0.01
Party national	0.20	0.38	−1.10	0.10	0.40	0.17	0.00
Party local/regional	−0.51	−0.89	−0.69	0.45	0.37	0.66	−0.13

Notes: Zero is the mean value for all respondents and has to be interpreted as an average importance of this category. For party names, see Table 14.1; SR: small right parties, that is, RPF, GPV, and SGP.

Table 14.5 *Personal qualities and their importance for the final ranking on the party list, 1994 (mean factor scores)*

	GL	PvdA	D66	CDA	VVD	SR	All
Acquired qualities	0.14	−0.11	−0.13	−0.12	0.01	−0.07	−0.05
"Inherited" qualities	0.14	−0.25	−0.61	−0.59	0.12	−0.06	−0.23
Local orientation	0.00	0.69	0.16	−0.49	−0.28	0.61	0.10
Religion/Values	−0.47	−0.73	−0.83	0.97	−0.28	1.42	−0.06
Political experience	0.18	0.97	−0.60	0.48	−0.32	−0.13	0.09
Miscellaneous	−0.57	0.03	0.05	0.09	−0.47	0.14	−0.12

Note: See Table 14.4.

and the right-wing parties: candidates on the left of the political spectrum rate the influence of local and regional party officials clearly below average, while those on the right indicate a high level of influence. The influence of associations of employers and employees is concentrated in the parties with the highest level of political power; the Labor party (PvdA), the Christian Democratic party (CDA), and the Liberal party (VVD), the biggest parties in the Netherlands which formed the various coalition governments in the last five decades.

Besides our questions about the influence of all kinds of people and groups on the selection process, we invited the candidates to rate the importance of a number of personal qualities with respect to their final ranking on the list of candidates. Again, factor analysis of nineteen of these qualities yields a structure of six underlying factors explaining 62 percent of the variance. These factors and the qualities underlying them are as follows (Table 14.5):

(1) acquired characteristics: good speaker, specific expertise, personal energy and enthusiasm, knowledgeability on issues;
(2) "inherited" characteristics: sex, age, ethnic descent, favorable personal appearance;
(3) local orientation: commitment to district, local prominence, connections with party supporters and civic organizations;
(4) religion, norms, values: religion, stable home life;
(5) political experience: political experience, experienced party worker;
(6) miscellaneous: support of groups' views, national prominence.

The mean factor scores lead us to the following main conclusions. first, "inherited" characteristics are not very important for most parties: only VVD and Green Left candidates rank them above average. Acquired qualities seem to be of even less importance: they played a positive role only in the selection process of the Green Left party. In the two most important parties, PvdA and CDA, special significance is attached to political experience. For the other parties, this factor seems to be (far) less relevant. Not surprisingly, the religious parties—CDA and the orthodox parties of the right—favor candidates on the basis of their religion and support of the family norm.

Table 14.6   *Most important reasons for candidacy, 1994 (weighted mean scores)*

	GL	PvdA	D66	CDA	VVD	SR	All
Asked to be a candidate	1.9	1.2	0.4	2.0	1.3	2.1	1.5
To become an MP	1.4	1.2	2.1	1.2	1.6	0.9	1.4
Support my party	1.9	1.3	1.4	0.9	1.2	2.0	1.4
Was reelectable as an incumbent	0.2	1.8	0.4	0.9	0.7	0.4	0.7
To promote political career	0.4	0.1	0.4	0.3	0.8	0.6	0.5

We will now analyze the most important reasons why the candidates for the 1994 elections ran for Parliament. Respondents were offered five possible reasons: support their own party; were asked to be a candidate; promote own political career; become an MP; were an incumbent. Respondents were asked to indicate their first, second, and third most important reasons. When we weigh the responses (first choice = three points, third choice = one point), we can calculate the mean scores for the candidates for each of the parties separately (see Table 14.6).

The most important reasons were "to be asked to be a candidate," "to become an MP," and "to support my party." The breakdown of the mean score for the various parties shows, however, more variation. Candidates running for Parliament because they were asked to, were more commonly among the religious parties (CDA and small right parties) and the extreme Green Left party—and not common among the liberal democrats (D66). To support their own party seems to be related to the size of the party: candidates of the smaller parties rank this reason higher than their colleagues of the main parties. Political career opportunities are the least important of all reasons, slightly more for liberal candidates (VVD) than for others.

Living off Politics

Since January 1997 MPs get an annual (gross) salary of €68,000 and they are allowed to earn around €8,160 a year from other sources of income. When more is earned, this amount is subtracted from the annual salary. Some MPs, like the Speaker of the House, or the leaders of the parliamentary groups, get an additional bonus. Apart from their annual income, Members of the Second Chamber get an allowance for traveling, accommodation, and general expenses (€1,900).

When membership of the Second Chamber is terminated, for whatever reason, one does not end in the poorhouse, because the law on pensions for political personnel provides a rather nice financial cushion. Each ex-MP receives a payment for the same number of years he or she has served in Parliament, but with a minimum of 2 years and a maximum of 6 years. If an MP has been less than 3 months in the Second Chamber, payment can only be received for 6 months. However, when leaving the Parliament at the age of 50 or older, and when having served the country for more than 10 years, MPs receive this payment—under a special provision—until they are 65 years old. In the first year they get 80 percent of the previous annual salary, in the second year 70, and then 60 percent. At 65 a pension is paid, amounting to about 70 percent of the previous annual salary. Obviously, MPs of the Second Chamber are well provided for. The level of income is competitive with jobs that also require highly educated professional people, and there is certainly no need for the individual legislator to accept all kinds of other positions in order to increase his or her income.

In contrast, members of the First Chamber do neither receive a salary like the members of the Second Chamber nor is there a financial arrangement for the "years after". Membership of the Senate is viewed as an additional job and members are expected to be in the Senate only for one day a week. However, senators do receive an annual allowance of €13,636 and an amount of about €1,800 for expenses. The Second Chamber's own administrative apparatus has been growing, especially during the last few decades. Now there are about 600 people working in five divisions, managed by an executive secretary (*griffier*). The level of administrative support for the First Chamber is very modest, around fifty staff members.

From 1966 onwards the parliamentary groups have been publicly funded, and therefore, able to employ secretaries and research assistants. Apart from this, individual MPs in the Second Chamber are entitled to hire part-time assistants and, since 1979, these assistants can be employed full-time. Each MP receives about €20,000 annually and can use this for secretarial or personal assistance. In practice, two MPs share one full-time assistant.

THE POLITICAL CLASS AND INSTITUTIONAL REFORM

The debate on institutional reform reached its first peak in the 1960s. Some politicians pointed out that the Dutch political system did not even meet the minimal definition of democracy as formulated by Schumpeter: that the electorate should decide who was going to be in power. Because of the necessity to form a governing coalition, more than once the party which "won" the election with the largest number of seats was kept out of government. This led to a plea for "polarization," that is, that parties should form coalitions before the election so that the electorate would not only vote for a party, but also for a certain government coalition (Thijn 1967; Uyl 1967; Dittrich and Andeweg 1982). Other points of discussion at that time were the direct election of the Prime Minister and the introduction of a referendum. Since then, several parliamentary or expert committees have studied possible reforms of the system without reaching firm conclusions.

The 1990s saw a revival of the debate on institutional reforms, in reaction to the negative public image of politics and politicians. When turnout in the large cities decreased to between 45 and 50 percent at the local elections in 1990, politicians started to worry about the large gap between voters and representatives and the possible lack of legitimacy of the local political system. The chair of the Second Chamber established several reform committees which were to advise Parliament on such matters as: changing the system of proportional representation into, for example, the German mixed system; the possibility of a directly elected mayor instead of nomination by the cabinet; and the possible introduction of referendums. Although the recommendations from these committees were rather conservative, it became clear in the parliamentary debate in 1993 that a large majority was still unwilling to embrace the proposals for change. The only reform that gained some sympathy was an increase in the weight of preference votes for candidates.

However, this debate has not come to an end, and probably never will. The 1994 election produced the so-called "purple cabinet" consisting of three parties, PvdA, D66, and VVD. The Christian Democrats (CDA), who are ideologically positioned between D66 and VVD, were kept out of government, something that had not happened since 1917. During the strained coalition negotiations D66, which had always promoted a radical reform of the political system, insisted on the inclusion of institutional reforms in the coalition agreement.

The cabinet kept its promise in 1995 by submitting a proposal to Parliament for a radical change in the system of proportional representation, as well as the introduction of a corrective referendum (i.e. repeal of bills). The proposal suggested a mixed electoral system: half of the members of the Second Chamber would be elected by means of proportional representation and a party list system (the current system), while the other half should be elected in five districts. Parties would still submit lists within these districts, but with fewer candidates since only a total of fifteen seats could be gained in each district. This proposal was intended to produce closer ties between the electorate and its representatives by decreasing the physical distance. The proposal was defeated by the Parliament in 1996, but in 1998, right before the election, it was back on the agenda again. But in the end the cabinet did not submit a reform bill in order to change the electoral system.

In the cabinet appointed in August 1998, D66 had three ministers and lobbied strongly in favor of institutional reform. A bill was passed by the Second Chamber introducing a corrective referendum, but it was defeated in 1999 in the First Chamber by a majority of one vote. As we mentioned before, the cabinet was more successful with institutional changes at the local level. In 2002 a law was passed by both Chambers introducing a dualistic system at the local level, with, among others, more direct influence for citizens (of large cities) to elect the mayor.

Dissatisfaction with the traditional political mores and institutions reached a peak in the time before the parliamentary elections of May 2002. It became clear that the love between the three "purple parties" was over and that a divorce was at hand. The divorce proceedings were speeded up by the arrival of a new party, *Leefbaar Nederland* (LN). People who had been successful at the local level with independent, local parties, founded LN to give a signal of protest directed against the "purple government" parties. They challenged the lack of transparency in decision-making and the lack of decisiveness of the government as well as the inability of the "purple cabinet" to solve problems such as the waiting lists for hospital operations and the increasing figures on criminality. Further, the LN placed the issue of the presence of immigrants and especially the question of (the lack of) their integration in Dutch society high on the political agenda. The popularity of LN really increased with the selection of a party leader. They found Pim Fortuyn, a former professor in sociology and columnist willing to take on this role. His flamboyant performance and his way to speak clearly and directly turned out be very successful. Pim Fortuyn had one problem, however, he was also a very individualistic person and not willing to walk on the leash of the party organization.

In February 2002 this led to a climax after he declared, in a newspaper interview (in the *Volkskrant*), the Islam culture as backward and asked for an abolition of the constitutional ban on discrimination. Immediately the board of the LN outvoted Fortuyn as their leader. Fortuyn, by now convinced of his electoral attraction given the highly successful polling results, founded his own party List Pim Fortuyn (*Lijst Pim Fortuyn*, LPF) and submitted a list of candidates for the election of May 2002. Fortuyn was then murdered 9 days before the parliamentary elections by an environmental and animal rights activist. The effects of all this on the election results are described by Andeweg and Irwin:

This first murder of a political figure in 330 years sent a shockwave through the country and led to an unprecedented public display of mourning. Amidst accusations that by "demonizing" Mr. Fortuyn the Left and the media had created a climate of opinion that made the assassination possible, the elections went ahead as scheduled on 15 May. Exit polls show that the murder changed the preference of 12 percent of the voters. Some voters used the ballot box to send a message of condolence, but other voters, apparently fearful that polarization would destabilize the country, produced a last-minute swing towards the Christian Democrats. (Andeweg and Irwin 2002: 99)

As expected and predicted by the polls, the three "purple parties" got severely beaten in the elections. The PvdA went from 29 to 15 percent (23 seats), the VVD from 25 to 16 percent (24 seats), and D66 from 9 to 5 percent. The opposition party CDA as well as the LPF were the alternatives for many voters. Not ever in history has a new party gained so many votes: LPF received 17 percent of the total vote and was represented in Parliament with 26 seats. The CDA became the largest party with 28 percent (43 seats). In August 2002 a CDA-VVD-LPF cabinet was formed, headed by CDA-party leader Balkenende.

The arrival of the LPF on the stage has shaken the Dutch party system. Pim Fortuyn appealed to a sense of unease that had been steadily growing: insecurity, feelings of powerlessness, and a loss of confidence in the government and in politics, in general. Dissatisfaction was also aimed at the behavior of politicians. Politics had become too professional and the politicians had isolated themselves from the voters. Being interviewed by the media, government ministers, MPs or party leaders never seemed to give straight answers, nor were able to admit to failures. The straightforward way of communicating by Fortuyn, visible in the many televised debates during the campaign for the election of 2002, was a welcome distraction from the somewhat arrogant attitude of the "old" political male leaders.

The relatively huge electoral success of a newcomer in parliamentary politics, the LPF, changed the composition of the Parliament: fewer women, fewer young MPs, fewer experienced MPs willing to play according to the rules. Especially the latter fact, the inexperience of LPF MPs and also of LPF cabinet ministers led to many internal quarrels. Members of the parliamentary party accused each other of abuse of power, the parliamentary leader of the LPF group was replaced and after several months, two LPF representatives left the parliamentary group and formed an independent party group. Inside the cabinet a similar situation happened with two LPF ministers accusing each other openly of power abuse and mismanagement. All this led to a very premature fall of the cabinet Balkenende, after being 87 days in office. Another consequence of the unexpected huge loss of the "purple parties" was the resignation of many former cabinet ministers and junior ministers from the parliamentary group. Since many of them were known with the general public, all these former government ministers had been placed high on the lists of candidates, and were thus, elected to Parliament. A majority of them, however, had no intention to stay another 4 years in Parliament and announced their resignation. This, of course, caused a debate in the media on the deceit of electors and blemished the "purple parties" even more.

In the end, the wave of reform that swept through Parliament under the "purple cabinet" did not last long. Before the 1994 election, the relationship between cabinet and Parliament could be described as static: a monistic relationship between government and the governmental parties, which were very disciplined as far as voting in Parliament was concerned. Bills submitted by the cabinet were sometimes amended, but almost always passed Parliament. Under the "purple cabinet" parliamentary behavior did change. The VVD parliamentary group and, less often, the PvdA and D66 parliamentary parties, did not automatically follow their own cabinet members, and several times the cabinet failed to gain a majority for its plans. Much more often than used to be the case, roll calls were necessary, and it seemed that the traditional split between government and opposition parties was not so clear-cut anymore and that Parliament was gaining influence again. But, with the Parliament that started in 2002 these "new" relations ended and again MPs obediently voted according to their role: government party or not. In addition, the electorate became confronted with MPs of the LPF parliamentary group accusing and fighting each other. Despite of all the pressures and debates on institutional reform Parliament has yet not succeeded in regaining trust and involvement of Dutch citizens.

REFERENCES

Andeweg, Rudy B. (1992). "Executive-Legislative Relations in the Netherlands: Consecutive and Coexisting Pattern". *Legislative Studies Quarterly*, 17: 161–82.
——and Irwin, Galen A. (2002). *Governance and Politics of the Netherlands*. New York: Palgrave.
Berg, Johannes Th. J. van den (1983). *De toegang tot het Binnenhof: de maatschappelijke herkomst van de Tweede-Kamerleden tussen 1849 en 1970*. Weesp: Van Holkema.
Dittrich, Karl, and Andeweg, Rudy B. (1982). "De mythologie van het meerderheidsdenken". *Socialisme en Democratie*, 39: 324–32.

Franssen, Hubertus M., and Schagen, J. A. van (1990). *Over de orde mijnheer de voorzitter: Werkwijze van de Tweede Kamer.* The Hague: SDU.

Hillebrand, Ron (1992). *The Antichambre van het parlement.* Leiden: DSWO Press.

Koole, Ruud (1992). *De opkomst van de moderne kaderpartij.* Zwolle: Spectrum.

——and Leijenaar, Monique H. (1988). "The Netherlands: The Predominance of Regionalism", in M. Gallagher and M. Marsh (eds), *Candidate Selection in Comparative Perspective.* London: Sage, pp. 190–209.

Leijenaar, Monique H. (1993). "A Battle for Power: Selecting Candidates in the Netherlands", in J. Lovenduski and P. Norris (eds), *Gender and Party Politics.* London: Sage, pp. 219–39.

—— and Niemöller, Kees (1997). "The Netherlands", in P. Norris (ed.), *Passages to Power: Legislative Recruitment in Advanced Democracies.* Cambridge: Cambridge University Press, pp. 114–36.

Mitchell, Brian R. (1992). *International Historical Statistics, Europe 1750–1988.* New York: Stockton Press.

Pitkin, Hanna F. (1967). *The Concept of Representation.* Berkeley: University of California Press.

Raalte, Ernst van (1995). *Het Nederlandse Parlement,* 8th edition. Deventer: Kluwer.

——(2000). *Het Nederlandse Parlement,* 9th edition. Deventer: Kluwer.

Thijn, Ed van (1967). "Van partijen naar stembusaccoorden", in E. Jurgens *et al.* (eds), *Partijvernieuwing.* Amsterdam: Arbeiderspers.

Thomassen, Jacques, Schendelen, Rinus van, and Zielonka-Goei, Mei-Lan (1992). *Geachte Afgevaardigde.* Muiderberg: Coutinho.

Uyl, Joop den (1967). "Een stem die telt", in E. Jurgens *et al.* (eds), *Partijvernieuwing.* Amsterdam: Arbeiderspers.

Velde, Hella van de (1994). *Vrouwen van de partij.* Leiden: DSWO Press.

Visscher, Gerard (1994). *Parlementaire invloed op wetgeving.* Den Haag: SDU.

15

New Zealand: Parliamentary Careers and Electoral Reform

ELIZABETH MCLEAY

The relatively small New Zealand political class is composed primarily of central government elected politicians from whom the members of the political executive, the Ministers of the Crown, are drawn. Although the Members of Parliament (MPs) are professionalized politicians aware of their common interests, thus constituting a political class, this term is seldom used in New Zealand, either as a shorthand method of identifying a particular group within the socio-political structure or as a pejorative term. But "politicians" have been the subject of mounting distrust and skepticism. It is widely held that there are too many of them and that they cost the taxpayers far too much. The public concern is about those who live "off" politics and are paid by the state.

POLITICAL PROFESSIONALIZATION IN HISTORICAL PERSPECTIVE

In 1840 the British Crown signed the Treaty of Waitangi with the leaders of the indigenous people, the Maori. On 24 May 1854 Parliament first met and responsible government began 2 years later. Thus, New Zealand is one of the world's oldest democracies. In 1852 all men who met a minimum property-owning qualification were enfranchised; in 1875 enfranchisement included all men who met residential requirements; and in 1893 women gained the vote (although they could not stand for Parliament until 1919).

Popular control is exercised through regular and frequent elections. Until 1879 the maximum term of Parliament was 5 years. Since then it has been 3 years, although this has been temporarily extended four times (McGee 1994: 128–9). In 1967 and 1990 voters overwhelmingly rejected proposals to extend the parliamentary term by

I wish to thank Jens Borchert for inviting me to write this chapter and for raising funds for paying for my visit to the University of Goettingen. I should also like to thank the Foundation for Research, Science and Technology for its eight-year grant to enable the New Zealand Political Change Project to proceed. This chapter was researched with its help. Thanks are also due to my colleagues on the Project: Jonathan Boston, Stephen Levine, and Nigel Roberts. I particularly wish to thank Leigh Ward for all her help.

1 year. In the absence of other institutional constraints—such as an upper house, judicial review, or federalism—electors constricted the duration of tenure of the political class. Indeed, turnover has been quite high. A comparative analysis of legislative turnover rates during the six general elections between 1978 and 1993 placed New Zealand at about the mid-point of twenty-five countries—not as high as in many proportional representation (PR) states but higher than other single member constituency, simple plurality systems (except for Canada), probably a reflection of the frequency of New Zealand elections (Matland and Studlar 1996). The turnover rate measured as a percentage of incumbents returned was 72.5 percent. New Zealand was in ninth position with the mean at 68.9 percent. In the first PR Parliament elected in October 1996, with its enhanced minor party representation, and therefore, increased number of new entrants, 61.7 percent were incumbents, rising to 73.3 percent in 1999 (McLeay 2000*a*) and 75 percent in 2002. It is too early to tell whether PR will have a lasting impact on the incumbency of New Zealand legislators.

The professionalization of elected politicians was a gradual process, especially concerning remuneration. Between 1854 and 1892 MPs were paid a sessional honorarium to help them meet expenses incurred through their absences from home and their normal occupations. As von Tunzelman explains, "Because of the twin principles on which payment was based, that it should be such as to not exclude even the poorest man from entering Parliament but should include no income element, the rate reflected an average labourer's wage" (von Tunzelman 1979: 61–2). The payment crept up until it compared with that paid the Clerk of the House (although MPs were still being paid on the basis of the parliamentary sessions rather than the full working year).

Throughout the nineteenth century MPs debated whether they should be paid salaries or merely be recompensated for expenses. The advocates of salaries argued that, among other things, unpaid MPs were in danger of bribery. There was also discontent with the mode of determination: through the annual debates on the Estimates of Expenditure. In 1884, therefore, the Parliamentary Honorarium and Privileges Bill was passed, to be succeeded by the Payment of Members Act 1892. Annual payments now recognized that parliamentary duties extended to constituency tasks. It is at this stage that "members had begun to see their remuneration in the light of the nature of the job and its comparability with other occupations" (von Tunzelman 1979: 68). Comparisons with labourers and tradesmen were no longer seen as appropriate; politicians were becoming professionals (salaries went down at times, however, when the country was in economic retrenchment). In 1944 legislation separated income from allowances. Dissatisfaction with the process of deciding upon MPs' remuneration and expenses continued. Plainly, it was both inappropriate and politically uncomfortable for MPs to determine their own salaries. The Civil List Act 1920 had provided for a royal commission to inquire into parliamentary salaries and also had enabled a commission to fix the rate of payments for ministers, parliamentary under-secretaries, the Speaker of the House, and the Chairman of Committees (now called the Deputy Speaker). From 1951 until 1973 the commission also decided upon MPs' remuneration. It took written evidence, employed statistical data, compared the emoluments of other Commonwealth parliamentarians, and considered changes in the cost of living. The reports were tabled in the House and an Order in Council (an executive order determined by ministers meeting with the Governor-General) was required to implement the commission's recommendations. Thus, political elements remained in the determination process.

From 1974, the independent Higher Salaries Commission—not dependent on an Order of Council—decided on the remuneration of MPs. Four assumptions guided its decisions: "(a) that the occupation of a MP should be regarded as virtually full-time and professional in nature; (b) that it should be assumed that a MP has no other income; (c) that it should be accepted that members are married with family commitments; and (d) that regard should be had to the sacrifices a member and spouse have to make in respect of their enjoyment and family life" (von Tunzelman 1979: 98). A parliamentary select committee was established in 1945 to examine superannuation, and a contributory scheme, similar to that of public servants, was established in 1947. Thus, the risks of a political career were somewhat offset by the benefits of a post-career income and allowances.

Politicians had always relied on voluntary and cheap labor to cope with their workloads, both in the legislature and in the constituency. Party workers bore part of the load; wives (for there were scarcely any politicians' husbands) took most of it. In 1955 only one typist was allocated to each parliamentary party. The number was increased to five per party in 1968 and the ratio was increased in 1968 (von Tunzelman 1979: 111). As recently as the 1970s two MPs were allocated one secretary to be shared, and there was no specific funding for electorate offices either; MPs had to pay for help out of their basic electorate allowances. In 1984, however, funding was allocated for helping MPs staff their electorate offices (McGee 1994: 31). Gradually, also, MPs had accumulated other entitlements: postal budgets, telephone expenses, and travel costs of members and spouses. Hence, the state gradually increased its contribution for administrative help and, also, payment for policy and political advice. The party research units were set up as a consequence of the 1970 Royal Commission on Parliamentary Salaries and Allowances (McGee 1994: 31). Before that, parties relied on a handful of researchers paid by the parties themselves, or on private secretaries made part-time researchers, or on individuals within the leaders' offices used as researchers (Klinkum 1995).

Overall, in the past couple of decades Parliament has become a more sophisticated, specialized, and policy-focused legislature. First, the parliamentary sessions have become regularized, although, because they are not controlled by statute, their duration largely depends on the government's legislative program. Under parliamentary Standing Orders Parliament must sit for about 90 days a year (Standing Orders Committee 1999). Second, there have been administrative changes. In 1985 the former Legislative Department was replaced by the Parliamentary Service. The Parliamentary Service Act was reviewed in 1998/9 (Review Team 1999) and a new act passed in 2000. There is also the Office of the Clerk of the House of Representatives, created in 1988. Thus, the Parliament is managed by two bodies, each with its own budget.

Third, the numbers servicing the political class have increased. Because of the structural and reporting changes named above, it is difficult to obtain figures tracing the numbers of those employed by the Office of the Clerk and the Parliamentary Service through time. In the financial year that ended 31 March 1988, there were thirty-eight people in the Office of the Clerk, and by 2000/2001 there were eighty-six (OC 2001: 50). The work of MPs is also supported by staff in each of the MPs' offices and by the party research units. Secretarial staff increased in number. In 2000/2001 there were 511 full-time equivalent staff employed by the Parliamentary Service, from messengers to librarians (PSC 2001: 6).

The historical costs of supporting Parliament's activities are also difficult to discern. In the financial year 1986/87, the total cost (excluding ministerial and cabinet costs) was NZ$26.095 million (approx. €13.0 million).[1] In the financial year 1995/96 the Office of the Clerk spent NZ$9,675,000 (€4.8 million) and Parliamentary Service NZ$33,753,000 (€16.8 million; OC 1987, 1991, 1996; PSC 1996). By 2001, the Office of the Clerk was reporting expenditure of NZ$13, 299,000 (€6.6 million; OC 2001: 44) and the Parliamentary Commission had spent NZ$32,813,000 (€16.3 million; PSC 2001: 49). Thus, the costs of maintaining representative democracy have been rising for some years; electoral system reform, with its growth in the number of MPs and the increased number of party leaders and researchers, accelerated the upward trend.

A major expansion of ministerial staffers occurred under Labour (1984–90). "Between 1985–1986 and 1989–90 the number of staff employed by Ministers [...] increased by about 40 percent from 146 to 205" (Boston 1990: 77). Also, before 1984 staffers were mostly "career public servants either on secondment from government departments or part of the corps of ministerial private secretaries operated and funded through the Department of Internal Affairs" (Boston 1990: 77). From then on, following overseas trends, many were recruited from the private sector to work on contract for ministers. In 1990 there were about 178 staffers servicing the political executive, and in 2001 there were 218 (Department of Internal Affairs 2001: 24). Since the 1975–84 National government's establishment of an eight-person "think-tank," there has also been a policy advice system for the Prime Minister—as distinct from a private office dealing mainly with the PM's appointments and media communications. Professionalization of the political executive, interestingly, had coincided with the radical economic and public sector reforms during the 1980s and 1990s.

Thus, in New Zealand, politicians came to see themselves as professionals who devote their full lives to politics. Indeed, the public now, and perhaps earlier, expect this, as demonstrated by the disapproval of business involvement and other activities such as running radio talk-back shows. The expectation that those who live "off" politics should treat it as a full-time job is partly to do with perceived conflicts of interest. It is also related to the belief that, since politicians are paid well, they should devote themselves to serving the people. Hence, professionalization and the changing role of the political representative have been mutually reinforcing trends. Further,

---

[1] Conversions from NZ$ to Euro are based on the exchange rate of 6 December 2002 (NZ$1 = €0.4975).

because politics is a full-time profession, the politician, like any other professional, needed proper, expert assistance. By the 1970s, New Zealand MPs had become a political class, professionalized, and conscious of its own identity and interests, as shown in the working environment and conditions it had created for itself. Moreover, aided by the small size of the House, there were well established norms and values of parliamentary life affecting apprenticeship criteria and institutional behavior that crossed party boundaries (McLeay 1978).

THE INSTITUTIONAL CONTEXT

Like most former colonial societies, New Zealand inherited its basic political structure from elsewhere. Indeed, the transfer of the Westminster system of government was often said to have resulted in a better example of that particular variant of a parliamentary system of government than is the British system itself. New Zealand has cabinet government, with the ministers responsible to and entirely drawn from the House of Representatives (McLeay 1995, 2001).[2] The constitution is not fully codified and Parliament has been unicameral since the (appointed) Legislative Council was abolished in 1951.

Between 1935 and 1993 Parliament was dominated by two political parties divided primarily on socio-economic issues: the Labour and National parties. The simple plurality, single-member constituency (or "first-past-the-post"—FPTP or FPP) electoral system in use until the 1996 general election encouraged the dominantly two-party system: it was particularly difficult for minor parties to gain legislative entry. Under FPTP New Zealand had a very low score on comparative effective representativeness between elections (Powell 1989: 126). New Zealand was a model of majoritarian government (Lijphart 1984, 1994; Powell 1981, 1989). These systemic factors strongly influenced the nature—and behavior—of New Zealand's political class. In particular its members shared the belief in the virtues of alternating majority party government; most MPs opposed proportional representation.

Despite its majoritarianism, however, New Zealand has been an interesting example of systemic variation to encompass the political rights of the indigenous minority, the Maori, and include that minority in the political class, albeit unfairly in terms of proportionality. In 1867 four Maori electorates were created in a 78-seat Parliament. They were originally a temporary measure but have remained ever since (Jackson and Wood 1963–65; Ward 1976; McLeay 1980; Chapman 1986; Royal Commission on the Electoral System 1986; Sorrenson 1986).

Majoritarianism was challenged when New Zealanders voted to change the electoral system from FPTP to an additional member system, known in New Zealand as the mixed member proportional system (MMP) (Levine and Roberts 1994; Vowles *et al.* 1995; Boston *et al.* 1996a,b; Jackson and McRobie 1998). The new rules are

---

[2] Further modifications of the British model have been: the triennial parliamentary term; the neutral Representation Commission which automatically redraws the electoral boundaries after each five-yearly census according to very strict criteria including a 5% permitted population variance; and referendums have been held more frequently than in Britain. On the FPTP electoral system, see Harris 1992.

modeled on the German electoral system but with national rather than regional party lists. The choice of MMP accelerated the shift from a political class characterized by party duopoly to one more characteristic of multi-party parliamentary politics (Barker and McLeay 2000; Barker *et al.* 2001).

Between 1935 and 1993, as well as exhibiting two-party dominance, there was a high degree of parliamentary party cohesion (McLeay 1978; Jackson 1987). Cabinet dominated both its own party and Parliament (Mulgan 1992, 1995; McLeay 1995). Hence, Parliament had weak policy capability. Nevertheless, since the 1970s there has been substantial reform (McLeay 2000*b*) as explained below, and Parliament now has an influential committee system. In 2002 there were thirteen subject committees plus others such as the Officers of Parliament, Regulations Review, Standing Orders, and Privileges committees. As a consequence of the 1996 Standing Orders changes a power-ful Business Committee decides on the parliamentary program, working within the government's legislative and budgetary priorities. Since 1996, proportionality has been respected in the allocation of party seats on the committees. The National/New Zealand First majority party coalition formed in November 1996 (with 61 out of 120 seats), together with its supporting party, ACT New Zealand, held all the committee chairs except for Regulations Review (chaired by an opposition MP since 1985). Similarly, the Labour/Alliance minority government formed after the 1999 election held all the chairs except for one that went to its supporting party, the Greens, and the Regulations Review Chair which went to National. After the July 2002 election, however, opposition parties received more chairs than they had previously.

The advent of proportional representation only slightly modified executive dom-inance over Parliament under the National/New Zealand First coalition government. The balance of power between political executive and legislature then shifted quite substan-tially after the coalition lost its majority in July 1998. One month later New Zealand First left the coalition. From that time until the general election in November 1999, National led a minority government that included some former New Zealand First MPs as inde-pendents, several of whom later joined the new Mauri Pacific party. The government was maintained in power by the votes of ACT and the one United MP. Parliament con-tinued to be influential after 1999, with the minority government's dependence on the Greens and sometimes New Zealand First to pass its legislation. Another minority gov-ernment was formed after the 2002 election. Labour and the Progressive Coalition nego-tiated with United Future to support the government on confidence and supply, and the Greens agreed to cooperate with the government on some legislative issues. With minor-ity governments, Parliament has become more influential.

Another change has been in the representation of outside interests. The New Zealand Parliament, like the British House of Commons (Norton 1990: 26), has shown a marked increase in the frequency of interaction between pressure groups and politicians. Lobbying has become professionalized.[3] The parliamentary commit-tees provide a major focus for the activities of groups.

---

[3] There are an estimated 20–30 individuals involved (but this figure needs verification). Firm figures are difficult to obtain because Parliament does not require registration of lobbyists.

Besides asserting its scrutiny and policy roles through committee reform, revised Standing Orders, and legislation,[4] Parliament has become a highly institutionalized legislature, fulfilling the criteria of having established: a defined organizational structure which is autonomous; a high degree of formality (in its rules and procedures); regular procedures of leadership selection and conflict management; organizational complexity; and defined links to its constituencies (Patterson and Copeland 1994). Institutionalization, however, has also increased the number of those who live "off" politics in order to support the political class, and this has attracted adverse public comment.

Although the state pays the parliamentary party researchers (see above), the parties themselves have to pay for their organizers and are run mostly by volunteers. To illustrate, the parties which gained representation in the 1966 general election, with their numbers of full-time paid employees in 1997, were ACT New Zealand, two (in party headquarters); Alliance, two (in party headquarters); Labour, eight; and National, twelve (six in headquarters and the rest in the regions). New Zealand First declined to provide the information (there were probably no full-time party workers), and United had no paid employees outside Parliament. Of the Alliance's five (until late 1997) constituent parties, the Green Party was run by volunteers, the Democrats had one employee plus a half-time president, and New Labour had one full-time employee. Figures for Mana Motuhake, a Maori civil rights party, were unavailable. Clearly, there is a difference in resources between the old parties and the new. The numbers of paid employees rise slightly during election campaigns which in general have become increasingly sophisticated and reliant on public opinion polling firms working on contract. But it can be seen that New Zealand parties are run by a tiny group of organizers; the extra-parliamentary parties remain essentially amateur organizations.

Thus, state funding of political parties is largely confined to the salaries and allowances given to MPs, including the extra support provided for parliamentary party leaders' officers (see below) and the parliamentary party research services. There is a third source of public funding, however: the limited help given to parties for campaigning through broadcasting at general elections. The Broadcasting Amendment Act 1996 stipulates the criteria by which parties are allocated air time and funds for broadcasting election ads. The decisions are taken by the (independent) Electoral Commission, which also educates citizens about the electoral system and registers political parties which are to be eligible for the party list vote. In 1999 the Commission spent merely NZ$1.85 million (approx. €0.9 million; excluding Goods and Services Taxes) on twenty-two parties (Electoral Commission 2001: 33).

It can be seen that state funding for political parties in New Zealand is not generous. There is a strong case for increasing these state subsidies, thus improving the chances of legislative entry of newer parties, reducing party dependence on business

---

[4] The Public Finance Act 1989, for example, strengthened the financial accountability of public agencies to Parliament; and the Fiscal Responsibility Act 1994 set out principles of responsible fiscal management and required governments to state their fiscal objectives and progress.

donations, and helping the policy capabilities of parties which now might find them-selves negotiating coalition agreements in the government formation process.

THE POLITICAL CLASS

Size and Composition

Because New Zealand has unitary government—local government institutions are entirely dependent on Parliament for their structures and power—with weak local and (more recently) regional government, the political class is concentrated in the capital city of Wellington. Local government is not unimportant, for it deals with planning issues, waste disposal, community facilities such as libraries and parks, local roading, and, at the regional level, water resources. Indeed, the large cities, although scarcely comparable to many other cities in the world, have substantial budgets. But although local government collects taxes based on property values, it carries out no social services except (for a few cities) some public housing. The state's social services are not devolved to the local level or administered by local authorities. Despite the plethora of local bodies, their representatives do not constitute a "political class" in the sense that their colleagues in central government do. Their careers are much less structured, and the role played by political parties is a very minor one. Moreover, apart from most of the mayors who receive annual salaries, other members are generally paid only allowances. Most are not professional politicians; they live "for" politics rather than "off" politics.

Who, then, comprises the total political class? If all those who fulfill the two con-ditions of living "off" politics and being paid by the state are categorized, we find there are two major groups. First, there are the elected politicians: national politi-cians and mayors. Second, there are the parliamentary, party, and political executive support staff discussed above. This section, however, focuses on the national parlia-mentarians, the core of the political class.

Parliament has grown from 37 to 120 MPs (for a population in the early twenty-first century of four million). Between 1900 and 1965 there were eighty. In 1965 the total number of seats in the House was linked with the increase in population (with the South Island, losing population to the North, guaranteed a minimum of twenty-five members). By 1993, the year in which New Zealand voted to change its electoral system and the year of the last election under the FPTP rules, there were ninety-nine MPs. These totals included the four MPs representing the four Maori elec-torates (a fixed number, unlike the rest of the seats). The Electoral Act 1993 determined there would be 120 MPs, including an indeterminate number of Maori seats linked to the number of Maori who chose to register on the Maori roll. The 120 total was the recommendation of the Royal Commission on the Electoral System (which actually preferred 140).

The Royal Commission had argued for an increase in the number of MPs whether or not the electoral system was changed: "to make the system of parliamentary committees more effective, to enlarge the pool of ministerial talent and to allow for an increase in the number of Ministers." The Commission added that "an enlarged House could provide more independence in caucus and improve the quality of parliamentary debate" (Royal Commission on the Electoral System 1986: 126). Such was the hostility of the public towards an increase in the number of politicians that, even though campaigners for electoral system reform preferred a larger legislature, they made submissions during the passage of the Electoral Act 1993 for a House of 100. They felt that voters would be likely to oppose electoral system change for the wrong reasons were they to be faced with two different sets of rules for electing a parliament of the same size. The parliamentarians, however, opted for 120, perhaps precisely because they saw a House of 120 MPs as a disincentive for voters to choose change and perhaps to increase their own chances of retaining their positions in the new House with its reduced number of constituency seats.

The debate about the size of Parliament did not abate after the first MMP election. From "letters to the editor" to speeches by MPs themselves, there were criticisms of the increased number. The discontented and acrimonious 1997 Parliament was seen as partly the consequence of too many, underworked MPs. Party lists MPs were the focus of particular criticism (Ward 1998). At the 1999 general election, a Citizens' Initiated Referendum (non-binding) was held that asked voters whether they wanted a Parliament of 99 or 120 MPs, and 81.5 percent chose the reduced number (Church 2000). By 2002, however, government had not acted on this result, partly to protect political careers, but also perhaps because of the deleterious effects reduction would have on minority and women's representation (Shaw 1999). There were also good reasons for retaining the expanded House. Political scientists had recommended an increased House well before proportional representation was on the political agenda, for the reasons given by the Royal Commission (although many would not want a larger political executive).

After the first MMP election in 1996 the party composition of the New Zealand elected political class changed dramatically, with increased representation of minor parties (Table 15.1). The newer parties, however, are dependent on the party lists for most of their caucus members, whilst the two older parties continue to dominate the constituency seats.

The MMP electoral system also had an impact on Parliament's gender and ethnic composition. Like all legislatures with FPTP electoral systems, the House had been male-dominated. Fewer women were available for selection, and women more than men were selected for hopeless or marginal seats (McLeay 1993). Nevertheless, despite women's social and structural disadvantages, there is no evidence of voters discriminating against women candidates (Hill and Roberts 1990). By 1975 there were still only four female MPs (4.6 percent). After the 1984 general election, however, there were twelve (12.6 percent); and after 1993 there were twenty-one (21.2 percent), a better result than in other FPTP systems (McLeay 1993). In part this was the result of feminists moving into the Labour Party during the 1970s, deliberately targeting leadership positions and affecting the selection process. The Alliance also emphasized gender equality. Thus, there has been a real difference in the

Table 15.1 *New Zealand parliamentary parties after the 1993, 1996, 1999, and 2002 elections*

	1993[a]	1996[a]	1999[a]	2002
Alliance[b]	2	13	10	0
Progressive Coalition	—	—	—	2
Green[c]	—	—	7	9
Labour	45	37	49	52
United[d]	—	1	1	8
New Zealand First	2	17	5	13
National	50	44	39	27
ACT	—	8	9	9
Total number of MPs	99	120	120	120

[a] The 1993, 1996, and 1999 elections were followed by party defections and fragmentation.

[b] The Alliance split during the 1999–2002 parliamentary term into the Alliance and the Progressive Coalition.

[c] The Greens left the Alliance to fight the 1999 election on their own.

[d] United joined with another (Christian-based) party and contested the 2002 general election as United Future.

recruitment criteria of parties of the left and the right in New Zealand. The share of women rose to 29 percent after the first MMP election, to 31 percent after the second (McLeay 2000*b*), and declined to 28 percent in 2002. This was a consequence of the wider range of parties in Parliament, plus parties' list recruitment criteria. Maori also benefited from MMP. When the party lists were compiled for the first MMP election, parties felt compelled to present "balanced" lists that included Maori. For the first time Maori were represented in the legislature in comparable proportions to their numbers in the general population (Table 15.2). After the 2002 election nineteen out of 120 MPs were Maori.

In the period between 1935 and 1975, the mean age of National Members was 44.9 years and of Labour 42.9 years (McLeay 1978). The mean age of MPs in the first MMP Parliament was 45.6. Over the years, more MPs have entered Parliament in their twenties, but this has not affected the average age of the political class.

Farmers, lawyers, and businessmen have always been important for the National party and its predecessors; the entry of Labour into the political class brought in a wider range of backgrounds including teachers and unionists (Webb 1944). Even in the 1935–75 period, however, only 10.9 percent of Labour MPs had been trade union officials, whilst 15.4 percent were blue-collar workers. The numbers in these latter categories have declined since 1935 (McLeay 1978). Table 15.2 describes the composition of the first MMP-elected Parliament. As can be seen, the historic differences between the parties of the left (Labour and Alliance) and the right (National and ACT New Zealand) were played out again in the proportional representation parliament. New Zealand First, a centrist party, has an appropriately mixed intake but

McLeay

Table 15.2 *Social and career characteristics of New Zealand parliamentary parties after the 1996 election*

	Alliance	Labour	NZ First	National	ACT NZ	% of Parl.
Sex						
Male	6	24	13	36	5	71.0
Female	7	13	4	8	3	29.0
Ethnicity						
Maori	2	4	7	1	1	12.5
Others	11	33	10	43	7	87.5
Occupation						
Professional	2	3	1	11	2	15.8
Company/ managing director	1	3	4	11	2	17.5
Small business	2	2	4	1	2	9.2
Farming	1	2	0	11	1	12.5
Teacher/lecturer	1	7	2	3	0	10.8
Unionist	1	8	0	1	0	9.2
Public servant	1	4	1	1	0	5.8
Others[a]	4	8	5	5	1	19.2
Education						
Some tertiary	1	4	1	8	1	12.5
University degree	3	8	4	13	3	25.8
Postgrad. qualifications	3	10	7	13	4	30.8
Political experience						
Local govt.	3	5	2	7	1	17.5
Party	11	28	9	32	4	70.8
Voluntary organizations	6	20	7	16	2	26.7
Unions/sectoral organizations	5	23	9	28	4	58.3
Total[b]	13	37	17	44	8	100.0

[a] This group includes "lower professionals," for example, librarians, researchers, administrators, and social workers, sales managers, a party worker, and an unemployed person.

[b] The totals include the sole United Party MP.

strongly represents the business sector (for 1993 figures and a survey of desired qualities of candidates, see Catt 1997).

The New Zealand elected political class has become much better educated in recent years, reflecting both the democratization of education and the rising expectations about the desired levels of MPs' expertise and experience. Contrast the 1935–1975 period, with only 23 percent with university degrees and a further 12.2 percent with some tertiary education with the 1996 Parliament (see Table 15.2): the majority of MPs were tertiary trained. In today's society, the political class is expected to be educated.

Political Recruitment and Political Careers

The conjunction of the FPTP electoral system with the institutional characteristics of centralized, unitary, and parliamentary government constricted sharply the career patterns of the political class. Whether an aspirant was ambitious for political power, or anxious to achieve policy change, or both, he or she had really only one decision to make in New Zealand: whether to join the Labour or the National party and seek nomination for a winnable parliamentary seat.

The Labour Party, formed in 1916, took office in 1935. The following year the former Liberal-United and Reform parties combined to form the National Party (Milne 1966; Gustafson 1986). Labour and National each developed organizations based on branch memberships and electorate and regional structures. Labour dominated first, but after 1949 it was National's turn; between then and 1996, Labour won only four general elections compared with National's twelve. For the truly ambitious—those who wanted a ministerial post—National was a better choice than Labour. Labour with its affiliated trade unions was on the center–left, attracting the support of the poorer urban voters and of Maori. National was on the center–right, based on votes from the countryside and the wealthier urban areas. Under FPTP, the major electoral battlegrounds were the marginal seats of the towns and the socially mixed urban areas. Political careers were securely built in the safe seats of each party or more precariously in the marginal ones. Once in Parliament in a secure seat, providing one's party became the government, promotion into cabinet was not difficult to achieve.

Despite the two-party dominance of the opportunity structure for politicians (or perhaps because of it) minor parties sprang into existence and attracted a growing percentage of the total vote (Aimer 1992; Boston et al. 1996a: 43–4). Social Credit, which contested its first election in 1954, was the first significant challenger to two-party hegemony. Later it split, forming the Democrats (later part of the Alliance) and a splinter group retaining the Social Credit label. Other important parties formed before 1993 were: the Values Party (the world's first green party), Mana Motuhake, a Maori-rights party which went into the Alliance; the Green Party, in the Alliance until 1997; the New Zealand Party; and New Labour, a splinter from Labour and the core of the Alliance. Anticipating the new world of MMP, political entrepreneurs formed other new parties between 1993 and 1996. Several were created by dissident and disgruntled MPs faced with insecure political careers. Party fractionalization continued after 1996 when New Zealand First split and the (electorally unsuccessful) Mauri Pacific party was formed. The party splitting led to a change in the Standing Orders in relation to how a parliamentary party should be defined and recognized (Standing Orders Committee 1999). Despite this, and legislation passed in 2001 to dissuade MPs leaving their parties by compelling resignation in certain circumstances, in early 2002 the Alliance, the junior coalition partner, divided into two ideological groupings. Its leader (and Deputy Prime Minister) was expelled from the party, along with others, but controversially remained in Parliament and in cabinet.

Meanwhile, an alternative vehicle for them, the Progressive Coalition, was formed to allow them to compete at the 2002 election.

Both Labour and National have closed recruitment systems; participation in selection is restricted to party activists (Catt 1997). Labour's selection of electorate MPs is decentralized in that the actual choice is made by a small committee of delegates at electorate meetings, although the Party's national interests are represented by participants from the central party organization, and they have some influence in ensuring a balanced ticket nation-wide (Street 1997; Sheppard 1998). National's system is more decentralized since the choice is in the hands of the local activists who elect delegates to form a selection committee that chooses the electorate candidate (Gustafson 1997). The newer parties use a range of selection methods (Jesson 1997; Miller 1997). After the adoption of MMP, the parties had to construct methods of choosing their party lists. Generally members voted for regional lists and then a national committee of delegates "knitted" them together. The Greens were the only party to have a quota for women. New Zealand First, unlike Labour or National, required all its candidates to stand for both an electorate and the party list. The latter was constructed using a complex and secretive balloting process.

When we turn to the careers of the political class, we find that what was true of earlier cohorts (McLeay 1978) is still true today: MPs are expected to have served pre-parliamentary political apprenticeships. Experience can be demonstrated in a variety of ways: by party activism, interest group involvement, or in local government (see Table 15.2). Many MPs have been involved in a whole range of activities before entering the political class. Because Parliament is small its career patterns are only partially structured: most ministers have served as chairs of parliamentary or caucus committees (McLeay 1987).

The recent decision to reward select committee chairpersons with increased salaries (see below) might alter this situation. Provided one was a loyal member of one's party, and had served a minimum of 3 years, MPs had an excellent chance of becoming ministers.[5] This was the pattern until 1996 when New Zealand First became part of the government and MPs without previous parliamentary experience became ministers. Given the poor performance of several of these ministers and the larger supply of experienced aspirants as the new parties become established, it is not surprising that only one minister in the 1999 Labour/Alliance government went immediately into cabinet (and she was a former Labour party president).

There are almost no restrictions on MPs in terms of the public or private offices they may hold at the same time they perform their parliamentary duties except that the Electoral Act 1993 (as did earlier legislation) prohibits public servants from sitting in Parliament. If they wish to stand for Parliament they must take leave for the period of their candidacies and mandates. Otherwise, MPs may continue their usual occupations, although they are now expected to devote their full-time attention to

[5] "Loyalty" could mean one of two different things, because in the National Party the Prime Minister chooses ministers whilst in Labour the caucus elects them. In both parties the Prime Minister allocates the portfolios, and in Labour the positions outside cabinet are in the patronage of the Prime Minister.

their political duties. Furthermore, Parliament itself does not hold a register of past and present non-parliamentary paid activities. There are no prohibitions on MPs holding office in local or regional government, and some have done so. But it has become usual for MPs to resign (perhaps at the time of the next general election) if they become mayors. But again, these pressures are moral and political rather than legal.

MPs remain in the House of Representatives whilst they hold executive office; they are not required to vacate their seats. MPs may only receive one salary and set of allowances, however, for their parliamentary or executive tasks. There are more restrictions on ministers than on MPs. Ministers are required by the Cabinet Manual to register their pecuniary interests in a document that is tabled in the House and are required also to perform their duties full-time.

Does the cost of politics prevent poorer members of society entering the political class? Certainly there are personal costs in lobbying for candidacy and campaigning, but these costs are kept relatively low. Indeed, there are legal ceilings on both individual and party expenditure and donations to both, if above a certain limit, must be declared.

Living off Politics

The independent, three-person Higher Salaries Commission, appointed by the Governor-General for 3 years, determines MPs' salaries and allowances. The terms of the Higher Salaries Commission Act 1997 require it to take into account, "the need to achieve and maintain fair relativity with the levels of remuneration received elsewhere; the need to be fair, on the one hand, to the person whose remuneration it determines and, on the other, to the taxpayer; and the need to recruit and retain competent people" (HSC 1997: 13). The Commission also decides on the salaries of members of the judiciary and of some other statutory officers. Parliamentary salaries are not appropriated annually by Parliament but are permanently charged on government expenditure.

In its 1997 determination, the Commission argued that it is not its task to evaluate MPs: "The task is to determine a rate for the job, no matter who happens to hold it" (HSC 1997: 13). This comment was aimed at public discontent with the new, party list MPs. The Commission produced a discussion paper, received many submissions and met with "interested parties" (HSC 1997: 14). Surveys of conditions in the market place were used which in 1997 showed large salary increases in senior positions. The Commission noted that any increase in salaries could stimulate public disapproval but that it was concerned that MPs' salaries had generally remained behind those of the market "even allowing for a discount against that market to reflect the element of public service which is involved" (HSC 1997: 14).

In 2001, MPs' salaries, having been raised considerably in recent years, were NZ$90,500 per annum (€45,020; *The Dominion*, 14 December 2001). Constituency MPs had higher allowances than list MPs: on top of the basic expense allowances of NZ$7,000 (€3,480) they received an average of NZ$14,000 (€6,960), depending on the size of their electoral district. All MPs were eligible for claiming "day" and "night" allowances to cover travel expenses when engaged in parliamentary business. Wellington accommodation allowances were also paid to members who normally lived outside the Wellington commuting area. Further allowances permitted MPs to claim reimbursement for travel on business requested by ministers and for car expenses. MPs who chaired select committees received a higher salary, as did, also, whips, party leaders and deputies, and parliamentary speakers. The Speaker was paid NZ$162,600 (€80,890). Cabinet ministers received salaries of NZ$162,600 (€80,890) and basic allowances of NZ$12,000 (€5,970), whilst the Prime Minister's salary was NZ$244,100 (€121,430), plus allowances. All members of the executive also received house and travelling allowances. In comparison, the permanent head of Treasury was paid between NZ$390,000 and $399,999 (€194,000–€198,980) in 2001. The allowances of MPs have been especially controversial in recent years. A review was undertaken which reported that the allowances should be included in salaries and be subject to income tax, and that allowances should not be granted automatically.[6] The government committed itself to promoting legislation to change the arrangements but by the end of 2002 it appeared that few changes would be made.

Superannuation benefits, also determined by the Higher Salaries Commission, are quite substantial. MPs who were in Parliament on 30 June 1992 must contribute 11 percent of their salaries (8 percent after 20 years) to the parliamentary part of the Government Superannuation scheme which was cut off to all new Members on that date (McGee 1994: 25–6). Members who serve for more than 9 years (not necessarily continuously) receive better benefits than those who do not, increasing the incentive to stay in Parliament. MPs elected after June 1992 have no specific superannuation scheme although there is a public subsidy given to MPs who join other (registered) schemes (McGee 1994: 26–7). The political class have thus successfully secured their post-politics financial futures.

THE POLITICAL CLASS AND INSTITUTIONAL REFORMS

Institutional reform in the past few decades has had both endogenous and exogenous origins. Since the mid-1980s, there has been substantial reform of Parliament initiated by MPs. Stimulated by reformers in the new Labour Government elected in 1984, MPs changed the committee system and improved the budgetary and scrutiny processes. There was another major review of Parliament's operations in 1995 which led to the revised Standing Orders in preparation for the MMP multi-party parliament (Standing Orders Committee 1995). This was particularly interesting, because a committee of the House toured PR countries in order to learn from them. In the

---

[6] The allowances and privileges of former politicians have not been discussed in this paper, although they certainly contribute to the cost of the political class. In 1995/96, for example, domestic travel subsidies for former MPs and their spouses amounted to NZ$199,300 (€99,140) and international travel subsidies to $704,890 (€350,650; *Dominion*, 29 March 1997: 2).

last two decades, therefore, Parliament reinforced its effectiveness and legitimacy by enhancing its capacity for policy and scrutiny activities. The endogenously generated changes outlined above were all consensually based, receiving cross-party support. In 1997, and again in 1999, as New Zealand and its Parliament became accustomed to the consequences of electoral system change, MPs instituted further changes. A committee initiated discussion on a possible parliamentary code of conduct, although nothing had been produced by 2002.

In contrast to the above reforms, electoral system change was exogenous in its impetus, although its roots lay in the Royal Commission set up by the 1984–90 Labour Government which was dissatisfied by the fact that in both 1978 and 1981 National had won the most seats in the House although Labour had won the most nationwide votes. Like many other countries, New Zealand experienced a profound transformation in public attitudes towards the political class. Citizens' attitudes have been manifest in three major ways: voting volatility, including a shift towards minor-party support; decreased faith in the ability and trustworthiness of politicians demonstrated in successive public opinion polls and in survey research; and a readiness to embrace electoral system reform to make politicians more accountable for their actions. The story of how New Zealanders actually came to be offered the opportunity to change their electoral system is a complex one, involving intensive pressure group activity, adversary party politics, a couple of strategic errors by political leaders, and a rear guard action by politicians to halt the change process (Jackson and McRobie 1998). The members of the political class were strongly against changing a system that had delivered them their positions. Likewise, except for the trade unions, the key sectoral interests identified with the interests of the political class by campaigning for the status quo.

There were two formal stages to the change process. First, there was an indicative (non-binding) referendum in 1992.[7] Voters were asked, first, whether or not they wished to retain FPTP. Whatever they chose they could also vote for their preferred system from amongst MMP, FPTP, STV, preferential voting, and an supplementary Member system. Of all registered voters, 55 percent participated, nearly 85 percent voting to change the electoral system. Over 70 percent chose MMP. Parliament then constructed the Electoral Act 1993. This provided the basis for the vote between FPTP and MMP at the 1993 general election.[8] It is at this point that the politicians—mostly against change—attempted to reshape the reform agenda. The electoral threshold became 5 percent for all parties, making it difficult for minor parties to gain legislative entry. This followed the German system, making the policy transfer a more complete emulation than the 4 percent proposed by the Royal Commission. If a political party gains one constituency seat, even if it does not reach the threshold, then that party is entitled to its share of the party list vote (a provision that has helped increase

[7] Since 1956 the electoral rules, like the parliamentary term, have been entrenched; they can be changed only by a majority referendum vote or a 75% majority vote in the House.

[8] At the time the legislation was shaped and passed the composition of Parliament was dominated by the two major parties. National had a large majority, although several MPs had left National for new parties (but had not left Parliament) by 1993. There was also one New Labour MP; the rest were Labour.

parliamentary party fragmentation). At the first general election held under MMP rules in 1996, there were 60 general constituency seats, 5 Maori seats, and 55 party list seats; and by the 2002 election the figures were 62, 7, and 51, respectively.

Responding to Maori wishes, Parliament rejected the Royal Commission's recommendation that the Maori seats be abolished. Retention might have pleased Maori, but equally it could be said to be designed to influence voters against electoral change (Vowles *et al.* 1995: 184). The number of Maori seats rises or falls according to the numbers on the Maori electoral roll—there were seven by the 2002 election. Following the recommendation of the Royal Commission, the party vote was nationwide and the party lists were closed (there had been a campaign for open lists). Thus, during the legislative process the political class—faced with disruption to political careers through the reduction of the number of constituencies and with the prospect of probably never holding the full reins of political power again—had reinterpreted the German model to suit their own goals, an example of joint institutional manipulation (Dunleavy and Ward 1991; McLeay 1996).

Electoral reform impacted on the political executive. Instead of the winning party taking all the positions in the political executive, the major parties, National and Labour, have had to share the political executive posts with politicians from minor parties. Furthermore, the minority governments that became the norm in the first terms after MMP was adopted had to share some power with non-government, support parties. However, minor parties have had difficulty adjusting to the constraints of shared government, as shown by the dissension within the two junior coalition partners between 1996 and 2002, New Zealand First and the Alliance.

During the second parliamentary term after electoral reform, as required by the Electoral Act 1993, a parliamentary select committee reviewed the new electoral system, reporting in 2001. Operating under a unanimity rule, the MMP Review Committee could not agree on recommendations for change (Church and McLeay 2003; Vowles *et al.* 2002). Nevertheless, opinion polls from 1997 onwards showed considerable discontent with the new system, although approval tended to rise and fall in conjunction with attitudes to the government of the day.

Electoral system reform has impacted on the political profession by diminishing the two-party dominance over career paths on the one hand and, on the other hand, by expanding opportunities through other parties. The composition and the identity of the political class in New Zealand has been changed. Questions remain, however, about its public legitimacy.

REFERENCES

Aimer, Peter (1992). "The Changing Party System", in H. Gold (ed.), *New Zealand Politics in Perspective*, 3rd edition. Auckland: Longman Paul, 326–41.

Barker, Fiona, and McLeay, Elizabeth (2000). "How Much Change? An Analysis of the Initial Impact of Proportional Representation on the New Zealand Parliamentary Party System". *Party Politics*, 6: 131–54.

——, Boston, Jonathan, Levine, Stephen, McLeay, Elizabeth, and Roberts, Nigel (2001). "An Initial Assessment of the Consequences of MMP", in M. Shugart and M. Wattenberg (eds), *Mixed-Member Electoral Systems: The Best of Both Worlds?* New York: Oxford University Press, 297–322.

Boston, Jonathan (1990). "The Cabinet and Policy Making", in J. Boston and M. Holland (eds.), *The Fourth Labour Government: Politics and Policy in New Zealand*, 2nd edition. Auckland: Oxford University Press, 62–82.

——, Levine, Stephen, McLeay, Elizabeth, and Roberts, Nigel S. (1996*a*). *New Zealand Under MMP: A New Politics?* Auckland: Auckland University Press/Bridget Williams.

————————(1996*b*). "Why did New Zealand adopt German-style Proportional Representation?" *Representation*, 33: 134–40.

Catt, Helena (1997). "New Zealand", in P. Norris (ed.), *Passages to Power: Legislative Recruitment in Advanced Democracies*. Cambridge: Cambridge University Press, 137–57.

Chapman, Robert (1986). "Voting in the Maori Political Sub-System, 1935–1984", in Royal Commission on the Electoral System, *Report of the Royal Commission on the Electoral System*. Wellington: Government Printer, B-83–108.

Church, Stephen (2000). "Crime and Punishment: The Referenda to Reform the Criminal Justice System and Reduce the Size of Parliament", in J. Boston, S. Church, S. Levine, E. McLeay, and N. S. Roberts (eds), *Left Turn: The New Zealand General Election of 1999*. Wellington: Victoria University Press, 203–16.

Church, Stephen, and McLeay, Elizabeth (2003). "The Parliamentary Review of MMP in New Zealand", *Represenation*, forthcoming.

Department of Internal Affairs (2001). *Annual Report for the Year Ended June 2001*. Wellington.

Dunleavy, Patrick, and Ward, Hugh (1991). "Party Competition: The Preference-Shaping Model", in P. Dunleavy (ed.), *Democracy, Bureaucracy and Public Choice*. Hemel Hempstead: Harvester Wheatsheaf, 112–44.

Electoral Commission (2001). *Electoral Commission Annual Report for the Year ended 30 June 2001*. Wellington.

Gustafson, Barry (1986). *The First 50 Years: A History of the New Zealand National Party*. Auckland: Reed Methuen.

——(1997). "The National Party", in R. Miller (ed.), *New Zealand Politics in Transition*. Auckland: Oxford University Press, 137–46.

Harris, Paul (1992). "The Electoral System", in M. M. Holland (ed.), *Electoral Behaviour in New Zealand*. Auckland: Oxford University Press, 1–24.

HSC (Higher Salaries Commission) (1997). *Parliamentary Salaries and Allowances Determination 1997*. Wellington.

Hill, Roberta, and Roberts, Nigel (1990). "Success, Swing and Gender: The Performance of Women Candidates for Parliament in New Zealand, 1946–87". *Politics*, 25: 62–80.

Jackson, Keith (1987). *The Dilemma of Parliament*. Wellington: Allen and Unwin/Port Nicholson Press.

——and McRobie, Alan (1998). *New Zealand Adopts Proportional Representation*. Aldershot: Ashgate.

Jackson, William K., and Wood, G. A. (1963–65). "The New Zealand Parliament and Maori Representation". *Historical Studies*, 11: 383–96.

Jesson, Bruce (1997). "The Alliance", in R. Miller (ed.), *New Zealand Politics in Transition*. Auckland: Oxford University Press, 156–64.

Klinkum, Grant (1995). "Pre State Funding Research Services for Parliamentarians in New Zealand", unpublished manuscript, presented at the New Zealand Political Studies Association Conference, Wellington.

Levine, Stephen, and Roberts, Nigel S. (1994). "The New Zealand Electoral Referendum and the General Election of 1993". *Electoral Studies*, 13: 240–54.

Lijphart, Arend (1984). *Democracies*. New Haven: Yale University Press.

—— (1994). "Democracies: Forms, Performance, and Constitutional Engineering". *European Journal of Political Research*, 25: 1–17.

Matland, Richard E., and Studlar, Donald T. (1996). 'Party Systems and Legislative Turnover: A Cross-National Analysis', unpublished manuscript, presented at the European Consortium for Political Research, Oslo, Norway.

McGee, David (1994). *Parliamentary Practice in New Zealand*. Wellington: GP Publications.

McLeay, Elizabeth M. (1978). 'Parliamentary Careers in a Two-Party System: Cabinet Selection in New Zealand', unpublished Ph.D. thesis, Auckland: University of Auckland.

—— (1980). "Political Argument about Representation: The Case of the Maori Seats". *Political Studies*, 28: 43–62.

—— (1987). "Selection Versus Election: Choosing Cabinets in New Zealand", in H. D. Clarke and M. M. Czudnowski (eds), *Political Elites in Anglo-American Democracies*. DeKalb: Northern Illinois University Press, 280–306.

—— (1993). "Women's Parliamentary Representation: A Comparative Perspective", in H. Catt and E. M. McLeay (eds), *Women and Politics in New Zealand*. Wellington: Victoria University Press, 40–62.

—— (1995). *The Cabinet and Political Power in New Zealand*. Auckland: Oxford University Press.

—— (1996). "Restructuring the State and the Electoral System in New Zealand: Public Choice Theory and Elite Behaviour", unpublished manuscript, presented at the 'Shaping Political Behaviour' Workshop, European Consortium of Political Research, Oslo, Norway.

—— (2000*a*). "The New Parliament", in J. Boston, S. Church, S. Levine, E. McLeay, and N. S. Roberts (eds), *Left Turn: The New Zealand General Election of 1999*. Wellington: Victoria University Press, 203–16.

—— (2000*b*). "The New Zealand Parliament after Electoral System Reform: Sorting out the Variables", unpublished manuscript, presented at the International Political Science Association Conference, Quebec City, Canada.

—— (2001). "Cabinet", in R. Miller (ed.), *New Zealand Government and Politics*. Auckland: Oxford University Press, 88–105.

Miller, Raymond (1997). "The New Zealand First Party", in E. Miller (ed.), *New Zealand Politics in Transition*. Auckland: Oxford University Press, 165–76.

Milne, Robert S. (1966). *Political Parties in New Zealand*. London: Oxford University Press.

Mulgan, Richard (1992). "The Elective Dictatorship in New Zealand", in H. Gold (ed.), *New Zealand Politics in Perspective*, 3rd edition. Auckland: Longman Paul, 513–32.

—— (1995). "The Democratic Failure of Single-Party Government: The New Zealand Experience". *Australian Journal of Political Science*, 30: 82–96.

Norton, Philip (1990). "Parliament in the United Kingdom: Balancing Effectiveness and Consent?". *West European Politics*, 13: 10–31.

OC (Office of the Clerk of the House of Representatives) (1987). *Report of the Clerk of the House of Representatives for the Year ended 30 June 1987*. Wellington.

—— (1991). *Report of the Clerk of the House of Representatives for the Year ended 30 June 1991*. Wellington.

—— (2001). *Report of the Clerk of the House of Representatives for the Year ended 30 June 2001*. Wellington.

PSC (Parliamentary Service Commission) (1996). *Report of the Parliamentary Service Commission for the Year ended 30 June 1996*. Wellington.

—— (2001). *Report of the Parliamentary Service Commission for the Year ended 30 June 2001*. Wellington.

Patterson, Samuel C., and Copeland, Gary W. (1994). "Parliaments in the Twenty-first Century", in S. C. Patterson and G. W. Copeland (eds), *Parliaments in the Modern World*. Ann Arbor: University of Michigan Press, 1–12.

Powell, J. Bingham (1981). "Party Systems and Political System Performance". *American Political Science Review*, 75: 861–79.

—— (1989). "Constitutional Design and Citizen Electoral Control". *Journal of Theoretical Politics*, 1: 107–30.

Review Team (1999). *A Review of the Parliamentary Service Act to the Parliamentary Service Commission*. Wellington.

Royal Commission on the Electoral System (1986). *Report of the Royal Commission on the Electoral System: Towards a better Democracy*. Wellington: Government Printer.

Shaw, Richard (1999). "What's That You Say, Mrs Robertson? The Citizens' Initiated Referendum and the 1999 General Election". *Legislative Studies*, 14: 62–79.

Sheppard, Simon (1998). "The Struggle for the Agenda: New Zealand Labour Party Candidate Selections 1987–93". *Political Science*, 49: 198–228.

Sorrenson, Maurice P. K. (1986). "A History of Maori Representation in Parliament", in Royal Commission on the Electoral System, *Report of the Royal Commission on the Electoral System*. Wellington: Government Printer, B1–82.

Standing Orders Committee (1995). *Report of the Standing Orders Committee: Review of Standing Orders*. Wellington: New Zealand House of Representatives.

—— (1999). *Report of the Standing Orders Committee: Review of Standing Orders*. Wellington: New Zealand House of Representatives.

Street, Maryan (1997). "The Labour Party", in R. Miller (ed.), *New Zealand Politics in Transition*. Auckland: Oxford University Press, 147–55.

von Tunzelman, A. (1979). *Membership of the New Zealand Parliament: A Study of Conditions 1854–1978*. Victoria University of Wellington, Master of Public Policy Research Paper.

Vowles, Jack, Aimer, Peter, Catt, Helena, Lamare, Jim, and Miller, Raymond (1995). *Towards Consensus? The 1993 Election in New Zealand and the Transition to Proportional Representation*. Auckland: Auckland University Press.

——, Aimer, Peter, Karp, Jeffrey, Banducci, Susan, Miller, Raymond, and Sullivan, Ann (2002). *Proportional Representation on Trial: The 1999 New Zealand General Election and the Fate of MMP*. Auckland. Auckland University Press.

Ward, Alan D. (1976). *A Show of Justice: Racial "Amalgamation" in Nineteenth Century New Zealand*. Canberra: Australian National University Press.

Ward, L. J. (1998). "Second-Class MPs? New Zealand's Adaptation to Mixed-Member Parliamentary Representation". *Political Science*, 49: 125–52.

Webb, Leicester (1944). *Government in New Zealand*. Wellington: Department of Internal Affairs.

16

Norway: Professionalization— Party-oriented and Constituency-based

HANNE MARTHE NARUD

The process of political professionalization in Norway has been analyzed most notably by Kjell Eliassen and Mogens Pedersen (1978) in their comparative article on political recruitment in Denmark and Norway (see also Eliassen 1985). They point to three ways of interpreting the professionalization of political elites. First, it may be perceived as an aspect of the *increasing workload* of legislators. Or, professionalization may be interpreted as *changes in the role* of legislators, in the sense that the orientation, perceptions, and total outlook of legislators will be more like those of professionals (e.g. lawyers or others of the liberal professions). Finally, professionalization may refer to *changes in recruitment patterns* of legislators, in which political experience, political achievements, and power positions in the political hierarchy become major assets for the prospective legislator. In their work, Eliassen and Pedersen (1978: 292–3) do not single out one of these interpretations; instead, they choose to treat the question of professionalization as a synthesis of the three. In the present chapter I will use a similar approach, and discuss how the historical process, political institutions, and changes in the recruitment patterns of political parties have contributed to the professionalization of the Norwegian legislature. More specifically, I shall focus on how these factors have shaped the outlook of the "political class." Here, two factors are of particular significance, the local "link" to the constituency and the role of the political party.

POLITICAL PROFESSIONALIZATION IN HISTORICAL PERSPECTIVE

The Parliament created by the Constitutional Assembly of 1814 was called the *Storting*, a name with historical connotations.[1] The Norwegian constitution of 1814

I would like to thank Bernt Aardal, Trond Nordby, Paul Thyness, and Henry Valen for valuable suggestions to the manuscript, and Svein Gunnar Berntzen at the Administrative Affairs Department of the *Storting* for providing helpful information on the economic benefits of the MPs.

[1] In the Middle Ages before the union with Denmark the *ting* was an assembly consisting of all free men, which met regularly and functioned partly as a legislative body and partly as a court. The word *Storting* means the *ting* of the whole nation.

is currently the oldest written constitution in Europe and indeed second only to that of the United States in the democratic world. Unlike the other Scandinavian countries (see, e.g. Damgaard 1992), Norway has not fundamentally overhauled and updated its constitution since the Second World War. Consequently, the Norwegian constitution is silent on many aspects of modern governance (such as parliamentarism), and on other issues there are major discrepancies between formal constitutional provisions and contemporary practice. Though Norway has in effect been a parliamentary democracy since 1905, the written constitution gives no recognition to this practice.[2] It is important to note, however, that long-standing practice has given parliamentary government the status of a constitutional convention (*sedvanerett*) (cf. Andenæs 1981; Nordby 1996). Moreover, Norway does conform to the concept of pure parliamentarism in the sense that Members of Parliament (MP) are the only national agents elected by the people.

The Constitutional Assembly of 1814 adopted the principle of separation of powers. The *Storting* was empowered with legislative authority while the executive power was vested in the King. During the first few decades after 1814 the *Storting* formed the arena for the defense of the constitution and of national independence, and in the subsequent process of political modernization opposition to the regime was promoted through the *Storting* (Kaartvedt, Danielsen, and Greve 1964; Rokkan 1967). The personal power of the King gradually declined, and since the dissolution of the Union with Sweden in 1905, royal power has been almost negligible. The state bureaucracy, which right from the start in 1814 held a powerful position, gradually assumed full control of the executive branch of government. The practice of parliamentary government, however, meant an end to the principle of separation of powers. Remnants of this principle, however, still prevail in the system, most notably concerning incompatibility rules for membership in the executive and the legislature (Lane and Narud 1994).

As in Sweden and Denmark, the Norwegian parties originated in the 1880s and around 1920 formed what has been called "the Scandinavian five-party model." The parties have been politically defined around six dimensions of cleavage, determined by economic, geographical, and historical circumstances (Rokkan and Valen 1964; Rokkan 1970; Valen and Rokkan 1974). Ranging from left to right on the socio-economic class dimension, the parties that developed around 1920 were the Communist Party, Labor, the Liberals, the Agrarian Party (later the Center Party), and the Conservative Party. The first deviation from this model occurred in 1933, when a religious faction broke away from the Liberals and founded the Christian People's Party. In addition, a left-wing faction split from Labor in 1961 and formed the Socialist People's Party (later the Socialist Left Party after merging with the Communists), over disagreement within the Labor Party on foreign policy issues

---

[2] Trond Nordby (1998: 163) argues that the government formed in 1884 did not represent a change of regime, as has often been claimed in previous studies (e.g. Hernes and Nergaard 1989). Rather, in the Norwegian case the principle of parliamentarism was adopted first in 1905, after also the Conservative party had accepted the decision of the *Storting* that the King could not go against a government supported by Parliament.

(NATO membership). In 1973 a new party on the right wing emerged: Anders Lange's Party, named after its founder. This right-wing populist party called for strong reduction of taxes and public expenditure. It later changed its name to the Progress Party.

Manhood suffrage was introduced in 1898 and universal suffrage in 1913. At the level of local politics, however, the right to participate arose as early as 1840 (Eliassen and Pedersen 1978: 297). Hence, in a comparative perspective formal rights of participation were given early to Norwegian citizens at the level of local politics, and from the beginning of the twentieth century MPs could be recruited from a pool consisting of all adult citizens. Until 1952, however, the rule of *bostandsbånd* (residential ties) required that all candidates should live in the constituency where they were to be nominated.[3] As we shall see, the local connection of Norwegian MPs is a major feature of the system and contributes to the professional outlook and the recruitment profile of the *Storting*. It is also a predominant element in the development of the electoral laws in Norway, a factor to be considered in the last section of this article.

As a general principle, everybody who is entitled to vote at *Storting* elections also can be elected. One notable exception to this rule should be observed, however. Civil servants employed in government offices, at the Royal Court, in the foreign services as well as higher military officers are not eligible. This rule, which was explicitly stated in the Constitution of 1814, derived from the principle of separation of powers. Recruitment to the two branches of government should be kept separate in order to avoid undue influences between them. Obviously, members of the *Storting* could not simultaneously be members of the government. This rule has always been maintained, even after the introduction of parliamentarism (Hernes and Nergaard 1989; Lane and Narud 1994).

As a consequence of parliamentarism members of the government are required to attend the *Storting*, but have no right to vote there. They may also be asked to attend hearings in committees in order to provide information about government policies. Moreover, the government is free to recruit its cabinet and junior ministers from Parliament or outside of Parliament. But if a representative is invited to join the government, he or she will have to give up the seat as long as occupying a government position, and a deputy representative will take the seat temporarily.[4] In the most recent government, Bondevik II (2001–), seven out of nineteen ministers were recruited from outside Parliament.

THE INSTITUTIONAL CONTEXT

The *Storting* is a strange combination of a unicameral and a bicameral parliament. It is unicameral in the sense that all representatives are elected in one single election

[3] Exceptions were made for former cabinet ministers.
[4] Until 1884 an elected representative was forced to give up his seat for the entire electoral period when recruited to the government as a cabinet minister.

and under identical suffrage requirements. Elections are held regularly every fourth year, and unlike most parliamentary systems there is no provision for an early dissolution of Parliament. There is, thus, no possibility of recall before the end of the regular term. There are also no term limits. The bicameral structure is constituted by an arrangement of the *Storting* in two divisions, *Odelsting* and *Lagting*, consisting of three-fourths and one-fourth of the assembly, respectively. This structure was originally created for two main purposes: impeachment and legislative procedures. In constituting itself after the election the *Storting* decides who shall be a member of each of the two chambers. The rule of proportionality among the parties is strictly observed in the composition of the two divisions.[5]

When constituting itself, the new *Storting* is not only concerned with the composition of the *Odelsting* and the *Lagting*; it also decides upon formal organization and the distribution of leadership positions for the next 4 years. Most important in this respect is the election of the presidents and vice-presidents as well as that of the chairpersons of the standing committees. The highest officer is the President of the *Storting*. In addition, a Vice-President of the *Storting* and a President and a Vice-President for the *Odelsting* and the *Lagting*, respectively, together serve as an institutional board and control the agenda. The President and the Vice-President alternate monthly in chairing their respective assembly. The positions of the presidency as well as those of the committee chairs are distributed among the parties in approximate proportion to their strength.

The committee system is a distinguishing feature of the *Storting* and is the most important factor supporting the professionalization of the political elites. Currently, the system consists of twelve standing committees. The division of topics used to correspond roughly to that of the government ministries, but since the committee reform of 1993 this is no longer the case. The main intentions of the reform were to even out the workload, which previously varied substantially between the various committees, to reduce the influence of specialized interests, and to improve coordination by establishing a new committee structure (Rommetvedt 1996). In addition, the *Storting* may establish *ad hoc* committees to deal with specific topics. All members of the *Storting*, except the President, are required to serve in *one*, and only one, standing committee, normally remaining there for the full 4-year term of the *Storting*. The parties are represented in the committees in proportion to their strength in the legislature. The floor management of committee reports rotates between the committees' members and, thus, contributes to the activation of the representatives. Policy expertise is concentrated among the members of the standing committees, and most often representatives are members of the same committee for several parliamentary terms. Hence, the committees serve as agencies of specialization, both in terms of policy-making and for the individual representative. Moreover, the committee system works as a vehicle for compromise and decision-making and serves to integrate the opposition into the power structures of the state. Under a

---

[5] Both chambers must deal with any policy issue coming up in the *Storting* in order to ensure proper treatment.

system of minority government, which has become the norm for government formation in Norway (see, e.g. Strøm 1990; Narud 1996; Narud and Strøm 2000), the committees are the most important channels for power integration and "power sharing" between the government and the *Storting* (Hernes and Nergaard 1989; Rommetvedt 1991).

In addition, compared to most other parliaments, and particularly the British House of Commons, the *Storting* cannot be classified as a "debating" parliament. Debates are few and not characterized by much eloquence. The relevant committees first deal with virtually all questions that reach the *Storting* and the individual representative spends a major part of his/her time there. Consequently, except for major issues the actual decisions are made by the committees in the sense that the *Storting* without much debate quite often accepts committee reports and recommendations.

The fact that committee meetings are not open to the public makes them conducive to compromise across party lines. The public is not admitted even when hearings are arranged with interest organizations.[6] However, an information channel to the public is established during parliamentary question time, which are arranged regularly every week when the *Storting* is in session. These opportunities are important for individual representatives who want to highlight specific interests related to their respective constituencies (Rasch 1994).

The preferred committees of the MPs vary according to their occupational background, party affiliation, district interest, etc. (Hernes 1971; Rommetvedt 1992). These wishes are taken into consideration when party leaders make their decision with respect to committee assignments. In a long-term perspective the predominant trend has been that committee members retain rather than change their membership (Rommetvedt 1995). From the late 1980s on, however, turnover in the committees has increased rather dramatically. Rommetvedt (1995: 255) notes that in 1989 only 14 percent of the MPs retained their committee membership as compared to 1953 and 1977 when the corresponding figures were 45 and 34 percent, respectively.

Two important consequences may result from this development. First, specialization and possible segmentation may decrease. And second, it would seem to increase the power of the party leadership. Formally, it is the group meeting that decides on the assignments of individual representatives to the committees. In reality, however, the party leadership decides and makes use of that power to distribute rewards and punishments (Hernes 1977; Heidar 1995a). In addition, the resources of the parliamentary parties have grown substantially compared to those of the committees. These developments contribute to weaken the relative significance of individual representatives to the advantage of the party leadership.

Given the institutional arrangement described above, the question of the role of the parliamentary parties is crucial for the understanding of political professionalization. The main and most effective counter-force against specialization and sectoral interests within the *Storting* are the party groups (see, e.g. Stavang 1964;

---

[6] In 1995 it was decided to introduce open hearings as a test case, and in February 2002 the *Storting* decided to make public hearings permanent (see section 21a in the *Storting's* Rules of Procedure).

Heidar 2000). Group meetings are held regularly every week when the Parliament is in session, and almost without exception the representatives attend these meetings.[7] Party discipline is very high in all the parties for two main reasons. First, representatives are expected to follow their respective party platforms, which are normally a result of broad discussions throughout the party organization, and thus, carry a strong moral force. Second, there is a commonly held belief that internal divisions are a sure way to a loss of voter confidence. The group meetings decide what the party's position should be in cases when the platform is not very specific or when entirely new matters have arrived on the agenda since the last election. However, in most cases the debates in the group meetings will take place on the basis of reports made by representatives from the relevant committees. If full agreement cannot be reached, it is expected that those who want to dissent clarify their positions and inform the party leadership *before* the issue comes up for a vote in the house. The cultural pressure against dissenting, however, is fairly strong in all parties, and overall, there is a high degree of party cohesiveness in parliamentary votes (Bjurulf and Glans 1976; Shaffer 1991; Teigum 1995).

We have already noticed the role of the standing committees as agencies for developing special skills within the *Storting* framework. Through the committee work representatives become spokesmen of their party in matters dealt with in their respective committees. Specialization, however, tends to counteract the generalism that is the basis for the *Storting's* main claim to political legitimacy, and is balanced by the party groups, which serve as the major generalist forces within the parliament. The party fractions from the committees must win acceptance for their views from the party groups, that is, harmonize the specialized policies with party programs and current party tactics, before the party's position is finalized in the committee (Heidar 1995*b*: 11). These two aspects of parliamentary party behavior—party discipline on the one hand and party coordination and procedures on the other—are central features of the *Storting*.

Dissent on local issues is the easiest for the party leadership to tolerate. The party leadership recognizes the importance of local ties, and all parties accept the political practice of building local or regional alliances to promote district interests. Apart from the odd local issue, there are few structural opportunities available to the representatives for influencing political decision-making outside the realm of the party. The coordination undertaken and the discipline enforced by the party groups are considered vital for the effective functioning of the Norwegian parliamentarian system (Stavang 1964), and are thus, a necessary precondition for following a parliamentary career.

In Norway, the rules by which MPs are selected and held accountable are embodied in rules of different status. Some of these rules are part of the constitution; others are spelled out in ordinary legislation, such as the election law and the nomination law

---

[7] In his book *Der er det godt å sitte* (It is good to be there), Guttorm Hansen (1984: 68–99), former President of the *Storting* and former parliamentary leader of the Labor Party, has described vividly the activities and practices of the parliamentary parties. See also the presentation of the activity of the parliamentary parties in *Stortingets Historie* (The History of the Storting), 1964, vol. IV: t.

(Valen 1985, 1988). Since 1920, Norwegian elections have taken place according to the rules of proportional representation (PR). Specifically, Norway currently uses a two-tier modified St. Laguë system, with 157 first-tier seats and a pool of eight national second-tier seats. From 2005 on, the total number of seats will be 169, with 150 first-tier seats and a pool of nineteen national second-tier seats. Obviously, the electoral system—together with the nomination system—restricts the structure of opportunity available to political professionals (see pp. 313–4).

THE POLITICAL CLASS

Size and Composition

In the postwar period the size of the legislature was changed three times. The first change occurred in 1973 when the number of seats was increased from 150 to 155. In 1985 their number was further increased to 157, and finally, in 1989, to 165 seats. In Norway, as in most other western nations, the composition of the political class has changed rather dramatically over the years. In addition, and like virtually all other national assemblies (see, e.g. Norris 1996), the *Storting* differs signific-antly from the population at large, as the socio-economic status of the political representatives lies well above that of the average voter in terms of gender, class, age, and education (Hellevik 1969; Eliassen 1985; Matthews and Valen 1999; Narud and Valen 2000).

In their comparative analysis of Denmark and Norway, Eliassen and Pedersen (1978: 315–16) point out that the professionalization of the Norwegian political elites—as opposed to those in Denmark—is closely linked to the electoral mobilization of the population. A rapid and lasting increase in the recruitment of legislators with political experience before parliamentary entry appeared as early as the middle of the nineteenth century, well before the establishment of the party system. This recruitment occurred in close correspondence with the electoral mobilization of the peasant population.

In a long-term perspective the predominant post Second World War trend has been the replacement of farmers and blue-collar workers with career-politicians (Eliassen and Pedersen 1978; Heidar 1988; Matthews and Valen 1999; Narud and Valen 2000). Table 16.1 reflects this development quite clearly. Furthermore, the political professional was more frequently found in the urban and rural mass parties than in the other types of parties. In contrast to many other countries the number of lawyers has never been extensive in the Norwegian legislature. In fact, Table 16.1 reveals that in the period between 1989 and 1997 this group of professionals was not represented at all in the *Storting*.[8] Possibly, the tendency for lawyers to be absent may be related to the level of income. Compared to the income opportunities of most

---

[8] This observation may, however, be disputed. In the present chapter I have chosen to categorize the MPs by their actual job, not by their education. For example, if an MP is a university professor in law or a journalist with a law degree, he/she is categorized as a "teacher" or a "journalist," not as a "lawyer." Hence, by this strict definition only people practicing law are included in the group of "lawyers."

Table 16.1 *Occupational background of Norwegian MPs, 1945–2001 (%)*

Election year	1945	1949	1953	1957	1961	1965	1969	1973	1977	1981	1985	1989	1993	1997	2001	Average
Blue-collar	12	11	11	9	7	5	5	8	6	4	1	2	5	7	5	6.5
White-collar	35	35	35	33	30	33	35	31	34	34	41	38	35	31	32	34
Teacher	9	9	4	5	9	11	15	21	19	17	17	15	12	13	9	12
Farm/fish[a]	23	26	28	27	25	20	14	13	12	14	9	7	7	3	3	15.5
Lawyer	5	2	5	5	3	3	3	2	1	2	1	—	—	—	1	2
Journalist	5	7	7	5	7	7	9	8	7	5	5	2	1	2	2	5
Party work[b]	3	3	4	5	4	5	4	6	5	4	7	16	21	29	31	10
Other[c]	8	6	7	11	15	16	15	12	16	20	18	19	19	15	17	14
N	150	150	150	150	150	150	150	155	155	155	157	165	165	165	165	—

[a] Includes also those MPs who combine farming with other type of work.
[b] Includes MPs employed in the party organization or with full-time positions at the local or provincial level (e.g. mayors), as well as ministers and secretaries of state.
[c] Includes students, housewives, self-employed, organizational workers (e.g. in labor unions) and other free professions.

Table 16.2 *Social and demographic composition of the Norwegian Storting, 1997–2001 (%)*

Gender	(N = 165)
Male	64
Female	36
Age group	(N = 138)
18–35	13
36–44	16
45–54	38
55+	33
Economic sector[a]	(N = 154)
Public	53
Private	47
Education[b]	(N = 165)
Low	1
Middle	36
High	63

[a] The sectoral classifications of the representatives refer to the time when they were first elected to Parliament. Included in the category of 'private' are also various sorts of organizations.
[b] The classification of educational level is based on the following Norwegian categories: 'low' (*barneskole, ungdomsskole*) 'middle' (*gymnas 1, gymnas 2*), 'high' (*universitet 1, universitet 2, universitet 3, forsker*). This classification implies that the 'middle' category is everything between compulsory education (low) and all types of started university education (high).

Sources: The figures concerning sector, gender and education are based upon biographical data, whereas the figures for age are based upon interview data in the Norwegian *Storting* (the Democracy and Power Studies, 1998–2003. Response rate = 84%).

lawyers, the salary of Norwegian MPs has been rather low. The most remarkable change manifest in the Table, however, concerns the increase in the number of MPs in the 1980s and 1990s whose occupational background is to be found in party or party-related work (as opposed to the more general category of "political experience"). In their analysis based on data from 1985 Matthews and Valen (1999) noted that the tendency towards greater professionalization may most easily be observed among younger and more highly educated members, who are almost all experienced public or party office holders.

Another striking feature is what Eliassen has called the intellectual professionalization of the Norwegian legislature. This development is expressed by the MPs' level of education. In the period from 1945 to 1961, 34 percent of the MPs had a higher education, whereas this percentage had increased to 46 percent between 1961 and 1985 (Eliassen 1985: 120). Table 16.2 indicates that in the 1997–2001 session as many as 63 percent of the legislators had a higher education.

As can be seen in the table, highly educated middle-aged men with a white-collar background dominate the Norwegian *Storting*. The public sector is slightly over-represented compared to the private sector, and women are under-represented. However, in relation to most other western legislatures, the Norwegian figures for female representation are rather high and second only to Sweden (Norris 1996). In the last two or three decades there has been a substantial increase in the number of women elected to the national legislature as well as to government (see Skjeie 1992). One of the reasons for the increasing number of female MPs since the late 1970s is related to the nomination procedures of the parties, in which the balancing of the list involves women's quotas (Valen, Narud, and Skare 2002).

Another striking feature is the high number of representatives with local experience, a factor pointed out also by Eliassen and Pedersen (1978) in their comparative study of Norway and Denmark. Hence, constituency work is an important avenue to become a member of the "national political class." One reason for this tendency, as we shall see, is the control exercised by the local party branches over the nomination process.

Political Recruitment and Political Careers

The Norwegian Nomination Act, incorporated in the Election Act of 1985, has regulated candidate selection since it was introduced in 1920. The electoral law requires that the parties present lists of candidates in the nineteen constituencies. The candidates on each list are ranked in the order in which the parties wish to see them elected. The voters are permitted to change the list by crossing out the name of one or more of the nominated candidates, but, in fact, the voters have never successfully changed the parties' rank ordering at *Storting* elections (Valen 1988: 211). Furthermore, it is important to note that political parties play a critical role in the recruitment process. Successful independents are very rare in Norwegian politics; since the Second World War only two candidates not affiliated to an established party have been elected to the *Storting*.[9]

In June 2002 a majority of the *Storting* decided to abolish the Nomination Act.[10] At the present stage it is too soon to say whether this change will have any consequences for the nomination procedures of the different parties. For this reason, the subsequent discussion will be based upon the nomination practices as they have been until now. The Nomination Act urged all parties to select their candidates in each constituency or "province" by conventions of delegates elected by the parties'

[9] The independents have been Anders Aune and Steinar Bastesen. Aune was in 1989 elected as a representative of a local non-partisan slate (*Folkeaksjonen Fremtid for Finnmark*) in the province of Finnmark. He did not run for reelection in 1993. Bastesen, a controversial and outspoken whaling captain, was elected from Nordland on the slate of the Coastal Peoples Party (*Kystpartiet*) in 1997 and again in 2001. Interestingly, both independents have been elected from northern provinces, a fact that may reflect a peripheral protest vote.

[10] See http://www.odin.dep.no/krd/norsk/publ/otprp/016001-050016/index001-b-n-a.html for a detailed description of the proposal (in Norwegian).

dues-paying members in the province's local subdivisions. Observe that the Nomination Act has not been mandatory, but if the party used the procedure described there, the national government would have funded the provincial conventions. In general, the parties have tended to follow the law, with the exception of the capital, Oslo, where distances are so small that expenses for nomination meetings are negligible (Valen 1988: 212).

Only party members have been allowed to participate in candidate selection meetings. For many years about 15 percent of the electorate paid their dues to parties, according to reports from party headquarters (Svåsand 1985: 49–53), but information from the national election surveys indicates that party membership by the turn of the century has declined to around 10 percent. Of these, only one out of three participates in the nomination process.

The Nomination Act stated that electoral lists are decided by party conventions in each constituency. The decisions were to be final and could not be over-ruled by public authorities or by national party bodies. The law permitted the conventions to submit the list to a referendum among party members, albeit such a referendum has never been held (Valen 1988: 212).

The organizational procedures for candidate selection have not differed much from one party to another. Henry Valen (Valen 1988: 213) points out that the selection process in Norway must be characterized as a highly decentralized one, and there is little or no acceptance of interference of the central party leadership.[11] In each locality the delegates are elected by a majority vote. Before the meetings, which are normally held 6–9 months before an election, the constituency nomination committee asks local party organizations to discuss potential nominees. In all parties it is common for nomination committees to ask whether incumbents are available for renomination. Note, however, that the request from the nomination committee is no guarantee that the incumbent candidate will be renominated. Normally, the first draft from the nomination committee is sent out to the local branches for comments.

Many similarities exist among the parties concerning selection criteria. The most important device is a system of group representation or "ticket-balancing" that is applied with varying rigidity from one party to the next. A set of three basic groups seems to occur in all parties: territorial groups, women, and youth. In addition, a number of other occupational and cultural groups are represented on the party list on the basis of ideology and electoral platform. Labor and the Left Socialists, for instance, tend to emphasize the representation of trade unions and workers on the list, while in the Christian People's Party several religious organizations are important (Valen 1988; Valen, Narud, and Skare 2002).

---

[11] Observe, however, that this does not exclude the possibility that national leaders might occasionally exert influence although they tend to deny doing so. Public debate in recent years suggests that the Progress Party deviates somewhat from other parties in this respect. The national leader of the Progress Party, Carl I. Hagen, has been accused by the mass media and even by his own party activists of intervening in the nomination process at the constituency level. An attempt was made at the party's national congress of May 2001 to alter party statutes regarding nominations to the effect that if the chairman or deputy chairman sought nomination, they should automatically receive the top place on the list. However, the party congress defeated this proposal.

The personal characteristics required of a candidate have been remarkably stable throughout the years. When comparing the evaluations of party "gate-keepers" between 1957 and 1985, Valen (1966, 1988) reports that on the one hand, political and professional competence was strongly emphasized as a requirement for nomination in both years (see also Valen and Katz 1964). Moral qualities and party loyalty, on the other hand, which were important criteria in 1957, were mentioned less frequently in 1985. The most striking difference between the two years, however, was a strong increase in the number of respondents mentioning public performance qualities (including charisma, eloquence, ability to perform in the mass media, being a communicator). No doubt, the increased significance of these qualities reflects a trend in modern politics towards greater visibility of political leaders. Since 1965 media interest in the question of candidate selection has increased dramatically, and the personal characteristics of individual candidates are being scrutinized to a larger extent than before (Narud 1991, 1994). Moreover, over the years the parties seem to have become more similar in terms of desired qualities (Valen 1988: 221).

Perhaps the most important criterion for candidate selection is political experience, that is, service in local or provincial government. Matthews and Valen (1999) report that between 85 and 92 percent of the MPs have served as members of municipal councils in every *Storting* session since 1945; between 56 and 79 percent served as party officials. In recent years from a quarter to a half have served in provincial councils (*fylkesting*), and over a quarter in national party leadership positions. "Combine this," Matthews and Valen (1999: 136) argue, "with the fact that today's members have spent many more years in schools and universities than their predecessors and are elected to the *Storting* earlier in life, and you have today a legislature of mostly career politicians."

District representation is linked to the local political interests of the constituency, for example, the construction of roads and other facilities for public transport, location of schools and hospitals, and the attraction of new industries. Therefore, geographical balancing is not only concerned with the number of candidates; it also affects the ranking on the lists. This means that ticket-balancing is a question of representing the various territorial districts within the province, reflecting the organizational strength of the local party units as well as that of significant local organizations. In addition to being devoted representatives of their party we, therefore, find strong local ties in the representative focus of Norwegian parliamentarians.

Interestingly, recent studies indicate that there is a dilemma between the constituency links on the one hand and following a parliamentary career on the other (Bauna 1997). The latter is associated with leadership positions in committees, membership on the board of presidents, the party leadership, or even the government, and extensive parliamentary experience is normally required in order to achieve these positions. At the same time, when MPs acquire more varied experience, it may be hard to maintain the local focus. Particularly, working in committees basically dealing with nation-oriented or international issues tends to make the "localist" representative turn "cosmopolitan" (Hernes 1983).

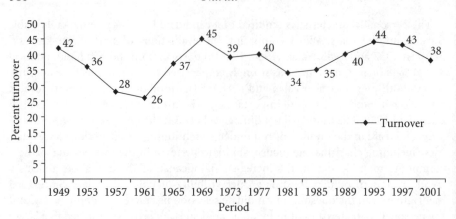

Figure 16.1 *Turnover at* Storting *elections, 1949–2001*

As in most parties in other countries (Ranney 1981), incumbency is an important criterion for reselection in all parties. Here, the record has traditionally been quite favorable from the point of view of Norwegian politicians. Their major obstacle has been getting the party's nod, and most party organizations have let interested parliamentarians accumulate up to three or four (4-year) terms of seniority. Recently, however, this picture has changed. In the run-up to the September 1997 and 2001 elections, several leading parliamentarians were either deselected or given less favorable ballot placements than they had previously enjoyed. A number of commentators interpreted these events as a tendency towards stronger "regionalization" and "localization" of the recruitment process.[12] Altogether, 26 percent of the incumbent *Storting* politicians were not reelected in 2001, either because of voluntary retirement, death or illness, internal party strife, or as a result of preferences for some competing candidate (Valen, Narud, and Skare 2002). The parties have no formal rules concerning retirement age, but it is customary that the incumbents do not seek renomination if they will reach 70 in the subsequent term.

The parties alone, however, do not control the overall rate of turnover. In addition to the above reasons, the political careers of MPs may end as a result of the voters' choice at general elections. Voter fluctuations have increased substantially for the last three or four decades (see, e.g. Valen 1981; Aardal and Valen 1995), creating great uncertainty over "who" will be defeated in the next election. Figure 16.1 shows the turnover rates for the postwar period.

The figure reveals that great variations exist from one election to the next. In a long-term perspective turnover has been steadily increasing in the postwar period. The turnover rate went down continually between 1945 and 1961, when the trend was reversed and then turnover increased substantially. This change reflects the generational shift in political leadership at the time. Turnover reached an all time high

---

[12] See, for example, Guttorm Hansen, *Aftenposten*, 11 December 1996.

in 1969 and again in 1993. In the 2001 election the overall rate of turnover was 38 percent; 12 percent was due to the election result (Valen, Narud, and Skare 2002).

Living off Politics

Few studies exist concerning the question of material rewards for being in Norwegian politics. Gunnar Hoff (1964) gives an historical account of the remuneration system, whereas the Parliamentary Commissions for Salaries of 1991 and 1996 have discussed the question of more recent legislative salaries. The 1991 commission was appointed by the presidency of the *Storting* to "evaluate the salaries and other benefits received by the parliamentary representatives and the members of government" (Innst. 1992). The background for appointing the commission were changes in the income rates of superior judges and the introduction of a new salary system for civil servants. Compared to these groups, it was argued (Innst.: 17), the salaries of MPs had been steadily declining, and hence, an income revision was called for.

The *Storting* determines the salaries of the members of the government, the MPs, as well as the salaries of the judges of the Supreme Court. Financial compensation for travel costs and meals was granted to parliamentary representatives from the very beginning in 1814, but they did not receive *per diem* compensation for expenses related to their legislative duties until 1954. Until 1845 the *Storting* had to provide the MPs with accommodation and daily meals, but after the introduction of annual *Stortings* in 1871 this liability was transferred to each individual representative. In 1954 a fixed monthly salary was established, supplemented by a *per diem* compensation. The latter amount was calculated on the basis of how far the MP was located from the capital (Oslo), and was intended to cover extra expenses incurred by district representatives in respect of accommodation in Oslo.

Until 1991 the salaries of members of the Supreme Court were tied to those of the members of government, whereas the MPs' salaries were calculated in relation to those of certain groups within the Civil Service. In 1991, this practice was departed from, and a separate increase in salary was given to members of the Supreme Court. This reform was partly due to problems in recruiting lawyers to official positions, a tendency we have observed also in relation to the *Storting* (cf. Table 16.1).

In a comparative perspective, the legislative salary of Norwegian MPs has been rather low. However, Table 16.3 indicates that in the last 10 years the salaries have been raised substantially.

Observe, however, that in 1991 these figures refer to the basic salary of MPs. In addition, they received *per diem* compensation for expenses in relation to their work (between 15 and 30 percent of the basic salary), reimbursement for among other things journal and newspaper subscriptions, and they also had their domestic travel costs reimbursed. From 1996 most of these compensations were included in the basic salary of the MPs, a reform which resulted in a nominal, but not real increase of their salary (see Innst. S. Nr. 94, Innst. S. Nr. 282). In 2001 MPs received NOK520,000 (approx. €71,100),[13] members of government NOK760,000 (€104,000), whereas

---

[13] Conversions from NOK to Euro are based on the exchange rate of 1 January 2003 (NOK1 = €0.137).

Table 16.3 *Salaries of politicians, judges, and administrative executives (in NOK)*

	2001	1991
Prime Minister	925,000	436,988
Minister	760,000	408,971
Member of Parliament	520,000	271,984
Judge of Supreme Court	785,000	555,000
Higher administrative executive	770,000[a]	364,000

[a] The figure is based upon the category D2 in the 'system of salaries for leaders.' The system divides the basic salaries for higher civil servants into five categories (A–E) which vary between NOK520,000 and NOK830,000. In addition, the system allows for individual rises up to 30% of the salaries defined by these categories (correspondence with the Ministry of Labor and Administration, 24 September 2001).

Sources: Recommendation from the Parliamentary Commission for Salaries 1991, 45; Innst. S nr. 7 (2001–02); Innst. S no. 8 (2001–02), the Norwegian *Storting*.

the Prime Minister received NOK925,000 (€126,500). Furthermore, members of the presidency receive an additional sum to cover representation costs, amounting to about 25 percent (the President), 17 percent (the Vice-President), and 8 percent (the Presidents/Vice-Presidents of the *Odels-* and *Lagting*) of their basic income.

A Pension Act for MPs was introduced in 1951. The Act required that MPs should have served two 4-year periods in Parliament. The present arrangement gives full pension (66 percent of the basic salary) to MPs who have served for 12 years in the *Storting*. Retirement age is 65 years.[14]

In contrast to the United States and certain European countries, no formal restrictions exist on the receipt of outside income by individual MPs.[15] A government minister, however, may not receive additional income from interest organizations or other institutions. Throughout the years the question of extra income by parliamentarians has been discussed on several occasions and a register was established for charting the financial situation of MPs at the beginning of the 1990s. Registration is not mandatory—it is up to each individual MP to decide whether he (or she) wants to be listed in the register.

To my knowledge, no extensive studies exist that deal with the individual legislator's job prospects after his or her political career ends. A general impression is that

[14] According to the Pension Act for Members of Parliament of 1981 (June 12, nr. 61), an MP may retire earlier and receive a full pension, if the sum of his (or her) age and seniority is 75 years (e.g. an MP at the age of 55, who has served in the *Storting* for 20 years).

[15] However, certain restrictions exist after retirement. If the salary of a former MP exceeds the full pension, the latter will be partly cut.

quite a lot of MPs feel uncertain about their future professional career.[16] A handful of parliamentarians are granted a secure retreat to a position as provincial governors (*fylkesmenn*), and there has recently been a tendency towards recruiting former politicians as professional "advisors" or lobbyists for private companies and organizations. However, anonymous lives without particular benefits seem to be the destiny of many former MPs. In accordance with the rules for bonus payment, the individual MP/minister is granted the basic salary for an additional period of 1 month after ending his or her political career. In case of no other income source, salary will be provided for 3 months by the presidency.

THE POLITICAL CLASS AND INSTITUTIONAL REFORM

So far, we have seen that two different, yet interrelated, factors shape the political class in Norway: parties and territory. Two sets of institutional reforms have been particularly important for promoting this development. One affects the electoral system and the strong concern for territorial representation. The other has to do with the development of party finance and the effect of increased resources for staff.

The electoral system introduced in 1814 was based on indirect elections and lasted until 1905, when it was replaced by direct plurality runoff elections. The transition to single-member constituencies narrowed the competition to only one candidate per party, and the parties applied quite frequently a system of primary elections (*prøvevalg*) where voters could display their candidate preferences quite freely (Valen and Narud 1999; Aardal 2002). This system lasted until 1919, when proportional elections were introduced. The call for PR was partly a result of pressures from below: the growing working-class represented by the radical Labor Party wanted to lower the threshold for representation. Partly it was a result of pressures from above, where the old parties wanted protection from the growing number of new voters surging from the introduction of universal suffrage (Rokkan 1970: 157). Based on the recommendations made by the 1917 Election Reform Commission, list elections in multi-member constituencies were preferred. Calculations of seats from votes were to be done according to the d'Hondt method.[17]

Three principles established by the constitutional assembly in 1814 had a lasting effect upon the development of the electoral system (Valen 1981, 1998). First of all, the basic principles of the system, the boundaries of constituencies and the number of seats for each constituency, were defined in the constitution. And since constitutional amendments require a two-thirds majority in the *Storting*, this made it very difficult to change the system. Second, the constitutional assembly decided that peripheral regions should be relatively over-represented compared to central areas,

[16] See, for example, *Aftenposten*, 14 June 1997.
[17] Bernt Aardal (2002) notes that, at the time, this was the method most frequently used in Europe. Since the method clearly favors the largest party and does not lower the threshold very much in small constituencies with few representatives and few party lists, it appealed to the established parties.

and third, the assembly decided that urban and rural areas should vote separately, with a seat allocation ratio of 1 : 2. This so-called "peasant's clause" was abolished in 1952 together with the replacement of the d'Hondt formula by the modified version of the Sainte Laguë method. From then on, each province became a separate constituency, including both urban and rural areas. Finally, some moderate adjustments were made to seat allocation among provinces.

The demand for equity of representation was the main argument in the *Storting* debates when *listeforbund* (list alliances) were re-introduced in 1985, after they first had been abolished in 1949 (Valen 1994). This reform greatly benefited the non-socialist coalition parties, who joined forces in the subsequent election. It was revoked again in 1989 and this time prohibited for the future by a constitutional amendment, when eight nationwide adjustment seats were introduced in addition to the 157 seats elected on a constituency basis.[18]

It should be observed, however, that overrepresentation for peripheral regions has always been accepted in Norway. Demands for equal size of constituencies have until recently not been raised, not even in the period of majority election in single-member constituencies (Valen 1998). Interestingly, the symbolic importance of territorial representation is mirrored in the seating arrangement of the *Storting*. In contrast to most other parliamentarian systems, where the seats of the MPs are organized party-wise, the seats of the Norwegian MPs are organized constituency-wise. This fact probably helps to reinforce the local ties of the party representatives.

In October 1997 the government appointed an Electoral Reform Commission to revise the electoral system. In the spring of 2002 the government presented several reform proposals to the *Storting* based on the Commission's recommendations. Since some of them involved constitutional amendments, they required a two-thirds majority. In June 2002 the parts of the Act concerning the local election rules as well as the abolition of the Nomination Act were passed by a majority vote. The government proposals also provided for an increase in the number of adjustment seats from eight to nineteen, an addition of four seats to the *Storting* (bringing the total to 169), and a new allocation of seats between the electoral districts, reducing the overrepresentation of peripheral areas and thus increasing the overall proportionality of the system. On 26 May 2003 this part of the law was passed, becoming effective with the 2005 election. The third major reform proposal, introducing personal votes in national elections, too, was submitted to the *Storting* on 4 June 2003, but did not gain a majority. The latest election reform implies that only principles for the allocation of seats between the electoral districts remain specified in the Constitution. Prior to each *Storting* election an adjustment will take place to accommodate changes in the distribution of the population.

For the potential "entry" to the political class, the question of financial resources is crucial, yet not easy to encompass in empirical analysis. For a number of reasons, many parties are reluctant to reveal their private sources of income (see, e.g. Svåsand

---

[18] Adjustment seats, allocated to parties that are underrepresented on the basis of constituency representation, are assigned to provinces in which the respective parties have the highest quotients of "unused" votes. The highest quotients tend to be found in large and underrepresented constituencies.

1991). In Norway there were four steps in the development of state finance to political parties (Svåsand 1991: 127–32). At first, from 1970 to 1975 state finance applied only to the national party organizations. From 1975 onwards it was extended also to the local party organizations, and finally, in 1978 to the youth organizations. Parallel to these extensions of public subsidies limitations were also introduced: state subsidies can only be given to parties with at least 2.5 percent of the votes at general elections. Moreover, financial support today is restricted to parties that have nominated candidates in at least half of the constituencies at the last parliamentary election. In addition to the direct state subventions of parties, Svåsand (1991: 136) points out that there are three forms of public support that are not directed to the parties *per se*, but which in reality must be considered as such: support for parliamentary groups, support for the party press, and support for educational associations.

To sum up, the activity of Norwegian parties could hardly have been carried out without the benefit of state subsidies, since they have tended to become more and more dependent on one source of financial support, the state itself (Svåsand 1991: 120). This steady increase in public funding, which indeed has made the parties wealthier, has brought about an important change to the "political class": the increase in party staff.

The party groups have received financial support since 1964. Two types of support are handed out, one directly to the parliamentary groups, the other indirectly by providing secretarial assistance and administrative capacity at the disposal of the parties. The latter has increased substantially since the late 1960s (Rommetvedt 1995), most notably in relation to the committee resources. Nevertheless, compared to the Swedish *Riksdag* and the US Congress, for instance, the resources available to the members of the legislative body are relatively limited.[19] Most of the resources are to be found in the public services, and the government branches have therefore considerable influence on parliamentary decision-making.

However, the amount of direct support given to parliamentary groups, which has increased substantially since 1964, is determined on the basis of the number of elected representatives for each party. These economic resources are by and large controlled by the party groups and have given them the opportunity to hire additional staff for secretarial and political purposes. Moreover, it gives the party groups considerable power *vis-à-vis* individual representatives. The result has been a substantial increase in party staff. Between 1971 and 1994 the number of party employees increased by 122 percent (Rommetvedt 1995). This development has not only contributed to a more extensive division of labor among the group secretaries and, hence, a greater potential for specialization. It has also increased the number of alternative career paths available to party professionals. Yet, the recruitment to these positions seems to a larger extent than before to be based on professional qualifications, not on long-term experience from party work. Traditionally, the group secretaries were hand-picked from the party organizations (or from organizations close to the party). Today many of these positions are advertised in the press (Rommetvedt 1995: 273).

---

[19] Earlier, the party groups were granted one secretary for ten representatives. In 1993 the relative proportion changed to one secretary for every five MPs.

CONCLUSION

The main concern of this chapter has been to discuss the political professionalization of the Norwegian *Storting*. The principal focus has been on the various institutional constraints of Norwegian MPs and on the importance of the recruitment structures for providing access to the "political class." These mechanisms constitute a system in which ordinary citizens have very limited opportunities to affect candidate selection or to sanction representatives once they have been elected. The absence of preference voting, primary elections, or recall mechanisms contributes to that situation. Parties are in a strong position to control their representatives, since ballot access is so much under their control.

Here, the role of the constituency party branch is crucial. Because local councils are the training ground for future parliamentarians, because of the decentralized character of the nomination process, and because of the political legitimacy of pursuing local interests, you rarely get to be a member of the "political class" without going through the local network provided by the constituency party. Overall, the present documentation indicates that Norwegian parliamentarians are actors on two different, yet interrelated arenas, the local arena and the parliamentary arena. As party politicians they play the parliamentary role game, as district representatives they are constrained by constituency demands.

Once elected to Parliament, the parliamentary party is the most important organizational structure to which the representatives relate. First of all, individual representatives have few incentives for "free votes" in parliamentary behavior. Party discipline is strictly upheld, and the representatives are constrained by the party program and the decisions taken by the party groups. On the other hand, through the specialization that takes place in the committee system, individual representatives may have a decisive influence upon party decisions on specific fields of policy. The policy expertise the MPs gain from the kind of issues they are dealing with in their committees gives the committee members of a party (and hence, the individual representatives) considerable influence *vis-à-vis* the parliamentary party. In addition, through their contact with interest group representatives, committee members have access to information and the possibility to pursue the interests of their particular sector. The increased level of committee turnover, however, seems to have increased the relative significance of the party as compared to that of the committee.

The trend pointed to by other scholars (Eliassen and Pedersen 1978; Matthews and Valen 1999) towards intellectual professionalization of the legislature is stronger today than it was one or two decades ago. It is reflected by the increased level of education among the MPs. By the turn of the millennium almost 70 percent of them had acquired higher education. Another striking feature is the increase in the number of parliamentarians whose occupational background is to be found in party or party-related work. Finally, the entry of women in politics has changed considerably the outlook and the composition of the "political class." The interesting theoretical question is how this development is going to affect the character of representative democracy and political decision-making. A group of professional and competent politicians, well equipped to meet the demands of a modern and complex society—how capable are they of representing the interests and meeting the demands of the ordinary voters?

REFERENCES

Aardal, Bernt (2002). "Electoral Systems in Norway", in B. Grofman and A. Lijphart (eds), *The Evolution of Electoral Systems and Party Systems in the Nordic Countries*. New York: Agathon Press, pp. 167–224.

Aardal, Bernt, and Valen, Henry (1995). *Konflikt og Opinion*. Oslo: NKS-forlaget.

Andenæs, Johs (1981). *Statsforfatningen i Norge*. Oslo: Tanum-Nordli.

Bauna, Lars (1997). "Å Slåss for Oslo Blir Man ikke Kirke- og Undervisningsminister av", unpublished M.A. thesis, Oslo: Department of Political Science, University of Oslo.

Bjurulf, Bo, and Glans, Ingemar (1976). "Från Tvåblocksystem till Fraktionalisering: Partigruppers och Ledamöters Röstning i Norska Stortinget 1969–1974". *Statsvetenskaplig Tidsskrift*, 79: 231–53.

Damgaard, Erik (ed.) (1992). *Parliamentary Change in the Nordic Countries*. Oslo: Scandinavian University Press.

Eliassen, Kjell A. (1985). "Rekrutteringen til Stortinget og Regjeringen 1945–1985", in T. Nordby (ed.), *Storting og Regjering 1945–1985*. Oslo: Kunnskapsforlaget, pp. 109–30.

Eliassen, Kjell, and Pedersen, Mogens (1978). "Professionalization of Legislatures: Long-Term Change in Political Recruitment in Denmark and Norway." *Comparative Studies in Society and History*, 20: 286–318.

Hansen, Guttorm (1984). *Der er det godt å sitte*. Oslo: Aschehoug.

Heidar, Knut (1988). *Partidemokrati på Prøve*. Oslo: Universitetsforlaget.

——(1995a). "Partigruppene på Stortinget". *Norsk Statsvitenskapelig Tidsskrift*, 11: 277–97.

——(1995b). "Norwegian Parliamentarians: what do we Know and how do we Know It?", unpublished manuscript, presented at the conference The Political Roles of MPs in West European Countries, Vienna.

——(2000). "Parliamentary Party Groups", in P. Esaiasson and K. Heidar (eds), *Beyond Westminister and Congress*. Columbus: Ohio State University Press, pp. 183–209.

Hellevik, Ottar (1969). *Stortinget—en sosial elite?* Oslo: Pax Forlag.

Hernes, Gudmund (1971). "Interest, Influence and Cooperation: A Study of the Norwegian Parliament", unpublished Ph.D. dissertation, Baltimore: Johns Hopkins University.

Hernes, Gudmund (1977) "Interests and the Structure of Influence: Some Aspects of the Norwegian Storting in the 1960s", in W. Aydelotte (ed.), *The History of Parliamentary Behavior*. Princeton, NJ: Princeton University Press, pp. 274–307.

——(1983). *Makt og Styring*. Oslo: Gyldendal.

——and Nergaard, Kristine (1989). *Oss i Mellom*. Oslo: FAFO.

Hoff, Gunnar (1964). "Representantenes Godtgjørelse og Boligforhold". *Det Norske Storting gjennom 150 År*, 4: 394–443.

Innst. (1992). (Innstilling fra Stortingets Lønnskommisjon av 1991) [Recommendation from the Parliamentary Commision for Salaries of 1991]. Oslo.

——S. nr. 282 (1995–1996), *Innstilling fra Stortingets presidentskap om godtgjørelser m.v. for stortingsrepresentantene og regjeringens medlemmer*.

Innst. S. nr. 94 (1996–1997). *Innstilling fra Stortingets presidentskap om godtgjørelser for stortingsrepresentantene og regjeringens medlemmer.*

—— S. Nr. 7 (2001–2002). *Innstilling fra Stortingets presidentskap om regulering av lønnen for Høyesteretts medlemmer.*

—— S. Nr. 8 (2001–2002). *Innstilling fra Stortingets presidentskap om regulering av lønnen for stortingsrepresentantene og regjeringens medlemmer.*

Kaartvedt, Alf, Danielsen, Rolf, and Greve, Tim (eds) (1964). *Det Norske Storting gjennom 150 År*, vol. 3. Oslo: Gyldendal.

Lane, Jan-Erik, and Narud, Hanne Marthe (1994). "Maktfordelingsprinsippet og den Konstitusjonelle Teori: Spørsmålet om Bemanning av Statsmaktene", in K. Midgaard and B. Rasch (eds), *Representativt Demokrati*. Oslo: Universitetsforlaget, pp. 155–82.

Matthews, Donald, and Valen, Henry (1999). *Parliamentary Representation: The Case of the Norwegian Storting*. Columbus: Ohio State University Press.

Narud, Hanne Marthe (1991). "Fra Oppgjør på Kammerset til Spill for Åpen Scene: Rekruttering av Kandidater til Stortingsvalg". *Norsk Statsvitenskapelig Tidsskrift*, 7: 155–72.

—— (1994). "Nominasjoner og Pressen", in L. Svåsand and K. Heidar (eds), *Partiene i en Brytningstid*. Bergen: Alma Mater, pp. 287–326.

—— (1996). "Voters, Parties and Governments", doctoral dissertation, published as Report no. 7/96, Oslo: Institute for Social Research.

—— and Strøm, Kaare (2000). "Norway: A Fragile Coalitional Order", in W. Müller and K. Strøm (eds), *Coalition Governments in Western Europe*. Oxford: Oxford University Press, pp. 158–91.

—— and Valen, Henry (2000). "Does Background Matter? Social Representation and Political Attitudes", in P. Esaiasson and K. Heidar (eds), *Beyond Westminister and Congress*. Columbus: Ohio State University Press, pp. 83–106.

Nordby, Trond (1996). "Brøl løve". *Nytt Norsk Tidsskrift*, 13: 249–64.

—— (1998). "Parlamentarismen i krise?". *Nytt Norsk Tidsskrift*, 15: 161–68.

Norris, Pippa (1996). "Legislative Recruitment", in L. LeDuc, R. Niemi, and P. Norris (eds), *Comparing Democracies*. California: Sage, pp. 184–215.

Ranney, Austin (1981). "Candidate Selection", in D. Butler, H. Penniman, and A. Ranney (eds), *Democracy at the Polls*. Washington, DC: AEI Publications, pp. 75–106.

Rasch, Bjørn Erik (1994). "Question Time in the Norwegian Storting", in M. Wiberg (ed.), *Parliamentary Control in the Nordic Countries*. Helsinki: Finnish Political Science Association, pp. 247–75.

Rokkan, Stein (1967). "Geography, Religion and Social Class: Crosscutting Cleavages in Norwegian Politics", in S. M. Lipset and S. Rokkan (eds), *Party Systems and Voter Alignment*. New York: Free Press, pp. 367–444.

—— (1970). *Citizens, Elections, Parties*. New York: McKay.

—— and Valen, Henry (1964). "Regional Contrasts in Norwegian Politics", in E. Allardt and Y. Littunen (eds), *Cleavages, Ideologies and Party Systems*. Helsinki: Westermarck Society, pp. 162–238.

Rommetvedt, Hilmar (1991). "Partiavstand og Partikoalisjoner", unpublished doctoral dissertation, Bergen: University of Bergen.

—— (1992). "The Norwegian Storting: The Central Assembly of the Periphery". *Scandinavian Political Studies*, 15: 79–97.

—— (1995). *Personellressurser, aktivitetsnivå og innflytelsesmuligheter i et Storting i vekst.* Bergen: LOS-senteret.

—— (1996). "Norwegian Parliamentary Committees: Performance, Structural Change and External Relations", unpublished manuscript, presented at the International Conference on The Changing Roles of Parliamentary Committees, Budapest, June 20–22.

Shaffer, William (1991). "Interparty Spatial Relationships in Norwegian Roll Call Votes". *Scandinavian Political Studies*, 14: 59–83.

Skjeie, Hege (1992). Den Politiske Betydningen av Kjønn", doctoral dissertation, published as Report 11/92, Oslo: Institute for Social Research.

Stavang, Per (1964). "Parlamentarisme og Maktbalanse", *Stortingets Historie* (1964), vol. IV. Oslo: Universitetsforlaget.

Strøm, Kaare (1984). "Minority Governments in Parliamentary Democracies". *Comparative Political Studies*, 17: 199–227.

—— (1990). *Minority Government and Majority Rule.* Cambridge: Cambridge University Press.

Svåsand, Lars (1985). *Politiske Partier.* Oslo: Tiden.

—— (1991). "State Subventions for Political Parties in Norway", in M. Wiberg (ed.), *The Public Purse and Political Parties.* Helsinki: The Finnish Political Science Association, pp. 119–46.

Teigum, Hanne Marit (1995). "Representasjon i en Flerdimensjonal Konfliktstruktur", unpublished M.A. thesis, Bergen: Department of Comparative Politics, University of Bergen.

Valen, Henry (1966). "The Recruitment of Parliamentary Nominees in Norway". *Scandinavian Political Studies*, 1: 121–66.

—— (1981). *Valg og Politikk.* Oslo: NKS-forlaget.

—— (1985). "Valgsystemet", in T. Nordby (ed.), *Storting og regjering 1945–1985: Institusjoner-rekruttering.* Oslo: Kunnskapsforlaget, pp. 47–56.

—— (1988). "Norway: Decentralization and Group Representation", in M. Gallagher and M. Marsh (eds), *Candidate Selection in Comparative Pespective.* London: Sage, pp. 210–35.

—— (1994). "List Alliances: An Experiment in Political Representation", in K. Jennings and T. Mann (eds), *Elections at Home and Abroad.* Ann Arbor: University of Michigan Press, pp. 289–321.

—— (1998). "Equity of Representation: Party versus Territory", in H. Valen and H. M. Narud (ed.), *Professionalization, Political Representation, and Geography.* Oslo: Institute for Social Research, pp. 41–55.

—— and Katz, Daniel (1964). *Political Parties in Norway.* Oslo: Universitetsforlaget.

—— and Narud, Hanne Marthe (1999). "Nomination Systems and their Consequences", unpublished manuscript, presented at the ECPR Joint Sessions of Workshops, Mannheim, March 26–31.

—— Narud, Hanne Marthe, and Skare, Audun (2002). "Norway: Party Dominance and Decentralized Decisionmaking", in H. M. Narud, M. Pedersen, and H. Valen (eds), *Party Sovereignty and Citizen Control.* Odense: Odense University Press.

—— and Rokkan, Stein (1974). "Norway: Conflict Structure and Mass Politics in a European Periphery", in R. Rose (ed.), *Electoral Behavior.* London: Free Press, pp. 315–70.

17

Portugal: The Patrimonial Heritage and the Emergence of a Democratic Political Class

JOSÉ M. MAGONE

One of the major features of the political class in Southern Europe is the historical discontinuity of its formation as a class. The Portuguese case is in this respect no exception to the rule. The process of democratization started in the nineteenth century and was fully completed only after the founding elections for the Constituent Assembly on 25 April 1975. Until 1974 the political culture of patrimonial exclusionary behavior was the dominant feature of political class formation. Since then we see, for the first time, the formation of a democratic political class, resembling Bachrach's (1969) elite democracy. Indeed, the weakness of civil society, due to a still persistent low level of education within the democratic structures, still prevents a stronger democratization of this political class.

One can probably say that 29 years of democracy have led to the establishment of a political class as a "class for itself," even if the Portuguese class was able to skip some of the typical historical phases of development which normally occur within a democratic framework by jumping from an institutional context dominated by emerging mass parties at the beginning of the twentieth century to a context of postmodern, "Americanized" parties after 1974. This "Americanization of European politics" becomes especially pronounced in the states of Southern and Eastern Europe, which lack any or just have scarce genuine democratic competitive structures of opportunity and have to adjust to the postmodern reality of light party structures and the multimedia possibilities (Beyme 1996a: 140). In the Portuguese case the structure of opportunities—meaning the nature of the parties and the party system—was first built according to the model which was dominant in the late phase of modern welfare statism in the late 1970s. Then it had to cope with its fast transformation into a

I want to thank Heinrich Best as the main discussant of the paper and the editors of this volume for insightful comments. Also thanks are due to Maria do Rosário Paiva Boléo of the Administrative and Financing Services of the Assembly of the Republic, Mrs Conceicao Henriques from the Office of the Secretary General of the Assembly of the Republic, the judge secretary Pedro Gonsalves Mourão, and José Eduardo Sapateiro of the *Conselho Superior da Magistratura* for very detailed information on the salaries of the MPs, ministers, and judges in Portugal.

model of competitive statism widespread in Western Europe, which intentionally directed its efforts to subcontract most of the public services as well as privatize public enterprises. This transformation of state structures also led to the emergence of a more individualistic oriented political field, and thus, to a crisis of the catch-all party. Instead the cartelization of parties as well as political marketing became increasingly important strategies to adjust to the growing tendency towards individualism in society. In this sense, the new democratic structures in Portugal were challenged by the double process of domestic and global restructuring.

Political class can only be fully understood, if one realizes that a specific position of a country within the modern world system will lead to a specific kind of political class.[1] After the collapse of the authoritarian regime, the new democracy had difficulties to overcome past cultural traits related to patrimonial behavior, meaning essentially a special access of certain privileged groups to politics and public goods (Aguiar 1985; Magone 1998: 217–21; Magone 2003).

A problem of democracies is to lower uncertainty in the process of recruitment and selection of new members to the political class. It is this process of establishing formal/informal rules of the game, which makes the study of newly emerging democracies quite challenging. The study of Bernard Silberman on the establishment of selection and recruitment procedures to offices in German, Japanese, British, French, and American bureaucracies shows that the Weberian model of bureaucratization has to be revised in many ways. While Max Weber assumed the development of modern, non-partisan bureaucracies as inevitable, Silberman shows that this process is a struggle between various elites, surmounted incrementally by establishing rules and procedures—resulting in a reduction of uncertainty in the process of recruitment and selection (Silberman 1993). This was also visible in Portugal, where the political class integrated several persons who were part of the former regime into its core, in spite of a revolutionary process that was highly critical of the pre-1974 authoritarian regime.

POLITICAL PROFESSIONALIZATION IN HISTORICAL PERSPECTIVE: THE PERSISTENCE OF PATRIMONIAL POLITICS

The political class in Portugal is characterized by a history of authoritarianism and electoral exclusion of the larger part of the population. Basically, the development towards universal suffrage paralleled those of other West European countries, but while in the latter this expansion of the vote became quite a common figure, in Portugal the different political regimes of the twentieth century attempted to freeze

---

[1] I have discussed this aspect for the Portuguese and Spanish case in my book *The Changing Architecture of Iberian Politics, 1974–1992* (Magone 1996). Using the world systems approach, one has to distinguish between political classes in core, semiperipheral, and peripheral countries. The Portuguese political class is clearly a semiperipheral one. This implies that it is highly dominated by the middle classes coming mainly from academia and with a negligible share of people coming from the working-class.

this development on a low level. Furthermore, the delay of full democratization is also related to a high level of illiteracy and the lack of migration from the rural areas to the urban centers (Magone 1996). One could say that in nineteenth century Portugal no political class existed. What existed was a power elite or ruling class, living for politics and setting power above the public interest. The system of *rotativismo* in the second half of the nineteenth century clearly showed that in the Chamber of Peers (*Camara de Pares*) of the Portuguese Parliament (*Cortes*) the power of the government was very much based on its ability to sell offices, the so called *fornada*: the nomination of a large number of peers by the government after elections. It was a means to keep the electoral machine going, based on patronage and clientelism (Monica 1994: 141–4).

The *rotativismo* system rested on an alternation of governance between the two major parties, which tended to use an extensive electoral machine based on a restricted electoral system. It was supported by local *caciques* (bosses), who offered blocks of votes to the representatives of the governing party in exchange for favors, thus acting as intermediaries of voters' interests. This structure of the electoral machine was kept throughout until the early twentieth century; even when in the last decades of the constitutional monarchy the level of corruption increased over time, because other parties were increasingly successful in winning parliamentary seats (Sobral and Tavares de Almeida 1982: 661–9). Although the constitutional monarchy was affected by political instability and violence, the ruling class was quite stable. Due to the restricted electoral system and the small number of eligible people, the perpetual election of the same members to the *Cortes* became more pronounced over time. Some seats were inherited within families, blurring the distinction between the private and the public sphere. Recruitment became very much the business of people who could afford to enter and stay in politics. Most members of the government had previous experience in Parliament, but this was not a prerequisite.

The ruling class of *rotativismo* was very homogeneous. Even when the importance of the liberal professions increased over time, the aristocracy remained of salient significance. Due to government's importance in "making" elections, the majority of Members of the Parliament (MPs) were related to the government in some way. This symbiosis between the executive and the legislative created a very small ruling class— defined by the social closure of elite recruitment. Most of its members were urban and well educated (Tavares de Almeida 1991).

The Republican Revolution of 1910 did not lead to a substantial change in the pattern of elite recruitment. The level of political instability and violence increased even more: *coup d'états*, political assassinations, and even temporary dictatorships characterized this period. Elite recruitment became very closed and the electoral system was quite restricted, even more than in the late phase of the constitutional monarchy. Personalism and factionalism were major features of parliamentarism in the First Republic (Wheeler 1978). The main reason for the restricted electoral system was to prevent that the rural *caciques* would be able to influence the political process. Therefore, the Republican elite emphasized literacy as a precondition to vote. In this period, we witness a movement from "living for politics" to "living off politics," but the self-interest still dominated over professionalism.

The political structures were changing or toppled down during the whole period until 1926, and the instability of government and parliament created a situation preventing the routinization of patterns of behavior, thus making it difficult for politicians to create a class for itself. In the end, personal likes and dislikes dominated politics in the First Republic. The majority of the professional politicians belonged to the middle classes (Marques 1980; Lopes 1994). In this sense, the pattern of recruitment during the constitutional monarchy—reproduction of the same ruling class— was also valid for the Republic. Only the rural *caciques* were replaced by members of the middle classes during the First Republic.

After the *coup d'état* of Afonso da Costa on 28 May 1926, a military dictatorship was established, changing into an authoritarian civilian one during the following 5 years. Dictator Antonio Oliveira Salazar established the *Estado Novo*, wanting to create a corporatist state. Although the suffrage was extended, eventually the manipulation of electoral campaigns created results that were positive for the government. In fact, according to Manuel Braga da Cruz (Cruz 1988) and Philippe Schmitter (Schmitter 1977), the regime tended to elect civil servants by civil servants—thus, reproducing itself. In the end, the same reproductive patterns of elite recruitment could be found in the authoritarian regime that had been common in the previous regimes. The 48 years of authoritarianism prevented a regeneration of the ruling class. It is important to notice that rural elites were quite dominant in Salazar's Portugal in the beginning, and only in the 1960s gained an emerging industrial elite a stronger influence on the regime's administration (Makler 1979).

In the 1960s and 1970s the regime came under pressure to change. The new middle classes were growing, demanding similar conditions as elsewhere in Europe; mass media, tourism, and emigration created an increasingly mobile society, which was more demanding in political terms. The liberalization initiated by Marcelo Caetano in 1968 came abruptly to a halt in 1972 because of resistance from the hard-line Salazarist faction. Caetano became a prisoner of the different economic and political groups, which once Salazar was able to control against each other (Makler 1979). Political inertia and the unpopular colonial wars were then the major short-term factors leading to the regime's collapse (Passos 1987).

The standard-bearers of the Portuguese "Revolution of the Carnations" on 25 April 1974 were middle-ranking officers, forming the so-called "Movement of Armed Forces" (*Movimento das Forças Armadas*, MFA). They overwhelmingly came from the lower middle classes. In contrast, the political class of professional politicians elected to the Constituent Assembly on 25 April 1975 was dominated by the higher or new middle classes (Gallagher 1983: 215), coming largely from the liberal professions. Only the Communist Party had over 50 percent of its members in the Constituent Assembly originating from the working-class. In the end, the political elite of the transition period was very heterogeneous and fragmented. Even the MFA collapsed in the summer of 1974, leading to the emergence of three factions, each presenting a different political design: apart from a "people's democracy model" and a model of "people's power democracy," orientated on examples of people's democracies in the "Third World," a group of officers under Melo Antunes and Vitor Alves presented a "democratic socialist" model. This one came close to the notions of the majority of professional politicians in the two main parties, the Socialist Party (*Partido Socialista*, PS) and the People's Democratic Party (*Partido Popular Democrático*, PPD, since 1976 *Partido Social-Democrata*, PSD; Magone 1996: 321–2). The outcome was the very eclectic constitution of 1976, integrating elements from all possible political designs presented during the revolution. So the categories of the new political system remained quite undefined until 1985. The struggle between advocates of different political designs made it difficult to create a "political class for itself." It was not until the second half of the 1980s that the categories of the political system got clearer and professionalization and routinization became major factors in establishing a political class for itself. In spite of that, a continually high level of turnover was not conducive to a strong role for the Portuguese Parliament (Magone 2000: 365).

The discontinuity of the regimes makes it very difficult to discern long-term trends in legislative salaries, the time-budget of legislators (length of sessions), and incumbency (legislative tenure/years in professional politics). While the constitutional monarchy and the First Republic were characterized by political instability, thus preventing the establishment of a professional political class, during the authoritarian regime the professionalization of the parliamentary elite was naturally conditioned by the repressive nature of Salazarism.

THE INSTITUTIONAL CONTEXT

The Portuguese institutional context has changed over time. The present political system had to deal with the transformation from a centralized, patrimonial authoritarian state structure to a decentralized, universalistic, and democratic one. This transformation had major implications for resource allocations. Despite the provision in the constitution that Portugal has a three-tiered state structure, comprising the central, regional, and local levels, the so called "administrative regions" were never established. There has been a general debate about their implementation, culminating in a referendum on 8 November 1998 in which a two-third majority voted against regionalization. Therefore, Portugal is currently a highly centralized, unitarian state with two main tiers: national and local. However, since 1976 a steady deconcentration of competencies from the center to the periphery has taken place, which became quite pronounced during the Cavaco Silva era (1985–95) and continued during the subsequent Socialist government. But it has not been accompanied by a corresponding transfer of resources and decision-making powers (Magone 1997: 74–8). This means that until now subsequent governments were not able to deconcentrate effectively public administration and resources away from Lisbon and Oporto to other parts of Portugal.

In terms of the political class, one can see a kind of division of labor between the central and the local level. Apart from the more prestigious positions in the main urban areas, where being a mayor may smooth the way into higher state positions, most of the elected local politicians tend to remain in local politics over a long period of time. Recruitment for the central level is done mainly by the parties without considering aspects of experience in local politics (Cruz 1995: 158–9). The main recruitment criteria is the expertise in a particular policy area that the respective person can bring into the office (Cruz and Antunes 1990).

The role of the national legislature in Portugal is not different from other European countries. Indeed, the *Assembleia da República*—consisting of only one chamber with 230 MPs—is dominated by the executive, which drafts most of the legislation. Government bills have increased over time, while private bills are mostly submitted by the smaller parties, the Communist Party (*Partido Comunista Portugues*, PCP) and the conservative Social-Democratic Center-People's Party (*Centro Democrático Social-Partido Popular*, CDS-PP). The policy dominance of the executive became quite evident when the PSD led the government between 1987 and 1995 with an absolute majority and therefore controlled the agenda-setting. However, since the mid-1980s, due to the increased stability and length of governments, the Parliament could gradually develop procedures, which make a stronger standing *vis-à-vis* the government possible. The level of professionalization has increased, new procedures have become more entrenched, the parliamentary committees have been more successful in monitoring the policies of the different ministries, and the flow of information between government and Parliament has improved substantially. Still, the major problem for parliamentary independence is the lack of human and material resources when compared to the government (Bandeira 1995, 2000; Magalhães 1995*a*).

Although the *Assembleia* gained in influence in the past decade, it is not regarded as a very prestigious institution by the population, its public standing even declining during the era of absolute majorities under Cavaco Silva (Bandeira 1996: 25–39). The parliamentary groups are normally the mouthpieces of their respective political parties and regularly have to rely on the expertise of their parties' research departments (Cruz 1995: 194).

It seems that seniority and experience are the two categories which make legislators move upwards in Portugal. Quite an important phenomenon until the mid-1990s was that MPs had substitutes to replace them while they were pursuing their regular jobs. Substitutes normally received the salary designated for the MPs. In the 5th legislature (1987–91), 452 substitutions took place: 225 in the first legislative session, eighty-nine in the second, eighty-three in the third and fifty-five in the fourth (Assembleia da República 1992). This modality led to a lack of knowledge of the people who are really in Parliament. In the second half of the 1990s, the practice of substitution was better regulated and organized, so improving the quality of parliamentarism in Portugal. The Statute of MPs (article 5) clearly defines the reasons for temporary substitution which cannot exceed a period of 10 months for any given legislative period. The whole process of substitution is now overseen and controlled by the parliamentary Ethical Commission. This development indicates a growing professionalization and routinization of parliamentary work.

The Portuguese electoral system is a proportional one and the seats are distributed using the d'Hondt system which tends to favor the larger and penalize the smaller

parties. The selection of candidates—which for the most part have no direct connection to their constituencies—is controlled by the national party centers. MPs are
elected in twenty-two districts, eighteen in continental Portugal, two in the islands of
Madeira and the Acores, and two outside Portugal for Portuguese citizens in
European and non-European states. The number of MPs to be elected per district
ranges from four to fifty-six (Ramos and Torres 1992: 15–6). A recent revision of the
constitution in 1997 intended to increase the overall number of uninominal constituencies to assure a stronger linkage of MPs to the population, but such reform
was not successful due to a lack of consensus.

For the moment, one has to acknowledge that most of the Portuguese parties are
cartel parties, meaning that they are highly dependent on state subsidies. The PS,
PSD, and CDS-PP were never able to build up a mass-membership, they remained
parties of cadres. During the Cavaco Silva period the PSD was able to increase its
membership, but lost a large part of it again in the elections of October 1995. Other
sources of income are quite restricted: in Portugal, political finance is regulated by a
law adopted in December 1993, which limits donations that can be raised from private donors. All donations have to be accompanied by a written declaration and the
parties' accounts are subject to periodic controls by the Constitutional Court
(*Expresso*, 20 November 1993). Indeed, a first general report by the Court, related to
the expenditure of parties in the years 1994/95, found that no party did declare all its
income and they did not state the finances of their local branches. Until 1993, party
finances were not checked by any auditing institution, leading to cases of illicit party
financing (Biezen 1998; Sousa 2001).

Thus, Portuguese parties are very interested in improving their electoral results, so
they can increase the state subsidies. In this respect, the PCP is an exception to the
rule, because it still maintains the traditional claim to be a mass party (Biezen 1998:
51, 56). One aspect less studied is the sphere of illicit party financing, which was quite
predominant in the Socialist and Communist parties during the 1970s and 1980s.
The Socialist party could rely on some of the connections with the Socialist
International and the American government; the Communist Party was subsidized
by the Soviet Union until the late 1980s. While the CDS-PP received funds from
European Christian-Democratic parties until it became an eurosceptic party in the
early 1990s, the PSD has received only sporadically some international funding until
the 1990s (Mateus 1996; Cunha 1997: 27; Frain 1998: 45–9).

Interest groups have become major political players. Particularly, the symbiotic rela-
tionship between the PS and PSD and the labor union umbrella organization *União
Geral dos Trabalhadores* (UGT) on the one hand, and the PCP and the General
Confederation of Portuguese Workers (*Confederação Geral dos Trabalhadores
Portugueses-Intersindical Nacional*—CGTP-IN) on the other results in interlocking posi-
tions of the political class with economic and social interest groups. Correspondingly,
a close relationship exists between the business organization *Confederação da Industria
Portuguesa* (CIP) and the PSD (Magone 1997: 122–5; Magone 2001).

Overall, considering the structures of opportunity, the Portuguese members of the
political class fit in the backbencher prototype suggested by Jens Borchert (see the

introductory chapter, this volume): The state structure is unitary, while the role of the legislature is weak. The Portuguese Parliament is unicameral, dominated by the parties, with weak committees, and the independence of the legislators is negligible. The electoral system is a proportional one. However, in contrast to the prototype, the parties are quite weak outside the state structures, because they depend highly on public subsidies. Moreover, interest groups are quite fragmented along ideological lines. Last but not least, campaign financing is regulated by law, but the controlling institutions are still learning to deal with the accountability procedures. All in all, the structures are affected by the youthfulness of the Portuguese political system, which is still in an steady process of democratization of all partial regimes previously regulated by patrimonial forms of behavior. What we find today is a mixture of some regimes permeated by a democratic logic, while in other cases patrimonialism still persists.

THE POLITICAL CLASS

Size and Composition

The definition of "political class" is rather blurred. According to Klaus von Beyme the "political class" in western democracies is characterized particularly by the linkage to parties and their relation to the state (Beyme 1996*b*: 68–9). Because of the predominance of parties in Western Europe, the concept of the political class can be brought very close to what has been characterized as *partitocrazia* in the Italian context, particularly before the collapse of the "First Republic" in 1992. In this respect, modern/postmodern Portugal is not very different: the political class is linked to the predominance of parties as political actors in state and society. The powers of selection and appointment really define the political class' boundaries in the Portuguese system—the selectors as well as the selected belong to it. In this sense, the "political class for itself" implies the internalization of this logic of the party state. The essence of *partyocracy* is that the boundaries are shifting or expanding all the time. This was quite evident in western democracies until the 1970s, when the welfare state reached its zenith. Postmodern democracies have even increased the dependency of the parties on the state in terms of subsidies. The cartel parties have tended to colonize media positions in the attempt to influence voters.

If one looks at the Portuguese case, it is very easy to identify the core of this *partyocracy*. The legislature, the government, the President, the politically appointed members of the Constitutional Court and Auditing Court are all part of the political class. One could also include in an extended notion of political class the more important elected offices in the large cities of Lisbon and Oporto. In the case of the legislature, one has to take into account the substitutes of MPs and in the executive the politically appointed secretaries of state and civil servants. The periphery of the political class includes positions in the modern media, party appointees in top positions of the public sector, incumbents of both party and interest groups positions at

Table 17.1   *Size of the core political class since 1976 (ranges)*

Government [a]	55–100
Legislature [b]	230–350
Constitutional Court	10
Auditing Court	3–5
Local political class Lisbon/Oporto	20–30
Total	318–495

[a] Includes ministers, secretaries of state, and sub-secretaries of state.
[b] Includes MPs and substitutes.

the same time (particularly in the Communist Party and the Communist trade union confederation CGTP-IN, as well as in the Socialist party and the Socialist-Social-Democratic Trade Union Confederation UGT), and the local political class outside Lisbon and Oporto. This distinction is quite important, because it emphasizes the difference between the "core political class" as setting the broad parameters of the party state, and the "peripheral political class" as acting under the conditions thus created, thereby sustaining and reproducing them (Table 17.1).

If we take a longitudinal perspective of the political class since 1974, not only looking at one legislative period at a time, and include positions in the peripheral political class, we see a cumulative network made up of about 6,000–8,000 persons. This would naturally include former members of the central political class: incumbents of positions which were strongly linked to the dominant political parties, who still play an important interlocking role in the political system after quitting active politics and now occupy new positions in the territory between politics, economy, and society. They are responsible for the expansion of the network and further the diffusion of the peripheral political class into all sectors of society.

Political Recruitment and Political Careers

Despite the fact that recruitment and career paths have hardly been studied in Portugal, some empirical comments can be made. Recruitment has been so far monopolized by the parties. According to the constitution, the party is the sole gatekeeper of the selection and nomination of candidates for the *Assembleia da República*. Nevertheless, the fourth revision of the constitution in 1997 introduced the possibility that citizen lists may be formed.

The strong overdominance of the political parties becomes evident by looking at the career patterns of Portuguese Members of the European Parliament (MEPs). The now twenty-five seats in the EP are regarded as very prestigious because of their remuneration and international dimension. There is a high level of competition within the political class to be nominated for these positions and the nominated candidates have a long history within party or state structures. Indeed, 62.5 percent of the Portuguese MEPs elected in 1989 had previous experience in the Assembly of the

Republic, 29 percent had previous governmental experience, and over 58 percent belonged to the higher echelons of the parties (Magone 1993: 11).

In this sense, one can recognize a ranking of positions in the political system and beyond it, which indicates a career hierarchy. A political career can—but need not—start in local politics. The selection or nomination for positions in national politics does not necessarily require experience in local politics. It is rather cultural or social capital (Bourdieu 1984), that is education or professional experience, than political experience that is required for the increasingly specialized positions in the legislatures. Even the Communist Party (PCP), which tended to allocate half of its seats to working-class candidates, had to include more lawyers and experts in their parliamentary group over the years (Cruz and Antunes 1990; Magone 2000: 359). The Assembly of the Republic may be regarded as the school of professional politicians in the Portuguese case. Some may remain within the legislature and pursue a career in committees and higher parliamentary positions. Other move on to government positions—even if governmental positions do not require membership of Parliament.

But other experiences, for example, within the party hierarchy or in professional life, tend to be just as important for the recruitment into government positions (Portas and Valente 1990). Quite important is that governmental positions are linked to the level of cultural capital (education) of a professional politician: the previous Socialist government had a vast number of academics in its cabinet. This interlocking of academia and politics is quite pronounced in the Portuguese case, due to the fact that cultural capital is probably the most important asset to move up in Portuguese society. This is reinforced by the ability to collect social and symbolic capital on the career path; so one could speak of a kind of "academocracy" dominating the Portuguese political class.

On average, the share of female MPs was around 10 percent in most legislatures until 1995. During the second Socialist legislative period between 1995 and 2002 it had increased to 28.7 percent. In the present 9th legislature (2002) it declined substantially to 21.3 percent. In terms of professional composition, MPs come predominantly from academia or are lawyers (together on average 40 percent of each legislature), even if in the 7th legislature (1995–99) the number of people coming from liberal and manual professions had increased (Magone 2000: 359).

The Constitutional and Auditing Courts require excellent representatives from the legal profession. Even if they are nominated politically, it is always a compromise between the parties, so that one could until now prevent the introduction of partiality in the Courts (Magalhães 1995*b*; Magone 1997: 51–3).

Even if in the beginning of the new democratic political system one could find some cases of cumulation of mandates, today a specialization takes place. There is naturally a simultaneous incumbency of party offices and legislative/governmental offices in Portuguese politics, but the accumulation of public offices, both horizontally or vertically, has been reduced over time. This leads to a separation between a local and a central political class. Some academics tend to continue to teach in their universities while they hold a public office, as was the case with Antonio Sousa Franco, the former president of the Auditing Court in 1993. This led to a controversy between the government and the opposition. Prime Minister Cavaco Silva wanted to make this simultaneity incompatible, but the main opposition party PS did not see any wrongdoing in this practice—Sousa Franco was, however, regarded as being close to the Socialist Party.

Overall, the Portuguese political class is already a class "for itself." A lack of studies makes it difficult to give a final assessment. Nevertheless, one can at least conclude that cultural and social capital are very important assets in moving up on the career ladder of Portuguese politics.

Living off Politics

Low income of the MPs has been one of the reasons for the large number of substitutes in the *Assembleia*. Many professional politicians continue their job as university teacher or work in their businesses. What we see is a parliament which provides the possibility for many people to learn the rules of the games of Portuguese politics.

In 2002 MPs received a monthly income of €3,449 before tax, which is quite low compared to judges of the Supreme Court of Justice (*Supremo Tribunal de Justiça*) receiving €5,542. Normal parliamentarians have the right to an additional monthly representation allowance, amounting to 10 percent of their respective salary, at the moment fixed at €345. MPs in special positions get higher allowances: the Vice-President of the *Assembleia* gets another 25 percent of the basic salary (€862), the leaders of the parliamentary groups 20 percent (€690), and their deputies 15 percent (€517). In addition, the MPs receive travel cost benefits depending on the place where they live (€0.33 per kilometer; monthly social public transport card €21; travel costs for political work in Europe €4,960; for political work outside Europe €11,821). They are also entitled to a daily reimbursement of subsistence costs (outside Lisbon €60; in Lisbon €20, and abroad €145). Being in a special position, the President of the *Assembleia*—who is at the same time Vice-President of the Republic—earns €5,518 per month, which corresponds to 80 percent of the President of the Republic's salary. He is also entitled to a higher allowance of €2,207.

The lack of space in the Assembly of the Republic led to the allocation of one office for two MPs. There is secretarial support for each parliamentary group according to their share of the vote, that is, their share of seats. The parliamentary groups are also entitled to research assistants or the commissioning of research studies for their parliamentary work.

Financially, less problematic is a governmental position. In 2002, the Prime Minister earned €5,174 per month and was entitled to €2,069 representation allowance, while a minister had a monthly salary of €4,484 and an allowance of €1,794. Apart from its salary and prestige, an executive position is also an excellent opportunity to gain managing experience. Later on, such a position may lead to high assignments in the public sector or to other public offices. Therefore, a position inside the government may lay the base for subsequent importance in the peripheral political class, which tends to sustain the categories of the general political class.

THE POLITICAL CLASS AND INSTITUTIONAL REFORM

According to the Eurobarometer data between 1985 and 1999, the Portuguese seem to have become more content with the political system. While in 1985 only 30 percent of them were satisfied with democracy, the number changed to 70 percent in 1991, 54 percent in 1993, and 57 percent in 1999 (Morlino and Montero 1995: 239; *Eurobarometer* 51, 1999: 6). Portuguese democracy is regarded as legitimate, because professional politicians were able to create a more stable democratic environment over time. The ideological rigidity of the first decade has been replaced by a more issue oriented approach since 1987. The absolute majority of Cavaco Silva after the 1987 and 1991 general elections brought a more technocratic element into politics. Nevertheless, the decline of satisfaction between 1991 and 1993 shows that the longevity of government led to the appearance of several scandals, alleged corruption, and a growing political alienation of the population towards the government. During the Cavaco Silva government several irregularities in the allocation of public contracts or cases of illegal party financing occurred. Another aspect was the dominance of interest groups in certain ministries, a good example being the strong position of agricultural interests in the Ministry of Agriculture or the misuse of the European Social Fund grants in the Ministry of Employment and Security (Magone 2003). A kind of general mistrust in professional politicians could also be observed by another study on political culture in the 1980s. In general terms there was, and is, a feeling of cynicism in relation to the world of politics (Heimer, Vala, and Viegas 1990). Indeed, the level of abstentionism in legislative elections has reached almost 40 percent in the past two elections (Freire 2000). A recent study commissioned by the previous government clearly states that the Portuguese population does not feel represented by the current parties and has a low esteem for government and Parliament (*Expresso*, 5 October 2001).

The best example of the lack of accountability in Portuguese politics is the case of the High Authority Against Corruption. This institution was founded on 6 October 1983 by the two main government parties at that time, the PS and the PSD. Costa Brás was nominated High Commissioner. His role was to investigate irregularities concerning public officeholders, but the main parties decided to give only weak competencies to this new body. After 9 years the High Commission was abolished in October 1992, having collected one and a half million pages of reports on corruption in Portugal. These were sent to the *Torre do Tombo*, the Portuguese National Archives, to be stored without public access for the next 20 years, so that people working in the public or private sector are protected against any acts of blackmail. Consequently, the corruption of the 1980s will only be known in the year 2013 (Magone 1994: 759–61).

The Portuguese case displays the major difficulty that professional politicians are facing in a new democracy, where a culture of patrimonialism has to be transformed into a culture of democratic universals and accountability: until the latter stage is reached, there will be a *mixtum compositum* comprising both cultural features. The building of a new democratic regime requires the establishment and implementation of a democratic legal framework, whereas its optimal functioning may be achieved only over a longer period of time and in a situation of political, economic, and institutional stability.

The Portuguese case clearly demonstrates that democracies need time to mature, to create their own rules of the game and live by them. A "political class for itself" can only emerge when patterns of behavior and expectations have become more stabilized. The Portuguese political class is now more cohesive than ever. One major reason is that the two main parties are ideologically not very distinct from each other—both PS and PSD occupy the center. This has led to the initiation of reforms of the political system through bargaining and compromise, the two main parties dominating the discussion. In recent years, one can recognize intentions to reform the system in the four relations defined by Borchert (see the introductory chapter, this volume):

(1) *Between the electorate and the elected.* In the discussion on constitutional revisions a change in the electoral system and in the relationship between the electorate and the elected was contemplated. Thus, during the last constitutional reform in 1997 the constituencies were aligned to the administrative districts. There was also the intention to enhance the connection of the MP to his or her constituency. This reform attempt failed due to a lack of compromise between the two main parties (Cruz 2000). Nevertheless, the discussion was restarted in 2001 once again, so that in the next revision of the constitution it will be on the agenda again.

(2) *Between the legislators and the legislature.* Over the years the Assembly of the Republic was able to improve its public standing; nevertheless, it is still not regarded as very prestigious among more senior politicians. Due to the fact that parties are the dominant actors, the relationship between legislators and the legislature will always be dependent on the role that the government assigns to the Parliament. Strong majority governments are disposed to neglect the parliamentary arena, even if the preceding Socialist government tended to take the opposition more seriously. In contrast, minority governments in the first decade of the new democracy were more dependent on Parliament's support. A reform of the legislature would be the most appropriate measure to strengthen the parliamentary accountability of government. The individual MPs need more resources—until now allocated to the parliamentary groups—to play a more active role in parliamentary politics and to be more independent of their groups.

(3) *Between the parties and the state.* In recent years one could observe attempts to regulate the relationship of parties and the state, being especially important in the relationship between government and administration. Political appointments in the administration are one of the most delicate questions. New procedures were designed and implemented since the beginning of the 1990s.

(4) *Between center and periphery (state and/or local level).* "Administrative regions" as defined in the constitution would introduce a new tier of government. The main idea is to achieve a better coordination of development efforts in Portugal and decentralize power away from Lisbon and Oporto. This would lead to a deconcentration of

governmental power. Regionalism has no tradition in Portugal, which became evident again in the last referendum on 8 November 1998 explicitly rejecting regionalization (Mira 1999; Baum and Freire 2001).

On the whole, for the near future one can expect a major change in the structure of opportunities for professional politicians. The external pressures coming from the European Union further reinforce the process of decentralization and democratization. Though, one can assert that democratization of the structure of opportunities has not led yet to a democratization of the political class—today it still is "academocratic" and predominantly from the middle classes.

CONCLUSION

The Portuguese political class has become more coherent over the years and the lack of ideological differences between the parties has led to a convergence of common interests. The negotiation of political and institutional reform is now the rule. It is a highly educated political class coming predominantly from academia or the liberal professions, while the working-class has been under-represented.

The historical development of the political class was characterized by a patrimonial structure of opportunities. The democratization of Portugal after 1974 had to overcome these past experiences and the redrawing of the structure of opportunities is still going on. It clearly brings to the fore that democracy is essentially a process, democratization. The political class, one has to acknowledge *sine ira et studio*, has become quite cohesive and stable over time. It is ideologically sustained by the peripheral political class in the mass media, the public sector, the local political class, and other adjacent fields occupied by former members of the core political class.

REFERENCES

Aguiar, Joaquim (1985). "Partidos, estruturas patrimonialistas e poder funcional: A crise de legitimidade". *Análise Social*, 21: 759–83.

Assembleia da República (1992). *Memória da V Legislatura*. Lisbon: Assembleia da Republica.

Bachrach, Peter (1969). *The Theory of Democratic Elitism: A Critique*. London: University of London Press.

Bandeira, Cristina Leston (1995). "Controlo Parlamentar Na Assembleia da República". *Legislação*, 12: 121–51.

——(1996). *The Portuguese Parliament in the Cavaco Silva Era*. Hull: Centre for Legislative Studies, University of Hull.

——(2000). "A Assembleia da República 1976 a 1999: Da legislacao à legitimação". *Análise Social*, 35 (154/155): 175–205.

Baum, Michael A, and Freire, A. (2001). "Political Parties, Cleavage Structures and Referendum Voting: Electoral Behaviour in the Portuguese Regionalization Referendum 1998". *South European Society and Politics*, 6: 1–26.

Beyme, Klaus von (1996*a*). "Party Leadership and Change in Party Systems: Towards a Postmodern Party State?". *Government and Opposition*, 31: 135–59.

—— (1996*b*). "The Concept of Political Class: A New Dimension of Research on Elites?". *West European Politics*, 19/1: 68–87.

Biezen, Ingrid van (1998). "Building Party Organisations and the Relevance of Past Models: The Communist and Socialist Parties in Spain and Portugal". *West European Politics*, 21/2: 32–62.

Bourdieu, Pierre (1984). *Distinction: A Social Critique of the Judgement of Taste*. London: Routledge.

Cruz, Manuel Braga da (1988). *O Partido e o Estado no Salazarismo*. Lisbon: Presença.

—— (1995). *Instituições Políticas e Processos Sociais*. Lisbon: Bertrand.

—— (2000). "A revisão falhada do sistema eleitoral". *Análise Social*, XXXV (154/155): 45–53.

—— and Antunes, Miguel Lobo (1990). "Revolutionary Transition and Problems of Parliamentary Institutionalisation: The Case of the Portuguese National Assembly", in U. Liebert and M. Cotta (eds), *Parliament and Democratic Consolidation in Southern Europe*. London: Pinter, pp. 154–83.

Cunha, Carlos (1997). "The Portuguese Communist Party", in Th. Bruneau (ed.), *Political Parties and Democracy in Portugal*. Boulder: Westview Press, pp. 23–54.

Frain, Maritherese (1998). *PPD/PSD e a consolidação do regime democrático*. Lisbon: Editorial Noticias.

Freire, André (2000). "Participação e abstenção nas eleições legislativas portuguesas 1975 a 1995". *Análise Social*, 25 (154/155): 115–45.

Gallagher, Tom (1983). *Portugal: A Twentieth Century Interpretation*. Manchester: Manchester University Press.

Heimer, Franz Wilhelm, Vala, Jorge, and Viegas, José M. L. (1990). "Padrões de Cultura Política e Portugal: Atitudes Face a Democracia". *Análise Social*, 25 (105/106): 31–56.

Lopes, Fernando Farelo (1994). *Poder Político e Caciquismo na 1a República Portuguesa*. Lisbon: Editorial Estampa.

Magalhães, Pedro Coutinho (1995*a*). "A actividade legislativa da Assembleia da República e o seu papel no sistema politico". *Cadernos de Ciencia da Legislação*, 12 (Janeiro/Marco): 87–119.

—— (1995*b*). "Democratização e Independencia Judicial em Portugal". *Análise Social*, 30/1: 51–90.

Magone, José M. (1993). *The Iberian Members of the European Parliament and European Integration*. Bristol: Centre for Mediterranean Studies.

—— (1994). "Democratic Consolidation and Political Corruption in the Southern European Semi-Periphery: some Research Notes on the Portuguese Case, 1974–1993". *Contemporary Political Studies*, 2: 751–64.

—— (1996). *The Changing Architecture of Iberian Politics, 1974–1992: An Investigation on the Structuring of Democratic Political Systemic Culture in Semiperipheral Southern European Societies*. Lewiston, NY: Mellen University Press.

—— (1997). *European Portugal: The Difficult Road to Sustainable Democracy*. Basingstoke: Macmillan.

—— (1998). "The Logics of Party System Change in Southern Europe", in P. Pennings and J. Lane (eds), *Comparing Party System Change*. London: Routledge, pp. 217–40.

—— (2000). "Political Recruitment and Elite Transformatiom in Modern Portugal 1870–1999: The Late Arrival of Mass Representation", in H. Best and M. Cotta (eds), *Parliamentary Representatives in Europe 1848–2000*. Oxford: Oxford University Press, pp. 341–70.

—— (2001). *Iberian Trade Unionism: Democratization Under the Impact of the European Union.* New Brunswick, NJ: Transactions Publishers.

—— (2003). "Political Corruption in Portugal", in M. Bull and J. Newell (eds), *Political Corruption in Contemporary Politics.* Basingstoke: Macmillan, pp. 120–31.

Makler, Harry M. (1979). "The Portuguese Industrial Elite and its Corporative Relations", in L. Graham and H. Makler (eds), *Contemporary Portugal.* Austin: University of Texas Press, pp. 123–65.

Marques, A. H. Oliveira (1980). *A Primeira República Portuguesa.* Lisbon: Livros Horizonte.

Mateus, Rui (1996). *Contos Proibidos: Memórias de um PS Desconhecido.* Lisbon: Dom Quixote.

Mira, Alvaro Xosé Lopez (1999). "Portugal: Resistance to Change in the State Model". *Regional and Federal Studies,* 9: 98–115.

Monica, Maria Filomena (1994). "A lenta morte da Camâra dos Pares, 1878–1896". *Análise Social,* 24 (125/126): 121–52.

Morlino, Leonardo, and Montero, Jose Ramon, (1995). "Legitimacy and Democracy in Southern Europe", in R. Gunther, P. Diamandouros, and H.-J. Puhle (eds), *The Politics of Democratic Consolidation.* Baltimore: Johns Hopkins University Press, pp. 231–60.

Passos, Marcelino dos (1987). *Der Niedergang des Faschismus in Portugal.* Marburg: Verlag für Arbeiterbewegung und Gesellschaftswissenschaft.

Portas, Paulo, and Valente, Vasco Pulido (1990). "O Primeiro-Ministro: Estudo sobre o Poder Executivo em Portugal". *Análise Social,* 25 (107): 333–49.

Ramos, Isabel, and Torres, Luis (1992). "Analise dos Sistemas Eleitorais dos Estados Membros da Comunidade Europeia". *Eleições,* July/3: 11–25.

Schmitter, Philippe (1977). "Portée et signification des elections dans le Portugal autoritaire, 1933–1974". *Revue Francaise de Science Politique,* 27: 92–122.

Silberman, Bernard S. (1993). *Cages of Reason: The Rise of the Rational State in France, Japan, the United States and Great Britain.* Chicago: University of Chicago Press.

Sobral, Jose Manuel, and Tavares De Almeida, Pedro G. (1982). "Caciquismo e Poder Politico: Reflexões em torno das eleições de 1901". *Análise Social,* 18 (72–74): 649–71.

Sousa, Luis de (2001). "Political Parties and Corruption in Portugal". *West European Politics,* 24/1: 157–80.

Tavares De Almeida, Pedro G. (1991). *Eleições e Caciquismo no Portugal Oitocentista, 1868–1890.* Lisbon: Difel.

Wheeler, Douglas L. (1978). *Republican Portugal: A Political History, 1910–1926.* Madison: University of Wisconsin Press.

18

Spain: A Textbook Case of Partitocracy

PETER MATUSCHEK

POLITICAL PROFESSIONALIZATION IN
HISTORICAL PERSPECTIVE

It was only in the mid-1970s that democracy definitely took roots in Spain and became incrementally consolidated in the years to follow. As one of the countries that passed from authoritarian rule to democracy during the so-called "Third Wave" of democratization, Spain was—besides Portugal and Greece—one of the South European latecomers in providing a democratic polity in which political careers could be pursued. This peculiarity has to be taken into account when analyzing the role and the nature of the Spanish political class. One important consequence is its discontinuity since the nineteenth century. However, it is possible to detect some early trends even in the system of the monarchic "Restoration" (*Restauración*) at the beginning of the twentieth century and later on during the II Republic, which can be considered as first, albeit timid, steps towards a professionalization of politics. During the system of the "Restoration," which was built upon the new constitution of 1876 and put an end to a long period of political turmoil throughout the nineteenth century, politics was characterized as politics of notables.[1] This system brought nearly 60 years of political stability, also preventing military intrusions into politics. Political parties were constituted on the parliamentary level, while extra-parliamentary parties hardly existed. Political life was characterized by the so-called *turno pacífico*, an invention of the party leaders Cánovas and Sagasta, which meant the peaceful alternation in power of the two dynastic parties (Conservatives and Liberals) without having to rely on support of military officers which would carry out the familiar *pronunciamientos* (Linz, Gangas, and Jerez Mir 2000: 382–3).

The Spanish answer to the extension of the suffrage was neither the development of mass parties nor the establishment of linkages with society via ancillary organizations (like in the case of the British Tories or the German *Zentrum*), but systematic electoral fraud (Esteban and López Guerra 1982: 28). This fraud was carried out by

---

[1] Although these "notables" sociologically differed from the model of "notables" in other European countries, as many of them came from the administrative realm. This is in contrast to a pattern of notables as members of the professions or land-owners (Linz, Gangas, and Jerez Mir 2000: 382).

the state machinery, particularly the ministry of the interior and the civil governors, which *de facto* established the results (*encasillado*). The local pieces of this machinery were the so-called *caciques* (local bosses) who used to depend on the civil governor. The system of the *turno* guaranteed this right to manipulate the result both to the Conservatives and the Liberals alternatively (Esteban and López Guerra: 29), marginalizing the parties not integrated into the system, like the Socialists, Republicans, or Carlists. Politicians in the two chambers of the Spanish *Cortes* (Parliament) were accordingly notables who gathered once a year and did not receive any salary for their office. The first small step towards a partial professionalization coincided with the crisis and decay of the system of the "Restoration" at the beginning of the 1920s. Had the first attempt to reform the rules of the *Cortes* (*Reglamento*) failed in 1918 and the introduction of salaries been rejected by the Parliament, since 1921, however, the deputies enjoyed a monthly compensation (called *indemnización mensual por franquicia*) which signified a hidden form of state payment. In 1922, a monthly income was proposed—and later approved after a lively discussion—which could be cut in case of non-attendance (Arranz and Cabrera 1995: 81–2).

The coup of the general Primo de Rivera in 1923 and the establishment of a dictatorial regime put an end both to the system of the "Restoration" and of the *caciquismo* and meant a break with the political class of the former regime. This break was even more visible with the emergence of the II Republic in 1931 in whose freely elected parliament very few politicians of the restoration period could be found (Linz, Gangas, and Jerez Mir 2000: 399–401). A new electoral system and a different social context led to a clear reduction of *caciquismo*, and at least two mass parties emerged with the Socialist PSOE (*Partido Socialista Obrero Español*) and the right-wing CEDA (*Confederación Española de Derechas Autónomas*). Parliament during the II Republic was characterized by a high turnover of its members in the three elections taking place in 1931, 1933, and 1936. Parliamentary work became more regulated in comparison with the system of the "Restoration" with the parliamentary groups being formally recognized in the Constitution and the *Reglamento* of the Congress (Sallès Bonastre 1995: 116–17). In general, politics had not yet become a full-time activity for all Members of Parliament (MPs), and the Members of the *Cortes* (which consisted of only one chamber during the Republic) could only partly be called professional politicians as not all of them depended on their parliamentary revenue. The majority of the Socialist Members of Parliament (MPs) certainly did, whereas most of the members of the CEDA group or the Republican parties of the center did not (Linz, Gangas, and Jerez Mir 2000: 421). The outbreak of the Civil War and the following installation of the Franco regime led to a purge of former Republican representatives within the state system. In the Francoist undemocratic and corporative *Cortes* only 3.1 percent of its—appointed—members had been elected to Parliament during the II Republic.

It was only after nearly 40 years of dictatorship that a new democratic political class emerged with the celebration of the 1977 general elections. The break of the new political class with the former democratic period is obvious given the long duration of the dictatorial regime. Only five members of the newly elected *Cortes*

(Congress and Senate) in 1977 had belonged to the Parliament during the II Republic (Morán 1989: 67).[2] However, the peculiarity of the Spanish transition, which did not mean the abolition of the Franco regime by a military coup (as in Portugal) nor its institutional breakdown, but a reform carried out within the Francoist institutions and initially respecting the Francoist legality (Nohlen and Huneeus 1984: 349), favored a certain continuity within the political elite. This was true in case of the right-wing parties AP and UCD, where some Francoist *caciques* survived, especially on the local level (Hopkin 2001: 119–20). Altogether, seventy-seven members of the first *Cortes* (both chambers) had been *procuradores* in the Francoist *Cortes*, forty-four during the second legislature 1979–82 (Morán 1989: 73), although in general a remarkable renovation took place: 168 of 350 seats in the Congress were won by anti-Francoist parties (Hopkin 2001: 118).

It is noteworthy that with the emergence of democracy in Spain in the mid-1970s, a definite transformation took place from a politics of notables or semi-professionals to a politics of professionals. A decisive factor in this development is the different role of political parties as a consequence of a leap-frogging process in a newly established democracy. Parties have immediately monopolized the position of intermediating actors between political system and society. Their predominant role was further enhanced by the generous provision of state subsidies and parties' prominent position in the institutions of state and society.

THE INSTITUTIONAL CONTEXT

One of the demands of the anti-Francoist opposition had been the *decentralization* of the highly centralized Spanish state as an essential part of an overall democratization process. The process of devolution started with the so-called historical regions Catalonia, the Basque Country, and Galicia and finally led to the design of an overall framework for the Spanish state with the establishment of the "State of the Autonomous Communities" in 1983. The Spanish state is divided into seventeen Autonomous Communities, which are provided with high levels of autonomy and self-regulation and reproduce the institutions found on the national level. The model of Spain can be called "asymmetrical federalism" with some Communities being conceded more competences than others (Agranoff 1994). This structure has led to the emergence of political subsystems on the regional level and has opened up new channels and opportunities for professional politicians.

The bicameral Spanish Parliament (*Cortes*) is composed of the upper house (*Senado*) and the lower house (*Congreso de los Diputados*). The Senate consists of 257 members, the major part (208) being elected by majority vote simultaneously with the Congress, while a minor part (49) is appointed by the governments of the Autonomous Communities according to their population size. The Congress consists

---

[2] The great attention paid to the "historic" members of the Constituent *Cortes*, like in the case of the legendary communist leader Dolores Ibárruri ("La Pasionaria"), only underlines their exceptional status.

of 350 deputies who are elected by a system of proportional representation. The legal framework clearly favors the Congress over the Senate which is attributed only an almost symbolic role; although laws have to pass the Senate after being approved in the Congress, the Senate has no power to stop legislation as any veto can be overridden by the Congress. Although denominated chamber of "territorial representation," the Senate does not act as intermediary between regions and the central administration: government bills concerning the Autonomous Communities are not subject to prior examination in the Senate (Capo Giol *et al.* 1990: 114–15). Moreover, as both chambers are elected at the same time, the party composition usually coincides to a large degree which tends to guarantee consensus. The minor role of the Senate in the institutional framework makes it a rather unattractive target for any political career, which is reflected in its composition, which makes it resemble a forum for retired politicians.[3]

The Spanish constitution opts for a strong executive *vis-à-vis* the Parliament as an essential provision to assure governability (Capo Giol *et al.* 1990: 100). The position of the Prime Minister is particularly strong: he is elected with a simple majority of the Congress, but in order to replace him, a vote of "no confidence" with an absolute majority is required. The Prime Minister has the right to dissolve the Parliament with few restrictions and his predominant role is further symbolized by own institutions like the Ministry of the Presidency (Barrios 1997: 561). All ministers are appointed exclusively by the Prime Minister and do not need the support of the Parliament. The government's role is further reinforced by the possibility of passing decree-laws (*decreto-leyes*) that do not need parliamentarian approval (Barrios 1997: 566). Apart from the legal provisions, strong party control guarantees governmental dominance over Parliament, as the parliamentary majority coincides with the parties in government (with the exception of some minority governments).

Laws are written almost exclusively in the ministerial administration. The link between government and majority party, together with strongly hierarchical procedures lead to a clear dominance of the administration. Another factor is the lack of expertise in Parliament for formulating propositions. Some provisions in the *Reglamento* of the Congress strengthen the executive: governmental bills have priority in the parliamentarian process (Capo Giol *et al.* 1990: 111; Barrios 1997), especially if the urgency procedure is applied (Paniagua Soto 1997: 412). About 90 percent of the laws passed in Congress are proposed by the executive (López Nieto 1998: 62).

The members of nearly all important national institutions are appointed by the Parliament. Of the twelve judges forming the Constitutional Court, four are elected each by Congress and Senate with a three-fifths majority. Two judges are appointed by the government, two by the General Council of the Judiciary (Barrios 1997: 578; Capo Giol *et al.* 1990: 21). All twenty members of the latter organ are elected by the *Cortes* as well, ten by each chamber (Barrios 1997; Capo Gios *et al.* 1990). The same

---

[3] No leading Spanish politician can be found among its Members (Capo Giol *et al.* 1990: 114–15).

is true for the Ombudsman (*defensor del pueblo*) and the members of the council of the state-owned television and radio network RTVE (Barrios 1997: 577).

The committees in the Spanish Parliament can be roughly divided into four groups according to two criteria: permanent committees vs. non-permanent committees, and legislative committees vs. non-legislative committees (Oñate 2000*a*: 85). Among these, there is a clear dominance of the permanent legislative committees. These can be attributed complete legislative competence, a provision otherwise only existent in Italy and Japan (Paniagua Soto 1997: 412). Another peculiarity of the Spanish case are the so-called *ponencias* (sub-committees). While sessions in the committees are open to the public via mass media (unless there is an explicit contrary vote of the majority), the *ponencias* work under discretion and have become the actual place of negotiation (Oñate 2000*a*: 87). Committees and sub-committees are composed proportionally to the representation of party groups in the Parliament, with the groups having the right to replace their members which occurs frequently (Oñate 2000*a*: 88). Due to the high turnover in the committees and the irrelevance of expertise as decisions are taken by a smaller group of MPs in the sub-committees, there is little specialization, and no "niches" for individual MPs arise. The selection of committee members is carried out by the heads of the parliamentary groups and criteria of seniority are of no importance (Liebert 1995: 271–2). A structural disadvantage of the parliamentary minority becomes evident in the case of committees of investigation whose installation requires a majority vote of the plenary (Barrios 1997: 555). It is obvious that legal and political circumstances prevent the committees from becoming potential arenas for individual MPs to pursue their political career.

The absolute dominance of the parties in political life becomes manifest in the parliamentary procedures which are strongly biased in favor of the parties. First of all, the rules of the *Reglamento del Congreso* strengthen the role of the political groups *vis-à-vis* the individual MPs: the latter have to belong to a group and in case of leaving it, they automatically pass to the Mixed Group (*Grupo Mixto*) which means a considerable loss of rights as a parliamentarian (Oñate 2000*b*: 123; *El País*, 24 August 1997). Another source able to guarantee the subordination of the single MPs to the parliamentary group are the provisions in the individual *reglamento* of each group.[4] At the same time, parliamentary groups are clearly subordinated to the extra-parliamentary parties. This is true both for the selection of personnel and the behavior of the MPs in Congress.[5] Another aspect that illustrates the strong interdependence between parliamentary groups and parties is the common rule that MPs are "expected" to pay part of their income to the party (Biezen 2000: 401). A very important factor that enhances

---

[4] In the case of the PP group, for instance, any activity within the parliamentary group requires the consent of the speaker, and MPs are not allowed to make any public statements about the content of proposals of the party (Oñate, 2000*b*: 113–14).

[5] In the PSOE, the party executive "appoints" the members of the presidency (*Mesa*) of the Congress; in the case of the United Left (IU), the members of the Committees require the ratification of the party executive committee (Oñate 2000*b*: 119), the most extreme case of subordination being the Basque Nationalist Party (PNV): the representatives for all functions within the group are appointed by the party executive and for every vote in Congress, a directive by the party executive is needed (Oñate 2000*b*: 122–3).

discipline of individual MPs is the exclusive selection of candidates for Parliament by the party leaderships (Paniagua Soto 1997: 415).

The electoral system established by royal decree in March 1977 and confirmed in an Organic Law in 1985 aims at maintaining a balance between the representation of a wide range of political groups and the need to create a party system conducive to stable government (Gunther 1989: 837). In general terms one can talk of a system of proportional representation, with a minimum threshold of votes required for parliamentary representation. The electoral districts would normally coincide with the fifty provinces while each province is entitled to a minimum number of representatives (two). The d'Hondt highest average method of seat allocation is employed. Inherent in the system we find two sources of representational bias: the overrepresentation of small provinces in the Congress and the combination of many small districts with the d'Hondt system of seat allocation (Gunther 1989: 838). The systematical effects of both are a bias towards the bigger parties at the expense of the smaller ones and considerable over-representation of the former in Congress. Regional parties concentrating their votes in some electoral districts benefit from the system and are granted representation whereas small parties with equal representation throughout the country are severely punished by the electoral system as in the case of the United Left (*Izquierda Unida*). Distortions in Spain are stronger than in any other western industrialized society, and as strong as those in some single-member constituency systems (Gunther 1989: 840).[6] The system of closed and rigid party lists on the provincial level and highly centralized selection procedures enforce the dependence of MPs on the party organization and make a political career outside parties virtually impossible (Montabes and Ortega 1999: 2).

While the relationship between politicians and interest groups is very weak, the role of the *parties* as vehicles for a political career is decisive. The omnipotence of political parties in Spain as indicated above also implies the strong penetration of state and society: this includes the central administration, the judiciary, the public television, and positions in public (or semi-public) companies. As a heritage of the Franco era there exists an overlap of administrative elite, political class, and economic executives, especially in state-owned firms and big banks (Barrios 1997: 563).[7] This is true both at the national and at the regional level where the public administration is equally politicized (Matas 1995; Mesa and Novo 2000). This is regularly revealed in the high degree of personnel turnover after electoral defeats.[8]

From the very beginning of the new democratic times, political parties in Spain found themselves in a somewhat privileged position as they were being granted public money (Castillo 1985; Biezen 1998: 43). While until the mid-1980s no explicit law existed on this matter, in 1987 the *Ley Orgánica* 3/1987 was approved which

[6] Proportionality in Spain during the first four elections was between 81% and 87% (Gunther 1989: 841).

[7] Most public firms once belonged to the public holding INI, founded by Juan Antonio Suanzes in the 1940s in order to push Spain's "state capitalism" (Beyme 1971: 163). INI was dissolved in the 1990s but left a couple of big companies which provide a receptive environment for deserving former politicians.

[8] Out of 322 higher positions in the national public administration (secretaries of state, under state secretaries, and directors general), 91% were replaced after the change in government in 1996 (*El País*, 6 April 1997).

considerably increased public resources for the parties, as there are public subsidies for the maintenance of the party organization, for electoral campaign costs, and the work of the parliamentary groups. With the development of the State of Autonomous Communities, public financing has become more decentralized, providing part of the contributions to the regional party branches (García-Guereta Rodríguez 2001: 331). The parliamentary groups and the MPs are also funded by the budget of the Congress while the contributions for the groups go directly or indirectly to the party. Thus, the employment of personnel by the parliamentary groups actually serves the extra-parliamentary party. A common rule is the practice that MPs "voluntarily" and with written "consent" transfer part of their revenues to the party (Martínez Sospedra 2001: 181).

Considering all the variables mentioned above, the Spanish type of professional politician beyond any doubt comes very close to the ideal type of the *backbencher*: the dominance of political parties does not leave much room for individual maneuver. A political career is virtually impossible without being a party loyalist. All the indicators mentioned above lead in one direction with the quasi-federal structure being the only exception. Nevertheless, the latter does not really help breaking with the overall pattern of the backbencher because the model of party dominance is reproduced on the regional level, and parties—with some exceptions in case of the nationalist parties—serve as a link between the national and the regional level.

THE POLITICAL CLASS

Size and Composition

Defining the boundaries of the political class is a rather difficult task in the Spanish case, as one has to distinguish between an inner circle of the political class and an outer circle where the degree of politicization is more difficult to determine. The inner core of the political class can be described as composed by the Prime Minister, the ministers of the national cabinet, the politicized administrative elite (secretaries of state, the under-secretaries of state, the general secretaries, and the directors-general), the elected Members of Congress and Senate, the presidents of the Autonomous Communities and their cabinet members, the Members of Parliament of the Autonomous Communities (at least partly), the mayors of the bigger cities, the members of the Constitutional Court, the politically appointed members of the General Council of the Judiciary, the director of the Auditing Court (*Tribunal de Cuentas*), the attorney general and the general director of the state-owned television and radio network (RTVE). The larger circle is composed by a wide range of members in public or semi-private companies, public institutions like universities, or in the cultural area.[9]

A characteristic feature of the political class in Spain is the degree to which its members are interwoven. There is a significant overlap between different positions,

---

[9] To mention only a few, the directors of public theaters, the director of the National Dance Company, or the director of the National Library.

the political parties being the decisive agents connecting the different spheres. Personnel overlap occurs in several dimensions: both horizontally and vertically, and between public and party positions. The most significant overlap can be detected between public office-holders and the party executive on the national level (Oñate 2000*b*: 105, 113).[10] This cumulation of offices can be also found on the regional and on the local levels (Morata 1992: 270–3). The cumulation of public positions both horizontally and vertically is allowed with some exceptions. Ministers are usually members of Congress although this is not as frequent as in other countries (Botella 1997: 152). Secretaries of state are also allowed to be MPs, and there are a few cases where MPs in Congress combine their parliamentary task with the office of a mayor,[11] although this is far from being the rule. More frequent is the combination of a public position on the national level and membership in the party executive on the regional or provincial level.[12]

Political Recruitment and Political Careers

As mentioned above, a professional political career in Spain is virtually impossible outside the political parties, as the parties are the agents who select the candidates for public offices (Capo Giol *et al.* 1990: 119). Recruitment strategies of the parties (the party executives) usually do not involve finding the candidate best suited for the provincial electorate but rather emphasize the party's interests. The "ideal" candidate ought to have previous party experience and should have proved to be disciplined (Montabes and Ortega 1999: 5).

Table 18.1 gives an overview about the first area of political activity for the Members of Congress in the 7th Legislature (2000–): Nearly 45 percent started their political career on the local level (municipal and provincial), 20 percent on the regional level, and 13 percent on the national level; 9 percent made their first political experience in the party's youth organization. It is evident that the most common starting point of professional politicians remains the local arena with the regional level becoming increasingly important.[13]

One of the most striking features of the political class in Spain is the high fluctuation between different positions within the institutional framework. This is indicated by the high turnover rates in the Spanish Parliament, both in the Senate and the Congress (Table 18.2).

[10] For instance, in the case of the *Partido Popular*, there has never been a lower degree than 60% of public office holders in the party executive, reaching an 85% in the National Executive Committee in 1998 (Biezen 2000: 404). Particularly striking is the case of the Socialist politician *Alfonso Guerra* in the 1980s as he combined the positions of the vice-secretary general of the party, Deputy Prime Minister, and Speaker of the PSOE group in Congress.

[11] There have been two cases in the last two legislatures with the PP deputies Villalobos and Martínez combining their seat with the office of mayor of Málaga and Cádiz, respectively.

[12] In 1993, the PP established several incompatibility rules, which limit the excessive accumulation of both public and party positions.

[13] For the PP, a clear tendency can be traced indicating a growing importance of the regional level as a recruitment arena for national deputies in Congress (García-Guereta Rodríguez 2001: 456).

Turnover among members of the different committees is even higher than the overall turnover which is especially striking in the case of committee chairpersons where the
turnover rate is above 50 percent (Oñate 2000a: 89–91). The average number of MPs
remaining in one committee in the 5th and 6th legislature was 32 percent (López Nieto
1998: 55). The same phenomenon also occurs on the regional level, in the Parliaments
of the Autonomous Communities (Delgado 2000: 298). The almost complete absence of
any principle of "seniority" prevents MPs from cultivating their "niche" within parliament and thereby strengthen their own position which would help promoting their
career. Again, the PP illustrates this pattern: of all its Members in Congress between 1977
and 1996, 57.8 percent served one legislature, 21.8 percent two, 12.9 percent three,
5.9 percent four, 1.1 percent five, 0.5 percent six, and no one served seven legislatures.[14]

Although at the beginning of a professional career there is a clear tendency from
the local to the national level, political careers in Spain take multidirectional paths.
The national Parliament, especially the Congress, can definitely be called the epi-
center of the political class, insofar as it takes the most important decisions and as
it unites large parts of the political class. However, it is far from being the culmination
point of a political career but often rather a transitional station.

Table 18.1 *First political experience of Congress Members, 7th Legislature 2000–2004*

	MPs	%
Local level[a]	157	44.9
Regional level[a]	71	20.2
National level[a]	45	12.9
Youth organization	32	9.1
Trade union	6	1.7
Party advisor/assistant of parliamentary group	6	1.7
Other functions	5	1.4
No political experience	9	2.6
No information	19	5.4
Total	350	100

[a] Both party organization and public office.

Source: Own calculations based on data from the *Congreso de los Diputados*; Menéndez and Fontes (2002).

Table 18.2 *Number of legislatures served by Members of
the Congress, 1977–2000 (N = 1.585)*

Number of legislatures	1	2	3	4	5	6	7	8
% of members	52.9	24.2	11.2	5.6	3.8	2.0	0.7	0.4

Source: Menéndez and Fontes (2002: 7–8).

[14] In the Senate, 64% served one, 21.8% two, 10.3% three, 3.5% four, none five or six, and 0.4% seven
legislatures. In the European Parliament, 61.4% served one, 31.8% two, and 6.8% three legislatures
whereas in the Autonomous Parliaments 65.9% served one, 23.3% two, 8.7% three, and 2.1% four
legislatures (García-Guereta Rodríguez 2001: 446).

This is further illustrated by a stable number of MPs who are leaving Congress during a legislature: eleven (3 percent) in the Constituent, forty-eight (14 percent) in the first legislature, forty (11 percent) in the second, forty-four (13 percent) in the third, nineteen (5 percent) in the fourth, fifty-seven (16 percent) in the fifth, fifty-nine (17 percent) in the sixth, and so far forty (11 percent) in the current seventh (2002–) term (López Nieto 1998: 54; Congreso de los Diputados).

Where do these MPs go to? One path goes down to the regional level: a number of MPs are leaving their seat in order to run for elections in one of the Autonomous Communities.[15] Another destination for members of the governing party is the central administration. This was the case under the PSOE in 1982/83, but especially with the newly formed PP government in 1996 and again in 2000: The parliamentary group served as a reservoir above all for secretaries of state but also for other higher positions in the administration. But there is also the reverse career pattern. Former ministers or secretaries of state are often "rewarded" with a seat in Congress through a safe place on one of the party lists (Morán 1996: 19).[16]

Thanks to the opportunities on the regional (and local) level and the relatively high degree of politicization of the public administration, exit options and alternative career opportunities for MPs leaving Congress are abundant. Both the members being replaced during a legislature and those who do not run again often remain within the political class. Of the PP parliamentarians leaving Congress, a majority has obtained a different function within the party elite: 54 percent of these MPs did so after the 4th Legislature (1989–93) and 61 percent after the fifth (1993–96). The rest obtains other positions: in 1986, 22 percent passed on to the Senate and 22 percent to regional parliaments. In 1989, 30 percent proceeded to the Senate and 50 percent to regional parliaments. In 1996, 18 percent moved to the Senate, 18 percent to regional parliaments, and 14 percent to executive posts in regional governments, while 40 percent took over positions on the provincial level (García-Guereta Rodríguez 2001: 449).

As mentioned above, the Senate seems to become a common retirement place for active politicians (Capo Giol *et al.* 1990: 115). Apart from the politicized positions in the public administration (above all the ministerial bureaucracy),[17] fall-back options exist in the realm of the public or semi-public enterprises.[18]

[15] This occurred in 1983 when the PSOE group in Congress lost 13% of its members, many becoming presidents of one of the newly founded *Comunidades Autónomas* or a Member of the Autonomous Parliament. The same happened to the PP in the 1990s, when it became more successful in regional elections. The group of the PP in the 5th legislature (1993–96) lost many members who ran for the European election in 1994 and especially the regional (and municipal) elections in 1995.

[16] A striking example is the case of those former ministers of the PSOE government who had not been MPs before, but entered Congress after losing the elections in 1996. The same happened to the former ministers Josep Piqué, Margarita Mariscal de Gante, and Javier Arenas in 2000 (all belonging to the PP).

[17] We ought not forget the ambassador positions, which are highly politicized. In 2000, the long-served PP deputies Javier Rupérez and Elena Pisonero were rewarded with ambassador posts in the United States of America and before the OECD (*Diario Vasco*, 10 December 2000).

[18] Under the PSOE-government, the Socialist MP Fernández Ordoñez left Congress when he was appointed director of the *Banco Exterior de España*. The MP Garrido Guzmán was named director general of the public INEAM, Luis Solana was named president of the not yet privatized *Telefónica*, and Elena Vázquez became member of the Administration Council of RTVE (Menéndez and Fontes 2002). In the

We find similar patterns of political careers and the phenomenon of a "recycling" of members of the political class on the regional level, too. In Catalonia, the politicization in the administration has increased during the 1980s up to the mid-1990s (Matas 1995: 6–7). In Andalusia, the Canary Islands, and the Basque Country, 80 percent of the administrative elite had occupied political positions on the regional level and 18 percent on the local level (Mesa and Novo 2000: 12). The most frequent career path to the Autonomous Parliaments seems to be from the local to the regional level, with 50 percent of the MPs of the regional Parliaments maintaining a position on the local level while serving regionally (Morata 1992: 273). The case of Catalonia shows tendencies of the emergence of a distinct and highly autonomous political class on the regional level. Here, the Spanish Parliament has been used by many Catalan politicians as a springboard to regional office, and the regional level obviously has become "a career arena in its own right" (Stolz 1999)—a tendency which is particularly pronounced for members of the regionalist parties.

Living off Politics

The income of Spanish MPs is one of the lowest in Western Europe and very modest compared to the opportunities in the private sector (Botella 1997: 146). In 2001, the MPs received a basis salary of ESP498,381 (€2,995)[19] per month plus ESP138,771 (€834) for those thirty-four MPs living in Madrid to cover extra costs. Those MPs living outside the capital receive an extra ESP290,733 (€1,747) (*El País*, 17 June 2001). MPs travel free of charge in the state airlines and railways (Morán 1999: 452). The chairmen of the parliamentary committees receive an additional ESP250,000 (€1,502) per month while the presidents of Congress and Senate earn ESP2,083,333 (€12,521) per month each. Ministers, MPs, and members of the public administration (the higher ranks) enjoy a compensation contribution during two years after leaving their post equivalent to 80 percent of their latest income (*El País*, 17 June 2001).

The chambers of the *Cortes* provide the parliamentary groups with means to cover technical and material assistance (Morán 1999: 452), but there is no individual assistance service for each MP. The number of assistants of the parliamentary groups is very low with three MPs sharing one assistant (*El País*, 17 June 2001). The income of the members of the government varies: while the Prime Minister is paid ESP1,088,306 (€6,540) per month, the ministers receive a salary of ESP960,201 (€5,770) (besides their revenues in case of being MPs), the secretaries of state ESP874,012 (€5,252), the sub-secretaries ESP764,331 (€4,593), and a director general ESP643,732 (€3,868). The President of the General Council of the Judiciary earns ESP1,735,925 (€10,433), almost the same amount as the President of the

---

1996–2000 legislature, the MP Martín Villa (PP) left his seat when named president of the public energy company ENDESA (*ABC*, 18 October 1997) while the MP López Amor was appointed director of the state radio and television network RTVE. In the following legislature, the PP deputy Juan Ignacio Barrero became president of the state-owned *Empresa Nacional de Celolosas* while the PP deputy Ramón Aguirre was named president of the *Instituto de Crédito Oficial* (*Diario Vasco*, 10 December 2000).

[19] Converted according to the fixed EMU rate (ESP1 = €0,00601012).

Constitutional Court. The President of the Auditing Court is paid ESP1,418,308 (€8,524) per month.

On the regional level, the situation varies from region to region: in the lead are the presidents of the Autonomous Communities of Madrid and Catalonia with ESP1,166,666 (€7,011) per month, while the Autonomous MPs receive between ESP500,000 (€3,005) in Valencia and nearly ESP750,000 (€4,507) in the Basque Country. The income of the mayors of the major cities equals roughly that of the Presidents of the Autonomous Communities, from monthly some ESP 916,666 (€5,509) up to ESP1,031,360 (€6,198) in Madrid (*El País*, 17 June 2001).

In the Spanish Congress, the *Reglamento* establishes that it is up to up to the presidency of the Congress (*Mesa*) to fix the amount of the MPs' benefits every year within the budget of the Congress (*Reglamento del Congreso de los Diputados*, Título I., Capítulo Primero, Art. 8). This mechanism enables the members of the political class to decide on their own income. Nevertheless, in spite of the widely recognized deficiencies in the material and financial provision of the MPs, there are no serious attempts to change this situation by raising the contributions to individual parliamentarians because of fear of negative repercussions on behalf of public opinion. The only measure taken is the annually adaptation of the salaries to inflation, which means a rather modest increase (of 2 percent in 2001). Instead, MPs prefer demanding more material support for the groups in Congress and more assistants (*El País*, 19 September 2001).

As far as additional sources of income besides their salary as MP are concerned, both the electoral law (Art. 157 and 159) and the *Reglamento* of the Congress (Art. 17) establish rather severe incompatibility rules which prohibit many paid activities in the public and the private sphere. However, there exist some exceptions and the possibility for every MP to exercise additional professional activities prior examination of the latter on behalf of a special committee of the Congress (*Comisión del Estatuto del Diputado*). The individual MP has to apply for a permission of compatibility which he is hardly denied in practice by the *Comisión* (*El País*, 31 October 2002). In the current seventh legislature (2000–), fifty-three out of 350 Members of Congress have been conceded the permission to work for private companies while being an MP (*El País*, 7 November 2002).

THE POLITICAL CLASS AND INSTITUTIONAL REFORMS

In spite of belonging to the European societies with a rather short democratic experience, Spain is no exception as far as the phenomenon of political disenchantment with the political class is concerned. While surveys show a high level of support for the democratic system in general, political parties and members of the political class reach only poor approval ratings.[20] Besides the general skepticism of the Spanish

[20] See for instance the opinions expressed in the regularly published "barometers" of the *Centro de Investigaciones Sociológicas* (2000).

public *vis-à-vis* their politicians, a wave of scandals during the 1990s led to an even greater distance towards the representatives. According to Heywood one can categorize the scandals that occurred during the 1990s into (1) greed-motivated scandals which blur the boundaries between public and private sphere;[21] (2) "political" scandals, like the case of the GAL (the death squads who acted against ETA during the 1980s with consent of members within the national government); and (3) illegal party funding[22] (Heywood 1995: 726–36).

The occurrence of the wave of scandals has gone along with an increased sensitivity of the Spanish public towards the phenomenon, being heavily influenced and fuelled by the media, especially some newly emerged newspapers like the Madrid daily *El Mundo*, founded in 1990, which has been developing an almost missionary passion for investigative journalism and uncovering scandals. Another change in the Spanish media market was the opening to private television at the end of the 1980s, putting an end to the monopoly of the public *Televisión Española* (TVE), heavily controlled by the government of the day. Now the private channels *Antena 3* and *Tele 5* have a broadcasting license and are competing with TVE.

In the mid-1990s, political scandals had affected political parties to the extent that some 52 percent of the public related parties directly with corruption in 1994 (Heywood 1995: 733). In spite of defects in all of the dimensions mentioned by Borchert (see introduction to this volume)—in the relation between elected and electors, between MPs and Parliament, between parties and the state, and between center and periphery—the prime source for reforms is disenchantment of the electorate with the political class and hence the first dimension.

One of the first reactions to the scandals of the 1990s was the establishment of an "ethical code" on behalf of the then opposition party *Partido Popular* for its public officeholders, and the approval of internal incompatibility rules, severely restricting the accumulation of posts within the party and in public office.[23] Another inner party reform, intended to regain credibility in public opinion and to broaden the options of political participation, was the introduction of the instrument of the "primaries" for the candidates in public office in the Socialist Party (PSOE) in 1998. The "primaries" allow the participation of all party members and had a certain mobilizing effect when practiced for the first time for the 2000 elections of Josep Borrell as prime ministerial candidate (although he resigned only one year later). The new instrument has been used on the national and the regional level as a means to make participation within the party more attractive and to break up the oligarchic tradition of the party.

---

[21] The most prominent was the so-called "Guerra case" which led to the demission of Deputy Prime Minister Alfonso Guerra as a consequence of the misuse of party and government infrastructure for private interests on behalf of his brother.

[22] The most prominent cases were the "Filesa" case on behalf of the Socialist Party and the "Naseiro" case of the PP.

[23] Beyond any doubt these measures had a highly electoral component and were part of a political strategy facing both the scandals occurred in the own party, and particularly, those of the political opponent.

Concerning the relation between MPs and the Congress, some modifications have been introduced in the 1997 *Reglamento* in order to stimulate debate during the plenary sessions by changing some provisions of the generally very rigid procedures of question and answer between government and opposition. The Prime Minister is obliged to answer three questions from the opposition, and this procedure is established as an obligation in the *Reglamento*, not as a mere custom. Furthermore, the individual MP is conceded more freedom in plenary debates about legal propositions: up to ten different MPs of one group are allowed to expose their views which may differ from those maintained by the speaker of the group (*El País*, 1 May 1997).

As mentioned at the beginning, Spain constitutes a peculiar case within Western European democracies given its late democratization during the 1970s. The emergence of democracy, however, has been accompanied by a definite transition to political professionalism. In the process of professionalization the role of the political parties has been decisive. Heavily centralized and hierarchically organized as they are, they have—for the first time in Spanish history—become the dominant actors in public life. They have succeeded in virtually monopolizing the position of intermediating actors between the political system and society. All the institutional variables in the Spanish case push the professional politicians towards the ideal type of the backbencher with the parties being the gatekeepers to a political career.

A characteristic feature of the political class is the significant overlap of different positions and the high fluctuation of professional politicians between positions in the institutional framework. Politicians usually start their political careers on the local level as elsewhere, but once they have entered the inner circle of the political class, careers may take many different paths with the national Parliament often being a rather transitional station. Abundant fall-back options exist thanks to the high degree of politicization in large spheres of state and society. The parties' control of this politicized sphere guarantees a constant "recycling" of the political class and provide the individual politician with a high degree of professional security in the Spanish partitocracy.

REFERENCES

Agranoff, Robert (1994). "Asymmetrical Federalism in Spain: Designs and Outcomes", unpublished manuscript, presented at the XVI World Congress, IPSA, Berlin.

Arranz, Luis, and Cabrera, Mercedes (1995). "El Parlamento de la Restauración". *Hispania* 55: 67–98.

Barrios, Harald (1997). "Das politische System Spaniens", in W. Ismayr (ed.), *Die politischen Systeme Westeuropas im Vergleich*. Opladen: Leske + Budrich, pp. 549–87.

Beyme, Klaus von (1971). *Vom Faschismus zur Entwicklungsdiktatur: Machtelite und Opposition in Spanien*. Munich: Piper.

Biezen, Ingrid van (1998). "Building Party Organisations and the Relevance of Past Models: The Communist and Socialist Parties in Spain and Portugal". *West European Politics*, 21/2: 32–62.

—— (2000). "On the Internal Balance of Party Power: Party Organizations in New Democracies". *Party Politics*, 6: 395–417.

Botella, Joan (1997). "Parlamento y carreras políticas", in M. Ramírez (ed.), *El Parlamento a debate*. Madrid: Trotta, pp. 145–53.

Capo Giol, Jordi, Cotarelo, Ramon, López Garrido, D., and Subirats, Joan (1990). "By Consociationalism to a Majoritarian Parliamentary System: The Rise and Decline of the Spanish Cortes," in U. Liebert and M. Cotta (eds), *Parliament and Democratic Consolidation in Southern Europe*. London: Pinter, pp. 92–130.

Castillo, Vera Pilar del (1985). *La financiación de partidos y candidatos en las democracias occidentales*. Madrid: Centro de Investigaciones Sociológicas; Siglo Veintiuno de España Editores.

Centro de Investigaciones Sociológicas (2000). "Barómetro de marzo". *Cultura Política*, Estudio no. 2,387, Madrid: CIS.

Delgado, Irene (2000). "Elites políticas y vida parlamentaria: actividades y motivaciones de los diputados españoles", in A. Martínez (ed.), *El Congreso de los Diputados en España*. Madrid: Tecnos, pp. 295–341.

Esteban, Jorge de, and López Guerra, Luis (1982). *Los partidos políticos en la España actual*. Barcelona: Planeta.

García-Guereta Rodríguez, Elena María (2001). *Factores externos e internos en la transformación de los partidos políticos: el caso de AP-PP*. Madrid: Centro de Estudios Avanzados en Ciencias Sociales.

Gunther, Richard (1989). "Electoral Laws, Party Systems, and Elites: The Case of Spain". *American Political Science Review*, 83: 835–58.

Heywood, Paul (1995). "Sleaze in Spain". *Parliamentary Affairs*, 48: 726–37.

Hopkin, Jonathan (2001). "A 'Southern Model' of Electoral Mobilisation? Clientelism and Electoral Politics in Spain". *West European Politics*, 24: 115–36.

Liebert, Ulrike (1995). *Modelle demokratischer Konsolidierung: Parlamente und organisierte Interessen in der Bundesrepublik Deutschland, Italien und Spanien (1948–1990)*. Opladen: Leske + Budrich.

Linz, Juan J., Gangas, Pilar, and Jerez Mir, Miguel (2000). "Spanish *Diputados*: From the 1876 Restoration to Consolidated Democracy", in H. Best and M. Cotta (eds), *Parliamentary Representatives in Europe 1848–2000*. Oxford: Oxford University Press, pp. 371–462.

López Nieto, Lourdes (1998). "Representación y funciones del Congreso de los Diputados español: 1977–1996". *Revista Mexicana de Sociología*, 60/2: 45–69.

Martínez Sospedra, Manuel (2001). "La jaula de hierro: La posición del parlamentario en el grupo". *Corts. Anuario de Derecho Parlamentario*, 10/2001 (Extraordinario): pp. 161–88.

Matas, Jordi (1995). "Public Administration and the Recruitment of Political Elites: Formal and Material Politicization in Catalonia", Universitat de Barcelona, Working Paper no. 104, Barcelona.

Menéndez Gijón, Manuel Ángel, and Fontes, Ignacio (2002). *Quién es Quién: sus señorías los diputados. Atlas de la democracia parlamentaria española*. Madrid: Ediciones Foca.

Mesa, Adela, and Novo, Ainoa (2000). "The Political-administrative Elite at Regional Level: The Case of the Autonomous Communities in Spain", unpublished manuscript, presented at the World Congress of the International Political Science Association (IPSA), Quebec.

Montabes, Juan, and Ortega, Carmen (1999). "Candidate Selection in Two Rigid List Systems: Spain and Portugal", unpublished manuscript, presented at the ECPR Joint Sessions, Mannheim.

Morán, María Luz (1989). "Un intento de análisis de la 'clase parlamentaria' española: elementos de renovación y de permanencia (1977–1986)". *Revista Española de Investigaciones Sociológicas*, 45: 61–84.

—— (1996). *Renewal and Permanency of the Spanish Members of Parliament (1977–1993): Reflections on the Institutionalization of the Spanish Parliament.* Estudio/Working Paper 1996/81, Fundación March, Madrid.

—— (1999). "Spanien: Übergang zur Demokratie und politische Professionalisierung", in J. Borchert (ed.), *Politik als Beruf.* Opladen: Leske + Budrich, pp. 439–55.

Morata, Francesc (1992). "Institucionalización y rendimiento político del estado autonómico: Un estudio comparado Andalucía, Cataluña, Galicia y Comunidad Valenciana". *Revista de Estudios Políticos (Nueva Época)*, 76: 255–97.

Nohlen, Dieter, and Huneeus, Carlos (1984). "Elitenwettbewerb in der Spätphase des Franco-Regimes: Der Kampf um die politische Reform", in P. Waldmann and W. L. Bernecker (ed.), *Sozialer Wandel und Herrschaft im Spanien Francos.* Paderborn: Schöningh, pp. 349–69.

Oñate, Pablo (2000*a*). "La organización del Congreso de los Diputados", in A. Martínez (ed.), *El Congreso de los Diputados en España.* Madrid: Tecnos, pp. 69–94.

—— (2000*b*): "Congreso, grupos parlamentarios y partidos", in A. Martínez (ed.), *El Congreso de los Diputados en España.* Madrid: Tecnos, pp. 95–139.

Paniagua Soto, Juan L. (1997). "Spain: A Fledgling Parliament 1977–1997". *Parliamentary Affairs*, 50: 410–22.

Sallès Bonastre, Anna (1995). "El sistema parlamentario durante la Segunda República". *Hispania*, 55/1: 99–124.

Stolz, Klaus (1999). "Political Careers in Newly Established Regional Parliaments: Scotland and Catalonia", unpublished manuscript, presented at the Annual meeting of the American Political Science Association, Atlanta.

19

Sweden: Between Participation Ideal and Professionalism

MAGNUS HAGEVI

POLITICAL PROFESSIONALIZATION IN HISTORICAL PERSPECTIVE

To a considerable extent, Swedish representative democracy is affected by the same participation ideal that John Stuart Mill favored in "On Representative Government" (1861). Mill argued that all citizens ought to be appointed to a public office at least once in a lifetime. That would increase the ability of the individuals not only to be responsible for themselves, but also to consider other citizens and the whole of society. Mill also held that political participation will make it possible for all opinions and different interests to be represented and heard. According to Mill, that was important because if the holders of an opinion failed to participate in politics, that opinion would not be accommodated when the decisions were made.

This participation ideal has affected Swedish politics in many ways. High voter turnout has always been an important and rather successfully pursued goal. Using Maurice Duverger's famous concepts, all traditional Swedish parties fall in the categories of mass parties, even the parties with predominantly middle class voters (Duverger 1954; Bäck and Möller 1992). The important level of local government contains a number of public offices which the holder is supposed to take care of during his or her spare time. It is easy to recognize the intention of Mill: all Swedish citizens should have the experience of serving in a public office at least once in a lifetime.

As the modernization of society proceeded, the development of politics put stress on the realization of the participation ideal. In the complex modern society, different tasks and occupations have been more and more specialized. As complexity increased, politics, too, ought to be affected by specialization. For example, the public sphere has increased its domain since the democratic breakthrough around the 1920s. This means that the politicians of the late twentieth century need to control more government operations compared to their early twentieth century colleagues.

I would like to thank Anna Karlsson and Ylva Norén Bretzer, both Göteborg University, for their comments.

The extensive and heterogeneous activities in the politically controlled sector of today makes it probably more difficult for the individual citizen to hold a public office during his or her spare time than before. Presumably, this means that politics becomes specialized, a task handled by professionals. Just as Max Weber (1946) observed in the early twentieth century, politics has become an occupation.

The professional politician is not at all embraced by the participation ideal. Instead, the opposite seems to be the case. Instead of a relatively high turnover, the professionalization of politics is supposed to result in long-term careers and low rotation of public officeholders. More professional politicians probably also mean that fewer citizens will have a chance to become public officeholders. Instead of a mass participatory engagement in public affairs drawn from all segments in society, these tasks are presumably delegated to a growing group of political professionals. As mass participation declines, recruitment to the political occupations is concentrated to elite segments of society, largely excluding the working-class.

Even though Weber described the rise of professional politicians more than 80 years ago, and professional politicians hardly are a new phenomenon, there is no comprehensive study of a political class in Sweden. We do not know in what way the professionalization of politics has affected representative democracy in Sweden. What is the effect of professional politicians on the participation ideal? Is it possible to identify a political class in Sweden? To what degree are the preconditions for a political class— that is, a reliable source of income, mechanisms of career maintenance, and opportunities for career advancement (see Chapter 1, this volume)—established in Sweden?

Politics had not always been professionalized in the Parliament. When the Swedish Parliament—the *Riksdag*—reformed from the old four estates to a bicameral structure in 1867, the members of the aristocratic first chamber had no salary. Only the members of the farmer-dominated second chamber enjoyed an annual remuneration. Not until 1909 were the members of the first chamber granted the same benefits. However, the amount of the remuneration from 1867—1,200 Swedish crowns (SEK)—remained at the same level for several years, which reduced the value of the reform because of inflation.

The *Riksdag* acknowledged this during the democratic breakthrough in 1918. At the same time, it also recognized that the enlarged franchise meant that new social classes had gained entrance to the Parliament. This meant that not all citizens could afford a public office, even if they were eligible. Accordingly, the *Riksdag* held that the amount of the salary must take into regard the many members who lose their ordinary salary during the parliamentary sessions (Committee on the Constitution 1918). This decision meant that an individual could be fully employed as a *Riksdag* member, at least during the parliamentary sessions. In the same *Riksdag* session, the local and regional councils were granted the authority to distribute remunerations among its members. Since these decisions, Parliament has adjusted the fee of its members to the rising cost of living, but also added compensations for other expenses.

In the years after 1945, three important steps toward more professional politicians in the *Riksdag* were taken: the salaries were raised, the sessions (which is the only period that the representatives were paid) got longer and now cover most of the year, and the first special pension system for retired *Riksdag* members was introduced. In the late 1960s, some major events occurred which affected political professionalization. On the local level, several amalgamations of municipalities took place and the services provided by local authorities were expanding. This resulted in the creation of full-time municipal mayors, supported by non-political civil servants (Strömberg and Westerståhl 1984). On the national level, the number of the political staff supporting the government expanded since the mid 1970s. The *Riksdag* also started to hire civil servants during the 1960s. From 1970 until now, their number has doubled. During the 1970s, the *Riksdag* was established as a fully professionalized place of work with both professional politicians and a professional staff (Ahlbäck 1994).

Among researchers, the existence of a Swedish political class is a question of disagreement. In a comparative study of local politicians in Sweden, the Netherlands, and the United States of America, the authors concluded that the Swedish local politicians are the most closed group of the three countries in the study (Eldersvel, Strömberg, and Derksen 1995). Others state that the turnover of politicians on the local level is very low (Petersson *et al.* 1997). Two journalists have come to similar conclusions in several investigations of ministers and the political staff in the Swedish government. Their inference is that a political class exists in Sweden (Isaksson 1986; Isaksson and Jonsson 1992, 1996).

It is not uncommon that political scientists are less drastic in their conclusions compared to conclusions drawn by journalists. They emphasize that the social representativeness of Swedish politicians is fairly good, at least by international comparison (Esaiasson and Holmberg 1996; Petersson *et al.* 1997). Almost every second politician is a woman, and the social background does not seem to be so important. Yet professional politicians do diverge from normal citizens: as in many other countries, they have a higher level of education, more prestigious occupations, a higher income and other things that are associated with a social elite. It is also notable that few are immigrants and that about two-thirds of the politicians—regardless if on the local, regional, or national level—are between 46 and 65 years old. And indeed, a substantial indication of a political class is found in every study of professional politicians: local, regional, and national politicians are more similar to each other than to the voters (Peterson *et al.* 1997).

In a report about the state of Swedish democracy, the authors find that a political career in Sweden demands a long faithful and often professional service in order to be successful. And Swedish politicians occupy their positions a fairly long time. The conclusion is that the gate to Swedish politics is rather wide, but the corridor is long. The authors think that the situation in the United States is the opposite of the Swedish circumstances. In the United States of America the gate is small, but the corridor is short. A sane Swede without political experience would not say: "I think I'll run for mayor next year." But it would also be peculiar if an American working-class woman with little education made the same declaration (Petersson *et al.* 1997).

THE INSTITUTIONAL CONTEXT

Sweden has been a stable democracy since the 1920s. Today, the population of the country is about 9 million. Politically, Sweden is a unitary state with a parliamentary system. "Swedish democracy is founded on the free formation of opinion and on universal and equal suffrage. It shall be realized through a representative and parliamentary polity and through local self-government." (The Swedish Instrument of Government, part of the first paragraph.) In order to correspond to this situation the old bicameral *Riksdag* was reformed to an unicameral one in 1970 (together with other important constitutional changes). The main reason for the introduction of unicameralism was that the will of the people should affect the composition of the *Riksdag* and the government without any interference from an extra chamber, as was the case in the old bicameral system.

On the national level, another important institution besides the *Riksdag* employs politicians: the government. According to the Instrument of Government (the main law of the constitution), the government is responsible to the *Riksdag*. It is the Parliament which decides who will be Prime Minister and forms the government. But as in most parliamentary systems, the institution with the most influence in reality is the government. Yet the modern *Riksdag* is quite a strong and working parliament with the ambition to be powerful, and the tendency is that it becomes more and more successful in its effort to influence politics (Sannerstedt 1992; Sjölin 1993; Hagevi 1998).

Despite Sweden's non-federal structure, some of the administration is decentralized to the 289 municipal councils and 20 county councils. This means that Swedish politics is structured in three levels: local (municipalities), county, and national. General elections are held at all three levels at one and the same time every fourth year (between 1970 and 1994 every third year). The mandates are distributed between parties in order to achieve proportional representation. Since Sweden became a member of the European Union (EU) in 1995, the country's share of public offices in the EU can be added as an European level.

It is important to note the significance of local and county politics in Sweden, especially concerning social welfare. The local municipalities and the counties have the right to extract income tax from their citizens. The amount depends on the municipality and county you live in, but on average it is about 31 percent. In the municipalities, the tax will finance primary and secondary schools, measures for improving the environment, childcare, social care, care for the elderly, culture and recreation, and the local infrastructure among many other things. The county councils are most concerned with health care. Municipal councils also have a limited right to make local regulations.

Before we go any further, the importance of political parties must be stressed. To some extent, it is possible to make a professional political career within a party organization, without being submitted to a public election. This possibility is greater in large parties, but it is also important in other party organizations. Traditionally,

356   *Hagevi*

the Swedish party system is a good representative of the so called "Scandinavian five-party model" (see Chapter 16, this volume). Between the democratic breakthrough and the late 1980s, there have been five parties in the Swedish *Riksdag* (with some temporary splinter parties during the 1920s). Since 1988, however, new parties have managed to gather enough votes to cross the 4 percent threshold that is required to be represented in the Parliament. Since 1991, seven parties have been represented in the *Riksdag*. In Table 19.1 the number of *Riksdag* mandates each party has won in the elections during the unicameral period is depicted.

Looking at the table, we find that the electoral volatility of the parties, and hence electoral turnover has increased during the 1990s. The main reason is the breakdown of the traditional five-party system. It is more usual now that new parties enter the *Riksdag* than ever before during the democratic era. This will probably result in a growing turnover among individual MPs: members lose their seat to members of new parties.

The power to decide who will occupy the *Riksdag* seats of the party is in the hands of the regional party organizations in each of the twenty-nine constituencies. They decide which candidates are facing the voters during the general election. Because the procedure is an internal party affair, it varies between different parties and constituencies. Lately, the power of the regional party organizations has diminished. Since the *Riksdag* elections of 1998, the voters have the possibility to change the preferential order on the list of candidates on the ballot. However, this system seldom

Table 19.1   *Distribution of seats in the Swedish* Riksdag, *1970–2002*

Party	Year of election										
	1970	1973	1976	1979	1982	1985	1988	1991	1994	1998	2002
Left Party	17	19	17	20	20	19	21	16	22	43	30
Greens	—	—	—	—	—	—	20	—	18	16	17
Social Democrats	163	156	152	154	166	159	156	138	161	131	144
Center Party	71	90	86	64	56	44	42	31	27	18	22
Liberals	58	34	39	38	21	51	44	33	26	17	48
Christian Democrats	—	—	—	—	—	—	—	26	15	42	33
Moderates (Conservativ.)	41	51	55	73	86	76	66	80	80	82	55
New Democracy	—	—	—	—	—	—	—	25	—	—	—
Total	350	350	349	349	349	349	349	349	349	349	349

Note: Swedish party names. Center Party—*Centerpartiet*; Christian Democrats—*Kristdemokraterna* (before 1994 *Kristdemokratiska samhällspartiet, kds*); Greens—*Miljöpartiet de gröna*; Liberals—*Folkpartiet liberalerna*; Moderates—*Moderata samlingspartiet*; New Democracy—*Ny demokrati*; Social Democrats—*Sveriges socialdemokratiska arbetareparti*; Left Party—*Vänsterpartiet* (before 1994 *Vänsterpartiet kommunisterna, vpk*).

changes the original order as decided by the regional party organizations. In the election of 1998, only 14 of 349 members were elected due to the new system of personal vote. Nevertheless, the existence of a voter influence on the order of the candidate list is a step away from party influence towards a more direct appeal from the politicians to the voters.

In the *Riksdag*, party cohesion is very strong; according to Rice's index of cohesion it is 98 percent. Public policies are formulated within the parties. To a considerable extent, the right to formulate party policies has moved from the party organization to the parliamentary party or the government ministries (when the party controls them). The extra-parliamentary party organizations tends to adjust their political positions to the decisions made by professional politicians on the national level (Albinsson 1986; Pierre 1986; Hagevi 1997; Teorell 1998).

One reason for the diminishing importance of the extra-parliamentary party is that professional politicians are less dependent on support from the dues-paying members of the party. Instead, both the extra-parliamentary party organizations and the parliamentary party groups are given large subsidiaries from the national state budget. Therefore, it seems that the traditional Swedish mass party has been transformed into a version of a cartel party (Katz and Mair 1995; Hagevi and Jahn 1999). The cartel parties are strongly linked to the state. According to the concept of cartel party, the political parties have a common interest in the state subsidies which finance all parties, disregarding who is in government. The system makes it possible for all the parties to survive, and to secure these benefits they form a cartel and collaborate with parties they normally compete with.

Large state subsidies probably result in a lower value given to party membership by ordinary citizens, at the same time as professional politicians perceive the party members as less important than before. Furthermore, the citizens, maybe, perceive the party members' lack of influence on professional politicians. If this is so, it seems more rational for ordinary citizens to seek more effective and less costly alternatives to achieve political influence than joining a party (Petersson *et al.* 1998).

If party membership is reduced in value, the number of party members ought to decline over time. Figure 19.1 shows the percentage of the Swedish voters who are party members from 1960 to 2001. As can be seen, the share of party members has declined since 1982. A huge drop occurred when the Social Democrats abolished the collective membership affiliation with the labor unions in 1991, but also if the collective membership is disregarded, the share of party membership among the electorate has declined. This supports the notion that party membership in general is regarded as less valuable among Swedish citizens. In turn this is in line with the hypothesis that the political parties of Sweden are transforming into cartel parties.

The growing rift between professional politicians and other citizens, which is indicated by the decrease in the number of party members, could affect the citizens' trust in their political representatives. If the citizens feel that the politicians are a remote group, alienated from society at large, the mistrust of politicians ought to increase. We can study the change in mistrust of politicians by analyzing the attitudes with regard to a statement that repeatedly has been mentioned in the Swedish election studies since 1968: "Those who make decisions in the *Riksdag* do not take any notice of ordinary people's point of view" (see Fig. 19.2).

A growing mistrust among the citizens is a challenge to the Swedish political system. During the last 30 years, the percentage of respondents who agree to distrust the intentions of the *Riksdag* Members has increased from 46 to 75 percent. There is no sign of reversal of this development. Thus, we may infer a growing division between ordinary citizens and the political representatives, which puts the political system under stress.

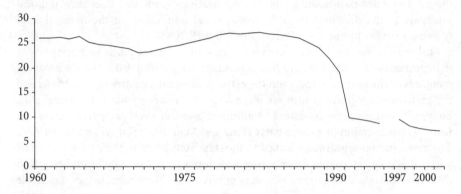

Figure 19.1   *Party members in Sweden, 1960–2001 (% of electorate)*

Source: Widfeldt (1997: 102). The data for 1997–2001 is from yearly surveys conducted by the SOM Institute, Göteborg University (see Holmberg and Weibull 2001 for details).

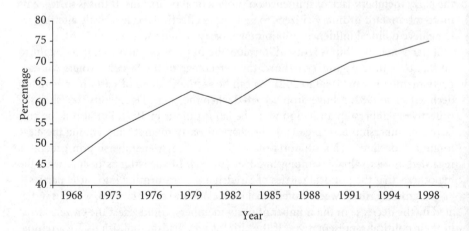

Figure 19.2   *Mistrust of* Riksdag *members, 1968–98 (%)*

Note: Percentage who very much agree or agree with the statement cited above.

Source: Holmberg (2000: 34).

Political parties and representative bodies are not the only important organizations in Swedish politics. Strong interest organizations have an equally long tradition as parliamentary democracy and have had a great impact on political decisions. The involvement of interest organizations in state affairs has been so forceful that the Swedish model has been labeled as corporatism, even though it is not as corporatist as for example the Austrian system. The strongest interest organizations are the Swedish Employers' Confederation and the Swedish Trade Union Confederation, and also to some extent the Swedish Confederation of Professional Employees. The rate of unionization in the employees' organizations is over 80 percent. During the 1990s, the Swedish Employers' Confederation began to doubt that their participation in the corporatist system benefited the employers. They decided to leave all corporatist bodies, and thus, terminate the corporatist system. Today, political science publications announce "the fall of corporatism" or ask "what happened to Swedish corporatism?" (Lewin 1992; Hermansson, Svensson, and Öberg 1997; Rothstein and Bergström 1999). The difference between the state arena and the interest organizations is more distinct than before, but the interest organizations are still important agents in Swedish politics.

THE POLITICAL CLASS

Size and Composition

The elected professionals of Sweden can be found on four different political levels: local (municipalities), county, national (the *Riksdag* and the government), and the European level (EU). To this we can add the staff members within party organizations, the parliamentary party groups, and the government ministries. Let us say that these groups constitute professional politics in Sweden. Estimates of the number of professional politicians in Sweden count about 2,500 fully employed individuals (SOU 1991: 80; DS 1994: 31; Isaksson and Jonsson 1996; Petersson *et al.* 1997; Hagevi 2000). Here, the professional politicians in the municipalities, the government, and especially in the *Riksdag* will be analyzed.

Most Swedish politicians are not professionals. They are citizens with an "ordinary" job, reserving some of their spare time for political duties. This is part of the participation ideal of Swedish representative democracy. To enable such participation, there are numerous non-professional public offices on the local and county level. In the course of the modernization of politics, these political assignments may be threatened. In a professionalized polity, full-time politicians and administrative experts take over what before was done by "laymen politicians." If so, the number of public offices on the county and local levels could be expected to decline. Accordingly, professional politicians would be more common on these levels. On the county level, we do not know the number of public offices, but on the local level they have been counted several times.

The number of public offices on the local level has diminished, and professional politicians are more common than ever before. In 1971, a municipal reform was implemented which reduced the number of municipalities from 464 to 274 (Strömberg and Westerståhl 1984). Before this reform the number of offices on the local level was over 187,000, but after the reform the number was reduced to less than 75,000 (Strömberg and Westerståhl 1984). In the last 10 years the local level has experienced a new wave of streamlining. Since 1989 the number of political offices on the local level has decreased from 83,000 to 68,000 assignments in 1999. In this year, 40 percent of the officeholders were women. About 44,500 local politicians held at least one public office on the local level in 1999 (Hagevi 2000).

In 1954 only fifteen municipalities employed full-time politicians, in 1974 about 200 did, and in 1999 out of a total of 289 municipalities 279 had at least one fully employed politician. Of those fully employed politicians on the local level 28 percent were women (Hagevi 2000). It seems like Swedish local politics is more professionalized than ever before, and this development has occurred at the expense of the participation ideal. We can relate this development to the number of party members and the political distrust among citizens. Fewer party members, fewer laymen politicians and an increased number of professional politicians correlate with a growing distrust in politicians among citizens.

Let us turn to professional politicians in Sweden on the national level. The participation ideal has never had a stronghold on this level. Yet, until the 1960s, the number of politically employed government staff members was hardly more than one or two at a time. All other employees were civil servants. This changed in 1966, when the government ministries started to employ a dozen political press secretaries. The next milestone was in 1976, when the first non-Social Democratic government in over 30 years employed so called political experts. Today, about 150 professional politicians are working in the government, including about 20–22 ministers and 20–22 state secretaries. About half of them are women, almost all have studied at the university level (89 percent), and 52 percent were professional politicians prior to their current office (Larsson 1990: 210–12; Isaksson and Jonsson 1992: 6, 10–11).

On the national level, most professional politicians are found in the *Riksdag*. Let us take a closer look at them: what kind of people are working in politics? If a large part of the polity is professionalized, a greater share of the parliamentarians should have a prior career as professional politicians, before they are elected to the *Riksdag*. A related question is what other occupational groups are replaced by the emerging political profession. Figure 19.3 presents the share of professional politicians in the *Riksdag*, together with the share of white-collar and blue-collar workers and farmers between 1906 and 1994.

As suspected, the share of professional politicians has increased over the years. The farmers paid the costs for the advancement of the professionals in Swedish politics. However, the farmers' shrinking representation in the *Riksdag* corresponds with similar changes in society at large. What is more interesting is that the democratic breakthrough around the year 1920 hardly had any lasting effect on the biased recruitment of many white-collar and few blue-collar professionals. An initial increase of blue-collar workers ended in 1933, when the first generation of democratically elected workers retired. From this date on, professional politicians also replaced the

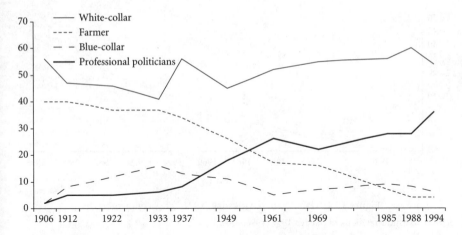

Figure 19.3 *Professional background of Swedish MPs, 1906–94 (% of members)*

Note: Between 1906 and 1969, the results refer to the second chamber of the *Riksdag*. For the years 1985–94, the results refer to the occupation the MPs had when first entering Parliament. For previous years, the members' profession is their last occupation.

Source: Data for 1906–88: Esaiasson and Holmberg (1996: 27). Sköld and Halvarson (1966) have originally collected the data of the years between 1906 and 1961. The 1994 data is collected from *Fakta om folkvalda 1994–1998* (1995).

Members of Parliament (MPs) with a blue-collar background. The share of blue-collar members is about the same now as during the pre-democratic period.

The significant pre-parliamentary experience of professional politics is also an indication that politics has become a lifetime career. Long political careers do not promote the participation ideal; and it seems to be a growing advantage to be a professional politician if you want to be a *Riksdag* member.

An important constitutional reform that made the democratic system effective was the women's right of suffrage and eligibility. The first women were elected to the *Riksdag* in 1921, and slowly the number of female members has grown. After the election of 2002, there are 45 percent women in the Parliament (see Fig. 19.4). This means that the Swedish *Riksdag* has the highest share of female parliamentarians in the world. It is notable that this tendency is corresponding to the participation ideal: opinions of all segments of society must be represented in order to be heard in political decision-making.

Compared to the voters, the MPs have always been highly educated. Yet not until the late 1980s had a majority of them a university education. During the last 25 years, the number of university-educated MPs has grown sharply, from 25 to 65 percent (Hagevi 1998). Regarding the level of education, there are great differences between the parties. Most MPs of the Moderates, Liberals, Greens, and the Left Party have studied at an university, but only about half of the members of the Social Democrats and the Center Party have the same experience (Esaiasson and Holmberg 1996).

In Sweden, there are no laws about term limits or similar regulations. Yet, there are strong informal norms stating that a person who is about 65 years old ought to retire

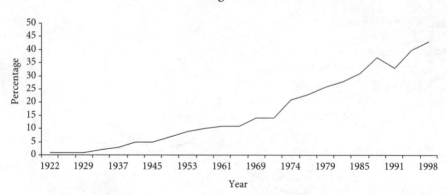

Figure 19.4 *Women in the* Riksdag, *1922–98 (% of members)*
Source: Statistical Yearbook of Sweden 1999 (1998: 424).

and not run for reelection. Before the election of 1998, no MP was older than 65 years. This custom was criticized intensively by senior citizens' organizations. Some parties responded to the demand and nominated older persons for the *Riksdag*. After the election of 1998, about 10 of the 349 Members are older than 65 years. Another demand— made in several election campaigns—was to increase the number of women. This requirement resulted in more women elected to the *Riksdag* (see earlier). However, the female freshmen were relatively young. This and the young age of many MPs from the new parties (especially the Greens) contributed to a lower mean age.

Political Recruitment and Political Careers

An indication of a political class is the existence of institutionalized career paths. A first thought could be that the career path should lead from the local via the regional to the national level. This suggestion overlooks the existence of several positions with very different status and prestige on each level. A prestigious position on the local level could be higher up on the career ladder than a low prestige assignment on the national level. This is summarized by the statement of Göran Persson—the current Swedish Prime Minister—when he voluntarily left the *Riksdag* to become a mayor in the small municipality of Katrineholm: "It is better to be a big fish in a small pond as Katrineholm than a small fish in a big pond as Stockholm." Accordingly, the Foreign Minister Anna Lindh had left the national Parliament for a position as mayor before entering the government. What is the prestige of different political positions in the Swedish polity? A good indicator for the prestige of political positions is found in a *Riksdag* survey from 1994. The MPs were asked: "What status/prestige do you think the following positions have among the *Riksdag* members in general?" The answers could vary on an eleven-point scale between zero ("very low status/prestige") and ten ("very high status/prestige"). By studying the answers, we will have some information how professional politicians perceive different political positions as part of a career ladder. The result is presented in Table 19.2.

Table 19.2 Riksdag *members' ranking of the status/prestige of political positions, 1994 (mean)*

Rank	Position	Mean of status/prestige	N
1	Minister of the government	9.1	322
2	EU Commissioner	8.9	321
3	Speaker of the *Riksdag*	8.7	321
4	Parliamentary party leader	7.9	321
5	Standing committee chairman of the *Riksdag*	7.4	321
6	Ambassador	7.2	319
7	Member of the European Parliament	7.0	321
8	County governor	6.5	320
9	Director-general of public authority/enterprise	6.3	313
10	Member of national party leadership	5.9	311
11	Municipal mayor	5.9	312
12	UN delegate	5.8	320
13	Member of government political staff	5.2	312
14	Full member of *Riksdag* standing committee	4.3	313

Note: For details about how the survey was conducted, see Esaiasson, Holmberg, and Brothén 1995.

Source: *Riksdag Survey 1994*. Department of Political Science, Göteborg University.

Let us first conclude that professional politicians in Sweden do perceive—and rather unanimously so—that political positions carry different status and prestige, and that these positions form a structure for political careers. It is not so that professional politicians always perceive positions on the national level as being higher than positions on the local level. Yet the seven positions with the highest prestige are all on the national or European levels. Despite this, it is interesting to note that the assignment most MPs occupy—full member of a *Riksdag* committee—is ranked only on fourteenth and last place by themselves. Other positions on the national level that are considered as less prestigious than regional or local positions are membership of the national party leadership or government staff. Note also that those typical retreat offices as ambassador, county governor, or director-general of public authorities/enterprises all have fairly high status. Attractive positions to fall back on simplify matters if the ordinary political career should come to an end. This means that the top professional politicians do not need to go to the extreme to fight for their political survival when it is threatened by electoral defeat, or something equally threatening. He or she knows that there is hope for life after political death.

Still, there are better prospects for a professionalized political career on the national or European than on the regional level, and better chances on the regional than on the local level. According to Table 19.3, the share of professional politicians gets larger as the unit of representation increases. Of the municipal councilors, only a third have a history of politics as a profession. Of the county councilors, six of ten have experience as professional politicians. However, all of the MPs and Member European Parliament (MEPs) are professional politicians.

Table 19.3   *Experience in professional politics, 1997 (%)*

Number of years	Municipal councilors	County councilors	*Riksdag* members	MEPs
None	71	59	0	0
1–10	20	26	54	56
11 and more	8	16	46	44

Note: Numbers do not add up to 100 because of rounding error.
Source: Petersson *et al.* (1997: 110).

Also the time spent as a professional politician increases with a higher level of government. Every twelfth municipal councilor has been a professional politician for more than 10 years. Among the members of the European Parliament, almost half have been professionally involved in politics for more than 10 years (see Table 19.3).

What about job security? To be able to judge how secure a position on the national level is, we can investigate the turnover among MPs. If the turnover is high, one may suspect that the position as a representative is relatively unsafe. It is difficult to judge what constitutes a high or low turnover, but it is possible either to compare levels of turnover between national parliaments or to analyze changes over time. Here, we will focus on changes over time: has the turnover of Swedish parliamentarians decreased or increased? Figure 19.5 displays the turnover as the share of freshmen in the *Riksdag* between 1922 and 1998.

The figure shows that the turnover of MPs has increased during the 1990s. Between 1922 to 1988, the share of freshmen was between 10 and 20 percent.[1] Since 1991, about 30 percent of the members were freshmen. One reason for the increase is the relatively large exchange of voters among the parties during the 1990s (see Table 19.1). Another reason is the successful attempt of party organizations to substitute the male dominated *Riksdag* with a more representative Parliament (see Fig. 19.4). All together, this means that the national Parliament is a less secure place of employment during the 1990s than before.

Connected to the turnover among the *Riksdag* members is their average tenure (see Fig. 19.6). The combination of long political career paths and the previously mentioned norm of retirement is likely to create relatively short time periods of *Riksdag* service. The mean seniority of the MPs shows a clear tendency towards decline. In 1945, the mean seniority was 11.4 years, but in 1994 it was only 6.5 years. Also if we consider the shorter election periods of only 3 years between 1970 and 1994—compared to the otherwise 4-year periods before and after—the *Riksdag* members' ability or ambition to remain in office has decreased.

[1] In 1970, the number of *Riksdag* members was reduced from 384 to 350, later to 349. When this change occurred, more senior members than usual chose to resign voluntarily and the number of freshmen increased. However, already after the next election the number of freshmen was at about the same level as before the reform. This indicates that the reduced number of MPs did not have any great impact on the number of freshmen.

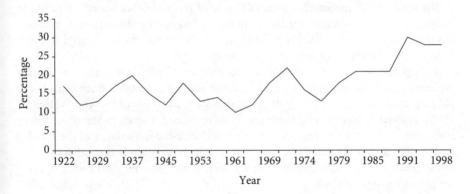

Figure 19.5 *Turnover of Swedish* Riksdag *Members, 1922–98 (% of freshmen)*
Source: For 1922–94: Brothén (1996: 44); for 1998 *Riksdagen i siffror 1998/99* (1999).

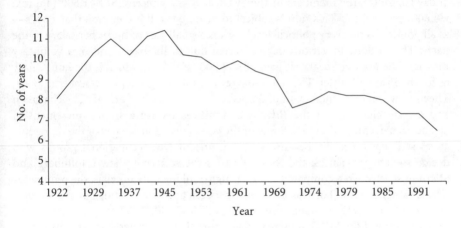

Figure 19.6 *Mean seniority of* Riksdag *Members, 1922–94 (years)*
Source: Brothén (1996: 44).

Local and regional politics is the most important recruitment base of MPs. Almost all of them have some experience in local or regional politics (Petersson *et al.* 1997). More than half of the national parliamentarians have been municipal councilors. Since politics has become more professionalized and specialized than before, it seems to be more difficult to hold positions on both the local/regional and the national level concurrently. In 1994, 16 percent of the MPs, most of them newly elected, also were municipal councilors, while most of the members focused on their parliamentary career.

In Sweden, the *Riksdag* elects the Prime Minister, which could be a reason why the Prime Minister has always been selected from within the Parliament since the democratic breakthrough. Concerning the ministers of the government, it is the Prime Minister alone who appoints them, without any interference from the *Riksdag*. The MPs can remove the already appointed ministers by a vote of no confidence. When addressed to single ministers, a successful vote of no confidence would result in the resignation of the particular minister in question, but not the rest of the government. However, such a vote could also be addressed to the Prime Minister, and if the vote is successful, the whole government must resign.

In opposite to what is the rule in the mother of all parliaments, the British Parliament, it is increasingly common that ministers are recruited from outside the *Riksdag*: in the 1970s, less then half of the ministers, today about two-thirds (Hagevi 1995). Instead, it has become more common to recruit mayors to the government (see above). This could be regarded as a sign of decreasing importance of the *Riksdag* and of the status of its members. An alternative interpretation is that other political units—such as the municipalities—have changed and become valid career options for professional politicians.

Living off Politics

Today (in 2002), the members of the Swedish *Riksdag* receive SEK41,500 (approx. €4,600) per month.[2] This sum is subject to income tax. It is common that a MPs— as all politicians on every political level—gives a small part of his or her salary to the party. This is done to various degrees, according to the party, and in a voluntary manner. The *Riksdag* Speaker is paid SEK97,000 (€10,740), which is the same salary as for the Prime Minister. The economic reward for being a deputy Speaker is lower. They receive an extra increment of 30 percent of the salary of an MP. The chairmen and deputy chairmen of the *Riksdag* committees receive a similar increment of 20 and 15 percent, respectively. Some of the voters may find the pay of the representatives striking, especially because they are one of few occupational groups who decide their own salaries: the *Riksdag* settles the salaries by law (Holmberg and Stjernquist 1998). Yet, compared to other high-ranking state officials, the remuneration is rather modest. For reasons of comparison, an ordinary judge of the Swedish Supreme Court (*Högsta domstolen*) receives SEK65,000 (€7,200) per month. The remuneration of the MPs has increased no more than the general level of the cost of living. In fact, during some periods the remuneration has been lagging behind the increased cost of living.

A travel allowance is granted if an official journey demands an overnight stay at least 50 km from the member's home residence. This allowance is taxable according to the usual rules, and amounts to SEK320 (€35) a day in 2002. In order to meet certain expenses, compensation is paid to the members, such as secretarial help, postal costs, and representation. This compensation amounts to SEK3,600 (€400) a month and is subject to income tax, too.

Since 1947, the *Riksdag* is paying retirement pensions to its former Members. This pension is a complement to the basic pension and the national supplementary pension paid by the state. To receive a retirement pension, the MP must have reached the

---

[2] Conversions from SEK to Euro are based on the exchange rate of 26 November 2002 (SEK1 = €0.11076).

age of 50 and been in the *Riksdag* for at least 6 years. Full pension requires at least 12 years of service. The pension is normally paid from the age of 65. Up to a certain level of income (in 2002 that amount was SEK282,750 a year, that is, around €31,320) the MPs receive their pensions from the same public system as all other citizens. This public pension is complemented by a retirement pension from the *Riksdag* that amounts to 11.5 percent of the pensionable income, and 65 percent of any pensionable income exceeding SEK282,750. The retirement pension is based on the pensionable income made up of an average of the pay during the last 5 years before leaving the *Riksdag*.

The *Riksdag* always guarantees a former member having at least 3 years of continuous service a certain level of monthly income. A life annuity is settled for those who do not become entitled to a retirement pension. Income received from other sources reduces the guaranteed income according to certain rules. A full guaranteed income of 66 percent of the income is payable to members who have served at least 12 years, except for the first year after retirement or reaching the age of 65, when it is 80 percent. For those who have served between 6 and 12 years the guaranteed income is reduced even further after the first year. For those who have served between 3 and 6 years consecutively, the guaranteed income is paid only for the first year. For MPs who have served for 6 years or more the length of time for which the guaranteed income is paid depends on their age. This also means that the need for professional politicians to fight for their political career is reduced.

Since the mid-1960s the dominant source of income for the political parties has been public financial assistance. The state and the *Riksdag* as well as municipal and county councils provide financial assistance to the parties that have gained seats in the various elections. There are special phasing-out rules for parties that lose their seats in the elected assemblies. Currently the contribution from the state and the *Riksdag* amounts to about SEK255 million (€28.2 million) annually (see Table 19.4). There is no public supervision of how the means are used.

Public financial assistance to party organizations (Table 19.4, first row) consists of party and office assistance. Party assistance is paid as a contribution per seat in the *Riksdag*, taking into consideration the election results in the two latest elections. Currently, the party assistance amounts to SEK282,450 (€31,280) per seat. Party assistance is also paid to parties which have not obtained seats, on the condition that they have obtained more than 2.5 percent of the vote cast in either of the two latest elections. Office assistance is paid to all *Riksdag* parties partly as a basic contribution and partly as a supplementary contribution. It is given to each party that has received 4 percent of the votes cast in the latest election to the *Riksdag*. It amounts to about SEK4.93 million (€546,100) per party. The supplementary contribution amounts to SEK13,850 (€1,534) per seat for a government party and SEK20,650 (€2,290) per seat for the opposition parties.

The *Riksdag* financial assistance to parliamentary party groups (Table 19.4, second row) is given by three means. First, contributions to the party secretariats are given partly as a basic support to each party, partly as a compensation for each MP. The basic support (Table 19.4, third row) amounts to SEK3.4 million (€376,600) for

---

Table 19.4 *Financial assistance to the parties, 2002 (millions)*

	Party							
	Left	Greens	Soc. Dem	Center	Liberals	Christ. Dem	Moderates	Total
Party organizations	17.1	9.8	45.1	11.0	10.6	16.5	29.8	140.0
(in €)	(1.9)	(1.1)	(5.0)	(1.2)	(1.2)	(1.8)	(3.3)	(15.5)
Parliamentary party groups	14.9	7.7	36.7	8.2	7.8	14.6	25.2	115.1
(in €)	(1.7)	(0.9)	(4.1)	(0.9)	(0.9)	(1.6)	(2.8)	(12.8)
Basic support	3.4	3.4	1.7	3.4	3.4	3.4	3.4	22.1
Add. support	2.4	0.9	7.5	1.0	1.0	2.4	4.7	19.9
Pol. secretaries	8.9	3.3	27.1	3.7	3.3	8.7	16.8	71.9
Foreign travel	0.2	0.1	0.4	0.1	0.1	0.1	0.3	1.2
Total	32.0	17.5	81.8	19.2	18.5	31.1	55.0	255.1
(in €)	(3.6)	(1.9)	(9.1)	(2.1)	(2.1)	(3.5)	(6.1)	(28.3)

Source: Riksdagen i siffror 2001/02 (2002).

parties in opposition and SEK1.7 million (€188,290) for parties in government. The additional compensation (Table 19.4, fourth row) for each member amounts to SEK57,000 (€6,310). Second, contributions for members' personal assistants are intended to cover cost for secretarial and research assistance (Table 19.4, fifth row). The amount of the contribution is calculated on the basis of one assistant for every two members—SEK34,500 (€3,820) per month including employer contributions. Each member also is reimbursed for some foreign travels (Table 19.4, sixth row). Third, the party groups also receive indirect assistance in the form of free office space and technical equipment in the *Riksdag* building.

Each municipal and county council may give financial assistance and other types of support to political parties, and all municipal and county councils do so. In 1999 the financial assistance from the municipalities amounted to about SEK290 million (€32.1 million), whereas the assistance from the counties amounted to about SEK155 million (€17.2 million). This means that local and regional politicians have considerable financial resources (Gidlund and Koole 2001).

Clearly, the political profession is financed by the public sector. Swedish parties are a good example of cartel parties. Together with the already mentioned retreat positions of high prestige, the rules of retirement form a social security net for formerly successful politicians. Economic conditions as these are the main requirements for the emergence of a political class.

THE POLITICAL CLASS AND INSTITUTIONAL REFORM

Money is only one aspect of an attractive occupation. There are also other aspects that concern the working conditions. The worker must feel some job satisfaction.

This could be the case if the work has a purpose, a meaning. In politics, one purpose is probably access to power. Let us investigate if the MPs increased their quality of work by securing a greater access to power. This could be attained by creating a more powerful Parliament and construct institutions that decentralize influence to individual members.

It is a common view among parliamentary researchers that the power of the Swedish *Riksdag* has increased at least in relation to the government (Arter 1990; Sannerstedt 1992; Sjölin 1993; Hagevi 1998). Between 1945 and 1970, the government mostly controlled the political decision-making alone, sometimes involving negotiations between the government and other extra-parliamentary actors. Mostly, the *Riksdag* and its members had to accept these deals as they were presented to them.

During the 1970s, the importance of Parliament expanded. One reason for this is a weaker position of the government in the *Riksdag*. Minority governments have always been common, but during the 1980s it was more difficult than before for the government to get support from the friendlier part of the opposition in Parliament. At the same time, committee work has become increasingly important. The difficulties of majority-building are forcing the government party in the *Riksdag* to negotiate with the opposition. These negotiations are mostly held among the standing committee members that consider the government proposal in question. The committee members are negotiating in the name of their own parties. This work of bargaining has made the assignments of the MPs more interesting.

To this, we can add the creation of a more potent Parliament. The old bicameral *Riksdag* was replaced with a new unicameral one together with the new committee system in 1971. The new committee system—which still is mostly intact—has sixteen committees mainly corresponding to the government ministries and specialized according to subject-matter. Almost every committee (except one) handles both statutes and appropriations. For the individual member, the committee assignment is important for the specialization of parliamentary work. The party groups of the *Riksdag* have organized their internal work so that the members' influence is greater now than before. In each party, small groups of parliamentarians formulate the party line within the policy area of their committee. This means that the MP of today has a relatively great influence on the official policy of the party within the jurisdiction of his or her committee. This also means that the quality of parliamentary work is more significant than before.

If committee assignments are important for the work of MPs, it is rational that they should try to increase the access to those assignments. In 1971, the number of MPs decreased from 384 to 350. Since 1976, the number of seats is 349. At the same time, the number of internal assignments increased. For example, the number of committee seats increased from 192 in 1969 to 272 in 1994. In a longer time perspective this change is even greater: There were ninety-six committee seats in the beginning of the bicameral *Riksdag* in 1867 (Hagevi 1998).

The trend to more committee seats is international (Westefield 1974; Gertzog 1976; Sinclair 1989; Hibbing 1991). One cause is probably members' demand of good committee assignments. Both the tendency of fewer amateur politicians and more professional politicians on the local level (see above) and the demand for better assignments among MPs indicate that professional politicians want to have an occupation with more satisfying qualities. In this case it means more influence to professional politicians and less influence to laymen politicians or to members of the extra-parliamentary party organization, but also less power for the government.

We can notice that the development of professional politics results in different tendencies on the local and the national level. On the local level, increased professionalization has the effect that more power is accumulated by fewer people—the professional politicians. However, in the fully professionalized environment of the national level the same development results in a decentralization of power: from the government to the larger body—the *Riksdag*.

CONCLUSION

There is a strong tendency towards political professionalization in Sweden, together with several signs of a possible political class. Among Swedish politicians, quite a few are professionals with a considerable income. It is also possible to track a professional career. Career positions differ with regard to status and to level of government: local, regional, national, and European. On each level, there are positions of high prestige that are attractive to most politicians on any of the other levels. About 40 percent of the freshmen in the Swedish Parliament are already professional politicians before they are elected. We also find a safety-net for politicians who lost their mandate in the form of retirement pensions and non-elective positions with high status.

Looking at the Swedish MPs as a group, they are clearly recruited from social groups with a higher status now than 30 years ago as indicated by a higher level of education. Compared to ordinary citizens, RMs may have a rather high income, but if we compare it to other high status positions such as a judge of the Swedish Supreme Court, the parliamentarians turn out not to be paid so well. Clearly, Swedish politicians are not among the highest paid in world.

Not all signs of a political class are possible to detect. There is no hard evidence of a real class interest among professional politicians. This could be a lack of measurement resources, but also an indication of a weakly developed political class in Sweden. Yet the professional politicians seem to have created an occupation with more satisfying qualities: they have created political institutions that grant the majority of them more influence and a safer career. Nevertheless, it is doubtful if all signs of a political class are visible.

With regard to the participation ideal—that all citizens ought to serve in a public office at least once in a lifetime—the professionalization of politics has had a negative impact. As politicians became more professionalized, the participation of citizens in public offices or as party members has declined. Simultaneously, we notice negative effects on the trust in politicians. Citizen distrust in politicians is growing, indicating an increasing division between the representatives and the represented. A possible causal relationship is that reduced citizen participation as party members and laymen politicians result in less communication between citizens and politicians.

This could create alienation from and a distrust in politicians among the citizens. Looking at the future, it seems likely that the ongoing professionalization of politics will result in the demise of the participation ideal.

Is the political establishment at all accountable to the reactions among the citizens regarding political professionalization? Could they—if they wanted to—go on to pursue only their own career? Or do they perceive demands for political renewal from the voters? To some extent, the parties are sensitive to what they perceive as demands from voters to renew the political personnel. It seems like the voters are sending a sign to the political managers that they want new blood in the business. Old parties had tried to adapt to the perceived demands and to present both more women and more younger politicians. Despite these efforts, the voters are switching parties between elections more often than before. Many of the voters support new, rather unestablished parties. Both the efforts of old parties and the success of new parties result in a higher turnover and a lower mean age of representatives in Sweden. Thus, voter reaction can hinder the unrestrained development of a political class pursuing only its self-interest.

REFERENCES

Ahlbäck, Shirin (1994). "Riksdagen—politikermakt eller tjänstemann-avälde?". *Statsvetenskaplig Tidskrift*, 97: 113–39.
Albinsson, Per (1986). *Skiftningar i blått. Förändringar i Moderata Samlingspartiets Riksorganisation 1960–1985*. Lund: Kommunfakta förlag.
Arter, David (1990). "The Swedish Riksdag: The Case of a Strong Policy-Influencing Assembly". *West European Politics*, 13: 120–42.
Brothén, Martin (1996). "Anciennitetsprincipen i Sveriges riksdag". *Statsvetenskaplig Tidskrift*, 98: 37–52.
Bäck, Mats, and Möller, Tommy (1992). *Partier och organisationer*, 2nd edition. Stockholm: Publica. Committee on the Constitution (Konstitutionsutskottet) (1918). *C 20, 5: 7*. Stockholm: Sveriges Riksdag.
DS (Departementserien) (1994). *Det offentliga stödet till partierna. Inriktning och omfattning*. Stockholm: Fritzes.
Duverger, Maurice (1954). *Political Parties*. London: Methuen.
Eldersveld, Samuel J., Strömberg, Lars, and Derksen, Wim (1995). *Local Elites in Western Democracies: A Comparative Analysis of Urban Political Leaders in the U.S., Sweden, and the Netherlands*. Boulder: Westview Press.
Esaiasson, Peter, and Holmberg, Sören (1996). *Representation from Above: Members of Parliament and Representative Democracy in Sweden*. Aldershot: Dartmouth.
—— and Brothén, Martin (1995). "Riksdagsenkät 1994", documentation paper, Göteborg: Department of Political Science, Göteborg University.
Fakta om folkvalda Riksdagen 1994–1998 (1995). Stockholm: Riksdagens förvaltningskontor.
Gertzog, Irwin N. (1976). "The Routinization of Committee Assignments in the U.S. House of Representatives", *American Journal of Political Science*, 20: 693–712.
Gidlund, Gullan, and Koole, Ruud (2001). "Political Finance in the North of Europe: The Netherlands and Sweden", in Karl-Heinz Nassmacher (ed.), *Foundations for Democracy*. Baden-Baden: Nomos.

Hagevi, Magnus (1997). "Liberal säkerhetspolitik: Från samförstånd till profilering". *Frisinnad Tidskrift*, 6/7: 152–6.

—— (1998). *Bakom riksdagens fasad.* Göteborg: Akademiförlaget Corona.

—— (2000). "Professionalisering och deltagande i den lokala representativa demokratin: En analys av kommunala förtroendeuppdrag 1999", *Cefos rapport*, 13: Göteborg Center For Public Sector Research (Cefos), Göteborg University.

—— and Jahn, Detlef (1999). "Parteien und Fraktionen in Schweden: Entwicklungen zur Kartellpartei", in Ludger Helms (ed.), *Parteien und Fraktionen.* Opladen: Leske + Budrich, pp. 145–69.

Hermansson, Jörgen, Svensson, Torsten, and Öberg, PerOla (1997). "Vad blev det av den svenska korporativismen?". *Politica*, 29: 365–84.

Hibbing, John R. (1991). *Congressional Careers: Contours of Life in the U.S. House of Representatives.* Chapel Hill: University of North Carolina Press.

Holmberg, Erik, and Stjernquist, Nils (1998). *Vår författning*, 11th edition. Stockholm: Norstedts juridik.

Holmberg, Sören (2000). *Välja parti.* Stockholm: Norstedts juridik.

—— and Weibull, Lennart (eds) (2001). *Land, Du välsignade.* SOM-rapport: 26, Göteborg: SOM Institute, Göteborg University.

Isaksson, Anders (1986). "Den politiska klassen". *Veckans affärer*, 48: 54–65.

—— and Jonsson, Anders (1992). "Den borgerliga makteliten". *Dagens industri*, 1 July 1992: 6–11.

—— (1996). "Di granskar den politiska eliten". *Dagens industri*, 28 October 1996: 16–21.

Katz, Richard, and Mair, Peter (1995). "Changing Models of Party Organization and Party Democracy: The Emergence of the Cartel Party". *Party Politics*, 1: 5–28.

Larsson, Ulf (1990). "Människorna i kanslihuset", in *Departementshistoriekommittén. Att styra riket. Regeringskansliet 1840–1990.* Stockholm: Almänna Förlaget, pp. 190–221.

Lewin, Leif (1992). *Samhället och de organiserade intresserna.* Stockholm: Norstedts.

Mill, John Stuart (1992 [1861]). "Considerations On Representative Government", in J. S. Mill, *On Liberty And Other Essays.* Oxford: Oxford University Press, pp. 202–467.

Petersson, Olof, Hermansson, Jörgen, Micheletti, Michele, and Westholm, Anders (1997). *Demokratirådets rapport 1997: Demokrati och ledarskap.* Stockholm: SNS förlag.

——,Teorell, Jan, and Westholm, Anders (1998). *Demokratirådets rapport 1998: Demokrati och medborgarskap.* Stockholm: SNS förlag.

Pierre, Jon (1986). *Partikongresser och regeringspolitik: En studie om socialdemokratiska partikongressens beslutsfattande och inflytande 1948–1978.* Lund: Kommunfakta förlag.

Riksdagen i siffror 1998/99 (1999). Stockholm: Riksdagens förvaltningskontor.

Riksdagen i siffror 2001/02 (2002). Stockholm: Riksdagens förvaltningskontor.

Rothstein, Bo, and Bergström, Jonas (1999). *Korporatismens fall och den svenska modellens kris.* Stockholm: SNS förlag.

Sannerstedt, Anders (1992). *Förhandlingar i riksdagen.* Lund: Lund University Press.

Sinclair, Barbara (1989). *The Transformation of the U.S. Senate.* Baltimore: Johns Hopkins University Press.

Sjölin, Mats (1993). *Coalition Politics and Parliamentary Power.* Lund: Lund University Press.

Sköld, Lars, and Halvarson, Arne (1966). "Riksdagens sociala sammansättning under hundra år", *Samhälle och riksdag.* 1: Stockholm, Almqvist & Wiksell, pp. 375–493.

SOU (Statens offentliga utredningar) (1991). *Kommunalt partistöd. Betänkande av partistödsutredningen.* 80: Stockholm, Allmänna Förlaget.

Statistical Yearbook of Sweden 1999 (1998). Örebro: SCB.

Strömberg, Lars, and Westerståhl, Jörgen (1984). *The New Swedish Communes: A Summary of Local Government Research.* Stockholm: Liber.

Teorell, Jan (1998). *Demokrati eller fåtalsvälde? Om beslutsfattande i partiorganisationer.* Uppsala: Acta Universitatis Upsaliensis.

Weber, Max (1946 [1918]). "Politics as Vocation", in C. W. Mills and H. Gerth (eds), *From Max Weber: Essays in Sociology.* Oxford: Oxford University Press, pp. 77–128.

Westefield, Louis P. (1974). "Majority Party Leadership and Committee System in the House of Representatives". *American Political Science Review,* 68: 1593–1604.

Widfeldt, Anders (1997). *Linking Parties with People? Party Membership in Sweden 1960–1994.* Göteborg: Göteborg Studies in Politics.

20

Switzerland: The Militia Myth and Incomplete Professionalization

RETO WIESLI

According to experts, four features characterize Swiss politics: direct democracy, federalism, consociationalism, and the militia ideal.[1] They are highly valued in the political system and shape the country's political culture and thus its political class. In this chapter, I refer to the definition of political class by Borchert and Golsch (1995: 614) which states that the concept is twofold: a combination of Max Weber's "living off politics" with Karl Marx' class acting "for itself". Hence the political class is a group structurally shaped by professionalization and at the same time a collective actor. On this basis professional politicians can be analyzed using the category of political class. In all western democracies, the focal point of this political class is the Parliament.

However, for Switzerland the concept does not seem to fit, because the Federal Assembly (*Bundesversammlung*)[2] is not a professional parliament. Hence, what influence do this fact and the aforementioned aspects (direct democracy, federalism, consociationalism, and the militia principle) have on the political class?

I will trace that question in the first part, where the history of the militia principle as well as the historical process of professionalization in Parliament, associations, and parties are developed. In the following section I will comment on the institutional conditions needed for the development of a political class and define the Swiss political class in relation to the four aspects. The political class and the public perception of the militia system will be described in the third part. Finally I will judge the possibilities of an institutional reform and sum up the application of the political class concept to Switzerland.

---

[1] A fifth characteristic, neutrality, is often added, but it is less important for the discussion at issue (see Klöti 1988; Linder 1994).

[2] The Federal Assembly consists of two chambers with equal powers, the National Council (*Nationalrat*; 200 members), representing the people, and the Council of States (*Ständerat*; 46 members), representing the Cantons. The Federal Council (*Bundesrat*) is the government. Throughout the text, the German versions of proper names are given.

MILITIA PRINCIPLE AND POLITICAL
PROFESSIONALIZATION IN HISTORICAL PERSPECTIVE

First it is useful to clarify the development, extension, and growth of the militia principle: historically and etymologically the idea and even the term stands for the armed peasant at the frontier of the Roman Empire, voluntarily protecting his country and its people. After the retreat of the Romans from the Rhine overlapping influences and the specific conditions of particular local economic forms (alpine, rural, urban) led to the formation of cooperative municipalities with mercantile–cooperative or social arrangements which utilized and maintained their economic space together (called *Gemeinwerk*; see Niederer 1996). On this basis, more structured regional authorities developed since the twelfth and thirteenth century, and they began to constitute their own administrative bodies and to articulate themselves politically.

To the present day the autonomous municipalities have remained the link between family and society as a whole. In particular the smaller rural and mountain municipalities continue to be the decisive social and institutional connection and are, therefore, identity-building collectives (Niederer 1996: 268). Here, citizens still possess, administer, and use their common goods collectively; they also grant the right of citizenship and each citizen participates in town meetings. Where citizens know the administrators as relatives, friends, or neighbors, the identification of inhabitants with their municipality is given and the common performance of rights and obligations still usual. The militia principle was historically formed through the *Gemeinwerk* as well as by the inherent participation and official duties. It then developed further—due to the modernization of the Helvetic period (1798–1803)—into today's militia administration (Im Hof 1991: 263).

Democratic self-government has remained the ideal, serving as an orientation for the entire public administration (Bäumlin 1961: 75). Ideally, there is no contrast between state and society: the state's administration is taken care of by citizens as a secondary occupation and the people's sovereignty is the political maxim. Even if this may apply to the beginning of the federal state, 150 years later things have changed. The constitutional powers are overshadowed by the associational system whose administration of particular interests has replaced the general formation of a public will and political self-government (Linder 1983: 369).

Nevertheless, the militia system remains present: the majority of the authorities in Swiss municipalities are militia administrations. That implies a form of public organization that is based on non-professional roles, wherein any citizen takes over executive functions in politics and administration during a limited term of office for a small remuneration and besides his regular occupation. On the basis of egalitarian values and a decentralized balance of power, the militia system strives for a variety of opportunities for democratic participation and the prevention of an independent elite that is only considering its own special interests. From an economic and technical point of view, the advantage of this system consists in the fact that the construction of a differentiated and specialized administrative apparatus becomes possible despite the modest means of a small society. However, contradictory consequences may result from the two objectives of effectiveness and participation, which, in the case of the priority of economic motives, can lead to a transformation into a regime of notables (Geser 1987a).

Particularly because of three reasons, the limits of the militia system become more and more evident (Klöti 1988: 8–9): First of all, political problems are becoming ever more numerous and complex, hence demanding special knowledge and professional experts. Secondly, the development of the political system has its limits, due to fact that the formulation and implementation of political solutions increasingly require time and energy which volunteers can hardly provide anymore. Thirdly, the scarcity of compensation and individual satisfaction leads to a lack of interest in the cumulation of different militia positions and therefore reinforces the need for further professionalization. Besides restricted temporal availability, limited motivation, and inadequate qualification, Geser (1987a: 19) also lists the incomplete autonomy as a disadvantage. These problems are especially salient in small municipalities with limited recruitment bases and close social networks; they can be partly compensated by the creation of collective bodies which neutralize the deficiencies of single individuals (Geser 1987a).

The administration has differentiated itself with the progressing economic and social development (Linder 1983), but this has not necessarily led to the disappearance of the militia system. Municipalities simultaneously increase their bureaucracy and the number of militia committees and therefore facilitate civic participation in specific administrative areas. On all state levels (confederation, Cantons, and municipalities) there is a tendency to establish a stable relationship of functional complementarity between militia and professional bodies (Geser 1987b: 320). Generally speaking, Parliament, associations, and parties also follow the same course of development (Germann 1996: 79), as will be shown in the following.

The founders of the Federal State in 1848 agreed on a compromise between centralism and federalism and therefore created a federal level with modest powers and few instruments: the entire federal administration consisted of hardly fifty full-time civil servants which administered a budget of about 5 million Francs. The activity of federal authorities and the Federal Assembly was mainly based on the militia system which was customary in the Cantons and the municipalities. As actual self-government on the federal level was utopian even at that time, other solutions for diminishing the distance between state and society have been searched for. The lack of a constitutional court, the denomination of the Federal Assembly (*Bundesversammlung*; the legislative) as the highest power of the Confederation, the principle of collegiality, the term limits for public officials and members of the Federal Council (*Bundesrat*; the Swiss executive), as well as the federalist administrative arrangement, are all an expression of a strong democratic control of the administration and thus of an understanding of democracy as self-government by the people (Bäumlin 1961).

At the beginning, the first 155 parliamentarians, 111 in the National Council and forty-four in the Council of States (two per Canton), met twice a year for 2–3 weeks in Berne, only receiving a modest daily remuneration. At that time they represented a new generation of the bourgeoisie and originated particularly from three socio-professional groups: leading cantonal authorities, lawyers, and entrepreneurs from industry and trade—thus a classical Parliament of notables. Members with politics-related professions, that is, full-time officials of the executive and judicial administrations at the lower state level, already made up nearly one third of the first National Council and thereby formed the largest single occupational group. Another occupational group practiced such a political function in combination with their private occupation (among them three as editors). The absolute size of this group remained the same in the following years, but their relative share decreased as the National Council constantly included more and more members.[3]

In 1863, for the first time there was more than one actual professional politician (these were normally editors of party publications). Their number has only begun to increase at the end of the last century with the rise of associations and political parties. In 1896 there were thirty-two National Councilors with full-time administrative positions and three with solely political functions, in addition to thirty-two in a dual function, three of them within political associations. Before the First World War this development made a leap to one third of parliamentarians holding a political or official function (1911). With the change from a majoritarian to a proportional electoral system at the end of the First World War the process even accelerated: In 1917 only twenty-four full-time politicians were elected to the National Council; in 1919 their number already reached thirty-six, while the number of cantonal and municipal officials remained constant. Thus, the National Council of 1919 registered an accurate division in two parts: one half of the members were active in a full-time political or official function, the other half were not (Gruner and Frei 1966: 247).

For the development since then, Gruner (1970) has analyzed three points in time more precisely: 1920, 1944, and 1968. Over the whole period the number of full-time professional politicians increased from thirty-six to forty-seven, the number of regional and local officials from forty-seven to fifty-two. Also the number of representatives with additional political occupations—usually members of the liberal professions— rose from fifty-six to seventy. In the Council of States (*Ständerat*) these additional political occupations are usually functions in cantonal or municipal authorities, in the National Council functions in political associations or parties (Table 20.1).

Thus, the tendency we have already observed in the National Council elected under a majoritarian system can also be noticed after the switch to a proportional system: the combination of a primary civil profession with an additional official or political occupation becomes increasingly common. Likewise, the total number of political occupations within the Federal Assembly rises. We can say that already in 1968 the National Council had changed from a militia parliament to a professional politicians' parliament. Two thirds (127) of its members had political occupations as their main or additional job.[4]

---

[3] Because of the increase in population and the rule to elect one representative per 20,000 inhabitants, the number of National Councilors increased constantly: 111 in 1848, 120 from 1851 onwards, 128 since 1863, 135 since 1872, 145 since 1881, 147 since 1890, 167 from 1902 onwards, 189 since 1911, 198 from 1922 on, 187 since 1931, 194 since 1943, 196 since 1951, and 200 from 1963 onwards.

[4] Unfortunately, parliamentary sociology has not been continued in the same way since Gruner's study, which prevents us from making any detailed longitudinal analysis. Where new studies exist, I have cited them in the text.

Table 20.1 *Political occupations among MPs (National Council/Council of States)*

	1920	1944	1968
Professional political position (besides mandate)	36 (34/2)	46 (45/1)	47 (43/4)
Cantonal or municipal office	47 (39/8)	50 (36/14)	52 (43/9)
Other political occupation as second job	56 (42/14)	70 (55/15)	70 (60/10)
Total political occupations	139	166	169
Total militia	94 (74/20)	72 (58/14)	75 (54/21)
Total	233 (189/44)	238 (194/44)	244 (200/44)

Source: Gruner (1970).

The crucial nuance is that these are not professional parliamentarians but professional politicians: their main political focus is not the federal capital, Berne, but on the city or cantonal (executive) level, within the association or party, or maybe in an editorship (Gruner 1970: 27). These are the people who, due to their political occupations, are substantially more available for any political activity than others and finally cumulate several roles:

The parliamentarians, who go to Berne four times a year for three weeks, have been called political seasonal workers. Yet, even this seasonal work must produce some gains. The honorary parliamentarian devotes himself to this work, hoping for another kind of "reward", namely jobs and appointments which may be more profitable than the mandate itself. One of the most important mechanisms in this respect is membership in key committees. Once installed in *influential positions*, one will be rewarded with financially *attractive jobs*, with chairs of associations, and seats on boards of directors. Thus, the number of jobs will gradually increase, resulting in an accumulation of roles which is observable in several ways. In fact, this promotes the honorary into a full-time parliamentarian and thus makes it difficult to identify the real distribution of power. Political conflicts are not openly pursued like in Anglo-Saxon countries, where one can recognize what parliamentarians stand for. Since conflicts of interests are more ore less hidden, it is also complicated to identify the channels through which compromises can be reached. (Gruner 1973: 97)

Information about these channels can not only be obtained by considering the number of primary and additional political occupations, but also by looking at parliamentarians with seats on boards of directors: between 1920 and 1968 their share increased from 58 to 83 percent. The cumulation of roles is indicated by the number of positions per parliamentarian: the percentage of those with four to nine seats rises from 19 to 30, the share of those with over nine posts from 0.5 to 10 percent! At the end of the 1980s the average number of seats on boards of directors amounted to 5.6 per parliamentarian (Kriesi 1995: 194). In 1996 nearly 150 parliamentarians still had at least one of these positions (*Neue Zürcher Zeitung*, 30 October 1996). Since the implementation of a new stock law, however, there seems to be a decline, because now boards of directors are held more accountable for the prosperity of their company and thereby political relations become secondary.

The intertwinement of state and economics is not restricted to board of directors' seats held by Members of Parliament, but concerns in particular the associations (Linder 1999). In the spirit of the liberal founding fathers of 1848, the state rather sought the assistance of economic associations than creating its own institutions. Problems arising in the course of modernization were—according to the principle of subsidiarity—first tackled by private organizations. In Switzerland, the transfer of functions from society to the state followed the liberal model, resulting in a state structure that has substantially been influenced by solutions proposed by the associations. In particular during periods of crisis like the First and Second World War and the 1930s, the state strongly relied on the assistance of associations to carry out its tasks and thus integrated at least the leading associations in its economic and social policies. The central role of the economic associations was institutionalized in 1947 by formal acknowledgement in the federal constitution. Since then, they managed to expand their standing in the decision-making process and to build up their own para-statal administration (Farago 1987). Accordingly, to answer the "question" about the existence of a political class in Switzerland, one has to recognize the professionalization within associations and especially among those functionaries who perform political tasks.

Due to the structure of the political system, associational interests are well represented in Parliament. However, just like the number of parliamentarians on boards of directors, this does barely say anything about the actual political weight of interests—but it can serve as a rough indicator and is useful for the assessment of an MP's time budget. In 1920, 130 associational spokespersons were present in the Federal Assembly and in 1968 this figure had reached 176. At first, farmers and employers were particularly well represented, but this situation was outweighed in later years by an increasing number of other associational representatives. Even though Parliament reduced its bias for some interests, at the same time the amount of associational representatives who belonged to several interest groups grew from 11 to 22 percent (cf. Gruner 1970: 123). With a total number of 1,000 organizations we can estimate the number of political organization's employees at about 2,000 people (Kriesi 1995: 225).

It could be argued that weak national parties are a result of federalism. The national party system is fragmented with respect to the number of parties and their internal coherence. The financial situation is precarious (Brändle 2002): the SPS (see Table 20.2 for abbreviations) for example derives more than 50 percent of its income from membership contributions and MPs' payments, the FDP derives up to 60 percent of its income from donations. The government only pays about 4.6 million Switzerland Francs (CHF; approx. €3.16 mio) annually to the various parliamentary groups.[5] In addition, the role of the parties is limited by the governmental system: first, there is no actual party government, and secondly, the system makes dissident

---

[5] Conversions from CHF to Euro are based on the exchange rate of 30 December 2002 (CHF1 = €0.687).

Table 20.2 *Full-time jobs in parties, national, and cantonal level*

Party	Level	1960	1970	1980	1990	1998
FDP	National party	3.5	7.0	9.5	13.5	12.1
	Cantonal parties	5.0 (7)	12.4 (11)	23.4 (15)	24.5 (18)	27.9 (22)
CVP	National party	*	*	*	*	12.6
	Cantonal parties	2.8 (2)	8.1 (7)	8.6 (11)	17.0 (16)	16.5 (18)
SVP	National party	*	*	5.5	6.0	8.1
	Cantonal parties	6.0 (4)	5.7 (5)	6.0 (5)	7.6 (6)	8.0 (8)
SPS	National party	*	*	*	*	11.9
	Cantonal parties	3.9 (5)	5.8 (6)	10.1 (11)	19.1 (17)	21.7 (20)
Others	National party	*	*	*	*	6.0
	Cantonal parties	5.6 (5)	7.0 (7)	13.4 (11)	18.3 (20)	15.4 (18)
Total	National party	*	*	*	*	50.7
	Cantonal parties	23.3 (23)	39.0 (36)	61.5 (53)	86.5 (77)	89.5 (86)

* = no positions or no data available.

Notes: The numbers are equivalents of full-time positions at national and cantonal party level, that is, they include part-time positions. Given in brackets is the number of cantonal parties with full-time positions. FDP = *Freisinnig-demokratische Partei* (Radical Democrats); CVP = *Christlich-demokratische Volkspartei* (Christian Democrats); SVP = *Schweizerische Volkspartei* (Swiss People's Party); SPS = *Sozialdemokratische Partei der Schweiz* (Social Democrats).

Source: Data provided by Andreas Ladner, Institute of Political Science, University of Berne, 1999.

behavior without sanction possible for individual MPs. Yet, the nature of modern politics in a media-oriented environment strengthens the parties' headquarters and thereby provides a certain balancing effect.

It is not especially surprising that the parties on the national level are only accounting for about fifty full-time jobs in their main party and parliamentary offices. Concerning the individual Cantons the situation looks more promising: Already in 1970 there were thirty-six cantonal parties providing thirty-nine jobs and in 1998 there were eighty-six cantonal parties providing ninety full-time positions. Especially the parties present in the Federal Council (*Bundesrat*) have displayed a small increase in professionalization.

THE INSTITUTIONAL CONTEXT

The Swiss federal system (cf. Linder 1994; 1999) has fundamental implications for the political class: By international comparison, there are many executive, legislative, and judicial positions to be filled on the municipal and cantonal level. However, such a small state as Switzerland can only afford that many positions thanks to the militia system and a restriction of specialization.

On the federal level, however, the high degree of autonomy for the cantons and municipalities signifies a basic limitation to the scope of action available to the cent-ral state itself. To be effective at all, the political class depends on the coopera-tion with the Cantons and associations. As we have seen, the personnel requirements for such a co-operation on the parliamentary level are mostly met in the form of a functional integration.

The Federal Assembly (*Bundesversammlung*) consists of two chambers: the National Council (*Nationalrat*) as a lower house with 200 members and the Council of States (*Ständerat*) as an upper chamber with forty-six members—the first one being a people's assembly (elected, as far as possible, by proportional representation), the second one an assembly of the cantonal representatives (elected by the citizens of the Cantons). Both chambers are treated as equals. The modern day Parliament has lost a lot of influence compared with the institutional power envisioned by the original founders in 1848. As a result of increasing complexity of the political process, its dependence on the Federal Council (*Bundesrat*), the administration, and para-statal organizations has grown stronger. The parliamentary control of govern-ment and bureaucracy, for example, by extended parliamentary staff, is entirely utopian due to an increasing lack of resources. Additionally, by adhering to the ide-ologically based maintenance of the militia system the Federal Assembly deprives itself of the possibilities to compensate the relative shortcomings of time, informa-tion, and competence compared to the federal administration. Moreover, there are other serious consequences: Riklin and Möckli (1991) stated that the maintenance of a mythical militia Parliament leads to a distorted representation and that large parts of the elect-orate are deprived of their right to be elected, which is very dubious in a democratic context. Only the alternatives offered by a pure militia parliament or an entirely professional parliament could promise to deliver democratically satisfactory results.

Furthermore, the power of Parliament is limited by consociationalism and direct democracy. The optional referendum strengthens the pre-parliamentary phase at the expense of Parliament and has, as an option always available to the tentative losers in the democratic process, a strong influence on parliamentary debates. By anticipating potential referendums, the Swiss Parliament appears to be very cautious and not very eager to suggest legislative projects (Kriesi 1995: 173). Likewise, consocia-tional democracy—as an elaborated power-sharing system—demands attention to minority groups and thus adds to the restricting effects of direct democracy on Parliament.

THE POLITICAL CLASS

Size and Composition

According to Borchert and Golsch (1995), the appropriate focus for research on the political class is the national Parliament, which in western democracies usually is pro-fessionalized. In the case of Switzerland, we can actually speak of a semi-professional parliament. The members spend an average of 57 percent of their working time on parliamentary activities, 10 percent on other secondary political activities, and 33 percent on non-political activities (from which they obtain 54 percent of their income!). Thus, parliamentarians on the federal level are professional politicians just about two thirds of their time, with the remaining third being as well paid as their political time. Besides, this is another indication that a parliamentary mandate provides extra value on the employment market and hence offers the chance of an additional income. A parliamentary seat yields about CHF50,000 (€34,340; for details see Section 20.3.3), with the average total income of MPs being about CHF150,000 (€103,020) a year (this figure is subject to considerable variations; see Riklin and Möckli 1991: 150).

Kerr (1981: 245) observed the following connection: the more a deputy devotes him- or herself to political work, the more he or she risks a loss of income from other sources. This could be compensated by other non-political, profitable activities, which would then leave less time for political activities related to the parliamentary mandate and eventually would induce a feeling of work overload. Correspondingly, MPs classified their parliamentary activities in a survey quite critically: especially the functions related to executive and administrative control, to matters of foreign affairs and the legislative process, as well as the capacity to provide a forum for the nation were assessed as being not or only barely accomplished (Riklin and Möckli 1991: 160–1).

Apart from the members of the Federal Assembly—as well as the members of the Federal Council the concept of the political class also includes the staff working for Parliament and its members. Yet, in Switzerland the number of these employees is small. In 1990 only thirty-three MPs had their own staff, and in 1994 only 115 people worked in the parliamentary service (which was set up as late as 1972).

The Swiss cantonal Parliaments comprise 2,929 parliamentarians in total. In comparison to members of the Federal Assembly they have a much lower workload. On average they use only 18 days a year for parliamentary meetings and are remunerated with about CHF4,000 Francs (€2,750) per year for their duty. The differences of time spent are huge between individual Cantons: for example in the half-Canton Appenzell Inner Rhodes only 5 days are scheduled for meetings annually, whereas the same position in the Canton Vaud requires 45 days a year, and this does not include committee work. Correspondingly, the remuneration in eight cantons is about CHF4,000 (€2,750) and only in four Cantons does it rise to CHF8,000 (€5,490) or more (Berne, Vaud, Valais, Ticino). Therefore the number of parliamentary service positions is small and the number of political jobs even smaller.

What other political offices are available on the cantonal or municipal level? In all twenty-six Cantons in 1994 there was a total of 162 executive positions which were predominantly full-time jobs and offered a remuneration of about CHF195,000 (€133,930). There are 120–150 full-time Municipal Presidents, more than half of which are located in the Canton St. Gall. Further full-time political positions are only to be found in larger cities. The eight largest cities (without Basel, which forms the half-Canton "Basel City") offer a total of fifty-four executive positions and 608 legislative seats. However, only the executive posts provide a sufficient income to live on. Since there are only sixteen cities with more than 30,000 inhabitants, but a large number of very small municipalities, it is evident that the requirements of local politics are mostly met by the militia system. An examination of the 115 municipalities with over 10,000 inhabitants reveals that only 14 percent out of the existing 880 executive posts are full-time positions; 109 are filled by men and eighteen by women. Additionally, there are eighty-five positions which are remunerated with between 50 and 90 percent of a full-time salary (Bundesamt für Statistik 1997: 21).

In contrast to their weakness on the national level, parties play an important role at the local level. They are usually responsible for filling political positions, at least in those two thirds of municipalities where local parties exist (the remaining third are mostly small municipalities with less than 500 inhabitants; Ladner 1996: 10).

Municipal Parliaments exist in about 500 municipalities, especially in the French speaking part (Western Switzerland) and the Ticino. In the German speaking region a municipal Parliament is only established if the local community has at least 8,000 to 10,000 inhabitants. The number of municipal parliamentarians can be estimated at 18,000; they mainly work in honorary positions and therefore cannot be classified as belonging to the political class. On the other hand, they represent a large part of the personnel pool from which the political class is recruited.

Political Recruitment and Political Careers

Based on the results of the study by Riklin and Möckli (1991) one can argue that at least the Federal Assembly has an extremely small, economically restrained recruitment basis. In order to be able to afford such a "half-day" position, one has to be either self-employed or to work for a highly flexible employer. The fact that only 8 percent of the population, but more than half of the elected MPs are self-employed, confirms this impression (Riklin and Möckli 1991: 163). The massive over-representation of the first and third sectors—among the latter especially lawyers and public administration employees—is another result of this opportunity structure.

Further indicators are provided by looking at the legislative representation of various groups. Foreigners are obviously not represented, since only Swiss citizens have the right to vote—consequently, about 20 percent of the population is excluded. Another large discrepancy occurs in the representation of different age groups (see Table 20.3). The average age of the population (39.8 years) is considerably lower than the average age in the lower house (51 years) and the upper house (53.8 years). The age structure has been more representative, whenever in the course of a period of political change a gradual renewal of Parliament took place. This was the case at the beginning of the Federal State, during the debates concerning the total revision of the Federal Constitution in 1872, and then after the change to proportional representation for the lower chamber in 1920.

Neither are women represented according to their share of the population: Up to 1971 women had no voting rights at all. After the introduction of female suffrage

Table 20.3 *Representation according to age and sex*

	Population (2001)	National Council (1999)	Council of States (1999)
Age (%)			
Up to 19 years	22.9	0.0	0.0
20–39 years	28.6	7.0	0.0
40–59 years	28.0	84.5	84.8
Over 60 years	20.5	8.5	15.2
Average age (years)	39.8	51	53.8
Women (%)	51.1	23.0	19.5

Source: Bundesamt für Statistik 2002.

they became increasingly represented. In 1999 they made up 23.0 percent of the lower chamber and 19.5 percent of the upper house (see Table 20.3).

Local parties—and especially the sections of the four government parties—are very influential when it comes to political recruitment, and political (as well as conomic) careers (Sciarini *et al.* 1994; Liebig 1997: 253). A further observation concerns the occupational status. Members of the party elite often belong to occupational categories which enjoy the highest social standing, for example, company directors, teachers, and other professionals such as doctors and lawyers. Furthermore, certain professions are over-represented in some parties, as are teachers in the SPS and farmers in the SVP. Regarding school education, the elite of the FDP and CVP—in comparison to the SPS and SVP—includes a higher number of functionaries with a high level of educational attainment.

A person's profession is very decisive for his or her political career: high affinity to the political sector, frequent contact to political protagonists, and a large amount of leeway in the time budget are central requirements for anyone wishing to pursue a political career. The significance of these prerequisites increased between 1978 and 1989. During this period the number of parliamentarians employed in public administration has risen, as has the number of those who represent economic associations. This was, in the case of public administration, attributed to the increased "feminization" of Parliament. In the case of associations, the development was caused by an increased interdependence of parties and economic interests, by a more professionalized organization of interest groups, and by growing demands on the militia system.

The family as a factor of availability affects mainly women. However, they have in fact the better chances once they have opted for a political career. On average, women achieve a parliamentary position after 14 years of political work, after 12 years of party membership, and at the age of 44. Men, on the other hand, achieve the same positions only after 17 years of being active in politics and at the age of 46. For a political career a large extent of political party work and professional requirements are demanded from both men and women (Liebig 1997).

As a typical career in politics starts at the local level, studies of municipalities are particularly useful. The beginning of political activities is usually combined with joining a local party and then leads to an unpaid honorary or secondary position. The municipal militia office is a point of entry where aptitude and inclination to a political career can be put to test. Starting from this position, parliamentary seats and administrative offices on the cantonal and federal level become accessible if the particular candidate proves him- or herself worthy (Geser 1987*a*: 21–2).

At the level of municipal executives, various observations can be made that allow us to draw conclusions regarding the recruitment process. Eighty to 90 percent of municipal militia posts are filled by middle-aged men; women, young people, and old people are very much under-represented (*Traktandum* 3/96; Bundesamt für Statistik 1997). The men are mostly married, have already established careers in their various professions, often carry the rank of an officer, and have high-level educational qualifications. They are elected, because their social status promises the authority (Geser 1987*b*: 323).

The office of Municipal President is restricted to those people whose professions enable flexible working hours: farmers, traders, and employees in leading positions (mostly civil servants). If the presidential office is a full-time position, it is regarded as being equivalent to the role of a leading civil servant. This is confirmed by the frequent recruitment of Municipal Presidents from public administration.

Once established in local militia positions, moving upwards to the cantonal Parliament is the next logical step. From there at some point usually a candidacy for the National Council follows. This opens up the path to either a cantonal or an urban full-time executive position—or even to the upper chamber, assuming that the political career is still pursued. A federal government post is only accessible in exceptional cases, due to the various proportional representation rules (concerning party, language, and Canton). In addition, the path into the Council of States and into cantonal and urban executive positions is blocked for most politicians: The number of seats is low and open seats are rare. Moreover, parties know how to defend open seats by nominating established and well-known members. In short, the path leading from local political offices to the cantonal and then federal level, and then Parliament is still the usual route taken by male politicians (more seldom by their female counterparts) in Switzerland. This is confirmed by a look at the lower chamber of the Federal Assembly (in 1997). Only twenty-seven members entered directly into parliament and even these succeeded only after being active either as an entrepreneur, trade union official, associational representative, expert, or journalist. In some exceptional cases a person can find his or her way to a parliamentary seat directly by taking one of the few seats won by a newly founded "protest party". In the case of the upper house, all members except two law professors gained their seats by working their way up from the municipal or cantonal level—or in most cases through both.

Such long-standing service is rewarded by the voters: Less than 10 percent of MPs are voted out, and these are usually cases of a short career in Parliament. The average number of terms for members of the lower house not being reelected in 1995 amounted to less than one legislative period, while those individuals reelected had already served nearly two legislative terms (an average of 7.7 years). The share of newly elected members in the lower house was a third, while two thirds were reelected—as was the case four years earlier.

In the young federal state it was common for a citizen to cumulate several roles, especially in the context of the prevailing liberalism at that time. Often a single person was parliamentarian, industrial leader, businessman, and army colonel at the same time. If we take the *Vorort* (which is the colloquial name for the Swiss Federation of Commerce and Industry) as an example, we can see that between 1883 and 1914, out of its fifteen to nineteen leaders between four and six sat in Parliament permanently, among which were all of its presidents and the leaders of the *Vorort* offices. Later this practice of representation by the associational top officials changed, because the parliamentary seat increasingly became a time burden and also questioned the autonomy of the associational management. However, some directors of the *Vorort* and the Chamber of Commerce still occupy a seat in Parliament. With the intensive contact to the group "trade and industry" of the Federal Assembly, the representation of the *Vorort's* interests is guaranteed even without the direct presence of officials. This system of interest representation operates by giving parliamentarians the possibility to enroll in semi-official parliamentary groups according to their interests at the beginning of a legislative term; the groups' offices are then mostly provided by interest groups.

Based on these facts concerning the integration of state and associations, one wonders how the persistence of the false public impression of a militia Parliament can be explained? One reason could be the lack of openness. The public notification of parliamentarians' commitments was only introduced in 1984. Since then, each member entering Parliament for the first time has to provide a detailed, written account of his various commitments, that is, his professional activity, any leadership or director's roles in Swiss or foreign organizations, institutes, or foundations, as well as advisory positions held for any association, and any involvement in commissions or other federal governmental bodies. The register containing all these details is open to the public, with the office of the respective parliamentary chamber overseeing the member's disclosure practice. However, collisions of interests only have moderate consequences: instead of completely abstaining, it is only expected that the concerned parliamentarian declares his or her interests before giving a statement in a commission or council (Année politique suisse 1983: 24; *Federal Law Gazette* 1984, I: 892–3). Representation of interests is therefore nothing reprehensible but rather taken for granted. The formal declaration of interests is not an actual duty but a voluntary act: no sanctions exist in case of defiance, and professional secrets still remain undisclosed, even if a MP lately, after having acceded to the presidency of the National Council, had to retire from a business position. Indeed the ideal of a responsible militia Parliament has not been touched by such rulings. Furthermore, strict rulings concerning the declaration of interests would hardly be possible, as the amalgamation of interests is considered an intrinsic part of the system.

According to the study by Sciarini *et al.* (1994) party functionaries are, compared to normal citizens, more involved in associations, a majority of them in three or more organizations and frequently occupying high positions. The different ways of participating in a party and in an association rather complement than exclude each other. Membership in associations and parties can be considered as two manifestations of the same relationship to the community and as an expression of a traditional, non-individualistic understanding of politics as a collective commitment—obviously this is typical for the political class. Liebig (1997: 252–3) confirms that the integration in professional organizations is an important basic condition for professional and political success. Most of the executives questioned by Liebig belonged to several of these professional associations which act as recruiting ground and networks for establishing further contacts between the economic and political elites. In this system, political parties play an important part by providing a social frame for communication between position holders in central areas of society.

In the governing parties one witnesses a correlation between the cumulation of offices within the party and the intensity of involvement in associations or organizations (Sciarini *et al.* 1994: 96). There are, however, differences between the government parties. The elite of the SPS is only superficially involved in association. This corresponds to the position of the SPS within the political system, in which the party is highly integrated but nevertheless kept away from the most important decision-making centers. Thus, the SPS is under-represented in extra-parliamentary commissions and the federal administration. In the case of the FDP we find the strongest correlation between frequency of activity in political offices and involvement as leading members in some association or organization. The somewhat modest commitment of the party elite to external organizations is balanced by an even higher integration of the more active party officials.

Considering the fact that Parliament certainly is not characterized by a pure militia system, one could be inclined to speak of a myth. In Parliament more than a third of the members can be considered professional politicians and only about 2.5 percent can be regarded as pure militia politicians (Riklin and Möckli 1991: 157). Gruner used the term "ideology of disguise" ("*Verhüllungsideologie*") for the continuing emphasis on the militia character of Parliament (Gruner 1977: 356). It is still not acceptable to question this ideology: A bill introduced by the Parliament in 1992, which was intended to serve as a large step towards professionalization, failed in a referendum, partly because it violated the ideological taboo. This was confirmed by the motto of the committee organized to oppose the parliamentary reform: "No to the masked introduction of a professional parliament".

In this campaign the supposed division between the people and their representatives came to the fore and has remained a contentious issue ever since. But one has to differentiate—the study by Sciarini and Trechsel (1996: 226–7) showed that the support of the *elite* by the people did not decrease. Simultaneously, the VOX analysis of the December 1996 plebiscite (Hardmeier 1997) concludes that mistrust in *government* has already been increasing since 1991. This critical attitude towards government is apparent in all social and political groups, but can have various causes and meanings.

The tradition of self-determination is obviously anchored quite solidly within society. According to this concept, the idea of representation is only a less-than-ideal solution and therefore the power of Parliament or the bureaucracy should not be further expanded (Bäumlin 1961; Hardmeier 1993). This was also ascertained by the VOX analysis of the referendum on 9 June 1996, when the "government and administrative organization laws" were rejected (Hug, Marquis, and Wernli 1996). The main motive behind the large "No" vote was the prevention of additional costs for the proposed state secretary positions and the avoidance of further bureaucratization. Again, the name of the referendum committee is illustrative: "Committee against an inflated federal administration with superfluous state secretaries". The group of citizens voting "No" also lacked confidence in government most strongly.

Decreasing confidence in the Swiss authorities since 1989 was not only shown by the VOX analyses, but also by studies conducted in the context of the "World Values Survey" carried out by the University of Geneva: It verifies the massive loss of trust in political actors and institutions compared to 1989 (Brunner and Sgier 1997: 107).

The gap between the fictional and the real political system in public opinion confirms the persistence of the so-called "ideology of disguise". Actually, the professionalization of Parliament is a given fact, but the final steps towards acknowledging a professional parliament are prevented by ideological reasons.

Living off Politics

The possibility to live off a legislative seat alone was not given in the Swiss Parliament until now. In 2003, parliamentarians will get CHF30,000 (€20,600) tax free a year for expenses and inconveniences and CHF24,000 (€16,480) per year (taxable) for preparatory work. In addition they receive a daily allowance of CHF400 (€275) during parliamentary sessions as well as various other expense allowances, which add up to an annual (taxable) income of about CHF80,000 (€54,940). This corresponds to about half of the salary of a higher level cantonal judge, a higher level civil servant, or a university professor.

The history of parliamentary pay rises has been long and troublesome. In 49 years and eleven debates on pay rises between 1923 and 1972 the lower chamber only raised the daily remuneration for parliamentarians from 30 to 70 Francs. Accordingly, it was exceptional that in September 1992 a draft bill was submitted to the National Council, which intended to raise the existing remuneration and even planned to introduce funding to hire personal assistants for MPs. The bill, however, was rejected by a referendum and the lower chamber has approached this question with great reservation ever since.

In contrast, the motion by a Green Party MP for appropriate pensions for members was passed by both chambers, requiring the Federal Council to submit a bill or to act directly. Pensions for members had never been a controversial issue and the legal requirement to provide a welfare scheme for retirement was obviously valid for parliamentarians, too. Another non-binding motion with respect to the remuneration of travelling expenses was first submitted to the Federal Council by the Green Party in

October 1995 as a postulate. The fact that a political party which is not part of the government selected the topic of remuneration as a central theme is no coincidence: there are no lucrative posts available for its members in the Swiss consociational democracy.

These demands were endorsed by the office of the National Council and led to a change in the federal remuneration law in March 1996. The Federal Council expressed a positive attitude towards the changes and even praised the modesty of Parliament. The bill, which was introduced into the lower chamber in June 1996, was accompanied by an article in the press highlighting the dilemma of regulating one's own income (*Tages-Anzeiger*, 17 June 1996: 7).

The remuneration law, which was rejected in September 1992 as part of the referendum package, had been passed in a slightly revised version in October 1996. That decision avoided any controversial raising of parliamentary remunerations and thus managed to avoid a referendum—only the pension contribution and the allowance for overnight stays were increased. A second revision in 2001, based on a scientific report about the important role and the insufficient payment of political parties, raised the payments to the parliamentary groups by 50 percent. At the same time, the daily remuneration went up to CHF400 (€275). Finally in 2002, the new constitution and a parliamentary initiative led to a Parliamentary Law (*Bundesblatt* 2002, 3985–4000): In order to support the MPs, they were granted CHF24,000 (€16,480) per year to employ personal assistants. Yet, despite these increases parliamentarians still have to look outside Parliament to supplement their income.

THE POLITICAL CLASS AND INSTITUTIONAL REFORM

Since the early 1990s, attempts to strengthen the position of government and Parliament at the cost of administration and interest groups have been frequently undertaken. Today, after a modest constitutional revision and the creation of a Parliamentary Law, the institutional position of Parliament is strengthened. A governmental reform, a judicial reform, as well as a federal reform concerning the distribution of tasks between government and individual Cantons will be completed within the next years. However, constitutional revisions by individual cantons went beyond mere adaptations and have been met with much more public enthusiasm.

In spite of all efforts and recommendations from judicial and political science experts, and despite all political discussions, it cannot be ignored that the Swiss consociational system is very strongly based on informal rules and procedures. Therefore a reform could be short-lived indeed and is exclusively dependent on political will (Kriesi 1995: 223). This observation is confirmed in the latest study about parliamentary reform: "As long as the political protagonists can somehow adapt to the existing institutions, these institutions are very resistant to any reforms" (Lüthi 1997: 198). Not a situation of collective bargaining but rather a mutual blockade of more encompassing reforms is observable. Indeed, the latest substantial reform in Parliament—concerning the committee system—needed 13 years from initiation to realization (Lüthi 1997).

CONCLUSION

The factors militia, direct democracy, federalism, and consociationalism have indeed a strong influence on the structure of the political class in Switzerland. We can speak—due to ideological reasons—of an incomplete professionalization of the political class. The militia principle along with the federal character of the Swiss political system leads to a kind of pyramid: On the top of it are the real professional politicians, surrounded by secondary, part-time politicians who have, depending on their standing in the hierarchy of the federal state, less money and time available for politics. The actual threshold between the members of the political class who are able to live off their political activities and those whose office is only secondary, is difficult to define. The Swiss political arena is shaped by federalism, direct democracy, and the pivotal role of associations (*Verbändestaat*) in such a way that it is no longer possible to determine a center of the political class. If greater reforms are to be achieved, this is only feasible with pressure from below or from the outside, as Kriesi (1995) was able to show. On the other hand, inter-party co-operation exists, but more on the basis of mutual advantages which politicians discover in the course of frequent contacts (Axelrod 1991).

A categorization of Swiss politicians and hence the definition of a political class is indeed possible, but only with certain qualifications. The political class in Switzerland is fragmented due to federalism and due to the multi-level nature of professionalization. It is easier to speak of a small elite cluster rather than an explicit coherent political class acting co-operatively. For Switzerland, the concept of political class, as we have defined it at the beginning, would have to be based more on Max Weber than on Karl Marx: Swiss politicians "live off politics"—but they rarely act jointly as a "class for itself".

REFERENCES

Année politique suisse (1983). University of Berne: Forschungszentrum für Schweizerische Politik.

Axelrod, Robert (1991). *Die Evolution der Kooperation*. Munich: Oldenbourg.

Bäumlin, Richard (1961). "Verfassung und Verwaltung in der Schweiz", in *Verfassungsrecht und Verfassungswirklichkeit*. Berne: Stämpfli, pp. 69–93.

Borchert, Jens, and Golsch, Lutz (1995). "Die politische Klasse in westlichen Demokratien: Rekrutierung, Karriereinteressen und institutioneller Wandel". *Politische Vierteljahresschrift*, 36: 609–29.

Brändle, Michael (2002). *Strategien der Förderung politischer Parteien: Eine vergleichende Untersuchung der Parteienförderung in der Schweiz, Grossbritannien und den Niederlanden*. Berne: Paul Haupt.

Brunner, Matthias, and Sgier, Lea (1997). "Crise de confiance dans les institutions politiques suisses? Quelques résultats d"une enquête d"opinion". *Swiss Political Science Review*, 3: 105–13.

Bundesamt für Statistik (1997). *Die Frauen in den Exekutiven der Schweizer Gemeinden 1997*. Berne.

—— (2002). *Statistisches Jahrbuch der Schweiz 2002*. Zurich: NZZ Verlag.

Farago, Peter (1987). *Verbände als Träger öffentlicher Politik*. Grüsch: Rüegger.

Germann, Raimund E. (1996). *Administration publique en Suisse*, Vol. 1. Berne: Paul Haupt.

Geser, Hans (1987*a*). "Einleitung", in H. Geser, P. Farago, R. Fluder, and E. Gräub, *Gemeindepolitik zwischen Milizorganisation und Berufsverwaltung*. Berne: Paul Haupt, pp. 3–78.

—— (1987*b*). "Zusammenfassende Schlussbetrachtungen", in H. Geser, P. Farago, R. Fluder, and E. Gräub, *Gemeindepolitik zwischen Milizorganisation und Berufsverwaltung*. Berne: Paul Haupt, pp. 317–32.

Gruner, Erich (1970). *Die schweizerische Bundesversammlung 1920–1968*. Berne: Francke.

—— (1973). *Politische Führungsgruppen im Bundesstaat*. Berne: Francke.

—— (1977). "Die eidgenössische Bundesversammlung als Milizparlament". *Zeitschrift für Parlamentsfragen*, 8: 351–6.

—— and Frei, Karl (1966). *Die schweizerische Bundesversammlung 1848–1920*, Vol. 2. Berne: Francke.

Hardmeier, Sibylle (1993). *Analyse der eidgenössischen Abstimmungen vom 27. September 1992*. VOX No. 46 (VOX-Analysen eidgenössischer Urnengänge). Berne: GfS and University of Berne, February 1993.

—— (1997). *Analyse der eidgenössischen Abstimmungen vom 1. Dezember 1996*. VOX No. 60 (VOX-Analysen eidgenössischer Urnengänge). Zurich: GfS and University of. Zurich, February 1997.

Hug, Simon, Marquis, Lionel, and Wernli, Boris (1996). *Analyse der eidgenössischen Abstimmungen vom 9. Juni 1996*. VOX No. 59 (VOX-Analysen eidgenössischer Urnengänge). Geneva: GfS University of Geneva, September 1996.

Im Hof, Ulrich (1991). *Mythos Schweiz*. Zurich: Verlag Neue Zürcher Zeitung.

Kerr, Henry H. (1981). *Parlement et société en Suisse: Une analyse en profondeur de la démocratie représentative helvétique*. Saint-Saphorin: Editions Georgi.

Klöti, Ulrich (ed.) (1988). *Milizverwaltung in den Gemeinden*. s.l.: s.n.

Kriesi, Hanspeter (1995). *Le système politique suisse*. Paris: Edition Economica.

Ladner, Andreas (1996). "Die Schweizer Lokalparteien im Wandel: Aktuelle Entwicklungstendenzen gefährden die politische Stabilität". *Swiss Political Science Review*, 2: 1–22.

Liebig, Brigitte (1997). *Geschlossene Gesellschaft: Aspekte der Geschlechterungleichheit in wirtschaftlichen und politischen Führungsgremien der Schweiz*. Chur: Rüegger.

Linder, Wolf (1983). "Entwicklung, Strukturen und Funktionen des Wirtschafts- und Sozialstaates in der Schweiz", in A. Riklin (ed.), *Handbuch Politisches System der Schweiz*, Vol. 1. Berne: Paul Haupt, pp. 255–382.

—— (1994). *Swiss Democracy: Possible Solutions to Conflict in Multicultural Societies*. New York: St. Martin's Press.

—— (1999). *Schweizerische Demokratie: Institutionen—Prozesse—Perspektiven*. Berne: Paul Haupt.

Lüthi, Ruth (1997). *Die Legislativkommissionen der Schweizerischen Bundesversammlung*. Berne: Paul Haupt.

Niederer, Arnold (1996). *Alpine Alltagskultur zwischen Beharrung und Wandel.* Berne: Paul Haupt.

Riklin, Alois, and Möckli, Silvano (1991). "Milizparlament?", in M. Bovey-Lechner *et al.* (eds), *Das Parlament—Oberste Gewalt des Bundes"?* Berne: Paul Haupt, pp. 154–63.

Sciarini, Pascal, Finger, Matthias, Ayberk, Ural, and Garcia, Carlos (1994). *Die Kader der Schweizer Parteien.* Zürich: Seismo.

——and Trechsel, Alexandre H. (1996). "Démocratie directe en Suisse: L'élite politique victime des droits populaires?" *Swiss Political Science Review,* 2: 201–32.

21

United States: A Political Class of Entrepreneurs

JENS BORCHERT AND GARY COPELAND

POLITICAL PROFESSIONALIZATION IN HISTORICAL PERSPECTIVE

In the early days of the American Republic two factors in particular prevented a professionalization of Congress and of politics more generally. On the one hand, Americans have expressed an ambivalence toward professionalism in the political realm from the very beginning. The leaders of the American Revolution and the founders of the constitutional system had a profound distrust of a governing class. The distrust ran so deep that under the Articles of Confederation legislators could sit no more than 3 years in a 6-year period. George Washington's two-term precedent demonstrated the belief that rotation in office is a desirable goal.

Members of Congress largely followed the same pattern of limited service. On the local and state level there often existed clear norms—partly based on custom, partly even legally fixed—that limited the number of terms anybody could serve (Kernell 1977: 675–7, 685–8; Brady, Buckley, and Rivers 1999: 498–9). Thus, throughout the nineteenth century one-third to one-half of the members of the House of Representatives, at any given time, were in their first term and the mean number of terms served did not reach three until the twentieth century (Polsby 1968). The idea that politicians should be recruited from among the citizenry for short periods of time and then—after fulfilling their civic duty—should return to their civil occupation is an important part of classical American republicanism, of what is called the "American ideology" (cf. Petracca 1992; Will 1992). Nonetheless many American citizens today have gotten the impression that their polity is being run by exactly those professional politicians their Founding Fathers sought to avoid—a paradox to which we shall return.

Jens Borchert would like to thank Klaus Stolz and Juergen Zeiss as well as the participants of the staff seminar of the University of Oklahoma's Carl Albert Congressional Research and Studies Center. His share in the article is based on research he conducted while being financed by the German Marshall Fund of the United States.

There is, however, a second and more profane set of reasons for short terms in the early Republic. Scholars are quick to point out that rather than being driven solely by principle there were several practical reasons promoting high turnover in the Congress: Washington was an inhospitable place to live, those being there exercised little power, and there was no certainty that staying in Washington would pay dividends over the long term.

When the third Congress convened in the capital district of Washington for the first time, most accounts depict it as an unpleasant city. Its population was less than sixteen thousand and it lacked the advantages of some of the larger American cities (Josephy 1979: 119). Henry Clay—who chose to stay much longer than most—described Pennsylvania Avenue, the main thoroughfare, as being "frequently so muddy as to be impassable"—a condition that lasted well into the presidency of Abraham Lincoln (see Will 1992: 11). The new leaders lived in boardinghouses (Young 1966) and battled mosquitoes as Washington tended to resemble a swamp. The nation's capital, then, lacked desirability as a place to live for most people leading few to value a legislative career.

Those who did come to Washington in the nineteenth century found themselves in a less than powerful position. The size and responsibility of the government based in Washington were both quite limited. In 1792, the federal government spent US$5 million.[1] It did not spend more than US$1 billion until the First World War, which never accounted for more than 5 percent of the GNP until that time. Initially, the federal government exercised limited authority, focusing on defense and foreign affairs, and having little say in domestic and economic policies. Distributive, regulatory, and redistributive policy-making did not become common until much later. In short, early members of Congress exercised little policy influence, had few benefits to distribute, and had virtually no patronage to offer (see also Hibbing 1991: 2–4).

Finally, there was no certain reward for longevity of service. The seniority system did not develop until the end of the nineteenth century. Long service did not guarantee achieving a formal position of power so investment of time had its risks (Abram and Cooper 1968; Polsby, Gallagher, and Rundquist 1969; Price 1971). Freshmen became committee chairs and even Speaker of the House while those who had served longer—which some members always did—sat and watched.

Congressional terms became longer when—nearly simultaneously—all three inhibiting factors changed: the quality of life in Washington improved notably, Washington became the center of power and patronage, and the seniority system developed as a mechanism for allocating positions of influence within Congress. Figure 21.1 shows the turnover rates in each Congress. The figure indicates that in the first several decades the turnover rate was routinely in the 30–40 percent range, but that it increased steadily beginning in the 1830s. A slow decrease in turnover rates began in the 1860s, but seriously accelerated toward the end of the century. With the exception of the last few elections it declined steadily from that point to the present.

---

[1] US$ are not converted to Euro in this chapter because of the near parity between the two currencies in 2002.

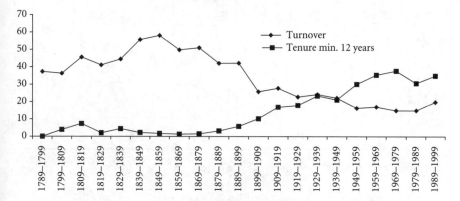

Figure 21.1 *Turnover and tenure in the House of Representatives*
(% of all representatives)

Note: Turnover means the share of newcomers. Tenure indicates the length of uninterrupted servings in
the House of Representatives. For the latter, only Members were included which belonged at least 12 years
to the House at given time. The figures are the average numbers for five Congresses (10 years).

Source: Own calculation based on Will (1992: 73, 78–80) and updated by authors.

Only in the 1990s there was an increase. The other line that shows the share of members
belonging to the House for at least 12 years displays a similar pattern: The number of
these members was very small in the last century while today it is close to 30 percent.

Apart from tenure and turnover, one also has to look at the material rewards available to legislators. Legislative salaries on a per diem basis were present from the first
Congress on. In the beginning this constituted hardly a base of income one could live
on. Since the per diems were changed to annual salaries for good in 1856—an earlier
decision to that effect had been reached in 1816 but had been revoked the year
after—the income situation of representatives improved quickly. Salaries rose to
about than US$60,000 (in 2000 dollars) even before the Civil War. In 1872, they were
above US$100,000 before declining some, and throughout most of the twentieth cen-
tury they have been over the US$100,000 threshold (own calculations based on
Fisher 1755–56, 1995, see Fig. 21.2). While there are plenty of historical testimonies
from Congressmen complaining to their families and friends (and voters) how little
income they had and that they hardly could get by (cf. Rothman 1966: 139–40,
147–8), the fact is that Congressmen—at least from the 1880s on—received what has
to be considered a professional income by any measure.

Yet American politicians in the late nineteenth century were not merely legislators
but rather party politicians who very often held numerous public and party offices
on the federal, state, and local levels successively and sometimes even concurrently.
Hierarchically organized party machines on the local and state level worked as a
coordinating device for these professional political careers. They tended to monopol-
ize all the political offices in their realm and handed them over to their adherents.
The Senate was regarded as a "federation of state bosses" (Dobson 1972: 33)—a kind
of "central committee" of the emerging political class in the United States. The reason

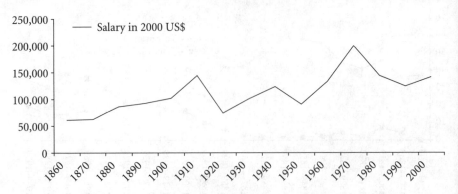

Figure 21.2. *Congressional salaries, 1860–2000 (in 2000 US$)*

Source: Own calculations based on Fisher (1995: 1755–56).

for this prominent position was the Senate's control over federal patronage and thus its key role in the reproduction of party machines. At this point in history, the United States definitely seemed to be heading towards an entirely different kind of professionalism than prevails today.

The turning point came in the Progressive Era when particularly electoral reforms (introduction of the "Australian ballot" and of direct primaries) undermined the control of parties over nomination and voting behavior. Direct primaries took away the parties' control over candidacy while the Australian ballot created the opportunity for split-ticket voting (Brady, Douglas, and Rivers 1999: 500). These reforms started in the West and then gradually expanded throughout the country. Figure 21.1 shows the tremendous impact of these reforms on the structure of the House membership.

Both a result and a culmination of electoral reforms was the end that reform-minded members of Congress put to the era of strong Speakers of the House in 1910/11. From that blow (and the introduction of direct election of Senators in 1913) party government in Congress never quite recovered. It was replaced with the politically neutral rights of seniority. With the party machines substantially weakened in all but a few places in the United States, politicians and would-be politicians developed their own political organization. The political entrepreneur planning and running his or her own career was born. What was at the time hailed as a success of the reform movement against corrupt politicians in fact had created a new type of politician—exactly that type against which today's criticism and reform movements are directed.

Even though some criticism had been raised against the professionalization of Congress, during the 1960s and 1970s there was a broad movement, especially among academic advisors, favoring the professionalization of the state legislatures according to the Congressional model (cf. Rosenthal 1998: 49–67). The exact level of turnover and its counterpart, careerism in the states, is not readily documented, but the pattern is widely agreed upon. Traditionally, turnover in the states has been high and with it professionalism has been considered low. Undoubtedly, turnover has varied from state to state, but no state approached the level of careerism that was found in the US Congress.

Historical analyses show a reduction by half of turnover between the 1930s and the 1970s and 80s when the numbers were 24 percent turnover for state senates and 28 percent for the lower houses (Shin and Jackson 1979; Jewell and Patterson 1986; Niemi and Winsky 1987).[2] This trend has continued since (Moncrief *et al.* 1992), with term limits, however, providing the base for a counter-movement (cf. Rosenthal 1998: 72–7). Looking at the likely consequences of an 8-year term limit, Opheim (1994) found that about half of lower chamber Members normally remained after 8 years and over 60 percent of those in upper chambers. More significantly, using Squire's classification system (1988), she discovered that those percentages were highest for legislatures that provide career opportunities, and are higher for springboard legislatures than dead-end institutions (Opheim 1994: 57–8). It is indisputable that state legislatures have changed dramatically in the last two to three decades. They have become more professional and state legislative service has become a career for more individuals.

However in 1997 only 28 percent of the state senators and 16 percent of the state legislators who had been in office in 1990 still held that position (Rosenthal 1998: 73–4). Hence there seems to be a current tendency which turns the state legislatures into just one step within professional political careers. Yet this should not be confused with deprofessionalization. It remains to be seen which changes for political careers—and for the legislatures thus affected—will result from that development. Although most political scientists regard long tenure ("careerism") as an important indicator of professionalized institutions, this should remind us that the two categorically as well as empirically are distinct phenomena (also cf. Moncrief 1994 and the introductory chapter to this volume).

In sum, there is no simple explanation for the growth of professionalism in the United States, but several factors appear to have made major contributions. First, and foremost, the responsibilities of the legislatures increased. As the federal government, and later the states, became responsible for larger budgets and a wider range of policy decisions, the stakes increased as did the potential rewards for service (cf. Berkman, De Boef, and Poggione 1995). As a further consequence of the growth of legislative action, there was also an increased attention given to the capacity of the institution, particularly in its relationship with the executive. As the importance of these positions grew, there followed an increase in the various benefits of the offices. Salaries and pensions grew as did other perquisites of office. Similarly, legislators sought to insure the rewards of service by institutionalizing rules that worked to the advantage of those who had served the longest. The seniority system in the Congress became virtually inviolable (Matthews 1960; Polsby, Gallagher, and Rundquist 1969).

---

[2] All states except unicameral Nebraska have two chambers in their legislatures.

Simultaneously the institutionalization of Congress and other legislatures made important positions dependent upon length of service and thus provided a link between professionalization and institutional development.

While legislative positions, especially in the Congress, became more desirable, the ability to continue in office remained at the whim of the public. The next step in the evolution of the political class included actions that enhanced the likelihood of electoral success for incumbents (cf. Mayhew 1974; Fiorina 1977; Alford and Hibbing 1986; Dawes and Bacot 1998). First, members of Congress successfully moved to establish themselves as independent political enterprises (Loomis 1979; Salisbury and Shepsle 1981). They supplied themselves with a generous staff who could serve their political needs. They also provided themselves with the resources to communicate with their constituents: the franking privilege for mail back to the district, long-distance telephone calls, and an increasingly generous travel allocation (Cain, Ferejohn, and Fiorina 1987).

At the same time they resisted efforts to limit their individual discretion by insuring weak parties and weak leadership and by increasingly decentralizing authority within the Congress (Ansolabehere and Gerber 1997; Adler 2002). Thus, political scientists' recurring dream of a party democracy in European style (cf. APSA 1950) remained blocked. The organization of primaries and the advantage of incumbents in campaign finance produced an increasingly safe re-election for all those incumbents seeking it. Hence, in the House of Representatives more than 90 percent of incumbents running again can count on their being sent to DC. Under this system parties are reduced to a dual yet rather modest role: they provide the organizational frame (the party labels) and are one influence on legislators among others. The professionalization pattern that has evolved since the Progressive Era has proven remarkably resistant to change—precisely because it is directly linked to the collective preferences of professional politicians, the American political class.

THE INSTITUTIONAL CONTEXT

The essential features of the American polity as we know it today are federalism with its abundance of electoral offices, a strong, bicameral legislature, and weak parties. Together these three elements provide a most hospitable environment for the political entrepreneur whose aspirations center on Congress and some highly professionalized state legislatures.

Federalism provides for several attractive and largely autonomous political arenas that may also serve as a frame of reference for political careers. The exceedingly high number of electoral offices (more than 500,000) guarantees multiple points of access to the system. This includes legislative and executive positions on the local and state levels. Additionally, law school graduates have the opportunity to enter politics by way of an electoral position in the judiciary, as a judge or district attorney—a pattern that partly explains the over-representation of lawyers in American politics. Another institution that serves as a possible starting-point for political careers is the local school board.

The attractiveness of Congress is enhanced by its high degree of professionalization and its important role in policy-making. No other democratic Parliament comes even remotely close to Congress in that regard. Democrats and Republicans "organize" Congress, that is, they form a majority and a minority and distribute the positions the institution provides. Their power as parties, however, is very limited. Individual representatives are very independent-minded and act in their own interest and according to their own conception of the public good (Wattenberg 1998; Rohde 1991). The committees and subcommittees constitute the main arena of Congressional politics. It is here that most of the legislative work is done and where most decisions are made.

The weakness of parties results from their inability to control the distribution of political offices ever since the Progressive Era. Thus, party patronage is mostly absent, and there is no safe fall-back position if one is not reelected or if a bid for higher office fails. Therefore American politicians tend to be rather reluctant to change offices and levels of government. It is these strategic considerations and the imponderabilities of career-planning that tend to limit the size of the otherwise excessively big pool of potential candidates for political office. This also explains a certain ambivalence of American politicians between risk-averseness and ambition: On the one hand they want to avoid the risk of running for another office and thus choose one level of government very early on. On the other they perceive the unlimited universe of opportunities around them and are constantly tempted to run for some other office.

Interest groups are highly fragmented; central associations play only a minor role. Nevertheless these groups have a strong influence on policy-making, the material base of which is in campaign finance (Clawson, Neustadtl, and Weller 1998; Gierzynski 1999). As political careers are dependent upon reelection, the influence of those who can provide financial resources to deter challengers and secure reelection is obvious. American interest groups finance electoral campaigns by way of their Political Action Committees (PACs), usually representing rather narrow economic interests. PACs collect donations and then either give them to candidates—which is limited to US$5,000 per candidate and election—or run independent campaigns for or against certain candidates—which is now legally limited in a variety of ways. Currently, there are about 4,500 PACs who in the 1999/2000 electoral cycle spent about US$580 million.[3]

The first-past-the-post electoral system in electoral districts of equal size and with direct primaries (of various types) also favors the individual political entrepreneur, as it works against any effort to unite local candidates behind a national cause. The primaries guarantee that the first, and often most bitter fight takes place among the competing candidates within the parties. Under these conditions a unified party platform would be counter-productive as it would make it more difficult for individual candidates to gain a profile with the electorate. Accordingly the system favors candidates which are particularly independent from their parties.

[3] Data from the Federal Election Commission; cf. http://fedweb1.fec.gov/press/053101pacfund/053101pacfund. html.

THE POLITICAL CLASS

Size and Composition

It is obvious that politics in the United States has become more professionalized and that American legislatures, both Congress and in the states, are increasingly populated by those who live off politics. The question remains, though, as to who is part of the political class in the United States. This question refers on the one hand to political professionalization; on the other hand the more difficult problem is to find out who of the professional politicians belongs to the political class, or rather to its core. Here we have to move toward subjective criteria to determine the boundaries of the political class.

The task of identifying who is part of the American political class will be greatly eased by identifying the focal point of those careers—the legislatures. This also is the prevailing perspective in American research on political careers. Thus, Prinz (1993: 34) suggests that "[p]erhaps the single best place to study the career paths of elected officials is the United States Congress." The reason for that supposition is simple: Members of Congress for the most part have long careers and their safety at reelection is particularly high. A second notable advantage of a focus on Congress is that many other professional politicians at some point in their careers run for Congress or even serve there.

Congress, however, also is a good starting-point to study the subjective component of political class formation and reproduction. Studies of the Senate, for example, long ago revealed the club-like character of that institution with clearly laid-out, if informal rules and the strong propensity to re-socialize newcomers into accepting the numerous written and unwritten rules (cf. Matthews 1960). Even if the character of the Senate and the rules of conduct have changed quite dramatically since (cf. Sinclair 1989; Schiller 2000; Campbell and Rae 2001), the adherence to clear boundaries to the outside and to a special atmosphere of community within remains. In the House of Representatives the sense of community is reinforced by the style of decision-making that as often as not relies on ad-hoc coalitions. The often-described mechanisms of coalition-building like "logrolling" contribute to a perception of common interests over the given partisan divide (cf. Arnold 1981). Contrary the parliamentary democracies in Europe, the split between government party and opposition is absent. What is produced in Europe by way of "cartel parties" (Katz and Mair 1995) is simply given under the American political system.

In a similar way, there are many advantages to looking at the legislative bodies in the states for other signs of professional politicians. Those state legislatures, obviously, serve as a training ground for many who wish to move to the Congress,[4] but for many they are a place where they can happily serve and live off politics. These state legislatures, as shown above, have changed dramatically since Wahlke and his

---

[4] Squire (1993: 146) indicates that in 1987 one-half of House Members had previously served in a state legislature and over one-third of the Senators had.

colleagues (1962: 76) found only 4 percent of the state legislators they surveyed identified their occupation as "politician" or "legislator". In the late 1960s and the 1970s there was a real wave of professionalization on the state level.

Today still around thirty-five state legislatures have to be regarded as non-professional or at most partly professionalized on the base of the legislative salary provide and the time-budget they require (cf. Sollars 1994; Squire 1992). In the others a living off politics is provided. This is based on the salary (like in California, New York, Michigan, and Massachusetts, among others), but also on extra income earned outside the legislature which is still legal in many states—contrary to Congress. In some states it is also possible to reallocate unspent campaign donations to the private funds of representatives. It is hard, however, to generalize findings in this area, as divergence is the most prominent feature of state politics: Some states only have few electoral offices, others have a lot. Some have rather small legislatures, others are surprisingly large. For example, Nebraska has 1.6 million inhabitants and a unicameral legislature of forty-nine members, New Hampshire has 1.1 million people, but 400 members in the State House alone, with twenty-four Senators on top of that.

This divergence makes it difficult to clearly count the holders of particular offices among the political class. The members of Congress, however, definitely belong to the political class. Even the newly elected Republicans in the "revolutionary" 104th Congress (1995–97), while strongly supporting the "Contract with America" with its anti-professionalism rhetoric that brought them to Washington, shunned the very contents of the "contract" and did not enact federal term limits once they had discovered the virtues of office (cf. Rae 1998). Thus, the power of its socialization effects and the integrative force of the American political class became particularly visible during this attack on its conditions of existence.

Some in the federal executive branch are also unequivocally part of the political class, including the President, Vice President, and some of the cabinet. The American cabinet is generally a mix of people who have made their living off politics for a long time and some from the private sector—many of whom return to the private sector upon termination of their government service. More difficult is the drawing of boundaries in the case of the judiciary. Federal judges are appointed according to political criteria, but they are not per se politicians. On the other hand, especially the Supreme Court has been politicized in recent times. And even in the other federal courts one can find careers like that of Abner Mikva—Democratic Congressman (1969–73; 1975–79), judge and Chief Judge of the US Court of Appeals (1979–94), advisor of the Clinton administration (1994–95). State and local courts are politicized by way of the election of judges as are some attorneyships.

At the state level, many or most state governors, the lieutenant governors, and some other statewide elected officials are part of the political class. The 7,424 state legislators do not form a coherent group, but rather have to be divided into professional and non-professional politicians. But even non-professional state legislators may share a political class outlook due to their progressive career ambitions. Among local politicians big-city mayors have to be named. The mayors of New York City have often held other political offices before or after their stint at Gracie Mansion.

A new trend can be observed in those states that have introduced term limits: Willie Brown, long-term state legislator and veteran Speaker of the California Assembly for 15 years, successfully ran for mayor of San Francisco when term limits threatened to end his career on the state level. Brown, a powerful figure in California, was astute enough to have himself elected into the best-paid political position in California at the time (*Los Angeles Times*, 27 March 1998).[5]

An issue in itself is the under-representation of women. In Congress currently there are only sixty-one women in the House of Representatives (14 percent) and thirteen in the Senate (13 percent). Ethnic minorities as well have fewer representatives than their share of the population would suggest. The reasons for both phenomena have to be sought in the electoral system and the necessity to build one's own organization and campaign funds. Demands for descriptive representation don't find much of a hold in an electoral system that does not know any mechanisms of balancing inequalities in representation.

Political Recruitment and Political Careers

In the United States there is neither any one typical career path prior to becoming part of the political class nor *a* typical career path within the class. The two most salient reasons for this are, first, the lack of a clear hierarchical linkage between the different levels of government combined with the constitutional separation of powers on any one level, and, second, the self-recruitment of candidates without any clearly designated intermediary institution. The first factor creates a great supply of political offices which may be linked in any imaginable line of succession, or political career pattern. The second factor increases the number of potential candidates by making the decision to run largely an individual one. The more important and professionalized an office is, the higher the financial resources needed and the requirements of the candidate during the campaign.

While there is no way to delineate a few clearly defined careers paths, one sensible approach to understanding them is to look at the career backgrounds of those who are part of the political class. Specifically, if we begin by accepting that the Congress is at least one of the focal points for a political career in the United States we can examine the career background of members to gain some insights into career patterns. Table 21.1 provides that information for three different periods of time. As we can see, there appears to be a pattern of increasing experience by representatives prior to assuming office. The number of Members coming from state legislatures has grown from 29 percent in the early period, through 37 percent in 1980, to 43 percent for the 104th Congress (1995). In fact, confirming Squire's finding, in that latter year another 6.2 percent of members had served in the state legislature at some earlier stage in their career making the total with state legislative experience approximately

[5] After his election as mayor, Brown made US$143,000 per year with the California Governor having only US$131,000. Shortly thereafter, the California Citizens Compensation Commission gave the Governor a pay rise to US$165,000.

Table 21.1. *Penultimate office prior to election to the House of Representatives (%)*

Position	1948–66	1980	1995
State legislature	29.3	36.8	43.1
Local office	10.6	10.6	14.5
District or prosecuting attorney	6.3	4.6	2.5
Judicial	6.3	*	1.2
Administrative/federal executive	5.9	4.6	2.1
Congressional office/legislative aide	3.4	4.6	3.4
Higher office/state executive	1.8	6.4	3.4
Law enforcement	0.7	*	3.4
Party ranks	*	3.0	1.4
No prior political experience			
Business	—	10.8	12.4
Attorney	—	10.1	8.3
Academia	—	3.2	2.3
Media/publisher	—	2.5	2.1
Local political organization	—	1.1	*
Medical doctor	—	*	1.2
School teacher/principal	—	*	1.2
Union	—	*	*
Widow of former Representative	—	*	*
Minister (church)	—	*	*
Total without prior political experience	35.8	29.5	27.5

* Indicates less than one per cent; — no data available.

Source: For 1948–66: Mezey 1970; for 1980: Prinz 1993: 33; for 1995: own analysis based on Barone and Ujifusa 1995.

50 percent. The importance of local office-holding experience also seems to have grown.[6] The other clear trend is that fewer people enter the Congress without previous political experience.[7]

Among the conclusions from an examination of Table 21.1 is the difficulty of identifying a standard career path to the Congress. Still that analysis does begin to provide some insights into the nature of the career path. Previous electoral experience is

[6] A note of caution (as well as a theoretical point) is appropriate here. Because of the plethora of positions held by representatives prior to taking office, coding is quite difficult when it comes to all but the most obvious positions. Since the data in Table 21.1 have been coded by at least three different researchers at quite different times, we recommend not reading too much into any specific figure (with the exception of state legislature which is a clear category). The theoretical point is that coding these data reinforces the sense of great variation in the American political career and in the opportunity structure from state to state. Also see the classical study by Schlesinger (1966).

[7] In fact, even the 27.5% figure for 1995 found in Table 21.1 misrepresents the reality. That figure refers to those who were not holding a political position just prior to ascending to Congress. In fact, a substantial majority of those individuals did have some previous experience in public life. We report the data in this form to be consistent with the previous researchers, but the reader should understand that "no prior experience" refers only to the immediate pre-election time-frame.

sufficiently important that a substantial majority of new members of the House have had it. State legislative service is the route most often traveled to Congress. It is not only the learning of certain techniques and the making of contacts that qualifies state legislators to run for Congress. Even more importantly, they can recruit supporters and donors who will also support them when they run for an office in DC. Also, (former) state legislators will have already represented part of the Congressional district they are contesting and thus are known to voters—probably the most important resource of all. Yet the differences between states are huge: In some states nearly all members of Congress have served in the state legislature while in some the number is zero. For some members the path to the Congress has been short and straightforward and for others it has been quite long and winding.

In many ways it is reasonable to say that there is little that interferes with the direct link between voters and office-holders in the United States. Few constitutional constraints limit whether one is eligible for office. Neither parties nor other organizations are very effective at either blocking or promoting candidacies. And, elections are generally highly personal contests. Party voting, never very high, has declined dramatically with personal voting taking its place.

But while the American political system is unusually permeable, success remains difficult to achieve, especially against an incumbent seeking reelection. Congressional reelection rates stand at more than 90 percent—with the state legislatures on average not being far behind (cf. National Conference of State Legislatures, http://www.ncsl.org/statevote98/incmb1.htm). That renders the choice of the right moment to run and the right office to compete for the decisive element in any promising campaign. Every election thus is turned into a process of selection by self-deselection: just as ambitious and talented individuals self-start, ambitious and talented individuals themselves opt out of the competition. In many ways, the most significant factor in the link between voters and office-holders is the choice of individuals to make themselves available for office (cf. Fowler 1993).

Those who seriously aspire to higher office make strategic decisions about seeking elections that are based largely on the context in which they operate (Rohde 1979; Jacobson and Kernell 1981; Maisel and Stone 1997; Powell 2000). Kazee (1994: 12–4) summarizes the contextual factors that influence a potential candidate's decision to seek election to the Congress and the competitiveness of the campaign he or she will run: formal and informal eligibility, party strength, chances of winning, financial resources, structural context, and personal costs.

Kazee's summary is important for several reasons. First it accents the social nature of the decision to seek public office. In nearly all cases decisions to seek office are made by individuals in consultation with their families and a relatively small number of critical advisers. The context, described by Kazee, shapes that decision-making process. But the decision is completely in the hands of the potential candidate. Second it suggests the factors that affect the nature of the link between office-holders and votes. We know that once an individual gains office, voters are likely to ratify a continuation of that relationship for as long as the incumbent offers herself or himself for reelection. So, when considering the context, the presence or absence of an incumbent tends to dominate whether a potential candidate opts to seek office.

The other significant conclusion from the Kazee discussion is that potential campaign contributors have become the most significant gatekeepers to the pursuit of office. It is a rare American politician who runs for office without considering the cost of the campaign, how much of her or his own resources he or she is willing to put as risk, and from where the rest of the money will come from. It is common for potential candidates to announce an exploratory bid for office, meaning they will talk to potential contributors to gain some confidence in their ability to raise the necessary funds. Often, those campaigns do not receive the assurances hoped for and thus end before the public campaign ever begins. Many candidates, of course, ignore the fact that they will not raise sufficient funds to win and run anyway. The consequence of that decision is obvious—they lose. So either way, the willingness of people with financial resources to back a particular candidate may well play the most substantial gatekeeping role in contemporary American politics. Unfortunately, we know little of the consequences of this evolving pattern of gatekeeping and its consequences, but it is surely an important component of the contemporary American political scene.

In many ways, the political class in the United States must see these as the best of times. Those in the political class are certainly quite comfortable by most interpretations and their successes are notable. The vagaries of elections are minimized to the extent possible. Electoral rules have been structured to work to their advantage in wide range of ways including campaign financing, districting, and weakening parties. The financial and fringe benefits of office tend to be relatively generous. The salaries and pensions allow a comfortable lifestyle both while in office and beyond. Moreover, they have structured rules and norms to allow themselves to seek and hold lucrative and powerful positions when they move out of electoral office. The number of individuals who leave politics upon losing office is generally relatively small. Yet, a few do lose and others voluntarily step aside. When they do, some move to appointed positions while others attract very generous salaries as lobbyists (Herrick and Nixon 1996).

Yet, in many ways it is also the worst of times for the political class. Low public opinion of public officials and a sense of distrust and alienation by the American public place the class in a precarious position (cf. Craig 1993, 1996; Hibbing and Theiss-Morse 1995, 2001; Mackenzie 1996; Davidson 1999). What the class has gained in other areas, it has lost in terms of esteem and legitimation. This is also linked to the public's perception of a growing number of political scandals.

Many charges of unethical behavior truly would be considered scandalous by most standards of judgment. Sleeping with an underage page or campaign worker might be examples of behavior that evoke widespread disdain. But in other areas scandals are, at least in part, the reflection of a conflict between the values and norms of the class and those of the public at large. Many areas where politicians come under fire are behaviors that are legal or, at worst, in gray areas. The Congressional bad check scandal that broke prior to the 1992 elections is an example. In that case, as a matter of formal policy, the bank of the House of Representatives covered checks that were written on accounts that had insufficient funds rather than return those checks to the recipient of the "hot" check. Some banks in the United States offer that overdraft protection to their best customers or to any customer who pays a fee. Members accepted this perquisite as normal and fair. Many, evidently, rarely bothered to balance their checkbooks and, therefore, routinely wrote checks when their funds were not sufficient. The checks, though, were ultimately made good by members; yet, when the public found out about it many saw it as outrageous behavior that lacked any moral justification and simply reinforced their views of members as irresponsible spendthrifts. The public perception of the institution and its members declined. Many of the worst users (abusers) of the system were defeated in their reelection efforts. Here, the institution and its members were tainted because the norms of the political class and the general public diverged.

Campaign finance practices is another area where the public is routinely outraged by the actions of both contributors and candidates. Even purely legal practices raise the eyebrows of the public. When candidates systematically seek out the legal loopholes, for example, soft money, or operate in gray areas the public is even more astounded. In this case the difference is not as much a question of norms, but rather that political candidates must operate on the edges of legality to succeed. In fact, by operating in those areas, they are more likely to succeed. Perversely, the very actions that the American public questions actually work to insure that candidates are above consequences of those actions. Moreover, if they do not operate in the gray areas, a challenger might emerge which could endanger the electability of the candidate scrupulously following the law. The American public, then, is frustrated and the views of the politicians and political institutions suffer.

In many ways, what we see is a direct consequence of the actions of the political class acting as such—consciously aware of common interests and working actively to protect themselves. It should surely not come as a surprise that the public perceives them as self-interested, putting their own above the public's well-being. Paradoxically, as the public becomes more and more unhappy with the behavior of the political class and the performance of the institutions which it controls, individual incumbents must work harder to differentiate themselves from the class (in the minds of their voters) by running against the Washington "establishment." In doing that they tend to increase the public's discontent in three ways at once: they themselves—especially as newcomers—criticize the system thus further lowering its legitimacy; once elected they are seen as mainly acting according to their particularized reelection interest; and finally the combination of both stances is regarded as hypocrisy.

The underlying paradox is that those politicians who initially succeed running on a platform of protest against the system as it stands—like the 1974 class of Democrats or the 1994 Republicans (cf. Loomis 1988; Rae 1998: 176–82)—are particularly dependent upon the mechanisms of career maintenance, as their districts tend to be marginal and thus hotly contested. While this behavior often is successful in electoral terms, it simultaneously raises widespread feelings of cynicism and political alienation resulting in a distrust of democratic institutions more generally. If you want to be (re)elected, you cannot practice a different form of political representation; if you practice a different form of representation, you will be held accountable and not be reelected—that's the paradoxical reality of American political careers.

Living off Politics

American national legislators have the highest income of all their colleagues in the advanced capitalist countries. The drawback to this can be seen in the severe limits imposed on other income most of which is considered unethical. Honoraria are illegal, and extra income may not surpass 15 percent of the salary (Davidson and Oleszek 1998: 145). Thus, the separation of political offices and of levels of government which makes the prototypical American politician a professional legislator is reflected in his being restricted to legislative activities.

The income of about US$150,000 a year is complemented with a rather generous pension plan, providing a maximum of 80 percent of the legislative salary (at age 60 and after 32 years of service). Since the Ethics Act of 1989 (cf. Thompson 1995), legislative salaries are adjusted to inflation annually by way of so-called "cost-of-living adjustments" (COLAs), giving members an automatic pay raise unless they specifically vote against it.

Also, Congressmen have access to what is generally referred to as "perks", which includes above all the franking privilege (on average US$163,000 per year and member), and a number of staffers that is unique by international standards (almost 24,000 in 2000, including support agencies). Each representative may hire up to eighteen full-time staffers; the average hired was fourteen in 2000. For the Senate, the average was thirty-four for each Senator (www.c-span.org/questions/weekly35.asp).

THE POLITICAL CLASS AND INSTITUTIONAL REFORM

The idea of a political class does not necessarily imply that its members are removed from society but it certainly raises the question of accountability. Which mechanisms could guarantee the democratic control of the political class? Parker's (1992) suggestion to regard its members as discretion maximizers may be an appropriate way to approach the issue. Members gain that discretion (over the fate of their class) by providing benefits for their constituents. In fact, Beyme (1996: 85–6) suggests that members are increasingly forced to be responsive to the needs of their constituents who are becoming ever more sophisticated and demanding. Thus, public pressure increases representatives' responsiveness at the same time as the political class severs its ties with the electorate. This schizophrenic behavior of superficially and symbolically fulfilling the demands of the citizenry—for example, in terms of constituency service—while keeping the political realm closed off is very rational in the short run. In the long run it leads to a legitimation crisis of representative democracy in the United States—and not only there.

The concept of political class might also help us integrate a range of theories relating to institutional reform. In an earlier work Peters, Copeland, and Mott (1994) suggested that reform results from intentionality, reaction to a grievance, and values to be achieved. They did not use the words, but the suggestion is that the political class reforms when it serves their needs as a class. In that case, reform is internally motivated. Other work (e.g. Copeland 1994; Dodd 1994) examines external factors that lead to legislative reform. That genre of work considers pressures from outside the institution as the primary impetus for reform. Little has been done to integrate these two strains of reform research (but cf. Dodd 1977; Schickler 2001), but the concept of political class offers an opportunity to do just that. In both cases, reform occurs when it is in the interest of the class to do so. In the first case they are the force behind reform because they want to (and can) enhance their quality of life (or rather, work). In the second case, they react to external pressures to protect the class from external threats.

But, it should not be assumed that any of these mechanisms of balance exist or that a balance ensues. Katz and Mair (1995) argue that "democracy ceases to be seen as a process by which limitations or controls are imposed on the state by civil society, becoming instead a service provided by the state for civil society" (22). As we explore propositions such as these and seek ways to protect American democratic institutions, understanding the operations of the political class is central to the success of those efforts.

With disaffection so evident among the American public, it is not surprising that there are widespread cries for reform. But, it should also be evident that the rule-makers live under the rules, structure them, and structure them to their advantage. Reform efforts are challenging. It would not be too much of an exaggeration to claim that Congressional reforms, throughout the twentieth century, can be understood as efforts to meet the needs of the political class at the expense of other interests, such as parties or the general public. The revolt against Speaker Canon and the Legislative Reform Act of 1946 can—in their consequences, if not in their intentions—be understood as meeting the needs of individual members in contrast to a more narrow leadership group (cf. Borchert 1987).

The events of 1910/11 were on the one hand a reaction to the growing chances of staying in the House and having a career there—chances that increased as a result of the 1896 realignment dividing up regions among parties and thus making more seats safe for one party. On the other hand the rebellion may be attributed to regionally diverging patterns of recruitment (cf. Swenson 1982). The Legislative Reorganization Act of 1946 started as an attempt by Congress to restore its power *vis-à-vis* an executive that had gained the supremacy during the New Deal and the Second World War. It ended as a further instance of decentralizing power in favor of the committee chairmen (cf. Davidson 1990).

The set of Congressional reforms in the 1970s most clearly illustrates our thesis. Members rebelled against a set of rules that concentrated power and influence in the hands of a relatively small number of members, the committee chairs. More junior members felt that they were being prevented from adequately serving the needs of their constituents both in the policy realm and in their ability to provide direct benefits to their constituencies. They simply were not central enough to the Washington establishment and, by not being a part of that system, they could not sufficiently work the system to their advantage. This, however, had adverse effects upon their opportunity for credit-claiming and hence on their prospects for reelection. Only by decentralizing the institution could they spread the advantages around. As a consequence, the rights of subcommittees and of individual representatives were enhanced (cf. Davidson and Oleszek 1976; Dodd 1977).

Other practices as well serve the collective security of the cartel of incumbents (Stein and Bickers 1995). The provision of office perquisites allows the political class to protect itself and their careers. Low rates of turnover not only provide job security to members of the class but also enhance the likelihood of socializing new members into the norms of the class. The campaign finance system promotes the same protection of the class though its biases toward incumbency or candidates who are "quality" challengers. Collusion among those who, in the public eyes, are opponents is another area where we see the consequences of the political class operating in American politics. A clear illustration of that pattern is found in redistricting practices that are often followed at reapportionment. In many instances, the redrawing of district lines takes on a clear partisan tone, but it also true that we often find patterns of incumbent-protection gerrymandering (Kousser 1996). In fact, there is some evidence that there has been an evolution in that direction and away from the bitterness that develops when we see partisan gerrymandering such as took place in California or Indiana after the 1980 census (Copeland and McDonald 1987).

In recent years four issues have figured most prominently in the debate on institutional reforms. These debates are partly connected to each other, but partly are led besides and against each other. The issues are:

- the American system of government,
- the internal structure of Congress,
- campaign finance,
- the introduction of term limits.

The debate on a reform of the governmental system aims at nothing less than a constitutional reform (cf. Sundquist 1992). Critics bemoan the "gridlock" that results from having different parties control Congress and the Presidency. What they would prefer generally is some sort of parliamentary democracy, or at least some steps in that direction. Thus, House terms should be prolonged and Senate terms shortened to reach congruence with Presidential terms. Some even argue for a cabinet recruited from Congress. But this debate remains a purely academic one. Nothing would suggest that Americans are prepared to give up the sacred principles of their Constitution in order to adopt a "foreign" system.

There has been no shortage of attempts to reform the structure of Congress. In 1993—like several times before in the twentieth century—a Joint Committee on the Organization of Congress was installed to devise a concept for reform (cf. Evans and Oleszek 1997). The plan the committee had reported failed because of the resistance of some influential Democrats in the House. When the Republicans won the Congressional elections of 1994, they introduced their own reform plan. This plan had as its prime goal the centralization of power in the hands of the Speaker and the party leaderships. The Speaker got back the right to appoint committee chairpersons while the number of subcommittees was reduced and the number of their staff cut by one third—to name but a few of the rather encompassing changes (Evans and

Oleszek 1997: 83–114). But the powers of the Speaker once again retreated with the demise of Speaker Gingrich.

The idea behind this reform was Newt Gingrich's conception to restore party government American style, as it had been in place at the beginning of the twentieth century. Gingrich aimed at the very structure of Congress. The boundaries of his plan, however, lay in the parties' very limited control over the nomination and (re)election of their Congressional candidates. When Gingrich resigned after the bad results of the Republicans in the 1998 election, he remained true to his concept of party government. Yet his resignation also marked the definite failure of his reform. His unpopularity in the American public may be traced back just as much to his alien institutional understanding of American politics as to his personality. After his displacement a return to normality, that is, creeping decentralization of the decision-making structure in Congress has been under way. Party government is not going to happen any time soon.

Campaign finance reform has been a perennial issue in American politics. Its permanence is based on the seeming futility of attempts to effectively regulate the influx of money into politics. Partisan proposals are regularly obstructed by the other side. The lowest common denominator of bipartisan reform efforts is the protection of incumbents. This, however, was almost perfectly achieved under the post-1974 system which impeded any reform enthusiasm. Proposals to limit campaign spending, especially, run straight into the face of incumbents' interest to benefit from their superior resources. Only after a major scandal did Congress act by making modest changes in the system. The successful bipartisan initiative, sponsored by Representatives Shays and Meehan on the House side and Senators McCain and Feingold on the Senate side, primarily attacks soft money—unlimited and unregulated money filtered through the national parties. It also increases what individuals can contribute to campaigns and limits the capacity of corporations, unions, and nonprofits to run independent "issue" advertisements. These reforms, while perhaps having value, seem unlikely to hurt incumbents while putting a halt to the growing importance of national parties in the campaign finance system.

The campaign for term limits is an outside attempt to challenge the ground-rules of the political game by referring to time-honored traditions (cf. Benjamin and Malbin 1992; Will 1992; Copeland 1994). At heart, this is a campaign to undo the professionalization of politics and bring back the citizen legislator. The enormous popularity of the proposal to limit the terms of politicians on all levels of the political system rests on two qualities in particular: it is seductively simple and it draws on deeply engrained traditions and resentments in American politics. Anti-professionalism in the political sphere—as opposed to the high regard in which the liberal professions generally are held in the United States—can count on a populist suspicion of politicians that is part of the political culture.

The success of the term limit campaign has been remarkable. Between 1990 and 1995 eighteen states enacted term limits for their state legislatures—usually via referendum (Rosenthal 1998: 75).[8] The attempt to apply term limits to members of

---

[8] After that, only Nebraska followed suit in 2000.

Congress as well did not pass the Supreme Court who considered that a state infringement upon federal rights. Congress itself has failed to enact term limits even though this was a key item in the Republican "Contract with America." It quickly became clear, however, that when pre-election pledges and post-election ambition collided, usually the latter won out. But on the state level term limits have become a reality that has already had a deep impact on political careers and even more so on career-planning (cf. Carey, Niemi, and Powell 2000). Congressional candidates have in some places come under increasing pressure to voluntarily term-limit themselves by way of a contractual arrangement with their voters.

The consequences federal term limits would have on American politics are yet unforeseeable. It is highly unlikely, however, that term limits would mean the end of professional politics in the United States. At a minimum, supporters should take into account the conclusions of an analysis on term limited Costa Rican politics by Carey (1996) who finds that professional politicians will find a way to perpetuate and protect themselves even under severe term limits—a result that is confirmed by a first look at term-limited states in the United States. The consequences of term limits, or any reform, can only be imagined by realistically taking into account what the political class would make of the reform in order to meet their own needs.

Under term limits a new path to political professionalism could evolve which then replaces the dominance of the professional legislator model. Rather, we could see a professional politician holding a variety of political jobs over time—very much like in the late nineteenth century. A model like that would have to be based on either parties or interest groups serving as a clearing-house and coordinating political careers. But then a major overhaul of the system is highly unlikely—given how firmly the American political class has entrenched itself within a time-honored polity that is rather resistant to change. Professional politics may be considered un-American and a violation of the founding spirit by some, but it is here to stay. Hence the failure of the widely popular term limits movement is just the latest evidence of the power of the political class in the United States.

REFERENCES

Abram, Michael, and Cooper, Joseph (1968). "The Rise of Seniority in the House of Representatives". *Polity*, 1: 52–85.

Adler, Scott (2002). *Why Congressional Reforms Fail.* Chicago: University of Chicago Press.

Alford, John R., and Hibbing, John (1986). "Increased Incumbency Advantage in the House". *Journal of Politics*, 43: 1042–61.

Ansolabehere, Stephen, and Gerber, Alan (1997). "Incumbency Advantage and the Persistence of Legislative Majorities". *Legislative Studies Quarterly*, 22: 61–77.

APSA (American Political Science Association) (1950). *Toward a More Responsible Two-Party System.* Washington: APSA.

Arnold, Douglas R. (1981). "The Local Roots of Domestic Policy", in T. Mann and N. Ornstein (eds), *The New Congress.* Washington: American Enterprise Institute, pp. 250–87.

Barone, Michael, and Ujifusa, Grant (1995). *The Almanac of American Politics 1996*. Washington: National Journal.

Benjamin, Gerald, and Malbin, Michael (eds) (1992). *Limiting Legislative Terms*. Washington: Congressional Quarterly.

Berkman, Michael, De Boef, Suzanna, and Poggione, Sarah (1995). "Legislative Modernization in Comparative Perspective", unpublished manuscript, presented at the APSA, Chicago.

Beyme, Klaus von (1996). "The Concept of Political Class: A New Dimension of Research on Elites?". *West European Politics*, 19: 68–87.

Borchert, Jens (1987). *Legitimation und partikulare Interessen*. Frankfort: Peter Lang.

Brady, David, Buckley, Kara, and Rivers, Douglas (1999). "The Roots of Careerism in the U.S. House of Representatives". *Legislative Studies Quarterly*. 24: 489–510.

Cain, Bruce E., Ferejohn, John, and Fiorina, Morris (1987). *The Personal Vote: Constituency Service and Electoral Independence*. Cambridge: Harvard University Press.

Campbell, Colton C., and Rae, Nicol C. (2001). *The Contentious Senate: Partisanship, Ideology, and the Myth of Cool Judgement*. Lanham, MD: Rowman and Littlefield.

Carey, John M. (1996). *Term Limits and Legislative Representation*. New York: Cambridge University Press.

—— Niemi, Richard G., and Powell, Lynda W. (2000). *Term Limits in the State Legislatures*. Ann Arbor: University of Michigan Press.

Clawson, Dan, Neustadtl, Alan, and Weller, Mark (1998). *Dollars and Votes*. Philadelphia: Temple University Press.

Copeland, Gary W. (1994). "Legislative Term Limits as Legislative Reform", unpublished manuscript, presented at the APSA, New York.

—— and McDonald, Jean G. (1987). "Reapportionment and Partisan Competition: When Does Reapportionment Matter?". *Political Behavior*, 9: 160–73.

Craig, Stephen C. (1993). *The Malevolent Leaders*. Boulder: Westview.

—— (ed.) (1996). *Broken Contract*. Boulder: Westview.

Davidson, Roger H. (1990). "The Legislative Reorganization Act of 1946", *Legislative Studies Quarterly*, 15: 357–73.

—— (1999). "Congress and Public Trust: Is Congress its Own Worst Enemy?", in J. Cooper (ed.), *Congress and the Decline of Public Trust*. Boulder: Westview Press, pp. 65–78.

—— and Oleszek, Walter J. (1976). "Adaptation and Consolidation: Structural Innovation in the House of Representatives". *Legislative Studies Quarterly*, 1: 37–66.

—— —— (1998). *Congress and its Members*, 6th edition. Washington: Congressional Quarterly.

Dawes, Roy A., and Bacot, A. Hunter (1998). "Electoral Career Patterns and Incumbency Advantage in the U.S. House of Representatives". *Legislative Studies Quarterly*, 23: 575–83.

Dobson, John (1972). *Politics in the Gilded Age*. New York: Praeger.

Dodd, Lawrence C. (1977). "Congress and the Quest for Power", in L. Dodd and B. Oppenheimer (eds), *Congress Reconsidered*. New York: Praeger, pp. 269–307.

—— (1994). "Political Learning and Political Change: Understanding Development Across Time", in L. Dodd and C. Jillson (eds), *The Dynamics of American Politics*. Boulder: Westview Press, pp. 331–64.

Evans, C. Lawrence, and Oleszek, Walter J. (1997). *Congress Under Fire: Reform Politics and the Republican Majority*. Boston: Houghton Mifflin.

Fiorina, Morris (1977). *Congress: Keystone of the Washington Establishment*. New Haven: Yale University Press.

Fisher, Louis (1995). "Salaries", in D. Bacon, R. Davidson, and M. Keller (eds), *The Encyclopedia of the United States Congress*, Vol. 4. New York: Simon & Schuster, pp. 1752–6.

Fowler, Linda L. (1993). *Candidates, Congress, and the American Democracy.* Ann Arbor: University of Michigan Press.

Gierzynski, Anthony (1999). *Money Rules: Financing Elections in America.* Boulder: Westview.

Herrick, Rebekah, and Nixon, David L. (1996). "Is There Life After Congress? Patterns and Determinants of Post-congressional Careers". *Legislative Studies Quarterly,* 21: 489–99.

Hibbing, John R. (1991). *Congressional Careers: Contours of Life in the U.S. House of Representatives.* Chapel Hill: University of North Carolina Press.

—— and Theiss-Morse, Elizabeth (1995). *Congress as Public Enemy.* Cambridge: Cambridge University Press.

—— —— (eds) (2001). *What is it about Government that Americans Dislike?* Cambridge: Cambridge University Press.

Jacobson, Gary C., and Kernell, Samuel (1981). *Strategy and Choice in Congressional Elections.* New Haven: Yale University Press.

Jewell, Malcolm E. and Patterson, Samuel C. (1986). *The Legislative Process in the United States,* 4th edition. New York: Random House.

Josephy, Alvin M., Jr. (1979). *On the Hill: A History of the American Congress.* New York: Simon & Schuster.

Katz, Richard S., and Mair, Peter (1995). "Changing Models of Party Organization and Party Democracy". *Party Politics,* 1: 5–28.

Kazee, Thomas A. (1994). "The Emergence of Congressional Candidates", in T. Kazee (ed.), *Who Runs for Congress?* Washington, DC: Congressional Quarterly.

Kernell, Samuel (1977). "Toward Understanding 19th Century Congressional Careers". *American Journal of Political Science,* 21: 669–93.

Kousser, J. Morgan (1996). "Estimating the Partisan Consequences of Redistricting Plans Simply". *Legislative Studies Quarterly,* 21: 521–41.

Loomis, Burdett A. (1979). "The Congressional Offices as a Small (?) Business: New Members Set Up Shop". *Publius,* 9: 35–55.

—— (1988). *The New American Politician.* New York: Basic Books.

Mackenzie, G. Calvin (1996). *The Irony of Reform: Roots of American Political Disenchantment.* Boulder: Westview.

Maisel, L. Sandy, and Stone, Walter J. (1997). "Determinants of Candidate Emergence in U.S. House Elections: An Exploratory Study". *Legislative Studies Quarterly,* 22: 79–96.

Matthews, Donald R. (1960). *U.S. Senators and Their World.* Chapel Hill: University of North Carolina Press.

Mayhew, David (1974). *Congress: The Electoral Connection.* New Haven: Yale University Press.

Mezey, Michael (1970). "Ambition Theory and the Office of Congressman". *Journal of Politics,* 32, 563–79.

Moncrief, Gary F. (1994). "Professionalism and Careerism in Canadian Provincial Assemblies: Comparison to U.S. State Legislatures". *Legislative Studies Quarterly,* 19, 33–48.

—— Thompson, Joel A., Haddon, Michael, and Hoyer, Robert (1992). "For Whom the Bell Tolls: Term Limits and State Legislatures". *Legislative Studies Quarterly,* 17, 37–48.

Niemi, Richard G., and Winsky, Laura R. (1987). "Membership Turnover in U.S. State Legislatures: Trends and Effects of Districting". *Legislative Studies Quarterly,* 12, 115–24.

Opheim, Cynthia (1994). "The Effect of U.S. State Term Limits Revisited". *Legislative Studies Quarterly,* 19, 49–59.

Parker, Glenn R. (1992). *Institutional Change, Discretion, and the Making of Modern Congress.* Ann Arbor: University of Michigan Press.

Peters, Ronald M., Jr., Copeland, Gary W., and Mott, Jonathon (1994). "Turnover and Reform in the US House of Representatives: A Historical and Conceptual Analysis", paper presented at the Annual Meeting of the Southwestern Political Science Association, San Antonio.

Petracca, Mark P. (1992). "Rotation in Office: The History of an Idea", in G. Benjamin and M. Malbin, (eds), *Limiting Legislative Terms*. Washington, DC: Congressional Quarterly, pp. 19–51.

Polsby, Nelson W. (1968). "The Institutionalization of the U.S. House of Representatives". *American Political Science Review*, 62, 144–68.

—— Gallagher, Miriam, and Rundquist, Barry (1969). "The Growth of the Seniority System in the U.S. House of Representatives". *American Political Science Review*, 63, 787–807.

Powell, Richard J. (2000). "The Impact of Term Limits on the Candidacy Decisions of State Legislators in U.S. House Elections". *Legislative Studies Quarterly*, 25, 645–62.

Price, H. Douglas (1971). "The Congressional Career, Then and Now", in N. Polsby (ed.), *Congressional Behavior*. New York: Random House, pp. 14–27.

Prinz, Timothy S. (1993). "The Career Paths of Elected Politicians: A Review and Prospectus", in S. Williams and E. Lascher (eds), *Ambition and Beyond*. Berkeley: Institute of Governmental Studies Press, pp. 11–63.

Rae, Nicol C. (1998). *Conservative Reformers: The Republican Freshmen and the Lessons of the 104th Congress*. Armonk: M.E. Sharpe.

Rohde, David W. (1979). "Risk-Bearing and Progressive Ambition: The Case of Members of the United States House of Representatives". *American Journal of Political Science*, 23: 1–26.

—— (1991). *Parties and Leaders in the Postreform House*. Chicago: University of Chicago Press.

Rosenthal, Alan (1998). *The Decline of Representative Democracy*. Washington: Congressional Quarterly.

Rothman, David J. (1966). *Politics and Power: The United States Senate 1869–1901*. Cambridge: Harvard University Press.

Salisbury, Robert H., and Shepsle, Kenneth A. (1981). "U.S. Congressmen as Enterprise". *Legislative Studies Quarterly*, 6, 559–76.

Schickler, Eric (2001). *Disjointed Pluralism: Institutional Innovation and the Development of the U.S. Congress*. Princeton: Princeton University Press.

Schiller, Wendy J. (2000). *Partners and Rivals: Representation in U.S. Senate Delegations*. Princeton: Princeton University Press.

Schlesinger, Joseph A. (1966). *Ambition and Politics*. Chicago: Rand McNally.

Shin, Kwang S., and Jackson III, John S. (1979). "Membership Turnover in U.S. State Legislatures, 1931–1976". *Legislative Studies Quarterly*, 4, 95–104.

Sinclair, Barbara (1989). *The Transformation of the U.S. Senate*. Baltimore: Johns Hopkins University Press.

Sollars, David L. (1994). "Institutional Rules and State Legislator Compensation". *Legislative Studies Quarterly*, 19, 507–20.

Squire, Peverill (1988). "Career Opportunities and Membership Stability in Legislatures". *Legislative Studies Quarterly*. 13, 65–82.

—— (1992). "Legislative Professionalization and Membership Diversity in State Legislatures". *Legislative Studies Quarterly*, 17, 69–79.

—— (1993). "State Legislative Careers", in S. Williams and E. Lascher (eds), *Ambition and Beyond*. Berkeley: Institute of Governmental Studies Press, pp. 145–66.

Stein, Robert M., and Bickers, Kenneth N. (1995). *Perpetuating the Pork Barrel: Policy Subsystems and American Democracy*. Cambridge: Cambridge University Press.

Sundquist, James L. (1992). *Constitutional Reform and Effective Government*, 2nd edition. Washington: Brookings.

Swenson, Peter (1982). "The Influence of Recruitment on the Structure of Power in the U.S. House, 1870–1940". *Legislative Studies Quarterly*, 7: 7–36.

Thompson, Dennis F. (1995). *Ethics in Congress*. Washington: Brookings.

Wahlke, John C., Eulau, Heinz, Buchanan, William, and Ferguson, Leroy C. (1962). *The Legislative System*. New York: Wiley.

Wattenberg, Martin (1998). *The Decline of American Political Parties, 1952–1996* (revised edn.). Cambridge: Harvard University Press.

Will, George F. (1992). *Restoration: Congress, Term Limits, and the Recovery of Deliberative Democracy*. New York: Free Press.

Young, James S. (1966). *The Washington Community, 1800–1828*. New York: Columbia University Press.

Subject Index

age of representatives
  in Australia 35
  in Belgium 54, 60
  in Canada 73, 75
  in Denmark 93–4
  in Israel 213
  in Italy 231
  in Japan 253–4
  in Netherlands 267–8
  in New Zealand 287
  in Norway 304, 306
  in Sweden 362
  in Switzerland 383
asymmetrical federalism 338
Australia 26–43
  Democrats 35
  electoral systems of 29–30
  ethical standards 41–2
  House of Representatives 29, 33–35
  Labor Party 30, 36
  Liberal Party 30
  Members of Parliament income of 40
  multiculturalism, policy of 36
  National Party 30
  Parliament 28–9
  party
    discipline 33, 37, 39
    service 39
  Senate 34–5, 38
  state and territory governments pattern, of 29
  Tasmania 29, 33
  voter conversion 32
  Westminister model 32–3
Austria 21, 359
authoritarianism 321

backbenchers (or professional party politicians)
    15, 60, 147, 152, 159–61, 177, 180, 182
  in Canada 78–81
  in Great Britain 169, 176
  in Ireland 189, 196, 200
  in Portugal 326
  in Spain 342
Belgium 27, 45–64, 259
  Christian Democrats 52, 55, 62
  College of Questors 60, 62
  constitutional reform 48
  constitutional revision of 1920 46
  cumul local 57, 62

  Flemish Liberals (VLD—*Vlaamse Liberalen en Democraten*) 55
  House of Representatives 45
  legislation on public financing of parties 51
  linguistic communities 48
  Members of Parliament (MPs) 45, 51, 57–9
    income 46–7, 57–8, 62
    pensions 60
    reward structure for 61
    socio-political background of 54
  Parliament
    allowances 58–60
    parliamentary work 47
    role in decision-making 49–51
    party income sources 52
  Senate 49
  socio-economic categories 52
  unitary state 48

campaigning techniques, modern 32
Canada 28, 67–81
  demographic profile of 72
  double-dipping 79
  House of Commons 69–70, 79
  legislative behavior 80–1
  legislative salaries 69
  Parliament 70, 79
    executive-centered 77
    number of sitting days 68
    salaries 77
  Prime Ministers 72
  privileges of political class 69
  shadow cabinet 75
  sub-national and national assemblies 74
  traditionally dominant political
    parties 73
candidate selectors 193
career
  advancement 8
  interests of individual politicians 15
  maintenance, mechanisms of 8
cartel party model 5, 231
centrality of political parties 37
central party organizations 49
Chaplainocracy 144
classe politica 2, 110, 228
  post-parliamentary career destinies 235
"class in itself" and "class for itself" 4
compulsory voting 27, 31–2